FOR ALL OUR GRANDFAT

BY
DAVID BAXTER AND NORMA HART
Co. Authors and self publishers

WE DEDICATE THIS BOOK
TO OUR PARENTS

For the love and support they gave us through the traumatic encounters
that life threw at them in war and peace

AND ALL OUR GRANDPARENTS

We listened, motionless and still,
The music in our hearts we bore,
Long after it was heard no more.

From "The Reaper"

*To Mike & Shelia
Love & Best Wishes
from David &
Norma*

FOR ALL OUR GRANDFATHERS
BY
DAVID BAXTER AND NORMA HART

Co. Authors and self publishers

ISBN 978-0-9557980-0-9
Published by Ancient Family Roots Ltd.
Date first published in Great Britain 2009
Printed by York Publishing Services York
Distributed by York Publishing Services York
First Edition
British Serial rights

The publishers with the assistance of the authors have earnestly tried to trace the owners of all copyright material, sometimes without success, and we are grateful to the authorities named for permission to use their material. We apologize for any omissions; should these be made known proper acknowledgments will be made in future editions.

ACKNOWLEDGEMENTS

We extend our grateful thanks to Gill McKenna of "Family Research" for the many hours spent researching our family history, to long-suffering families and friends for support and tolerance with our obsession. To N.C.H. Harris, translator, P. Rutledge archivist for help with an ancient petition from Thomas Bulwer/Dalling to the Duke of Gloucester. The Norwich and Yarmouth Libraries Archives/Computer sections for helpful information, and various Registry Offices for their help and assistance in tracing and issuing certificates.

To Lord David Cobbold and his son, also Lady Hermione Cobbold [nee Bulwer his mother] of Knebworth Park; the archivists at Knebworth for their co-operation and permission to use photographs from the Knebworth collection. [More information on the Knebworth Families can be found on the Knebworth web site [www.knebworthhouse.com].

Jane Preston of Dorchester [archivist and author], for information particularly in respect of the tapestry embroidered by Louisa/Lorina Bulwer of Great Yarmouth, Norfolk [sold by Christies 19th November 2003; information listed later] and for using our chart regarding de Dalling/ Bulwer's in her book 'Squires of Heydon Hall'.

Sir Edmund Lacon Bt. of Ormsby, for the Lacon Family History of the 1800's. Mr. Kevil Davis retired owner of Lacon Breweries, [another branch of the Lacon families] for excellent photographs of the Ward family. Whitbread Brewery for supplying information from Lacon Brewery records, including repair bill for the sloop "Eagle" used for transportation of ales.

The Watchtower Bible and Tract Society of New York Inc. for information taken from their book 'Insight on the Scriptures' 1988. The Eastern Evening News and Daily Press, Norwich for permission to use photographs and their assistance in locating our 2nd cousin Barbara Palmer in Scotland, where she now lives. The Star Hotel Great Yarmouth for help in respect of late owner Mr. Goate.

To Alka Parquet of Authors Supermarket New Authors Agency For Publication Assistance and Editor James Mcnicholas.

We extend a special thank-you to Cousin Peter Green who did much research on the Williment's and their related families. To the late Cyril Ramsey our ex-neighbour for his account of personal war experiences. Richard Robinson, Mark Norris, Rodney Mason our computer wizards, also Jessica Robinson and Mason her brother, who provided some of the computer technical hitches and Finley Robinson for mental torment. To these we can now add a little girl named Verity Robinson.

We would like to extend our grateful thanks to Laurence Gardner; without guidance from his extensive knowledge of ancient family lineage's contained in his book 'Bloodline of the Holy Grail' [ISBN N0 1-85230870-2] we would never have achieved such a comprehensive survey of our earliest ancestors from their ancient roots.

To all others offering help; our Grateful thanks to you all

FAMILIES THAT FORM THE FRAMEWORK OF THIS BOOK

It is important to understand that this book starts with a historical study from the beginning of time, as we understand it and follows the earliest tribes from Adam that spread across the continents. We follow the line from Adam and Japheth in Europe. The two wives of Rollo [Giselle and Popae] start two distinctive family lines; Popae leads to our mother's Bulwer branch and his other wife Giselle leads to William Longsword whose two marriages 1st to Emma creates the Royal line [Kings of England] and 2nd wife Sporta creates nobility [that we believe to be our father's line]. It is these and associated lines we will concentrate on.

Chart 1

PROGRESS CHART TO 2008

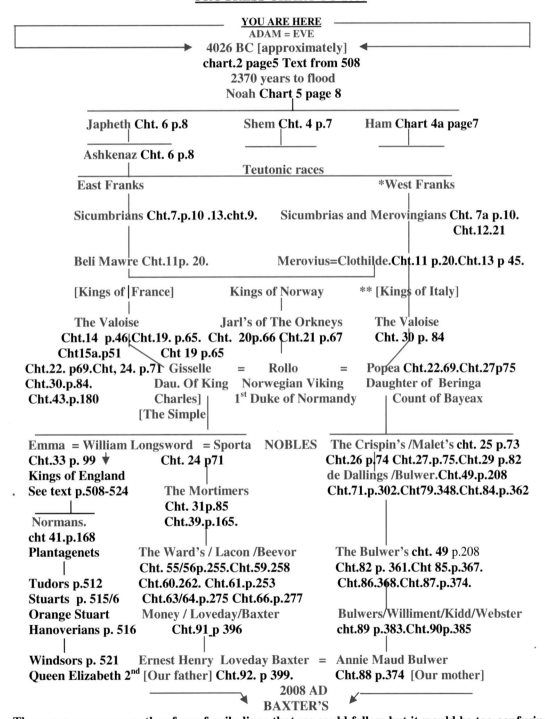

YOU ARE HERE
ADAM = EVE
4026 BC [approximately]
chart.2 page5 Text from 508
2370 years to flood
Noah Chart 5 page 8

Japheth Cht. 6 p.8   Shem Cht. 4 p.7   Ham Chart 4a page7

Ashkenaz Cht. 6 p.8

Teutonic races

East Franks   *West Franks

Sicumbrians Cht.7.p.10 .13.cht.9.   Sicumbrias and Merovingians Cht. 7a p.10.
                                                                                    Cht.12.21

Beli Mawre Cht.11p. 20.   Merovius=Clothilde.Cht.11 p.20.Cht.13 p 45.

[Kings of France]   Kings of Norway   ** [Kings of Italy]

The Valoise   Jarl's of The Orkneys   The Valoise
Cht.14 p.46 Cht.19. p.65. Cht. 20p.66 Cht.21 p.67   Cht. 30 p. 84
Cht15a.p51   Cht 19 p.65
Cht.22. p69.Cht, 24. p.71 Gisselle   =   Rollo   =   Popea Cht.22.69.Cht.27p75
Cht.30.p.84.   Dau. Of King Norwegian Viking Daughter of Beringa
Cht.43.p.180   Charles]   1st Duke of Normandy   Count of Bayeax
                       [The Simple

Emma = William Longsword = Sporta   NOBLES   The Crispin's /Malet's cht. 25 p.73
Cht.33 p. 99   Cht. 24 p71   Cht.26 p.74 Cht.27.p.75.Cht.29 p.82
Kings of England   de Dallings /Bulwer.Cht.49.p.208
See text p.508-524   The Mortimers   Cht.71.p.302.Cht79.348.Cht.84.p.362
                        Cht. 31p.85
Normans.   Cht.39.p.165.
cht 41.p.168
Plantagenets   The Ward's / Lacon /Beevor   The Bulwer's cht. 49 p.208
                        Cht. 55/56p.255.Cht.59.258   Cht.82 p. 361.Cht 85.p.367.
Tudors p.512   Cht.60.262. Cht.61.p.253   Cht.86.368.Cht.87.p.374.
Stuarts p. 515/6   Cht.63/64.p.275 Cht.66.p.277
Orange Stuart   Money / Loveday/Baxter   Bulwers/Williment/Kidd/Webster
Hanoverians p. 516   Cht.91 p 396   cht.89 p.383.Cht.90p.385

Windsors p. 521   Ernest Henry Loveday Baxter = Annie Maud Bulwer
Queen Elizabeth 2nd [Our father] Cht.92. p 399.   Cht.88 p.374 [Our mother]
                                    2008 AD
                                    BAXTER'S

There are numerous paths of our family lines that we could follow but it would be too confusing to include them all. Rollo Ragnavaldsson is the common ancestor to both our parents, when they married both lines conjoined.

FAMILY OR ASSOCIATED FAMILY LINEAGE CHARTS
CHARTS A, B C AND D ARE CONSRUCTED TO SHOW AN EXPLICIT FLOW OF OUR FAMILY LINEAGE

FAMILY OR ASSOCIATED FAMILY LINEAGE CHARTS
[CONTINUED]

PLATES

PLATES

CHRONOLOGY

Note; - Some chronology is out of date order due to subject matter in the text.

INTRODUCTION AND FOREWORD

T I M E!
It is true that...**T I M E**...waits for no man! Sadly when we started researching our family history [1986] all of the older generation had died.

T I M E... for us too, was at a premium if we were going to gather all the recollections of our childhood; it had to be done now to put all our memories into print.

IT WAS TIME! We felt compelled to do this not realizing the full implication of this decision.

Many years have passed since we as children waited with baited breath to hear stories told by many generations of our family; these have lain dormant in our hearts and minds. We realized that we would have to gather together recollections of all that had been said and so decided to put into print these intriguing stories of the past and include our own life and times, for the enjoyment of present generations and those yet to come.

Initially this book was written to prove our family lineage, but due to the exciting facts we discovered during our research studying numerous manuscripts and books, to our amazement we were constructing a family tree that led back from the present family to ***Joseph of Arimathea.** We knew from studies that he was the [reputed] uncle of Mary the mother of Jesus Christ and through these two we could trace this lineage in the bible right back to Adam; we could hardly believe it ourselves. With facts we have provided, the reader will be able to confirm our findings and we also consider that this book will be of great interest to both historians and families of today;

We started by explaining with the aid of the oldest historical record, the bible, to show how the nations derived from **Noah's** three sons and their family units that expanded and spread into various lands. The book concentrates on our lineage from **Japheth,** son of **Noah** and the father of the European nations to **Joseph of Arimathea** and his daughter **Anna** who married a druid **Bran Bron**. This lineage continues through Saxon, Merovingian, Sicambrian Franks to **Rollo,** [a Norman Viking] who was married 1st to **Gissell Valoise** [daughter of the king of France] and 2nd to **Popea Valoise** [daughter of the king of Italy] and explaining how the power struggle in Europe developed, to prove that their lineage came through a Messianic descent.

On the progress chart you will note that **Rollo** is common ancestor to our mother's and the royal lineage [we also believe this to be true of our fathers]. **Rollo's** descendant William invaded England 1066 with the **Crispin's Mortimer's** and other relations including **Turold Crispin** our forbear and his relation **William Warrenna / Mortimer**.

This book is full of human interest, of religious upheaval, the reformation, and the Huguenots, involving much of Europe including humour and tragedies, such as King William [Duke of Normandy] who kept his friends and enemies on the run from birth to his macabre burial, or when **David** took the Duchess of Kent on an unplanned tour to the basement while the dignitaries waited for her on the 6th floor, asking "Where is the Duchess".

Our book relates to people, local events murders, mayhem and family tragedy such as a shipwreck that made our great great grandmother Ann Furrence an orphan or our grandfather Baxter, who we discovered was a foundling. As children we lived through a tragic year with the death of our brother, eviction, demolition of our family home, father's bankruptcy and our parents struggle to raise their young family with no aid as today. Our grandfathers' efforts to get our family out from that poverty trap.

Nostalgic memories of wartorn Britain and the experience of a war that involved aerial combat and the terror of the blitzkrieg. Even that had its humorous side. The mass evacuation of the nation's children to the countryside and overseas, some never to return. Starvation by blockade and sinking of merchant ships were also mixed with lots of laughs and comradeship among our friends and neighbours. We continue life through to **David** and his wife **Heather** secret involvement in 1970 with test tube babies that have helped many childless couples. Our story continues from youth, marriage and children to the present day. These are events we will never forget and have put into text for you to enjoy as much as we have researching into our past.

One story more than any other, has lingered in our minds, told to us by our mother as we sat in the firelight of a war torn Britain so many years ago. It concerns a particular grandfather in the **Bulwer** line, his existence spoken of by relatives as if there was something to hide, but what it was, no one would say. It was this intriguing story with its unanswered questions that prompted us to research into who he was and why his past seemed so secretive. The original family seat of Wood Dalling Hall had been owned by the Bulwer family since the the time of our anscestor **Turold de Dalling Bulver,** who lived in the time of [and was related to] William the Conqueror. Later this had to sold to pay the debts of the estate.

When **Edward Bulwer** of Heydon Hall Norfolk died in 1934 there were issues over the estate, which our grandfather and his brothers wished to discuss [one traveled from Australia], endeavoring to prove their family relationship. Records were not so readily available in those times so their claim against the estate failed. Our research has found the proof they earnestly sought linking the families.

As if by fate, this mysterious grandfather in our mother's family line brought another story to our minds. We remembered that our mother spoke of mystery in the Ward/Lacon families through our grandmother [in our father's lineage] that had a connection with a brewery in Yarmouth; this made us widen our research.

As there had been a Lacon's Brewery there we made a start by looking in Bloomfield's "Norfolk" and *Palmers "Perlustrations", both refer to a Senator Laco. Another ancient scribe Dio also mentioned a certain Laco who Emperor Claudius summoned to England. We were astonished when these books amazingly led us on a trail from the time when the Romans walked the earth to the present family of today.

It seems certain that the **Laco** families later settled near Wem, Shropshire, in a little village bearing the name of **Lacon** where the ancient Lords of **Lacon** had their seat [The oldest recorded family in Britain from Roman times]. This was to us staggering information, as it tied up with the eventual story of a marriage linking a brewing family in Yarmouth to the **Lacon's** of Shropshire.

During our research it was ironic that we found that the families developed into two family lines that conjoined again (possibly) after about two thousand years with the marriage of our parents, [see chart 1 page 3]. You will note that all family members in the text and some important events are highlighted in black **bold print.** The the major charts are highlighted in **blue** to help you follow our family lineage but in order to reduce costs we had to use other means to identify the continueing family lines such as capital letters. We have also formulated 'Progress Charts' so you can associate the events of that time period to the text.

We achieved the proof we sought of our mother's lineage beyond doubt, but could not prove our father's line due to missing records.

*C.J.Palmer [married to Graham Lacon's sister] stated "It is not improbable that the Romans when they occupied Shropshire left many memorials, and may have given their name to the small township of Lacon. The Lacon's were Lords there in the time of King Edward.

CHAPTER 1.
THE BEGINNING OF TIME AS WE UNDERSTAND IT
The start of all the Nations of the Earth

TIME is an interesting discussion point in its own right that none of us can escape from, so the calendar was invented to measure its passing and life in todays world would not be possible without it. Several forms of time measurement evolved to regulate peoples lives until we arrived at the clock system we use today, which has organized our lives ever since.

The ancient calendars seem to be based on the interval of sunrise and sunset and between new moons [29.5 day's], which gave rise to measuring *religious periods of time. Farming also dictated that calendar's had essentialy a seasonal base [the solar year]. Sun dial's were used and the the shadow cast by the sun on a marked plate told the time.. In c195 BC an astronomer devised the 24 hour day, which was later sub-divided into minutes and seconds. Mechanical clocks were first used in the 14th century.

Some historical data began by recording facts with wall paintings, written statements or even tapestries of personal, family, local or national occurrences of disasters or achievements. A large amount was recorded by various clerics or monks in the monastries but most of these documents have been either lost or destroyed. Those saved were pieced together and made into some form of recorded history usually long after the events took place; family structures were no exception. Britain has an ancient written history of about 2000 years that started seriously again after the invasion by Julius Caesar in 55 BC. Unfortunately most of the data concerning Roman times in Britain is considered unreliable and scarce due to the ravages of the invading Teutonic tribes that followed the Roman evacuation of this country

T I M E...again was in question where to start? So much information! What was the focal point? History stretches back into infinity, we had to start somewhere! What had started as a little jaunt to find a missing grandfather had resulted in an incredible journey back through time. The genealogy we uncovered went far back; so far back we couldn't believe that anyone would possibly accept this as truth, we still feel uncertain about the history of these early years, but we can only relate stated facts that we have researched from historical records. The book Mrs. McKenna our researcher recommended "Bloodline of the Holy Grail" by Laurence Gardner who had been granted privilege access to European sovereign and noble archives. These contained generations of family lines, several of which blended into our own family history.

* i.e. Stonehenge

THE BIBLE AND HISTORY
Chart.2

THE FORMING OF TRIBES OF ISRAEL AND THE LINE LEADING TO THE CHRIST

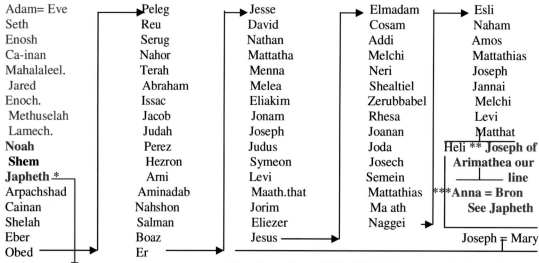

Adam= Eve	Peleg	Jesse	Elmadam	Esli
Seth	Reu	David	Cosam	Naham
Enosh	Serug	Nathan	Addi	Amos
Ca-inan	Nahor	Mattatha	Melchi	Mattathias
Mahalaleel.	Terah	Menna	Neri	Joseph
Jared	Abraham	Melea	Shealtiel	Jannai
Enoch.	Issac	Eliakim	Zerubbabel	Melchi
Methuselah	Jacob	Jonam	Rhesa	Levi
Lamech.	Judah	Joseph	Joanan	Matthat
Noah	Perez	Judus	Joda	Heli ** Joseph of
Shem	Hezron	Symeon	Josech	Arimathea our
Japheth *	Arni	Levi	Semein	line
Arpachshad	Aminadab	Maath.that	Mattathias	***Anna = Bron
Cainan	Nahshon	Jorim	Ma ath	See Japheth
Shelah	Salman	Eliezer	Naggei	
Eber	Boaz	Jesus		
Obed	Er			Joseph = Mary

European-Judaic lines   Line from Jesus, [The Christ] blank, ****Jesus d 33 AD
Other family line's come from his brothers & sisters

conjoin. Arch Druid Bran/ Bron***=Anna daughter of Joseph of Arimathea. The names listed above are taken from Luke chapter 3 verses 23-28. The following text ***according to legend **Joseph of Arimathea was the uncle of Mary; he took them into his care when Joseph father of Jesus died. If correct, his family through bible chronology would go back through Judah to Abraham and Adam. Joseph a rich merchant trading in tin for the Romans again by legend came to Britain and engraved a stone that was eventually set into the wall of St. Mary's Chapel Glastonbury found in Cressy's Church History. James later arrived in England with Jesus the Justice, son of Mary Magdalene. The hymn "Did those feet in ancient times" is related to this event. Ham is not mentioned above, as he was not in the lineage for Christ, see p. 7

Joseph of Arimathea a Hebrew descended from the line of Judah lived in Arimathea, Judea, possibly a relation of Jesus, as were some of the disciples. **Joseph** in whose tomb Jesus was buried. When an order from Caesar Augustus required people to register in their own city, the family of Jesus had to go to Jerusalem. ****Jesus [The Christ son of Joseph a poor carpenter] was born soon after in Bethlehem Judea in October 2 B.C; six months after the birth of John the Baptist, [born April, 2 BC.] King Herod; alarmed at the rumour that a new king of the Jews had been born tried to kill Jesus by ordering all boys under the age of two to be murdered. Joseph was forewarned, and escaped with Jesus to Egypt. They later returned to their homeland and went to live in Nazareth in Galilee. People who lived there at this time were called Nazarenes and were very much looked down upon.

Bible chronology does not give much detailed history of nations apart from the Hebrews and the most prominent world powers that were fighting with or against the Jews. The records are very vague and scarce because of warring tribes; little is known about them. ****Jesus [the Christ] although he was born from the tribe of Judah, the higher class and richer tribe of Israel worked and lived in Galilee where the ordinary poor class of people lived. *+**+*** "Watchtower Bible and Tract Society New York Inc Insight into the Scriptures Also Joseph of Arimathea is known as the great uncle of Jesus, mothers side,.**+***+**** See also Chart. A [20] p.11 for further information of lines conjoining. Note; As this is a very complicated situation we strongly suggest that you read Laurence Gardner's book Bloodline of the Holy Grail pages 138/140.

The time period can be pinpointed by 15th year of the reign of Tiberius Caesar and the district rulers living then, which determines the date of 29AD; [see Luke chap.3 v.1-3]. Our research shows the start of John the Baptist ministry began in April of that year; Jesus ministry, six months later both aged 30 years [an age when priests were ordained]. On King Herod's birthday his wife arranged for Salome; their daughter, to dance. This pleased the king who asked what she would like as a reward. Mother and daughter requested the head of John the Baptist on a platter; Herod reluctantly agreed. John was killed, and Jesus Christ was put to death six months after. His ministry of 3½ years brings us roughly to April 33.AD making Jesus about 33 years old at his death.

Using our chart below proceed to Bran/Bron=Anna] daughter of Joseph of Arimathea. Mary Magdalene according to the chart in Laurence Gardner's book married a man called Jesus. [There were many with the name Jesus/Joshua]; the first son named Jesus [*The Justice born 37AD], and a grandson **Galain/Alain** [b. 37AD. Another son was called Joseph [The Rama-Theo ; b 44AD] whose son Jossue started a line of kings [called the Messianic line] We have mentioned this, because it caused strife during later periods of history in Europe; particularly relating to our own ancestors. Aminadab's marriage to Eugen conjoined family lines; We leave others to make up their minds about these earlier generations as we can only relate what we have found.

EARLY TIMES 1st – 7th CENTURY

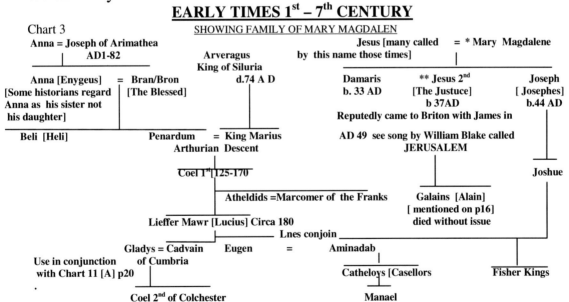

Directly after the Romans defeated the Iceni tribe in Briton *James and Jesus the Justice reputedly came to England to set up a church at Glastonbury in spite of Roman imperialism. The chart is derived from the chart "Messianic Decent of Britain and Europe" "Bloodline of the Holy Grail by Laurence Gardner with information from p 140 para; 1 p 3 of the same book, and Arthurian Legend. There is no positive statement in the bible as to the relationship of Joseph of Arimathea to what was termed the Messianic line we refer you to the statement above chart. **Saint James, whose gold silver and jewel encrusted tomb is in San Diego cathedral see note * For further information at end of lineage shown for the Christ p 5. Children of Mary Magdalene and her husband born several years after Jesus the Christ died. [See above chart. and para 1].

START OF LINE LEADING TO CHRIST
TRIBES ORIGINATING FROM *SHEM   Chart 4

2nd BORN SON OF NOAH
Name means fame – The chosen one
Founder of 26 Nations [See Gen. Chapter 10 v. 1-5 & 21]

Asshur [1st to be king]	Lud	Aparshed	Aram	Elam and others mostly Middle
Assyria 2nd World Power		Shelar		Eastern tribes and their offshoots.
Was made to be subject to	Lydians	Eber	Arameans	SE. Mesopotamias merged also
Arcadian Empire 2000BC			& Syrians	with Japhetic nations.
Conquered again by Ur then		Joktan	Peleg **languages were confused in these days	
by Babylon 3rd World Power.			and through the lack of communication the nations	
Assyria recovered in about 135 BC			scattered all over the earth. Gen.11 v. 1-9	

Line to Christ as shown in the bible. See our page 5 Also Mathew chapter 1. 1-16 and Luke Chapter 3. 23-28

TRIBES ORIGINATING FROM HAM
Third and youngest son of Noah
See Gen; 9-25 – 30 Nations

After the flood there were three main branches from Ham who was the originator of most of the dark skinned races. Canaan did not produce any Negro descendants but was the forebear of the various Canaanite tribes of Palestine [see Genesis 9.v 22-25 and 10.v 9 in the bible, also 'Insight into the Scriptures' volume 1 Cush].

Chart 4[a]   Ham

***Canaan	Cush	Mizraim		Put
was cursed by Noah				Possibly Libyans of
for base conduct		Egypt 1st World Power		North Africa

Seba	Havliah	Ramah	Nimrod [means rebel]	Sabiteca
			**** Rebel against God	Southern Arabia
East Africa	Saba	Dedan	Gen. 10 v. 8-10	
Sabeans				Rama

Hivites	*****Heth	Amorites	Girgamites	******Arkites	Zemites
Palestine		Palestine	Palestine	Palestine	

* Start of line leading to Christ **Language confused

Note:- ***Canaan was cursed by Noah; all the children of Canaan died out as to name, by disease, famine, migration and by being taken over and absorbed by families of other nations. This curse [Gen:9 v 25-27] stated let Canaan become a slave to his brothers'. [See story on Japheth p.10-13]

Note: **** Nimrod built the tower-stepped ziggurat and also built the city of Babylon/Iraq capital of mans first political empire. His father Cush was involved, given the name Bel and worshiped like a god. Probably this was the start of Bal-al. worship on earth. The tower was rebuilt in the time of Skarkalisha King of Argade

***** +******Arkites founded Akkad and were responsible with his father and grandfather in building the tower of Babel [see above under Nimrod] Gen.11.1-4 *See also Insight on the Scriptures 1988 [Ham & Shem] "Watchtower Bible and Tract Society New York Inc". ****Heth founded an empire, which lasted until 1120 BC then it was destroyed and cities burned by the Phrygians. Note: *** See Japheth, 1st born son of Noah 1st paragraph next page.

THE BIBLICAL ACCOUNT
OF THE HISTORY FROM JAPHETH LEADING TO THE FIRST EUROPEANS

Chart 5

*ADAM	KENNAN	ENOCH	NOAH [The time of the flood]
SETH	METHALALEEL	METHUSELLAR	**JAPHETH
ENOSH	JARED	LAMECH	

**First-born son of Noah, Japheth [14 nations issue from him see Gen. Chap: 9 v 27] his name means 'may he grant space' historically he was the start of modern Aryan/Indo races. Japheth did enlarge his tents, illustrating how white races have taken land of others to build up large empires. [For more information see Insight into the scriptures vol. 1 Japheth].

The blessing from Noah shows that Japheth would dwell in the tents of Shem. This still holds true today as the Western/European nations [Japheth's descendants] still remain sympathetic to modern day Israel. All this could explain the present situation in the Middle East, which is still in turmoil, and in Gen. 10 v 6-20 it states that Nimrod, a descendant of Ham was a rebel against Jehovah.

The above information seems to clarify the present situation in what is now called Iraq [Babylon] Genesis 10v 6 –20] ancient enemy of Israel from time of King Nebuchadnezzar.

JAPHETH

Chart 6

GOMER	Magog	Madia	Javan	Tubal	Meshschel	Tiras
.	Sythians probably	Medes related	Greek			Associated. with
	related to Causica and Russia	to Persians	Islands			Togarmash

Riplath	Togamash	*** ASHKENAZ		Elisha	Tarshish
Very little	settled in Tyre	↓			Ancient Spain

Riplath   Togamash   *** **ASHKENAZ**   Elisha   Tarshish
Very little   settled in Tyre   ↓   Ancient Spain
is known   and remote parts Eldest son of Gomer, [son of Japheth]. In Jewish writings of medieval
about these   of the north   times and even later the name **Ashkenaz** was given to the Teutonic races
tribes who   Jeremiah 5-27 says the Kingdom of Ashkenaz fought on the side of the enemies of
were known   Babylon, Territories lay between the Caspian and Black Sea; ***this name also
to live in the   applied to the early Cythian's. We found no names of leaders or specific people for
region of the   this time though there was a confederation of German tribes called Franks. Around
Red Sea.   the area of the **Rhine. The Teutonic Ashkenaz nations captured what is now
            France, Italy and European nations started to form.

Note. According to the bible, the oldest record of mans history in existence, begins with *Adam and Eve; we also start at this point of time because as you will see it does tie up with later text. The bible and secular history agree that after the flood. Noah's descendant's settled in the Plain of Shinar, and the first mention of separate nations is found in the book of Genesis chap. 11 v 2. Many people find the bible hard to accept but we have found some of the names mentioned in the early part of our book do connect with people in both bible and secular history too. Although bible chronology does not include many secular records regarding leaders of nations [other than the Hebrews and races of the Middle East]. The start of mankind as we know it, from Adam and Eve has developed into a number of tribes, some to the European races from Japheth and * Ashkenaz who we will concentrate on and their descendents each under their own name. **See 'Insight on the Scriptures' 1988 p192 "Watchtower Bible and Tract Society New York Inc**

Chart showing general migration of nations from the Plain of Shinar

Plate 1.

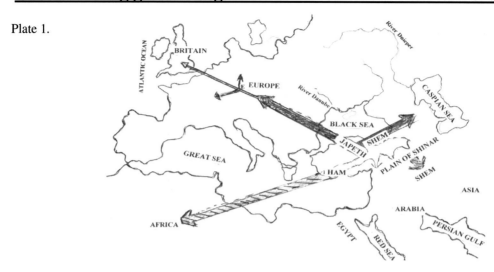

The sons of Noah, [Shem, Ham and Japheth] led their tribes from the plains of Shinar in separate directions to form independent nations. Shem to Asia, Ham to Africa, and Japheth to Europe.

The bible is the only book that gives a clear line of descent for early man, concentrating on the Hebrews developing the line leading to the Christ. Our own family line [from the tribe of Japheth] conjoins with the line of Joseph of Arimathea [from Shem] eventually going through the Saxons, Vikings, and Normans following a completely different path to Europe. An interesting reference found regarding the many languages spoken today [Genesis chap.1v.4] shows how the languages became confused. Nations began to separate through lack of communication developing their own culture, traits and religions.

The three main branches from the sons of Noah enlarged into 70 nations, and though these clues do give us links to prehistoric history, we looked at secular records too to find the particular events we needed for our book. We will not be dogmatic as previously stated, so much time has passed, secular records of those days were muddled, very scarce and vague because of the warring tribes, so very little is known about them apart from a few records of major events and some very fanciful stories.

Early records in the bible show that the Teutonic [European] races started with *__Ashkenaz__ grandson of **Japheth** and great–grandson of **Noah**. As we are particularly interested in the European nations we have made a chart to combine this early information. The lineage on the chart 5 p.8 from **Ashkenaz** [who is mentioned in the bible], was difficult to trace as there were no individual names after this for a long time, though we found his descendants as tribes that began the Teutonic nations.

Note; although this map shows the general direction of the tribes, Gomer and *Ashkenaz sons of Japheth [first lived in the area north of the Black Sea]

SOME OF THE TRIBES FROM JAPHETH [EUROPEANS]

and the area's they lived
Chart 7

Japheth Aryan branch of speech [Indo/European] fourteen families]

Japheth and Gomer	Lived in the area North of the Black Sea.
*Ashkenaz	South – East of the Black Sea.
Ripath	[Paphlagonians]
Togamah	[Armenians]
Magog	
Madai [Medes]	South of the Caspian Sea; associated with the Persians.
Javan	[Ionians, and Greeks south east Europe]
Elishah	[near Greece]
Tarshish	Pre-Spanish [South West Europe]
Kittim	Cyprus
Rodanim	Rhodes
Aegean	Islands [Aegean Sea]
Tubal	Asia Minor
Meshech	Phygians Asia Minor
Tiras [Tyrrhenians]	Aegean Islands and coast lands

As we are mainly interested in descent from Japheth [European descent] we will not include the nations that issued from Shem or Ham from this point on unless they intermarry into these lines. As mentioned no more names are listed in the European line for a long time; nations began to build and they were made up of people of one language and related by blood. They were also subjected to their own governmental control and had a defined place to live; **Japheth continued to exploit territories and as you can see, mostly at the expense of his brothers.

The East Franks   The West Franks   Chart 7[a]

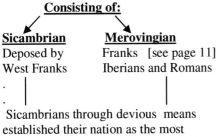

Consisting of:

Notes

Sicambrian	**Merovingian**	**The Celts** The Teutonic and Belgae were deposed by
Deposed by	Franks [see page 11]	the Burundians, Visigoths, Scandinavians
West Franks	Iberians and Romans	Normans [under Rollo the Norwegian.
		Viking [From this line later] came
		William the Conqueror]

Sicambrians through devious means established their nation as the most dominant by absorbing the Merovingians.

Celts	**Italics**	**British Isles**
Irish	Romans	Before the Stone Age, Britain is thought to
Manx	Spanish	have been joined to the continent of Europe
Highlands	Portuguese	by an alluvial plain now a broad shelf of
Scot	Latin America	land 300 feet average depth under the sea.
Welsh		
Breton		
Cornish		

See p.13 cht. 9 [11B.C. Francus/Franco] + Also see Insight on the Scriptures 1988 [p192 Ashkenaz] "Watchtower Bible and Tract Society New York Inc". [Theological Dictionary of the Old Testament.]**

The **Celts** started to settle in Briton from 700 BC and later joined by other tribes such as the Belgi. Then there was a long gap to 132 BC [chart 12A.p.20] and restarts with **Belli Mawre.** In some text or charts he was known as Bili/Billi or Helli who became in the 1st century, Great Sovereign Lord of the Celtic Britons and the Eastern section of the Sicambrian Franks and as you can see integrated with the nations of Shem, [**Noah's** second son].

You will note this chart show that Belli Mawre was the grandfather of Arch druid Bran/Bron the Blessed and son in law of Joseph of Arimathea. We could not establish the origins of **Beli Mawre** but the written accounts which we have included above gives a fair indication of his family genealogy. [See chart.6 p.8. **Ashkenaz**].

One important fact we discovered during our research, by looking at the details of the Merovingian and the Sicambrian Franks we noted [as on the previous page], in the dynasty of the Merovingian's, most royal lines considered their family stemmed from a Messianic source and gained this not by appointment or coronation, but by claiming Messianic right through kings of past generations from the succession of King Faramund. Retaining this right caused serious disputes, and intrigue and violence between them and the Sicambrian who eventually displaced the Merovingian's as the power base of the Kings of the Franks.

We have included all we have managed to find but would be grateful for any further information to add to this. From c 450 – 750AD, national and international struggles for power, raids and invasions created the wholesale destruction of historical records, which would have been priceless today.

This with widespread illiteracy, the lack of cultural activity, disease [especially the black plagues] and war, the western nations lost ties with their eastern brothers. This period became known as the 'Dark Ages' and has clouded memory; even the most formidable leaders of this time are not known. There are several different accounts of these early historical writings depending of the allegiance of the writer and conflicting historical accounts we therefore have tried to keep as far as possible to proven facts using Manor Rolls and other reliable sources of information.

We have accepted accounts that seem to fit the time and circumstance of the subject concerned but do realize that many historians will have strong leanings to one account or the other depending on their point of view, and the various sources where they acquired their information and we respect their opinions.

FIRST PROGRESS CHART
Chart 8
You are here

*ADAM = EVE
4026 BC [approximately]

2370 years to flood
Noah p.8 cht. 5

Japheth	Shem	Ham.
Ashkenaz	Issue	Issue

East Franks   Teutonic races see p. 10 chart 7   *West Franks
also page13

Sicambrian Franks   Sicambrian
and Merovingian's Franks

Beli Mawre   Merovius

[Kings of France]   Kings of Norway/ Sweden   ** [Kings of Italy]

The Valoise   Jarl's of The Orkneys   The Valoise

Gisselle	=	***Rollo	=	Popea
daughter of Of King		Norwegian Viking		daughter of Beringa
Charles [The Simple]		and 1st Duke of Normandy		Count of Bayeaux

Emma = William Longsword = Sporta   The Crispin's /Malet's

Kings & Queens   The Mortimers   de Dallings /Bulwer
of England

The Ward's / Lacon chts.   The Bulwer's Hainford
Money/Loveday / Baxter   Bulwers / Williment

Ernest Henry Loveday Baxter = Annie Maud Bulwer
[Our father]   [Our mother]

2007 AD
Queen Elizabeth 2nd   The Baxter's
Chapters nine and ten

The only record of ancient names we could find was in the bible, until the time of Beli Mawre [Lord of the Celtic Britons]. Historical records are unable to follow the Celtic main family lines because of tribal warfare that raged across the European scene until just before the time of Christ and the arrival of Beli Mawre whose descendant married the daughter of Joseph of Arimathea. From the time of Beli Mawre the lines become contemporary. [See our main chart.11A. p.20]

Note; The chart above is not complete, as there was not enough space * for full account of first recorded names see page 5 chart 2
Note; list of developing nations from Ham Shem and Japheth see pages 7,10,13

Sicambrian tribes who changed name to Franks in 11 BC
[See Francus below]   Chart 9

Antenor   [d 443BC] was King of the Cimmerians of Scythia in the region of the Back Sea] .
.   decendant. from the Royal Trojan dynasty

Marcomer   [d 412 BC] moved the Cimmerians from the Black Sea to West Friesland and Holland, .
.   across the Rhine to conquer Northern Gaul

Antenor   [d 385 BC] married Cambra a tribal Queen after whom the Sicambri were named

Priamus   [d 358 BC] introduced the new covenant [Newnige] and the Saxon language

Helenus   [d339 BC] priest of the Arcadian sea god Pallas

Diocles   [d300 BC] aided Saxons against the Goths and southern Gaul

Bassanus   [d 250 BC] built the city of Bassanburge

Magnus   = Norwegian Princess

Clodimer   [d 232 BC] assisted the Saxons and Thuringians against the Gauls

Nicanor   [d 198 BC] married daughter of British chief Elidure.

Marcomer   [d 170 BC] defeated Romans, Gaul's and Goths

Clodius   [d 159 BC] withstood further invasions by Romans and Gaul's

Antenor   [d 143 BC] concluded a piece treaty with the Gaul's

Clodimer   [d 123 BC] Gaul's broke treaty but further incursions were repelled

Merovius   [d 95 BC] Led army of 22,000 against Roman centers in Italy and over through Bohemia

Cassandra [d 74 BC] fought alongside King Hamecus of Thuringa and King Arabius

Antharius [d 39BC] withstood invasions by Julius Caesar

Francus   [d 11 BC] issued an order changing the tribal name from Sicambri to Franks, and led a
[Francio]   Frankish-Saxon army of 300,000 against the Roman's. Made a perpetual league with
            the German Princes

Clodius   [d 20 AD continued to withstand Roman invasions, drove Nero's Legions out of Metz and
            Trier
Antenor   [d 69 AD]

Ratherus   [90AD] ratified league with Germans and Saxons

Richemer   [d 114 AD] continued war against Romans and Goths

Odomar   [d 128 AD] had peace treaty with Romans and Goths

See chart 11page 20 for continuation from Odmar

We started in 1986 in total ignorance in what lay before us, and have checked and rechecked a vast amount of historical data, some of which has lain undetected or used as specialist material in a variety of places. It has provided us with many hours/years! In fact more than twenty-one years, of amusing, very difficult and frustrating, but exciting research. As you can imagine it has caused many heated discussions, sometimes at 3am in the morning [much to the disgust of our disgruntled spouses] in order to research and co-ordinate all the facts we found.

To be able to follow this text and fully understand the sequence of all the family structures we think it is important when reading the text you carefully study the charts. In the next few pages we have outlined the structure of the book so it can be more easily followed through the various stages of these lineages.

Due to the many families concerned, we have followed just a few of the numerous families that were listed and dealt with each main branch separately. We have tried as far as possible to keep these individual families grouped together and also to show how our various ancestors relate by marriage. Due to the numerous paths one could follow in our family lineage charts, to assist you in searching for your own connections the lineage we have used we have highlighted [the main charts only] in **blue** and others in different font. In the text our ancestor's names are in **black** bold print [when we remembered to do this!]

Our first lineage charts will be of collective families and royal lineage, but later there are two charts that give a single line from Joseph of Arimathea through Rollo the Norman Viking to our present family. It is an example of the many different families that can be followed through various grandparents. Coming down to mediaeval times, documents were available in which references were made to earlier writings.

One thing we gleaned about medieval times was there were no official registers of births marriages or deaths; those that were recorded were done unofficially by many of the leading families in the areas in which they lived. Some of these can still be found in the missals and Psalters of the fifteenth century; it was an entirely personal affair.

Most of these records were destroyed when King Henry the 8th made a break with the Catholic Church to obtain his divorce from Catherine of Aragon. He destroyed buildings and seized the wealth that was owned by the monasteries and churches. During the 1530's Thomas Cromwell a Londoner of humble origin [who worked for Henry 8th under the minister Cardinal Wolsey], revolutionized national administrative procedures and recordings.

Thomas Cromwell Earl of Essex
1452 – 1540
The start of modern archives

Thomas Cromwell saw that monks could no longer be protected by the Pope when Henry became head of the Church of England, and could seize their land and treasures. Cromwell also brought in the official register by injunction in 1538 AD when an order was made for religious leaders in every parish to keep a record of these events. In recent times all the manorial and court registers were instruments of genealogical records, which were collated to be kept in municipal government archives.

Thomas Cromwell   Plate 2
Artist's impression

Today, the head of every family is responsible by law to register births, marriages and deaths. Modern registrars make use of census and electoral rolls. Private firms also conduct surveys to evaluate lifestyles and eating habits to ascertain the present material needs of the population to forecast future production targets. Thomas Cromwell established a corps of civil servants to administer efficient record keeping but after promoting Henry's marriage to Anne of Cleves in 1540 he was convicted of treason and beheaded.

At first, you might wonder why we have included what seems a great amount of national and local history. We have deliberately done this, first of all it links in with our families, made it more interesting and it also explains how and why our, and perhaps your, ancestors arrived on these shores and added new names to our family tree. So we have decided to start from the beginning assisted by the comments contained in books, like "Bloodline of the Holy Grail", Inquisitions, Manor Rolls, Pipe Rolls, Wills and other reliable sources.

As you will see it was very difficult to keep trace of family lines during some periods of time, particularly after the Norman invasion when name changes took place to deliberately deceive the King and those in authority, mostly to avoid paying taxes or punishment when opposing his rule. We apologise for the fact that we have at times not used date order in our text but this was unavoidable due to the history of families that co-existed at the same period of time. There were also times of plagues and civil war etc. The further back in time the more difficult it became, as a real detective story, needing the same type of approach, presenting a huge mammoth task of letter writing and research.

Reading and constantly re-assuring the Bedford and Norwich librarians that the many history books that we had on loan for **oh'so** many years were still in existence. Visits to public buildings and graveyards for clues where local communities with dutiful suspicion eyed these strangers who were studying details of their residents long departed.

Gathering the facts was a long hard grind, though we did find help through a very able researcher, Mrs. G. McKenna (Family Research) who earned our grateful thanks. We sincerely hope you will track them using the charts as we have done, and enjoy reading about these families.

We must emphasize again these should be used with the written account to find the time period and the people mentioned, also help you to assess how these particular events must have affected those who lived then. It also gives us a rough idea of the actions and decisions they took that affect our lives today, and perhaps you could visit the historical sites where people once lived, loved, laughed, cried, then faded into history.

There are four principal family charts in this book marked A, B, C. and D. Chart 11A page 20 starts with Beli Mawr the Celtic Lord of the of the Britons, which leads to Faramund and the French royal families; Chart 13B p.45 continues with the Merovingian Kings and the Carolingian line; Chart 17 C page 63 continues bringing us to the marriage of Rollo [Norway] and his two wives Giselle [French royal line] and Popae [Italian royal line] Chart 22 page 69 splits into two separate lines leading to Giselle [what we believe to be our fathers line; not yet proved] and Popae our mothers line.

As can be seen by consulting chart A. page 20 the first recognizable names start to appear showing British descent down to the Arthurian line. In the 4th century the Sicambrian Franks were in the Rhineland where they had moved from Pannonia in 388 AD. Their chiefs were Genobaud, Marcomer [deposed. 414], and Sunno [deposed.414].

These leaders established their seat in Cologne in the region of Germania, over the next century their armies invaded Roman Gaul then overran Belgium and Northern France. The charts on pages 25-13 are the early accounts of nations as detailed in "Insight on the Scriptures" 1988 The Watchtower Bible and Tract Society of New York.

*See chart for the Dynasty of Saxe Coburgh and Gotha. Page 51 chart 15

'Bloodline of the Holy Grail'
By Laurence Gardner
Definition of the various lines leading down into our own

Laurence Gardner is prior of the Celtic Church's Sacred Kindred of St. Columba and internationally known sovereign and Chivalric. He has produced the above book that contains charts, which are extremely intriguing, and are of great value to all historians and genealogists today; we recommend that it should be used in conjunction with our book.

He made use of his access to a variety of records and state annals, describing how the Sicambrian line of the Franks from whom France got its name, [by acquiring it from the Chief Francio who died in 11 BC]. The city of Paris named after him was established by the 6th century Merovingian's and bears the name of Prince Paris, the son of Priam of Troy who caused the Trojan War because of his liaison with Helen of Sparta.

This book "Bloodline of the Holy Grail" has been a valuable guide for us with all of its charts and the ancient written history of mankind. From this book we have derived our own charts using some of his extensive information with our research, some devised from early biblical history. This was purposely done to show how our family flows from one chart to another; in a continuous lineage that ultimately converge into two major Valoise families from three separate royal lines.

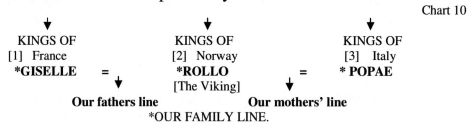

Chart 10

KINGS OF	KINGS OF	KINGS OF
[1] France	[2] Norway	[3] Italy
*GISELLE =	*ROLLO	* POPAE
	[The Viking]	
Our fathers line		Our mothers' line

*OUR FAMILY LINE.

The chart above show these three family lines that will in later pages conjoin once again with the marriage of our own parents. There are many family names in our charts like Mortimer, Crispin, Dalling, Bulwer, Valoise, Earl, Wiggett, Elwin, Paul, Fearnly, Johnson, Billing, Malet, Bintree, Shrimpling, Rook, Dickerson, Godred, Ferrer, Roper, Ward, Wodehouse, Smith, Plowright, Rice, Chapman, Williment, Claxton, Money, Loveday, Hart, Willimott, Hill, Carter, Thompson, Moore, White, Webster, Rix and yes, even Baxter and many more.

We have also included extended family branches, hoping it will enable many more people to link into our family tree and discover their own ancestors. We think it will prove an exhilarating journey, full of stories, excitement and surprises.

TRIBES THAT LIVED IN
SAXON BRITON

We briefly leave the discussion of the buildup of individual tribes and their sources, to begin the examination of national events and the roles individuals and family members played in these. The main flow of the story starts here.

*The Belgae, who started to arrive in 200 BC were fine craftsmen, had a tribal aristocracy and were ruled by hereditary chiefs. Homer the Greek philosopher sang their tribal songs, and the stories of King Arthur stemmed from them. The Celts, who probably originated from the Steppes of Russia, were a people of mixed origin, settling in Europe before 1 BC and were in the majority there forming large numbers of independent tribes. No distinction was made between men and women in the roles they played in their communities, they were all warriors.

Plate 3

Tribal Location; these were the main tribes that settled here but the tribe that interested us most was the Iceni who occupied East Anglia

Our country at this time was subjected to the influx of other tribes marauding, plundering and stealing mostly along the coast. Successful bands of these raiders stayed to lay claim to the territory that they took, jealously guarding their spoils, always fighting and formed tribes keeping the names they had before.

King Lud, grandfather of the mighty **Cymbeline** [father of Caracticus] was Pendragon head and King of Briton during the life of Jesus. [See our chart A11.p.20] these kings were appointed by Druid elders and were not dynastic. Caracticus was the governor of the Belgic Celtic and all the other tribes the Catuvellaun. He ruled from his his seat at Colchester, which they named Camulod [Belgic], this name Camulod meant curved light. Later it came to be known as the city fort [also called a court where the king resided]. It was the most impressive Iron Age fort in the land and similar to the one described in the tales of King Arthur.

*See chart A 11 page 20 for Penarden and Cymbeline.

THE ICENI TRIBE

The name Iceni / Eceni, whichever way you prefer to say it, means the tribe of the sharp swordsmen, which tells us that they knew how to use iron and were the largest and most powerful tribe in East Anglia. They were one of the many tribes that came from the continent and were descendants of Cymbeline. [See our chart 11A page 20] from High King Beli Mawre Lord of the Celtic Britons].

The Iceni were a splendid looking race, red/ blonde hair (Titan), tall with vivid blue eyes, large limbs, courageous and taking pride in their strength. Historian Amminiaus Marcillainius said, a whole troop of men would not be able to withstand a single Gaul if he called his wife to assist him, swelling her neck, gnashing her teeth, brandishing her arms and flexing them to enormous size, striking blows and kicks like so many missiles from the string of a catapult.

Iceni costume   Plate 4

Our research has shown there were various conflicting accounts regarding the Iceni tribe, who are said to have made their large and principal encampment in an *area of fertile very open land between what is now Norwich and Stoke Holy Cross [known as Caistor St. Edmund] and also occupying large tracts of East Anglia. They lived apart from the other clans and had their own government and laws. These tribes fought between themselves and were isolated from Europe by the sea, but soon envious eyes would alter their way of life.

They were reputed to be very skilled horsemen, equine breeders and charioteers, which was later reflected in their style of warfare using this ability to cut to pieces a whole Roman legion. The Saxons also found this form of transport suited their way of fighting, fast and high above the foot soldier. As you will read the Roman's defeated all these tribes, including

Iceni Chariot   Plate 4 [a]

the Iceni who became a client kingdom of the Roman Empire, but this was not to last.

*Caistor St. Edmund is only five miles from where we lived as children and we spent many happy hours swimming in the river at the spot where, in all probability those Iceni and Romans did the same, all those years ago

CHART A; MAIN FAMILY LINEAGE FROM EARLY TIMES

See chart 6 Japheth page 8   <u>Use in conjunction with cht.B.p.45</u>   **Chart 11**

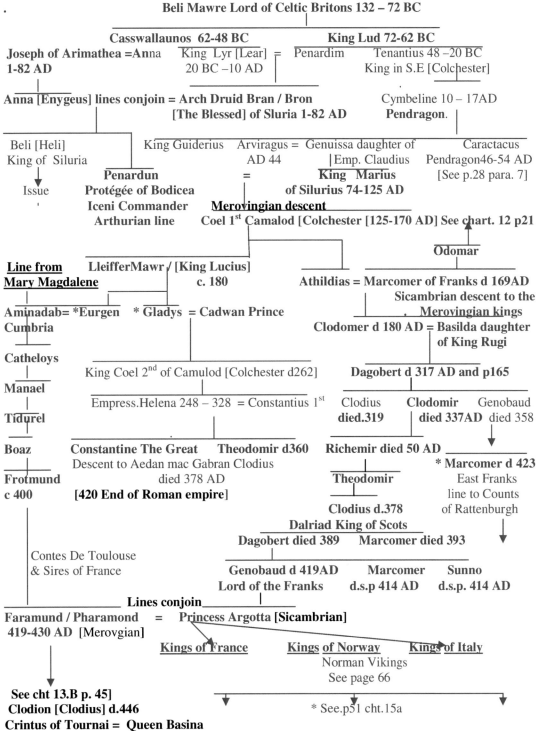

Beli Mawre Lord of Celtic Britons 132 – 72 BC

Casswallaunos 62-48 BC   King Lud 72-62 BC

Joseph of Arimathea =Anna   King Lyr [Lear] = Penardim   Tenantius 48 –20 BC
1-82 AD   20 BC –10 AD   King in S.E [Colchester]

Anna [Enygeus] lines conjoin = Arch Druid Bran / Bron   Cymbeline 10 – 17AD
                 [The Blessed] of Sluria 1-82 AD   Pendragon.

Beli [Heli]   King Guiderius   Arviragus = Genuissa daughter of   Caractacus
King of Siluria   AD 44 | Emp. Claudius   Pendragon46-54 AD
                                   King Marius   [See p.28 para. 7]
Issue   Penardun   of Silurius 74-125 AD
           Protégée of Bodicea   **Merovingian descent**
           Iceni Commander   Coel 1st Camalod [Colchester [125-170 AD] See chart. 12 p21
           Arthurian line
                                                              Odomar
Line from   LleifferMawr / [King Lucius]
Mary Magdalene   c. 180   Athildias = Marcomer of Franks d 169AD
                                              Sicambrian descent to the
Aminadab= *Eurgen   * Gladys = Cadwan Prince   . Merovingian kings
Cumbria   Clodomer d 180 AD = Basilda daughter
                                                    of King Rugi
Catheloys
          King Coel 2nd of Camulod [Colchester d262]   Dagobert d 317 AD and p165
Manael
          Empress.Helena 248 – 328 = Constantius 1st   Clodius Clodomir Genobaud
Tidurel   died.319 died 337AD died 358
Boaz   Constantine The Great   Theodomir d360   Richemir died 50 AD
        Descent to Aedan mac Gabran Clodius   * Marcomer d 423
Frotmund   died 378 AD   Theodomir   East Franks
c 400   [420 End of Roman empire]   line to Counts
                                          Clodius d.378   of Rattenburgh
                                       Dalriad King of Scots
                                  Dagobert died 389 Marcomer died 393
        Contes De Toulouse
        & Sires of France   Genobaud d 419AD   Marcomer   Sunno
                              Lord of the Franks d.s.p 414 AD d.s.p 414 AD
                    Lines conjoin
Faramund / Pharamond = Princess Argotta [Sicambrian]
419-430 AD [Merovgian]
                   <u>Kings of France</u> <u>Kings of Norway</u> <u>Kings of Italy</u>
                                   Norman Vikings
                                   See page 66
See cht 13.B p. 45]
Clodion [Clodius] d.446   * See.p51 cht.15a
Crintus of Tournai = Queen Basina
Note; - We have emphasised our family line in bold blue and show the interlinking of families by
marriage [sometimes names are omitted due to lack of space] The above chart is a derivation
from charts in Laurence Gardner's book p.236 and p197 For family of Eugen = Aminodab also
family of Mary Magdalene continued from chart. 3. p.6. of our book. Note;-* Line down from
Genobaud d 358 include Dagobert d 379, Clodius d 389, Marcomer d.404, Marcomer d.423 Lord
of the East Franks, leads down to the counts of Rattenberg on *Chart B.16. p.45. to King Clovis.
This chart also shows many different paths all leading to our present family and therefore all in
blue.

By studying our chart 11. [A] page 20 we find three family lines, one starting with Odomar whose son the Sicambrian chief Marcomer, Lord of the Franks [eighth in descent from Francio c130AD. d169 AD [Arimathaic line], married Athildais sister to King Lucius. Eurgen of the Royal descent married Aminidab [Christine line] son of Joshue.

Another Sicambrian descendant was Genobaud whose daughter Argotta married King Faramund/Pharamund 419/430 and was a descendant of Boaz Anfortus also on chart A.11 p.20

The Merovingian heritage was strictly adhered to and Faramund was cited to be the true Patriarch of the French Monarchy mentioned again later, which merges into the *Allyne/Alleyne/Elwyn families.

Chart 12

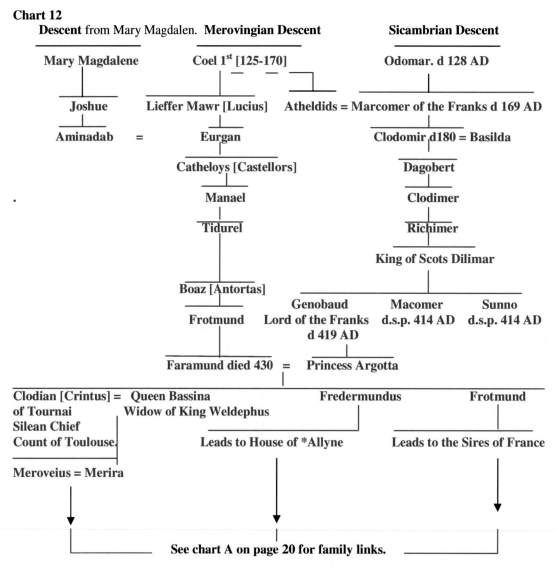

*Ancient house [in bold print] later to marry into the Bulwer family

The chart on the previous page describes the family line for the house of **Alains/Allyne/Elwyn Alains** whose descendant later became King **Alleyn** of the Bretons d.580 AD. Among his descendants were Lancelot and Galahad, other lines of this family are included in the kings of Scotland Wales and France which also mentions the names of Caractacus son of Cymbeline, [on chart A]. Bodicea and Alleyn, the ancient house mentioned when **Jone Alleyn/Elwyn** married **Simon Bulwer** in 1510 AD.

Chart B p.45 includes **Charles Martel** [reputed to be son of **Pepin 2nd**] and their related families from King and Emperor Charlemagne to King of France, **Charles the Simple** whose daughter **Giselle** married **Rollo.** We have concluded this probably is our father's line, which shows how several families' lines link together. In later historical records we found so much to intrigue us in our own history involving Kings and other VIPs living in Norfolk, such as **Thurold/Turold** [Sheriff of Buckenham also later Lincolnshire] our mother's lineage. **Hereward the Wake, William Dalling, Turold's** sister **Lady Godiva** and many others**.**

King Edmund who lived at Reedham, King Harold Godwin, [not relatives] who in their own times created so much history that we feel no one can ever again say, "Nothing ever happened in Norfolk". Much of the text might seem irrelevant to you at the moment but it is deliberately included, as you will find it forms the written history of part of our family line, or has close connection with them and links with other lineage's.

CHRONOLOGY 700BC - 616 AD
THE FORMING OF EUROPE

700BC   Celtic tribes [Kelts] arrived from central Europe and settled in Briton developing their culture through the Iron Age and expanded their tribes till they controlled most of Briton renaming it B'tithain meaning covenant land.

400BC   Invasion of Europe by the Celts.

200BC   Belgae tribes arrive.

132 BC   The beginning of the house of **Sax-Coburgh**.

The Roman Involvement in Britain

55 BC   Julius Caesar sent Giuis Volusenus to assess the shoreline to find suitable anchorage and beaches for disembarking troops.

54 BC   Julius Caesar invades landing at Deal in Kent.

33AD   **Joseph of Arimathea** arrived in Glastonbury Briton in 49AD and a stone can be seen in the south wall of St. Mary's Chapel commemorating this. He died c 82AD. It is reputed that Jesus/ Justice the son of Mary Magdalene also came with him and the hymn "And did those feet in ancient times" originated from this story.

9AD   Germanic nations start to form preceding the fall of Rome.

37-41AD   Emperor Caligula planned an invasion of Britain but never attacked.

43-45AD.   Claudius Caesar sends an expedition to Briton to assess its wealth and plans full-scale invasion. Claudius invades using General Thanet, [born in Lyons 10 BC] to direct troops; in 55BC summoned **Laco** the Procurator of Gaul to join him

61 AD   Revolt against the Roman occupation by the Iceni tribe resulting in catastrophe for the Iceni. Their village at Caistor St. Edmonds near Norwich was destroyed; the Roman's built a fortress on it and named it Venta Icenorum.

69AD   The year of the four Emperors in Rome.

120 AD.   **Allyne** conquered most of Europe.

121-122.AD Building of Hadrian's Wall started.

125 AD.   Venta the Roman fort [near Norwich] now boasted a Roman Basilica, public baths etc. and became the administration centre for the region responsible only to London.

150 AD.   The population of Britain was greatly reduced.

376 AD.   The Huns ravage Europe. In fourth century AD, Franks established themselves in Germania and in the fifth century invaded Belgium and Northern France.

379AD   The decline of the Roman Empire, their army started to depart our shores. Only a nominal force remained.

409 AD.   **Allyne** conquered Spain.

410 AD   Final withdrawal of Roman troops four centuries after Julius Caesar landed in Britain. The main body of Roman soldiers had left Britain and there were new invasions by the Celts. No specific dates can be stated, as there was always some form of intrusion onto the British mainland, sometimes by small bands and occasionally in great numbers. Picts and Scots gain prominence in England and start to attack the South. They settle and started to attract other immigrants; large communities built up. Then came men of three Germanic tribes, Angles, and Old Saxons [Old is a term used for the original tribes of Saxons who invaded our shores] and Jute's. The emergence of Genobaud, Marcomer and Sunno also Pharamund and the nation of France. Goths invade Rome. In Britain, Scots had established tribes and with the Picts overwhelmed Hadrian's Wall. Men from Britain went to Rome seeking help against the Picts and Scot's but were refused because of the attacks on Rome from Attila the Hun who had started invasions all over Europe.

Goths and Visigoths defeat Rome. There was no single Kingship in England as each tribe had their own king. The Jute's held Kent and the Isle of Wight; the Old Saxons became known as the East Saxons and West Saxons. Later becoming shortened to Essex and Wessex. From the Angles came East Angles, Middle Angles, Mercian's, at first all the tribes of the Northumbrians drove way their king's enemies.

CHRONOLOGY DURING TIME OF THE SAXON KING'S 41O-611 AD

434 AD   Jutish mercenaries were invited to defend Britain by King Vortigern (a British King). Led by Hengest and Horsa they arrived in three ships landing at Ebbesfleet in Kent and were given southeastern Briton as a reward on condition they fought off the Picts, which they did successfully. King Vortigern killed. Horsa gave his son Hengest the Kingdom. Anglo Saxon advance halted early in the sixth century, but they won a decisive victory after which there were fifty years of relative peace.

495 AD. Cerdic the Saxon settled in East Anglia, on the island of Jairmud [Cerdic Land now Great Yarmouth]. Goths lose most of Gaul, and Franks gain ascendancy over Northern Tribes.

507 AD. The Franks were the most successful of the barbaric tribes led by Attila the Hun and under **King Clovis** they quickly established a strong nation in northern Gaul, conquering most of the tribes through a succession of outstanding leaders.

517AD. By the end of the century a distinctive Anglo Saxon Britain emerged.

519. AD More Mercian's come to England. **Leofric's** ancestors start to develop tribes.

572 AD Lombard's rule Italy and become powerful, but are defeated by **Charles the Great of** France initiating [the start of the **Valoise** families of France and Italy from which Rollo choose his two wives].

616 AD. Radwald was High King of East Anglia until his death in 624. [High King meant one having authority over other Anglo Saxon-Kings]. He established Edwin as King of Northumbria; Edinburgh Castle which is named after him (Edwin's' burgh) was at this time still part of Northumbria. In the summer of 1939 excavations revealed one of the most significant archaeological discoveries ever found at Sutton Hoo England; the Sutton Hoo ship burial, a treasure trove that had lain undiscovered for 1300 years, which was almost certainly the grave of Radwald.

SEA TRANSPORTATION OF MEN AND MATERIALS
And their means of communication

The enquiring mind, ingenuity, a sense of adventure and the necessities to maintain succession drives mankind to move home many times, which was comparatively easy across a continent. To move a whole tribe or army across the sea in those times was another matter, as the weight of men, horses, food and all the fighting equipment must have been carefully estimated, especially when at war. It demonstrates the skills and endeavors of men to risk their lives to overcome the forces of nature, with all the dangers involved.

These vessels, with their beautiful ornate carving of a swan's head on the stern, were constructed of wood without the use of modern tools and materials designed to withstand the might of the sea, are astounding. Each beam of wood was carefully chosen and hand cut to make a watertight seal using animal's hair, which they compressed between every plank.

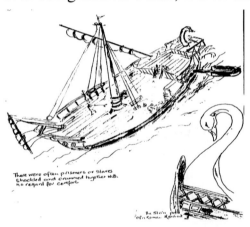

There were often prisoners or slaves shackled and crammed together with no regard for comfort

The Stern of a Roman Merchant

2nd Century Roman Cargo Ship Plate 5

In the second century the crew and other members of the ships company were efficient, well trained and ready to do battle. The strategy of their attacks was well planned and co-ordinated. The Romans not only utilised ships for their conquests they also constructed them to carry a wide range of goods to establish trade links throughout-out the known world of that time, which were bartered for food, weapons or clothing.

Some carried enough grain for a year at sea. The larger merchant ships carried up to 280 people and had a large passenger cabin at the stern where the Roman elite could shelter and rest while their slaves and others toiled, often shackled and crammed together with no regard to the weather conditions, comfort or hygiene.

The easiest job on board was the lead swinger who swung and dropped a lead weight on the end of a rope to judge the depth of water beneath the ship for a safe passage; hence the term used today "He's swinging the lead". They had no communication between ships as we have, once out of sight over the horizon they were alone. Close contact had to be maintained in daylight and darkness when travelling in convoy. High ground was sought after disembarking on land and light beacons maintained communication between groups.

CHAPTER 11

THE ROMANS
Julius Caesar Decides To Reconnoitre Britain55 BC

Julius Caesar was a powerful and an able administrator, but many of his retinue had taken advantage of their positions at court to squander money from the public purse. Immorality and degeneration were affecting life at court, with ambition and jealousy running rampant. This led to many assassinations in Rome over the next hundred and fifty years.

Julius Caesar had money problems   **Inspecting his troops**
Plt.6
Conglomerate of pictures derived from various sources and adapted to fit text.

The conquests of Julius Caesar were the result of the brilliant mind of the man and the strategy he cleverly employed to obtain the wealth of others. He was dictator of Rome four times but he never became an Emperor.

With the national wealth declining in 55 BC he needed to expand his boundaries and decided to reconnoitre Briton and see what assets he could seize by force. He sent Giuis Volusenus, a military officer, in a single ship to scout the English coasts to find suitable beaches and a good anchorage. Giuis reported back that he found the region of Deal most suitable. If he had travelled a few miles further he would have found a more sheltered harbour by the Isle of Thanet [which Claudius would use a century later].

As it turned out the choice of Deal was a bad mistake as on two occasions Caesar's invasion ships were wrecked by bad weather leaving his army stranded. On one such raid, Commius whom Caesar had sent as an envoy to win over the tribes by negotiation, failed in his task and was taken prisoner. Initially these raids were mere forays to see what they could take, never intending to stay, as there was too much unrest in Gaul.

Some information above from * 'See Roman Briton' by Leonard Cottrell and 'The Roman Invasion of Britain' by Graham Webster

The reports Julius Caesar received were ideal for his purposes, the tribes appeared to be very wealthy, had little communication between each other, and acted independently against enemies whilst constantly warring, which made them vulnerable to attack. He decided his visit had to be a precursor for future large-scale invasion, so returned to Rome to mobilize his armies.

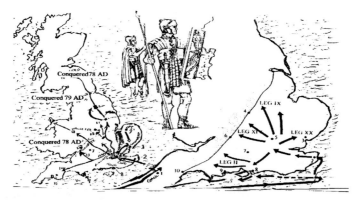

The Roman invasion army quickly penetrated deep inland and crushed resistance   Plate 7
A conglomerate of pictures derived from various sources and adapted to fit Text

*In 54 BC he intended to invade and attacked with five legions of soldiers (one legion = ten cohorts = 4,800 men = six centurion's = 480 men = total of 20,000. The first cohort was different as it had five double centurions). The estuary at the mouth of the River Yare at Yarmouth, Norfolk was much larger than it is today and considered to be of great importance to routes inland, invaluable for surprise attacks against the tribes who had their main towns along its banks. There was also a very large lake in the vicinity of what is presently called Lakenham and Venta [Caistor St. Edmund] both places near what would later be known as Norwich.

The Roman armies were at that time the best fighting force in the world, well organized with each man knowing his function; the ranks in accession were roughly equivalent to a modern army. Milites Gregarius were ordinary Privates, Immunis equivalent to a Lance Corporal, Tesserarius a Sergeant, Optio a Lieutenant, Signifer a Colour Bearer, Beneficiarius a Sergeant promoted by recommendation, Cornicularius in charge of administration. A Centurion was a commissioned officer and company commander of about eighty to a hundred men.

A few soldiers rose through the ranks by achievement, all others by direct appointment such as the position of a Senior Centurion, Primus Pilus, similar to a Colonel or Brigadier who wore shoes instead of sandals, carried swagger sticks and was almost certainly of noble rank or very close to Caesar.

Some of this information taken from 'Seeing Roman Britain' by Leonard Cottrell

There was serious trouble with the Gauls and the army had to return to France but before leaving Britain the Romans extracted promises that the tribute would continue to be paid regularly and tried to persuade the tribes to live peacefully. Then taking a few slaves with them they departed these shores.

Caesar's assumption of dictatorial powers created fear and distaste within a senatorial group and a plot was hatched for his assassination. Servillus Casca cut him down at the foot of the statue of Pompey on the Ides [15th March 44 BC] in a Senate's meeting room where other plotters Brutus and Cassius stabbed him repeatedly. Octavius Caesar who changed his name to Augustus Caesar, succeeded as ruler aged only 19 years old and died (29/33 AD) shortly after taking the census of Jews.

Tiberius his stepson took over from him and was in power when Jesus was put to death. His fanatically suspicious nature over possible assassination plots caused others to die but helped him to survive. With all the murders and intrigues in the court of Rome it was not surprising that Claudius was reluctant to be next in power.

EMPEROR CLAUDIUS
[b.10 BC-54 AD]

Approximately one hundred years had elapsed since Julius Caesar returned home, tribute from Britain had ceased and all the old inter-tribal warfare had re-started. This was noticed by Rome, who feared this fighting would result in the emergence of one powerful leader, which was decidedly not in their interests as divide and rule was their policy.

The bad situation existing in Rome before the Claudian invasion of Britain was caused by deliberate acts of treachery. Those with power created deceit, betrayal, adultery, greed and a lust for more control; this was craftily driven by the ambitions of their wives. Added to this, Emperor Claudius was in need of both money and a victory to bolster his image, so took action and sent Roman general Aulus Plautius to Britain with several legions of soldiers. Claudius who was in Gaul at the time arrived shortly after with reinforcements, 24,000 men of the 2nd 9th and 20th Legions.

Landing in the Southeast they were confronted by *Caractacus and Togodumnus his brother, princes of the land of the Catuvellauni who fought a hard battle but were defeated. Among Senators in the Claudian invasion party was Decimus Valerius Asiaticus, immensely wealthy and the first Gaul to be made Consul who was too powerful to remove, but too dangerous to leave behind when they invaded Britain.

* 'Seeing Roman' Britain' by Leonard Cottrell. Also see chart p.20 son of Cymbeline descent from Beli Mawre Lord of Celts.

LACO TO BRITAIN

Adulterous family problems and the fear and suspicion of each other put Claudius in a difficult situation. Claudius did not capture all of Britain as the Celts disappeared into the hills and mountains of Scotland, Wales, and Cornwall so most of the population of the lower lands came from the invaders.

After the defeat of *Caractacus and the capture of Camulodunum /Colchester, Vespasian was put in command of the 2nd legion, to subdue what is now equal to the modern counties of Somerset and Dorset. Aulus Plautius was made Governor with a Procurator under him to collect taxes in the former Catuvellauni capital Camulodunum.

We noted with great interest that the Roman Emperor Claudius summoned **Laco/Lacon** the **Procurator of ***Gaul to do duty in Britain with a large group of advisors and Senators. This was to be the war council that made tactical decisions on the future of this country.

Laco had been most helpful to General Aulus Plautius in the invasion, as he was familiar with all the ports of embarkation in that area. **Laco** as procurator was also given the task to report on law and order and as he was familiar with the tax system and had control over financial matters so he could have been indirectly involved with the financial crisis connected with Queen Boudica. We hesitate to mention that this possible relative of ours was one of the first official tax collectors in this country! Sorry but someone had to do it!

Most of the tribes who were defeated lost all of their possessions and independence. The Iceni and Trinovantes sued for peace and although they paid tribute to the invaders, kept their wealth, ruled themselves and were obliged to stop intertribal fighting. Claudius stayed only 16 days returning to Rome to sort out national and domestic problems.

Messalina the wife of Claudius became involved with the nephew of an important man called Pallus; for some reason she poisoned the mind of Claudius against Pallus's nephew who was executed with Asiaticus and Vinicus. Other Senator's also fell foul of the greed and jealousy of Messalina.

* 'Seeing Roman' Britain" by Leonard Cottrell
** Ancient scribe, Dio who also mentioned a certain Laco who had been Praefectus of Gaul at the time of the invasion.
See also "The Roman Invasion of Britain" by Graham Webster
***An area north of Italy and southern France. Heavily populated by Italian immigrants and annexed to Italy in 42 BC. A very productive region prosperous from the time of Julius Caesar].

The Emperor no doubt fed up with her intrigues took a new wife Agrippina. Many had reason to assassinate Claudius including his new wife; her secret ambition was to install her son Nero as Emperor.

Junius had married Claudius's daughter Octavia and was legally next in line to be Emperor but the plotting of Agrippina against Junius unjustly made Claudius turn against him and Junius committed suicide. Claudius's natural son Brittanicus was too young at this time. It was the fulfillment of Agrippina's conniving mind that having persuaded Claudius to name Nero as his successor, when Claudius returned home she arranged for him to be poisoned. Having rid herself of Junius, and, now Claudius, gained her ambition when her son Nero became Emperor. The Roman General Aulus Plautius was left in charge of mopping up operations in Britain.

CAESAR NERO 37-68 AD
Storm Clouds Gather Humiliation and a sad fate awaits the Iceni's

The Druids were systematically killed off by the Romans at the beginning of 59AD and the land around Colchester/Camulodunum was allotted mainly to veterans of the legion who in return were expected to report any signs of revolt or resistance to Roman rule. The new Emperor, 17 year old Nero lacked confidence and reluctantly took advice from Seneca the Philosopher and Burus a Praetorian Prefect. However his natural disposition resented this and he dismissed anyone who tried to assist or in the slightest way opposed his will. Due to Nero's habits of gross debauchery and profligate spending, even after having grabbed national wealth, he started to look elsewhere for funds to make up the deficit. Once more attention was drawn towards the Iceni tribes in Britain who he knew were very rich.

*Boudica, Queen of the Iceni's was tall, and in appearance terrifying, her eyes fierce, her voice harsh. A strong stubborn woman married to a weak husband [King Prasutagus] who the Romans treated harshly to extract details of his wealth causing him to commit suicide. It was common practice that legacies were acquired by the Emperor, including a share in one's will and by Roman law on intestacy all the deceased's property went to the state. In contrast Queen Cartimandua of the Brigantes in the north betrayed her people, signed a treaty with the Romans and handed over Caratacus of the Catuvellauni who had been resisting the invasion of Romans into Wales, earning her the name of traitor among the British. Caractacus was later paraded through the streets of Rome in chains.

*In various history books or inscriptions, the name of the Iceni Queen is spelt Bodicea / Boudica. The variation in the spelling is due to a misprint of the text of Tacitus during its transmission from Roman times and has no direct association with the Queen of the Iceni Tribe.[From 'Roman Britain' by Peter Salway. P113 footnote ISBN 0-19-821717]

Obviously the Emperor sensed there was much more wealth for the taking and considered that he had not received his fair share of the late King Prasutagus estate. He sent the District Procurator to find out more about the real riches of the Queen but she refused to answer their questions and reaped the terrible consequence. Nero who was a cruel grasping man ordered his men to beat her; and rape her daughters before her eyes. The Queen and her tribe were so incensed that it drove them and Trinovantes to a plan of action that would rid them of Roman tyranny.

While the other tribes were gloating over her downfall Boudica was ready to avenge her children who could have married powerful nobles, restoring the sovereignty and freedom of the Iceni Tribe. Calling her army before her she stood in her chariot, the air was charged with emotion as she described the evil events done to her family and their Queen. Knowing that life under the Romans would never be the same, she reminded them what it would be like if the invaders were permitted to stay. She goaded them on, their anger and grief joining with hers.

The early morning sun catching the red/gold of her hair, falling in great swathes down to her waist, turning it into a blaze of light around her head, she looked every inch a Queen. Proud, full of courage, she commanded her men vowed to win their freedom, and believed they had every chance of doing so. Boudica, knowing the Roman General was away quelling trouble in the *north was aware that the soldiers left in the garrison of Camulodunum (Colchester) would be unprepared and disorganised. The time was ripe, so seizing this opportunity she marched her army to attack, yelling her famous war cry * *"Y-gwir erbyn y Byd"* [the truth against the world].

With blind hatred in their hearts for the 2,000 people, including army veterans and pro Roman Britons, who were living there at the time, the fury and sheer numbers of those ranged against them overwhelmed the city. The Roman 1X Hispania legion stationed at Nene marched to defend Camulodunum, but they were ambushed and cut to pieces by Boudica's army who caught the Romans completely off guard. They broke ranks, fleeing the rage of the Iceni and their chariots. They took no prisoners, the Iceni's looted, burned and destroyed. Emboldened with success they marched on to St. Albans and London leaving them both in flames. Their jubilation was short lived however when the Romans swept back with a full legion of the X1V Germania from South Wales, a **12,000 strong, well armed, experienced fighting machine under the command of Suetonius Paulinus, Governor of Britain, prepared for retribution.

***From "Seeing Roman Britain" by Leonard Cottrell ** Stated in various sources ** The numbers involved we noticed varied considerably in various history books.**

DE-FEET OF THE ICENI TRIBE
Their Last Battle

There is no certainty as to the location of the site for this final battle, which took place somewhere in the Midland's or the accuracy of the numbers involved. A leading authority on this subject suggested that it could have taken place in Leicestershire to the South East of Atherstone and close to the line of Watling Street.

**The Iceni's Brave Stand Against A Well Trained And
Equipped Roman Army**

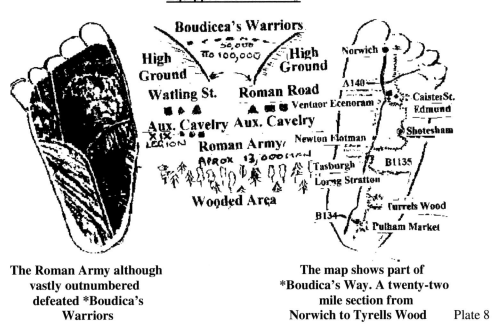

The Roman Army although vastly outnumbered defeated *Boudica's Warriors

The map shows part of *Boudica's Way. A twenty-two mile section from Norwich to Tyrells Wood   Plate 8

The Iceni warriors were defeated and seemed finished as a tribe. The Romans terrorized them in the most barbaric ways possible, fearsome in revenge, adopting a scorched eath policy" they destroyed everything including crops, habitations and possessions. These once proud people were now either slaves, in hiding or dead, very few of their men returned home again to their families and friends; Queen Boudica seeing their torment took poison and died.

The Romans, though cruel in battle were usually kind to those they made slaves and although times were often hard, the Iceni's that did survive regained status quo after about ten years. It was never easy for the Romans, as there was always unrest in Rome and the Middle East. Continual fighting in North Wales and Cornwall together with the 61AD rebellion that occurred in this country had all drained Nero's resources.

Note;-It was directly after this event that Joseph of Arimathea came to England to set up his church at Glastonbury, in spite of the Roman imperialism

* The correct spelling is Boudica but is sometimes spelt Bodicea The variation in the spelling is due to a misprint of the text of Tacitus during its transmission from Roman times and has no direct association with the Queen of the Iceni Tribe

It is possible that before the Iceni rebellion and the ransacking of Colchester, the Roman administration including the Procurators moved from there to London as gold smelting activity was discovered on the site of the latter and an official iron punch used for Gold marking was also found. The Roman's deliberately moved their Procurator's around the country to effectively stop any fraternization. Being tax collectors it was not in the best interest of the Emperor for Procurator's to get friendly with those around them, so **Senator Laco/Lacon** must have moved about a bit before settling in Shropshire using London as a base.

In conclusion, in respect of the above events, after their initial invasion the Roman army defeated most of the tribes, and gave the Iceni's their freedom to avoid further trouble, but when the conquerors greed went too far the Iceni people reacted violently. It was at this time that Nero set fire to Rome in order to build his Golden Palace, which he planned to cover half of the city, not only to impress his subjects and visitors, but also to occupy the imported population in building the palace, as these people were becoming restless.

Tons of stone transported by ship and cart, often from distant shores was used to build his new palace. Marble of rich colours from Africa, France and elsewhere was obtained with only primitive means of haulage, using manual strength and ingenuity. This certainly did not allow for a Health and Safety Act! "Oh well, we've just lost another slave!" must have been their attitude. A huge lake was formed within a park where wild animals were allowed to roam which in later years was filled in and the Coliseum built on the spot.   Nero has gone down in history as a mad tyrant, one of the worst emperors and when the Praetorian Guard acclaimed Galba as Emperor, Nero committed suicide. It seems that he focused his life purely on his own self interest, cruelty and cowardice; most historians seem to find him contemptible.

We must remember that the Romans were the most advanced nation in the world at this time both culturally and materially; able to use their talents to make better lives for themselves. They constructed road networks using natural materials such as wood or granite blocks so that men and materials could be transported very much quicker, especially when the army needed to attend trouble spots.They must have experimented with all available natural resources to better their living environment and as a result form the basic concoctions and formulations of materials we use today. For example, an interesting fact of this time, they found by mixing lime, sand and Pozzolana rock from Northern Italy (a natural volcanic cement) that they had discovered a new building material we know today as concrete.

They put this to good use by pouring it between two walls of brick or stone, which made it immensely strong and gave it a pleasing mellow colour. Some buildings made from this material are still in use today.

*Even human excrement was put to good use for agricultural purposes and urine was used as an ingenious way to treat clothing materials. They discovered that by using stale urine before or at the end of cloth manufacture the ammonia in the urine degreased it, enabling the water based dyes to penetrate deeper into the fibre, also making it supple and less hairy giving the material a lasting colour and texture.

The process of dying cloth is very complex and their ingenuity must be noted; some dyes required a mordant, a chemical used to bind the dye to the cloth such as Alum [iron salts] which is part of the sulphate group. They also used a system of baking murex seashells that produced a chemical that made a purple dye, which they washed from the shells into the human stale urine; it was then heated to obtain a concentrated liquid later known as Royal Tyrian purple.

This important chemical Alum is widely used today in many products and processes such as purifying water, cooking, medicines and the arts. Other coloured dyes were derived from vegetation such as Madder or various Heathers [these materials were also used for bedding and making beer].

Dog excrement was also used as a dye [known as puer or pure] especially white dog poo which was a prized commodity as it had exceptional qualities for tanning. Urine and dog poo became collectable materials in great demand. Urinals were set up to collect the urine, which developed into a flourishing business, incentive payments were made for each bucketful, and the practice soon spread from Rome to Britain.

The Roman Emperor **Vespasian [ruled AD.69-79] reputed to be mean, was renowned for his ability to pocket other peoples cash and when his son criticised him for putting a tax on urine sales, he took a coin from his pocket and replied *"It does not smell bad to me"*.

***In England during Henry 8th's reign, urine was in such great demand the King made a law that urine had to be saved for collection. Even up to the 1800's buckets full of urine were collected by horsedrawn carts in London and elsewhere by collector's called Piss Harry's or Joe's. The incentive payment helped to pay for their next dinner or pint of ale; [men's urine was of better quality due to the hops contained in the beer].

* This section is our interpretation with the help by members of a professional team who kindly agreed to let us incorporate it in this book from a B.B.C. program 'Taking the P**ss Out of London' Radio 4   July 9th and September 28th 2003] **Sources Sueyonius, Vespasian chapter 23 ***From Encyclopedia International

Urine was also found to be an excellent method to obtain sparkling white teeth or removing unwanted wrinkles in women's faces, which gave a taut yet soft skin, but we expect the ladies lover or husband strongly disapproved of this practice. Later there was a shortage of urine during the time of the expansion of the wool industry and as the mills in the north of England became predominant, demand exceeded supply. Ships were used from various ports to transport it and when there were bad conditions at sea, the boats and crew became a floating sewage farm, some recipient ports refusing to welcome them.

To disguise their cargo shippers often labeled the barrels as wine but could not contain the odor and when asked from the jetty what their cargo was they shouted back *"wine"*. The reply from the shore was ***"Are you taking the Piss?"*** which is where this slang expression originated. Even up to the 1970's this [let us say chemical] was being used in some manufacturing processes and is probably still in use today.

You may be wondering as to why we have included this article but we wish to not only to make history and family genealogy more interesting but also to emphasize how man has enriched his life by the use of an enquiring mind and experiments which form a part of our lives today. Perhaps it was the simple act of throwing an article of urine soaked cloth on to the dying embers of a fire containing alum, and after seeing the material turn purple [and realizing he/she had not a health problem] decided to investigate further, made a larger quantity and dipped his clothes in it.

Of course some of the discoveries that we take for granted our ancestors had experimented with and used thousands of years ago, such as the extraction and manufacture of copper, which was probably made before 4000 B.C. The casting of bronze, a mixture of copper and tin, began about 3500-3000 B.C. but it was not until modern times [1825] that Aluminum was discovered, although it is 8% of the earths crust.

We understand [though we have not researched this fact] that many years ago, bark from the Willow tree was used for medicinal purposes and today forms the essential ingredient for a well known drug that many families use today on a daily basis for headache, heart problems etc.

These often primitive and simple experiments have led to great benefits for mankind and each new innovative idea leads into what we have today through the efforts and labours of our ancestors. Most have been for our benefit but some might lead to the path of our own possible destruction. It also proves that the past is always a part of the present.

VENTA ICENORUM
61-367 AD.

The rebellion in 61 AD brought utter subjection to what remained of the Iceni tribe. This cumulated in a final humiliation when the Romans decided to build a fort on the very location which had been their main dwelling place, using those survivors that were left as slave labour to do it.

Considering the scale of the project in building Venta, locating collecting and moving the colossal amount of flints, wood and other materials required without the aid of modern tools is quite impressive. What remains of the defensive walls can still be seen to this day.

The building of Venta a Roman Fort on the very place that the Iceni tribe had their principal settlement. It was a humiliation that the proud Queen and her tribe could not take   Plate .9

The legend goes that after a while the Romans relented in admiration for the late Queen, respecting the strong bond that existed between her and her people, also the brave men who gave their lives; they honoured them by naming the town Venta Icenorum.

Venta Icenoram was laid out in blocks, the streets in grid fashion, stone and brick mansions stood where once the native huts used to be. Later a forum (market place) was established and the town thrived as the centre for trade.

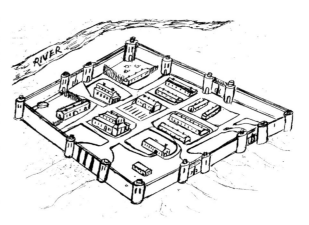

In 125 AD. A Basilica (town hall) was added, also public baths and surplus water was drained into the river Tass.

Typical layout for a Roman Garrison for this time   Plate.10

Venta Icenorum became the command centre for the whole district, responsible only to London, which controlled all Roman activity in Britain. We visited this site and found that it had not changed since we were children; a very marshy area surrounds the site on three sides and the area seemed quite desolate though the busy Norwich outer ring road is nearby.

Many cottage crafts and industries developed in this small town of Venta Icenorum and the surrounding villages. At some unknown date, walls 20ft high complete with towers were built and a ditch 80ft. wide was dug for protection around the perimeter. The main roads led to four gates with bridges into the town; yet by the fourth century the town had fallen into disrepair and decay.

In 150 AD the population of Britain had greatly decreased, those that were left after the plague and famine had to bury their wealth for safety, away from prying eyes and the thieving exploits of the Viking marauders. While Norfolk slowly recovered, Scotland and Wales were still in a state of war.

Venta Icenorum is now a listed historical site that is controlled by the Norfolk County Council and many tourists seek out this very important place just outside the city of Norwich where the ruined walls of the old Roman fort are clearly visible. So if you visit this site, stop and ponder all the things that must have

Recent photograph of section of Ventnor's Plate 11 happened there long ago when

Perimeter walls as it is today it started as a very primitive Iceni settlement and later became a bustling vibrant township with Roman soldier's riding through in armour at a time when Jesus walked the earth.

Before we leave Venta and its people, looking back from our own time we can see that there is much to thank the Roman's for as they not only brought their culture but left a large network of wide roads and trade routes that are still in place today linking our towns and cities. The road from Venta provided the beginning of a little settlement called Norwic, now the thriving city of Norwich. There is not much left of Venta now but an eerie silence remains, brooding on what used to be, and we remember too the happy hours we spent as children on that Tass river bank.

Caistor was a City when Norwich was none
Norwich was built with Caistor stone.
So goes an old Rhyme.

Some of the above information is taken from Reader Digest "When Where Why and How it Happened'.

Venta in the Days of Our Childhood
1940's

Going forward to the days of our childhood, one of our most favoured walking adventures during the hot summer holidays was to go to what we called Bluebell Wood which stood on a steep high hillock [four miles from Norwich]. It was thick with trees and when in season had a carpet of bluebells. The principal railway line to London cut a deep gorge through the middle of the wood, its main part being on the other side of Harford Viaduct.

Looking back we often wonder how we dared to cross the long viaduct to get to the wood, with express trains passing every few minutes. If our parents knew the dangerous risks we took they would have gone berserk.

Our home was about here X

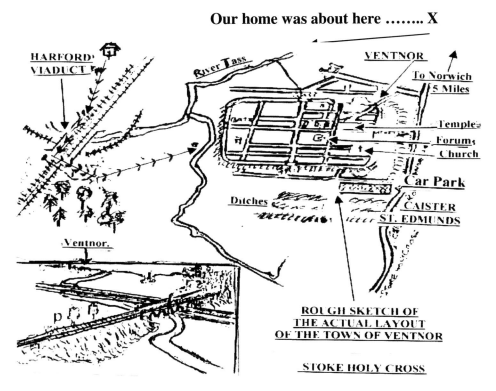

Rough sketch of the Harford Viaduct and the hazardous route the boys took.   Plate 12

Our walk went through a farmers meadow [who we nicknamed Bummy for obvious reasons], which was often flooded by the nearby river Tass and was very dangerous, pitted with deep mud filled holes from which farm animals often had to be pulled out.

There was an old iron railway bridge [which still exists spanning a river] that we eyed with awe; remembering the unfortunate fisherman enjoying the pleasures of fishing from this bridge until a train passed by and the passenger steps of the train removed his head.

Reaching the viaduct, the six arches towered above, spanning another railway line and a wide river. We climbed the steep bank to reach the brick wall of the railway viaduct where we hid in the soldiers' sand bagged trench and waited, listening for express trains to or from Norwich to pass. Sometimes we put a penny on the track and after the train had gone it was collected, squashed to twice its original size.

There was no need to wait long, as the familiar clanking noise became louder and louder. With a belch of steam and smoke the locomotive raced by just three feet away, shaking the ground as it thundered past just above our heads. With us holding our hands over our ears to keep out the deafening noise; in seconds it was gone.

Jumping from the trench we made the dash to reach the far end of the long bridge, falling into the other trench and waited. After the next train had passed we clambered out, crossed the line, up the bank and into the wood. We will always remember the beautiful sight that confronted us, a brilliant blue carpet of bluebells stretched down the slope of the hill, the warming sun casting the long shadows of late spring through the trees before us. Slowly making our way across the field to the riverbank we stripped off, and up to the knees in water, made for the other side with our sandwiches, after a while we paddled to the bend to where it was deep enough to swim.

On one occasion this did not go to plan when the four nude boys sat down on the bank to eat. Noting the look of horror on his brothers' faces, David looked down to see his lower half completely covered in ants as he had unfortunately sat on an anthill. His screams brought the young farmers' daughter running to the scene but she quickly retreated when confronted by the naked boys who quickly dressed themselves and returned home by the same route clutching armfuls of bluebells for their mother.

While spending those many happy hours on that riverbank, we did not realise that we were at the very place where Iceni children, Roman boys and probably **Laco** also did the same thing all those centuries before. Without knowing it we were actually within what had been the Iceni Camp and the Roman Fort of Venta Icenorum.

When we were children the six arches on the viaduct seemed to tower to a great height and remained so in our memory but on a recent visit we were amazed to see that these same arches, though still very high, were much smaller than we remembered in our minds as children. The ground was still marshland and obviously had areas of mud that presented a danger to the unwary walker or animal.

FOR TWO MAGICAL DAYS THE PAST IS REVEALED
Then Disappears Back Into Time

*Found In a Potato field

During July August 1996 there was a countrywide drought that Norfolk shared and the hot dry weather gave Archaeologist's their best opportunity since 1976 for aerial photography of ground markings. [Local authorities also use these conditions to check for any unauthorised building work].

In recent times there have been many media reports on mysterious surface shapes suddenly appearing in isolated fields, causing speculation about visitors from outer space, many are a hoax, but others are genuine aerial photographs that show where bygone settlements had been. One such amazing aerial picture was the image of the remains of a previously unknown Roman fort that they say may provide new thinking on the rebellion of Queen Boudica / Bodicea and her Iceni Tribe of about 2000 years ago. This fort straddled the Roman road (Peddar's Way) in central Norfolk.

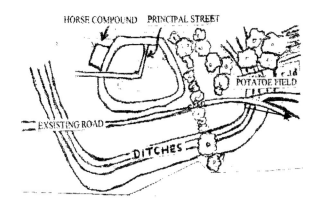

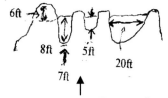

Ditch arrangement drawn from Aerial photograph showing a cross section of the ditches that were used on this site at this time.

Drawn from an aerial photograph of the site   Plate 13
Photo by Derek Edwards. Copyright Norfolk Museums and Archaeology Service.

The images of the original layout were clearly visible and gave up their secrets only because of the extra dry ground conditions at the time, then vanished again into history after two days. Also found in East Norfolk was an Iron Age long barrow and a superb image of the foundations of a Roman Villa. The exact location of this remarkable find has not as yet been revealed due to its probable plundering by souvenir hunters and treasure seekers. From the site layout it is considered to have housed a garrison of about 800 Legionnaires and Cavalry, built 60 – 61 AD to reinforce the Roman authority and repel the Iceni attacks.

*Featured in Eastern Evening News Summer 1996. [Ref. See William Warrenna and Doomsday f .1836 and 1bv i 349. also Freeman's B.E William the Conqueror].

THE ANCIENT GAME OF MERRILLS
Also Known As Nine Men's Morris

This is one of the oldest games in the world and boards have been found dating back 2000 years in Arab mosques. The Vikings and William the Conqueror's soldiers played it. Even sailors aboard Henry 8th ship the "Mary Rose" scratched the playing board on to the top of a barrel. It must have been a very popular pastime and has recently been revived with world championships, so why not give it a try as our ancestors did all those years ago.

How to play.

Take a board designed like the one below. Each player must have a set of nine counters, [each set of a different colour]. The game is played by two people placing counters in turn on the spots shown on the board the aim being to stop the other player getting three mill [counters in a straight line are called a mill]

The three counters must form a line vertically or horizontally

.   Artists impression   Plate. 14   only, diagonals do not count.

Each time a player makes a mill he can remove one of his opponent's counters as long as it is not part of a mill.

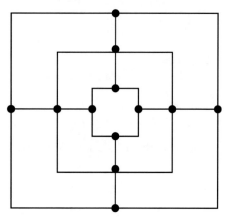

When both players have placed all the counters on the board they can start to move them around and attempt to win his/her opponent's counters each time a mill is made. Counters can only move to one dot at a time, only move along the marked lines and cannot land on his opponent's counters and once taken out of the game do not go back again.

Merrill Board   Plate 14 **a**   When one player has only three counters left she/he can move to any free spot on the board, the other player still has to move their counters one spot at a time. A player loses when either they cannot move or they are down to two counters. Learning to play the game is easy but winning takes many hours of practice.

VISIGOTHS EMERGE TO END THE ROMAN EMPIRE
410 AD

Continuing with our story of the Roman occupation of Britain which had now settled to a more peaceful time, a menacing force was about to erupt and strike a fatal blow to Rome itself. The Goths and Visigoth's were getting stronger and more aggressive and by 376 AD large numbers of Goths were allowed by Emperor Valens to settle near Rome to escape the Huns but were exploited by the citizens and grew very bitter over this treatment. The fanatical self-interest of those who held power in Rome at one stage led to several emperors reigning at the same time divided between Eastern and Western Emperors, the supervision floundered and soon all control was lost. Half a million soldiers and administrators were now needed to protect what was left of Rome's far-flung and declining empire, with their army so stretched out and financial income in chaos, Rome built up massive debts; taxes became intolerable with very little food available. Foreign elements and other imported labour at the very heart of the Roman Empire became very restive, took advantage of the confusion and assisted any attack on Roman rule.

The only solution for Rome to alleviate her problems was to shrink the empire and bring back those citizens that were true to Rome. *After 340AD they started to withdraw their main army from Britain, which was in effect the beginning of the decline of the Roman Empire. The nominal force they left behind soon lost control of the border tribes who became more aggressive. Among those who stayed in Britain must have been some of the descendants of **Senator Laco** who settled in Shropshire, a most difficult and dangerous time for them. The wealthy buried their riches, and as the years rolled by these hiding places were forgotten, today with modern technology the location of these treasures is more easily found, much to the delight and sometimes the dismay of modern historians.

Through lack of funds and manpower the forts and villas became dilapidated, open to attack from marauding tribes. **Hadrian's Wall was deserted and soon hordes of Picts invaded to loot and plunder. The Saxon's found easy access to Britain along the eastern and southern coast in their 'sea-steeds' or 'wave horses' as they called their ships, which were feared for their speed and barbarous attacks. This and the increased violence by the Visigoths in their own country prompted the eventual departure of the small Roman force left in Britain, so in 410 AD they finally withdrew and left to defend Rome itself.

Note: - * + **Emperor Hadrian in 121-122AD built a wall right across the land from Tyne to Solway [still in existence] that effectively held back the hoards of rebels that attacked from the north. 'Roman invasion of Briton by Graham Webster 1980' the Vigils of Rome mentioned on page 197 line 13 also mentioned in various other sources.

The Visigoths under the leadership of **Alaric** inflicted a final devastating attack and humiliating defeat on the Romans. At midnight on the 24th August 410 the City of Rome, after standing unchallenged for twelve centuries fell to Alaric and his army of Visigoths assisted by the many Goths living there that had been Roman slaves and the city was sacked. Roman/Celtic people left behind in Britain were frightened, as there was no protection. This not only caused problems for Rome but also for the people in Britain who sent a deputation to Italy asking for help. At his new capital in Ravenna the Western Roman Emperor Honourius refused their requests as they were also in difficulty. The Visigoths were now in control under Althaulf, [Alaric's brother in law] who took over leadership c.410 AD.

The powerful Roman army was defeated, their empire gone forever. Earlier, Emperor Honorous's sister Maria had married General Stilicho a Vandal and counted on his support. Another sister Galla Placida married General Constantinus later to become Emperor Constantinus III. The Visigoths encouraged the Roman citizens to rebuild their city. After seven years the scars in Rome were barely visible, only the emotional and mental ones remained but the sophisticated culture and the Roman way of life was badly affected by the barbaric ways and customs of their new overlords. Their bodily odours, the way they ate and their drunken parties were not conducive to peaceful living. The Western Empire lasted another sixty years, and then faded. During the next few centuries' new invaders overran Britain, the Celtic/Viking, Saxons' Jutes', Angles' and other invaders ravaged these shores causing turmoil and disputes amongst the various factions.

The Visigoths turned back from Italy and stayed in Gaul until King Euric declared independence and conquered much of Spain, but in 507 AD the Visigoths lost most of Gaul. The Franks were now the most successful of the barbarous Germanic tribes and led by Attila the Hun occupied much of the old Roman Empire. Under **King Clovis** [see p.45 chart 13 B Merovingian Franks] they quickly established a strong nation in northern Gaul, gaining ascendancy over the tribes with a succession of outstanding leaders.[their line of descent were the families of de Razes] heodoric became king in 419 and later many of the beautiful churches in Rome were constructed during his reign; when he died Sigebert (Comte) de Razes took over the Merovingian throne. [As on chart 13 B p.45]

Note The Visigoths under the leadership of Alaric had been demonstrating their power since 9AD, ravaging Media from AD 70 and Europe from 120 AD. In 409 AD they had settled in Spain. (One of their chieftains had been a leader in the Roman army, which invaded England under Julius Caesar 54.AD). The written histories of these times had few sources. One was the Saxon Chronicles that relied on the earlier writings of the Venerable Bede written between the evacuation of the Romans and 731AD, which are important sources of information.

CHRONOLOGY FROM 616 – 878 AD.
ROYAL FAMILY LINES START TO EVOLVE THOUGH FRANCE, ITALY AND NORWAY

616   **Charles the Great** crosses the Alps at Pope Adrian's request and annexes the whole of Lombardy. **Viking Norsemen from Norway**, attack England, Ireland and Europe. **Ingvald Ragnvaldsson** [The Ganger] Viking father to **Rollo** becomes Earl of Orkney (see chart for Norse descent)

796.   Death of King Offa (Mercian).

887   Saxons defeated by **Charlemagne** who claimed the Visigoth Empire from the Elbe to the Pyrenees. **Charlemagne** demanded the lands beyond from the North Sea to Central Italy and overcame the Saxons. **Rollo** [Norwegian/Swedish Viking common ancestor to our parents] marries **Giselle** daughter of **Charles 3rd** of France and is given the Dukedom of Normandy. The line of the Norman/English kings starts here.

ANGLO SAXON CHRONOLOGY DURING THE TIME OF THE KING'S OF WESSEX

519 /534 Cerdic first conquered Yarmouth [Garmud] Norfolk in 495 and later became King of Wessex. We have only mentioned part of this family tree, for a complete list see Bloodline of the Holy Grail by Laurence Gardner page 414.

825/858. By 825 King Egbert held sovereignty over most of England, with the exception of the areas held by the Danes. Later Danelaw was retaken, and again united with England. We are at this time particularly interested in the lines coming down from **Hengst and Horsa**. [See chart.15a.p.51. for The House of Saxe-Coburg and Gotha]. Their own people killed Pope Adrian and Aethelred King of Northumbria on April 19th. Ecgferth received the Mercian kingdom and died on the same date. Edwulf received the Northumbrian Kingdom on May 14th and was crowned King on May 16th at York.

839.   Aethelwulf.

858.   Eathelbald.

860.   Eathelbert.

866   Athelred 1st Invasion of Celts 400 BC-866 AD

878   The Danes were driven into East Anglia by Alfred the Great, where Edward the Elder conquered them in 917 AD. They never returned until 902. A balance of power was achieved with the Danes holding the Danelaw an area east of Watling Street [The Roman road from London to Chester]; Alfred held Mercia as overlord and King of Wessex; this was the time when Viking raids became more frequent.

CHART B.

Chart 13

MAIN FAMILY EUROPE 5th–8th CENTURY 446 – 8--AD

Merovingian Kings and the Carolingian line leading to Popae.

Cont. from Faramund cht A p20

*Clodion of Tornai d 446
=Queen Basina

Fredemundus   **Frotmund**

Leads to Comtes
de Toulouse and Sires
of France

Sigimer =	Meroveus = Mera	Alberic	Nascien 1st
dau. Of Roman	d.456Founder of the	Lord of Moselle	Prince of Septimanian
Senator Ferreolus	Merovingian Dynasty	=Arotta of the Ostrogaths	Midi

Childeric of Franks d 481   **Vaubert d.528**   **Celedoin**
= Basina 2nd Queen of Thuringa   = Lucilla [Roman]

Ferreolus   * See history of Carologian dynasty [Carloman]   **Nascien 2nd**
Lord of Moselle].   And surrounding pages in this book
= Dinteria [Roman]   **Merovingian Kings**   **King Chilperic of Burgundy d 504**

Clovis 1st   = [1] Evochild
d 511
         = [2] Clothilde of Burgundy d 550

Theuderic d 534	Chlodomer	Childebert 1st	Lother 1st	Clotilde
	d 524	d 558	d.561	King Almanic of

Theudebert d 548   **Theudebald d 555**   =Sisters = 1st] Ingund Visigoths
                                   = 2n Aregund

.   lines conjoin
Ansbert =... Blitidius		Charibert	Guntram	Sigebert 1stst d 575	Chilperic
d 570		d 567	d 593	= Brunhilde	= Fredegund
	Carloman			[Visgoth]	d584

Arnoald of Skelt = d. 601   of Brabant   [See cht. For Hengst and Horsa]
Austrasia d 647   Pepin 1st   Childebert 2nd   Lothar 2nd d 629
Princess Dua of Swabia   Lord of Brabant Mayor of+ Palace   d 595

                                        [Mistress] = Faileuba [wife]
Arnulf d.641
 King of Austrasia   2nd Theudebert   Thuderic 2n   Dagobert 1ST d 638
. Bishop of Metz   d. 612   d. 613   = 1ST Raintrude   .
= Dobo A Saxon   2nd = Nanthilda
            Lines conjoin
Ansegis	=	Begga	Grimoald	Sigbert 2nd	Clovis 2nd
d. 685		of Brabant	632 – 656	633 –656	d. 656
Lord of Brabant			Lord of Brabant	=Immachilde	= St.Batilde
Margrave of Skelt d 685			Mayor of Palace Nathilda	of Austrasia died 656	[Saxon]

                            [See story of kidnap of   lines conjoin
                              Dagobert 2nd
                                    * Dagobert 2nd = Blichilde = Childeric 2nd Theuderic 3rd
                                       d 679   = 1st Matilde   d 674
.   = 2nd Gizelle   Clovis 3rd Childbert 3rd
Pepin 2nd [The Fat] of Heristal = Alpais   Dau of Bera 2nd
Mayor of Palaces of   Conmte   Childeric 3rd   Dagobert 3rd d 715
Austrasta, Neustria, & Burgundy   de Razes   dep. 751 by   = Saxon princess
                                                   Pepin The Short
Charles [Carolus] Martel d 741   Cont. on chart C
Masyor of Palace &Nustrasia, & Burgundy   Princess Blanchefleur = Flora of Hungary
                                                      Lines cinjoin
            Lines cinjoin   Lines cinjoin
Carloman   Pepin 3rd [The Short] = Princess Bertha   Aldia   =   Theuderic 4th deposed
737 d 741   Mayor of the palace of   [Big Foot]
*New dynasty of French Kings   Neustria d.768
Heribert   * Bera   Theoderic   See chart. 17 C page 63 Text p 46-47

*Start of the Valoise dynasty.
Note; The Merovingian succession emanating from Faramund [father of *Clodian and husband of Argotta], was truly
desposynic Spanish Midi. [our book] undermined by Catholic church and Sicambrian Kings. [See p46-47 for text and
p.46.cht 14].

Sicambrian's fight Merovingian's for European Supremacy

From the time of Merovingian King Dagobert 1st there was an important change in the power base of Europe; their Dynastic rule was undermined by the Catholic Church and taken over by the Saxons [The Sicambrian line] helped along by war, intrigue, murder, and assassination. The Sicambrian's intermarried with Merovingian Princesses and so could legally claim all the titles and privileges the Merovingian's possessed, plus the right to assert descent from the Messianic line.

They seized their opportunity when *King Sigebert 3rd died. Mayor of the Palace,(a post like a Prime Minister) Grimoald the elder kidnapped Sigbert's son Dagobert 2nd, who was just five years old, sent him into exile in Ireland and placed his own son on the Austrasian throne Not expecting to see him again he told Queen Immachilde that her son was dead. Prince Dagobert was educated at Slane Monastery near Dublin and at the age of fifteen years he married the Celtic Princess Mathilde. He returned to France after Mathilde died, to the amazement of his mother who thought he was dead, now Grimoald was discredited.

Chart showing different family lines locked in battle with the Papacy and each other
With Murder intrigue and betrayal   Chart 14

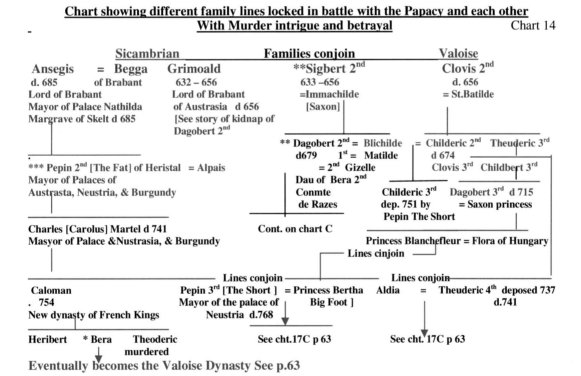

Dagobert then married Giselle de Razes niece of the Visigoth's King. After an absence of nearly 20 years he was reinstated as King in 674 AD. Though Dagobert's reign was short he centralised the Merovingian power centre, the Catholic organisation was in defiance of the so called Messianic inheritance as it overshadowed the Pope's authority.

*+ ** See Cht.13..B p.45 ** Also see specialist book by Laurence Gardner 'Bloodline of The Holy Grail' pages 173/174, 124/9 for more detailed information for ***Pepin the fat.

Dagobert's enemies included his own very influential and ambitious Mayor of the palace. The papal administration had full control of their Prime Minister then called the Mayor of the Austrasian Palace. Dagobert had to be deposed because of his toleration of Arian beliefs. Rome began to dismantle the Merovingian succession in Gaul: This situation continued for some time. *Pepin the Fat [Sicambrian] engineered the death of Dagobert 2nd [Merovingians Franks] when out hunting in the forest of Wepria one of his men lanced him to death by impaling him to a tree, two days before Christmas in 679.

The Church of Rome was quick to approve this assassination. The Mayor received the Merovingian administration in Austrasia and was succeeded by his illegitimate son **Charles Martel. In 679 following his father's murder Sigbert 4th was sent to his mother's home at Rennes le Chatateu in Languedoc. The official version of these histories were hidden or suppressed for a thousand years so the accounts of Dagobert's life were not discovered or made public in the chronicles, until it became known that Dagobert had a son called Sigbert who was removed from the grasp of the Mayors of the Palace. However in what was perhaps an act of at atonement the Catholic Church canonised Dagobert as a Saint in 872

Up to the time of the accession, [except for the time Grimoald put his son on the throne] the monarchy had been strictly dynastic [hereditary] and sacred. The Catholic Church had no formal jurisdiction at all so Rome grasped this opportunity to create kings by Papal authority. By the time of Childeric's death Sigbert 4th in 783 was made Count de Razes succeeding his maternal grandfather Visigoth Bera 2nd. Later the line from Sigbert included the famous crusader Godefroi de Boullion. In 751 **Pepin 3rd [The Short,** Sicambrian Franks cht C.17.p.63] with the aid of the catholic papal authority was crowned as king in place of Childeric [Merovingian] who was displaced and publicly humiliated by the catholic bishops by having his long hair tonsured. This was against the Nazarene tradition and he was forcibly detained in a monastery where he died.

Pepin [The Short] had made an agreement to set up a Jewish kingdom within the land of Burgundy, which would recognise the descendant of the Royal house of David. The pledge of allegiance made by the church with **King Clovis** and his descendants was broken; they then took over the ancient legacy of the Merovingian's by appointing their own kings.
So a new dynasty arose, the Carolingians named after **Charles Martel.** This kingdom was established in 768 from Nimes to the Spanish border and named Septimania [The Midi]. Theodoric 4th who was deposed by Charles Martel in 737 had previously governed this territory.
*+** This was a conspiracy between Pepin the Fat and the church of Rome to take over Merovingian administration.

Theodoric [married to **Pepin the Short's** sister Aldis] whose son William de Gellone Count of Toulouse then came to the throne uniting the two houses of **Pepin** and Merovia, to the chagrin of the Pope. Their son's were **Bernard** of Septimania, Heribert, *Bera and *Theodoric.

Bernard became imperial chamberlain and second in authority to the Carolingian Emperor and the leading Frankish statesman from 829 AD. He married Dhuoda the daughter of **Charlemagne,** producing two sons, William and Bernard 2nd [who held power and the reigns of Aquitaine even rivalling King Louis 2nd in the region]. More than two hundred years later the so called Davidic succession was still going in Midi but the kingdom had ceased to function as a state within a state.

Summary of events from the time of Charlemagne
King Charlemagne extended the Frankish territories and also became king of the Lombard's. In 800 he was crowned Emperor of the West by Pope Leo 3rd. By this strategy Rome inaugurated a new imperial dominion in control of territory that included much of western and central Europe. Rebellious sons undermined the unity of the empire in control of his son Louis so the kingdom was split into three by the treaty of Verdun. Louis 2nd held the Frankish Kingdom east of the Rhine, Lothar 1st was given North Italy and part of France and Belgium and Charles 2nd (the Bald) the Western Frankish Empire containing most of today's France.

In 843 the middle kingdom included Lorraine and Province in the east was Germany and in the west was France. Norsemen were allowed to establish a province in Normandy and the succession in France went to the Capetian dynasty which began in 987 and lasted to 1328 then German emperors contend with the papacy but this family line was defeated by a papal military allegiance in 1268. From then on the empire became the Holy Roman Empire and the emerging emperors were invariably Habsburgs (Hapsburgs) originating in 10th century Switzerland. From 1278 they were rulers of Austria. From 1516 they also inherited the Spanish crown. For five centuries they governed the Holy Roman Empire almost continually until 1806 when its sovereignty was abolished.

It can be seen from the above text that most of the power struggles in Europe at this time and future generation directly resulted in trying to prove descent from the Messianic line and having no respect in how they achieved it. Charlemagne established France as an imperial domain but later the incompetent Carolingian's allowed the Norsemen to invade and colonise northern France and **Rollo** became head of state of this province.

Note; According to information gained from the Internet we conclude that this Bera could be the father of Beringa de Senalis Count of Bayeux, who was the father of Popae. [Wife of Rollo and our mother's line]. Some of the information was taken from Blood Line of the Holy Grail. *See chart 17 C p.63.

PROGRESS CHART
Chart 15

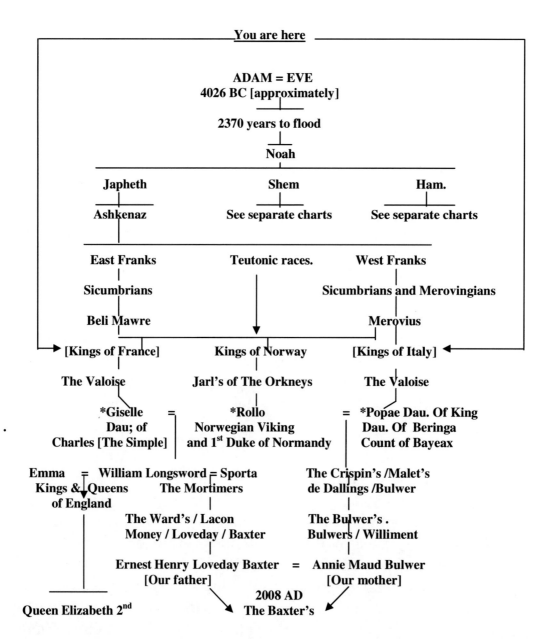

You are here

ADAM = EVE
4026 BC [approximately]

2370 years to flood

Noah

Japheth	Shem	Ham.
Ashkenaz	See separate charts	See separate charts

East Franks	Teutonic races.	West Franks
Sicumbrians		Sicumbrians and Merovingians
Beli Mawre		Merovius
[Kings of France]	Kings of Norway	[Kings of Italy]
The Valoise	Jarl's of The Orkneys	The Valoise

| *Giselle Dau; of Charles [The Simple] | = | *Rollo Norwegian Viking and 1st Duke of Normandy | = | *Popae Dau. Of King Dau. Of Beringa Count of Bayeax |

Emma = William Longsword = Sporta
Kings & Queens   The Mortimers
of England

The Crispin's /Malet's
de Dallings /Bulwer

The Ward's / Lacon
Money / Loveday / Baxter

The Bulwer's .
Bulwers / Williment

Ernest Henry Loveday Baxter = Annie Maud Bulwer
[Our father]   [Our mother]

2008 AD
The Baxter's

Queen Elizabeth 2nd

*At this point in time Rollo's marriages combined three important royal families; France [Giselle], Norway / Sweden [Rollo] and Italy [Popae]. His marriages joined both Valoise families of France and Italy and created a large power base, which gained great respect for his position that he took full advantage of.

These marriages also created a division between the two Valoise families and the Habsburg's that caused disputes and wars for many centuries. They all had a common ancestor Louis 1st the Pious b. 814-880. [See p. 63 chart C].

SAXON TIMES LEADING TO THE HOUSE OF WESSEX.
Early lines; contemporary with the Norwegian Vikings [From 350 AD].

The minor raids of Celtic/Viking, Saxons, Jutes and Angles, began putting pressure on the Romans in Briton in 350AD. Their employment of mercenary armies from the continent, with some settling and eventually over-running Britain, which caused much unrest and disputes among the native inhabitants. The Saxon raiders began colonising in larger numbers, and a few of their homesteads formed a village or settlement surrounded by woodland, which no stranger crossed without first sounding a horn. The old type feudal system came from these tribes as they established outposts and made their homes here; it was a murderous time of ethnic cleansing.

By 418 Vortigern was elected Pendragon [High King meaning senior to all other kings] after he seized and took full control of Powys [Wales] in 425AD, adopting the emblem of the red dragon, symbolising a mighty kingship, which later became the national flag of Wales. The chart for Hengest and Horsa [Golgotha and Saxa cht.15a.p.51on next page] show that King Vortigern invited Kings Hengest and Horsa to defend his realm [Briton] against the Picts, Scots and other invaders. This chart indicates the Sicambrian/Goths are predecessors of the Carolingians kings of Italy and France. They drove the British/Roman/Celtic tribes out into the mountainous regions of Scotland, Wales and Cornwall, some fleeing to Brittany during the years 455-456 and continuing during the time of the shadowy King Arthur and his Knights of the Round Table.

So many Angle's settled in the lands of Eastern England that it became known as East Anglia. Even more arrived to become the majority 449–500 AD and in the fifth century the House of Wessex was an Anglo Saxon kingdom in Southern England that encompassed land in South Wiltshire, Hampshire and Wessex, extending their territory through their various kings. Strong groups formed such as the Angles and Jutes, these were only halted during the 6th century during which time *Anglo Saxon England was established.

As there are so many family inter-marriages contrived to maintain a power base, it is harder to explain the many routes of lineage that can be followed, so we refer you to the chart p184-186 in Lawrence Gardner's specialist book, which shows that from Joseph of Arimathea down to the lineage of the Scots, two major lines of kings conjoin with the Merovingian descent. It is from one of the many lines that our ancestry continued through to **Rollo**, 1st Duke of Normandy [see chapter on Normandy] whose father **Ragnvald** was the Jarl of Orkney.

Note: - information from various sources. *See chronology and chart 8 page 49 for the Saxons.

HENGEST KING OF THE SAXONS.

OUR FAMILY LINE CONTINUED

From 434 AD These were contemporary with the Norwegian Vikings Chart 15 [a]

From the fall of Rome in 410 the Saxon Goths and Visigoths took over the world scene.
In 434 Hengest/Hengist became King of the Saxons on the death of his father   Horsa or Horstus
Witingislau [4th from Woden]. Upon the invitation of Vortigern, King of the Britain's sailed into Briton
asked him to assist against his northern enemies the Scots and Picts. He set sail   and was slain at
for Briton in 447 with his Angles [the first Englishmen] and landed in Thanet.   the battle of
It is said that he received the whole country of Kent and became king there   Ailsford,
on giving his daughter Rowena in marriage to King Vortigern. Hengest is said to
have died in 474 or 488. Father of Hadwker [or Audoacre] Father of Hattwigate
father of Hulderic Father of Bodicus, Father of Berthold, Father of Sighard, Father
of Dietrich Father of Wernkind who was father of Wittekind leading to Cerdic
[who landed at Yarmouth] is also connected to this line]

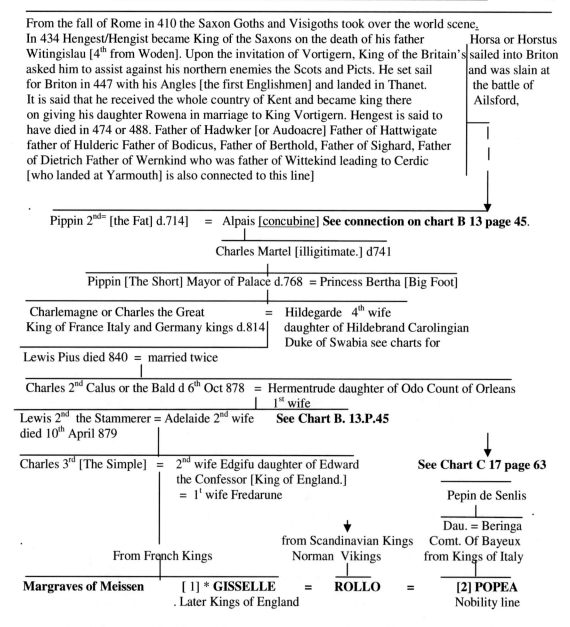

Pippin 2nd= [the Fat] d.714]   =   Alpais [concubine] **See connection on chart B 13 page 45.**

Charles Martel [illigitimate.] d741

Pippin [The Short] Mayor of Palace d.768 = Princess Bertha [Big Foot]

Charlemagne or Charles the Great   =   Hildegarde 4th wife
King of France Italy and Germany kings d.814| daughter of Hildebrand Carolingian
                                              Duke of Swabia see charts for
Lewis Pius died 840 = married twice

Charles 2nd Calus or the Bald d 6th Oct 878   = Hermentrude daughter of Odo Count of Orleans
                                                   1st wife
Lewis 2nd the Stammerer = Adelaide 2nd wife   **See Chart B. 13.P.45**
died 10th April 879

Charles 3rd [The Simple] = 2nd wife Edgifu daughter of Edward   **See Chart C 17 page 63**
                             the Confessor [King of England.]
                             = 1t wife Fredarune   Pepin de Senlis

                                          from Scandinavian Kings   Dau. = Beringa
                                          Norman Vikings   Comt. Of Bayeux
                     From French Kings   from Kings of Italy

Margraves of Meissen   [1] * **GISSELLE**   = **ROLLO** =   [2] **POPEA**
                . Later Kings of England   Nobility line

ALL NAMES ABOVE ARE OF FAMILY LINEAGE
**Note; *The historian Anderson makes Giselle the sister and not the daughter of Charles 3rd and
after more research we concluded as per chart. Any records of these times were either lost or
destroyed; few survived during the Danish/Viking invasions. As very little is known about this
time it made our research very difficult. This period, known as the Dark Ages continued between
the years 400-700. The monk's restarted records before the dark ages ended; even so these are
very scarce. The Viking raids gradually increased to armies that got more and more
overwhelming.
Chart 17C. p 63 shows the connection between the kings of Germany, France and Italy [and their
backgrounds] this shows the conflict between the Houses of Hapsburgh and   Valoise with the
division of the three kings Pepin King of Italy, Emperor. Charles of France and Louis 2nd of
Barvaria Germany] who became bitter enemies which was emphasized with the persecution of the
Huguenots p. 234 -236. Information above obtained from various sources See Chart B 13 p.45 See
descendents of Clodian**

THE NEW SAXON INVASION OF BRITON.
Forming A New Settlement They Called Garmud [Early Yarmouth 495 AD.]

When the Romans first arrived in 55 BC the fork in the river Yare made Yarmouth in Norfolk an Island, which they called Gariannonum and built forts there. One at Castor, [now known as Caister-on-Sea] that was at the left fork of the river, where the remains of a Roman town can still be seen and probably founded as a port. Other ruins can be found at Aylmerton; also the remains of a fort at Bure.

The break up of Roman domination in Britain was preceded by continual attacks from several sources, mainly from the North by Picts and Scots, also the self interest of the Roman army in Britain such as Constantine 3rd who set himself up as a rival to Emperor Honorius. After the Romans left Britain it was open to all prospective invaders.

There were already Saxon settlements in Briton but many more tribes invaded such as Angles and Jutes. The Saxons were a tribe who originated in West Germany, became active seafarers setting up small kingdoms in other lands; in Sussex 477AD and later Hampshire 495 AD [Wessex]. The history of the Old Saxons left behind in Germany has a very interesting story but due to space and time we will not expand on this.

The Saxon Cerdic's invasion into Briton 495AD was the most written about of the early raids and he was reputed to have descended from Woden which is doubtful, unless like Buddha, their gods were based on hero's amongst themselves. Other ancestors were Baldeag, Brand, Fresthegar, Wig, and Geiies.

Cerdic arrived at the island of Gariannonum that we know today as Great Yarmouth, with his son Cynric and their followers in five ships. They must have gained extensive knowledge about the weather, winds and tides of this area from men who had been there before, otherwise he would have had great difficulty in landing.

He settled on this island whose Saxon name was Gamud/ Jermud and re-named it as Cerdic Land or Shore from where he attacked the Iceni [still existing as a tribe]. The forces of nature dictated the position of the island each time the river changed its course.

Attacking and plundering nearby territories caused written records to be stopped once more. Before Cerdic left the area he built a new town on the watery fields, which proved unwholesome, so he started to move to the other side of the river where he solidified the sandbank against the sea and laid the foundations of a town.

After Cerdic moved to Wessex the history of the old town came to an end when the river changed its course, which was due to the fork of the river at Caister becoming blocked with sand, carried in on the swift incoming tides. This dried up estuary can still be clearly seen north of Yarmouth. Several families were left behind to continue building the town on the island starting a small community that gradually developed into the Great Yarmouth we know today, which as you will read later, has important family connections.

Bloomfield states in his entomology, in the actual history of Garmud / Jarmud that "Great" was added in Edward 1st reign to distinguish between the two other Yarmouth's, one in the Isle of Wight, the other in Suffolk. Cerdic was allied to **Hengest and Horsa** who had been given the West Saxon kingdom of Wessex as a reward for defeating the king's enemies.

Within six years Cerdic had defeated the West Saxon kingdom, but it took another 360 years for his descendants to conquer the Welsh. In 519 Cerdic received more land after being asked to fight with the Britons and the Royal Line of the house of Wessex. They ruled there and became very acquisitive, penetrating further and further inland.

After Cerdic, the next tribe/tribes of note to invade this country were the Mercian's, then came the Viking Norsemen, a mixture of Norwegians and Swedes. Many small bands of these tribes had already made settlements but now they came in larger numbers and could exert power and took what they could. From Cerdic's time, villages in Britain began to take the name of a family that lived there or to describe the area in which it was placed and contained the suffix Ham, Ing, or Ton. Many places are named in this way such as Ketteringham, the Ham [home] of the Kettering's.

As you will note later in the book surnames often linked occupations and places and that it is a fact that almost every name must have some reason, or story behind it. For example, a Dane who settled in Bedfordshire was a Wilhelm Holm, so the area became known as Wilhelm's Homestead, then Wilhelmstead and is now called Wilstead that still has a lane named Dane Lane. We visited this area, which is off the A6 near Bedford, it has been partially redeveloped but there was an open area of wet slightly marshy ground, which gave us some idea of how it could have appeared to Wilhelm the Dane.

We continue our story to give a brief outline of the future development of our family with the different royal families and their marriages [connected to our own] from their various countries and the environment in which they lived.

The Viking Ship

Terror that came from across the sea
See where the longship, proudly lies at anchor
Above the prow the gilded dragon rears its glowing head.

Poem by Harthacnut

These beautiful ships were a tribute to man's skill and determination to overcome the forces of nature. Using primitive tools the Viking's built

***Beautiful carved figure-heads of Viking ships**.
Artists impression   Plate 15

ships in several sizes; the smallest type was referred to as twenty roomed. This meant that it had twenty places for rowing and forty oarsmen, twenty-five roomed and thirty roomed ships were also common.

Often thirty-two roomed or even larger ships such as Earl Hakon's 'Orman Lange' [this will be mentioned later in the book] as being forty roomed with eighty oarsmen. The distance between the oars on the 'Gostad' was ninety-centimeters so the length of the "Oman Lange" can be estimated as forty-six meters.

.   **Viking ships at sea**   Plate 15 [a]
Artists Impression

They were of clinker construction [overlapping planks of oak] stuffed with animal hair mixed with tar along the seams to stop the seawater getting in. Wooden dowels or iron nails were used to attach the planks to the keel, wood being preferred as it did not rot so quickly and swelled when in the water.

The mast was placed centrally and supported coloured sails some blue for camouflage against the sea, others were striped, ropes around the stays secured all the sails. Fighting ships were called Long Ships or Skeid, usually narrower than other versions and built for speed. They were fitted with frightening detachable dragonheads, serpents, or war gods set up high on the prow; one such dragonhead was found in the estuary of the river Sheldt. The Kings ship was more ornate and often had sails of different colours, richly embroidered in colourful designs, pictures of them on tapestries from as early as the eighth century show lines running from the leaches to the sternpost taking the place of the betas.

There was usually a raised platform at the stern, which later designs developed into a castle type structure; these had a system of sheets in battens, designed to strengthen and tension the sails evenly. Fear must have struck into the hearts of those who sighted the Viking ships emerging from the mists of Breydon Water at the mouth of the river Yare. No sound came from the men in the boat the only noise would be the quiet splashing of the oars when there was no wind to fill their sail, vigorously pushing aside the waters of the estuary. Those watching would have seen at least sixteen men sitting each side of the boat with their shields hanging over the sides. It must have been a wonderful sight to see when in full sail; with the ripples of white foam being cut by the bow the golden dragons' head adorned its prow.

Beautiful, but deadly in its mission, there was a good reason for the locals to be consumed with fear as they knew these raider's were going to loot, murder, destroy, rape, and terrorise with sordid ferocious vengeance on their victims. The very sight of their arrival struck terror to those in the areas they raided, and there were few left alive after they departed.

Each attack was spearheaded by beserkers, hence the expression 'to go berserk'. Once unleashed on land these men from Norway or Denmark destroyed everything in their path. They lusted for blood and enjoyed killing for personal pleasure in the most barbaric sense. Nothing was spared, men, women, children or animals. They methodically destroyed hamlet after hamlet solely to kill, loot and set them ablaze. The main body of men usually made straight for the church or abbey, where they knew the gold and silver lay. What they did not want they destroyed or set fire to, including personal possessions, precious historical books, documents and other records, which had been preserved through centuries and would have been priceless today. The Wessex Kings resisted without much success.

With these people it was the common practice [primogeniture] for the eldest son to become heir and owner of the estate and property of a deceased father putting the rest of his siblings in the situation of having to seek their fortune elsewhere; many became Vikings. The Scandinavian side of our family started to form and we have endeavored to put the true names and locations to these individuals such as **Leofric** a Mercian and **Rollo Ragnvaldsson,** a Viking of mixed Norwegian/Swedish decent.

It was these vicious Viking raids that caused **King Charles 3rd** [as a peace offering] to give his daughter **Giselle** to **Rollo as a wife,** also transfering a large area of northern France to Rollo who adopted it as the Kingdom of Normandy [Carolingians descent] where Rollo took the title of Duke and later became a Christian.

THE VIKINGS COME TO ENGLAND IN FORCE.
The Wild Men of the North.

The term Viking was used for Scandinavian traders or raiders who were feared for their ruthless slaughter, these attacks were obviously made to better themselves by trading or plundering. The Norsemen were first [Swedes/Norwegians our ancestors] then Danish Vikings, the Swedish Vikings often travelled as far as Western Russia or Persia.

History, like time, never stands still, those in authority wanted more, having power meant more wealth and the easiest way to obtain this was to take it from others. As said previously the main reason behind the attacks was the fact that some families produced too many sons so when the inheritance went to the oldest son the younger ones roamed the known world taking what land, food and riches they could find by raiding other shores. Those that found easy pickings returned again and again to rob and terrorize these same victims.

It was about this time in the first decades of the 9th century that the Swedish/ Norwegian Vikings made occasional raids on the English coast and as these attacks increased they became more brutal. The first raiders came in small groups like the Mercian's who settled here.

The really serious Viking raiders were the Dane's who arrived in force on British soil in 780 AD. The terrified population tried to bribe these Vikings with gifts and coin to keep them away [later known as Dane money] this only encouraged them more. As stated by the elderly lady of ninety one years we met at Crowlands Abbey; -

"Much Wants More
And Greedy Wants the Lot."

These raids increased in size according to the resistance met, until the defenders had to raise an army of untrained men against hordes of well armed, organised and ruthless invaders. They usually attacked the Southeast where there were good landing areas and estuaries leading to rivers that enabled them to infiltrate deep inland; also the area at this time was the seat of kings.

People living along the North East Coast of Britain and East Anglia must have been aware of and in constant fear and danger of the Viking invasions. This situation made these counties very dangerous places in which to live and work. They must have been constantly listening and watching for intruders who would not only take their possessions but also their lives.

ESTABLISHMENT OF THE MERCIAN KINGDOM
KING OFFA OF THE MERCIANS 757-796.AD.
Early lines contemporary with the Norwegian Vikings

The English population during this period was decimated owing to plagues, famine, and attacks by the Vikings; those that were left hid their wealth from the new marauders. However they were often driven from their homes and killed so the hiding place for their riches was not known to anyone until perhaps many years later when it was found and called treasure trove.

The Saxon raiders began to arrive again in increasing numbers and started to settle into large tribes. The particular ones we found of interest were in the Meridian Kingdom *otherwise known as the Southumbrians. They began in c.500AD when Icel was vaguely named as their king [though Penda was positively dated as their first king in some charts]; they gradually gained control in central England and East Anglia, developing into four kingdoms, Central Mercia, Lindsey, East Anglia, and Essex.

Artist Impressions

Offa's Kingdom [of Mercia]
Plate.16

**Alleyn receiving Mercia as a gift
from William the Conqueror** Plate 16[a]

In Circa 700 these initial migrations ceased for a while, and from King Offa's time there was a peaceful era in which the population increased and people returned to their abandoned towns yet ruthlessly bullied surrounding kingdoms. Demanding they make formal obeisance to Offa; trade expanded and Christianity spread. King Offa's silver coins were the standard coinage issued in England and in use until the conquest. Offa was King of the central English kingdom for forty years and almost united England from 757 to 796AD. He was known as the self-styled king of the English, considered the strongest ruler since the Roman period and renowned throughout Europe.

*From 'The Making of Early England' by D, P. Kirby 1967

He founded a monastery to the memory of St. Alban who died in 303AD, and it was during his reign Britain formed a sphere of learning and culture that left its mark on the area controlled by the Mercian kingdom.

In 781 while traveling through Saxony on a pilgrimage to ask God for a son, Offa called on his cousin King Alkmund who lived in Nuremberg whose wife Queen Siwara was having a child. King Offa adopted the baby boy, and called him Edmund, then continued his journey to Jerusalem to complete his vows. On his way back he was taken violently ill at a place called St. Georges Arm. He sent for his council to state that Edmund would be his heir, sending his coronation ring to a Bishop to confirm this fact.

It was also the time when the second wave of Vikings again started to devastate the coasts of England, increasing in numbers and ferocity. Offa beheaded the King Aethelberhts of the East Angles in 794 then combined the kingdoms of Wessex and Northumbria whose rulers had become his son-in-laws and were all then dominated by Charlemagne.

He extended his power over Southern England and was particularly renowned for the construction of a defensive earthen barrier [Offa's Dyke 784-796] between Mercia and Wales that stopped the warring factions.

By 796 King Offa achieved political unity and very quickly established an improved relationship with Rome and Pope Adrian 1st but died in the same year aged 39 years at Offley Hertfordshire. Many years later the Medieval Chronicler Matthew Paris wrote that King Offa was buried by the river at Cauldwell Priory Bedford in the vicinity of the Castle but his chapel and tomb were destroyed when the river flooded.

The Angles went to Saxony demanding Edmund as their King, and brought him back to East Anglia landing at Hunstanton, continuing on to Attleborough. We are again able to the identify names and places associated with our ancestors in our charts such as Leofric 1st 746, Alfgar 757. [See chart for the Earls of Mercia]. These were the fore-runners to Leofric 3rd who married **Godifu** sister to **Turold Crispin/Bulver** our ancestor.

After Offa's death, the Southern Kingdom of Wessex grew at Mercia's expense. The King of Wessex Egfrith expanded his kingdom bonding it with Kent defeating a coalition of Welsh and Vikings and the centre of power shifted from Mercia to Wessex lasting for a hundred years. From then on the English kingdom moved toward a single monarchy. Its strongest leader was Alfred, Egfrith's grandson. A struggle then began between the Anglo-Saxons and invading Vikings mainly from Denmark.

Chart for the Earls of Mercia

Chart.16

Offa King of Mercian's ruled from 780-796 died aged 39
Contemporary of Charlemagne

Edmund [adopted son] King of East Anglia
Break in lineage but Mercian Kingdom continues from Leofric 1st

Early lines contemporises with the Norwegian Vikings

Leofric 1st Earl of Leicester 745-757AD

Alfgar 1st Earl of Lincoln and Leicester 757-839AD

Alfgar 11 Earl of Lincoln and Leicester 839-872AD

Leofric of Mercia Abbot of Coventry And Peterborough also was Thegn in court 1051	LEOFWINE Earl of Leicester 925 – 975	Edwin [killed by Welsh]	Norman [killed]

See lineage for **Popea/Rollo** page 63

Crispin families Text page73 to 75

	LEOFRIC 111 Inherited from his uncle Leofric the above Monasteries and the title of Earl of Mercia in the time of Canute and Edward the Confessor	=	LADY GODIGIFU [Godiva] Of Nursery Rhyme fame]. daughter Of Gibert Crispin	TUROLD Crispin /Bulver

Norman	Aelfgar Inherited title of Earl of Mercia on his father's death.	=	Aelgifa Malet sister to wife of Turold Crispin daughter of William Malet	Hereward the Wake [Turold's nephew]

Edwin Killed by his own men 1071-72	Morca Disinherited Count of Northumbria	Edith 1st = King Griffyd] [of Wales 2nd = Harold Godwin King of England	Lucy = Ivo Tailebois

Countess Lucia = 1st Roger Roumara = 2nd Rannulph Earl of Chester

Most of this family killed in battle of 1066

Issue down to the de Lacy families
See chart for de Lacey and the Earls of Lincoln

Note. *King Offa, contemporary of **Rollo Ragnavaldssonn** [British Library London] The **Lady Godigifu** was wife to Leofric 3rd , her brother was **Turold Crispin / Bulver,** and she had three sisters one married Godfrey leading to the St Clare Families, one married Robert Malet and the last married William Malet. Also see book 'Hereward' by Victor Head page 160 particularly last paragraph. See Complete Peerage. Vol. 7 Appendage J. read alongside Sir Francis Hills Book 'Medieval England'.

Note; Names in **large bold print** denotes family members, others associated families

In 798 the sudden visits of the Vikings was not to be a one off but a series of short violent assaults that left villages and large areas devastated. For a period these raids stopped as the invaders turned their attention to Ireland and they did not return until 835AD.

The Earls of Mercia had the main part of their land in the Kingdom of Lindsey [the old name for Lincoln, England], the rivers Witham and Fosdyke formed the boundary and the walled city of Lincoln was within this. The suburb of Wigford outside its bounds was to be the future Holland, [a name given to the low-lying terrain of marshes and fenland that belonged to the Middle Kingdom of East Anglia].

Early Ecclesiastical histories link the area in with Mercia; Cruthlac was a descendent of Hengest. According to the chart in Crowland Abbey, Cruthlac landed on the island of Croyland/Crowland in AD. 699, which was [and still is] in the Fens long before the Dutch drained it. The church was dedicated a little before 706 AD. and the abbey was founded on St. Bartholomew's day AD.716, which belonged to the Royal Mercian House and was the seat of the Mercian Kings until the time of William the Conqueror.

Leofric's family was Mercian, we know of his connection with the royal household through his position as Thane/Earl of Mercia and the fact he was made Abbot of Peterborough, which denotes nobility. It was his nephew **Leofric** who married the **Lady Godigifu [Godiva] Turold's** sister. This **Turold [Crispin/Bulver** of our line] will absorb our main attention as in this first part of our research into our Bulwer family and we can now link him with other family connections, which like a giant jigsaw puzzle, we found ourselves hooked into, forever searching for the next piece.

It is interesting to note the relationship of all those in power; how each person of national or local standing had some form of connection to a king by blood or marriage. The pivotal person at this time was **Rollo** who linked three of the nations of Europe, and stemming from him were the various Royal lines Dukes and Earls down to sheriff etc.

Norfolk has long been the home of most of our ancestors; Our family surname of Bulwer was originally Crispin who probably came with the nobles that Edward the Confessor brought over from France and was changed by **Turold Crispin** c.1066 to **Bulver**. This related to his position as being responsible for store's for the invasion. His descendants changed it to de Dalling, which described the area of Norfolk where they lived and finally changed back to Bulwer in 1530AD [p.303.chart 71].

KING EDMUND.
b. 781-d 870
King of East Anglia
855- 870.

Coat Of Arms
Azure A Cross Patance Or, Ethelwulf Given The Same Arms as Egbert, Ethelbold, Arms Repeated again. Gullim States That King Aethelred 1st Bore. The Shield Emblazoned "Azure Cross potent Fitchy or"

King Edmund succeeded to the throne as King of East Anglia in 855 following the death of his adoptive father King Offa. After the coronation he was handed the ring, which the king had bequeathed to him by the Bishop of that time. He lived for a while in Attleborough Norfolk, an ancient town of repute, which he re-fortified to repel attack from the Danes at Thetford. King Edmund later moved his palace ten miles from Reedham where he stayed.

During his reign, Lothric a young Danish nobleman, [the son of Ragnar Lothbrok the famous Viking Warrior] when out hunting and fishing around the coast of Denmark, was blown off course eventually being driven ashore on the East Coast of England. He was captured and taken to King Edmund in his palace near Reedham. Lothric formed a close friendship with the king, as both shared a love of hunting and fishing. Unfortunately King Edmund's huntsman Beerne became jealous of Lothric and the place he occupied in his in his masters affections, so he murdered him. It was said that Lothric's dog never left his masters' side.

When the body was discovered and the culprit located, Edmund ordered that the man be put in Lothric's boat and cast adrift. It so happened that the boat drifted on to the coast of Denmark and was recognized. The man was captured, taken to King Ragnar and faced trial by torture where he admitted Ragnar's son had been murdered, but blamed King Edmund. Iver and Halfdan, Lothric's brothers were there and heard this confession, resulting in terrible consequences for East Anglia.

In 865 a Danish Army of 20.000 men including Ivar [the boneless] and Halfdan the reputed sons of Ragnar came to ravish the countryside, leaving its principal townships in flames. King Edmund was brutally tortured and ritually sacrificed to their god Odin. The small East Anglia towns such as Norwich and Thetford expired with him in 870 AD. But these were later rebuilt. Edmund became one of the principal saints of the Anglo-Saxon Church. Bury St. Edmunds was known as Bedricsworth Monastery until King Edmunds body was exhumed and brought here forty five years later. [See full story on page 100].

THE ABBEY OF BURY ST. EDMUNDS.

The present building was built on a site that had been used for religious purposes since 633 and was considered of great importance to early churches. Apart from being centers of learning, monasteries were often used for administration in the 7th century and as the churches expanded these roles were eclipsed.

In Europe **Charlemagne** [of the Sicambrian Franks] was crowned king of the Franks/French, and the Holy Roman Empire which was founded on the premise of the Christ being married with children, and being included in this line caused many intrigues and murders, even wars. [See **Pepin** page 63 chart C] he established Christianity [771AD] but was immoral, accepting no restrictions on his private life. **Rollo** [the Viking b.870] became a Christian and [**Alleyne**/Alan **of Brittany established** a more correct version of the Vulgate (Latin Bible).

King Sigebert the first Christian King of the East Angles founded a religious community at Bury St. Edmund and entered it himself, but was slain when trying to repel the heathens, [the Mercian's under King Penda].

The main South door of this Abbey led to the great cemetery where in front of this door stands the tomb of [**Comte Alleyne of Bretteny/Count Alan of Brittany**] d.1089 who married William the Conquerors' daughter and was also known as the Earl of Richmond]. He held great estates in East Anglia and one of his descendants married into the **Bulwer** family. Bury St Edmund became a place of pilgrimage, and one of the biggest and richest abbey's in England, it is where later the Norfolk Barons met to discus ways to force King John to sign the Magna Carta. In 1381 during the Peasants rebellion the local population beheaded Abbot John de Cambridge, and left his body in the fields to rot.

In 1465 a plumber left a brazier burning in the West Tower while he took a lunch break and during his absence a wind arose starting a fire. This destroyed the whole of the church and refectory, which were damaged to such an extent the great pinnacle fell into the crossing. The palace was also burned, and the abbot's chapel collapsed.

Queen Mary, daughter of Henry 7th of England [who married Louis 12th of France] died in 1533 and was buried there in great state but she was later taken to St. Mary's. The Abbey was totally destroyed in the time of King Henry 8th when the monasteries were dissolved, the ruins sold for 403 pounds and used as a quarry by local builders.

The above information was obtained from various documents.

FAMILY LINEAGE THROUGH FRANCE NORMANDY AND ITALY
771 – 980 AD. Cont. from chart B page 45

CAROLINGIANS CHART C

Chart 17

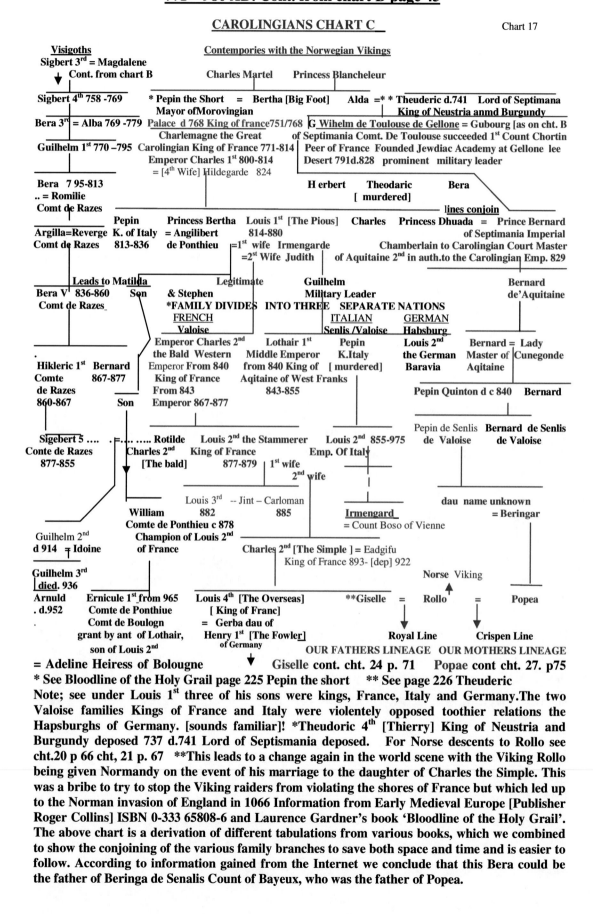

OUR FATHERS LINEAGE   OUR MOTHERS LINEAGE

= Adeline Heiress of Bolougne   Giselle cont. cht. 24 p. 71   Popae cont cht. 27. p75
* See Bloodline of the Holy Grail page 225 Pepin the short   ** See page 226 Theuderic
Note; see under Louis 1st three of his sons were kings, France, Italy and Germany. The two Valoise families Kings of France and Italy were violently opposed toothier relations the Hapsburghs of Germany. [sounds familiar]! *Theodoric 4th [Thierry] King of Neustria and Burgundy deposed 737 d.741 Lord of Septismania deposed.   For Norse descents to Rollo see cht.20 p 66 cht, 21 p. 67 **This leads to a change again in the world scene with the Viking Rollo being given Normandy on the event of his marriage to the daughter of Charles the Simple. This was a bribe to try to stop the Viking raiders from violating the shores of France but which led up to the Norman invasion of England in 1066 Information from Early Medieval Europe [Publisher Roger Collins] ISBN 0-333 65808-6 and Laurence Gardner's book 'Bloodline of the Holy Grail'. The above chart is a derivation of different tabulations from various books, which we combined to show the conjoining of the various family branches to save both space and time and is easier to follow. According to information gained from the Internet we conclude that this Bera could be the father of Beringa de Senalis Count of Bayeux, who was the father of Popea.

YOUR PROGRESS CHART THROUGH TIME

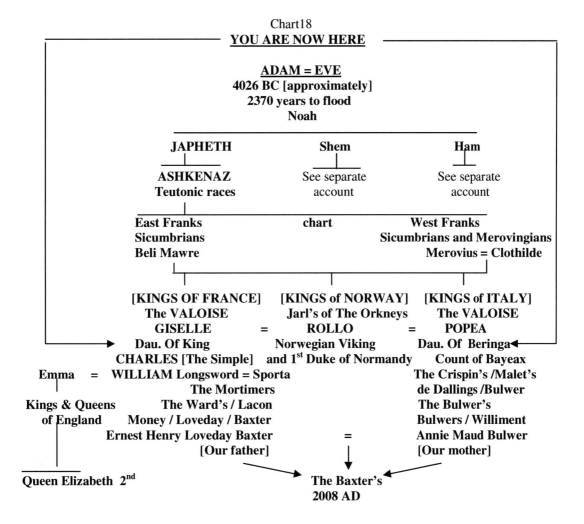

Chart18
YOU ARE NOW HERE

ADAM = EVE
4026 BC [approximately]
2370 years to flood
Noah

JAPHETH	Shem	Ham
ASHKENAZ	See separate	See separate
Teutonic races	account	account

East Franks	chart	West Franks
Sicumbrians		Sicumbrians and Merovingians
Beli Mawre		Merovius = Clothilde

[KINGS OF FRANCE]	[KINGS of NORWAY]	[KINGS of ITALY]
The VALOISE	Jarl's of The Orkneys	The VALOISE
GISELLE =	ROLLO =	POPEA
Dau. Of King	Norwegian Viking	Dau. Of Beringa
CHARLES [The Simple]	and 1st Duke of Normandy	Count of Bayeax

Emma   =   WILLIAM Longsword = Sporta   The Crispin's /Malet's

The Mortimers   de Dallings /Bulwer

Kings & Queens   The Ward's / Lacon   The Bulwer's

of England   Money / Loveday / Baxter   Bulwers / Williment

Ernest Henry Loveday Baxter   =   Annie Maud Bulwer

[Our father]   [Our mother]

Queen Elizabeth 2nd   The Baxter's
2008 AD

We have travelled back to a time when powerful armies of bloodthirsty Vikings roamed the known world to plunder, steal, and colonise, claiming land and settling to form new nations. In the next few pages you will read how the attitudes of this time period once more dictated the course of history. Kings felt compelled to hand their daughters in marriage to leaders of the attacking nations as a peace offering as in the case of Giselle [France] or have them taken as spoils of war i.e. Popae. [Italy].

Rollo was from the Orkney Islands [originally his ancestors were king's of Norway/Sweden] married both these women. Their descendants married the daughters of Herfast a Danish chieftain creating even more influence and power and bringing other nations into the family circle.

 Gilbert Crispin, his son **Turold Crispin/Bulver** and Richard Duke of Normandy, his half brother Rudolph and William Warrenna all married into the Malet family and their descendants; these families you will read about later.

CHAPTER 111
OUR FIVE MAJOR FAMILY LINES
Close Family Structures. [See p.66- 67 cht 21-22]

By the end of the century in the year of 911 the huge armies ravaging all over Europe were disintegrating into smaller raiding parties and nomadic tribes were still roaming over vast areas, subsisting on wild animals, fruits and stealing food from other communities. Most of these barbarians were finally overcome, absorbed by other nations, settled and became farmers. We will now concentrate on the five major family lines. Not all members of the family are mentioned in official charts, so we have used different sources to try to obtain a complete picture; the most interesting family lines have been used.

In the next few pages we will study the;

1]   Descendants of **Ingald** [The Wicked, King of Uppsala, Sweden] listed on chart 20/21.page 66/7 to the Viking **Rollo Ragnavaldsson** of Swedish/Norwegian and Jewish connections] we believe he is a common ancestor to both our parents

2] The descendants of **Rollo's** marriage to **Popae** ancestors to the Kings of Italy leading to the 200 barons and nobles of England and
.   eventually to the **Bulwer's**, [our mother's line] chart 27 page 75.

3]   The family of **Crispin's,** [chart 29 page 74 and our own family line], Descendants from **Rollo** through the female line also married into the Malet **family** [chart 27 page 75 and text page [73] also chart26 page 74

4]   Descendents of **Rollo's** marriage to **Giselle** daughter of King Charles 2nd of France [1st line of descent believed to be our fathers lineage] chart 24 page 71.

5]   Family descendants of **Herfast Malet** a Danish Chieftain whose sons and daughters intermarried with Norman and British nobility [chart 24 page 71 chart 27 page 75]

Rollo's Connections to Carolingian Kings   Chart 19

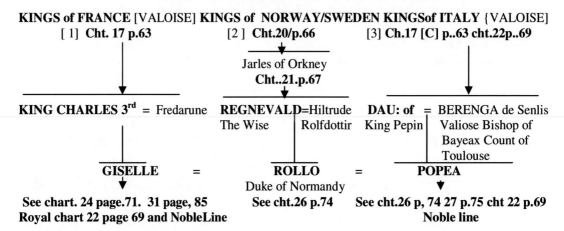

KINGS of FRANCE [VALOISE]	KINGS of NORWAY/SWEDEN	KINGSof ITALY {VALOISE}
[1] **Cht. 17 p.63**	[2] **Cht.20/p.66**	[3] **Ch.17 [C] p..63 cht.22p..69**
	Jarles of Orkney **Cht..21.p.67**	
KING CHARLES 3rd = Fredarune	**REGNEVALD**=Hiltrude The Wise Rolfdottir	**DAU: of** = BERENGA de Senlis King Pepin Valiose Bishop of Bayeax Count of Toulouse
GISELLE =	**ROLLO** = Duke of Normandy	**POPEA**
See chart. 24 page.71. 31 page, 85 Royal chart 22 page 69 and NobleLine	See cht.26 p.74	See cht.26 p, 74 27 p.75 cht 22 p.69 Noble line

KINGS OF NORWAY AND SWEDEN
LEADING TO THE JARLS OF ORKNEY VIKINGS

These are the antecedents of **Rollo** founder of Normandy, who was one of many sons of the Kings of Norway and Sweden who were forced to set out to seek their fortunes elsewhere as the eldest sons inherited all the wealth a titles of their fathers. The names of the Kings leading to **Rollo** that we found listed are as follows which goes back in a time span of 1380 years each with a life average of 60 years;

Chart 20

FAMILY LINEAGE FROM THE JARLS OF ORKNEY TO INGALD THE WICKED LEADING TO ROLLO

King Njord of Sweden c. 214.	Agni Dagssonn
King Yugu = Frey	Alrek Agnisson=Daggsdottir b466 Sweden
Fjolner Yugvi = Freysson	Yngvi Areikssos b 466 Sweden
Svegdi Fjulnersson	Jorund Yugvasson
Vanlandi Svegdasson	Aun the aged Jorund sson
Visbur Vanlandasson	Egilvendikraka Aunsson
DomaldiVisburbursson	Ottar Eglsson
Domar Domaldasson	Adils Ottarsson
Dyggvidonarsson	Eyestein Adilsson d 531
Dag Dyggvisson	Ynguar / Ingvar ? = Ysteinsson
	Brautonund Ingjaldsson d.565
	= Lady Braut-Onund Ingvarssond

Ingald the Wicked [Injaldbrut Onundsson] King Uppsala Sweden 7ᵗʰ Century]
Chart Continued on next page chart 21

In France two streams of colonists met and converged to explore, ravage and from this base attacked the inhabitants of Britain and Ireland. They also spread along the shores of Spain and Denmark. These were Norwegian/Swedish Vikings; some European countries had a fair sprinkling of Jutes and a great many Anglo/Romans from previous invasions. So Europe became intermixed [even more so today]. This made the definition of any of the very early European races from this time very difficult.

Ingald [The Wicked] King of Uppsala Sweden lived in the 7ᵗʰ century.
His descendant **Ranald Ragnavald [the Wise,** married **Hiltrude Rolfsdottir]** was a Norwegian/Norseman His sons were **Rollo** The Ganger [the walker] born about 870 and Gurim Ragnavaldsson born at Maer Norway. **Ranald** being one of the younger sons was forced to seek his fortune elsewhere so rebelled against this situation and against the Dacian King.

He left with his followers and sailed round the shores of what is now Scotland then occupied by the Picts [Bretons]; and stayed long enough to fight the local tribes and ransack the area. After leaving Scotland they traveled on and settled in the Isles of Orkney to become the 1ˢᵗ reigning Jarl where they still celebrate the feast of Uppsala [Sweden].

Continued from previous page

DESCENDANTS OF INGALD the WICKED   Chart 21
Norse descent to Somerled and St. Clair
[Lineage of both our parent's]
For connecting families see chart for Britain 1st-7th centuries and Merovingian Kings 5th-8th centuries

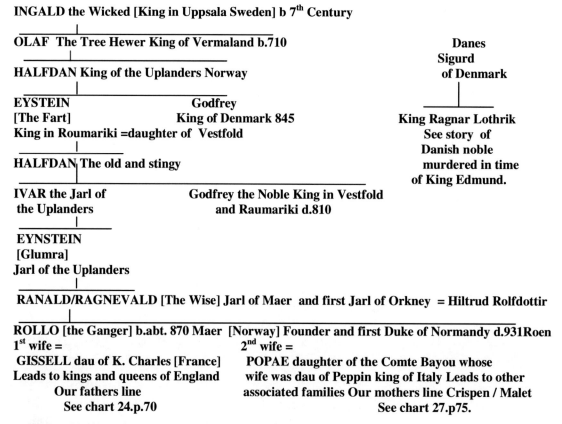

INGALD the Wicked [King in Uppsala Sweden] b 7th Century

OLAF The Tree Hewer King of Vermaland b.710   Danes
                                      Sigurd

HALFDAN King of the Uplanders Norway   of Denmark

EYSTEIN   Godfrey

[The Fart]   King of Denmark 845   King Ragnar Lothrik

King in Roumariki =daughter of Vestfold   See story of
                                      Danish noble

HALFDAN The old and stingy   murdered in time
                                     of King Edmund.

IVAR the Jarl of   Godfrey the Noble King in Vestfold

 the Uplanders   and Raumariki d.810

EYNSTEIN

[Glumra]

Jarl of the Uplanders

  RANALD/RAGNEVALD [The Wise] Jarl of Maer and first Jarl of Orkney = Hiltrud Rolfdottir

ROLLO [the Ganger] b.abt. 870 Maer [Norway] Founder and first Duke of Normandy d.931Roen

1st wife =   2nd wife =

 GISSELL dau of K. Charles [France]   POPAE daughter of the Comte Bayou whose

Leads to kings and queens of England   wife was dau of Peppin king of Italy Leads to other

       Our fathers line   associated families Our mothers line Crispen / Malet

        See chart 24.p.70   See chart 27.p75.

When **Ragnvald** died his sons **Rollo** and Gurim his brother were still in rebellion and were defeated by the King's army, Rollo sailed with those who remained loyal to him to exile. They first went to Jutland where the King of the Angles sued for peace by crowning **Rolfed/Rollo** as co-regent. **Rollo** was at this time disturbed by a prophetic dream and sought the help of his priest who took advantage of this and persuaded him to leave and invade France.

A historical treatise (The Book of Kells) written in Ireland about 802AD states that a tribe named Scott took advantage of the Viking destruction and moved north eastwards from Ireland during the Roman occupation and gave the name of their tribe to Scotland. From the time of Kenneth McAlpin in 844 the Scots royalty inherited their crown in accordance with Pictish custom, [through the female line]. The Pictish princess married the Scots King therefore maintaining the status quo and uniting the Picts and Scots.

Rollo was a very large man of whom it was said was too big even to ride a horse [the horses were smaller in those times] so was forced to walk everywhere, a man of extreme violence and insecurity.

It is from here careful thought must be given to the various family structures shown in this book, also important is the fact that **Rollo** is a common ancestor to [possibly] both our parents by his two marriage's. First to **Giselle** [this we believe is our fathers line] and then to **Popae/Popa** [that we have proved is our mothers line]; both of these European families shared the same surname of Valoise. Thus showing their common origin and from this point you will note that these two marriages provide the backbone for European, national and our own family lines.

These families produced some of the most influential characters that formed the structure of our society; some parts are with us today. Events that occurred in those days from the time of **Rollo's** two marriages seem to weave a fascinating story leading down to the present time, which provides the main framework of our book.

THE ANCESTORS OF POPAE AND HER MARRIAGE TO ROLLO

We discovered that **Popae's** mother; [name unknown] was daughter of **Pepin Quintin [de Valois] Senlis,** King of Italy. **Berenger, Popae's father** was harder to trace, but the historian Dudo wrote of a **Berenger Count of Senlis [Italy]** showing there could be Carolingian descent on both sides of **Popae's** family.

Poppa/Popae's name indicates descent from a dynastic heritage, which usually gave the name Poppo/Peppin to the second born of the family. *****Rollo's** marriage to **Popae** created a dynasty of Earls and Barons, as you will see later in our book. After reading the chapter on Gissing Manor, you will understand why there is so much confusion when tracing any lineage beyond a certain date.

We found from the Internet that one of the defenders of Bayeux [France] was a **Count **Berenger** who was killed in the fighting. His daughter Popae was taken prisoner and allotted to **Rollo** and proceeded to Danish marriage, which meant she would be married to him as long as he remained in the area [later Normandy] but it would become void if he moved away.

*Rollo descended from the Norwegian / Swedish kings and Popae his wife from the Italian kings
** Berenger, father of Popae is difficult to establish as to his positive origins but collated information from various sources to conclude as per chart and text.

Chart for the Decent of Popae and Giselle   Chart 22

Continued from chart 11 A p20 to cht. 13 B p. 45 to chart C 17 p.63
Carolingian / Valoise Descent of the kings of France and Italy [later Briton]

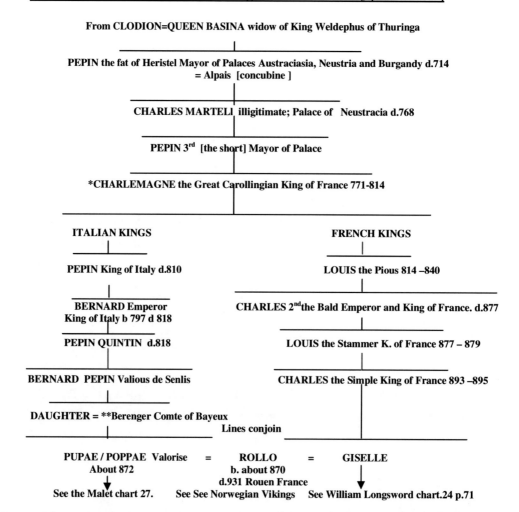

From CLODION=QUEEN BASINA widow of King Weldephus of Thuringa

PEPIN the fat of Heristel Mayor of Palaces Austraciasia, Neustria and Burgandy d.714
= Alpais [concubine]

CHARLES MARTELL illigitimate; Palace of Neustracia d.768

PEPIN 3rd [the short] Mayor of Palace

*CHARLEMAGNE the Great Carollingian King of France 771-814

ITALIAN KINGS	FRENCH KINGS
PEPIN King of Italy d.810	LOUIS the Pious 814 –840
BERNARD Emperor King of Italy b 797 d 818	CHARLES 2nd the Bald Emperor and King of France. d.877
PEPIN QUINTIN d.818	LOUIS the Stammer K. of France 877 – 879
BERNARD PEPIN Valious de Senlis	CHARLES the Simple King of France 893 –895
DAUGHTER = **Berenger Comte of Bayeux	Lines conjoin

PUPAE / POPPAE Valorise   =   ROLLO   =   GISELLE
About 872   b. about 870
                                        d.931 Rouen France
See the Malet chart 27.   See See Norwegian Vikings   See William Longsword chart.24 p.71

We found the lineage of **Berenger very difficult and almost impossible to trace as there were several people of this name, but as his wife was from the Valoise family it is logical to assume he was of noble birth. After much research we found a reference in Laurence Gardner's book on page 186 giving a Juhel de Berenger, [930-937] who was descended from Frodaldus Count of Bretagne. Other dates also seem to confirm this thought

Berenger on the same page of this book is included in the line that leads down to the Stuarts of Scotland. Another source indicates he was a child of Hierarch, but we consider that Berenger de Senlis [Italy] is probably the one that is mentioned at Bayeux.

* + ** Note. For the Valoise families England. [See Field Dalling] the Bulwer Histories are listed in Genealogy data on www. See p.4 of nine. More references are given on the Internet. As a matter of interest the Gladiolius Lily in the Judaic Fluer de Lys form adopted by Merovingian Kings then passed to Charlemange.

SAXON AND NORSE DESCENT
For our family line.

Chart 23

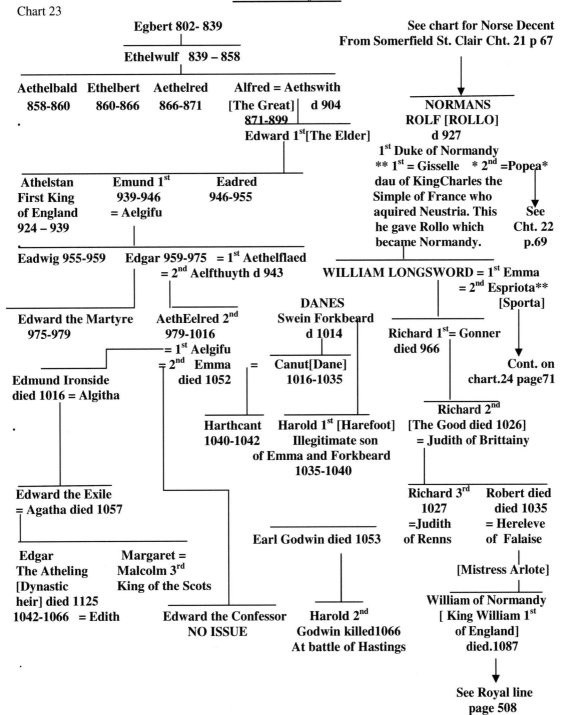

Egbert 802- 839

Ethelwulf 839 – 858

See chart for Norse Decent
From Somerfield St. Clair Cht. 21 p 67

Aethelbald 858-860	Ethelbert 860-866	Aethelred 866-871	Alfred = Aethswith [The Great] d 904 871-899

Edward 1st [The Elder]

NORMANS
ROLF [ROLLO]
d 927
1st Duke of Normandy
** 1st = Gisselle   * 2nd =Popea*
dau of KingCharles the
Simple of France who
aquired Neustria. This
he gave Rollo which
became Normandy.

See
Cht. 22
p.69

Athelstan First King of England 924 – 939	Emund 1st 939-946 = Aelgifu	Eadred 946-955

Eadwig 955-959   Edgar 959-975 = 1st Aethelflaed
= 2nd Aelfthuyth d 943

WILLIAM LONGSWORD = 1st Emma
= 2nd Espriota**
[Sporta]

DANES
Swein Forkbeard
d 1014

Edward the Martyre
975-979

AethEelred 2nd
979-1016
= 1st Aelgifu
= 2nd Emma
died 1052

Richard 1st= Gonner
died 966

Cont. on
chart.24 page71

Canut[Dane]
1016-1035

Edmund Ironside
died 1016 = Algitha

Harthcant
1040-1042

Harold 1st [Harefoot]
Illegitimate son
of Emma and Forkbeard
1035-1040

Richard 2nd
[The Good died 1026]
= Judith of Brittainy

Richard 3rd 1027 =Judith of Renns	Robert died died 1035 = Hereleve of Falaise

Edward the Exile
= Agatha died 1057

Earl Godwin died 1053

[Mistress Arlote]

Edgar The Atheling [Dynastic heir] died 1125 1042-1066 = Edith	Margaret = Malcolm 3rd King of the Scots

Edward the Confessor
NO ISSUE

Harold 2nd
Godwin killed1066
At battle of Hastings

William of Normandy
[King William 1st
of England]
died.1087

See Royal line
page 508

Note: - * + ** our parents lineage   * Mothers lineage proved   ** Fathers [not yet proved]

NORMANDY AND THE VIKING ROLLO [911-931 AD]
THE BEGINNING OF A STATE
Rollo Ragnavaldsson marries twice 1st Giselle daughter of King Charles the Simple.
Their son William Longsword's also married twice 2nd wife Sporta
[Our Fathers line probably through Sporta]

To reiterate a previous paragraph that has importance, the terror engendered by these invading berserkers led **King Charles** [the Simple] to concede the Cotentin Peninsula and Bressin in northern France to **Rollo**. This was later to be known as the Norseman Duchy [Nor'mand'y], also offering his daughter **Giselle** in marriage to Rollo. By the gift of this land **King Charles** Simplex [The Simple] hoped to create a buffer state against the raiders who plunderedhis domain and almost destroyed the city of Rouen.

The line from **Rollo's** marriage to **Giselle** and their son Duke **William Longsword** who was born c.895 at Notre **Dame** Normandy is the one we are now interested in. On the chart below, note he was married twice; 1st to Emma who produced Richard 1st [married to **Gonner Malet,** daughter of **Herfast**] starting the family lines of The Dukes of Normandy and the House of Clare, later to become Kings and Earls of England. It is **William Longsword's** 2nd wife **Sporta** that probably provides our father's lineage.

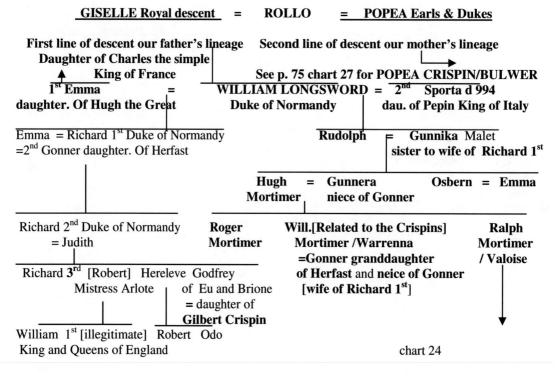

See p. 75 chart 27 for POPEA CRISPIN/BULWER

chart 24

Rollo's two marriages created three distinct important family lines. [a] The Royal line from his wife Giselle destined to rule Normandy and Britain, which determined the future of the whole of Europe. Their children Emma and William Longsword providing Kings, Queens and

Dukes. [b] Sporta and William Longsword, contributing Nobles, probably our fathers line and [c] his wife Popae our mothers line of Nobles. **Rollo** being the head of his new territory assumed the title of Duke and his people adopted their own version of the French language and integrated into a French/Norman state. They also used the same Frankish feudal law with a feudal type Government that was adopted by the French and were used as a vassal state.

By the end of the century these Norwegian Vikings became Catholic Christians but their Viking pagan worship compelled them to live for war and freed their conscience on account of it, later they were to rock this and many other European nations for years to come.

King Aethelstan of Britain gave assistance to **Rollo's** conquests and later invoked a pact between them to receive help against the English rebels; at the same time he presented Norway with the Western Isles of Moray, Shetland, Man and Orkney. Later in 1266 Magnus son of King Haarkon of Norway sold these Islands of the Hebrides back to Scotland.

You will note on the chart on the previous page, that in 993 William Longsword [later assassinated at Picquigni Somme] was married to 2nd wife **Sporta/Sprota** of the Bretagne Liutgard of Vermaoise, the daughter of **Pepin Valoise** from the line of Carolingian kings of Italy]. They produced a son **Rudolph Mortimer** who married Gunneka sister of Gunner [wife of Richard 1st **Rudolph's** half brother].

As can be seen from the same chart **Rudolph**, had two children**, Hugh** [Bishop of Constances] and **Emma** who married Osbern. Hugh married Gunnera [niece of Gonna wife of Richard 1st]. Hugh had three sons Ralph Mortimer, [alias/**Valayns/Valois/Valoynes** the old family name] and **William Mortimer** [alias **William Warrenna**] and **Roger Mortimer** [alias Wigmore/Mortimer/Percy we believe this is our father's line]. Again we apologise for this confusion in name changes creating a researcher's nightmare but it was one way they could hide from the anger of the king and add to his confusion and ours.

In 1066 Normandy was used as a springboard to attack Britain; the connection between Normandy and Britain existed long before Duke William came on to the scene [See chart from Alfred the Great to Henry the second for example].

Norman writers gave details of Aelthelstans friendly relationship with **Duke William Longsword** in 930AD. This was put on a more intimate footing by the marriages of the **Princess Emma**, first to Aethelred, then to Canute both Kings of England.

THE MALET AND CRISPIN FAMILIES
Their involvement and influence in the course of history
[See structure plan chart 1 p3 and lineage from Popae]

Herfast Malet from the early days was referred to, as an unknown Danish chieftain that we knew had owned vast lands in Normandy, he was very wealthy and influential. His daughters married into all the most important families, including the descendants of **Rollo** the Viking. These were the start of several important and powerful family lines. He became Chancellor in the Court of Edward the Confessor [the first to be mentioned as far as we know]. The surname of Herfast's children's we confirmed by charts was Malet so the surname of their father **Herfast** must also be **Malet** though we have not yet discovered which Danish family he was attached too. This family was later connected by marriage to Kings and nobility of Normandy and England.

FAMILY OF HERFAST MALET   Chart 25
HERFAST MALET

Fredrik Malet	Osborne Malet = Emma	**GONNER MALET** = Richard 1st	Gunnika = **RUDOLPH**
Killed by	dau.of	[BOTH SONS OF WILLIAM LONGSWORD]	
Swein Godwin	Hugh the great]	their other marriages to SPORTA and Emma	
.		made Richard and Rudoph half brothers	
	See charts for Osbornes	**See chart for Rollo**	**See charts for Warrenna**

LARGE PRINT DENOTES OUR LINAGE

It is important to note that on the chart of **Herfast,** Richard 1st and his half brother **Rudolph** married sisters, **Gonner and Gunika Malet,** daughters of **Herfast Malet.** Following the chart for **Rollo** through his wife **Popae** you will see that the **Male**t names are the most prominent of all from the time of **Gilbert Crispin** and **Gunner Malet,** who produced five children. All these **Malet** families were rich and of very high rank owning vast amounts of land in both England and France.

Though their origin is a bit obscure we have found some of the answers. [See **Malet** charts and history of the **Malet's**]. We will continue with the line of descent, from **Crispina** as it is a continuance of the **Malet** lineage and deals with the major line. You will see from the chart above that the female lines of the Crispin family from the fourth generation were cousins to Duke William [later King of England]. **Hesillia Crispin** married **William Malet** who later changed their name to Gissing and lived in the original Gissing Manor in Gissing Norfolk. Their two sons fought by William the Conqueror's side in the Battle of Hastings.

* + * and ** + **Same person
Note;-When Rollo married it was under Danish Law and probably due to his connection with the Danish Herfast.

Chart For Malet's And Crispin's

Chart 26

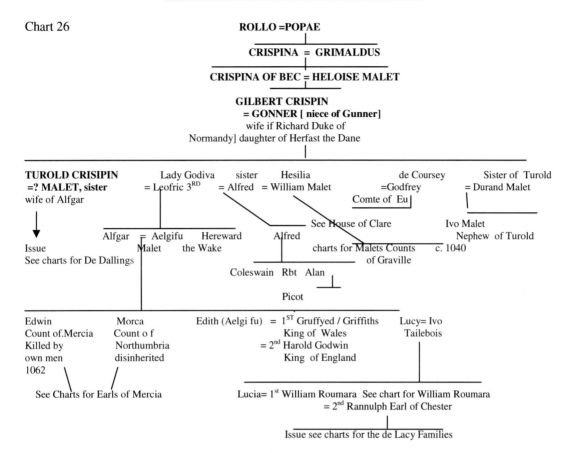

ROLLO =POPAE

CRISPINA = GRIMALDUS

CRISPINA OF BEC = HELOISE MALET

GILBERT CRISPIN
= GONNER [niece of Gunner]
wife if Richard Duke of
Normandy] daughter of Herfast the Dane

TUROLD CRISIPIN
=? MALET, sister
wife of Alfgar

Issue
See charts for De Dallings

Lady Godiva
= Leofric 3RD

sister
= Alfred

Hesilia
= William Malet

de Coursey
=Godfrey
Comte of Eu

Sister of Turold
= Durand Malet

Ivo Malet
Nephew of Turold
c. 1040

Alfgar = Aelgifu   Hereward
Malet   the Wake

Alfred

See House of Clare

charts for Malets Counts
of Graville

Coleswain Rbt Alan

Picot

Edwin
Count of.Mercia
Killed by
own men
1062

Morca
Count o f
Northumbria
disinherited

See Charts for Earls of Mercia

Edith (Aelgi fu) = 1ST Gruffyed / Griffiths
King of Wales
= 2nd Harold Godwin
King of England

Lucy= Ivo
Tailebois

Lucia= 1st William Roumara See chart for William Roumara
= 2nd Rannulph Earl of Chester

Issue see charts for the de Lacy Families

NOTE; CAPITAL LETTERS DENOTE OUR LINEAGE

William Roumara and Ranulph Earl of Chester lived and fought during the time of the civil war between King Steven and William the Conqueror's daughter Matilda to gain the crown of England.

The text gives you a picture of the **Malet** connection with the **Crispin** family through **Rollo and Popae**. We will now show the **Malet** connection through **Rollo and Gisselle**. Their son **William Longsword** as we have mentioned before also married twice; the resulting offspring of both marriages were related to **Herfast Malet.**

*Alfgar son of **Leofric** and **Godvia**, as stated by Lanfrec married **Algifue Malet** daughter of **William Malet,** who in 1064 was a valiant soldier. But after his rebellion against the King in 1070 returned to Normandy and lived out the remainder of his years as a monk in the Abbey of Bec [See item on "The Enigma of Conteville"].

We realize that many of these relationships we repeat but have done this deliberately for you to get a clear picture of the close marriages that enabled them to retain power.

*Turold Crispin was Godvia's brother and uncle to Alfgar
Note: - See chart for family of Herfast on previous page.

CRISPIN/MALET FAMILY LINEAGE CHARTS.

Second line of descent [Our mother's lineage] From Rollo Ragnavaldsson 2nd marriage to Popae daughter of Berenger Comte Bayeaux

Cont; from p.63.Cht.17 C   **Chart 27**

1st GISELLE [our fathers line] = ROLLO = POPEA 2nd Line of descent [our mothers line]
daughter of Chares King France   grand-daughter of Peppin King of Italy c. 872
    [The Simple]
    [See p. 71 cht. 24]   **CRISPINA = GRIMALDUS Duke of Monaco**

                                  CRISPINUS of Bec = HELISE MALET

GILBERT CRISPIN = GONNER	**Hesillia =William Malet**	**William Durand**

*TUROLD CRISPIN /BULVER	***GODIVIA daughter =Leofric =Englishman**	**Hesillia =William Malet**	**Gilbert Malet = de Courcel**	**Robert = Elise de Brione**
= dau W. Malet	**Alfgar= dau of W.Malet Alfred**			**Ivo = Margaret**

** William Durrand   **Hugh Fitchett =Bassilica**

    = sisters   **Robert William**   **Baldwin Malet Abbot of Buckenham]**   **Robert**

Alain Robert Coleswein Muriel Picot   **William Malet = Maude**   **Roger**
             =Robert   **[disinherited   Mortimer**   **de Graville**
             De Hayes]   **[France]**
             ISSUE

Gilbert   **Bartholomew**   **Walter**
Leading to Ann Boleyn   **traded inheritance**   **Paid King Henry one shilling**
Our researcher Mrs.Gill   **with brother Walter**   **to have name changed to Gissing.**
McKenna came from this line   **to go to crusades**   **Bought Gissing Manor,**
                    changed name to Suthfield   **entered on Pipe Rolls.**
                                         Descendants involved in the
                                       Peasants revolt in 1381. The
                                       Manor then came into the hands
SIR RALPH = LADY JUGA   **of the de Dalling families.**
                                         [See item on The de Granvilles]

William   Peter   ROGER de DALLING = AGNES VALOISE [widow of Adam   de Rattlesden]

William   **Roger [probably killed in Crusades]**   **SIR RALPH [alive 1203]**

PETER FRITZ RALPH   **Philip [of Field Dalling]**   **Reginald**

Con. Chart 49 p208 [Thomas = Lefguana]
Where families divide into three main branches
Family members in capital letters.
+ Brother and sister
Turold=into Malet family, Godvia [his sister] = into Mercian family. See text on following pages. Names of Atthil, Woodhouse, Ward, Warrenna, and de Bios all stem from Mortimer [see charts for Warrenna Bulwer] All the above are cousins linked by marriage. The chart also shows Rollo's second marriage to Popae and we have included the full Crispin/Mallet family with Gilbert Crispin's son Turold Crispin/Dalling/Bulver/Malet connection. This started our mother's Bulwer line. C. Waters Gundrada de Warrenne page 11 Archaeological Journal iii 7; Cont., Will. Jumieges viii 37 makes his mother a niece of Gonner.

Our mother's line came through **Rollo** and Popae down to Crispin de Dalling to **Turold Crispin/ de Dalling Bulver/Bulwer** and the surname **Bulwer** follows the family to the present day. Names below are on charts page75 chart 27 and 59, chart 16 are prominent in this part of our family story; it is less complicated to study a chart than discuss the relationship in detail.

Turold during the time of Edward the Confessor was the Sheriff of Bukenhale, Norfolk [now known as *Buckenham] and married a daughter of **William Malet** whose Christian name is unknown. **Turold's** sister **Godvia** married **Leofric 3ʳᵈ** [a Mercian family of nobles and earls who were elder's in the courts of Canute and Edward the Confessor].

Leofric 3ʳᵈ inherited the Abbey's of Peterborough and Coventry from his uncle, also named **Leofric** Earl of Leicester, [see p.59 for Mercian's]. Leofric and Godvia raised a son **Alfgar,** and two more sons; one was the famous **Hereward the Wake.** Before we continue with the lines of descent we will conclude this section of the **Crispin / Malet** families with a mention of their Manor at Gissing, which will feature in a later story, and was the background to **Gilbert Crispin's** association with the Abbey of Bec. If you use the charts provided, you will see there are many names we have mentioned before and will again, about lives long absorbed in time.

GISSING MANOR

This manor was the family seat of William Malet/Sire de Graville of Dawling from early times and remained so even after ***Gilbert Malet and his son William became involved [1381] in the rebellion with the Dukes of Bainard, [see p.187 and p273]. We were confused over this manor as a Gissing Manor was still standing in the village but found it was not the original one, which was sited some distance away from the present building. The Kemp's owned the hall in 1640 who left many memorials in St. Mary's **Church** Gissing. We find that Stephen Fitzwalter, one of the Lords of the Diss Hundreds enfeoffed Walter-le-Breton [in the service of several villeins of blood. See chart for Rollo].

It is this first Gissing Manor that sparked our interest, because of its long remarkable connection with the **Malet** family who owned it and lived there for centuries. We know it was moated and was nearer the village than the existing one but was destroyed then rebuilt after the peasant uprising and pillaged again during the civil war.

*Castle mound is still there but castle is a ruin. **+**+***http://oaks.nvg.org./abra10him/rollo [from Internet]. Sources; - 1Merian =Ahen 2 Ahnentafel Rubel-Blass from Internet Dudo of St. Quinten Internet. Other information from Books by Charles Crawford and Owen Feelizer 'The Conquest of Normandy. Note: - Edward the Confessors sister married Druex Count of Vexen. Note; -We appreciate the help from the present inhabitants of the village in locating the site of the original Gissing Hall.

Sadly all we found of it was one of its large barns, there was nothing left of the first house. Lacking a drawing of the original building, because of its association, we have included a photograph of the present Gissing Manor on page 79, which is still there today.

Gilbert Malet the son of William Malet and Maude Mortimer/Malet bought Gissing, his descendants had a share in important events right through its history. Both **William** and **Robert Malet** returned here after the Conquest [see battle of Hastings] and following King Harold's defeat and death in 1066, they were asked to bury him as his family was related by marriage.

The descendants of Helise and Robert Malet lead down to the Fitzwalter families; all are related and connected to Gissing. William Taylor bought the manor but the relatives continued in the Service of the hall with other free tenants who sold to Sir Hugh Hasting, he in turn sold to John Boyland [clerk], which his Aunts held until their deaths in 1283.

John Boyland's son Richard sold this hall to **Simon de Dalling and his wife Isobel,** who purchased the Manor of Gissing in1283 [whose surname was at that time Dawling]. On the same occasion they purchased an annuity from **Robert le-Breton [Simons'** uncle] of ten shillings rent, which he was to receive out of the Manor. Coming into the hands of the **Dalling** families, we now can confirm that they being landowners were descendants of the relatives of the king and of each other.

Soon after the Conquest, the Manor of Gissinghall in Roydon was added and this remained so until 1579 when other parcels of land were acquired. It was held partly in the honour of Eye and partly for the Abbot of Bury. Like many other old family manors, the actions of their owners often offended the contemporary kings so to avoid retribution they changed their surname to hide their real identity. After the Conquest the Lord of the Manor was in the hands of the Earl of Norfolk Ralph de Geuda until the rebellion of 1075, when his estates were passed on to Roger Bigot/Bigod.

Later **Hesillia Crispin** and **William Malet** lived in this manor and because of the offence of Robert [b1079] and his son William against the king they had to change their name to Gissing but still continued to live there. These name changes cause much confusion today when researching family history. **Gilbert Malet [Roberts's** father] was rich enough to have supplied his son with more than he required for his expedition to the Crusades and the rank of Banners that he assumed. **Robert,** Lord of Eye was banished while he was living in Gissing.

His son William [The **William Malet** who became a monk in the Abbey of Bec] behaved himself until his fathers' exile then **William** the son was exiled for his part in the rebellion and his participation with Earl Elias of Maine. After which, he fled back to Normandy where his father held the territory of Graville. **William** was the first **William Malet** who became the 1st Lord of Graville. [This is the opinion of the French authorities].

An interesting situation developed between Bartholomew Gissing and his younger brother Walter. Bartholomew who traded his inheritance with Walter possibly to finance his expedition to the Crusades and Walter paid the king one shilling to register the claim in the Pipe Rolls, demonstrating the respect that people held for these Rolls at the time.

Great emphasis was placed in this period on dress and refinements. William the Conqueror and his attendants returned to Normandy in 1067 with clothes made of gold tissue enriched with bullion; other garments were dyed in very bright colours; to make scarlet, a pigment was made from cockles, and a purple dye was obtained by crushing snails or other shells. People had found an interesting way to stain cloth [see p. 34] and like today there were many that envied the possessions of others and obtained them by fair means or foul. Those stealing from the king were harshly dealt with when caught, being blinded, having limbs severed or they were killed.

Simon de Dalling also had to complete the title, so he obtained a release from Isobel the Widow **of John de-Boyland. Simon and Isobel** had one child, **John de-Dalling** of Wode Dalling who in 1335 settled it on his wife Maude. Their only child named Cecily married William of Shimpling. [The village of Shimpling is adjacent to Gissing in Norfolk].

1381 Thomas Malet/Gissing used the Manor as a local headquarters in the Peasants Rebellion and as he was the ringleader for that area was later confined in the Tower of London where he was to stay for some time. **William Bulwer**, also a related descendant of the Malet family through the female line was charged with trespass in c. 1381when he led his prize bull together with its followers over the fields belonging to one of the Lords of the Manor.

Because the **Malet/Dalling/Bulwer's** had lived in the original Gissing Manor and had strong connections with royalists directly serving the Crown, the manor was pillaged and burnt at the end of the civil war. The present Gissing Hall [some parts probably Elizabethan] although ancient was not completed until the time of Queen Victoria and was probably not part of the great Manorial Estates but like many others in these days of excessive death duties, has ceased to be a family dwelling.

Today this imposing attractive building with its Elizabethan style frontage is presently being used as an 18-bedroom hotel. Its large and accommodating rooms are complete with an intriguing air of mystery and a sense of history lurks behind its façade of faded glory. At the time of our visit [2001] it was the home of the proprietor's William and Anne Brennan.

Gissing Hall today   **Plate 17**
[Not the original one owned by the Malet's]

THE KINGS PARDON

We return to the Gissing family for a moment to trace the movements of the elder **William Malet** who after offending the king became interested in Monastic life [see item on Conteville]. Ernest succeeded him to the Graville title, and in England another son took the surname of Fitchet. *This family is also the same one of **William Malet** whose descendants intermarried with the **Crispin/ de Dalling** families.

The family experienced the Kings' Political mercy when William bestowed Conteville on the **Abbey of Bec, the family not only received the assent of the King and Queen to this grant but also the nobles and the whole of the powerful religious Ecclesia were commanded to be there at its dedication.

1308-1335 Deeds Chart 28

Simon Mariote de Suffield   Robert de Suffield = Margaret

| = ?

John = Jone   Robert   Matilda   Jone   Letitia   Margaret   John = Agatha

Nicholas

Note; as a matter of interest the above family developed from one of the Malet female line.
*pp.C2. Bloomfield's Norfolk
**See Bloomfield's' History of Norfolk Beck Manor vol.1.x page 76

THE SITUATION OF GRAVILLES/MALETS IN ENGLAND

* "Lewis Graville of Bambri Draiton Oxfordshire married Margaret the daughter and heyre of a noble cauled Sye Gyles Aden. The wife of the which Syre Giles was named Philipe, and she likewise was a woman bourne to faire landes. So the possession of Sye Gyles and Philipe descended to Lewis Granville. Whose faire tumb is yet sene in Paroche church of Draiton. The son Lewis had to wife a daughter and hyre of one Corbet [related to the Wards and Lacunas] Court Rolls remain yet at Draiton ons by yer [were] 1,300 marks [blank supplied by Stow]".

The elder House of the Graville's/Malet's that settled in Oxen /Oxfordshire England [two miles from Bambri], originated the famous rhyme "Ride a cock horse to Banbury Cross" and of the **Lady Godiva/Godigifu [Turold's** sister]. According to the TV programme "One Foot in the Past' this ride took place, as a protest because she considered the taxes of **Leofric** her husband were cruel and too hard on the people at that time. The Time Team was called in to dig out more.

FITZ WALTER

Plate.18

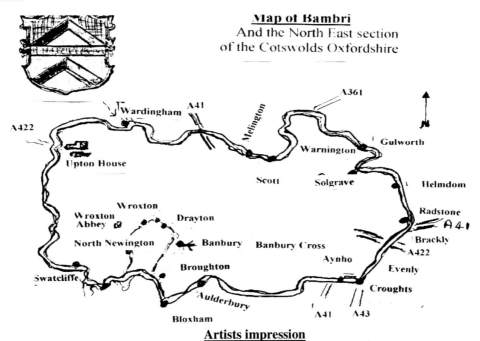

Artists impression

Bloomfield states: -

Sum the opinion that the Graville's cam originally in at the Conquest. These developed from the Malet's who adopted aliases after they offended the king. There was one of the Graville's of Draiton. After that they cum into great landes and much used these, and dyed in warfare. This Graville left one Somerton, a meane gentleman of Draiton in Oxfordshire a peace of whose lande is in a gate, yet remaineth to who he left his landes in a foment without declaration of will. Whereupon Somerton sold much of it, and converted the sum to his own hyres".

*Original text found in Leylands Initianary in England and Wales. Vol. ii 1535-1543, fol.16
Graville London Centaur Press Ltd., Edited by Lucy Toulon Smith.
Note: - See Chart Crispin/ Malet

The Malet Shields
Thetop two lines of shields show the shields Baldwin of Malet and Clare.

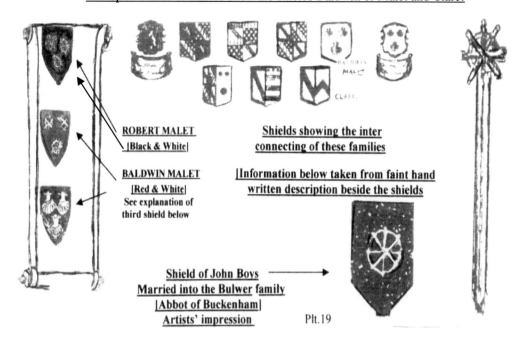

ROBERT MALET
[Black & White]

BALDWIN MALET
[Red & White]
See explanation of
third shield below

Shields showing the inter
connecting of these families

[Information below taken from faint hand
written description beside the shields

Shield of John Boys
Married into the Bulwer family
[Abbot of Buckenham]
Artists' impression

Plt.19

The Scrolled items deal solely with Malet shields. The first belonged to Robert Malet, the second to Baldwin Malet's family, the third to Baldwin as Abbot of the Priory at Bukenham. A sword was used by Crusaders who when isolated and without any church nearby they could stab the sword into the earth and use it as a place of worship. How the term Coat of Arms evolved is very interesting and became intertwined with heraldry. During the middle ages wars were almost continuous and more and more armour was added until the knight was protected from head to toe until they could not tell friend from foe.

This was overcome by wearing cloth surcoats over their armour or on their horses with symbols emblazoned for identity   purposes. Shields were also painted with the same designs. The very first arms were very simple but became more complex over time, then being given meanings of personal or family status; achievements, motto's etc were started. 1419 Henry 5th of England placed legal regulations over their use and forbade anyone to espouse arms unless by right of ancestry or as a gift from the crown. From the time of Henry 8th the Garter King of Arms made visitations around the country once in a generation to review which families were entitled to them.

Note: - To decipher the meaning of the various designs, colours or material that gave historical data about the family or the person who is displaying it, requires a study of specialist text on this subject and is interesting reading.The book "The Norman Conquest "had a note by Mr. Freeman vol.3. 1875 edition p. 600-1. And 1870 Edition collected information has helped us enormously to find much of the information on the house of Malet.

DECENT FROM
Robert Malet

[Cont. from page 75 chart 27]

ROBERT MALET = Sister of **GODIVIA CRISPIN**   **Chart 29**

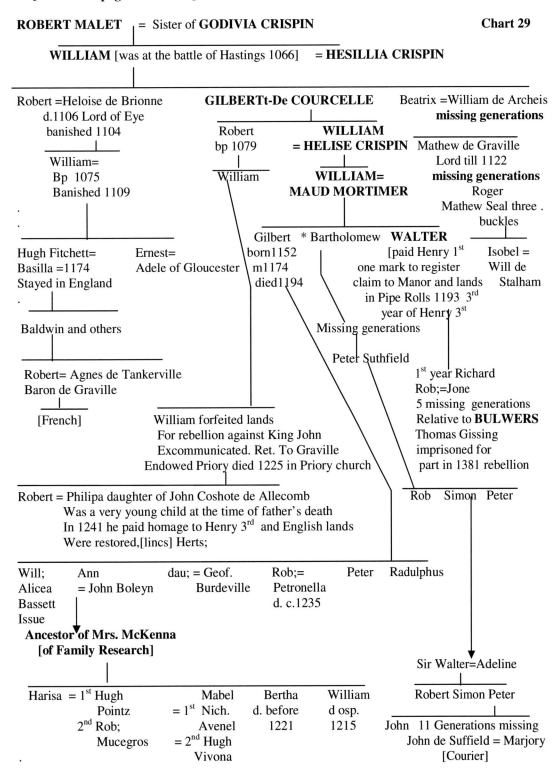

WILLIAM [was at the battle of Hastings 1066]   = **HESILLIA CRISPIN**

Robert =Heloise de Brionne   **GILBERTt-De COURCELLE**   Beatrix =William de Archeis
d.1106 Lord of Eye   **missing generations**
banished 1104   Robert   **WILLIAM**
                           bp 1079   **= HELISE CRISPIN**   Mathew de Graville
William=   Lord till 1122
Bp 1075   William   **WILLIAM=**   **missing generations**
Banished 1109   **MAUD MORTIMER**   Roger
                                                           Mathew Seal three .
.   Gilbert * Bartholomew **WALTER**   buckles
.   born1152   [paid Henry 1st   Isobel =
Hugh Fitchett=   Ernest=   m1174   one mark to register Will de
Basilla =1174   Adele of Gloucester died1194   claim to Manor and lands Stalham
Stayed in England   in Pipe Rolls 1193 3rd
.   year of Henry 3st
                                                  Missing generations
Baldwin and others
                                                  Peter Suthfield
   Robert= Agnes de Tankerville   1st year Richard
   Baron de Graville   Rob;=Jone
                                                           5 missing generations
      [French]   William forfeited lands   Relative to **BULWERS**
                      For rebellion against King John   Thomas Gissing
                      Excommunicated. Ret. To Graville   imprisoned for
                      Endowed Priory died 1225 in Priory church part in 1381 rebellion

Robert = Philipa daughter of John Coshote de Allecomb   Rob   Simon   Peter
         Was a very young child at the time of father's death
         In 1241 he paid homage to Henry 3rd and English lands
         Were restored,[lincs] Herts;

Will;   Ann   dau; = Geof.   Rob;=   Peter Radulphus
Alicea   = John Boleyn   Burdeville Petronella
Bassett   d. c.1235
Issue
Ancestor of Mrs. McKenna
[of Family Research]
                                                           Sir Walter=Adeline

                                                           Robert Simon Peter
Harisa = 1st Hugh   Mabel   Bertha   William
         Pointz   = 1st Nich.   d. before d osp.   John 11 Generations missing
      2nd Rob;   Avenel   1221   1215   John de Suffield = Marjory
         Mucegros   = 2nd Hugh   [Courier]
.   Vivona

* See written text page 78.
NOTE; - NAMES IN CAPITAL LETTERS INDICATE A FAMILY MEMBER OR A
RELATIVE. .

ENIGMA of CONTIVILLE
And The Abbey of Bec.

Our journey takes us back through time to a place in Normandy called Conteville (Seine int.; arr. Neufchatel Cant Aumale). When Robert [The Devil] Duke of Normandy died his illegitimate son, the young William now became Duke of Normandy [later king of England]. Robert's widow Harlette de Falase married the Count Harlevin de Conteville, an individual of genius who founded the Abbey of Bec. *Departing from the monastic role he allowed Lanfranc to open a school there for all comers.

They had many pupils who later distinguished themselves. Desiring to enter a religious career he joined a group of enthusiasts who formed a nucleus with those in the Abbey of Bec and three years later was appointed prior. **Gilbert Crispin** [an intellectual and father of **Turold,** our mother's line] wrote a book called "Victor Hellion".

The intellectual distinction of Bec is probably due to his teachings. Lanfranc himself, who had been Abbot of a monastery in Caen, was a teacher of European reputation who taught for a time at Avranches shortly after 1040. In the year 1076, **Gilbert Crispin** was installed as Bishop of Westminster and was responsible for a law that was instigated forbidding clergy to marry.

When Lanfranc died in 1077 he provided for the operation of Cannon Law that separated ecclesiastic courts, copies were made and sent to the greater English Churches. After Harlette died [widow of Robert of Normandy] the Count married Fresende and had a son Osbert de Conteville.

In the charter [temp. of William 1st], ** **Robert Malet** Lord of Eye at the request of Osbert de Conteville gave all the land that Osbert held in Occold [Acolte] Suffolk to Eye Priory. But there was no church there, so it cannot be related to the above place, especially as it belonged exclusively to the Abbey of Fecamp [France], and confirmed thereto. In 1196 **William Malet, Robert's** successor to Graville in Normandy gave Conteville to the Abbey of Bec (see item on William de Graville page 75-76).

---

*From the book 'History from the Life of Bec' Editors J. Armitage Robinson & Gilbert Crispin page 88.
**See complete Peerage p.569 footnote [n] Note Roville... 13th Century spelling is Rovilla. Roville Seine-inf: arr., Lr Havre cant. Bolbec. His lord Robert Malet confirmed gifts made by William Roville to Eye Priory. Roville is 14km.East of Elmallerville where another tenant lived. There is no other place of the same name in this part of Normandy.

It does appear from the charter that there was a confirmation in the reign of Henry 2nd, the gift included the Manor and Church with all attachments thereto; there were other problems such as another hamlet of Conteville. The hamlet of Paluel (Seine inf. Yvetot, cant Cany) is six miles north of Claville-en-Caux a **Malet,** and 8 miles Northwest of Crasville.

La Mallet could have been another which was confirmed by **Robert Malet** in his writings in a charter for Eye, which show him to have an under tenant Hugh de Avillers in Conteville who probably took the name for Auvilliers in Conteville. Odo, half brother of William the Conqueror had a son Turold [The monk knight from the abbey of Peterborough married to Eustachia] who also had a son named Odo who gave other gifts.

These were named in the same charter, which included a moiety of the church at Conteville; the other places mentioned show this to be "The Conteville". A similar situation happened in England, with the charters of **Valoise** in respect to the lands given by **Peter and Roger Valoise** his son covers the same lands and seemed to verify the promises from father to son, or one person to another. (See the charters of Valoise to Binham Priory).

Chart showing the de Valoise families.

Chart. 30

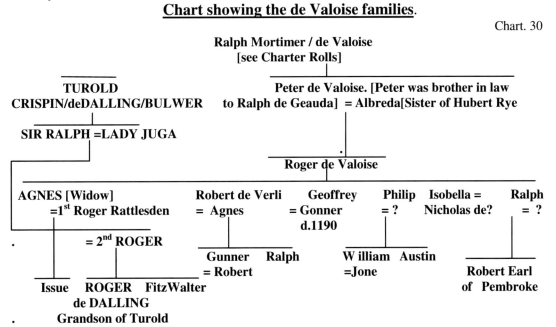

For extended charts see page 180 chart 43

Some of the research references attached to his notes refer to the Crispin families who conjoined with the Mallet's. This chart can be used in conjunction with the Crispin / Malet charts 26/27 p.74/75 p 82 cht 29. Much of the above information is taken from the research done by Arthur Malet and his brother ['Notices of the English branch of the Malet Families'] and gives his sources of information as taken from The book 'Norman Conquest' by Mr. Freeman.

NOTE;- ALL NAMES IN CAPITAL DENOTES OUT FAMILY MEMBER OR RELATIVE

THE FAMILY OF WILLIAM

To keep the story flowing, we will continue from 'The Beginning of a State' and remain in Normandy for a time to follow the family line to Richard 1st, who married **Gonner** daughter of **Herfast Malet,** a Danish chieftain. His half brothers and cousins, married into this family too making it very close knit indeed.

Royal and Noble descent   Chart 31
[We have included this chart again to show how individuals play a part in Williams's early life]

GISELLE Valoise [French]	= ROLLO =	POPAE Valoise [Italy]
Daughter of Charles the Simple	Ragnavaldsson	
King of France	Norwegian Viking	
Believed to be our father's lineage.		See chart for Crispin's
See full chart		Proved to be our mothers lineage

1st Emma   =   WILLIAM Longsword Duke of Normandy   =   2nd SPORTA d. 994
      ROYAL DESCENT   NOBLE DESCENT

Richard 1st Duke of Normandy   RUDOLPH = GUNNIKA Dau. of HERFAST
= Gonner daughter of Herfast   Sister of Gonner wife
                                                             of Richard 1st

Richard 2nd Duke of Normandy   HUGH = EMMA dau.of Osbert   Emma = Osborne
            = Judith   son of Herfast

                              Ralph Mortimer   *WILLIAM MORTIMER
                                 Valoise]   [Warrenna[
                                                  Earl of Hereford

Richard 3rd   Robert [the Devil] = Harlette = Herliuem   Leading to what we believe to
              Had association with   be our fathers line
                 Arlette

William   Adele   Robert   Odo   Ralph   Osborn
The Conqueror
Kings and Queens of England   Cont. on Chart 39 p.165

There will be names mentioned in the following text that you would need to remember. Osberne [son of Herfast] married **Emma** the daughter of **Rudolph/Ralph Mortimer** half brother to Richard 1st Duke of Normandy.

The eldest of **Rudolph's** grandsons was *****William Mortimer / Warrenna** who later was steward to William 1st and received large estates in England becoming Earl of Hereford shortly after 1086. [See chart above]. Osbern's nephew Osbert came to England before the Conquest and was the Bishop of Exeter in 1072.

NOTE;- Names in capitals indicate family lineage. [Our fathers lineage not proved]

Some of this text is repeated to show relationship to other families. Ralph de Geuda married the sister of Roger Mortimer/Beaumont in defiance of the Kings wishes and joined in the rebellion of the Barons against him. He was also closely linked to **Peter de Valoise** and the **de Dalling** families. **Alfgar,** son of **Leofric** was also a member of these families much to the chagrin of Godwin. Using the chart for **Rollo** [chart.31.p.85] follow the line down to Richard 2nd of Normandy, you will note that his son Robert the Devil married Harlette and had two sons Robert and Odo. His alliance to Arlette the daughter of a Tanner in 1027 produced an illegitimate son William 2nd [later King William 1st of England, The Conqueror] and also a daughter named Adeliser/Adele.

Before Robert set out on a pilgrimage he named this son William as his heir, causing uproar among the legitimate members of his family. Robert died while on this pilgrimage and his widow married Harlevin Count of Conteville. When she died he married Fresende resulting in a researcher's nightmare once more as they had sons Ralph and Osborn, which made them all closely related to the throne.

Jealousy and harsh treatment from his family because of his fathers' preference for him and his illegitimacy resulted in all of them being embittered with one another. Though very young William was astute in handling situations and affairs of state; evidently his father's controversial decision to name him as heir proved correct, he must have seen qualities in this boy his other offspring did not possess.

This jealousy cumulated in a plan to assassinate the young William, who was only eight years old at this time. The plot was overheard by Steward Roger Bigod while serving his **Lord William Mortimer/Warrenna** [the **Duke of Mortain**] who reported it. Among the disloyal people who betrayed him in 1047, were Vernon his cousin and childhood playmates, the Lords of Conten, Bessin and Conteville, also Gilbert de Brione who was brother in law to **Gilbert Crispin,** of our own family**.**

A plan to counter this plot was laid, and when they tried to carry out the murder, they found several protectors there to safeguard William's life; **Adele, Williams sister** had been poisoned prior to the attack. In the struggle Osberne Malet the brother of Gonner (wife of Richard 1st) was killed, along with **Gilbert of Brione.** This story was substantiated in a grant made to Holy Trinity at Rouen. William was snatched away by another of his mother's family and hidden in the house of a peasant. As Duke William grew older he showed his bravery and wisdom. Protectors such as Ralph de Lacey, who had slain Gilbert, grew in number. These loyal ones were [mainly French], but there were still those who were disloyal, such as the Scandinavian relatives who were in a state of rebellion against him. They took into account his illegitimacy and denied his fathers' right to make William the heir to Normandy. When he was old enough the young William chose the right moment to exact revenge on those that attempted to murder him. Firstly by disinheriting his uncle *William Mortimer/Warling/Warrenna the Comte of Mortain [Normandy] who held the Castle and its lands, which was situated in the modern section of la Marche of the Pax de Caux.

The title lands and Castle of Mort-en-mer en Brai was given to William's half brother Robert who became the Comt'e for that area and changed his name to accommodate the title becoming the Duke of Mortain. Many of the young and adventurous found Normandy too small with no scope or outlet for their energies so left for other lands. The rapid exodus from Normandy increased to a volume difficult to handle and to cope with this problem they considered expansion of their national boundaries. In 1054 Robert Curthose rebelled against his father William Duke of Normandy with **Ralph Mortimer** head of the Kings army who deserted and joined in the battle of Val-Es-Dunes on Robert's side.

*William Mortimer was also involved. They took shelter with his relative Roger Mortimer/Warrenna in the castle at Mortimer-en-brai, but were defeated by the king; both fled to England. William Mortimer/Warrenna went into disfavour for supporting Robert Curthose but was rehabilitated after a friend interceded on his behalf. From then onwards he became a staunch friend of King William 1st and was with him at his death. He was appointed Governor of Rouen in the district of Caux and the manuscript register at Lewes Priory dates his death 11th May 1138. He was buried with his father in the chapter house at Lewes.

Roger went to Wales founding the families of Mortimer and Wigmore. [The Lords of the Marches] where the family became very rich and powerful landowners. The Percy family was another Mortimer line that came from Roger and were involved in many intrigues later, including the Gunpowder Plot. **Ralph Mortimer** was disinherited and fled to his relatives the Osbornes, where he stayed for a long time. He changed his name to **Valoise** the ancient family name connected to the Kings of France and Italy; from there he came to Norfolk. An attempt was made on William's life at Valoygnes, but he evaded this and rode on alone to Rye and Falaise. He and Henry of France had defeated their enemies for the time being. The Mortimer's fled to the castle of Roger Mortimer their brother but having been discovered there returned to Britain.

*We found in reference books that William Mortimer changed his name to /Walyne / Warrenna. The surname Warrenna comes from a large fortress built on the banks of the river Varrenne [France] now called Bellacombre where the remains of the 11[th]century castle can still be seen.

William Mortimer became a loyal subject of the Duke after being disciplined and was one of the Lords consulted prior to the Conquest early 1066 at Lillebourne, later fighting for William at the battle of Hastings. After the Conquest he was rewarded with a responsible role in England, becoming a large landowner and King William offered him many privileges. Eventually his responsibility was the redistribution of lands that were made forfeit by knights and followers who had offended the King and these were given in trust to **William Mortimer** now called **Warrenna,** with the power to hand them out to whom he wished.

He held vast territories in his own hands, half of which were in Norfolk. His main residence was set in a woodland valley at Castle Acre North Norfolk. In the village are the remains of a Priory, and set on a green mound is the ruin of a castle [7th century] rebuilt by William Warrenna in 1067-80. He also owned a Mansion on St. Giles Street Norwich later called Mortimer's Hotel, which still exists today as a municipal building.

Castle Rising Norfolk [built by William Albini] was also held by **Warrenna.** It was later the scene of a great drama, both tragic and some would say romantic, [see item on Edward third]. Duke William ordered its destruction but the Castilian [at this time **William Crispin**) only yielded the place on William's express command. However the Governor of the county refused to give way, and garrisoned against the Duke. Eventually the Castle was taken set alight and the Governor banished. There were enterprising raids and expeditions into France and Henry 1st of France complained that the Fortress at Tillers was a nuisance to him; the Duke's councilors ordered its destruction.

CHRONOLOGY [from 732- 1066].

732	Archbishop's Egbert and Aethelbert 766, built up a fine library and established a flourishing school, Alcuin their student joined the court of Charlemagne in 782 and became one of the leading literary figures of the Carolingian renaissance. Anglo Saxons of the pre-Viking period shared a restricted literacy of the ancient world from the fifth and sixth centuries.
870	East Angles conquered by Vikings.
924	Athelstan king d.939.
939	King Edmund 1st [King Alfred's grandson] reigned six and a half years, died 946 [his brother Edwin reigned 955 -959]
959	Edgar [The Peaceful] d.946.
975	Edward [The Martyr, brother of Athelred] aged sixteen crowned King by St. Dunstan. Murdered 978 and Athelred crowned.

Danes in the Southeast, Sweyne's sister was killed 1002 AD. King Sweyn [Svein] attacks Norwich and Yarmouth, plunders and burns the whole borough. Major battle at Thetford, which Danes win; Thorkll Sweyne's brother becomes Lord of Attleborough. Danes invade England. Athelred flees to Normandy with his family. With the coming of the Danes, Norwic [Norwich] prospered, becoming a centre for trade which included fishing, as at that time the estuary reached as far as Norwich. The area was tidal and the surrounding land extremely wet, especially where the Cathedral was to be built in later years. During some of the more recent building work, the remains of the old curing houses have been found where they used to cure the fish when it was tidal. When the tide reaches the New Mills it stops due to a barrier and a drop in water level

1014   After death of Sweyne [Svein] Forkbeard, Athelred returns to England promising his people better leadership, breaks his word. War breaks out, then agrees to rule with Sweyne's son.

1016   Canute reigns over Northern England while the son of Athelred, Edmund Ironside rules the south, which he did in defiance of his father who still held the South East. Edrich Streaona arranged the assassination of the elders Morca and Sigeforth.

1016.   King Athelred dies, on the 4th of April 1016, Edmund Ironside and Canute fight for the crown.

1018.   King Edmund reconciled with Edrich Streaona, and battle is joined against Canute, but Edrich acts as a traitor. Although the battle was lost, agreement was reached on the areas each controlled. Suddenly Edmund dies and Canute becomes King of all England.

1035-40   King Canute dies. Harald Hardrada son of Canute reigns with Aelgifu of Northampton the daughter of Thorkill/Thirkill the Dane.

1035-41   Godwin murders Alfred. Edward flees back to Normandy. Reign of Canute's son Harald Harefoot whose mother was Emma, daughter of Richard 1st Duke of Normandy. Edward the Confessor son of Athelred and Emma (Princess of Normandy) becomes King there was bitterness between Edward and Godwin whom he later banished for a time.

1055   **Aelfgar** son of **Leofric** Earl of Mercia becomes involved in a feud with Earl Godwin. **Aelfgar** banished [it was said unjustly] for consorting with Gruffydd King of Wales, **Aelfgars** daughter marries Gruffydd. **Aelfgar** banished once more. **Gilbert Crispin** the father of **Turold** probably came to England, with Edward the Confessor and his family, and became Bishop of St.

Peters Westminster. During a quarrel with his father-in-law the Earl Godwin, Edward designates for consideration William, Duke of Normandy as his successor. After Earl Godwin's sudden death, Harold Godwin is made leader of the Army. Harold Godwin and William Duke of Normandy were considered for that kingship, as Edward the Confessor had no heirs. In this year it is thought that Aelfgar the son of Leofric died. Odo Bishop of Bayeux, Duke William's half brother, commissioned one of the best records of the events of this time, the Bayeux Tapestry to record history. Some think it was embroidered by William's wife Matilda and her ladies in waiting. Its designer could have been either Norman or English.

1066 5th January Edward the Confessor dies.

English Nobles crown Harold Godwin King in January 1066.

His brother Earl Tostig and King Harald Hardrada of Norway invade the north of England. On September 27th William Duke of Normandy and his army sailed for England and find the coast unguarded. Harold Godwin was in the north of England fighting King Harald and Tostig. Harold Godwin defeated them both and raced south only to be killed by Williams's forces at Hastings. William was crowned King of England on Christmas day 1066 in Westminster Abbey and the Saxons never regained the throne until recent times. William's victory at Hastings is displayed on the Bayeux Tapestry in Bayeux, Normandy. Further panels, now lost, probably took up the story from William's Coronation. The existing tapestry records the facts from the time of Harold's mission to William in 1064, to William's Coronation in 1066.

We noticed an interesting item recorded in the 'Doomsday Book,'which was initiated by William to assess his new Kingdom, about the thriving iron industry. Ironsmiths were valuable members of society in those days. There was a law that ordered every nobleman moving into a new district to take his Smith with him.

The Ironsmiths knew very well without their specialized ability, the farmer would possess no hooks or ploughshares and the seamstress would be without her needles although they had the alternative to use other materials such as bone or wood; in some places even the taxes were paid with iron-work. There were many other occupations that provided work for the ordinary folk and profit for their Lord, such as cloth, salt, and embroidery, some sold at home, and also traded abroad.

BUILD UP FOR THE FIGHT
TO CLAIM THE ENGLISH THRONE

We have to travel back in time again to 830AD so you can get a clear picture of events leading to the fight for the English crown by family members [or associated members] of various European nationalities. The Norwegian/Danish kings and their followers had settled in the Isle of Orkney, became Jarls there and will provide the mainspring of this part of our story. The Viking **Rollo Ragnavaldsson** [our ancestor and founder of Normandy in 911 [see chart 15a.p.51] was attacking England, Scotland and France. This was also the time when Charles 2nd of France [The Simple] lived who tried to avoid the constant Viking attacks by giving Normandy and his daughter Gissel as a wife to Rollo, which established another power base and problems for the future.

In Briton by 835 the Danish Vikings began attacking in force until their numbers grew sufficiently to overthrow the English Kingdom of Athelred 2nd. They took a great interest in a small hamlet called Norwic [now Norwich] adding a third community on the south side of the river to the two already there, naming it Westwick. By studying the Mercian chart on page 59 chart 16 you will note that Offa a Mercian had settled in England and adopted a son named Edmond. Leofwine had a son circa. 956, **Leofric 3rd** who married **Lady Godiva** sister of ***Turold Crispin;** Also by studying another chart [19] for The Mercian's, you will see that **Turold** is a Scandinavian descendant of the Viking **Rollo.**

In 978 **Aethelred/Ethelred 2nd became king and complications set in when he married first Elgifu producing Edmund Ironside. His second wife Princess Emma [daughter of Richard 1st of Normandy] bore Alfred, and Edward [later the Confessor]. During the Danish invasion in 1016 King Sweyn Forkbeard raped Emma who we believe produced Godwin father to Earl Godwin, and her marriage to Canute a Dane [Sweyn's son] produced Harald Harthcnut. Later Canute married Elgifu [ex wife of Aethelred] and had issue; we suggest you study the chart on p.92;

William Duke of Normandy descendant of Rollo who was directly related to Emma was half promised the crown by Edward the Confessor. Earl Harold Godwin though not of royal blood was related by marriage, and his brother Tostig who was a favourite of Edward, added to the coming problems when they all wanted to claim the crown of England

*See Crowlands Abbey ** Note; Anglo Saxon Letter AE in a name means this name is an ancient one that goes back to 580BC. Is known as the way the Anglo Saxons would have spelt it, though the A/E would have been almost joined together] **+**Constant refrain of Leber Eliensis and note 32 of Unification and conquest included in a book by Pauline Stafford p 57 and a more detailed account can be found in Sir Frank Stentons Book 'Anglo Saxon England' 2nd Edition

Eventually the families of these different nationalities having common mothers [Queen Emma and Elgifu] paved the destinies of nations, leading some to greatness others to obscurity. We have outlined these various royal families with multinational offspring that caused so much turmoil when each had the ambition to gain power. They could hardly be described as founder members of the United Nations, not that this is a good recommendation at times.

Jealousy bloodshed and war were created in the fight for the English throne, caused by the death of Edward the Confessor who left no issue. To try and explain the inter-relationship within the various royal families would be like trying to keep track of several rabbits in a soapbox, hence the necessity of using the charts.

CLOSE FAMILY RELATIONS FIGHT FOR THE ENGLISH CROWN

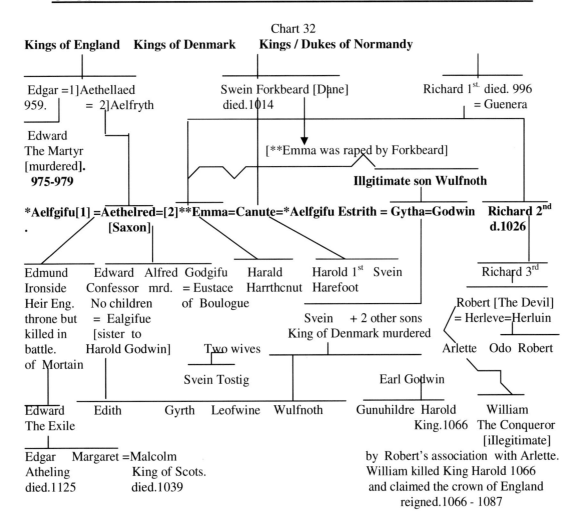

Chart 32

Kings of England   Kings of Denmark   Kings / Dukes of Normandy

+ Same person [Canute married Athelred's widow Aelfgifu].
**Emma also married twice 1Athelred 2 Canute [Swein and Harald Harefoot illig.] Chart 36 p, 123
Note: - Above chart shows how the various inter-marriages join not only families but also nations
   which caused confusion and bloodshed in the fight for the English crown?

DEATH OF KING EDGAR AND THE MURDER OF HIS SON
(959 – 978 AD.)

We have included this part of history to show the bitter struggles, and callous attitudes adopted in these times. Queen Alfthryth, second wife of King Edgar played the central female role in this classic family struggle working with others to make gains for her fraternal son at the expense of her stepson. Atheistic and his son Edgar were the first Kings of England to have full-anointed coronation services. This must have started around 638 when the Catholic Church in France overthrew the dynastic succession and grasped the opportunity to appoint Kings by Papal authority. It emphasized bonding the Church and King and gave the Catholic Church the legal right over both. [To compare times and origins of this ceremony, see the book 'Bloodline of the Holy Grail' p. 222-224].

Edgar's first marriage to Elfrida produced a son Edward [The martyr] and by his second wife Alfthryth a son Althelred. His chief advisor Dunstan, [Archbishop of Canterbury] recognized King Edgar as Gods instrument for controlling the government and played an important role in Edgar's reign. When King Edgar died 978 his oldest son, thirteen-year old Edward by his first marriage was expected to become the next king. A bitter dispute among members of the royal family and the English nobles as to who would succeed King Edgar erupted; Edward [who had alienated many by his bad manners and temper] or his stepbrother Athelred. When the next king was pronounced as Athelred, Edward became enraged.

A plan to remove Edward was hatched by Athelred's supporters including his stepmother. All seemed well when Edward paid a friendly call to see her and his half brother Athelred on the 15th March 978 at Corfe Castle Dorset. On his arrival Alfthryth his stepmother sent the retainers of her son Athelred to greet him with respect and to bed his horse. But before Edward could dismount his hands were seized, and he was murdered with such violence it was even shocking to those that were conditioned by it. The manner it was carried out on an innocent boy of thirteen shocked the nation and later he was made a martyr and Saint.

He was buried without any form of honour at Waxham Norfolk and Athelred, [Alfthryth's son] was crowned one month later. It was discovered one hundred years later that Alfthryth had arranged the murder to enable Athelred her son to become king. The death of any king allowed opportunities for others to express publicly their grievances, such as undoing agreements or reclaiming their land and possessions taken from them during previous reigns, especially the lands taken from the people and given to the churches. **Leofric** the Mercian tried to annul all the agreements made during this reign.

KING ATHELRED 2nd
(978 – 1016)
(Exiled to Normandy 1013 – 1014)

Coat of arms:

Athelred 2nd same as Edgar and Edmund Ironside "Azure a cross patance or "Canute the Great "Or a cross gule in the first and forth quarters, semee of hearts, a gule two lions passant guardant azure. Second and third quarters, a lion rampant, gule supporting a battle axe argent upon an escutcheon of pretence, azure three crowns, or".

It was now 978 AD and soon after his brother was murdered Athelred 2nd became king between the ages of 10/13 years supported by the Mercian's and of course his mother. He was indecisive unless the matter earned his strong feelings, then Althelred would suddenly erupt to force an issue. He was called the Unraed (Unready)] but as you will see for yourself the forces lined up against him from abroad were formidable and his power at home was constantly being undermined by those around him.

To be fair to this King of England, no other monarch had faced such constant ferocious organized attacks from so many foreign insurgents at the same time. Any leader would have been concerned not only how he could repulse the attacks, but also to sustain the courage of his army against the barbaric actions from enemies with much greater trained armies that came from across the sea.

Denmark was becoming a powerful nation emerging under the Danish King Harald Bluetooth, a strong and fearless commander, the conqueror of Norway, which as we will see was not good. He had forced Christianity on both these countries. In England the court regarded Althelred as the deputy of Christ on earth.

A series of Viking raids began again about one year after Althelred's succession to the throne in 978. The Danes and Norsemen occupied large tracts of land in northern and eastern England. In 991 AD instead of fighting, he preferred to raise huge sums of money called Danegeld that he gave as bribes to keep them away hoping to ensure peace. This only encouraged them more, resulting in even greater taxation.

In 993 the Danes turned again to England coming to the mouth of the River Humber, towns were plundered and destroyed. The Angles gathered a very large army and battle was joined but the English leaders Fraena, Frithegist and Godwin took flight. Abbots, Bishops and other religious leaders were not strangers to the battlefield and were often prominent members of an army. Two bishops were among the naval commanders of Althelred's fleet in 993.

King Athelred 2nd Marries Elgyfu (1st wife) of Northampton

Elgyfu [the niece of Canute and was probably daughter of Thorkill], produced sons, one was Edmond Ironsides. Although Athelred honoured her she was never accepted as queen. Between 997-1014 national morale crumbled, leaders changed sides and those that stayed loyal often later betrayed him. Within a year Athelred made a determined attempt to get the invading Danes out of the country and appointed Sheriff (**Turold**), Bishop Elfstan, Bishop Aeswig and Aelfric to lead the troops against them to destroy their ships, and instructed his councillors to gather all their own seaworthy ships at London.

Aelfric turned traitor, warned the Danes and they escaped. He fled that night to his own disgrace. Athelred ordered his own ships to sea and found the Danish fleet off East Anglia and London where they slaughtered the Danes and seized their ships complete with arms and equipment. Athelred took a second wife Emma a Norman Princess and the daughter of Duke Richard 1st of Normandy in 1002

Her Viking temperament leaned more to her Danish and Norse roots than to the English, as you will read later. This marriage proved important, not only to the future of British history but it entitled Athelred to a refugee status in Normandy that he took advantage of when he was later exiled.

By 1002 King Athelred 2nds subjects, tired of the constant attacks on their communities influenced him to take action. On the 13th November he sent an order that all Danish settlers were to be massacred. This order was executed, which brought dire consequences for the nation. Unfortunately among those murdered was the sister of King Swein Forkbeard son of Harald Bluetooth.

In 1004 the Viking's originally raided England in small groups but now came with well organized armies from a fort specially built by Harald Bluetooth [Sweyn's father] at Jomsborg at the mouth of the River Oder, in Germany. Its purpose was to train thousands of crack Danish soldiers to a very high standard ready to do battle at short notice and embark on waiting ships kept on a permanent war footing.

The raids became more regular, Devonshire, Cornwall and the entire coastline to Wales suffered. The Norwegians and Danes devastated the coast of Northumbria and Lindsey [Lincolnshire], these marauding invaders required large quantities of food, which they stole from the resident population. The harsh weather conditions in 1005 and the lack of time devoted to growing crops created a scarcity of food and the whole country was near to famine conditions.

In the same year Thorkill came again with an immense army to Sandwich. It was an interesting situation of divided loyalties when you consider that in some areas of Briton royal control was non-existent and relied on Athelred's sons and son in laws acting in Vice-royal status. Athelred not only had to deal with foreign attacks but also try and unite the bitter territorial rivalry between his son in laws, other principal dignitaries of his court and the local administration.

They used their power in unscrupulous ways to obtain wealth for themselves and as Athelred supported their actions this contributed to his perception as an unjust ruler. One of Athelred's daughters had married Edric Sterona who became Elder man of Mercia and caused much treachery. Another later married Ulfycetel Ealdorman of East Anglia and Mercia, and a third daughter was given in marriage to Waltheof of Bamburgh who will be spoken about later.

The Danes attacked once more and marched to Ringmere Pit near Thetford to the place where the brave commander of East Anglia Ulfceytel had stationed his men. Hearsay suggests that this battle was deliberately avoided on the advice of Edric Sterona and a tribute was paid, probably to give time for Ulfceytel, the Commander of the East Anglian troops, to raise a larger army from all over East Anglia. As William Mortimer and Turold were living at this time we expect they saw and probably were in some way involved with the problems and raids taking place in Norfolk.

In 1009 a great battle took place; the king's son in law Aethelstan and Osuri his son, Eadwig the brother of Aelfric and Wulfric [Leofwine's son] were killed. Many men defected. Ealdorman Ulfceytel led the East Anglian army, which put up a gallant fight, but most of the East Anglian leaders were killed and Ulfycetel was defeated when Canute came with Thorkell/Thirkil the Dane [brother of Sigvaldi, a companion of Swein and the commander of Jomsborg].

These revenge attacks still took place in retaliation for the murder of Sweyn's sister. In 1010 Thorkill landed at Ipswich; Sweyn made East Anglia the focal area and came with his fleet to Norwich burning it; the whole area suffered dreadfully from these attacks. Nothing was spared in their anger. Leaving the skies glowing red with fire and moved on to Thetford, the capital of East Anglia at that time, to do the same. The terror continued and a year later Olav Tryggvason of Norway and Sweyn of Denmark, joined forces to attack London with 94 ships, to burn it but they were repulsed so they ravaged the coastline from Essex to Hampshire instead.

Note: - Most information taken from the*Saxon Chronicles.

These raids caused serious problems for Athelred who although he had an army and navy, relied mainly on each local county, which could call up the population as needed.

*After the major defeat of the East Anglian army in the year 1009, by 1010 the English were confused about these raids and made matters worse for themselves by putting their own differences first in preference to the overall defense of the realm. Refusing to help each other when in need, which resulted in weaknesses in Athelred's defense.

The Danes who had a formidable army took advantage of this shortcoming and caused more confusion by avoiding battles, striking in unexpected places, and then disappearing by quickly slipping away back to their ships. When the English army arrived to defend the north the enemy attacked the south, when the English went to defend the south the enemy attacked the north; Athelred and his councilors sued for peace, and paid more tributes on condition the harassment would cease.

By 1012 after constant attacks from several foreign armies, King Athelred's influence over his nation had become very weak; he could not continue raising cash for an effective army. The Danes that had settled in the country assisted the invaders. Canterbury was captured; Archbishop Alfheath was seized, refusing to be ransomed. They took him to Greenwich London and probably on the site where Greenwich Church now stands; in a drunken stupor they murdered him on Saturday 19th April 1012 by pelting him with bones and cattle heads. Finally they struck him on the head with the back of an axe and killed him.

The Bishops Eadnoth and Aelfhun with others took the body with all honour and buried it in St. Paul's minister. When the church was built it was dedicated to St. Alfheath. Thorkill/Thirkil lost control of his men because he objected to this murder and their brutal behavior to their captives. In disgust he joined the English taking forty-five ships with him and the rebels returned home. In defiance they took some hostages, only to deposit them further along the coast minus their eyes, hands or feet.

**It is interesting to note that England evolved slowly into shires from about the time of Athelstan but became more prominent during the reign of Athelred with the kings representative called a reeve of the shire. Later known as the shire reeve [sheriff] who presided over the shire court whenever the ealdorman was not available, which was quite often, some Reeves took over the administration of a shire.

*All in Saxon Chronicles
* * 'The making of Early England' by D.P. Kirby

DANISH INVASION AND CONQUEST OF ENGLAND
King Sweyn, becomes King of England Denmark and Sweden

When the large invasion came in 1013 King Sweyn himself came for the last time determined to have conquest. Choosing the region of the Humber making their headquarters in Gainsborough, which was no accident as they anticipated the assistance of the Thegnes [landowners] of Dane law and were not disappointed.

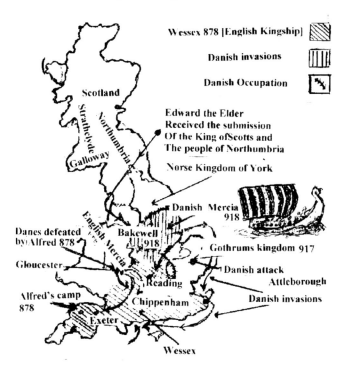

The Danish Invasion [Artists impression]   Plate 20

The men of five (later seven) boroughs were the chief lawmen and always acted together in ways similar to our own government and law system of today. The English leaders Fraena, Frithegist and Godwin again took flight and went out to meet their Viking Danish brothers. Athelred considered that to negotiate with a foreign power was treason. This explains why those lawmen were murdered [more about them later].

Among the Thegnes who came to join the Danes were Morca and Sigforth who gave their submissions as did Wessex, Oxford, Winchester and Bath with no opposition.

King Athelred with Thorkill, who had changed allegiance and gone over to him held only London. When Thorkill's loyalty to Athelred came into question, London submitted. Danelaw had broken down because King Athelred was a weak ruler who could not unite the fractionalized army and had lost the respect of the nation.

It was Christmas and celebrations were in full swing. Some reports state Athelred stayed behind to fight for his kingdom others say he stayed aboard his ship with his fleet on the Thames, by now it was a lost cause. When Thorkill fled it left King Athelred in big trouble so he sent his wife and children to be with her father Richard 1st in Normandy. Finally Athelred had to leave his kingdom too and went into exile in Normandy with his family, which left the Danes masters of most of the country.

The sons of Athelred 2nd and Emma, Alfred and Edward the exiled princes probably met William [later the Conqueror] at his fathers court where the hopes of the two young princes to regain the English crown were kept alive. William of Jumeiges claimed that William [later the Conquror] actually contemplated the invasion of England on Edward's behalf, so when Edward was invited back to England in 1042 as King, it must have looked to him as being a victory for the Norman connection.

After the invasion by the Danes not many Saxon churches or monasteries were left visible above ground. Only parts of the second monastery of North Elmham Norfolk [a Saxon Cathedral] are left. Valuable books and historical documents were destroyed and lost forever, which made the progress of learning almost impossible. During the time of the Danish rule the capital of Norfolk moved from Attleborough to Thetford. King Sweyn of Denmark and Sweden extended his kingdom over England but this lasted for only two months before he died. In conclusion the Chronicle's account of the wars of Athelred's reign is that he was conspicuous by his absence and never fought decisively against the Danes.

DANISH ROYAL FAMILY [Kings of England]

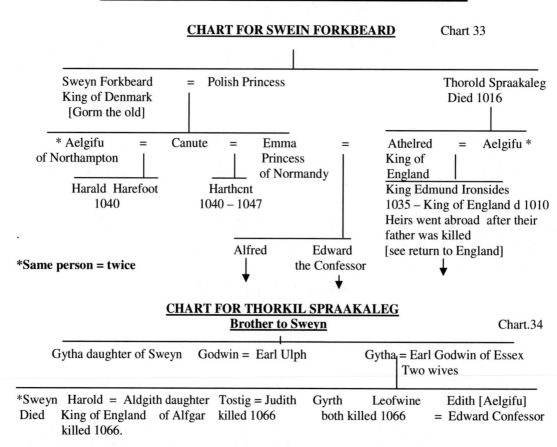

See; - Saxon Chronicles. The main characters that will feature in the next few years of our story are on page 120 / 122 *Sweyn and Tostig had different mothers' page 92 chart 32

KING SWEYN (SENIOR) DROWNS AT SEA

Canute is chosen by the army to be king of England

Mystery and legend surrounds the cause of King Sweyn's sudden death on February 3rd 1014 AD. Was it an accident?

A legend was created after the death of King Edmund [the adopted son of Offa who lived at [Rendelsham/Reedham]. He had been wrongly blamed for the death of Lothric a Danish nobleman [see story p.61] and was brutally killed by Danish arrows and then decapitated at Haegelisdun (Hellesdon near Norwich in 870]. The legend stated that miracles often took place at Hoxne and Sutton. The first miracle was a wolf crying out "here" which led to the recovery of the king's head; this made the monastery at Hoxne a place of pilgrimage.

In 903 Edmund King of East Anglia became a martyr and created a Saint as briefly referred too in the item on Bury St Edmund's. This says that in 945 or shortly after, the land surrounding Bedricsworth [now known as Bury St Edmunds] was given to the community and the murdered Edmund's remains were taken there. Upon the renewal of Danish raids they took his body to London for safety where it stayed for three years then returned to Bury. King Sweyn made demands for a ransom from St. Edmund's lands.

Rumours spread that "the Saints spear" brought increasing respect for his power at sea and caused King Sweyn's death. To atone for his father's lack of respect, *King Canute added a rotunda to the earlier church of St. Mary in 1020 and Bishop Ailwin of Elmhem granted freedom from Episcopal control, substituted twenty monks taken from St. Benet's near Horning and from Ely for the Secular Priesthood.

Even in later years Edward 1st dreamed that St. Edmund was making him into another Sweyn when he started infringing monastic rights in the town outside the abbey. A St Edmund memorial coin was issued which stimulated patriotic feelings, and caused the removal of the Saints body to a royal monastery; his shrine was placed behind the high alter at Bury. Edward the Confessor granted a mint in St. Edmunds Bury, the first use of this name. Sweyn's army still in England chose his 18-year old son **Canute as King of all England. Athelred learned of these events and sent his son Edward to negotiate with the English councillors to accept him back as their king, promising them his kingship would change.

*+**Canute, son of Sweyn Forkbeard was also known as Cnut. He raised a son Harthacnut and his half brother Harold Harefoot. Some information on these pages is from Saxon Chronicles translated by Ann Savage and various specialist history books on this period of time. One book 'The Making of Early England' by D. P. Kirby ISBN 9 3328 3297 30 is particularly recommended for study.

He returned to England to claim back his kingdom and intended to take revenge on those that had betrayed him. The five boroughs returned to their English allegiance and the two kings came to a truce agreeing to divide the kingdom between them, Canute ruled the north and Athelred the south.

After an uneasy peace was established the Danes made **Leofric** [the brother of **Leofwine**] Earl of Mercia. Athelred made Leofwine, the Earl of Harrow (this was the northwestern neighbour of the West Saxons in Warwickshire and Gloucestershire). These had their own royal dynasty and bishopric thought to be at Worcester) **Leofric**'s family were counted as being nobles in the court of Canute. At first the people rejoiced for the return of Athelred, but he soon he reverted back to his old ways.

War broke out once more, Athelred drove Canute up north chasing him out of Lindsey and paying 21,000 to Thorkill for his mercenaries to guard London. Canute went back to Gainsborough taking hostages from Lindsey and put to sea with these, leaving Thorkill behind. In 1015 King Athelred summoned a meeting of his council at Oxford and all the leading Danes from the Welland attended. (See item on Crowley for a more detailed account of the Welland seat of the Abbey).

Among those present included brothers **Leofric, Morcar* and **Sigforth** who had been judged as traitors, ringleaders for those collaborating with the Danish invaders, tricked by Edrich Sterona, taken into a side room and murdered on what looked like the orders of Athelred. These were the cousins of **Morca and Edwin** the sons of **Leofwine, Leofrics** brother.

On the order of Athelred all their possessions were confiscated with that of any other Dane who remained in his kingdom. In 1015 Alfred of Lincoln (**Leofric's** nephew) had a coin struck bearing the monogram of Alfred of Lincoln. Norwich became a mint city producing over 200 varieties of coins. So the whole of **Leofric's'** family may have moved from Attleborough at sometime just before this date.

Most buildings, domestic and personal items were made of wood [which was abundant] or cloth, unless these were stored, treasured or looked after in a reasonable environment they decayed. Of course they were also discarded and finally rotted away so that masses of ancient artifacts were lost forever. While staying at Malmsbury Athelred also ordered the widow of Sigforth to be brought before him, possibly to humiliate her. Edmund who by now was in rebellion against his father [some things never change] over the assassination of Sigforth and Morcar, took many decisions, forestalled

* See Saxon Chronicles page 160.

Athelred and took Sigforth's widow, married her and claimed all the possessions of both these men. This caused a dispute between Edmund and Edrich Sterona, who was annoyed over this marriage; it was decisive factor in changing his allegiance back to Canute's side. Under the favour of Canute, Godwin [senior] being unscrupulous in action rose to power as his advisor, which gave him political influence. He had a sense of aggrandizement, which stood him in good stead apparently. [His father was Wulfnoth Cilde, a Thegne of Essex who later in 1018 Canute created Earl].

When Godwin married Gytha sister of Olaf of Denmark, it brought him in close contact with the court where he and **Leofric** [junior] together with Thorkill and **Leofric** senior formed a committee of Thegnes or a circle of councilors from 1018-20. Godwin gained ascendancy with the two **Leofric's** as his chief advisors but it was the treachery of Edrich that would later cause Edmund's early death.

KING ATHELRED 2nd DIES
Edmund Becomes King of Southern England
1016

Canute returned once more pillaging the South East Coast like some wild animal and invading Wessex. Edmund raised an army with what he thought was the help of Edrich Streona but Edrich deserted him changing sides to fight with Canute's army which secured victory for the Danes.

The West Saxons had to submit leaving Edmund no help except for Uchtred of Northampton. Uchtred was lured by the treachery of Edrich to defend York and was assassinated. At this time Athelred, seemed to want to remain in London as he was unwell and probably dying; he withdrew from active participation and left Edmund to organize resistance as best he could.

King Athelred 2nd, the father of Edmund Ironside by Elgifu, and Edward the Confessor, Alfred and Godigfu by Emma died on 23rd April 1016 Edmund succeeded as king of Wessex and became the second King of Southern England. Canute was hailed as King of England but Edmund hotly contested this and he and Canute prepared for a battle. Canute's attack on London was a failure.

In the same year Edmund commanded ***Alfgar** to be blinded, no doubt in revenge for his part in accepting Danish rule at that time, and the betrayal of his father to the Danes in 1013. These times were full of selfish interests and self-preservation; loyalties were easily switched. Edmund was treacherously deceived for the last time when the armies met.

* Both Alfgar and Turold married daughters of William Malet, a powerful Dane.

The Chronicle states that the two armies met at Ashington; Edrich deserted to Canute with his men and fought against Edmund. Most of the nobility of England were killed among the Anglian troops Ulfcytel of East Anglia, Ealdorman Elfric of Hampshire, and the bishop of Dorchester. The Chronicle records that Edmund was defeated, yet amazingly he still took advice from Edrich who persuaded him that there was no hope he could defeat Canute and reluctantly Edmund agreed to give up more of his kingdom.

However Canute wanted even more and so the skirmishes continued. The fact that Edrich Sterona, Edmund's brother-in-law betrayed not only his country and the nation of his birth but his Lord, which provoked the disgust of the Chronicler. Edmund who had meanwhile taken Edrich into his confidence again was persuaded to face Canute at Alney, some say in personal one to one combat with an agreement to divide the country.

What happened to Edmund is not clear, some writers say he survived and by legend died later by the hand of Edrich. Whatever the outcome Edmund did not live for long after the meeting and died on St. Andrews's day 1016.

With no real leader the West Saxons accepted Canute as their King in 1017 AD and Edrich Streona is said to have counseled him to destroy the surviving sons of Athelred. One Edwig was slain; Athelred's widow Emma, escaped with Alfred and Edward to Normandy to be with her father Richard 1st Duke of Normandy and sending the children of Edmund to Hungary.

In Broomfield's historical writings it states Edrich was the ancestor of **Leofric's** family, but this is the only mention of this fact that we could find. There are many references to **Leofric** and associated members of his family not only because of its interesting local history, but the incidence of the name of **Turold** is the one that ties in with our own family regarding time and circumstances.

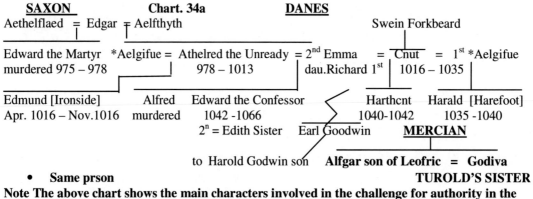

- **Same prson**

Note The above chart shows the main characters involved in the challenge for authority in the time of King Athelred

CANUTE THE DANE BECOMES FIRST KING OF ALL ENGLAND

After **C**anute succeeded to all the kingdom of England in 1017 he divided it into four. Following the way of the world, the powerful, and the devious are usually the ones that receive the rewards. For the treachery of Edrich the Danes initially rewarded him by making him Earl of Mercia and Eric (Blood axe) Earl of Northumbria. Canute claimed Wessex and set up his court of Earls including his two brothers Harkon 1019-26 and Eric Duke of Worcestershire who captured church estates there 1018-1023). Thorkill was made Earl of East Anglia, 1018-1020, and Eilaf the Viking leader 1018-1024 was also rewarded.

The significance of these dates is that from 1018 there is a gap in the series of charters of Canute's Earl's who had been prominent in the first part of his reign. When the series restarted the Scandinavian Earls who had been influential during this period had all disappeared. Sigward of Northumbria succeeded Eric of Normandy in 1075 then his son Waltheof received the Lordship; no new Danish Earls appear.

It is here that the inter-relationship between kings, queens and others gets complicated and needs to be thoroughly understood [see chart 32 p.92] as they start a series of events that later causes bloodshed and war between their offspring. Before the 1st August King Canute ordered that Emma, the widow of Athelred to be brought to him to be his wife. Canute had previously had an association with Elgyfu the first wife of Athelred and had issue, Harold and Swein.

In the marriage negotiation in 1017, agreement was reached between Emma, her father Duke Richard 1st of Normandy and her new husband Canute, who promised on oath that Edmund Ironside would succeed him and he would never set up a son of any other woman to rule England. This oath only applied to England, and this would bring yet more complications to the claims for the prospective heirs to the crown, as they later produced a child Harald Harthcnut.

Her other children by Athelred, [Alfred and Edward] appeared to be permanently exiled in the environment of the Norman Court, but this did not save Alfred, as you will read, even though their situation made them many Norman friends. In Norfolk there were other families of royal decent with Scandinavian and Norman origins, (see charts of **Rollo and Leofric**) that we can follow as we continue through the book. Canute was desperate to retain his dynasty. With all the intrigue and murders that surrounded royalty at this time there seems to be a logic of self-preservation behind his marriage to Emma.

Showing some of the descendants of Siward Earl of Northumbria And the Earldom of Huntingdon.

Chart 35

Siward Earl of Northumbria =Adele sister of William the 1st
1035

Osborne	Judith	=	Waltheof
Killed in Scotland	Niece of William 1st		became Count of Huntingdon
1054	King of England		1065 executed 1076

1st Simon 'de St Liz' 1st = Maude = 2nd David 1st King of Scotland
Became Earl of Huntingdon in or before 1090;

Simon de St.Liz 2nd	St Waltheof	Henry of Scotland Successor to Earldom of
C of Huntingdon	Abbot of Melrose	Huntingdon 1136-1139 After Scottish war
		resigned the Earldom in Huntingdon
Simon de St Liz 3rd		to become Earl of Northumberland
Count of Huntingdon		

Malcom	Wlliam the Lion	David of Scotland
King of Scotland	king of Scotland	became Earl of Huntingdon
	Earldom of Huntingdon	1185 d 1219
	In 1165 deprived	

As Emma belonged to a very powerful family Canutes marriage to her would deter others, such as the late Athelred's family, from attacking him. There were so many children of the same mothers Elgyfu and Emma [by different fathers] who were beyond his grasp. Canute had to find a way for giving his own offspring a clear path for the kingship.

He did not need to replace the English landowning class as he patronized the major landowners by giving them estates in their own localities and by establishing garrisons in major towns. Assuming the self-interest of these people would be sufficient for him to hold control over them. By the end of 1017 Canute's thought that he had achieved a safe situation and decided to remove the remaining Englishmen he distrusted, so on Christmas day Edrich Streona and several others were assassinated.

In Canute's last years, **Leofric Earl of Mercia** and Godwin Earl of Wessex were powerful men. Godwin [who was a Dane/Norman married to Gytha] and his sons were part Scandinavian [with Scandinavian names] but having no ancestral claim to the English crown, his cunning lies, deceitful maneuvering and treacherous violence began a power struggle with one eye on the throne.

Ultimately, the rivalry of Godwin and **Leofric** was a significant factor in weakening the possibility of united resistance against the impending invasions by the Norman's and killing one another. Canute on the death of his brother the King of Denmark in 1018 [till his own death in 1035] succeeded him as King, and in 1028-1029 he also became king of Norway.

However he was anxious to give England his main attention, so he sent back most of the Danish ships and fighters. The balance he left in England helped to make up a royal guard [Huscarles]. These were used for garrison duty and he took care to have a good administrative staff at his side in order not to offend the Anglo Saxon legal and administrative procedures, also insuring that he kept on good terms with the French and Italian Kings of the powerful **Valoise** families. Both were his relatives by marriage and part of the Holy Roman Empire.

The King outlawed Thorkill (The Tall) Earl of East Anglia on 11th November in the same year, though the Earl retained his position in East Anglia and still lived in Attleborough. Legend has it that the Canute took Thorkill's son under his protection in 1023. This was a pretext, the real reason was that he had sent Thorkill with his own son Harald Harthcnt to Denmark in order that the boy would be trained as king and to protect his own authority over the throne of Denmark. He retained Thorkill's son to ensure his will was carried out. On the 12th June 1021 monks were installed in the church of Bury St Edmund's, it was said that these were introduced there on Thorkill's authority.

In 1022 the Pope directed that **Leofric** senior and **Leofric** junior [son of his brother **Leofwine**, who Canute had unlawfully driven out of Ely] "Should be pardoned. Because the people of the land said they were upright and generous men" and were one of the few families to remain in power without using violence or aggression.

KING CANUTE DIES

CONTENDERS FOR THE CROWN STAKE THEIR CLAIM

King Canute's death on the 12th November 1035 precipitated a royal crisis as both his sons' [Harold Harefoot and Harald Harthcnt] contended for the crown of England; though both attained the throne, neither of reached the age of thirty. After Canute's death Harkon appears at Shire meetings in two other documents selling land with **Leofric** in an Eversham lease (S1423) and judging a lawsuit with Ealderman **Leofwine** and **Leofric** (S1460).

Leofwine's presence in court (S1460) may or may not indicate that Harkon was under his authority. Edmund Ironside, [son of King Athelred] had already been killed in battle and never attained the fruition of the succession, which had been agreed in the marriage contract between Canute and Emma. But there were other claimants waiting in the wings.

Note; - most of above is derived from the Saxon Chronicles   *See chart 36 page 123 for marriage of Godwin.

HARALD HAREFOOT TAKES THE THRONE FROM HARTHACNUT

(Son of Canute and Elgifu)   (1035-40   (Son of Canute and Emma)

BROTHERS IN A BOTHER

All the various options and the outcome as to who would be the next king of England did not always rest with succession or a chosen contender, sometimes in with the connivance or violence of those with power. King Canute had given Harthacnt Denmark so he had to remain there to stop an attack from Norway and dared not leave to claim England. Was this connivance by Elgyfu [widow of Canute and stepmother of Harthcnt] to keep Harthacnt tied down in Denmark while she and her son Harald Harefoot took possession of England and Winchester treasury?

Canute had intended that Harthacnut would become King of England and Denmark. It is very difficult to keep to plan in real life and certainly impossible to control a situation from the grave. Harald Harefoot and Elgyfu were given the guardianship of Norway, but he was considered illegitimate and did not have the right to rule and so was deposed and driven out of Norway to return to England, or was it a veiled voluntary move? A party led by **Leofric** Earl of Mercia, with strong Scandinavian connections helped them. There was a division in England 1035-6 that showed in the coinage when local mints struck coins simultaneously in names of Harold Harthcnt while others were minted in the name of Harald Harefoot.

The Kingship for Harold Harthcnt was agreed at Oxford attended by **Leofric** and men north of the Thames. Harald Godwin and the chief men of Wessex held out against him, supporting the fleet in London. His supporters pressed for him to be regent for his brother's share. Emma took the royal treasure and Wessex Regency. Godwin took control of the royal household troop but their power was short lived as Harald Harefoot was recognized as King throughout England and he then seized the royal treasure.

The Ambush of Alfred 1036 AD

In consideration of the previous information, matters became more complicated when the two sons of Athelred and Emma, Alfred and Edward [later King Edward the Confessor] were invited by a "letter" in Emma's name to visit her in Winchester. A simple natural thing to do but she claimed King Harald [we assume she meant Harald Harefoot] forged this letter, but in those times some mothers were dangerous people. Emma must have regarded the visit by her two sons as threatening, and for them to dare to visit England at this time indicated something serious was afoot as they were supposed to stay exiled in Normandy.

As mentioned previously, Emma had agreed with her husband Canute that Edmond Ironside by Athelred and Elgyfu would be the next king of England and her son Harold Harthcnut would succeed to the throne after Edmund Ironside's death. As this had already occurred in battle; no doubt Harald Harefoot wanted to get any other claimants to the throne in his clutches.

Edward reached Winchester but Earl Godwin [who was a close confident of Queen Emma's and probably aware of this situation, was evidently now a supporter of King Harald Harefoot); he had Alfred intercepted and captured at Guildford while on his way to confer with King Harald Harefoot. Godwin dispersed Alfred's friends, some into captivity others tortured, blinded or beheaded. Alfred was blinded and taken to the monks at Ely, who were renowned for their cruelty, where he died of head injuries.

Later **Osborne Malet** blamed Godwin and **Hereward the Wake** for this and his brother Frederick's death. After this despicable act, hatred festered between **Leofric, Alfgar, Osborne** and the Godwin's, causing them to take action to bring Earl Godwin to book. As the house of **Leofric** was connected to both the Norman and the Scandinavian royal houses it would explain why Godwin was so vindictive to those that came between him and his secret lust for power.

Harald Harefoot who obviously supported Godwin in this matter prosecuted the lying bishop of Worcester, who swore that the order for the death of Alfred came from Harald Godwin. Because of this intrigue Godwin was then exiled and his lands given to **Alfgar.** Godwin was later allowed back as King Harald feared his power as an enemy and in 1039 the King decided to restore him to favour. **Leofric** and some of his loyal contemporaries were against this as they probably saw the danger to **Alfgar.** Emma (mother of Harold Harthcnt) was expelled by Harald Harefoot and fled, not to her father in Normandy, as the situation there was unstable due to the fact that her nephew William Duke of Normandy's position in Normandy was in the minority so she went to Flanders instead.

In a short time all Alfred's sons were tracked down and killed leaving Harald Harefoot master of England. Hearing the news about his brother Alfred from his mother, Edward also fled. After ruling England for four years and sixteen weeks King Harald Harefoot died suddenly in Oxford 17th March 1040, embarrassing for many who had changed loyalties. Also threats were being made to young William Duke of Normandy who as you will read later, rather unexpectedly becomes King of all England.

Note – Most of this information derived from the Saxon Chronicle page 168

KING HARTHACNT
(1040 – 42 AD)

The English again sent for Harthacnt to become King, which was supported by **Leofric,** and many chief Thegnes but vigorously opposed by Godwin. There were many doubts about Harold Harthacnt as he had spent much of his time in Denmark.

A pact was made with King Magnus of Norway, to enable Harthacnt to return and take the throne of England that would unite the two kingdoms of England and Denmark. On his return he gave an order to exhume the body of his half brother [King Harald Harefoot], which they dragged through the mud and cast into the River Thames.

The sudden death of King Harald Harefoot, and the new king being half-brother to Alfred (who Godwin's eldest son Sweyn murdered), put Earl Godwin in an awkward situation; all his treachery had come to nothing so he had to try to make peace with the new King. The hatred for them at Court was considerable but the Godwin's somehow kept their hands on the reigns of power. It did seem at this time no one could remain in the path of the Godwin's for long, but powerful Thegnes found that they could block his ambitions by acting as a group, and **Leofwine** and **Leofric** were amongst these. Harthcnt imposed heavy taxation during his reign.

In the early part of the eleventh century Edward the Confessor and his brother Alfred were living under the protection of the Dukes of Normandy. The pressure of rivals seeking the throne and above all fear of attack from Normandy caused so much unrest that in 1041 Harthacnt, who suffered ill health, invited Edward (the son of Athelred and Emma) from exile to join him in England. Which was for him like walking into the lion's den. Edward was bold, well received and sworn in as King on April 5th 1041 during his half brother Harthacnt's lifetime.

*Harthacnt died on June 8th 1042 AD while taking part in a drinking match with his friends in Oxford suffering an alcoholic fit. Here the Godwin's excel again, as close advisors to Queen Emma who was of Viking blood. She did not want the Old Saxon regime back so the feud continued between the Godwin's and the families of **Leofric**. How much involvement she had with Godwin is not known but it seems quite considerable.

Merrymaking. Plate 21
By John Mathews

* Derived from Saxon Chronicles page 168

The reasons for the forthcoming battle of 1066 were mainly caused by the royal inter-marriages. The resulting children were of different nationalities that all had a claim to the throne, so you can see why we asked you to follow the charts carefully. In the previous chapters we have outlined the national course of events that have been gathered from ancient writings, and from these we have mentioned names of individuals that we can put into our own family structure.

The Danes like the Romans created many different settlements and three of these were formed in Norwic [Norwich] where the communities soon made paths and tracks that led to a common marketplace they called Tombland [which means open space] on the same side of the river as Conisford [Kings Ford]. These names are still used and the present road system in the old part of the city principally follow those ancient tracks today. An ancient church stood where the Norman church of St. Michael still stands but it has lost the interesting part of its name, which was St. Michael in the Mootstow [The place of meeting].

It is interesting to study the history of how the course of roads and territorial areas in the ancient town of Norwic came into existence, which was an important issue to our forefathers. Throughout time boundaries generally began and ended by the course of rivers which acted as a barrier to invaders. For example, in the 800's north-west Mercia and Northumbria were bounded by the river Mersey; the north east by the Humber. Mercia and Wessex were bounded by the Bristol Avon and Thames, Norfolk and Suffolk by the Waveney. The river was not only a means for traveling by boat, drinking and domestic requirements, but provided a defense for towns and villages

*There are numerous examples of these river boundaries. The road network was mainly established during the Roman period mostly for military reasons, which linked the population and strategic forts. The roads unlike the rivers were constructed on high ridges to avoid river crossings and served as a look out point. Watling Street acted as an important boundary between the Saxons and Danes and in the time of Alfred and Guthrum they regarded their boundary as being along the Thames to its source then a straight line to Bedford continuing along the river Ouse to Watling Street. As the population was very much smaller than today there were great areas of wooded countryside and villages were few and far between, any stranger who had lost his way and did not indicate his presence, was often harshly treated, assaulted or killed.

*A more detailed description of this can be found in D.P. Kirby's excellent book "The Making of Early England" [chapter 2]

THE SAXONS RETURN
TO CLAIM THE THRONE OF ENGLAND.

EDWARD THE CONFESSOR
[1042 – 1065 AD]
Alfgar v Godwin ----- He Who Dares Wins
(And a question of relativity)

The Coat Of Arms Assigned To Edward the Confessor
Azure "a cross patance between five martlets ore". Which Harold 2nd is supposed to have born:
Two bars between six leopards' faces all or".

When Edward the Confessor son of Athelred came to the throne 5th April 1042 he became sole King over all England, the Anglo Saxon Royal House regained the position it lost in 1016 and the Danish/Viking age in England had gone forever. He was about the age of forty and was named the "Confessor" because of his saintly nature.

Being majestic in appearance the defects in his character did not show too much, he was probably an albino. His virtues were mainly spiritual though reputed to be indolent and neglectful, unfitted for kingship, only showing his ability to rule when he had strong feelings on a matter, which may have resulted in violent fits of temper. Edward's nature allowed others to dominate and manipulate him to their advantage and again it was a group of the more powerful Thegnes who monopolised provincial government.

The Godwin family used their influence to override his courts, and the rise of Harold Godwin is an important fact in the politic history of England proceeding more slowly than historians realise.Throughout his reign Edward was surrounded in England by intrigue, deceit and betrayal from his own close relations and the ambitions of the Godwin family, who lusted for power at any cost. By connivance and intrigue they would remove anything that stood in their way to gain the throne of England, they did achieve this for a few months in later years. [King Harold 1066]. Before Edward came to the throne rumours started and continued during the years of 1051-2 regarding the death of his brother Alfred, most of the rumours connected to the Godwin family.

Edward's upbringing in Norman court circles reflected his loyalties during the first ten years of his reign as he still regarded Normandy his home where his relatives and friends lived. He kept contact with those he grew up with such as Ralph of Brittany (later the Earl of Norfolk), Lanfrac (later the Archbishop of Canterbury), **Osborn** and **William Mallet** our ancestor's. Many gained very high positions and were a great help to William the Conqueror in the Norman Conquest of 1066.

Duke William's father (Robert the Devil) and other near relations were Edward's friends and benefactors during his exile and as far as Edward was concerned were his nearest blood relations. The Norman connections that he promoted to the seats of power were not in the best interests of Earl Godwin who plotted to change the situation and gain control over others for himself and his family. This he achieved, his powers of influence were strong, something we would today call charisma.

His possessions were vast but scattered widely; his main strength laid in Southern England where his lands were and where the centre of national authority was. Unlike the Earls of Mercia he never had the combined resources of land in the Northwest Midlands, where the Earls of Mercia had no rivals*. No doubt he had in his mind that his future grandson would inherit the crown of England but alas like many things in life, this did not go to plan. Harold Godwin's older brother Sweyn became Earl of Mercia in 1043 but even after the promotion of his brother Tostig, in 1065 [to the Northumbrian Earldom] the house of **Leofric** was still more powerful than the house of Godwin.

Earl Godwin senior was always a thorn in Edward's crown especially later after his marriage to Godwin's daughter. We can only conclude, that it was as strange as it was obvious that Godwin, who was causing so many problems for Edward was allowed to hold great influence.

Edward's reactions show that he must have been afraid of the power that Godwin, his wife and his mother together commanded, or was there something else? Was he involved in the murder of his brother Alfred? His court had not forgotten this murder and regarded him with suspicion. Likewise Godwin knew that although treated with respect, he was far from Edward's favourite, the complex quarrel between the King and Godwin was turning to hatred and building to civil war. The Earl was trying everything to gain control, and the constant persecution of **Leofric's** family showed that he considered them a threat.

It seems that Godwin had a hold on Edward as each decision made against him was always reversed and Godwin always came out on top. To his credit, Edward upheld the dignity of the crown in what literally was a sea of trouble. There was no goodwill between them and to add more worry for Edward the three-way claim to the English throne was mounting. To make matters worse he discovered his mother Emma had leanings towards the Viking's in Normandy and a strong desire to remove him as King and to place her Norman blood relations on the throne.

*Derived from the book "Saxon England" by Sir Frank Stenton

The Norman's, although they implied that they were assisting Edward by closing their ports in Normandy to their Viking brothers, still offered them refuge and a base from which to make attacks on England until a truce was made.

King Edward's feelings toward his mother hardened in 1043 and he took action against her for conspiring with Godwin against **Leofric** and Siward, and being connected with the murder of his brother Alfred. Worse, he learned that she had put all her wealth at the disposal of Olaf, King of Norway and Sweden, possibly inviting him to invade England.

He punished his mothers' treacherous acts by sending three of his most senior Thegnes **Leofric**, Siward and another to carry out his orders. Confiscating her jewels, goods, wealth and properties; as he put it, she held them too close to her and as a result Godwin her close advisor was banished from her presence. The women in power had little mercy even for their own family so you can understand why Edward took no chances. Quite a little hornet's nest was stirred up but we will leave it there and not disturb their conscience.

The Chronicles also state that Sigmund the priest (another confidant) was deposed from his Bishopric and the king confiscated all his goods. Edward sent three of his most senior Thegnes to carry out his orders concerning his mother, **Leofric,** Siward and another that proved that they were his most trusted men. Envious eyes waited for a reason to attack Edward's throne and ambitions were raised as King Edward married Earl Godwin's daughter Algifu (Edith) in 1045. Godwin must have been most satisfied, it was his greatest achievement to gain power and a positive place in the royal family, and he became the kings' father-in-law!

The main threat of invasion was removed when his mothers intended invasion ally Magnus of Norway died in 1047.

Earls/Thegnes were chosen from the ranks of those of noble birth to represent trade in the Anglo Danish Monarchy. They acted as lawmen, defenders of the realm and advisors in the kings' court, and representatives of Edward in Angle/Danish monarchy. Their sons inherited these positions as titles, property; other assets were passed down in ambitious rivalry with one another. There was a lesser court of minor Thegnes, called Southwell, which judged the ordinary citizens.

Some of the pre conquest Lords such as **Gilbert Crispin** [when he was Abbot of St. Peters Westminster] kept large numbers of landless knight's and 25 houses for these men.

But there was an ulterior motive, as they could be called upon to fight for their Lord when the need arose, just as Edward used the help and loyalty of his most senior Thegnes (such as **Leofric** and Siward). **Leofric's** father **Leofwine** was of Danish/Mercian descent, a well-connected Danish noble a councilor of Canute's court. Godwin was especially jealous of this and **Leofric's** friendship with Ralph de Geuder [Edward's nephew].

Edward did not oppose Godwin knowing that to do so would enable his enemies to see weakness in his governmental system that could seriously affect the country and invite attack. The selfish ambition of Godwin to gain the throne of England spelt disaster for himself, his family and the nation. Edward and his wife Edith [Godwin's daughter] without a child made Godwin think his only hope was to create an incident to grab the throne, as he had no recognized royal blood relationship to make it legal.

In 1051 Eustace the count of Boulogne was involved in a dispute with the citizens of Dover, complained to the king and laid the blame on the people living there. As it was a part of Godwin's Earldom the king ordered him to punish the town. Godwin refused and was summoned to a council meeting, the Kings men arrived with a small force and found Godwin already assembling an army. **Leofric** saved them arriving with reinforcements to aid the King facing Godwin's army at Beverstone.

Edward never attacked, fearing Godwin would call upon his foreign friends who would be all too willing to use it as an excuse to invade England, so he negotiated a new meeting. Using the time lag Edward summoned his army from all over England. When some of Godwin's men defected and joined the king, Godwin tried to clear his name but failed.

After a discussion with no agreements reached, fearing enemies would seize this moment of indecision, Godwin fled to the coast, sending a message asking for their names to be cleared; but the king refused. Safe conduct was not granted to any Godwin's, or their close supporters all were ordered to leave within five days; the rebellion was over.

The rebels fled the country, Sweyn and Tostig to the Baldwin's in Flander's [*Tostig's future father-in-law descendant from **Charlemagne** King of France], Harald and another brother went to Ireland. Bitterly angry, Edward sent his own wife Edith, daughter of Godwin to the nunnery at Wherwell. All these circumstances left King Edward disillusioned and unhappy with the wrangling and bickering among his own nobles.

*This brought Tostig Godwin into the Royal circle. Most of the above information is derived from the Saxon Chronicles p.177-179

His lack of a successor became a worry. The sons of Earl Godwin had expected to be uncles to the next king and it was becoming clear that there would be no children of the marriage to reverse the king's intention towards William of Normandy receiving the crown. Edward had neither brother nor son, and all his near relations had either died or had been murdered.

While the Godwin's were in exile, Edward began to bring more and more nobles from Normandy, which the people did not like at all; neither did his mother Emma who did not want to return to the old Scandinavian regime with the involvement of Norman power. What association she had with Godwin's influence seeking murders and intrigues there is no way of telling. We do know, referring back, that under the previous King, the Godwin's had been her chief advisors and close confidants.

It was also during 1051 at the time of Godwin's expulsion that William Duke of Normandy was probably informed of Edward's thoughts about choosing him as his successor; perhaps this was the reason why William visited England. Edward still had the strength of **Leofric** and Siward to rely on, but fearing for the security of the realm he took the advice of his senior Thegnes allowing the Godwin's to return to England and regain all that had been taken from them. They were reinstated after negotiations, but this spelled trouble for **Aelfgar** son of **Leofric** who had been given their lands.

Time passed and by 1052 the Godwin's had grown so powerful they were confidant that their obsession for ultimate power was near to fruition. Edward became more introverted moving even closer in spirit to his relations in Normandy. It was at this time, according to Norman sources the Godwin's had to agree to accept the king's wishes that William Duke of Normandy would be his successor. Edward had officially nominated William Duke of Normandy to succeed him by sending Robert of Jumieges archbishop of Canterbury with the news.

Historians claim that the constant quarreling between Edward and the Godwin's made the king all the more determined that William should be his successor. He was apparently still very unsure of himself due to the circumstances that surrounded him while a boy and sought constant advice, but was very positive once he had made a decision. Although he was not able to see that the recommendations given were mostly in the interests of the advisers. When Earl Godwin (senior) died in April 1053 of a heart attack while at a banquet, the serious challenge to Edward was now removed though his sons still held prominent positions of power.

This was reduced further when Sweyn Godwin [the son] died in the same year while on a pilgrimage to Jerusalem, which left Harold Godwin to succeed to the title of Earl of Wessex. This was the only earldom in their hands from 1053-55, as Hertfordshire with Oxfordshire was given to the king's nephew Ralph the Timid, East Anglia was given to **Alfgar** the son of Leofric. **Alfgar** was outlawed in 1055, unjustly according to the chronicles but he succeeded to Mercia on his father's death in 1057, by this time Harold Godwin had become Edward's most influential baron though he was unable to prevent **Alfgar** returning later that year.

The Godwin brothers still held some of the most important positions in the land for a time, in spite of the fact there was intense hatred between them and Edward. The association between **Alfgar** and Gruffudd King of Wales was made even stronger by the marriage of his daughter to King Gruffudd. The firm friendship of Gruffudd and **Alfgar** lasted the rest of their lives but it brought them only trouble and disaster and proved a fatal mistake for both men when **Alfgar** was outlawed again.

Embittered by the treatment from the English, with the aid of king Gruffudd he collected together ships of the Irish Viking Fleet and attacked the English coasts creating a dangerous situation. This gave Godwin the opportunity he needed and he took full advantage to nail **Alfgar** once and for all, Godwin's constant smearing of Alfgar to the king paid off.

East Anglia was taken from **Alfgar** and given to Gyth, [Harold Godwin's younger brother]. **Alfgar** was in a difficult position, he was a broken man his political life destroyed and never regaining any prominence. Harold Godwin was now totally in command, always given the more dangerous tasks and was asked to remove the problem of **Alfgar** and King Gruffudd.

Sadly he was made a king's councillor and sent to negotiate with **Alfgar** and the Welsh king. At the meeting he came to an agreement that Alfgar would be restored and it had also been agreed by treaty in 1056 with **Leofric** in attendance, that the Welsh King Gruffudd would become an under-king to Edward. But this was a farce, by 1063 Harold and his brother Tostig attacked King Gruffudd's kingdom.

In the resulting battles that took place in Wales, the Welsh along with Thorkill and many others killed **Leofric's** brother **Edwin**. It was said that King Gruffudd's own men betrayed him, possibly to Harold Godwin who sent the severed head of Gruffudd together with his ships' figurehead to King Edward. According to statements, **Leofric's** grandson **Edwin** of Mercia [**Turold's** nephew] was not present at this attack due to his youth.

PROGRESS CHART

Chart 35[a]

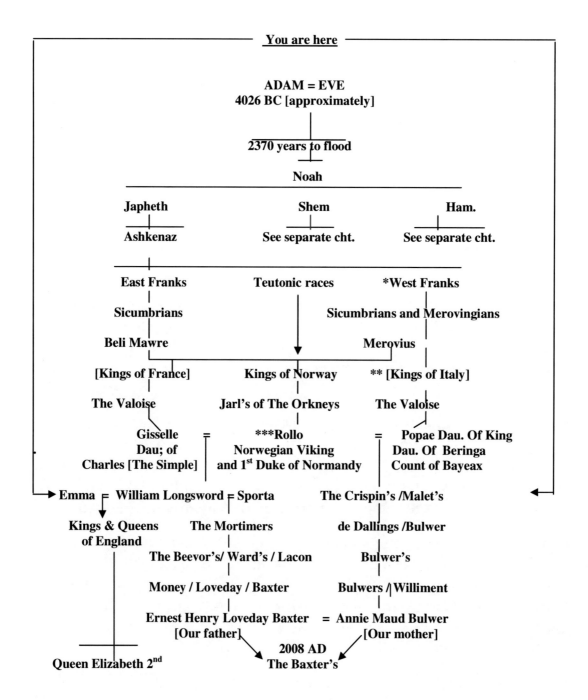

You are here

ADAM = EVE
4026 BC [approximately]

2370 years to flood

Noah

Japheth	**Shem**	**Ham.**
Ashkenaz	**See separate cht.**	**See separate cht.**

East Franks	**Teutonic races**	***West Franks**
Sicumbrians		**Sicumbrians and Merovingians**
Beli Mawre		**Merovius**
[Kings of France]	**Kings of Norway**	**** [Kings of Italy]**
The Valoise	**Jarl's of The Orkneys**	**The Valoise**

| **Gisselle Dau; of Charles [The Simple]** | = | ***Rollo Norwegian Viking and 1st Duke of Normandy** | = | **Popae Dau. Of King Dau. Of Beringa Count of Bayeax** |

Emma = **William Longsword** = **Sporta**   **The Crispin's /Malet's**

Kings & Queens of England	**The Mortimers**	**de Dallings /Bulwer**
	The Beevor's/ Ward's / Lacon	**Bulwer's**
	Money / Loveday / Baxter	**Bulwers /| Williment**
	Ernest Henry Loveday Baxter [Our father] =	**Annie Maud Bulwer [Our mother]**

2008 AD
The Baxter's

Queen Elizabeth 2nd

The last of Canute's Earls, **Leofric** the elder died in 1057, and left his nephew also named **Leofric** [3rd] the abbeys of Burton on Trent and Coventry [which he founded] together with inheritance and position. **Leofric 3rd** married **Godvia** the daughter of **Gilbert Crispin and Gunner [Malet]** and sister to **Turold Crispin.**

In Coventry there was a Saxon Church standing, long before it became the Cathedral [which was bombed during the 2nd World War]. Recently a vault was found in the graveyard, which is believed to be the burial place of Leofric and Godiva, as stated in the television broadcast by Time Team.

Turold [our direct ancestor and **Godiva's** brother] as we said previously, was part of the family of **Gilbert Crispin** and **Gunner. Gilbert Crispin** came from Normandy and was appointed the bishop of Winchester probably in the time of Edward the Confessor.

Further information can be obtained on **Gilbert Crispin** and **Lefranc** by combining the information gained from the item in this book "The Enigma of Contiville" and "The Norfolk Rebellion" with the chart for **Rollo.**

The daughter of **Alfgar** [**Algifu** who was the widow of King Gruffudd/Griffiths*] now married Harold Godwin who had killed him. He reasoned correctly that this would bring him in reach of the royal circle, humiliate her father, and increase his power and influence, but the breach between the two families of **Leofric** and Godwin never healed completely. The hostility amongst Edward's nobles was the main cause of his decision to choose William Duke of Normandy as the future king of England as we will describe later.

After the marriage of Algifu and Harold Godwin, William Duke of Normandy invited Harold Godwin and **William Malet** to be godfathers to his new daughter Adele which they both accepted. His excuse that it was in gratitude for Harold's help in 1064 for holding Normandy during the rebellion of his relatives. Being married to **William Malet's** granddaughter gave Harold enough standing to enable him to act as Godfather to the new arrival, otherwise the Duke would never have allowed him to enter any intimate relationship with his great Norman Barons for political reasons.

Information derived from the following books See Dugdale and Mon., Vol.3.p.206. Thorold, Sheriff of Lincolnshire; also called Thorold of Buckenhale, the brother of the Countess Godiva See Carmen de Hastings Praelio in Michels Chron., Anglo/Normandus 3 line 567. Quidam pavom Normanus p.27.et Anglus. Original Charter in Cotton Collection. xxx Appendix A.1. References: Complete Peerage Vol. 17 app. J and 1X p175 Earl Edmund read alongside Sir Francis Hill Medieval England. Introduction to Doomsday book and For the Pre-conquest Personal Names of Doomsday (Uppsala 1937) by Sir Henry Ellis Romuds Feudal England p140/142 (From the Readers Digest book "How Where and When) References William Malet described by Guy of Amiens as Norman/English gives an accumulation of evidence. Conclusively proving the existence of two previously unrecorded sisters of Turold and Godiva and that William and Durrant Malet were the sons of one of them.

So it was a fact that as William treated Harold as an equal in Normandy, the same applied in England. This statement gives full credence to the fact that a more than the commonplace affinity bound and tied both Duke and subject.

Apart from a relationship through his later marriage to a **Crispin** who was one of the descendants of **Rollo Ragnavaldson** 1st Duke of Normandy and the influential **Malet** family, Crispinus of Bec married Heloise Malet of Guynes and so they continued the line of the house of Clare. The son of Crispinus Crispin married Gunner [niece of the Gonner who was married to Richard 1st of Normandy].

Referring back to invitation from William 1st there was a more devious motive on William's part, as it was at this reception that Harold received a most unpleasant surprise and claimed later that he was tricked into swearing on sacred relics to support William's claim to the English throne.

On his return from Normandy he quickly dismissed the promised claim. But to William a promise was a promise not to be broken or forgotten. This error of judgment by Harold later brought fatal repercussions. King Edward was still in a dilemma although William of Normandy was his choice there were at least six other possible heirs to his throne. The chart 36 p123, portrays a very important part of our national history as it illustrates the turmoil culminating from the fact that Edward the Confessor had no issue thus leaving the throne very vulnerable.

The offspring of Emma, Algifu, Athelred, Canute, Forkbeard and others created many contestants to fight for their claim to the crown of England. The only living son's of the English royal house were Edward who was in exile and his son Edgar.

Craftily Harold Godwin had earlier persuaded the king to send the Bishop of Worcester abroad in 1054 to find any survivors of the royal house who had been scattered when Canute was crowned. His main aim was to bring back Edward the son of Edmund Ironside and his family (Margaret, Christina and Edgar the Aethling grandson of Edward Ironside) from exile in Hungry.

After three years of searching for Edward and Edgar they were found. It appears that Edgar, only twelve years of age lived in Scotland and an invitation was sent and accepted. Edward the Exile died shortly after arrival in England in 1057 before he could meet the king.

Was this a connivance between Godwin and the Queen, or were they playing for time knowing that Edward was not in good health, his death again left King Edward in a dilemma. Queen Emma, wife of two husbands, [Athelred Canute and raped by Swain] who's offspring represented several family lines that would later decide the fate of three nations, died in 1062. Fortunately she never lived to see her sons fighting and killing one another for the sake of power.

How much she contributed to the outcome is uncertain, but we suspect owing to the fact she associated with such men as Godwin and took his advice was danger in itself. This shows in the fact that after Alfgar's death c1062, and Godwin's rise to power, **William Malet** and his son in law **Turold** saw what was to come and fled the land taking young **Edwin**, **William Malet's** grandson with them.

Edward was preoccupied with religion and had Westminster Abbey planned according to his orders. He foolishly reduced the strength of his army, and sold his ships, probably to provide money for the building. Edward was still undecided! If he were to nominate Harold Godwin as his heir he would have to delay it until the last moment for fear of attack from Duke William whose position in Normandy was unstable.

Godwin was bitterly opposed to William being king and on Edward's short list. These Englishmen (though not of English royal blood) were Harold Godwin Earl of Wessex and his brother Tostig Earl of Northumbria, who was accused of being exceptionally harsh to his people, with the connivance of Queen Edith and by assassinating the Northumbrian Lords.

In 1065 the Northumbrian's revolted and invited **Morcar** brother of **Edwin** to become their Earl to replace Tostig who had become a Tyrant in their lands, [he had been given these lands after **Alfgar** had been disgraced]. Harold Godwin who tried to retain family power would not accept this and so tried to resolve it by force, but met a strong Northumbrian army at Northampton.

Harold had to concede on behalf of the king and appoint **Morcar** as Earl of Northumbria; the Godwin's for once had been humiliated. Tostig left for Flanders, as his brother wanted to stop his claim on the throne knowing that he had been a favourite of the king.

The two brothers now became bitter enemies and later in battle, one killed the other. Harald Godwin with no royal blood was the only possible Saxon that had the experience and the ability to stand against William, Duke of Normandy.

As there were no legal heirs to succeed to the throne, many could say they had an outside chance of royal connection but there was no direct royal link. Harold was now the most powerful English Earl nominated by the Witam and supported by the country. William of Normandy challenged this, claiming Harald had broken his promise to him, which was later to have a disastrous effect on him at the Battle of Hastings.

Life in England was very diverse at that time, almost in a different world, the country was covered in thick forest and large towns such as London only had about 15,000 inhabitants. Villages scattered around the country mostly near rivers or millstreams, small hamlets of a few families made up the total.

*England was divided into earldoms, earldoms into shires, and shires into hundreds. Hundred was a term used because this area once contained a hundred hides the amount of land that could support a family; this definition varied according to the area and time period which amounted to 40 plus acres. When the forest was cleared to allow more useable land, the area was still called a hundred although it could now support more than its original figure.

It must have been a daunting task to venture out of the safety of their homes to walk or travel by horse and cart with their goods to the next town. No sign posts to guide them only the sun, stars, and well worn tracks through the trees that might lead to the old Roman road with possibly thieves waiting to pounce from the dense woodland to steal their hard earned goods.

To understand what it was like to live in those times we have to look at the environment and structure of the realm to see what role each individual played. There was plenty of timber so their cabins or houses were constructed with wooden frames and walls of wattle, plastered with dried mud or clay, thatched roofs with a hole to let the smoke out unlike the grandeur of the Roman villa. They lived in one large room, where they cooked and ate round a central fire but had a separate room for sleeping. Those of higher rank had much the same houses but somewhat larger.

People often took a surname that described their trade or where they lived and so they did not confuse the elder's name with their children's; the offspring were given nicknames, which was extended as they established their place in life, each person was owned or belonged to another.

*These notes were derived from p14 & p19 '1066 The Year of the Conquest' by David Howarth 1981. Also [Penguin Books 1981] ISBN 00211845 9

At the bottom of the pile were the serfs or slaves who were usually those who had offended the laws of the land, not paid their tax, or were an enemy who had been captured. The slaves worked as labourer's doing what they were told with only food, drink and shelter as payment and as they were not wanted in the small villages, strangers were discouraged from staying.

Some were allowed to progress to the next part of the social structure, which were the cottagers or cotters that might have been the part time craftsman, miller, blacksmith, tinker, beekeeper, potter etc. Then the villeins [small farmers] who farmed up to about fifty acres, and the thanes [Earls] who drew rents in kind from them.

There were six earldoms each ruled by an Earl, who covered the country at this time, usually related to and representing the king. No one could claim they had absolute the right of land ownership. The villeins held land for the thanes, the thanes held it for the earl, church or king and the king held it all by Gods grace. To keep this arrangement each without exception owed duties in return to the others, above and below him.

The king ruled all, and the hierarchy of the church which had a similar structure, from village priests to Archbishops, ran in parallel to the state structure. Village people were by and large much more contented than those who lived in the larger towns. They were not as industrialized as the townsmen, who were open to disease [there was no sewage system]. Because people lived much too near each other these conditions bred more illness. They were also more prone to organized attacks by robbers looking for richer pickings.

Villages had close control of their environment ensuring as far as possible that they had enough food, firewood and space. Each person, man or women had a task to do in their town or village; everyone's wellbeing depended on each person doing his task well and each son was expected to follow his fathers' duties. As there were no schools each child had a job to do according to his ability.

There was a definite cast system, everyone knew his place in life from slave to king. The church was the main instigator of this and taught the poor that god decreed every man to his station. The earl was rarely seen in the villages, marriages were usually arranged for wealth or political reasons. After the endless drudgery to produce enough food, playing a form of football, a type of indoor cricket, or drafts and checkers, broke the boredom and exertion for existence. These games gave them a break from the endless drunken stupor. Apart from ill health, this was the time when they were most vulnerable to the attacks from rivals.

The days were long and their entertainment and sleep only took place after they were sure the main toils in the fields and other necessities of life were achieved and the store of food was secure. The Thane was the important man of the town or village, the only one that regularly left it for service to the king. He had to feed, escort the lord, his court and protect his lord's messengers, at least one day of the year and also look after the estates. He would attend at the hundreds court once a month, share in judgment on those in breach of the law and appear at the shire court to resolve and help to judge more serious crimes.

He was the communicator of the kings' directives bringing news from the outside world and obliged to give military service with his sons if they were old enough. A Thane was the mainstay of the fyrd, which was the kings' army governed by the earl on the king's behalf. While away his family would usually assume his role administrating village life.

KING EDWARD THE CONFESSOR DIES
January 5th 1066 with no heirs to the English throne

The news of the kings' impending death was speedily conveyed from village to village along the forest tracks, either by travelling merchants and traders, by the king's messengers, or Thanes. King Edward the Confessor, from whom under the power of god, all power flowed, was near to death. He had reigned a long time, a strange kingship that existed alongside, [particularly in his last years], the desire to be a monk. When King Edward died on the 5th January 1066 leaving no issue, it was the start of a long year, in which fate determined to change the course of the history of England. The outcome of this set a pattern, much of which affects us to this very day. The story so far gives the reasons behind the forthcoming battles that our ancestors were involved in and completes the scene when Edward the Confessor dies without issue.

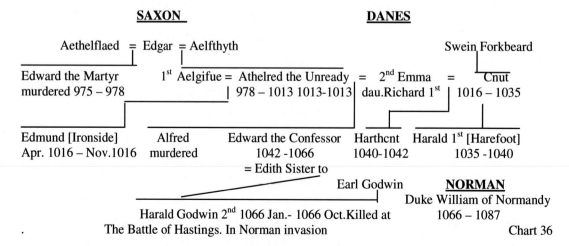

Chart 36

Note; the children of the inter-marriage's and other claimants have become adults and want to claim what they consider their right to the crown

The news soon spread to the contenders for the throne of England

1] Edgar; great grandson to King Athelred [married to Emma daughter of Richard of Normandy]

2] Harold Godwin; the Saxon Earl, son-in-law to King Edward considered he was rightful heir, had the advantage of already being in position and only had only to defend his place but had no royal blood..

3] Tostig Godwin; half-brother to Harold and also brother-in- law to the king who favoured him though he had no royal blood.

4] Svein of Denmark was a possible contender through Canute's marriage to Emma [Queen of England] but discounted by the Witan

5] William, [Duke of Normandy [later the Conqueror who was 5th in descent from **Rollo**]. William had been promised by King Athelred that he would succeed to the crown. Also his claim was supported by the fact that his great aunt Emma had married two kings of England which made him cousin to King Edward so he felt that his claim to the throne was safe and did not feel the necessity to prepare for war.

6] Harald Hardrada King of Norway [son of King Magnus], did not have a legitimate claim and was also discounted by the Witan but was persuaded by Earl Tostig to join in the fight [see story]. He was connected by of Canute's marriage to Emma [Queen of England]

Count Eustace of Boulogne had a better hereditary claim to the English throne than William of Normandy to whom he was related by marriage; his great aunt Emma had married two kings of England and was Edward the Confessors mother. Eustace had borne a grudge ever since being bundled out of Dover by Godwin. William of Normandy sought help from Eustace who promised to support him. William, fearing that Eustace might attack Normandy demanded his son be left as a surety, so Eustace did not dare make a claim for the throne.

The following charts are for Kings prior to the Conquest, cht.37. p.123.and 36.p.125. You can see why they and the Norwegians claimed the right to the throne of England. The one that opposed William's plan to invade was Count Conan of Brittany who wished him well, but stated he would take advantage of William's absence to invade Normandy as William was a bastard and usurper. The Count thought he was the rightful heir to Normandy; this outspoken Count was poisoned a few days later. The great fight for the English crown had started all over again; this time because of royal inter-relationships that gave all the main rivals what they considered a valid claim to the throne of England. As the storm clouds gathered new and interesting family branches emerge.

Some of these notes were derived from p 98 '1066 The Year of the Conquest' by David Howarth1981 [Penguin Books 1981]. ISBN 00211845. 9

CONTESTANTS TO THE THRONE OF ENGLAND
For full list see chart p.124.   Chart 37

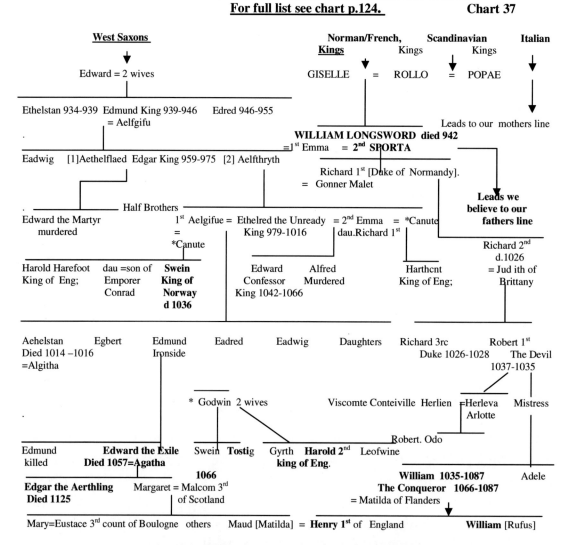

KINGS PRIOR TO THE CONQUEST

While Canute was still ruling as King of Norway, Denmark and England, just before his death he gave his son Harthcnt Denmark and Harold Harefoot [and his mother Algifu] the guardianship of Norway. As Harthcnt was considered illegitimate he did not have the right to rule Norway, so was supposedly driven out and returned to England once more and laid claim to the English throne. With Harold Hardrada of Norway, [not a legitimate claimant but was persuaded by Tostig to contend] this left only three contenders after Edwards death.

It was the ambition for those in powerful positions to make a claim of royal blood. On the continent [as you will have read] in the effort to be part of the blood line of the Holy Grail either by matrimony or direct descent caused intrigue, wars, power struggles and arranged marriages.

See page 191 chart 44 for more details.
NOTE; all names in capital letters are family lineage.

CHAPTER 1V
HAROLD GODWIN BECOMES KING.
January 6th 1066

King Edward the Confessor's death occurred in the morning on the 5th of January 1066, and on the same day, although they had grave misgivings over the propriety of naming a king with no royal blood, the council and the Witan confirmed Harold Godwin [brother of the Queen] as Edward's successor. He was the only Saxon successor that had the experience and ability needed to oppose William Duke of Normandy, who was relying on the promises of Edward the Confessor in 1064 and was so sure of his right to the throne that he thought that there was no necessity to prepare for war.

Harold was a popular choice for the English but this aroused the anger of the other contenders. His supporters wasted no time, seized the opportunity and on January 6th 1066 he was crowned King Harold 2nd of England in the newly completed Westminster Abbey. This was the same place that Edward had been buried a few hours earlier and which many claimed was indecent. After his coronation Harold rode to York, capital of the teenage Earls of Northumbria, [**Edwin** and **Morca**] to be proclaimed as their king and there is a story that it was then he married their sister Edith who was the daughter of **Aelfgar.**

Duke William of Normandy hearing the news that Harold had been crowned, realised he would have to work fast to get his army ready to take the kingdom by force and summoned a selected council of war at Lillebonne to plan the invasion of England. Most of his important Barons were at this meeting to listen to his grievances. One who attended was his half brother Robert [the Duke of Mortain]. William stated his case for an invasion even reintroducing the murder of Edward [Athelred's brother] that he claimed was by the hand of the Godwin's.

The council of war could not agree on many matters. Rumours circulated among senior members that their obligations to William were for domestic disturbances and the defense of Normandy not for very doubtful overseas missions for the sole benefit of William's ambitions, so the meeting broke in disarray. Instead of another collective meeting William saw them each in turn alone. The result was William Fitz Osberne instead of supporting his kin, suppressed all and sided with William.

As expected they were unable to match William's guile and power. With no available support, each succumbed to his persuasion with a written promise of certain rights and privileges as an inducement, together with his own displeasure if they declined.

He had won their minds but not their heart's to fight so they looked for reasons not to get themselves involved. Each one agreed to support him and with his consent preferred to stay in Normandy and send their sons and relations as their representatives in charge of the army. We suspect this was what most likely happened in Odo's [Williams's half brother] case when he sent his son Roger who was killed in the battle.

We expect that **Turold Crispin,** who was already in Normandy at this time, was designated to co-ordinate supplies and stores [a Bulver] and from then on took the name of **Turold Bulver** [man of the stores]

William's other half brother Robert, Duke of Mortain promised 200 ships, and the Counts of Mortain, the Comtes of Valoise and Caen all supported him with aid, materials and men. William himself had already collected together 2,000 knights, 8,000 vassals and contingents was ready for war; the army was standing by.

King Harold 2nd started to gather his supporters; of his brothers Swein had died [while on a pilgrimage] and in disgrace, Tostig was in opposition, with his own ambitions. Wulfnoth the youngest was imprisoned in Normandy, which left Gyrth and Leofwine the only ones who could help save Harold's new kingdom.

By Easter King Harold, aware of the danger had already started to defend his new realm and called up the thanes and their men on a war footing. The festivities of Easter had also began but many men were too tired to join in after their journey, or were wearily making their way south by the shortest path through wild spring flowers and budding tree's of the forest to the sea with their weapons of war.

William knowing of other claimants craftily waited for others to attack first, hoping they would tire the English out. If Tostig, King Harald Godwin's brother [who also wished to claim the crown] did attack, what he would hope to gain was unclear. He never had been accepted in his own earldom due to the harsh treatment of his charges, so he would never be accepted by the nation in any earldom. For him it would be certain death and another one out of the way for William.

Tostig gathered his inherited forlorn fleet of ships and called upon the Cinque Ports agreement to supply their ships and men as agreed. They were a poor assortment of cargo ships that would have been laughable beside the purpose built ships of Duke William. But even William's ships were not fit to carry the amount of stores and equipment for such an attack, and certainly not the amount of horses that would be required on a on a sea journey even in calm waters.

*As King Harold and his Witan were celebrating the Easter feast [April 24th 1066] on Thorney Island, they gazed up in awe at the bright light in the sky that trailed a hairy tail. This mysterious thing put fear into the hearts of all the nations and they took it as a warning of doom. In these days we would have known it possibly as Haley's Comet.

Soon after this Tostig Godwin and his ships appeared near the Isle of Wight having just arrived from Normandy, he had probably confided to William of his intention to take the crown of England. No doubt William was pleased to hear this and would use it in his independent carefully laid plans to overthrow Harold of England.

He did not want to even appear to associate with Tostig for the same reason as Harold Godwin, they both wanted to keep good a relationship with the English Earls who had Tostig exiled, so Tostig was turned away by William to do battle on his own. He then embarked on a mad nostalgic trip using the same route that he and his family took in the days of close family relationships.

Tostig landed on the Isle of Wight with armed men but soon left when he found that he was not welcome. He probably thought it was his last chance now Harold was king hoping all would be forgiven. Harold could not afford to forgive Tostig on behalf of the nation or to make peace with him. To even to allow this brother to stay would still amount to civil war no matter what his personal feelings were.

Tostig must have been bitterly disappointed at Harold's rejection and he moved from port to port each time being turned away with hostility by the bewildered defenders who were expecting a Norman invasion, some even paid him to go. He moved again fighting for provisions, taking ships and hostages.

Dejected he went back to Flanders, home of his in-laws and left his wife and children there. Handicapped by his stubborn temperament he started on his last mission. Putting to sea again, he traveled north with his supporters, not by choice but by the dictation of the wind and tides to the mouth of the Humber where he started to plunder the coastline.

The Northern Earls turned out against him and he was heavily defeated by Earls **Edwin** and **Morca**. Most of his men deserted him and he was left with only twelve ships, so he put to sea going further north to Scotland to request Malcolm king of Scots for a refuge but did not stay long.

*From the Saxon Chronicles

After seeking help, he was rejected by Denmark in February, Normandy in April, Isle of Wight and Scotland in May. In June he traveled on to Norway to consult with the Norwegian King Harald Hardrada, a giant of a man, with one eyebrow higher than the other which had been inflicted in one of his many battles. He was a national hero and a berserker. Harald Hardrada was Tostig's last hope for someone to assist him to attack England. Two summers had passed since Harald had a fight, it was because his love of war and killing that his ships and army were always ready for action at short notice.

Tostig cunningly, instead of trying to get help from King Harald of Norway, implied that English nobles wanted Harald as king and he would help Harald to claim the throne. Thus Tostig gained an accomplice and left to assemble what men he could, while Harald sailed with his son Olav to join his fleet of war.

Harald Hardrada landed in England, met up with Tostig and set about destroying the little fishing port of Scarborough for no real purpose but the fun he got out of it. After leaving it in flames they decided to attack the capital of Tostig's old Earldom of York. They sailed up the Humber as far as they could then rowed the rest of the way. Tostig's armies were disembarking from their ships to march on York, when the young brothers, **Earls Morca** and **Edwin** heard the news.

Unprepared the two young earls quickly assembled the local defenders and marched out of York to meet the invaders at Fulford where a short but bloody battle took place. Initially they had the invaders running, but their inexperience in battle contrasted with the experienced Harald who unfurled his white standard with a black raven and blew his horn. This brought his army of berserkers into the fray and resulted in a carpet of English dead. Tostig and Harald went into the city of York, which surrendered.

The atmosphere was hostile although Tostig knew he would not have been welcomed even before this intrusion. Rather than risk a confrontation they demanded five hundred hostages to be brought to them on Monday 25th September at Stamford Bridge then went back to their ships walking through the mass of dead left on the field of battle.

Communication in those days was slow and done by messenger, so the information William received on the happenings across the channel was that Harold had left the south to fight in the north of England and this was good news, so he loaded his ships for attack.

These notes were made from p 135 '1066 The Year of the Conquest' by David Howarth 1981. Penguin Books 1981] ISBN0 00211845 9 also *Saxon Chronicles page 194

*It was on the 19th September 1066 Harold Godwin received the news of the invasion and the fate of Scarborough; The most reliable sources say that he then marched out of London on the 20th September and was 10 miles from York on Sunday 24th. A remarkable achievement; on learning the fate of York he rode into the city. His army had swelled to a great number, but he made sure that his sudden appearance at Stamford Bridge would surprise his enemies. The tale goes that the first incident was before the Battle started.

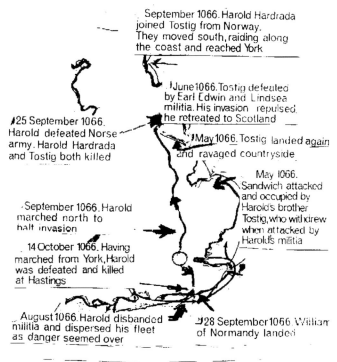

September 1066. Harold Hardrada joined Tostig from Norway. They moved south, raiding along the coast and reached York

June 1066. Tostig defeated by Earl Edwin and Lindsea militia. His invasion repulsed, he retreated to Scotland

25 September 1066. Harold defeated Norse army. Harold Hardrada and Tostig both killed

May 1066. Tostig landed again and ravaged countryside

May 1066. Sandwich attacked and occupied by Harold's brother Tostig, who withdrew when attacked by Harold's militia

September 1066. Harold marched north to halt invasion

14 October 1066. Having marched from York, Harold was defeated and killed at Hastings

August 1066. Harold disbanded militia and dispersed his fleet as danger seemed over

28 September 1066. William of Normandy landed

Astounding time scale of Harold's brave attempt to save his kindom   Artist impresstion Plate 22

On the 25th September Harald Hardrada divided his men into two sections, his son stayed behind with some others to protect the ships, Tostig and Harald took with them a very large army as they were expecting to meet their hostages at Stamford Bridge, and becoming very confidant, sure that the main fighting was over they left all their coats of mail behind and ambled along in the very warm weather carrying just shields and their weapons. Arriving at Stamford Bridge they were shocked, realizing what they thought was a rabble of hostages approaching was a sea of glittering shields and weapons. Harald Hardrada dismounted from his horse and King Harold of England not knowing who this giant of a man could be was informed that it was King Harold Hardrada of Norway.

Being near enough to speak, King Harold asked the Norwegian where Tostig was. His brother came forward and the two faced each other. Harold not wanting to identify himself, risked the wrath of others in order to test his brother for a peaceful settlement, telling Tostig that his brother sent him greetings and offered him all Northumbria rather than battle, and that he would give him one third of his kingdom. *If I accept", replied Tostig, "What would he offer Harald Hardrada?"

*These notes were derived from p 139 '1066 The Year of the Conquest' by David Howarth 1981. [Penguin Books ISBN0 00211845 9

He said something about six foot of English soil, or a bit more for such a big man'! At that Tostig replied that he should tell his King to prepare for battle. He knew all along that he was talking to his brother but preferred to keep up the pretense, knowing that if either showed their identity it would have certainly meant a personal fight between them to the death brother-killing brother.

One of the longest and bloodiest battles ever recorded in English history began. Even continuing after the brave old warrior Harald who had taken the role of a berserker had fallen dead with a single arrow in the throat. Harold made an attempt to stop the slaughter, by offering peace to his brother, but it was Tostig who picked up the banner refusing to give way.

When the rest of the Norse army arrived from the ships the fighting began again, but because they had run there in full armour they were too tired to fight. As darkness fell Tostig was killed and the survivors of his army fled to the ships. Many, many English died also, Olav the son of King Harald with the earls of Orkney [see **Regnavald**] surrendered and with a rare show of forgiveness in any battle Harold allowed them to go.

Prior to 1066 Athelred had given William of Normandy two Manors in England. One at Steyning with a large estate the other nearby at Rameslie on the Sussex coast so he was already well acquainted with the area. He had cunningly put this to good use by visiting the pro-Norman Abbey of Fecamp to plan with the Abbot in case he had to invade. Some monks may have been William's soldiers acting as spies, which provided William with vital information on Harold's troop movements in the north of England fighting Tostig leaving him to prepare his army. No doubt the Abbot found his position was very profitable.

Duke William of Normandy invades England

Due to the oncoming winter, Harold was sure that owing to the time of year and the mass of men and equipment William would need to transport, an invasion by sea would be madness. He considered there was no need to keep his army on a war footing and started to disband them.

William was carrying on regardless of time of the year, winds tides or weather; whatever he did William seemed to have the gods on his side. He had timed this invasion perfectly even the weather changed in his favour so he put to sea and headed for his intended landing place at Bulverhythe, Pevensey Bay on the south coast of England.

These notes were derived from p 139/40 '1066 The Year of the Conquest' by David Howarth 1981. [Penguin Books 1981] ISBN0 00211845 9

All went to plan until dawn broke on the morning of September 28th, when far into the English Channel he could not sight his ships or land. Lost at sea! To avoid panic William calmly told his crew to drop anchor and eat. While they sat eating to his relief his fleet arrived and he ordered his ship the "Mora" to sail. Owing to the delay, they had to find a landing quickly, or wait another day for the next tide. It must have been a nightmare for the pilots finding their way through the strong currents. They identified the walls of the Roman fortress of Pevensey, and the gap in the stony beach leading to the harbour.

In the meantime King Harold spent a few days in York and decided to give a great feast to celebrate their victory in his Northern Kingdom. The surrender of York and the great loss of life had caused **Edwin and Morca** to be unfairly disgraced, and as they were severely injured were out of action for some time.

Harold spent more time there in order to smooth out the recriminations over the loss of so many men, also to pacify the defeated Earls of Fulford but knew his biggest test in respect of William Duke of Normandy was yet to come thinking that he had a few months to prepare, not knowing that William was already on his doorstep.

Harold's celebration in York did not last long; while eating he received the news that William Duke of Normandy had invaded the very coastline that he had guarded all summer and was forced to leave quickly, after racing his men north to meet confront and defeat his brother. Now it was an urgent issue to get them back south to fight William so he spent some time in reassembling his army, building up provisions, recruiting more men and preparing them for the long walk back with many more joining them on this journey. The scale and distance covered was awe-inspiring especially after the battles they had fought previously.

The mighty Norman invasion fleet, after one or two mishaps reached the coast of England at Pevensey Bay at about 9am on September 28 1066. Duke William, the first man ashore, slipped and sprawled full length on the ground; a groan of despair went up from his army, this was not a good omen. The quick-witted Duke turned this to his advantage grabbing two handfuls of English soil saying. "By the splendour of God, the earth of England is in my two hands".

William had achieved what no invader has done since, a successful landing on English soil and soon completed much of his gigantic task of setting up camp and unloading the mass of stores without any pressure; his timing had been perfect so he began to block the road from London.

.

THE BATTLE OF HASTINGS 1066
AND THE DEATH OF KING HAROLD OF ENGLAND

The success of the invasion was one of the best-managed operations in military history considering the gigantic task. The Norman armada comprised of many hundreds of ships carrying more than 8000 fighting men, as well as sailors, supplies, horses, knights' archers, plus armoury, wagons and stores.

Pevensey Bay showing Bulverhythe, the Harbour and Battlefields
Williams landing place and battle area
Derived from other diagrams of similar nature

plate 23

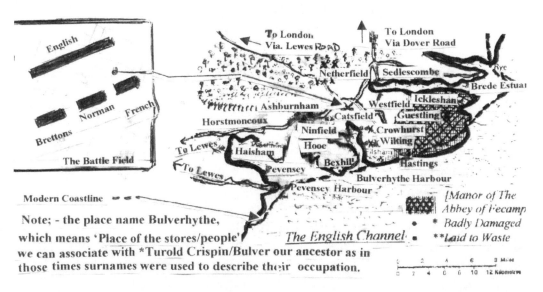

William led his troops to Hastings who were not all Normans but consisted of three main factions that included French and men from Brittany]. He ordered a timber castle to be built on a mound that would be used as a base for his operations. It was a prefabricated building brought from Normandy packed in boxes ready to be fitted together with pegs.

This was an early example of the prefabricated buildings we know today. Why William choose this particular area is probability because it was already Norman property and he received valuable tactical information from his monks in the Abbey of Fecamp.

It was a small isolated area by the river Brede to the north and a wide marshy valley that was bounded by the harbour of Bulverhythe to the west which was impassable except for a track round the head of Bulverhythe harbour used by his foot soldiers. He waited a week [others state a month] for his army to recover from the sea crossing and a stomach infection using this time to strengthen army fortifications and provide an escape route.

Harold's Brave Attempt to Retain the English Throne

Harold did not travel all the way to London with his men but diverted on his own to Waltham, where he had built and installed twelve cannons of Holy Rood [stone figures of Christ on the cross- encased in silver] this was of special significance to Harold. As a boy, he claimed that it was this that had cured his paralysis and we expect that he had come here to pray for his survival in the forthcoming battle. *He spent a whole day quietly praying by the shrine and after he had finished his spiritual necessities he resumed his journey to London.

Harold left London on 12th October 1066 and duly summoned the men of Sussex and Kent to meet at an apple tree on Calbec Hill outside Hastings arriving there himself on the 13th. The battle area chosen was uninhabited and Harold took the cross-ridge. The call went out and in the dawn of the 14th Harold King of England appeared on the battle scene with his most feared heavily armed Housecarls arranged in front wielding two headed axes. The most important fact Harold had to keep secret at this time was that the Pope had in the summer, judged him to be in the wrong and that he should respect his promise to William and surrender the crown.

If his army and the church found out that Harold had not accepted the papal judgment they would not have dared to support him. According to the "Roman de Rou", a rumour spread that the king had been ex-communicated and the same would happen to anyone who fought for him. Of course William must have known this and waited for the psychological moment to spread this rumour, which he hoped would be believed and cause Harold's army to desert him. When Harold arrived with his troops he sacked the whole area including the monastery where the monks paid dearly for their assistance to William.

Owing to the fact that Harold stole all the food in the surrounding area and destroyed what was left, William and his army now desperate, had to move fast or starve. Harold chose a commanding position on a hilltop, which dominated the battle area to face his enemy, seven miles west of the Norman's position at Hastings, called Seniac Hill (named Battle on modern maps).

The track that William and his army followed from their camp to the battlefield was long and narrow, and took from 9 am-11am to get the troops positioned. For the English looking down on this never ending trail of men and all the equipment must have been a nerve-racking time. For two hours they sat ready for battle.

Note; Map and Text [p157] derived from the book '1066 The Year of the Conquest' page 146 and 169 by David Howarth1981* [Penguin Books 1981] ISBN 00211845 9 and other historical documents.

If Harold had used the same delaying tactics his army would have swelled to four times the size, but he was too impatient to start. Many messages passed between various factions, stating reasons why they were claiming the English throne and why both thought the other should concede. Neither agreed; William labeled Harold a perjurer and a usurper. A message came to Harold delivered by a monk giving a devastating shock, destroying his self-confidence stating that William was to fight under the Papal Banner and that on his finger was the holy relic of St. Peter, round his neck would be relics on which Harold had sworn oaths in Normandy.

It was a terrific blow to Harold that either William or his half brother Bishop Odo would wear the Papal Bull of his excommunication. He learned also that in his absence the papal court without his knowledge or defense judged him guilty. One can only guess Harold's thoughts on what his army would do when they saw this at the start of the battle. It seems very likely that it was on the premise that he was a usurper. But the statement is only inference, having one piece of direct confirmation, the Roman De Rou.

Both armies prepared for battle with the archers in front; none of these men had any form of armour and carried just short bows and cross bows with heavy iron bolts. Next were the mailed foot soldiers that carried swords and pikes, behind these were mounted men with mail down to their knees, their horses being unprotected. Then followed helmeted knights carrying swords and spears some with lances and iron maces also on armoured horses. The brothers of King Harold [Gyrth and Leofwine] and their nephew Harkon, reappeared on the scene, and once more offered a plan that one of them should replace Harold in battle. Harold rejected the plan, which in hindsight could have won it for him when the evenly matched sides met with Duke William in the centre of his troops.

A man called Taillefer rode out alone from the Norman lines cantering across the valley into the English ranks and killed three of the enemy before being killed himself. This bravery cause the English army to double its front rank and overlap their shields to defend themselves from the Norman advancing archers who fired their first volley at fifty paces and the battle was joined.

References. Much of the information in this section of our book has been collated from several specialist books on the subject as "1066 The Year of the Conquest", by David Howarth1981. [Penguin Books1981] cross ref. with an ancient book "Heimskringla" or "The Lives of the Norse Kings" by an Icelandic poet and historian Snorri Sturlasson 1230 AD Carman de Hastings (the song of the battle of Hastings ascribed to Guy, the Bishop of Amiens. He wrote it probably within six months after the battle, and "Gesta Guillelmi", ("The Deeds of William") by the chaplain William Pointers backed up by detail on the Bayeux tapestry. Also "When, Where, Why and How it Happened" (Readers Digest]

All went well for Harold, the advantage he had on the hill at first caused chaos in the Norman lines. There was a moment of crisis when William's Breton soldiers started to desert him. The English, wielding their huge two headed axes were decapitating horses and hacking at their fallen riders, which must have presented a depressing sight to the Normans.

Early in the fighting William's left flank broke in terror, fleeing down the slope, their horses stumbling and falling over the steep hillocks. Panic increased as a rumour spread that William had been killed, but Eustace of Boulogne seized the Dukes banner and indicated that William was still alive.

William pulled back his visor, saying. "Look at me, well, I am still alive and by the grace of God I shall yet prove victor". This spurred his men on and during the Norman panic the Saxons continued to pursue, leaving their hilltop to chase the Norman retreat but it left them open and divided; seeing this William rallied his men to turn the rout to his advantage.

This pursuit was for the English side a costly mistake that William must have foreseen. When the English broke ranks, one end of their line became split into two factions and were cut down like wheat, whether it was planned by William or done on impulse is debatable, William had proved that he was still very much alive and an astute leader.

There are many conflicting reports as to how Harold Godwin died but most agree that he received a mortal wound to the head by an arrow. Some of his brothers fled into hiding, others were killed and the young **Earls Edwin** and **Morca** escaped the carnage as they were still recovering from wounds of the previous battle in York. The Saxons were defeated and William the Conqueror at the end of the battle is said to have pitched his tent where the fighting had been fiercest to eat a hearty meal untroubled by all the corpses around him.

Amid the dead and dying he commanded that an Abbey dedicated to St. Martin be built on the spot where king Harold died to be called *Battle-Abbey in memory of the Norman victory. The families and knights of William's' army were later rewarded according to their status, and for the support they extended to William in the battle of Hastings. William had to now prepare himself for the march to London, take the crown of England and win the battle for the minds of his new subjects.

Note.
*Anglo Saxon word Santlache] The Norman's changed the name sometime after 1140 to Senlac/Sanguelac (Lake of Blood) now known as Battle of Hastings For a few hours they waited and would have continued to do so if Harold had not seriously understimated the enemies' wiley nature. Refer to book 'The year of the Conquest' by David Howorth p169 also Douglas Peerage Ed Wood p.348. C.M. Bloomfield. Passim

Norman Nobles that accompanied William Conqueror to England

Peter de Valoynes the new Kings nephew was later amply rewarded for his part in the conquest with 57 Lordships in Essex Norfolk, Suffolk, Cambridge and Lincoln. He fathered six sons, and two daughters; these too you will meet later in this book.

To avoid he clutches of Harold Godwin who was envious of the Mercian estates ***William Mallet'** [an extremely wealthy man, Sheriff of Norfolk pre-Conquest] escaped with **Turold** his son in law, [Sheriff of Bukenham who lived in Bukenham Castle near Attleborough Norfolk now in ruins] to Normandy taking **Edwin** [**William Mallet's** grandson and **Turolds** nephew] with them. They returned in 1066 with William the Conqueror.

The Ducal Family

William son of Richard Everux, **Richard of Clare, son of Gilbert Brione**, Robert Count of Mortain, *Odo, Bishop of Bayeux [sent his son Roger]

House Officers

William Fitz-Osbourne, Hugh de Montfort, [later beheaded]. Hugh de Irrey, Ralph de-Tankerville, Girraldi the Marshall.

Unofficial Baronages

Thurstan son of Ralph de Troy, **William Warrenna** uncle to **Turold** [whose position was to afford protection against Danish invaders on the East Coast] made his home in Norwic [now Norwich.] and Castle Acre North Norfolk.

WILLIAM IS THE CONQUEROR AND KING OF ENGLAND
English and Norman Government and State

The route William took to London is as on the diagram on page 133. William wanted to wait until his wife Matilda arrived to accept the crown beside him but the urgency of the times impelled him to act quickly and was crowned as king on Xmas Day 1066. This was the start of the new royal line. While the ceremony took place, the mounted guard outside misunderstood the shouting of the crowd. Thinking the new king was under attack, in their panic they set fire to buildings around them, the ceremony was completed after the situation calmed down.

Note; - some of those above did not come to the battle sending their representatives, but arrived later*+* both of these had previously left Briton taking the young Earl Edwin to protect him from Godwin but returned with William the Conqueror.

King William stayed in London and **Ralph,** being the Earl of the county was under orders with Bishop Aelthelmer of Elmham and the Thegnes of Norfolk to deliver the lands and money from those who stood against the king in the invasion. They were responsible to the king for collection of rents for property held in trust, such as Wood Dalling and Binham, which were sub-enfeoffed to the knights and various tenants. This money was used to provide capital to pay for the redemption of estates for his friends and the relatives who had supported him.

Robert, [William's half brother] held lands for the king in Normandy. **Peter and Ralph Valoise** were entrusted with other lands for the king in Norfolk.

Malmsbury in the Cotswold.
Founded in 880 AD.

It would be prudent to mention that we found another Turold, [son of Odo the half brother to William 1st], a monk/knight who was given Malmsbury Abbey, for services rendered during the invasion of England in 1066. Kings often thought that their loot was safer hidden in churches or monasteries guarded by monks who had military training, as this was considered sacred ground, except by the vandal type individuals whose envious eyes wandered that way.

Malmsbury was one of England's oldest boroughs', granted a charter by Alfred the Great in 880. The river Avon almost encircles the town of golden coloured stone houses. The octagonal 15th century market cross still serves as a shelter, and the soaring nave is all that remains of the immense seventh century abbey which was burned down during Danish invasions, though the church still exists and is used today.

The full measure of William's achievement socially, economically and politically in one day should not be under estimated. The house of Godwin had been almost eliminated, except the young sons of Harold Godwin who had fled to Ireland with their mother.

Not one strong leader of this house was left alive. The people and those English Earls that were left still hankered after *Edgar Atheling, [grandson of Edmund Ironsides] already a sick man, as King Harold's successor.

*Edmund 2nd Ironside d.1016 = Algitha] was the son of Ethelred 2nd [979-1016 and 1st wife Alfgifu. They bore Edward the Exile d1057 = Agatha] who had s son *Edgar Atheling, d.1125 and a daughter Margaret who married Malcolm 3rd King of Scots.

THE WIND OF CHANGE THAT PARTED THE MISTS OF TIME
The Restructure of the State from 1066 AD.

William soon began to lay the foundations for his English kingdom. These were the beginnings of great social and economic change and a new way of life for people in this country, a revision of the social structure that was to last many years into the future. Some of these modifications still exist today.

Dukes in Normandy were hereditary; it was probably the same in East Anglia though the system was different in the five boroughs, authority rested on men of Scandinavian origin, some of noble birth or those that came from the previous settlers who lived in East Anglia, called Thegnes [a hereditary office].

These men were skilled in law and about twelve in number who presided over an open assembly representing the community, often as a collective body and in some districts they actually became chieftains.

William 1st originally intended that the leaders of the two countries to work together in government, as can be seen in a charter that was granted to the abbey of Peterborough. The witness list is interesting as it demonstrated his desire to rule through people of both nations. He proved this point by taking all the leading Thegnes back with him to Normandy as hostages and kept them there for the greater part of 1067 for training until 1069 when he returned to England.

*The Thegnes were then used as important cogs in the wheel of state and there was at this time a great combination of English and Norman Magnates. By using the English names first demonstrates William's earnest aspiration to use the Angles to keep jealousies at bay, but this later proved unsuccessful, as you will see. At first they kept the peace but the Normans had underestimated the wily nature of the English and their rebellious streak, which would not submit to any rule other than their own.

William hearing of this became angry, but was appeased by a bag of gold, and mediation. The people had to submit to William, **Edwin and **Morca** grandsons of **Leofric** and **Godvia** among them.

Note see p.134 "Some marks of Feudalism".
*Douglas? Peerage Edward IV p348 C.F. Broomfield Passim
** [Laud Chronicle [E] 1066.Lincoln. Douglass Peerage.ed.Wood.ii.p.348.C.F. Broomfield Norfolk. Turold's link with Doomsday transcript, by Munford [Norfolk only]. Sir Henry Spelman has taken most of this information derived from the "Saxon Chronicle" the book Norman England" and Freeman's book The Norman Conquest of England.volii.p216.

This is the main reason why William decided to restructure the positions of those he had given power, and also to create the Doomsday Book so that every one in the country would be accountable by name and possessions. After the Norman Conquest, even though William had increased his power, the custom of domestic warfare was so firmly rooted even he could not get rid of it.

For example a story of one of our ancestors proves this point, when Gilbert of Brione arranged a battle with his enemy. Noting that they were too evenly matched he went to arbitration and accepted a judgment from Duke Robert. The battle was canceled but in reality there was no effective control over errant Knights, if they wanted to war they went to war.

The Thegnes that were used as judges consisted of, Eldred Archbishop of York, Wulwig Bishop of Lincoln, Merlswein who was Sheriff in Lincolnshire at this time, [Ex-King Harold's representative in the North], Ulf, the son of Tope and Earl William Fitz-Osberne of Hereford.

William Malet, Lord of Attleborough had lived here before the Conquest, and later became the first Norman sheriff of York. Charters show that **Edwin, Morca** and Waltheof associated in council with Norman nobles such as Odo, Bishop of Bayeux, Geoffrey de Constances, Earl William Fitz Osberne and Robert Count of Mortain.

Some of their history can be seen in Cambridge, Stamford, York, and Chester museums [described as having sake and soke, occasionally having almost equal authority with the king]. Most existed in their positions until 1086, after this they acted as individuals but their descendants were certainly still there until 1275 and were mentioned in the Hundred Rolls, referred to as having ancestors who were of old time Judges.

*By the end of William the Conqueror's reign it was apparent that all the combined directive power of the judges was put into Norman hands. There was more than one reason for the disappearance of the great English landowners due to forfeitures, rebellions, and Crusades in which many were killed or made bankrupt, also the natural extinction of family lines due the birth of female rather than male heirs added to this problem.

Some went abroad because of the upheavals caused by the various rebellions, as they found no respite in the land they knew so well. Those who found no place in the new order of things just left, military families were eyed with suspicion, The better-known families were crowded out often being mistrusted, and offered no serious work or position.

*See item 'Fall of a Rebellious House' p 150

The two older men who presided there during the reign of Edward the Confessor were in the Diocese of Bath and Ramsey, both being the only ones which remained in English hands. Although the poor were not affected by most of this they did feel the painful restraint of a number of rulers and the penalties that they inflicted.

There was also much distrust because of traitor's and quislings, which were often even in their own families. The dividing of the country between foreign nobles organized for war was the first result of the conquest; this made the country more stable, the people more content with their lot and held the upper classes together by supplying military aid to the king when necessary.

Towards the end of William's reign nearly all the Scandinavian and Saxon names had gone and people who used them were considered eccentric, though this was more likely due to the coming retribution for their rebellion. Not to be outwitted, these names had been craftily changed by the use of aliases and other means to evade close inspection from the Norman's, although Anglo Saxon names can be traced back prior to this time they are open to question.

Nobles often ended up having as much, if not more material wealth and power than they did before. This was the reason why the government always seemed to be looking over their shoulders, and why William appointed no English persons to any See or Bishopric.

FEUDALISM
Lords and Vassal's

Feudalism was a system of organisational development found in Gaul in the eighth century used by the early Carolingians. It provided the king or ruler of that time with a large number of vassals who were obligated to do military service within a fief [the estates held by a lord] in return for the use of the kings/rulers land. A fief became the hub of military organisation for the whole country.

The European systems of feudal government and social relationships depend upon control in word and/or deed; both parties being usually of unequal rank or position from lords down to vassals [even the lord was regarded as a vassal]. The term feudalism was not fully recognised in England until the arrival of the Normans who extended this to established governmental, social and economic constitutions of England. This was known as becoming feudalised and lasted until the First World War of 1914-18; some of this structure is still in place.

Some of the marks of Feudalism

Governmental	Economic	Social
1] The King owned lands and enforced economic reform, structure of land and rentals.	2] Rented lands out to the Great Barons and to land Owners who sub let to the lesser Barons.	3] Relationships by Lord and vassals, and contracts made between them for support and aid in times of war.

One unit or Knights fee was equal to 2 caracates/100acres. This term simplified means an amount of land sufficient to keep an armed horseman with a following of retainers. [Latin Feodum /Old French /English fee].

Governmental Feudalism

This was the first recognized application of Feudal organization, but as people gained more material wealth, possessions became more abundant. Feudalism was applied more intensely in social relationships too i.e. class distinction increased.

Social and Economic Feudalism

The vassal like a faithful son owed his Lord fidelity [fealty] and was required to provide   material help or aid, which might require defending his Lords domain. [For example see item on **Turold** and **William Warrenna**].

Economic

Help could be financial defined by contract, and in return vassals received protection and maintenance in the courts. The rebellions from 1079 were the last straw, so King William gave orders for the Doomsday Book to be drawn up. He was compelled by events to change his mind on combined ruler-ship as he could no longer trust the native nobles, and started to remove them from power, **Edwin** and **Morca** among them.

Norman's were now the leading members of the Kings household and no one could see with a cursory glance, that William ever intended to continue his rule involving the nobility of England. However the Saxon form of Feudalism that stemmed from the barbaric kingdoms that followed the fall of the Roman Empire remained in place. Another ruse William began to adopt was the installation of loyal knights as monks in monasteries to keep an eye on his loot, and to ascertain the thoughts and mood of the masses.

References; Will of Pottiers [See Round, Geoffrey Manderville p.321 'The Invasion of England'. Iii Oderic.p.785 iv.ib. p.907]. Referred to in the book William the Conqueror by Freeman sees Oderic 658. See item "fall of a Rebellious House" page 150

WHAT`S IN A NAME

Usually in those times a man changed his name to describe his position, occupation, home or possessions or to hide his misdeeds and avoid the anger of the King. We believe it is important to understand the names given to people, as they will be used in this book and linked to the story of the families, describing their position in life or where they lived.

FAMILY NAMES AND ADOPTED NAMES [ALIAS]
And Their Meanings

Bulverhythe; Bulver is a key word in this book and provides our main family surname. As a point of interest the port named Bulverhythe was a suitable and sheltered port for King William to unload and store his heavy equipment and you may also note the associated name of Turold Crispin/Bulver this probably indicated that he was at some time responsible for storage.

Names

BULVER	Stores.
BULVERHYTH.	Port of the stores.
TUROLD BULVER.	Turold of the stores.
TUROLD de DALLING	Turold of the open fields with woods.
PETER de DALLING,	Peter of the open fields.
TOUT COURT	Without formality or explanation.
ENFEOFF.	To grant lands to, (In fee) or to invest with a fee for an estate
RALPH de DALLING,	Ralph of the open fields.
MORTAIN	Name of Norman estate given to Robert by his half brother William.
VALOISE.	Name of Castle and area where the Duke of Normandy [William 1ST of England] was born.

Titles

VILLEIN,	Pertaining to a villa, farmer, or freeborn peasant of inferior class of landowner, later in the 13th century the meaning changed.
BONDSMAN,	Landowner, householder, who tilled his own land or a freeman (word now means In Bonds / slave).
SERF,	(Pre- conquest) Saxon word for Slave-working land belonging to his master attached to the land, and conceived as being in a degrading humiliating position, similar as a villein although personally free, is bound by the land. He cannot leave without his master's consent and immediately sold with the land to which he is attached or a Tenure of land held by feudal rights.
THANE	[Saxon] where a holder pays rent instead of military service.

Note; we would like to mention the name changes made by individual families to escape being disciplined for misdemeanors against the King. For example William Mortimer and his sons who changed their name to Warrenna. There are many other examples for you to take into consideration.

ATTLEBOROUGH, NORFOLK AND THE FAMILIES WHO LIVED THERE
CAPITAL OF EAST ANGLIA FROM 979-1070]

The English Norman Connection.

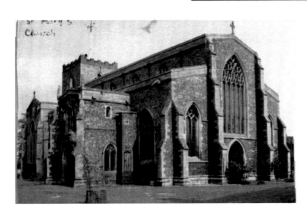

Attleborough Church   Plate 24

Photograph from unknown source.

We feel we have to mention to you the importance of the towns of Attleborough and Thetford, particularly as they appear to be the areas where we first found our traceable Norman ancestors who had settled there. We will outline the existence of these families and the Manors where they lived to give you an idea of their time, places and life styles.

The power struggles taking place in their lifetime decided what they did for themselves and their families. Atling, King of that province founded Attleborough; and the Attile/Attil part of the name did come from the king, though it was not only the name of the man but also a description of the place where he lived. This name also means 'burgh at the watery place' which speaks for itself. The name Attleborough, which came first? Like the chicken or the egg we do not know.

In the second year of Henry 2nd reign, a William Fossetto de Attleburc lived there; in old English the 'Atte' means a Dyke, now Dykes or Dix. One part of Attleborough contains Plassets Manor, the other part is adjacent to it, where the church and the Abbey stand [The Abbey has since almost disappeared]. The two communities of Attleborough and Thetford constantly fought for supremacy. From the time of King Athelred and after the last confrontation with the Danes, Attleborough was not only the capital but also the metropolis of Norfolk when the battle with the Danes was lost at Ringmere pit.

In 1023 Thorkill [brother of Canute] lived in Attleborough for a time, but was sent to Norway with King Canute's son Harald under the pretext that he was to be trained as king, while Canute held Thorkill's son as guarantee. Thetford was made the Capital until they recognized the strategic position that Norwich occupied, so the Norman's made this the Capital instead in 1070.

Note: - A monk named John Braeme who resided at Thetford, recorded much information on this area and has been quoted in various history books. Other information we gathered from Bloomfield's Norfolk. Mrs. McKenna of "Family Research" carried out even more research also Norfolk Libraries and research centers gave assistance.

Other lands in the area were divided between William Malet Turold's father-in-law, **Edwin,** son of Aelfgar and *Turold/Toradrea, who held Bukenham as Sheriff. After Alfgar's death they rescued the young Edwin from the grasping hands of Earl Godwin and took him to Normandy, which explains why **Turold** and **William Malet** disappeared from the Attleborough Norfolk area at this time, and reappeared again when William Duke of Normandy invaded in 1066.

We have no details of **Turold's** life in Normandy during this time or when he arrived back in England though he was listed as being in Norfolk before and after the battle of Hastings. In view of his name change from **Crispin to Bulver** [which means man of the Stores] the possibility of his stay in Normandy might partly be due to his involvement in the task of preparing the massive amount of equipment needed for Williams's invasion of England in 1066.

The Mortimer's contained a third part of the advowson (ecclesiastical benefit) in which the church was situated being a separate institution. This was the benifit of their family too, and was the capital of trade at this time. Before the rebellion in 1075 Ralph de Constable held lands here, and after he died his son also named Ralph but surnamed de Geuda held some of these Manors. He forfeited this right for his part in the rebellion in 1075 when they were handed on to William Albini and Roger Rainard a descendant of **Lucy,** niece of **Turold.**

On Rogers' death they reverted back to the crown. Others also held property there at various times including King Edward who during his reign owned a mansion in Attleburgh. Much later Oliver Cromwell owned part of this town and John Attleburgh was also owner of an estate in St. Bartholomew's Parish [Ber Street] in Norwich.

In the time of Turold, Attleburgh partly belonged to the crown and was held between William Warrenna [who later went to Norwich and was put in charge of the Norfolk Coast] and **William Malet** who was Lord of Attleburgh. It also came in part to the Mortimer's soon after the conquest that also held Stanford Park, Buckingham and Colton Norfolk.

You may wonder why we have included so much history in this write up, but the reason is our family was involved in many of these areas and events that shaped history. Other national and European situations also affected all who lived in those times too and also had its place in future lives that we will discuss later in this book. We leave Attleborough to look now at what was an important residence for one member of our family before the conquest.

Note; for Turold Crispin see chart for Crispin Mallet page 75 chart 27

OLD BUKENHAM, NORFOLK
Home of Turold

Bukenham was established before the conquest and received its name because of the large numbers of bucks, stags and other deer that lived in the surrounding woods. The Old was added when New Bukenham was formed after the Conquest.

Both Old and New Bukenham were connected and tied in with Attleborough, an ancient town and it was difficult to separate them as they were included in with the Manor. Although they belonged to the crown, they were always held by one of the Barons with the Sheriff **[Turold]** living in the Castle. Today they are separate and distinct, the written history of the area seems confused but today both the Bukenham's are a good walking distance away from Attleborough.

Buckenham Castle
This is an old world carving of probably the 2nd one built shown on walls of the Crown Public House as the first castle was a rectangle as shown below.

Plan of Castle and bridleways

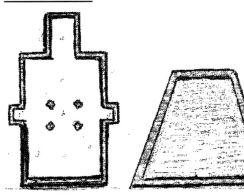 

Plan of the Church

Plan of the old castle

Plate.25

Artists impression of the view of the southwest ruins of Bukenham Castle

Turold was sheriff of the Manor before the Conquest, which confirmed he was of noble birth and a good indication that there was more information on him somewhere.

We were finding the hidden clues like detectives and fitting each fact into their rightful position, which in time gave us great satisfaction. It seems that even the ruins have all but disappeared for both castles but we could not get close enough to confirm this though from the road the mound looks as if it flattens out on top.

Before the conquest in the time of Edward the Confessor, there were three carucators (plowmen) in demesne, and woodland sufficient to maintain 162 swine 21 stockmen of his own and 43 under the protection of other men, all of which the Earl Godwin joined to his own Manor.

After **Turold** and **William** took **Edwin** and fled to Normandy, as mentioned earlier, it prevented Godwin eliminating **Edwin** [heir to the Earldom of Mercia] Godwin, frustrated, seized all **Edwin's** lands, which increased his power though **Edwin** still held extensive land and property in Normandy. When **Turold** returned to England either just before or during the Conquest, he did not return immediately to Norfolk but was appointed for a while as Sheriff of Lincoln. These entire situations are covered in the main stories of the families.

Bukenham was divided into two parishes, All Saints, and St. Andrews with the Castle that stood by the Abbey. Old Bukenham remained in the hands of its **Lord William Warrenna**.

NEW BUKENHAM, NORFOLK

New Bukenham was formed when William Albini founded the castle there after obtaining the land from The Bishop of the Norwich Manor called the Bishops Haugh. These Manors were one part of the Parish of St. Andrew. The tithes were paid to the rector of Eccles [originally this land belonged to the Manor]. The new town possessed a gallows and held a market every Saturday with a market court for which they had to pay five shillings.

There was an official called the 'Capital Steward who had the same power as the sheriff of the area. He attended the court every Saturday to judge weights and measures including debts and other incidentals contracted to the market. In fact everything connected to the market affected the residents of the burgh.

A large fair was held once a year that also held a court called the Warpound Court where all rents were paid on the same day as the courts sat. The going rate was one halfpenny for any type of freehold premises within the parish the total amount being three pence, which was a large sum of money in those days.

BACONSTHORPE, NORFOLK

A niece of **Lady Godiva** lived here at one time with her husband, an Englishman [name unknown], and her son Alfred. **Turold Crispin** who was Alfred's uncle lived in the Manor of Bukenham in the Confessors' reign. *The other Lordship belonged to Guard, a Dane and was held by Uluric/Wulric a freeman at the Conquest whose name reminds us that we discovered that Turold built a Cell at Crowland but which Crowland we are not sure as there are several of that name. One at least was in Norfolk but for obvious reasons we concluded it must be the Crowland in Lincolnshire.

The village is mentioned in Doomsday Book by the name Thorpe. To clarify it from all the others with that name, the additional family name of Bacon was added because the Bacon families were once the Lords there, a name thought to be in close relationship to the king.

Baconsthorpe Manor   Plate 26

At the time of the survey there were two Lordships, **William Warrenna** was Lord, until his death in the battle for Maine [France] and **Turold** was his Sheriff. **Turold** held the land with his nephew Alfred for a time after the demise of William Chettleburgh a freeman who held 60 acres of land.

This residence became the focal point of Queen Elizabeth's 1st anger when during her reign the demesne lands of John and Christopher Heydon at Baconsthorpe were despoiled as they had robbed the Queen of lands, [they were crooked solicitors]. It is in ruins now but must once have been a very beautiful place with a lake and a moat [still to be seen and well worth a visit]. There are some records of the Bulwer family being there at some time though we seem to have mislaid this account.

***Baconsthorpe came into the possession of Roger Bigot after the rebellion of the Norfolk Barons in 1068-75. Roger was the ancestor of some of the Earls of Norfolk and the Bacon family [according to Bloomfield's Norfolk]. He was also related to **William Warrenna** Earl of Surrey. These Barons lost their lands in the reign of King John but they were restored back to the family in 1216. The family of Heydon later held Baconsthorpe.

*+***As chronicle roll ser.vol; page 348-9 **See complete peerage page 586-9
***See Peerage and Pedigree vol.ii.page 30 and Chronicle Rolls ser, vol 1, page 348-9

CAWSTON MANOR, NORFOLK

In early times it was commonly called Caston and in the Confessor's survey was found to belong to Harold Godwin, Earl of East Anglia before he was killed at Hastings in 1066. William, The Conqueror seized the crown and took all Harold's possessions including Cawston [Caston], Manor that was an extensive building.

Illustration of the mace carried

By Erasmus Earle   Plate **27**

from Bloomfields.

The lower inscription on the left states:
This Mace is always carried before the Lord of the Manor of Cawston whenever a court is held there. The Brazen Hand or Gauntlet is the Rebus of John of Gaunt Great Duke of Lancaster and the Ploughshare of iron in it denotes the Manor to be held in Free Soccage and not in Capite. The present shafts of these Maces were fitted up in 1537 and adorned with the Cipher and Arms of Erasmus Earle Sergeant at Law friend and confederate to Oliver Cromwell who purchased the Manor.

As the inscriptions above state, the town is of ancient demean with many privileges that were associated with the Duchy of Lancaster and also being member but exempt from its jurisdiction by John of Gaunt, who was Duke of Lancaster. It had a peculiar custom where a Brazen Gauntlet (or hand) was carried before the Lord of the manor or his steward whenever the court was held there. It is interesting to note that the top left inscription says

'To Augustine Earle Esq. One of his Majesties Hon. Commissioners of Excis. Lord of y Manor of Cawston and Heydon in Norfolk, this plate is gratefully inscribed by his most obliged humble Serv'. Francis Bloomfield'

The inscription in the centre written in Latin is dated 1690 the lower inscription right states: -   *This Mace is carried before the Lord of the Manor of Cawston or his Steward at every court there. The top is iron and represents a bearded Arrow by wch Tenure part of the Town Hall of the Duchy of Lancaster in free Soccage.*

One explanation for this says `The manor to be held in free scutage (tax) and not capite (tenure). Another states that it was in the service of Champier to the Dukes of Lancaster and the office of the Gauntlet is a token of it being the very thing that challenges another to fight according to the laws laid down. If the challenged person picks up the Gauntlet thrown before him then a combat takes place. It was the way of accepting an honorable challenge. Hence the modern saying that `he threw down the Gauntlet` to challenge a rival.

THE FALL OF A REBELLIOUS HOUSE.
1070

After the massive national building program had started, trouble broke out early in the reign of William before the border between England and Scotland had been established. Edinburgh had been part of **King Edwin's** Mercian Kingdom of Northumbria and he gave the present city the name of Edwin's burgh/fort or Edinburgh [the earlier fortress was built there in 611 AD]. We are not sure if there was any connection with our family but as these lands were part of the Mercian kingdom there probably is.

Edwin's Castle Edinburgh [Artist Impression]
Plate 28

Like all recorded information careful consideration has to be made when writing an account of historical events as scribes in general write their own version according to what personal, political, national, or other allegiance they may have had. We have taken note of the common areas of text's where the scribes seemed to agree, and in other writings the most likely sequence of events. No one can be absolutely certain of what is fact, some writers actually contradict others over the same event. We have taken particular interest in Hereward the Wake, as he was the son of Leofric 3rd married to Lady Godvia the sister of Turold our ancestor, it makes Hereward one of our family ancestors [see chart for Mercian's].

While reading the many descriptive writings of his life and times it is difficult again to determine between facts and legends often used to bolster the deeds of this very determinedly brave man. It seems he was one of the very few Mercian or Saxon leaders to take a real stand against the Norman oppressors. We need to understand how Hereward became the rebel thorn in King William's side from early youth. It appears that his character was to be his own man and no one could rule or control him, not even his father, who had to turn him away from his house as his attitude toward the Norman overlords brought danger to them both.

He became homeless and went to live as a tenant in the Abbey at Ely, but would not even accept the possibility of losing a dispute and was callous to the extreme on those who lost the battle to him. This brought him many enemies and some admirers, who became his associates in the rebellions against the Norman's. His very high position within family structures obviously protected him from the punishment that would engulf lesser mortals. It now became clear that King William had to do something to control the Mercian threat.

Mercian Family   Chart 38

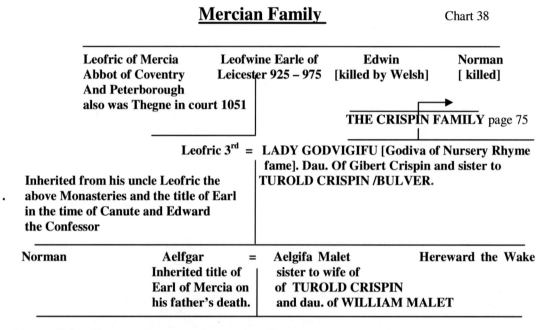

Note all family members are in capital letters

In 1068 the late King Harold's sons unexpectedly made a pirate raid from Ireland, and a year later Prince Edgar son of Edmund Ironsides came again with many hundreds of men thinking they could restore Danish rule. He joined troops that were hiding near the Humber to raid York, storming the Castle slaying hundreds of people, abducting the leading citizens and stealing wealth.

When in 1069 King William tried to take the land away from **Edwin** [the future Earl of Mercia] and give it to his brother Robert who was ruthless and brutal which caused anger among the people. The whole of the northern counties rose in rebellion and **Edwin** left the court of William for the North. The people once more longed for their Old Saxon rulers. Prince Edgar the youngest and the only remaining son of Edmund Ironsides in this country, was the last of the line of Cerdic [who founded Great Yarmouth 495 AD]. Edgar realized this situation, and came with all his nobles and a host of loyal supporters including Seigforth the son of Old Sigward. Others joined them including the Earl Waltheof husband of Judith [niece of King William].

In 1070 the Mercian's led by **Hereward, Edwin and Morca** [grandsons of Leofric], and many hundreds of men with other armed forces such as the Danes who were in guerrilla warfare against William, set out for York. Once there they burned York Castle and they slew everything that came before them. Added to this were the fiery Welshmen who stormed over Offa's dyke into the lands of Mercia. The battle was violent; many killed their own men. **Edwin** son of **Aelfgar** travelled northwards to join his brother **Morca** and the Fenmen as he intended to seek the help of the King of Scotland but was ambushed and killed. Three thousand died in this battle in one day; death came through clumsy weapons use or confusion when the English became blood crazed and vicious.

The Danes hearing of the unrest sailed into the Humber with Swein and also Harald King of Norway, and Tostig his half brother. The situation became more serious at Peterborough where invasion fever continued to be high. All those Danes who had settled here joined Prince Edgar with three other nobles who wanted to rid themselves of their captors. In Peterborough the Danes grabbed all the treasures in the Abbey killing hundreds, capturing others and taking them to their ships.

When King William had first heard of this he sent Turold of Malmsbury the son of Odo his half brother to sort things out. He arrived at the abbey with his fully armed and trained soldiers and found everything destroyed but took possession. King William casually remarked that as Turold fought more like a knight than a monk he would find him something to fight about, and appointed him abbot there.

William Warrenna with his army rushed to the district to lay waste the whole area, and accused two monks of conspiracy. The Danes had driven out all the French monks in Peterborough Abbey. After leaving the Abbey in ruins William immediately left to organise his army and set out for York, and after several forced marches, brought him to the scene; the weather turned bitter. The devastation that met his eyes and the news that the Danes were anchored in the Humber added more fuel to his burning anger. Witnessing all this and hearing more he exploded in full fury, unleashing his horsemen who struck down and trampled all before them.

With Edwin dead King William was determined to capture **William Malet, Morca**, Siward and most importantly **Hereward** who had escaped by taking a ship to flee to the Abbey at Ely. King William who had made so many enemies around the York area tried to regain popularity by protecting children, helping the sick, caring for the dying, and benefiting the poor in the districts where they resided. These actions in a subtle way gave more authority to the king.

The King bribed the Danish fleet, and though they took no more part in battle they remained in the Humber staying just off shore, so the mini rebellion died out. At first rather than oppress the masses of his reluctant subjects he brought in Norman priests to influence their opinion.

William Warrenna besieged the abbey and drove out **Hereward** and his followers who fled to the fens, a treacherous place of tall reeds, mud and marsh, ideal for guerrilla warfare. **Hereward's** extensive knowledge of the marshes made it possible for him to defend them. It was clear to the king he would have to give more attention to the Fenmen. Their Mercian leader, **Hereward the Wake** was proving to be a distinct thorn in his side and was a tenant of the Abbey, which Turold son of Odo recaptured.

[Artist impression]

Wooden causeways were built by the Normans at Ely in 1070 to attack their hideout   Plate.29

William Warrenna took a leading part in suppressing this rebellion as he had a special grudge against **Hereward** who had killed one of his relatives. William formed a ring of flat-bottomed boats that encircled the marsh sealing every exit, manning them day and night he then constructed wooden causeways into its heart. Despite **Hereward's** attacks at night and other various ruses it was just a matter of time before the trapped men of the marshes had to surrender. The Fen's area at that time was a very different terrain than now. [It was later drained by the Dutch and large towns formed].

A treacherous monk by name Y'ware the Sacristan, who stole all he could the night before from Peterborough Abbey, sought out Turold son of Odo and asked for protection. He betrayed the fact that the outlaws intended to come to Peterborough as he knew the monks in Ely wished to bring an end to this siege so informed the Norman's of a secret path through the marshes; the fate of the rebels was sealed.

Hundreds of attackers who did not know of the dangerous bog and quicksand must have sunk below the sea of mud around the fighting area of Aldreth and Stuntney and their remains could we suppose, still be found in full armour below its surface. **Hereward** was defeated but escaped by hacking his way through all that stood in his way like some Berserker using sheer force, and with a handful of men found safety in the forest of Brunswald [West Huntingdonshire]. He caused much trouble for King William striking from many counties but in the end became a homeless outlaw. **Hereward** had enemies who wanted to settle old scores such as **Earl Warrenna** and Ivo Taillebois [husband of Lucy] who had plotted against him.

Resistance soon collapsed which brought an end to the rebellion; then revenge came, bitter and severe. **William Warrenna** created a blackened barren landscape from the Humber to the Tyne. A scorched earth policy designed to prevent further insurrections. Not a building was left standing between York and Durham everything was flattened. Fences, walls, harvests, livestock and cowsheds were destroyed and burnt. The same was true for Derby and Chester [when the Doomsday Book was written, there was nothing to record for that area]. He then mopped up the other pockets of resistance at Peterborough; **Morca** was captured and imprisoned in Normandy, the other rebels were either killed or scattered to various prisons after loosing their hands and sometimes their eyes.

There are many written versions of the events for this period concerning **Hereward** but again nothing to prove this history. However we agree with the version of the pedigree of Du Gestis Herewardi as this fits in with the names and places already mentioned, such as Crowland and the **Earls of Mercia.** We concluded from various written accounts that Hereward, feeling very disillusioned with living like a hunted animal gave himself up and was imprisoned in Bedford Castle jail. *Here he struck up a friendship with the jailer, as described later in the book.

Some say that on being moved to Buckenham prison his escort was ambushed and his followers set him free. Later King William forgave **Hereward,** being aware of his high rank in Mercia and with the respect and affinity that exists between all fighting men, restored his lands in Lincoln, thus bringing an end to the years of rebellion and bloodshed.
Hereward converted from being a rebel to becoming a loyal subject of the realm with all possessions reinstated. Another version describes how his last years were spent living in fear from those who sought to kill him. He was finally attacked by several Frenchmen who he dispatched, then one of their number, Ralph de Dol from behind, struck **Hereward** who swung round breaking his sword on his assailant; both fell dead.

Earl Waltheof was the last great Saxons leader who until 1070 had held the Earldoms of Northampton and Huntingdon, where the Saxons were prevalent. He was one of the perpetrators of the uprising; however King William pardoned him by royal decree releasing him from prison. To keep his allegiance he was given the hand of William's niece Judith, [the daughter of his half sister Adelaide] who later betrayed him. The king also restored the lands his father had possessed before the Conquest. In addition, William made him Earl of Northumberland the title his father held before the conquest. **Unfortunately Waltheof became involved with the next uprising, this time with the Norfolk Barons.
*+** See page 184

CROWLANDS [OR CROYLAND] ABBEY
PRIDE OF THE MERCIAN KINGDOM

The Three Ways to No-where Bridge

There were four abbeys built on this site, the first was founded by Guthlac on 24th August AD 716, who landed on one of the islands that the existed among the muddy swamps of the fens. The Danes destroyed this original building in 870 AD including its many documents and records. King Sweyne then ransacked it in 1016. King Edred visited the 2nd abbey and was later a monk there and restored the buildings. More of these important properties were ransacked and burnt after the rebellion of the Norfolk Barons [1075-1090].

We found two conflicting reports on the abbey's destruction in 1091, one scribe states that it was destroyed by a fire accidentally by a plumber. The 2nd account states that it was revenge attack because Hereward had been in rebellion against King William the Conqueror; as a result the king and William Rufus were determined to destroy the House of Mercia including Crowlands Abbey. After the Barons revolt they took pleasure in venting their spleen by vandalizing and despoiling the Mercian House.

Most of the ancient library records, buildings, charters and manuscripts of Mercia were destroyed and with **Morca** being disinherited, this effectively ended the Mercian hold on the reigns of power. Quite a lot of the old histories and documents which the earlier Danish Vikings might have missed were reduced to ashes along with the Abbey. This included all the records of the Mercian royal line which has caused us so many problems tracing **Turold Crispin** and his ancestors.

The third new building to be constructed by Ingulphus 1110/1113 was commissioned by Henry 1st and built in the Norman style; unfortunately in 1118 AD an earthquake destroyed most of this.

Crowlands Abbey   Plate 30

Artist's impression of the ruins

The town grew around the ruins and Sigmund a Danish knight owing allegiance to Leofric held half of the township of Crowley. The other half belonged to the church and was coveted by Sigmund, when peaceful negotiations failed, he took it by force and fighting again devastated Crowlands Abbey.

The case came to court, Leofric intervened which resulted in a compromise and Sigmund gained a life interest in the half that belonged to the church providing he performed military service. Since the great disaster in 1090/1 mentioned above and further destruction by Henry 8th the abbey has steadily crumbled away, although some parts have weathered the ravages of time, such as the 13th century West Front and the 15th century aisle; it is now used as a parish church.

Trinity Bridge
The three ways to nowhere bridge   Plate 31

At Crowlands the monks built a curious shaped bridge situated at the point where the river Welland divided into two streams, one going past the abbey [at that time used for their sanitary and sewage purposes] with the main branch continuing towards Spalding.

Edward 4th traveled by boat on this river to Fotheringay Castle. The first bridge was constructed of timber and referred to in the charter of King Eldred's [AD 943] as the triangular bridge, which was used as a means of defining boundaries. The charter of King Ethelbald AD716 also speaks of a triangular bridge in Croyland. It must be remembered that prior to the draining of the fens, Crowlands were group of islands and its main streets were waterways. This present bridge was built c.1360/90 and the streams were probably diverted when he Dutch drained the fens. The course of the waterways still exist today but are dry, leaving us and the present day visitor in a state of curious bewilderment finding a bridge that apparently serves no useful purpose.

On the 6th of May 2002, we visited this small village community, and whilst walking along its narrow streets we sensed an air of mystery here belonging to another time period. That of a bygone age steeped in ancient history. Although no living person was near we found ourselves talking in whispers. It was a strange experience; even the ancient pub where we had a pleasant meal was very quiet. After walking over the bridge and upon reaching the abbey we had a conversation with a local lady aged 91, who remembered as a child, water flowing under this bridge. The Abbey itself contained many written references of the history of Crowlands and this is where we obtained much information.

Ref., M.S. Stevenson's book "Anglo Saxon England". p.262-265 an early enfeoffment dated 1066-87 has Thorold Papillio as witness. See Gissinghall Manor and Bloomfield's Norfolk p.173 from book "Mediaeval England" by Peter Cross "[Crowlands] by Stenton centres for English House of Wessex AD 802-1066

THE DOMESDAY BOOK
1085 AD.

In 1085 AD England was threatened for the last time with a Danish invasion when Canute, 4th son of Sweyn Erithson succeeded his brother Harold as King of the Denmark. It had always been his ambition to win fame in England and on becoming King he reasserted his claim, which his brother failed to do, by making his naval force overwhelming to others. William the Conqueror sensing danger removed all supplies that could have helped any invader from the English coast. In Denmark a violent dispute broke out among King Canute's men, resulting in his murder, this together with the matter of the serious rebellion of the English Barons urgently needed to be considered.

William called a meeting at Xmas 1085 in Gloucester in order to debate these issues, and the outcome of these talks caused him some deep thought which prompted him to take stock of the nations' wealth. He wanted to know exactly what assets individuals held. In order to achieve this, he created an inventory that later became known as the Domsday Book. This he did to protect himself and his kingdom and control the wealth of others; it was one of William's greatest achievements, the first survey/census ever taken by any European nation, not even lawmen were excused, everyone came under its scrutiny. The work was undertaken by Commissioners sent out by William, in two massive volumes written in Latin. These tomes took the skins of 800 sheep to provide the parchment for the Domsday Book which became the most quoted, detailed, misunderstood yet informative English historical document ever created.

Considered by some as a bible, a day of reckoning, a doomsday inventory that was hard on his subjects. It was efficiently compiled, unpopular and caused uproar. He then brought mercenaries into the country, and quartered them among his barons; according to the chronicle the number of men sent to each was strictly proportionate to the amount of land on each estate used. The order of billeting these men must have impressed all that took part, the information being supplied by the survey. If you remember in earlier chapters it was the mercenaries and slaves the Romans brought back to Rome that helped to destroy them.

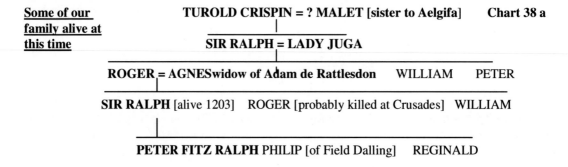

Some of our family alive at this time — TUROLD CRISPIN = ? MALET [sister to Aelgifa]   Chart 38 a

SIR RALPH = LADY JUGA

ROGER = AGNES widow of Adam de Rattlesdon   WILLIAM   PETER

SIR RALPH [alive 1203]   ROGER [probably killed at Crusades]   WILLIAM

PETER FITZ RALPH   PHILIP [of Field Dalling]   REGINALD

We suppose William took note of this possible problem, but decided keep track of them and the taxes due to him. No questions of his authority were allowed. The assessment of a Barons estate to Danegeld and other taxes became well known to the king's financial officers. As William inspected his own records he noticed the inaccuracies, an old Monk described William's thought patterns while this was being carried out. "You could almost see the look of disdain and the sarcastic curl of his lip as he asked 'What sort of men!' William openly expressed his disgust at the vagueness of the information returned by the Barons who were not always honest, causing him to hold a debate at Gloucester once more. He was furious at being thwarted at every turn.

Of the lawmen alive in 1066, only three remained in office two years later. William replaced two of these with Normans, and the successors inherited their lands. No stone was left unturned in William's search for the wealth of the nation, he insisted that every Ox, Pig, Goat Abbot and Earl's head would be counted along with the massed population, hides, buildings, the measurement of all lands, and who owned what. Its records like the Last Judgment were inevitable.

No doubt our ancestors such as Turold, the Malet's and others with vast land, wealth, titles and other possessions were less than happy to have their worldly gains exposed to the king in order for him to levy taxes accordingly. This depressed the English, especially the peasants and caused much unrest, they thought that it was a huge business concern designed to keep control them and the landed Saxon gentry. After the Doomsday Book there was a gap in the English records for three generations until the pipe rolls were started.

No one dared to cheat the King, although not everyone is mentioned by name, the great bulk of humans could just as well be cattle or swine, the whole country was counted. We can gain comfort from the thought that we must have been descended from the best people [they must have been, to get through all the troubles that were to descend upon them through the ages]. An estimate of the people living in 1086 in Britain was between one hundred million to one hundred and fifty million, with five thousand five hundred Knights, and less than 200 great landowners.

After the barons revolted many records were eradicated, another destruction of archives came with Henry 8th and the dissolution of the Monasteries where no care was taken to preserve ancient documents. Whole libraries, art, and many other priceless treasures that would have helped genealogists today were destroyed. However the possession of Harlexton by the Mortimer's does lead us through the maze to the time of Kings Richard and John.

THE FEAST AT NORWICH CASTLE
Ralph the Elder and his son Ralph de Geuda.

In those days most titles, positions and possessions were passed directly from father to eldest son, this has proved confusing as often they both had the same first names too. Time and lack of detail have obscured the information on the Elder Ralph whose birth occurred before 1011. He was known to be half Breton, which fits in with other information we have, whose granddaughter Arnice married William Beaumont [See chart 39 p165]

We have found that he was born in Norfolk, reputed to be the nephew of Edward the Confessor and son to Edward's sister, who married the Comte de Vexin. But there is some doubt about this. An extract from the complete Peerage states "Se ylca Raulf [Ralph] waes Brittisc in his moder healfe and his father was Englise Raulf Latte and was boren on Norfolce" *He attested charters in Brittany 1031-32, and was in England as Dapifer [Kings Steward] in **1060-66. Ralph the Elder also known as Ralph the Staller was stalre [constable] to Edward the Confessor 1062 as Regius Auctotitas; this was confirmed by numerous references in the Doomsday Book as [Stalra / Stalre]. This survey also shows he held extensive estates in Norfolk Suffolk, Lincoln and Cornwall whether by grant, inheritance or marriage to an English Heiress.

He was also in possession of the Barony of Gaul from which his son took his name. Before the conquest Ralph was the Earl of East Anglia. He was a minister in the government, and both he and his son attended the court of Edward the Confessor and were referred to as friends in a charter confirming gifts to St. Rachel in 1078. When a force of Norsemen invaded England and captured Norwich in 1069, Ralph de Guader [his son] routed them, his father died about this time and he inherited all his wealth and titles.

After the Conquest William the Conqueror favoured him, thus emphasizing the close bond of relationship to royalty by marriage. This tends to confirm that he must have descended through the royal lines of these two nations. Ralph is often referred too as a close relative of King William. He was summoned by the king with 60 others to advise him on affairs of state and appointed Joint Commissioner with William Bishop of London.

*Complete Peerage Vol.2
** In September 1065 Tostig was Earl of Northumbria and the king received news of a revolt in Northumbria demanding King Edward dismiss Earl Tostig as he had despoiled their churches and overtaxed them. They wanted a young boy of eighteen years of age named Morca as their Earl [brother to the Earl of Mercia] or they would attack the King. The king submitted and sent Tostig abroad sowing the seeds of further trouble but not knowing he was soon to die.

A Foiled Plot Against The king

The Keeper of Norwich Castle [the Castilian] about this time (1069) was Hubert de Rye, one of the knights granted lands who were required to live in the Castle on an alternating basis and provide troops to defend the kings' realm from both inside and outside of the country.

In 1075 Ralph de Geuda married the daughter of William, son of Osborne and although the relationship to our family is unclear [through his connection to the Alleyn's]; we found this wedding happened during an interesting period in the history of Norwich. There were many disconsolate Mercian and Saxon Nobles at this wedding feast, including Ralph de Geuda who had married against the Kings wishes and was starting to regret it. This led to his joining the rebellion of 1075, which is written about later.

The bridal feast was held at Norwich Castle where Ralph was the custodian and the occasion was sadly noted by an old Rhyme that says, "There was a bridal feast alas, through which death to many came to pass" When the nobles met, murmuring began and a plot to cause King William's downfall was formulated. Others overheard this conversation including Judith, the wife of Earl Waltheof who was also a niece of William 1st. Waltheof had been persuaded to join in with their plans much against his better judgment. It was rumoured Judith had her eyes on another man and wished to be rid of her husband, so probably reported the plot discreetly to William who returned to England from his Norman domain in a fury, swearing vengeance against the perpetrators.

Meantime William prepared to fight and built more castles and fortifications to protect him against the rebels. Feelings against him were still running high over the laying waste and complete brutalizing of the north. Treachery was in the air when the king was again away in Normandy addressing local affairs and had to return when he heard a devious plot by some of his nobles was being made against him.

The uprising was a failure and the guilty fled including Ralph de Guader who left his wife with some soldiers in Norwich Castle to face the results of his mistake. He and his men encountered vastly superior forces near Cambridge under the leadership of Odo the Bishop of Bayeux and the Earl of Constance. He retreated back to Norwich pursued by the Royal army; at the castle they continued the fight under the leadership of Ralph's wife, until she was able to make a deal with the king *she then left for Brittany where later her husband joined her.

* See Peerage and Pedigree Vol. ii page 30. and item from this book "Wedding feast at Norwich Castle"

Several of the rebel Barons made great efforts to regain William's favour in various ways. Before he left for France Ralph built a church in Norwich as a peace offering, which went unnoticed by the king. Robert Curthose of Mortain, half brother to William Conqueror traded his Dukedom in Normandy with his brother Henry to fund the Crusades and was later joined on a Crusade to Jerusalem by Ralph de Guader, his wife and Bishop Odo, [after Robert's defeat by Bishop Wulfstan].

*Ralph de Guader was deprived of all his English lands and Earldoms and Odo's high-flying career had also been in sharp decline between the dates of 1087-89. In mid winter the king judged the other rebels, some were blinded, others were outlawed and shamed in various loathsome ways; the rest fled to France.

Turold in trouble with the King

Turold, son of Gilbert Crispin had sold his lands at Bukenham to the Abbey after he and his son **Ralph** were involved in supporting Odo, [who had rebelled against the king], and went to join the rest of his family in Lincoln. **Turold's'** family was now very poor and the records show that whilst living in the Manor of Greetwell he did not pay the Danegeld [a tax originated by Athelred to pay tribute to the invading Vikings]. He then moved back to Norfolk before taking up a post as **William Warrenna's** man. Records in the Church of Rochester show that he started a litigation action to recover his lands and fortune; this must have had some success even before William Warrenna died, as you will see later.

Robert Curthose the king's son [Ralph's nephew] died on the way to Palermo in the vicinity of Antioch. This was also the last mission in which Ralph de Guader and his wife took part, as they were both killed in the course of a battle during the siege of Nicea leaving three sons. William the eldest son of Ralph succeeded his father and on the death of his uncle tried to claim his fief without success, dying shortly afterwards.

Ralph, second son of Ralph de Guader inherited from his brother William, attaining the honour of Brittany, which his daughter Amice carried to her husband Robert Earl of Leicester who was a Breton. The Breton Estates remained in the hands of Ralph third son of de Guader who also acquired the great estates and Barony of Laval so he must have been connected in to the House of Alleyn [**Alleyn of Brittany**] and to our own line. He was also given the estates in Mercia taken from the imprisoned **Morca** after the rebellion, [although **Morca** was released many years later].

*[from various volumes of Anglo/Norman studies]

The families and leaders of the Mercian Earls now disappeared from the history books, never to return. The Mercian **Lord Leofric** moved to Lincoln with his family as it was part of the lands of Mercia; he had probably also been involved in the rebellion.

Waltheof the Saxon Earl [husband of the kings' niece Judith] fled to France and from there pleaded with King William for forgiveness against the banishment order. The king seemed agreeable with this, but his Barons advised that there would never be peace while any Saxon remained in power.

In the following year 1076 Waltheof was brought back to England in chains and beheaded; to the Saxons he was a martyr and the monks of Crowland took his body to their Abbey in the Fens where his tomb was regarded as a shrine. It was said after Waltheof died his wife Judith suffering pangs of conscience, founded the Abbey of Elstow in Bedford. All that remains of this building is the Chapel.

England was still mainly covered in forests, woods and wild heath. Land outside the cultivated fields was called runacre or common land and was used by the ordinary people. During Saxon times their pigs fed on acorns and chickens and sheep could be kept there. The Norman nobles took these rights away and made this land forbidden territory so they could use them as hunting grounds. These prohibitions caused much resentment.

William now enlisted the aid of the bishops who had their appointments transferred from the quiet country districts to the larger towns. This enabled them to be more effective in gaining extra support for the king from his subjects and the ability to stop trouble before it began. Herbert de Losinga Bishop of Thetford received orders to move into Norwich, which by this time had become an important center for trade, and the largest town in East Anglia. Losinga was a Norman priest, and although born in England was brought up in the Abbey of Fecamp [the area where William first brought in his Norman knights disguised as monks prior to the invasion of England].

Losinga had the ways, ideals, speech, and the Norman way of thinking, loved power and fame, which was common to the religious people of his day. To this end in 1070AD he bribed King William, who had a love of money, to appoint him Bishop of Norwich

References: - (See Saxon Chronicles). Laud Chronicle E. 1070 page 205-206.Peterborough.
Sir Francis Hill's book Mediaeval England and the Chronicle Rolls ser, vol. pp.348-9.
Note From Calendar Documents preserved in France.page 108 York ii page 176-8 pp133-4.
Anglo Saxon England by Stenton p.168 Coleswein father of Picot was a benefactor of Lincoln Minster LCS.ii p CCXXXV Infra Chapter V

The Bishop then developed a conscience and pleaded with the Pope for forgiveness. He was told to return to office and spend his considerable fortune building as many fine churches as his money would allow. This is how Norwich Cathedral and the most beautiful Parish church of St. Nicholas Great Yarmouth came into existence. The land Losinga wanted to build his Cathedral in Norwich on was part of the Blofield Manor, for this he had to petition the king to be able to purchase it and permission was granted in 1096. The land was boggy and extremely wet so the foundations had to be laid on bales of wool. Losinga based his design on his old Abbey of Fecamp, which was still close to his heart, and had the finest white stone shipped from Caen in Normandy where it was hewn and shaped.

The people's market place was in Tombland, [meeting place] which the monks stole to incorporate it within the walls of the new Cathedral Close to the disgust of the community and bitterness grew; many battles were fought; hatred became so intense it soon exploded into full violence. Always the people lost out. After the Priors men robbed a city merchant the people went wild with anger; the monks had to retire behind the massive gates of the Abbey firing bolts from crossbows at those who ventured too near. The people piled wood against the doors and set them alight, then stormed through, wrecking and ransacking the priory. St. Ethelbert's church was destroyed during the fighting and many were killed.

Retribution came when the Norman's made the City repair the damage done and pay for a new gate. This was built where the church had stood and called St. Ethelbert's gate. The monks escaped without punishment, but the Prior was imprisoned. The building still stirred up hatred in the people, as it had no part of their lives and had forced them to use another market place in the *Magna Crofta, (Latin: great field) always under the watchful eyes of the Normans in the castle.

Norwich and Norfolk are steeped in national and local history with many fine old buildings still existing, these are well maintained each with its own particular story to tell of happenings long ago. The tranquil area of Phuls/Pilsbury Ferry is in complete contrast to the modern development one hundred yards away, containing the main railway station, Norwich City Football club, plus domestic and commercial interest

* The market place still used today.
Note; *A fine view of this ancient market can be seen from the battlements of Norwich Castle with its colourful array of stalls and goods for sale that has taken place for many centuries. There is a fine Church there called St. Peter Mancroft where Simon de Dalling [married to Margaret Mouney] was Bishop of Norwich c 1530. This church was used by other generations of Bulwer's.

PICTURES OF ITEMS MENTIONED IN TEXT

*Phuls [Pilsbury] Ferry
Still exsists in the heart of Norwich
*Well known to the people as Phuls Ferry

To build Norwich Cathedral a special water channel as in photograph had to be cut to allow the fully laden Wherries (sailing barges) to sail up to the Cathedral site. Of course there were various designs to suit their use i.e. goods or passenger   Plate 33

Wherries on the river during the Norwich Festival

Plate.34

The land Losinga wanted to build his Cathedral on was **boggy** and extremely wet so the foundations had to be laid on bales of wool.

He based the design on his old Abbey of Fecamp, and had the finest white stone shipped from Caen, hewn and shaped then loaded onto Wherries'

Norwich Cathedral   Plate 32

THIS CHART EXPLAINS SOME FAMILY RELATIONSHIPS IN THE FOLLOWING TEXT

Chart 39

Showing descent of WILLIAM WARRENNA/MORTIMER/WARD'S
From Rudolph half brother of Richard 1st. Duke of Normandy [Cont; from page 85 chart 31]

RUDOLPH [Son of WILLIAM LONGSWORD]
= GUNNER [sister to Gonner wife of Richard 1st

HUGH MORTIMER	ROGER MORTIMER [Descent to Wigmores of Wales]	RALPH MORTIMER/VALOISE

WILLIAM MORTIMER/WARRENNA Note; change of name
= 1st Gundred sister of Gerbal the Fleming niece of Gunner wife of Richard 1st
= 2nd sister of the Grand Earl of Chester

WILLIAM WARRENNA 2nd Supported Robert Curthose=Isobel Beaumont	Rainard Took part in death of Arch bishop Was disinherited	Edith = Adeline = Robert
WILLIAM WARRENNA 3rd = =Margaret		Gundred = Nigel Albini

WILLIAM WARRENNA 4th Was with King Stephens army. Took part in disturbance that broke out between Norman and Flemish Followers [i.e.Stephen and Matilda	Roger de Mowbray	Henry = Margaret Dau. Of Comte Montago
	Roger=dau; of Earl of Warwick	

Roger Beaumont   William Beaumont =Arnice dau of Ralph de Geuarda

Thomas Beaumont *[V] = Agnes dau; of Amauri Comte of Mortain

Robert Beaumont=Isobel Fought at Hastings Made Count of Leicester In 1801 was Count of Muelan		Henry Beaumont = Margaret Rotrou Earl of Warwick 1088 died 1119 issue

*Waleran [William]=dau; of Amauri * Robert le Bossu = Arnice daughter of Ralph de Gaul
de Montford Count   [name changed| to Wards]
of Muelan and Count of Mortain   Thomas = Isobel

Iissue leads down to WARDS when Simon Ward married Margaret Mortimer in 1391**
 Note; Important marriage connection and name changes found in Bloomfield's history of Norfolk listed under the Manor of Kirby Bedon.

***John Warde Lord of Kirby Bedon = Heir of John and Thomas de Bosco of Kirby Bedon

**John Warde [Gent] son and Heir =Katherine dau; of William Appleyard of Braconash and Dunston Norfolk. Will proven 27th Oct. 1445 ordered his body to be buried in Church of Kirby Bedon often called John Atttwood. John de Bosco He fought at the siege of Calias

Sir Thomas Warde = dau. of Elder son of Robert Kemp	John Warde Rector of Morley 1480	**Robert Ward [Gent] = -Alice

Robert Warde Esq; = daughter of Cobbledyke Esq.,

Robert Warde Esq., of Kirby Bedon = dau., of Sir Giles Cappel
*twins **See Wards of Broke and Yarmouth ***See Notes for this chart on next page
All capital letters are Mortimer families. Names leading to Ward family are on right hand side in Batan font.

References and notes below refer to the chart on previous page.

See **item on Kirstead Kirkly Manor p. 270 Simon Ward Living 20th June1391 married Margaret of the Noble family of Mortimer

See charter for Conference of gifts by Duke William to Sir Wanderville, witnesses include the name of Gilbert Crispin Hugh Bigod [EN 1154 before 1045].
William Warrenna [1] related to Turold through Rollo [Viking] also by marriage into Malet families

Note. The line from William Warrenna became extinct by 1347 but Mortimer names are still around Norfolk. The active life of the Castle at Lewes ceased with the depopulation of Sussex during the Black Death. In the years of recovery Arundel from the West and Bodian from the East became abandoned eclipsed by Lewes Castle and was ruinous, until the 19th century when efforts were made to preserve its Goel Gower of Percha [Goel Earl of Loctre] C Waters U.S. p.20 Bermondsy Annulsii 320. See Chronicle of William de Jumeiges de Immutations Ordinus Monischorium Oderic. E 1104 p.235-239. Bloomfield's Norfolk Kirkly Manor [Kirkly] For Vitals name changes Part in Latin. This leads to the family of Ward; from which we believe though unable to prove at this time our father's ancestry.

Names of Atthil, Woodhouse, Ward Warrenna, and de Bios all stem from Mortimer. See charts for Warrenna, Bulwer. [All the above are cousins linked by marriage].

YOUR PROGRESS CHART THROUGH TIME   Chart 40

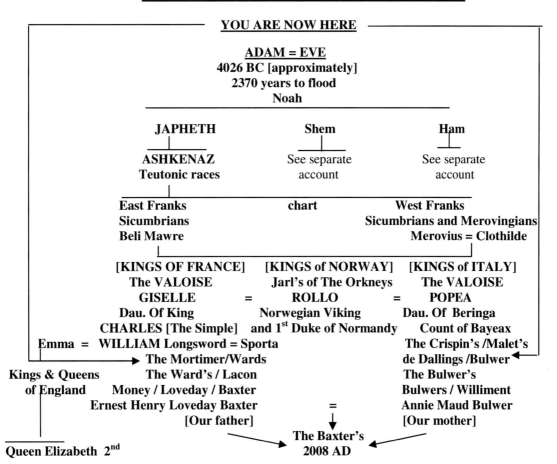

WILLIAM WARRENNAS' MANOR
North Pickenham
c1075.

There were two manors here, Huddlesford and Virleys. Huddlesford was William Lord Warrenna's Manor, which Osford held in the Confessors time. From Doomsday we find this village was a small Lordship/Hamlet that was part of the Manor of Sporle, and was valued with it. In this parish is a hamlet called Cotes, and **Ralph le Breton** relative to the **de-Dalling /Bulwer** families held lands there in the time of Henry the 3rd.

In the time of Edward 2nd, **Robert Ward** of Cotes conveyed lands and the *Old Hall there to Edmund. Osbert Pickenham who lived in Lynn; he was a Carmelite monk [the White Friars] who became a Prior of this order and was a great writer in the reign of Edward 2nd. William Pickenham was L.L. Dean of Stoke St. Clare Norfolk.

Huddlesford

Ribald brother of Alleyn of Richmond was Lord of Middleham in Yorkshire, but the male issue failed for this family, so it passed into the hands of others.

Turold Bulver/Crispin Becomes William Warrenna's Man in 1075

William Mortimer/Warrenna was the founder of the House of Warren, and possibly one of the original Norman Earls of Norfolk. At some time after the rebellion **Turold** returned to Norfolk and was sworn in as **William of Warrenna's** man by placing his hands between those of William as his Lord and swearing fealty/loyalty giving a fair indication that he might have been in great trouble.

His family connection brought him under **William Warrenna's** protection, as they were relatives by blood and by marriage. This was possibly after the feast at Norwich castle, where the plot was planned against King William, which he could have been involved in.

William Warrenna held lands in trust from the Norfolk Barons of that time who were also involved with the rebellion of 1075 and after his death Godric challenged the right of **Turold [William Warrenna's man]** to hold these lands. From 1050 to 1300 agricultural land became more profitable in respect that the horse was used for the transportation of goods as they were faster than an Ox. The two-year crop rotation was abandoned and replaced by the three year, which gave much bigger yields making food more abundant and increasing profits for the land owner; thus life was less harsh and the population soared.

*See *Manor of Kirby Bedon page 274

Turold had to forfeit some of the lands and the associated money, which reverted back to the King who then decided that as **Turold** had paid fees on some of the lands concerned returned them to him. The rest was given over to Godric, who farmed them for the King. **Alleyn,** Lord of Richmond held it from him. King William burnt and destroyed the Abbey at Crowlands in a revenge attack shortly after the death of **William Warrenna** [whose grave is in the church of St Andrew North Pickenham].

Chart Showing The Family Relationship Between William Warrenna and Turold Crispen/ de Dalling

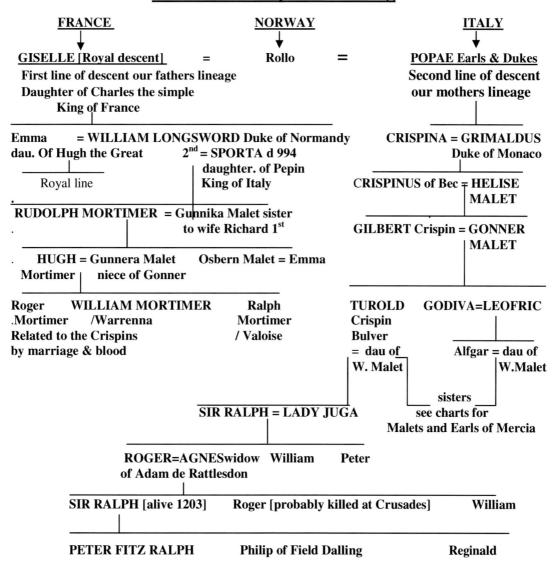

Chart 41

Turold Crispin and some of his sisters married into the Malet family and confirmation of the connection to Mortimer's by marriage and blood comes through our common ancestor **Rollo** the Viking Duke of Normandy. Also Rollo's two marriages first to **Gisele** [France] second to **Popae** [Italy]. Rollo therefore links three royal Dynasties of Europe, [Scandinavia, France and Italy].

TUROLD HOLDS LAND FROM WILLIAM WARRENNA
c1075

*****Turold** retained some lands [in total 30 parcels of land] after the death of his Lord **William Warrenna. Turold** spelt **Thorold/Toreadre** in the Doomsday Book holds Hackforth and Wood Dalling in exchange for Lewes. In Coltishall 110 acres of what had been Stigurd's land. [Man of **Leofric:** - see item on Crowlands].

Lands of Ralph the Constable.
After the rebellion of 1075 and his death and tribunal, these lands were given to Roger Bigot of Spalding Manor. **Turold** gave land titles to monks of Spalding Monastery, which held no Charters for **Turold;** these documents were destroyed in the great fire of Crowlands in 1091.

Land in Mortoft.
These lands are most likely to have been confiscated from rebels, and held in abeyance by **William Warrenna** before his death.

Ittering fifteen acres, Little Barningham 30 acres, Wickmere 24 acres, Mannington 17 acres Irmingham 8 acres, Tuttington 16 acres. Crackford 10 acres, Brampton 6 acres, Paston 30 acres. Sco Ruston 10 acres, Filby 9 acres, North Banningham 16 acres,

Roger Bigots lands.

Thorold holds Framingham Earl 20 acres, Mundham 6 acres he cannot rent or sell without permission. Seething 16 acres, Little Hockham 3 acres, Heckingham 26 Acres.

From Roger Morston.   Baconsthorpe 60 Acres.

Ralph Beaufors lands. **Thorold** holds Tunstall 60 acres.

Manor Rolls Roger son of Reinards Lands.

Thorold/Turold   Holds 28 acres and 30 acres of land that he held before the conquest. When he and **William Malet** his grandfather fled to Normandy, they took the young Edwin Earl of Mercia to protect him from Harold Godwin, and gave the lands of Bukenham and Attleborough to Bukenham Abbey [held by Baldwin Malet, his relative by marriage].

*Note; this evidence seems to clinch the identity of Turold/ Thorold/Toreadre and the descent of the Bulver's./Bulwers/Bulwars/etc

TWO DALLINGS AND A DALHAM

During the initial search we noted three Manors were mentioned, Dalham Dalling and Field Dalling [the pre-conquest name was Dallinga a Saxon name meaning watery dale or vale; two were in North Norfolk one in Suffolk. King William found it confusing so had them renamed. One was named as Wood Dalling, near Foulsham, another as Field Dalling near Bynham Priory, the last one as Dalham/Dawling, in Suffolk, later known as Gissing. After serious rebellions in 1069-1075 and again in 1090 the Saxon Lords were deprived of power and wealth and everything reverted back to the Normans, many changed names to avert punishment.

All lands were ultimately owned by the king but the Barons held them in fee to farm [enfeoffed] or rented them out [known as Grace and Favour residences]. The history relating to these manors is confusing as we found several Dallings/Dawling/Dalhams with no indication as to which ones they were or their location. John Bulwer and his wife Maude bought *Gissing in the time of the Black Prince but this branch of the family died out in the Bulwer name because lack of male heirs and the plague, which was still very active in those times. When their daughters married, the estates passed to the Shimpling family, so it was never easy to retain these holdings within one household.

Barons were often called before local committees made up of religious leaders and other influential Barons to assess wealth, ascertain their allegiance to the monarchy and check whether enough in the way of taxes and other levies had been paid. If these accounts proved inadequate they could lose part if not all of the estate, so it is clear why the church received many fine gifts.

William kept his Barons apart to stop any collusion, and they were never allowed to split any of the estate among family members, eldest sons took all and this caused bad blood between them and the younger brothers. Before the Norman invasion the English were rich making William's balancing books easy, taking taxation without leaving them poor.

People realized after the conquest and rebellions, every one of its Thanes had gone; there was now a foreign way of ruling, no one had the right to speak his mind. There were many prisons built for those not complying with the new regulations, even children were made aware of this new way of life yet these children never became Norman remaining stubbornly English with a new outlook on life.

References; See Doomsday Transcript by Mundford for more detail Oderic.vol. 11 p.163-4 Q.d.idem. Vol.ivp.330-410 *See item on Gissing and Peasants rebellion in 1381. Fortunes changed hands many times, through the king's displeasure, the committees' decisions and the cost of the Crusade caused much bankruptcy, and the plagues that often wiped out whole families.

WOOD DALLING

Turold exchanged Lewes for Wood Dalling with William Warrenna and the Manor of Wood Dalling was left to **Turold's** son **Ralph.** These manors are very mixed up in the history books but we have managed after an enormous amount of detective work, to sort out most of the information they give. The book "William the Conqueror" by Freeman, shows that Wood Dalling was spoken of as the original seat of **Turold.**

Woodalling Hall as it is today   Plt. 35

Freeman quotes, "Comes a mention of Godric a "Dapihier" showing how he reclaimed land for the King and goes on to say: -

*"A sokeman holds 8 acres of land value 20p, a man of Warran Hunc Tenuit Lenstow antessesor Telehi. T.R.E. et Radulphus eum quando foresfecit et est de soca, de Caustuna, Modo eum Tenuit Godricus sed **Turaldus** Homo Wilelmui de Warrenna eum saisivit super regum et tenuit eum per tre annos Modo derationatus et super eumet reddit **Turaldus** v solides de Cattallo regis et dedit vadem de justia facienda".*

The gist of this quotation being "Luestan Tiheli and Radulphus are past holders of the land which is in the jurisdiction of Cawston. Godric is claiming it, but **Turaldus,** [William of Warren's man] is now in possession, and had possession of it for three years as tenant paying a rent of five shillings of the king's currency. He gives a pledge of some sort." [Probably that he will comply with the court verdict]. We visited Woodalling, which is in a remote and flat part of Norfolk on a cold overcast day. To us it presented desolate picture; not a soul in sight either in the fields or around the scattering of houses that are some distance from the Hall. Perhaps this description is not fair to the place, a brighter day no doubt would have improved this scene from a bygone age.

*See Doomsday Transcript by Mundford for more detail Oderic.vol. 11 page 163-4 Q.d.idem. Vol.ivp.330-410*See item on Gissing and Peasants rebellion in 1381.

CONCLUSIONS ON THE FACTS GAINED ON TUROLD / CRISPIN / BULVER

1. **Turold** was the son of **Gilbert Crispin and Gunner Malet** [niece to Goner Malet who had married Richard 1st Duke of Normandy].
2. He was cousin to **William Warrenna;** both descended from Rollo.
3. Brother to the **Lady Godiva/Godigifu**, whose husband **Leofric** was the Earl of Mercia also an Elder in the courts of both King Canute and Edward the Confessor, who inherited the Abbeys' of Peterborough and Coventry from his Uncle **Leofric** Earl of Leicester. As a matter of interest, from written accounts she was the **Lady Godiva** of the famous nursery rhyme 'Ride a Cock Horse to Bambury Cross'. This story was discussed on one of televisions history programmes. She was reputed to have done this journey in the nude in protest against her husbands' high taxation of the people. The medieval cross in Bambury was destroyed by the Puritans in 1600 and replaced in 1859.
4. **Turold** was the sheriff of Bukenhale Norfolk [now known as Bukenham] during the time of Edward the Confessor [1042-1066]
5. He was Uncle to **Lucy** daughter of **Alfgar** who married Ivo Tailebois. Ivo inherited the office of Sheriff of Bukenham when **Turold and William Malet** fled to Normandy, [great uncle to **Lucia** the daughter of **Lucy** and Ivo Tailebois].
6. **Turold** married sister of Aelgifu Malet [**Alfgar** 's wife]. **Alfgar** died, and before Harold Godwin became King of England, **William Malet** [Grandfather] and **Turold** [Uncle] fled to Normandy with **Edwin** young Earl of Mercia in order to protect him from Harold Godwin
7. Before leaving and to avoid his land being confiscated **Turold** sold some of it to Bukenham and gave other parcels of it to the Abbott of Bukenham Abbey. **Edwin** and **Turold** returned. Later **Turold** and **William Malet** regained some of their possessions, but **Edwin,** who was subsequently killed by his own men, had nothing, his lands were forfeited for rebelling against William.

The historical facts of this particular **Turold** were difficult to establish, as there were several people of this name in the same associated families. Due to the different name changes that they adopted to evade punishment by the king or assuming the place name of where they lived made him difficult to place within our family tree. After collating all the facts and clues we could find; we finally proved our **Turold** originated from the **Crispin** family.

Note; Turold traded Lewes for the Manor of Wood Dalling, Norfolk with William Warrenna and later he became William of Warren's' man after the rebellion of 1075. Turolds' son Roger married Agnes Valoise widow of Roger Rattlesden. They lived at Field Dalling near Binham Abbey.

INFORMATION FOUND IN VARIOUS ROLLS

1202 Marsham had tenants at Field Dalling; he married **Cecile Noin** and had three daughters **Sabina, Joan and Agnes**. He also owned land at Bynham Priory and Great Ryeburgh. So in this instance Rye's Book of Norfolk Histories is incorrect when he states "No de **Dalling/Bulwer** families were to be found there. We did manage trace them but we have to admit they were very difficult to find. 12.6.17. Ref: to **Simon Bulwer** being seized of the land of Millers and Copers.

It is at Woodalling where the main lines of descent of **de-Dalling/Bulwer's** were to live for generations until a much later date. By that time one branch of the de Dalling's, changed their name to Bulwer by court deed, then the Wiggett Bulwer's merged into the Earl line and adopted the name of Bulwer. The family moved their seat to Heydon, but retained the old family residence, where other members of the family still lived at that time. [See item on Dalling]. Several of the families branch lines occupied other manors around this area.

Doomsday Transcript by Mundford [Norfolk Only].

Wood Dalling was re-enfeoffed to the de Dalling's again in 1530, when the name was officially changed to Bulwer and was affected by **Simon Dalling** "Tout Court" [No argument]. This was the main **Bulwer** family's seat until **William Wiggett Bulwer** married **Mary Earl** daughter of **Augustus Earl**, niece of **Erasmus Earl** Chief Lawman to Oliver Cromwell. After this the family seat was transferred to Heydon which was previously the home of the Earl family.

*****Thomas** [senior married to **Ann Fearnly**] leased out Wood-Dalling for twenty-one years, from 31st December 1799. Bulwer genealogy 11/317 states "From **William Earl Bulwer** to **Thomas Bulwer** [senior b.1728] farmer of Woodalling who died after two years of the lease in 1801. The 2nd lease for this property on 10th October 1809 for one year of promises to the poor of Woodalling from **Thomas Fearnly Bulwer** [son] b.1760 farmer 5/1 paid [Bulwer. 4/313]. **Thomas Fearnly** lived at Woodalling Hall with his family, and when he died in 1827 aged 67] his widow [Mary Johnson], in order to obtain more money to pay out legacies sold it back to **William Bulwer** of the main family.

*****Note:-**According to Bloomfield there was a break for some time probably when the family went to Thurning to live. Thomas Fearnly Bulwer of Hainford was half brother to John Bulwer [our line, [see chart and write up on p.360 Thomas and his family later.] This fact from the Doomsday Transcript is repeated and confirmed by Norfolk Visitation Book 1664. Oderic p.149. Ryes' Norfolk Miscellany. Doomsday Transcript. [Norfolk only] chronicle of Jumeiges de Ummutatiune of Oderic Charters of King William Monasticus. 244-245. Freeman's Norman Conquest vol.11v 47in 584-658 and ib vol vi Doomsday Book f. 1836.

Grants, appointments and offences, from the *Patent Rolls.
Dalling's and Bulwer's in trouble

1230. AD. William son of Turold [grandson of Bishop Odo, not our line; text written In Latin.]

12.10.1235 **Thomas Valoynes** and others appointed as wardens at Yarmouth fair. Court enquiry regarding **John** son of **Turold**, Robert Alewry killed. Decision self-defence. Pardoned. [Separate court] Complaint by Hugh de Fourn, that **High Knight William de Dalling and** others stole his ship and 60 tons of wine from Gravelings in Flanders, took it to Yarmouth and sold it. **William De Dalling** going beyond the seas on the king's service as letters nominating others as his attorneys' is granted protection for one year.

3.4.1313. Writ de intendo for **Simon de Dalling** whom Walter Waldeshire Kings Yeoman has appointed his deputy during his pleasure in parts of Lenne [Lynn] Kinkele and Blakeny

. Writ de Intendo for **Simon de Dalling** to be deputy in ports of Lenne Kinkele and Blakeny 26.6.1331. Protections for John Travers, Constable of Bordeaux for going to Aquitaine on the Kings service, with seven others include **William de Dalling.** Complaint re Prior of Wabron [Weybourne] that **Robert de Dalling** and others took two horses, and assaulted his servants at Kellyng and Sheringham.

30.8.1337 Simple protection for one year for **Master Bernard de Dalling** 28.10.39. **John de Dalling** and servant Robert arrested and imprisoned in the Norwich Castle for assault on the Norton Family who were on service to the fleet.

27.10.1339 Grant for losses over two years because of war. [See reign of Edward 3rd that includes John the Elder de Dalling Protection for Wool trade]. Merchant traders dare not come. November 1341 **Alice de Dalling** and **Ingulred** her son, among others at the assizes accused of unjustly de-seizing the Abbot of Louth Park of his free tenements at Louth.

Most Research done by Mrs. G. MacKenna of 'Family Research' on our behalf from documents stored at The Public Records Office London and Published by H.M.S.O.

Bacons Advice That Surety Should Be Given By Subsidy Men.

*"My humble duties remembered. Yor letter in behalf of Mr Patteson I received and made tryall by the best means I could, to further his suite to **Miss Elwynn** for marriage, and have prevailed nothing. For she had entered speech for marriage, with one **Mr. Bulwer** Her neighbour, who is likely to enjoy from his father 400'-500'By the year, beside his own personnel estate, and to this she grivet still acceptance, though it be not hitherto be finished.* [See chart this is our line].

25.1.1443 William Hempsted Mayor of Norwich planned an insurrection to force Thomas, Bishop of Norwich to abandon various actions against the city. He believed the city was too important for the King to Punish. Arrangements were made for John Gladman, a merchant, to ride a horse through the city wearing a crown and scepter and three unknown men [which included **Richard de Dalling**] acting as if they were valets to the king and urged the people to riot. After this protest they were all punished and excommunicated. The Mayor was imprisoned for three weeks and the city was fined. **Richard de Dalling** traded as a Cutler on St Andrews Hill Norwich, This shop is still there though it sells something totally different today, 541 years later in 2007.

*FIELD DALLING
Bloomfield's Norfolk. Feet of Fines. I.P.M. Copingers Manorial.

Peter Valoise, whose father adopted this old Carolingian name was nephew to William the Conqueror, [according to the legend on Bynham Priory], which stated **Peter de Valoise** was William's favourite. Bloomfield wrote that **Peter Valoise** was given this manor [Field Dalling] direct from the King and held it as one of 57 Lordships that were bestowed on him at the time of the conquest; he also held many parcels of land elsewhere. **Ralph de Valoynes/Valoise** and **William Warrenna** were descendants of **Rudolph** half brother of Richard 1st of Normandy; these two families were originally from the Mortimer family.

Turold's son Roger de Dalling married **Agnes Valoise [daughter of Peter Valoise] widow of Roger de Rattlesden. They lived at Field Dalling creating two different dynasties. The families of **Warrenna Valoise**, and **Crispin** were closely involved and related naturally by marriage. This marriage brought the two lines of **Mortimer** and **Crispin** together including their lands [see chart] We had to transgress a little into the future here to give you the general picture on these families.

* Field Dalling is in North Norfolk near Binham Priory.
 ** See chart 42 page 177

Later there was a dispute with the Rattlesden family and the Manor of Field Dalling passed over to their descendants. [See chart of the Rattlesden family]. Unfortunately not being able to read Latin [though we do have a rough translation], we have told only part of the story. However it does help to focus the mind on the various events of the time and gives the general outline and a fascinating glimpse into the shape of their lives.

The various Manor Rolls shed a great deal of information about these family members, although of high rank they were typical of a cross section of the community of their day. They were more than capable of misdemeanors and not entirely squeaky clean about these affairs either, causing the present day family much amusement over some of their antics.

De RATTLESDEN OF FIELD DALLING
And their families

*Sir Roger Rattlesden, born c1170 had Fine for one-third advowson of Bukenham Ferry 10.Ric.i 1198 Witnesses to grant advowson of Flixton to Lord of Beyton Suffolk, had one half fee of the Manor of Wood Hall Suffolk, of Hugh de Plaiz, temp Henry 3rd . Sir Roger married Agnes Valoise who held the Lordship of Saxlingham [near Binham Abbey] in the third year of Henry 3rd. and two knights fee's in Wood Dalling, Guestwick, and Little Ryeburgh, of the Barony of Valoise. This Manor was also known as Dallinga.

King William attached this Manor to the Lordship of Holt and Robert de Verli/de Valoise held it until he became a rebel against the king. The lands passed into the hands of **William Warrenna** and on his death to **Turold** [his man] along with thirty-three other parcels of land in great swathes, not all are mentioned in this book for lack of space.

Turold enfeoffed Field Dalling to his son **Sir Ralph Dalling**, who gave two parts of his tithes to Binham Priory, **Turold's** son **Roger** and his wife **Agnes Valoise** [her second husband] both confirmed this exchange and were witnesses included is a *paraphrased account Agnes held the Lordship of Saxlingham 3rd year of Henry 3rd and held two knights' fees in Wood Dalling, Guestwick, and Little Ryburgh, of the Barony of Valoise. There were many disputes over the ownership of these lands and you will see by the Manor Roll accounts that they eventually passed out of de-Dalling/Bulwer hands.

+ See family tree and charter of Rodger de Dalling on the following two pages.

Chart for the de Rattlesdens

Chart 42

John de Rattlesden son charged to repair ferry at Bukenham. Had property at West Acre 1316 = Margaret	Simon de Rattlesden born 1270. heir minor 1286 Held one-third knight fee of Barony of Valoynes in Wood Dalling 1315. Lord there in 1305 had two parts of Little Ryeburgh of the same Barony Lord of Capel St. and Suffolk. 1310 Lord of Bukenham Ferry Saxlingham, 14.Edward 2nd 1320. Returned as Manorial Lord, Norfolk1316 at Field Dalling Bukenham Ferry and Hassingham Died seised 14 Edward 2nd 1320] = Maude who presented to Hassingham 1319 lived 1305 1310/11 sold property to St Vedast Nch.1310/11

Sir John de Rattlesden b.1300 Lord of Wood Dalling 18 Edward [1344] and Bukenham Ferry, 1349. Held two parts fee of Little Ryburgh of Barony of Valoynes presented to Bukenham Ferry 1337, 1349, 1362, = Alianora [Liv. 1344]	Richard de Rattlesden In property deed with Luke Harman 1306 Nch deeds.

Philip de Rattlesden	John Rattlesden 1300 Lord of Wood Dalling 36 Edw. 3rd 1362 and of Fakenham Aspes Suffolk = ?
Lord of Bradfield 1393	Joan de Rattlesden b 1330 dau and Heir = 1st Robert Hovell = 2nd Robert Monceaux

Adam de Rattlesden married Agnes daughter of William de Reymes 1249-1250. Agnes sued Hugh de Reymes for possession of one quarter Knight fee in Overstrand and Northrepps 1231, which was successful by right of Duel, he quit and Agnes claimed for eighty marks [1250] and moiety of two fees Bukenham Ferry.

It intrigues us that with the vast area of the country that they had to cover, they managed to control the lands they possessed. How did they collect monies due with the absence of any form of banking system? It must have been very time consuming to collect and then pay the king his taxes. From peasant to Lord there must have been a very complicated money go round done on a regular basis and woe betides anyone who failed to pay.

Sources for chart -: Bloomfield's Norfolk. Feet of Fines. IPM. Copiers Manorial.
All the above families and others discussed in this book are all interrelated to the European families as you will see when studying the charts Valoise families are especially notable for their connection with the reformation.*See also chart for Valoise chart 43 page 180

THE CHARTER OF ROGER DE DALLING

*Roger** was the son of **Peter de Valoise** and the charter he signed was in favour of Bynham priory, originally part of his daughter **Agnes** inheritance, similar in content to the one signed by his father. It is of interest not only to genealogists but also to historians in general, showing the system of feudal grants. In it **Roger** greets friend's etc. and gives a reminder of his father **Peter Valoise** who made gifts of Berney and lands at Thursford.

It was given, he said for the souls of himself and his family, on the advice of many wise men [including the Archbishop of Canterbury]. He warned that a noble knight should not just give a fee of six knights, but the whole of knight's lands or more!

"If any mans' heyre [a subtle warning for **Agnes**] should try to take away these Alms, which are interposed as a bridge between his father and Paradise, he is disinheriting his father from the Kingdom of the Heavens. Thus effectively disinheriting himself also, since he who kills his father, has proved himself no son.

The one taking away these alms to Binham, his lot will be with Abiron, Dathan, and Judas the traitor in the depths of Hell. But he who confirms these alms to Bynham his lot will be in the lot of the elect, to enjoy eternal life".

'Food for many thoughts!'

The above is a very short paraphrased account of the charter, to show the general thought patterns of these arrangements after Bynham had been commissioned.

It is interesting to note that many of these families always seemed to have a common link through marriage. For instance Peter de Valoise was brother in law to Ralph de Guader. Agnes the daughter of Roger de Valoise married 1st Roger Rattlesden, 2nd Roger de Dalling/Bulwer grandson of Turold Crispin/Bulwer.

You will see from the Manor Rolls under Field Dalling that a bitter dispute took place between Agnes and the de Dalling families regarding ownership of Field Dalling in Norfolk. There are many other instances you might note as you read on.

All above on Valoise chart 43 page 180

BYNHAM PRIORY
Ralph and Peter Valoyne's founded Bynham Priory 1091.

After King William had secured his new domain of England he instigated the appointment of his most trusted followers to powerful positions. **Peter and Ralph Valoise** were entrusted lands for King William in Norfolk, Ralph being made the Earl of the county.

They were responsible to the king for collection of rents of property held in trust, such as Wood Dalling and Binham, which were sub-enfeoffed to the knights and various tenants. The King put **Ralph** under orders with Bishop Aelthelmer of Elmham and the Thegnes of Norfolk to deliver to him the lands of those who fought against him at Hastings.

Ralph Valoise founded the Abbey of Binham; **Peter Valoise** his son endowed it in 1091 and confirmed a grant to his Kinsman Walter Valoise before he was shorn on becoming a monk, sealing this by laying his knife upon the altar. **Peter** died soon after, and it was his son-in-law Roger who reaffirmed the alms that Walter de Valoyne's gave in exchange for the Lordship of Bynham, which was the gift of Berny with lands in Thursford. [See charter of Roger de Valoyne's].

During the reign of King John, Robert Fitz-Walter besieged the priory in the year 1212 He was a descendant of the Counts of Brione and grandson of Richard 1st of Normandy. He was also a friend of Thomas the Prior of Bynham at that time that had been removed from office for his continued defiance to the major priory of St Albans, the chief seat of the Benedictine order. King John, enraged sent an army to relieve the siege and Fitz-Walter fled.

These rebellions against the mother church continued until the time of Henry 8th, which gave the King valid reasons for demolishing the religious structures of this time and removing their wealth. Binham was not completed until the middle of the thirteenth century, and then Henry 8th probably had the roof removed contributing to its demise and ruin by letting the weather do most of the work.

The ruins were later damaged even more by Oliver Cromwell, you can still trace out its magnificent proportions, what remained has over time suffered from the weather and people taking away its stones to build other properties. In comparison to the size of the original Priory the church today it is approximately one fifth of its size. Seven bays remain so it still looks huge; there is more on this, see reign of King Henry 8th.

The years took their toll and the great windows at the front entrance became broken and ruined and were bricked up in 1809 but still give a glimpse of the beauty they once possessed. The building itself is similar to the mother church in St. Albans, which again is thought to be a copy of the cathedral in Rheims; In later years a great number of major repairs were carried out and today it is still used as a place of worship.

Chart showing the de Valoise families.

Chart 43

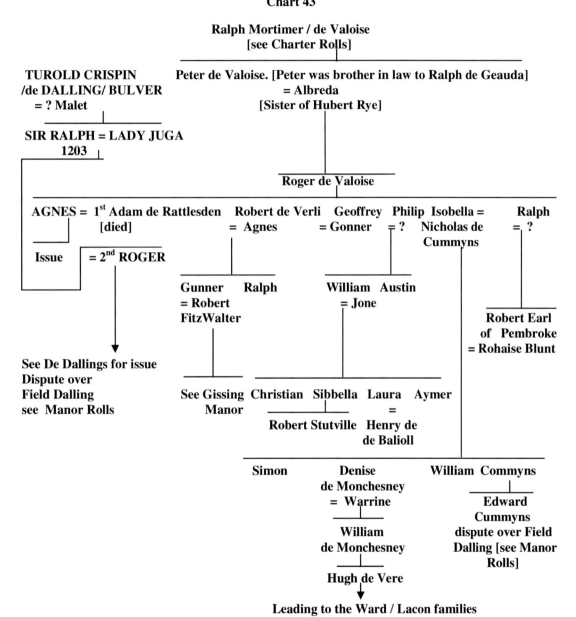

Note. This chart shows the de Dalling / Bulwer /Ward/ Lacon/ de Vere connection to the Valoise families. Detailed information on the Warrenna, /deValoise/de Veres. [See separate item on each family]

FAMILY MEMBERS IN CAPITAL LETTERS

THE VILLAGE OF BINHAM

The village of Binham [Norfolk], just over one hundred years ago contained around five hundred inhabitants including a blacksmith, but he had closed his forge by 1947.

The school closed in 1950 and in that year also, the annual fair [granted by Henry1ˢᵗ] finished too. There used to be a thriving community here, with the various trades and crafts all connected in some way to horses. Today there are barely one hundred people. It once boasted three public houses, but only one of them survives. It is called the Chequers and came into the ownership of the **Bulwer** family of Buxton when **Elizabeth White** the daughter of John White of Wisbeach married **Peter Bulwer.**

Chequers Today   Plate 36

Later this public house was sold by **Thomas Bulwer** of Buxton to Charles Weston who started the first bank in Norwich with the proviso that some of the profits of the public house went to the poor of Hainford. Another Public House that used to be in the village was also owned by the **Bulwer's** and was called the White Hart. These taverns were handed down in our family line for several generations; more of this later.

Curia Regis 1191-1231

1204   Adam Rattlesden versus **Roger de Dalling** regarding 2.2 acres of land, this issue arises again in the years 1205 and 1206 with the same people involved.

1208. **Hamo de Dalling** concerning Ecclesia vacant at Dalling. **Philip de Dalling** versus Roger Bacon. Decision made for de Dalling.

Gap in Records here from 1212-1220

1220   **Ralph de Dalling** "Opulit se Quarto die" Versus **Agnes** wife of **Roger de Dalling**.

1230   Two cases from **William de Dalling** one against **Peter de Dalling**.

1231. **Agnes** wife of **Hamo de Dalling** versus **William** son of Hamo and several petitions with the Priory of Blakney.

Patent Rolls

1228. **Hamo Valoyne's** mentioned.

1235. **Thomas** and others appointed Wardens at Norfolk fair.

1285. Grant to Eleanor the Kings Consort, of the custody of William Commyns, son and heir of William Commyns son and heir of Adam Rattlesden tenant in chief of the Manor of Dalling, late of Adam Rattlesden who held it of knights' service.

Feudal Aids

1301. Simon Rattlesden of Great Ryeburgh, mentioned as heir of Commyn [de Baronia Valoygnes].

1302. Reference to heirs of Simon Rattlesden.

1346. To Court comes Johannes de Rattlesden of Great Ryeburgh, and Johannes Ward heirs of Adam Rattlesden of Great Ryeburgh. The **Ward** family here seems to connect with the Rattlesdens also with the **de Dallings** and the **Valoynes.** Most of these families stem from the **Mortimer** side of the Norman families**.**

Manorial Lists 1316.

Field Dalling. Peter son of Philip de Dalling. Swainsthorpe, **Simon de Dalling**. Wood Dalling. Earl Warren, Simon de Rattlesden. John Newman. Ralph de Stinton.

Close Rolls 1231-1380.

1231 In Latin

1280 Enrollment of a grant by Roger son of William de Stalham to Sir Robert Burnell, Bishop of Bath and Wells, of his messuage in Thirning and Dalling, which he had from John son of Reginald de Thirning witness/ Philip de Dalling.

Documents Fine Rolls 1272-1380

An order for the escheater to take into the king's hands, the lands of the late Adam Rattlesden tenant of knight service of William Commyns 17 year's alias Valoynes son of Isobel Valoynes,

Inquisition Post Mortum 1272-1450 17.4.37. Henry 3rd 1253. Isobel Valoynes her son 16-17 years is heir to her lands in Dersingham.

Edward 3rd Dispute with Simon Rattlesden, as to lands in Saxlingham, Little Ryeburgh, Salle, and Wood Dalling. Agnes Rattlesden mentioned when they came into dispute, as she owned two knights fee in Thurning and Guestwick. Simon de Rattlesden and his wife Beatrix owned them jointly. Son John heir John de Rattlesden died on the Saturday before St. Nicholas in the 35th year of Edward 3rd in Windmill Manor of Dalling, rents at Guestwick

1333   Robert at nine months son of Robert Herve, husband of Jone Rattlesden is his heir. **Philip de Dalling** in the 30th year of Henry is found to hold half a fee. Eustice de Dalling, in the sixth year of Edward second had license for alienation of Mortain, by Justice to William Parson of Field Dalling. Nicolas Parmenter was found to hold half fee in Virleys, which Thomas Bacon had held before him. **Agnes Dalling** widow of **John Dalling** married Richard Blakeman. **Agnes** was involved in a legal battle with father-in-law, after a suite that involved the Assize of 'Novel Diseisson'. She established that **Richard Bulwer** a relative of her former husband 26.3.1335 should confirm her dower to her. This meant that half a messuage and twenty acres of land, which should remain the property of her new husband, if **Agnes** should die first instead of reverting back to the **Bulwer's.** June.1333 Grant of Land to **Walter Bulwer** chaplain,

17.4.1331. Richard son **of John Bulwer** releases land to John Richard Neale that he acquired from Edmund Otes.

10.1332. List of land acquired by Neil Family. **Agnes Bulwer** lands near Bondescroft 4.11.1323 **John Bulwer's** land 1 acre. **Walter Bulwer's** Land 17.4. 1331. **Richard Bulwer's** lands 1.11.1323 In addition to above I rod of **John Bulwer's** Land. Nicolas Parmenter was found to hold half a fee in Virleys, which Thomas Bacon had held before him. It went to the Heydons in Elizabeth's reign and the Harboards of Gunton; from there it went to Nicholas Minns in the twenty- fourth year of the reign of Elizabeth, being held in honour of Clare.

Court Documents

Reginald Turold brings action that **Richard,** priest of Morton pleaded in Christian court about his lay fief on condition he gave two acres of land by decision of the judicial sentence, and **Richard** says he had taken him to court over fourteen acres of land in the county, they agreed about the four acres of land, which remained for **Richard** himself, afterwards it seemed to **Reginald** that Richard had more land than he wished. He pleaded in the Episcopal court at Brudefield they agreed on condition two acres remained with **Richard** who would pay annually to **Reginald** one penny.

He takes to the High Court that had the greater right as tenant of those two acres from **Reginald** in demesne. Produces this in court, Reginald himself has writ to summon four knights for electing twelve knights and the day appointed for this was the fifteenth day [Canceled text **Richard** the priest produces in Episcopal court a warrant from Easter Sunday for one month].

THE DEATH OF KING WILLIAM 1ˢᵗ
And the farce of his funeral

We will now return to the Norman situation and the final chapter of William's life when he returned to Normandy in 1087 to protect his Duchy. After placing a saddle with a high pommel on a lighter horse, called a Palfrey, which was totally unsuitable for those in battle dress. It has been suggested his horse stumbled while traveling through a place that had been burnt and the pommel seriously injured him. He was carried back to Rouen, then on to St. Gervaise, a suburban church owned by the Abbey of Fecamp. Refusing to eat, his doctors gave up hope; he was sixty years old and had only five months to live.

Only the king's most dedicated friends and family remained by his side, those were his sons William Rufus and Henry, and his half brother Robert of Mortain plus two prelates, the Bishop of Lisle and Abbot Gunter. Knowing he was dying William ordered his servants to make an extensive inventory of all his wealth in the Rouen treasury, his household money, gold crowns and arms etc. Each family member was called to his side in turn.

King William was disappointed at the news his eldest son *Robert Curthose was absent consorting with his enemy Philip of France, and was prepared to dismiss him, but relented. Instead of the crown of England he gave Robert Normandy. Henry was bitterly disappointed at his lot (which really was a vast fortune) and left to supervise the weighing of his new wealth and to check the fortifications of the buildings that housed it. William Rufus was offered King William's sword, scepter and crown, and was ordered to England to safeguard it from French attack.

As he lay dying his half brother Robert of Mortain pleaded the cause of Bishop Odo his brother who had been punished for holding the Castle of Penvesey against King William from April to June 1087. This was in support of Robert Curthose when Bishop Wulfstan defeated the Earl of Shrewsbury, one of the main leaders. On his deathbed William reluctantly agreed to forgive Odo and gave him his freedom. The Bishop later joined Robert Curthose and others to go to the Crusades.The Bedford jailer petitioned on **Hereward's** behalf and persuaded King William let him go free. One scribe states that while **Hereward** was a rebel he captured Ivo Taillbois [Morca's brother-in-law] who had been given large estates by William] and used him as the instrument of negotiation for his own pardon. William confirmed his decision and ordered the release of **Hereward the Wake** [**Turold's** nephew] also King Harold's half brother Wulfnot, who had been imprisoned.

Note; There is more than one account of Hereward the Wake according to the writers view of events. * Start of dispute over the crown of England see page 188

It is said **Hereward** lived for many years and was buried in the Mercian Abbey of Crowlands, Norfolk. **Morca** the former Earl of Mercia had remained a prisoner in Normandy until freed by this royal decree. Things deteriorated from that moment, William Rufus left with the Kings blessing to lock up the family silver in England taking Earl Waltheof with him. Having given away all his earthly goods, William was left alone with his doctor's, servants and a few Barons waiting for death; Aisle the Abbot of Beck was summoned to the dying king's side, but fell ill on the way and never to reach there. The main chronicle by Orderic Vitalis of William's last hours mostly concurs on all these facts.

William 1st died 7th September 1087 leaving confusion in his wake and abandoning his supporters to fight for their status and wealth. He had lived most of his life in a state of turmoil and so it ended; the greater the leader the greater the void. It gave fresh hope to those with nothing and as they did then, so it happens today.

We would like to include from Orderic Vitalis's account our personal view of the serious, but in some ways humorous story of his burial. All the beneficiaries including the Barons had immediately rushed off to protect their estates not caring what they left behind. Their servants were now without supervision, their hour of glory had arrived. They stripped the corpse and the building bare stealing all they could carry to improve their lot. As there was little else to gain they left the body of poor William half naked and fled.

There was no one to carry out William's last wishes except a country knight, who at his own expense paid undertakers to take the corpse to a ship en route to Caen. The monks organized a procession from Rouen to Caen to take the body for burial at St. Stephens. Further problems ensued after docking. The procession to Caen was brought to a halt as it passed through the town when a serious fire broke out, and fearing premature cremation, most, including the monks again abandoned the corpse to put the fire out.

At last the body arrived at its destination but by this time rather larger than when it started; unfortunately, the time scale of decomposition had been overlooked the process was in progress and his bloated body was filling with gas. At the ill-attended ceremony, those present included his brother Odo, son Henry and the Bishops and Abbots of Normandy. After mass Bishop Gilbert of Everex gave the address praising King William. During his reign William had no serious external enemies but many internal ones that he had deprived of their assets and had only used the castles to protect his followers and imprison those who offended him.

The Bishop concluded by saying, "Any man whom William had offended, had to forgive the offense". To this remark a certain Ascelin Fitz Arthur, who could not contain his desperation, stepped forward with his neighbours to support his claim that the land they were standing on belonged to his father, and as William had robbed him of it, he forbade them to bury the body on his property. To avert this problem a collection was made from the clergy and Barons to raise sixty shillings for the price of the land, with a promise they would pay the rest later.

The burial proceeded, and the farce continued. With all the pomp and ceremony due to a king the corpse was lifted from the bier, to be placed in the sunken Sarcophagus. William, who was considered a giant of a man when alive, was by now, due to the decomposition gases very much larger, in fact too big to fit in the Sarcophagus. The body had to be squeezed, and then finally broken to get it in. Unfortunately the bowels full of putrefying gas exploded, those who saw this happen must have been petrified and forced by the stench to make an undignified exit.

Others who could not see the situation could certainly smell and probably blamed the unholy monk in front, until they too were forced to make a premature withdrawal via the nearest exit. The rest probably short of the seventh sense piled incense into the burners, which only enhanced the disgusting stench that no amount of fragrance could conceal. It must have been very trying to chant the Te-Diem at double speed, discreetly holding ones nose, and singing with the mouth closed.

The burial was quickly concluded. King William left this earth in the same way he lived, keeping everyone on the run in a dramatic fashion. His sons who followed in his steps had a difficult time to control and maintain their legacy, one was later murdered and the other had to struggle to hold on to the reigns of power.

In retrospect William [the illegitimate son of Robert the Devil], from a Norman point of view, could be considered as the rightful heir to the English crown and the nearest blood relation to King Edward who died childless. From a Saxon point of view they regarded Harold Godwin as the rightful heir and the only one that had the experience and qualities to make a king, not forgetting all the others who had this ambition.

But it was William who had the drive, cunning and some say good fortune to take the crown and England into an era of outstanding management, structure and progress. He was able to control a nation that he had taken by force yet instigated reform and a feudal system; some of his regulations and laws are with us today.

KING WILLIAM RUFUS.
Crowned 1087-1110

After William 1ˢᵗ died, his son William Rufus started to make a clean sweep of all the Saxon Lords in the following year 1088. **Morca,** [released by Williams royal decree] had been brought by William Rufus from France, was again given life imprisonment and later his lands were given to Ralph Payne, Sheriff of Yorkshire.

Obviously Rufus had not forgotten the charter of William 1ˢᵗ for Peterborough Abbey, which contain notes as to the rebellion of William Mallet of Gissing [in the story]. It also mentions that **Edwin and Morca** left the Kings Court for the north; It was after this the lands of all three were confiscated.

Also after William Rufus became king dissension arose between the Barons and the monarchy and continued throughout his reign cumulating in another rebellion planned at Bec Manor, Norfolk in the year 1110. Most plotters were punished or disinherited others went to the Crusades.

Bec Hall Manor held by the Clares

This building was among several held by the Clares [another branch of the Crispin family], and whilst looking for information in 'Bloomfield's Norfolk', we found this Manor also held facts that led directly to the **Ward** family as declared by our grandparents to be connected to our family on our father's line. Alid owned this Manor in the Confessors time later it was held by **Hereward the Wake,** then by Ralph and Geoffrey Bainard until 1098, when Geoffrey accused William of Eu, a kinsman of the Conqueror of treachery against King William Rufus.

For his pains King William 2ⁿᵈ had Geoffrey's eyes put out, and he was castrated. His cousin Ralph was hanged and his estates then went to William Fitz-Walter. **Lady Maude Boyland** also held fee here from whose Manor it was purchased. William Bainard conspired against the King with Elias the Earl of Maines and lost his Barony. Their chief seat was Bainard Castle, situated below St. Paul's church near the river Thames. Beck Hall then went to Robert Fitz-Gilbert of Clare, youngest son of Richard.

*1229 Cokefield held it for **Walter Fitz-Robert**

1325. The Official papers of Nathaniel Bacon state…"Robert Bainard with six others were assigned to make inquiries in the Counties of Norfolk and Suffolk regarding Felonies oppression and crimes". **Simon de Dalling** was among those reported.

*See Woodhouse Manor Kirby p.273/4 and chart for William Warrenna cht. 39 page 165 to see how some of these families link up with the Wards). Also 'Bloomfield's Norfolk'.

PEACE BREAKS OUT

Peace was established between King William Rufus and the two main Barons. **Ralph Mortimer** became a partner of Rufus and joined him in Normandy to fortify houses to repel the French army. **Ralph Mortimer** [alias Valoise] took no further part in the feudal strife, being too busy adding to his possessions in Normandy.

King William Rufus was disliked by his nobles and his death occurred in suspicious circumstances while hunting in the New Forest. Gilbert the son of Richard of Normandy, his brother Roger, and brother-in-law Walter Tyrrel, [the suspect], were in the royal hunting party, and met up with their uncle William Giffard. King William Rufus was found with an arrow straight through his heart. The wound was too accurate to be an accident and was highly questionable. Tyrrel was accused of the killing, which even on his deathbed he denied strongly, claiming to be in a different part of the forest at the time.

It was thought he was used as a scapegoat, or he was a very good actor. Being a stranger to Hampshire it would have been difficult for him to escape to the coast quickly, or to collect his own money without help. The actions of King William's [Rufus] brother *Henry were also suspect, as he was closely bound with two others to the outcome of a mysterious affair involving an accumulation of disappointments over his inheritance. One was **Gilbert of Clare**, married to Alice whose uncle William Giffard was Chancellor to the King.

Richard of Clare [Artist impression] Plate **37** Apparently his descendants were not too honest either. The other one of Henry's best friends, married to the sister of Alice and the eldest of three brothers was the rebel **Richard of Clare.**

The day after the fatal so-called accident, they both rode on with Henry to London where Henry gave appointments to these men [Giffard was appointed to the see of Winchester the richest in the country at that time]. When Henry was crowned King, **Richard of Clare,** at that time a monk in Bec Abbey was given See of Ely. Ten years later William Giffard of Clare was appointed to the lordship of the Shires of Cardigan. **Gilbert of Brione/Clare,** brother in law to the accused; twice before connived at the demise of William Rufus and was present when he was killed.

Note. Richard Clare's cousins the Crispin's were slowly dying out [by name i.e. replaced by Bulwer] as aliases were being used more and more, with the Old Saxon names disappearing from view. Their descendants are still around. The family of Lucia daughter of Lucy still exercised influence as she married the Earl of Chester *See item on Williams Death, i.e.* dispute over the claim for crown of England.

The House of Clare prospered spreading influence over Normandy and England. Richard of Clare inherited his father's vast wealth with extensive lands in Normandy and England also adding the Honour of Tonbridge in Kent with many Manors in Essex and Suffolk. His brother Baldwin Lord of Meuls became Sheriff of Exeter; this continued until the next generation; family records count for more than genealogical interest, they show the general direction and politics the powerful Norman dynasty displayed, unifying Anglo Saxon Kingdoms under their rulership.

CHAPTER V
Henry 1st, Stephen and Matilda 1100-1134

The Norman Barons being ambitious for power, opposed Henry 1st reign [he being the youngest son of William the Conqueror] to the point of open rebellion. There is more than one William Warrenna on the chart 39 p.165, and it was William Warrenna 2nd, [the second Earl of Surrey who supported Robert Curthose in the rebellion. He married the beautiful Isobel, widow of Robert Beaumont who died 1118 [it is said he carried her off while the husband was living]; she was the daughter of Hugh the Great, son of Henry 4th of France. [See Kirby Bedon p.275]. William Warrenna 4th rebelled against William Rufus, fought with Stephen and Theobalds [house of Blois chart. 47 p.197] army and his descendants changed their name several times.

In 1120 the most serious reverse of Henry 1st reign occurred when his natural son William drowned when the "White Ship" sank near the Normandy coast. His illegitimate son Richard also perished. **William Roumare*** [son of Lucia's 1st marriage] was to sail with them but refused to go because of the dissolute company and considered this a futile journey. This decision saved his life. Three hundred people drowned with only two survivors. The half-cousin to King Henry's son, Richard of Averanches went and was also drowned, so **Ranulph*** [son of Lucia's 2nd marriage] inherited the title of the Earl of Chester in his place, this incident concerned all of Europe because of the huge loss of life.

Being of vital interest to Western Christendom, even to the point that the disintegration of the Norman Dominion in the north could now be a consideration. We suggest that you study the charts to understand the family relationship of the contenders. Owing to the fact that both King Henry's sons William and Richard had died created a vacuum for the perpetuation of the English crown. Matilda, Henry's daughter who had married Geoffrey Plantagenet was the natural heir but Steven [Henry's nephew] was recognized by the nobles who wanted him as king.

*+**Disputed succession could have meant civil war in England and also jeopardize the political unity of Normandy as it impinged on the Royal Dynasty of the Capetion Valoise family from the Italian/French kings.*Family de Lacy See chart 46 page 194. See Earl's Mercia chart 16 page 59.

This power crisis remained until the Empire was restored in an enlarged form, under new direction. William son of Robert Curthose was discarded; being a protégéé of the French, but his favourite nephew Stephen of Blois was considered. The only disadvantage was Matilda [Also known as Maude and Stephens cousin] the widow of Holy Roman Emperor Henry 5th of *Germany. Now an Empress she remarried, her second husband was Geoffrey Plantagenet, heir to Count Falk of Anjou.

Both these marriages gave her land that stretched from Scotland to Loire in France. In view of this Henry 1st wanted Stephen of Blois to agree to Matilda being Queen, but when her father died the Barons craftily installed Stephen as king because he was easily manipulated, he also resented the idea of being under a woman's thumb.

By the end of the reign of Henry 1st most of the old Scandinavian names had completely disappeared and even the memory of them was fading fast. In 1140 Civil war ensued because Stephen had been crowned as King against the wishes of Matilda / [Maude]. **Randolph** the Earl of Chester**,** and his half brother **William Roumare** were fighting Matilda's cause and were under siege by King Stephen; [these were the sons of **Lucia** from her two marriages. She was the granddaughter of **Leofric** and the Lady **Godiva, Turold's** sister]. The two men sent for the Earl of Gloucester but his troops deserted them and fled.

Matilda had the military advantage at the time, she captured Stephen but after fourteen years of strife Matilda departed England for Normandy and Stephen was released in 1142 causing much mayhem. In France she bore a son who challenged Stephen's son Eustace for the throne but unfortunately Eustace died in 1153. Stephen submitted and recognised Henry [the son of the Duke of Anjou and Matilda] as King. Geoffrey Plantagenet of Anjou, Henry's father was recognised as the Duke of Normandy after 1144. Louis.7th [King of France] was forced to acknowledge the position of Count Geoffrey until 1150, all his wealth and possessions went to his son Henry, the future King of England.

Some concessions had to be made to the House of Blois, when William son of Stephen was confirmed in his vast wealth and possessions as Count of Bologna and Mortain through his marriage to **Isobel Warrenna**. King Stephen the last of the true Norman Kings died in 1154. After his death Henry [son of Matilda and Geoffrey] returned to claim the throne and became the first Plantagenet king.

Facts from Encyclopedia International Vol. 2 Matilda 1102 -67 Queen of England dau. Of Henry 1st married Emperor. Henry 5th of France 2nd Geoffrey Plantagenet was no friend of England. Their son became Henry 2nd of England. Her brother William heir apparent was drowned when the White Ship that his father had bought him for his birthday sank in a storm.

NORMANS AND ANGEVINS
Chart 44
Showing how lines conjoin again with Stephen and Matilda's marriage

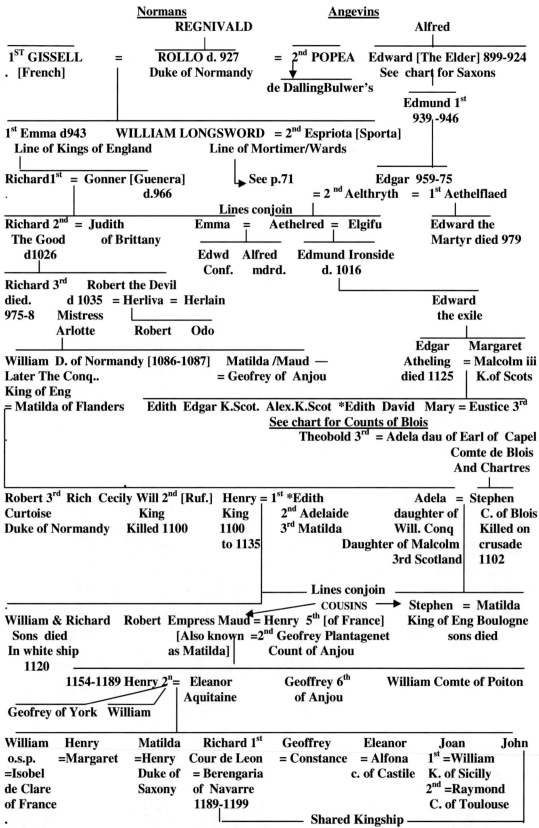

Normans   Angevins

REGNIVALD   Alfred

1ST GISSELL = ROLLO d. 927 = 2nd POPEA   Edward [The Elder] 899-924
. [French]   Duke of Normandy   See chart for Saxons

de DallingBulwer's

Edmund 1st
939-946

1st Emma d943   WILLIAM LONGSWORD = 2nd Espriota [Sporta]
Line of Kings of England   Line of Mortimer/Wards

Richard1st = Gonner [Guenera]   See p.71   Edgar 959-75
.   d.966   = 2nd Aelthryth = 1st Aethelflaed
Lines conjoin

Richard 2nd = Judith   Emma = Aethelred = Elgifu   Edward the
The Good   of Brittany   Martyr died 979
d1026   Edwd Alfred Edmund Ironside
   Conf. mdrd. d. 1016

Richard 3rd   Robert the Devil   Edward
died.   d 1035 = Herliva = Herlain   the exile
975-8   Mistress
   Arlotte   Robert Odo   Edgar Margaret
   Atheling = Malcolm iii
   died 1125 | K.of Scots

William D. of Normandy [1086-1087]   Matilda /Maud —
Later The Conq..   = Geofrey of Anjou
King of Eng
= Matilda of Flanders   Edith Edgar K.Scot. Alex.K.Scot *Edith David Mary = Eustice 3rd
   See chart for Counts of Blois
   Theobold 3rd = Adela dau of Earl of Capel
   Comte de Blois
   And Chartres

Robert 3rd Rich Cecily Will 2nd [Ruf.] Henry = 1st *Edith   Adela = Stephen
Curtoise   King   King 2nd Adelaide   daughter of   C. of Blois
Duke of Normandy   Killed 1100   1100 3rd Matilda   Will. Conq   Killed on
   to 1135   Daughter of Malcolm   crusade
   3rd Scotland   1102

Lines conjoin
COUSINS → Stephen = Matilda
William & Richard   Robert   Empress Maud = Henry 5th [of France]   King of Eng Boulogne
Sons died   [Also known =2nd Geofrey Plantagenet   sons died
In white ship   as Matilda]   Count of Anjou
1120

1154-1189 Henry 2n = Eleanor   Geoffrey 6th   William Comte of Poiton
   Aquitaine   of Anjou
Geofrey of York   William

William   Henry   Matilda   Richard 1st   Geoffrey   Eleanor   Joan   John
o.s.p. =Margaret =Henry Cour de Leon = Constance = Alfona 1st =William
=Isobel   Duke of = Berengaria   c. of Castile K. of Sicily
de Clare   Saxony   of Navarre   2nd =Raymond
of France   1189-1199   C. of Toulouse
.   Shared Kingship

Owing to the complicated lineage of these times we have included a few dates and coloured
kingship's in green.   *Same person. Names in capital letters are our family members.

Chart showing the connection of Emma and the Scandinavian interest in the succession to the English throne in 1042 and after.

Chart 45

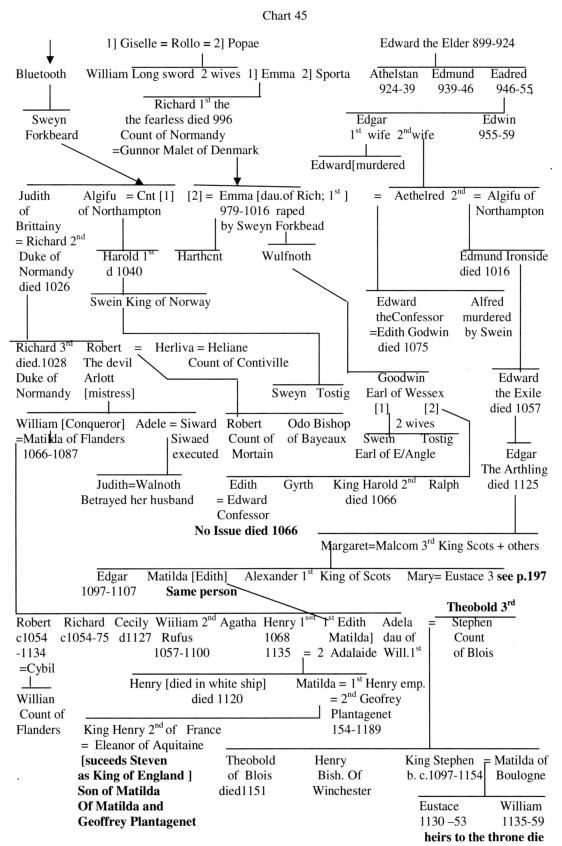

Note; chart showing how the different lines succeeded to the throne and title.

Lucy and her daughter the Countess Lucia
[Some of this text is repeated as it involves a connection with two different families].

Lucy, daughter of **Alfgar** [son of **Leofric** and the **Lady Godiva**], and her sister **Algifu/Edith** was the granddaughter of **William Malet].** If you recall in a previous chapter their great-uncle was

Lucia's Castle Lincoln. [from Bloomfield's] Plate 38 **Turold Crispin** [brother to the **Lady Godiva**] who vacated the office of Sheriff in Bukenham. We have included all this detailed information from various history books and Manor Rolls to show how Lucy his niece and her husband Ivo Tallebois came into possession of the large amount lands and titles that were held by them, which went with the office of sheriff and were not hereditary.

These were at first held by Gilbert of Gent and later passed to Ivo Tallebois, [sheriff] husband of Lucy, [Turold's niece] this would explain how Lucy came to inherit all this land when Turold left adding to her vast estate. It was then passed on to her daughter Lucia's two successive husbands, [who again were sheriffs] **1st William Roumare 2nd Ranulph** Earl of Chester. Lucia also inherited lands from her great-grandfather **William Mallet**, who was Lord of Attleborough. [Killed on the Marshes at Ely during the 1075 rebellion supporting **Hereward the Wake**].

Lucy's and Lucia's origins have always given genealogists real trouble, as most people believe these are one and the same person, but it seems more logical to us that they are mother and daughter. We discovered that the Peterborough Chronicle and Pseudo-Ingulf of Crowland both agree with this, and it seems to be far more aligned with with the truth considering all circumstances. Lucy the mother held Alkborough [Attleborough] and the daughter Lucia's claim to the castle of Lincoln came, through the facts that her father Ivo Tallebois and her great-uncle **Turold**, with her two husbands had all been sheriffs. This would have involved a close association with the chief Castellion of the county of Lincoln. [See charts for the de lacey families]

The family of William **Mallet** [grandfather on her mothers side], held land in the Bail [Lincoln], they also had estates in Derby, Lincoln and York. Lucia was also associated with the Lordship of Bolingbroke through her grandmother. A survey in 1068 showed adjoining patches of land as well as ditches, being let at rents with the North and West Dykes.

Note see cht 46 page 194 also Earls of Mercia chart 16 page 59

THE FAMILY OF DE LACY AND THE
EARLDOM OF LINCOLN

Chart 46

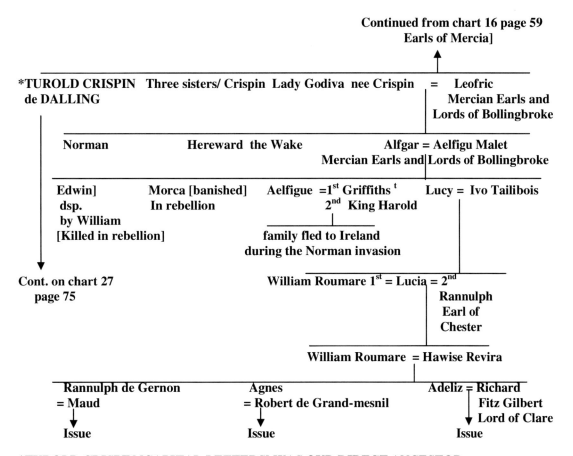

Continued from chart 16 page 59
Earls of Mercia]

*TUROLD CRISPIN Three sisters/ Crispin Lady Godiva nee Crispin = Leofric
de DALLING Mercian Earls and
Lords of Bollingbroke

Norman Hereward the Wake Alfgar = Aelfigu Malet
Mercian Earls and Lords of Bollingbroke

Edwin] Morca [banished] Aelfigue =1st Griffiths t Lucy = Ivo Tailibois
dsp. In rebellion 2nd King Harold
by William
[Killed in rebellion] family fled to Ireland
during the Norman invasion

Cont. on chart 27 William Roumare 1st = Lucia = 2nd
page 75 Rannulph
Earl of
Chester

William Roumare = Hawise Revira

Rannulph de Gernon Agnes Adeliz = Richard
= Maud = Robert de Grand-mesnil Fitz Gilbert
Lord of Clare
Issue Issue Issue

*TUROLD CRISPIN [CAPITAL LETTERS] WAS OUR DIRECT ANCESTOR

This chart illustrates the development of the de Lacy families from their original roots within the Earldom of Mercia. After inter marrying with other powerful families Lucia [daughter of Lucy] exercised influence after she married the Earl of Chester cumulating in the added Earldom of Lincoln and the large fortune left to her by her grandfather **William Malet.**

As previously stated Richard Clare's cousins the Crispin's were slowly dying out [by name] as they were using aliases more and more when patriarchs of these families started to rebel against the throne. The Old Norman names began disappearing from view, although their descendants are still around

Note; Full account of the de Lacey family by William Farrar is to be found in V. C. H. Lancs; Vol. 1 page 310

COLESWEIN/COLSUEN
Of Lincoln

Most of the Magnates that held lands and houses in Lincoln were not permanent residents and took no real part in city life, holding greater interests elsewhere. But there were a few tenants in chief that had more roots there and among these were **Coleswein** son of **Alfred** and grandson of **Leofric.**

One of the most interesting entries in Doomsday Account of Lincoln says of him:

"Coleswein held in the city of Lincoln four tofts of his nepos Coles lands. Outside the city he has 36 houses and two churches upon the wasteland that the king gave him, which was never before built upon. Now the king had all the custom from these tofts outside the city that he inherited, but those outside he received of the Kings favour though he had not endowed them".

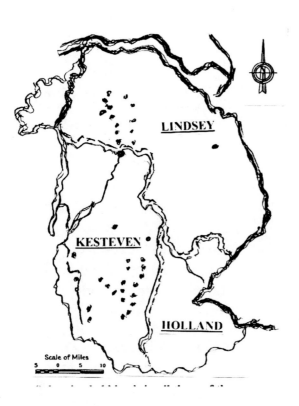

Many different thoughts surround this matter, in those times as he was one of the only two native land holders in the whole of England south of the Tees who owned Baronial estates of any size. He was accused of being a traitor.

According to the Doomsday account, not one of his lands and Manors were held at the time of the conquest. All his descendants seemed to have owed their duty of guard at Lincoln Castle and so must have had a very great deal of favour from William 1st to receive such treatment.

Map of extent of Coleswein held lands in these areas
Artists Impression   Plate 39

CHRONOLOGY 1100 – 1173 AD

1100 Henry 1st took interest in Norwich and started to replace the old wooden castle with the structure we can see today built of stone.

1101 – 1120 Henry 1st son and heir William, drowned at sea in the "White Ship", later set off a power struggle on Henry's death.

1122 Henry spent Xmas in Norwich.

1123 Rebellion of Waleran de Meulan, Amuary, Hugo de Monfort, **Ranulph** the Earl of Chester **and William of Roumare**. Many others turned away, to hold castles against the King almost all the borough of Lincoln was burned down and untold numbers of people were burned to death on May 19th of this year. The above Earls fled from Roger de Beaumont's Castle to another called Vateville.

1124 The king's army attacked; they fled once more, but were captured taken before the king. Waleran and Hugo sons of Gervaise were imprisoned in a castle in Rouen. Hugh son of Graviles and Valerian was reinstated.

1125 Matilda's 1st husband the Holy Roman Emperor Henry 5th died and she married Geoffrey Plantagenet of Anjou. Henry then had a difficult task to persuade the Barons to swear loyalty to his daughter and accept Matilda as the future Queen; according to custom of the time her new husband would become king and he was no friend of England.

1135 Henry 1st dies and the barons went back on their word [just as the king had expected]. Stephen of Bloise [Matilda's cousin] acted quickly to take the crown of England.

1135 Many influential people were in violent opposition to his rule, including the clergy, some even took arms against him.

1139 Matilda, daughter of Henry 1st returns and, captures Stephen who later regains his freedom. Matilda's son Henry comes to assert his right to the throne following the untimely death of Eustace.

1147 Shield of the Crusaders [Heydon family carried in procession]

1148 Defeat for Matilda; rejoined her husband Geoffrey in Normandy.

1153 The military pressure exerted by Henry caused Stephen to change his mind and recognize Henry as future King of England.

1154. Henry 2nd was forceful and ruthless, but less fortunate than his father; as William Shakespeare wrote in his play King Lear 'how sharper than a serpents tooth is to have a thankless child'.

1173 Henry's sons; Henry, Geoffrey, Richard and John in jealous dispute turned against their father which ended in their betrayal of him. The king's bias towards his favorite son John led to war. Their mother Queen Eleanor supported the other three sons who were defeated.

THE FAMILY OF BLOIS

Chart.47

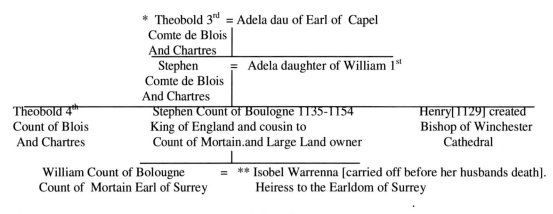

```
         * Theobold 3rd  = Adela dau of Earl of Capel
           Comte de Blois
           And Chartres
              Stephen       =  Adela daughter of William 1st
           Comte de Blois
           And Chartres
Theobold 4th        Stephen Count of Boulogne 1135-1154      Henry[1129] created
Count of Blois      King of England and cousin to            Bishop of Winchester
And Chartres        Count of Mortain.and Large Land owner         Cathedral

     William Count of Bolougne    = ** Isobel Warrenna [carried off before her husbands death].
     Count of Mortain Earl of Surrey      Heiress to the Earldom of Surrey
```

Counts of Anjou and associated families

Cht.48

```
                                              Norman's        Counts of
                                                 ↓            Boulogne
               Fulk 4th 'Ie Rechin = Bertada of   Robert      See chart above
               C.of Anjou          Montfort       The Devil
               C.of Touraine       later Queen of France
               d.1105
Fulk  Anjou C.of Maine =1st Eremberga d and heiress of     William the   * * **Theobold 3rd
King of                 Elias C of Maine                   Conq K. of  England
Jerusalem               =2nd Melisande d. of Baldwin 2nd    = Matilda
1131-1143               King of Jerusalem

               Emp. Of France Henry 1s =  Maude        Adela      = ** Stephen
               1135 King.of England     daughter.of   Daughter. of      of Blois
               Brother to K. Rufus      Malcome 3rd    William 1st  Count of  Anjou

Geoffrey 5th Plantagenet 2nd  husband of = ** *Empress Matilda [no English coronation]   William
Count of Anjou 1129-115                  1st marriage = Henry 5th              drowned at sea
. Count of Touraine5th                    Emperor of  Germany died 1125        in the White Ship
Duke of Normandy 1144-1151                civil war  breaks out in England           1120
[was no friend of England]                [also known as Maud]  .

       Henry 2nd of Eng.= Elenor of Aquitaine       King  Stephen of Blois and Eng
            1154 – 1189    Heiress of Aquitane and Q. of France  [Seized throne from his
       Count of Anjou 1151 [Repudiated wife of King Louis 7th]    Cousin Matilda [1135]
                            of France                             Duke of Normandy 1151
                                                                  and Count of Maine
       Richard [Lionheart]     John                               Duke of Aquitaine 1152
       1189 -1199              1199 -1216                          = Matilda of Boulougne

     King Henry  3rd  =  Eleanor of Provence 1216-1272    Eustace    and    William 1154
```

Heirs to throne die and Henry the son of Stephen's cousin Matilda is made King Henry 2nd of England

** Isabel Warrenna was kidnapped and he married her while her husband was still living.
***Matilda daughter and heir of Henry 1st.of England [after her brother was drowned in a shipwreck] were also known as the Empress Maud after marrying Henry 5th Emperor of Germany who died; she was remarried to Geoffrey Plantagenet. Although heir to the English crown and planned to be crowned she was so unpopular her coronation never took place. Stephen was released from prison and captured Matilda who again escaped and after a series of skirmishes Matilda returned to Anjou never to return. Stephen became King of England; both his sons die and crown of England reverts to Matilda's family decedents, the Plantagenet's.
**** See top chart

THE EARLS OF OXFORD.
The de Vere Families

This dynasty is connected by marriages into the **Malet, Valoise, Lacon and Ward families.** [See individual charts]. Castle Hedingham, Norfolk, dominated one of the many estates held in Anglia by the Earls of Oxford. The Hawe was part of Bec Manor, and when it was sold it passed with Winfarthing to the Mackenzie, de Veres' and other families.

This was not a Manor originally as it was a part of the demean of Beckhall*. In 1311 Sir Hugh de Vere married Denise/Dionasise Valoise a descendant of Peter [see Valoise family tree]. They owned the premise bought from Richard Forester of Hurling, Overhugh in Banham, called Banham Hugh, which came with Winfarthing but was sold in 1607.

The de Vere's had a turbulent medieval history, Richard de Vere fought for Simon de Montfort at the battle of Lewes 14th May 1265 in the civil war against Henry 2nd. ** In 1281 Robert de Vere Earl of Oxford lived in Hatfield Broad Oak, and has a memorial in Broad Oaks Church obituary 1311. In the wars of the Roses, the family fought for Lancaster against York without much success.

In February 1462 the Earl of Worcester executed John de Vere twelfth Earl and his son for treason. When Henry came to the throne, the family's revenge was sweet when they passed the death sentence on the Earl of Worcester and to read more on this, consult the ***Lleyland's initiary. This was the same de Vere, who after losing his way in April 1471, attacked his own side and lost the battle for Barnett and Lancaster.

Queen Elizabeth 1st made a grant to Edward de Vere Earl of Oxford in 1502 styling him Viscount Bulbede, Lord Badlesmere **** [Lord Scales].

Note see chart for de Valoise
***Bloomfield's Norfolk**
****Peerage App.G.51.**
***** Leyland's Initiary [Open Gate Press Inc. Centaur Press 1954]**
******Infra Supta pp, 8994**
Note Rolesditch Robert Grossette. R.L.S. p.20 See Parker Chartuary of the Augustine Priory of Frentham. In the Historical Collections of Staffordshire. William Small Arch, Society vol. xi p, 259-260. The de Veres were tenants of Lucy's family. They owned St Bartholomew's Church in Norwich West of the Castle

NORWICH GAINS A STONE CASTLE
Which replaced the original wood post conquest stockade of 1067 in 1125?
Which replaced the original wood post conquest stockade of 1067 in 1125?
During the reign of Henry 1st 1100-1135

At this time Norwich begins to wield influence as a city; it had grown in stature. A few decades had passed since the first attempt had been made to put a fortress on the mound that had swallowed up part of the old Roman road, [which had been a continuation of the road we know as Ber Street]. The castle, the pride of our city, still towers above, high on its mound overlooking the ancient roads and bustling market.

Much thought went into its preparation; it gave the Norman soldiers a view from the high point of the Castle to the coast at Yarmouth. The harbour twenty-two miles away could be seen on a clear day. It had a position of dominance over the city, and proved a good communication link to the Roman Castle at Caistor. Any provocative movements of the community would be seen for miles around. The Barons could no longer be trusted to co-operate with the king.

Henry 1st demolished the old worn wooden stockades and replaced them with very substantial stone fortifications for this Norman edifice in Norwich. In 1125 tunnels were dug under the castle to connect important buildings such as the Cathedrals monasteries they were also used as escape routes or for clandestine visits to the Nunneries.

Norwich Castle [built 1067] Plate 40

Though the tunnels still exist today they are much too dangerous to use. What stories and intrigues they must have witnessed. When the Castle was first built, the people were fearful as to its purpose especially seeing the great white stone walls continuing to rise above their heads, and feeling the sinister eyes of the Norman soldiers watching all the movements below.They could also see the Royal Heralds arrive at the gates to announce the coming of the king's marshals to test the weights and measures.

Knights who were granted lands and favours were required to serve their turn in guarding the Kings interests by living in the castle quarters and providing troops to protect and maintain it. Norwich Castle still stands proudly in the centre of the city and is used as very large museum and tourist attraction, which takes a whole day to fully explore including all the battlements and historical artifacts. The settlement for the Norman community was separate from the rest, and added a fourth community called the Magna Crofta, the new burgh or port, both names meaning town.

Sir Ralph and Lady Juga [son of Turold one the forerunners of the Bulwer families] were alive at this time and must have taken their share in this work. We wondered what it would have been like to live in Norwich then, to look down on the milling crowds in the market square. Did the Dalling family have to bargain for their goods like the rest, or were there maidservants to do this for them, what prices did they pay? There were no stalls as we have today; people just sat on bails of straw in the open market place, displaying their wares.

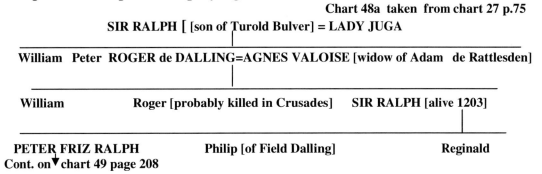

Chart 48a taken from chart 27 p.75

SIR RALPH [[son of Turold Bulver] = LADY JUGA

William   Peter   ROGER de DALLING=AGNES VALOISE [widow of Adam de Rattlesden]

William   Roger [probably killed in Crusades]   SIR RALPH [alive 1203]

PETER FRIZ RALPH   Philip [of Field Dalling]   Reginald

Cont. on ▼ chart 49 page 208

The area where the Normans first lived is still familiar to Norfolk people because their outstandingly beautiful Norman church of St. Peter Mancroft, which looks over their market place that is still used today. The original market place was in Tombland, [meeting place], which the Norman's moved, much to the disgust of the community, though they lost a great deal of this new market when monks stole land to incorporate it within the walls of the Cathedral Close.

Trade increased and luxuries were imported from abroad. Norman's regarded their Saxon neighbours as inferior because of their simple way of life compared to their own more cultured way of doing things. The Castle was hated as much as the new market place [which had been forced upon the people] and the Cathedral.

Both Saxon's and Norman's must have marveled at the colours in the dress of the knights and their ladies. The bright trapping on the horses and the gay colours of the city parades, all passing like a pageant before their eyes. At the same time some were being taken down into the dark dungeons of the Castle never to be seen again.

The mostly unseen watchers in the castle often witnessed degrading events. It must have presented a very moving picture of humanity. The building towered above the new cattle market where farmers congregated each Saturday to sell their animals by auction. **David** [co-author] and his brothers in their youth, spent many hours there fascinated by the bustle and willingly assisted the farmers to drive cattle [known as bullock whopping] through the streets of Norwich during the 1940/50's.

THE CRUSADES
c.1095

The Crusades were called enthusiastic military/religious enterprises against the infidels of the Holy Land. We do believe some of our family may have taken part but we have no proof to confirm this. European and Middle Eastern Kings formed armies to fight for what they believed. It was a romantic time full of valour and bravery.

The control of the holy places in Palestine by the Seljuk Turks combined with the rising population in Europe caused unrest and a great revival of religion during the eleventh century creating strong emotions. The challenge of the Crusades emanated from the Emperor of Byzantium, who appealed for help against the Turks. Pope Urban the 2nd and two hundred Bishops backed him up in 1095 AD during the time of William Rufus. Hundreds of knights responded, they wore the red crosses made of cloth from which the Crusaders took their name.

The first Crusade was called the peoples Crusade; the participants were all slain by the Turkish archers, it was a day of disaster, Christendom believed it was the "Day of Judgment", and indeed the blame rested squarely on their shoulders. On the seventh day of June 1099 AD, the Crusaders reached Jerusalem. This was a fearful battle, even disgusting to the soldiers taking part, lasting three days and creating a mass slaughter.

They successfully destroyed Jerusalem and Constantinople as religious centers. Jerusalem [still a cause of contention today] was only partly handed back to the Jews in recent times. In the twelfth century in order to guard Jerusalem, the Crusaders built a large Garrison Castle at the only pass from Tripoli to the Christian territory, and strategically this was like a knife-edge being held against the throat of the Saracens. Because of its positions and massive walls it stood for one and a half centuries.

We have no positive information regarding the Mortimer's involvement in the crusades but we do know that **Peter de Valois** and **Turold** both died in 1099 AD the same time as the battle for Jerusalem. There was a mass said for the soul of **Peter de Valois**, who previous to this date had displeased the king and had forfeited his lands. We suspect he like others had joined the Crusades to earn forgiveness.

There is a large green wooden shield in the church at Heydon, half has either rotted or been broken away caused by its use in fighting. It has a notation nearby that states that this was carried in the funeral procession of at least one of the Heydon family who died in the Crusades.

A notation on another crusaders shield in Heydon church states in chilling words:-

AS YOU ARE NOW.
SO WE ONCE WERE.
AS WE ARE NOW.
SO SHALL YOU BE.

There were many crusades, in the military sense they were all disasters for the West. The so-called Holy places remained in Muslim hands. The main advantage gained was the impact on cultural education and geographical knowledge obtained during these exploits.

SALADIN THE KURD

Saladin was born in a country known today as Iraq and was from a Kurdish family. He joined the Syrian army and rose to a prominent position. After their defeat of Egypt he assumed full command of the army. As the founder of the Ayyubid dynasty in Egypt and Syria he used his position to start a Muslim Holy war [Jihad] and swore to wipe out Christendom and the Jews as religious groups, all other religions apart from their own were referred too as infidels; this war still continues today.

Turkish Soldier Plate 42
Artists impression

The second Crusade took place in 1144 AD when the Turks considered Jerusalem as their own city and it did become theirs on Oct 2nd 1187 for a great number of years. The Crusaders returned home defeated, as it was to be the case so many times after. Saladin's many victories enabled him to obtain an armistice agreement when he agreed to retain all but a small strip of land in the Syrian coast to be held by the Crusaders.

The Turkish element was well equipped for war at this period and had a form of unusual dress. It certainly must have been a very frightening sight to confront them fighting in a war. Bows were hung round their neck, and arrows at their waist, an axe on their arm, curved daggers on their belt, a curved sword called a scimitar held in one hand and a shield in the other.

Saladin admired and respected King Richard as a very brave leader and if the situation had been different they perhaps would have been very good friends. Saladin took a major role in the Crusades and when in died 1193 they lost a very able leader. The Crusades continued on and off for about three hundred years with the Saracens having the advantage most of the time. An interesting children's crusade in 1212 AD is mentioned later.

In the eighth and last major crusade of 1270 like most of the others, trickery, deceit and ignorance started all sorts of trouble before the crusade even embarked.

When the Crusaders finally reached and entered inside the walled city of Carthage they became trapped and surrounded by the Turks. They were on the inside and the vital water supply outside resulting in thirst and unhygienic conditions making them have to sue for peace. Then the dreaded plague broke out amongst them and the luckless army returned home in disgrace spreading the disease right across Europe.

Also it was during this crusade, which was led by King Louis 9th of France they attempted to capture Tunis but Louis died of the plague outside its walls before the attack. It was this debacle that finally confirmed the futility of these holy wars and any others that followed were comparatively petty affairs.

KING HENRY 2nd
(1154-1189)
The Barons come to heel in the time of Sir Ralph [Turold's son]

While the Crusaders were still fighting abroad, in England Henry 2nd had become the first of the Angevin or Plantagenet kings. Henry had a strong personality that in time would control the barons. In addition to being the King of England he possessed more land in France than the French king. He displayed striking contrasts in character, being restless, energetic, and wanting more power for himself. His dominating personality restored order in England and regained authority for the crown.

Henry decided to restore the legal system his grandfather had introduced which involved trial by Jury to give ordinary people more justice. Previously guilt was determined by trial in combat and/or ordeal, which he considered barbaric. The Jury system he installed is similar to the one we use today with a judge and twelve Jurors who are sworn in.

The accused had the opportunity to appeal to a Royal Court if they felt there was an unjust verdict. Cardinal Thomas a'Becket assisted him in this and was Henry's chancellor, but much to Becket's disapproval Henry made him an Archbishop. This story is widely told in history books so we will not retell it here except that the outcome was that a'Becket was murdered while praying at his alter.

Henry reduced the power of the Barons and their profits, the Barons tired of fighting and plundering gave their support to the king whose reign was an epoch in English history as much as that of King William the Conqueror.

KING RICHARD AND KING JOHN

Richard and John were sons of King Henry 2nd and totally opposite in nature. John was King Henry's favourite until, like his brothers he took up arms against his father and earned his dying curses. For sixteen years Richard 1st Coeur de Leon [The Lionhearted] was either in rebellion against his father or at war with his eldest brother Henry.

His arrogance offended many people around him. King Henry 2nd died during the 3rd Crusade in 1189; his son Richard claimed the crown as his older brothers died before their father. Richard also went on the crusades, which made a hole in the nation's purse and crippled the country with high taxation. His brother John was left to sort this out and although he was described as a cruel and grasping man he was not entirely to blame.

Traveling across Europe King Richard led the Crusaders in a decisive victory over Saladin at Arsuf 1191, but on learning that his brother was challenging his government in England he hurried home. John desiring to be king engineered the capture of Richard who was held for a ransom. This was paid and when Richard arrived back in England in 1194 he extracted a submission from John who despite his treachery still recognized him as heir. Many of his senior religious leaders, the barons and wealthy landowners then took up arms against King Richard.

King Richard Gives Norwich Its Charter

Just over eight hundred years ago [1198] King Richard 1st presented Norwich with its Charter which is probably the most important and priceless document that it has ever owned, this he granted after returning from the crusades. Norwich became an independent city, self-governing, no longer tied to the king, and was granted a Manor Farm, paying a tax of one hundred and eight pounds per annum every Michaelmas. From then Norwich no longer was a part of Norfolk as it was to be counted as 'The County of The City of Norwic'. Soon after King Richard left England again to defend his possessions in France, he died on April 6th 1199 at Calais and John gained his ambition by becoming King.

In 1202 knights ceased to be effective when the longbow was invented, this implement had more power and longer range than the old short bow. Later the cannon was invented that made the bow and the sword extinct. **Sir Ralph** [son of **Turold**] married to **Lady Juga** [d 1203] had sons **William, Peter,** and **Roger** [married to **Agnes**, **Rattlesden**]. **Roger** lived in the manor of Field Dalling after his marriage, and maybe only **Roger** was alive to witness the events of this time period, as **William** and **Peter** were probably killed on the crusades; it was an exciting time for the rich.

National and local laws were being made or adjusted and the jockeying for personal possessions and assets became a necessity as these laws clearly defined who owned what by law to avoid any family disputes.

William Mortimer was a rebel who forfeited the title Earl of Mortain after the battle of Tinchebrai and sought protection in the house of his uncle, William Fitz-Osberne until the loss of Normandy in 1204. King John, to cover the cost of trying to protect his lands in France was desperate and ruthless and levied high taxes to raise money, this angered the Barons and Nobles who planned to get rid of him.

When one Baron died and his next of kin was not yet of age the usual practice of the king was to claim guardianship of the estate. He then used the proceeds in his own interests, which started serious moves to put rebellion plans into action. King John continued to spend national wealth on the Crusades and with all the troubles at home he abandoned Normandy completely in the same year. The efficient administrative machine inherited from their father helped to overcome many difficulties but the territories in France that Henry 2nd and Richard had worked so hard to defend were lost, and only Gascony and Poitou were retained.

In 1214 King John tried to invade France and regain what he had lost but failed. Odo the half brother of William 1st originally held the manor of Freebridge at Kings Lynn and after he was disinherited it passed to his butler whose family eventually died out. It reverted to the crown, back into King John's possession and while he was staying at this residence the barons finally revolted in protest at his high national taxes, which were needed for John's crusades and they went after him.He made a desperate attempt to escape by crossing the flat dunes of the Wash [Norfolk/Lincolnshire estuary] when the tide was out. People acquainted with this treacherous part of the coast would know of its dangerous tides.

He was caught as the tide turned when he was halfway across and had to run for his life, taking his and the nation's treasures with him. The crown jewels and the coach that carried them stuck fast in the wet sand, at the mercy of the sea and the incoming tide. He was lucky to escape with his life. The barons met at Bury St. Edmund's on 20th November 1214 to discuss the future of King John of England; Cardinal Langton and 25 Barons were instructed and swore to obtain justice from him. They revolted in 1215 and forced King John to attend a meeting at Runnymeade where they drew up the charter called the Magna Carta which included sanctions to curb the violence of the bullying knights. He was forced to sign as they accused him of squandering the country's wealth.

Note; from then on the monarch could govern but not rule.

<u>Some of the 25 Barons who met at Bury St Edmonds.</u>
<u>Those listed below in bold print were connected to our family</u>
[This issue failed]
Robert Fitz-Walter, Marshall of the Barons army.
Richard de Clare, Hertfordshire.
Gilbert de Clare, Gloucester [extinct].
John de Lacey Earl of Lincoln [extinct]
William Malet left two daughters.
John Fitz-Robert unknown today [see chart for **Warrenna**].
Roger Bigot E/Norfolk. Duke of St Albans
William Albini Baron of Belvior
Richard de Percy

The barons forced John to recognize the rights and liberties of the people; at first it was mainly for the rich but later ideas that he inserted were added; these were items involving all classes. This was done to avoid trouble, many disputes were settled, marriage wardship and military service included.

<u>There was a poem also on the tower that related.</u>
When this rude buttress totters to its fall,
And ivy mantles o'er its crumbling wall.
The once high altar's lonely resting place,
Let patriotic fancy muse awhile,
Amid the ruins of this ancient pile.
Six weary centuries have passed away,
Palace and Abbey molder in decay.
Cold death enshrouds the noble, and the brave.
Langton and Fitz-Walter slumber in the grave.
But still we read in deathless records,
The high souled priest confirmed the Barons vow.
And freedom unforgettable recites.
The second birthplace of our native rights.

John agreed to rule according to law, but broke his word and promptly, appealed to Pope Innocent to release him from this oath. Civil war began and King Philip de Valois of France seeing all the unrest, attacked. He said he would give England as a present to his son. Pope Innocent who had excommunicated John put England under interdict and made this country a Papal Fief due to John's long drawn out hostility towards him. The Pope gave his blessing to Philips intention. Another Crusade worth mentioning was the Children's Crusade in 1212 AD (the true version of the Pied Piper]. Thousands of children took part but most never survived the hazardous journey across Europe. Many disappeared on the way, others kidnapped to become slaves, few returned to relate their story.

King John never completed this struggle as he died in 1216 after eating his favourite dish of shrimps (historically known as the surfeit of lampreys) and left his son Henry 3rd an inheritance of civil war complicated by a French invasion. The Christian Crusades never achieved what they set out to do but caused heartbreak and bloodshed and cost a fortune.

HENRY 3RD 1216-1272.

It was at this time our side of the Mortimer families start to appear with the **Mortimer/Wigmore's** that came to Norfolk and grew rich and powerful. Their wealth grew to exceed that of the kings. When Sir **Roger Mortimer** took King Edwards 2nd wife and usurped his position, his castle and seniority were forfeit, together with his lands, which passed into the hands of William Warrenna, [see story page164]. Another Mortimer with an alias, **Ralph Mortimer** whose possessions and power in Wigmore were larger than any other follower of William Warrenna in England, was a very crafty person, laying claim to a number of things to which he was not entitled. His grandson Ralph succeeded to his father's titles, and served under his Uncle William Fitz Osberne, Earl of Hereford.

Robert Mortimer witnessed a charter of **William Warrenna** to Castle Acre Priory. King Henry wanted to give the hand of his daughter to him, Abbot Anslem objected owing to the close family relationship, both being descendants of Gonner. During the reign of Henry 3rd there was a quarrel between Richard de Clare the Earl of Gloucester and the Duke of Montfort [This continued into the reign of his son Edward] that resulted in Henry breaking all ties with the Montfort Party cumulating in a war at the battle of Lewes [1264] where Henry's son Edward was taken hostage.

The Barons wanted to negotiate reform with the king, De Montfort chose **Mortimer** as one of the twenty-four representatives to discuss terms. Edward the king's son escaped from De Montfort's hands and formed an opposition party. On 4th August 1265 AD at the battle of Evesham De Montfort was defeated; the Earl of Montfort was brutally tortured and killed and his head sent in a gruesome parcel to his wife Eleanor [sister of Henry 3rd].

In November 1281 the barons were forced to compromise and on December 7th Henry formally pardoned some of those that opposed him, **Ralph Mortimer** was on this list, henceforth he was obliged to stand by the King. **William de Mortimer** was ward of the Earl of Warren and in 1280 released all his estates in the Manor of Scoulton on the eighth of June 1294. With 60 others he was summoned to the king to advise him on the affairs of State.

* Note; we suggest you use charts as there are same names for different people of different generations which is confusing.

Bulwer / Dalling Line

Thomas [son of Peter Fitz Ralph] and Lefguana lived during the reign of Henry 3rd and witnessed several family and national historical events which are outlined in text.

Continued from chart 27 page75   **Chart 49**

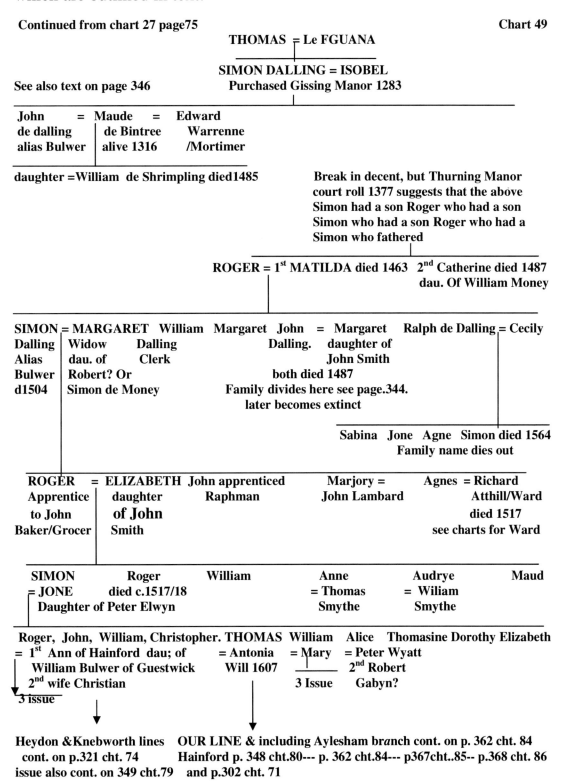

THOMAS = Le FGUANA

SIMON DALLING = ISOBEL
See also text on page 346   Purchased Gissing Manor 1283

John de dalling alias Bulwer	=	Maude de Bintree alive 1316	=	Edward Warrenne /Mortimer

daughter =William de Shrimpling died1485   Break in decent, but Thurning Manor court roll 1377 suggests that the above Simon had a son Roger who had a son Simon who had a son Roger who had a Simon who fathered

ROGER = 1st MATILDA died 1463   2nd Catherine died 1487 dau. Of William Money

SIMON Dalling Alias Bulwer d1504 = MARGARET Widow dau. of Robert? Or Simon de Money   William Dalling Clerk   Margaret   John Dalling. = Margaret daughter of John Smith both died 1487 Family divides here see page.344. later becomes extinct   Ralph de Dalling = Cecily

Sabina Jone Agne Simon died 1564
Family name dies out

ROGER Apprentice to John Baker/Grocer = ELIZABETH daughter **of John** Smith   John apprenticed Raphman   Marjory = John Lambard   Agnes = Richard Atthill/Ward died 1517 see charts for Ward

SIMON = JONE Daughter of Peter Elwyn   Roger died c.1517/18   William   Anne = Thomas Smythe   Audrye = Wiliam Smythe   Maud

Roger, John, William, Christopher. THOMAS William Alice Thomasine Dorothy Elizabeth
= 1st Ann of Hainford dau; of   = Antonia   = Mary   = Peter Wyatt
William Bulwer of Guestwick   Will 1607   2nd Robert
2nd wife Christian   3 Issue   Gabyn?
3 issue

Heydon &Knebworth lines cont. on p.321 cht. 74 issue also cont. on 349 cht.79   OUR LINE & including Aylesham branch cont. on p. 362 cht. 84 Hainford p. 348 cht.80--- p. 362 cht.84--- p367cht..85-- p. 368 cht. 86 and p.302 cht. 71

OUR LINEAGE IN CAPITAL LETTERS

Chronology of Events 1348-1674 AD.

1348   The first and worst of the great plagues.

1381   Wat Tyler in Peasants revolt, **William Bulwer** involved.

1430   The first important step forward was the provision of a clean water reservoir. [A tower was added and a pump installed in 1665 driven by a steam engine in Norwich. Improved in 1802].

1447   A procession held (with the shield of a Crusader) for members of Heydon family killed in the crusades.

1476   Printing introduced in England by William Caxton [printed in Bruges] in English language.

1549   Kett's Rebellion. Robert was hung from Norwich Castle 7th December his brother was hung from a church in Wymondham

1554   Wyatt's rebellion against marriage of Queen Mary to Philip of Spain.

1559   Oliver Cromwell formed the Roundheads (Parliamentarians) with **Bulwer** support v The Crown (Cavaliers or Royalists)

1604   April, Conspirators met May to plan Gunpowder plot; Thomas Percy rents John Wynyard's house next to the House of Lords posing as a caretaker. 11th Dec; plotters start to dig tunnel from this house to beneath the Lords chamber.

1605   7th Feb. postponement of Parliament – March tunnel idea abandoned. Another room found under The Lords Chamber Midnight 4th Nov. Guy Fawkes betrayed and arrested.

1606   Jan.-Parliament decreed the 5th Nov. should be day of public thanksgiving. 27th Jan. Guy and seven others sentenced to be hung, drawn [disembowelled) and cut into quarters but Guy deceived the executioner, jumped from the scaffold and broke his neck.

1640's   Oliver Cromwell appointed Erasmus Earl, his close friend and confident Sergeant at Law [equal today as Chief Queens Consul. **John Bulwer** is appointed Cromwell's Armourer.

1644   Battle of Marston Moor.

1645   Battle of Nasby; Royalists defeated.

1648   Oliver Cromwell defeated the Scottish Army at Preston.

1653   Dissolved [Rump] Parliament. Oliver becomes Lord Protector.

1667   Harold Bulwer who we know existed, but found no details on his life, so we have not included him in the family records yet.

1662   Recognition in the development of sign language John Wallis in competition for this honour with John Bulwer.

1674   **Thomas Bulwer** born in Saxthorpe.

1674   John Bulwer instigates sign language for the deaf.

NORWICH AN EXPANDING CITY

The Charter given by Richard 1st [1198] was important to the city, it gave the Elders more freedom to govern and these terms have not been altered since 1300AD. The councilors and aldermen are still controlled by its Mayor who has helped Norwich to prosper from about 1274, when roads extended beyond the city walls.

It can be seen from maps how rivers and bridges dictated how far the roads and settlements extended as water not only identified boundaries but also more importantly acted as a protection from invaders. The southern side of the city reached as far as the river at Harford, Catton Cringleford, Earlham, Hellesdon, Mousehold and part of Thorpe, where the river's Yare and Wensum meet.

In 1307 Edward 2nd succeeded to the throne and married Isabella who took a lover Sir Roger Mortimer [see p. 159, feast at Norwich Castle]. By 1334AD nearly fifty years after they had started building the city walls, they still did not form a continuous line round the city but were in two parts, one each side of the river which protected the gaps. By following the wall round the city you can identify the name of each gate with the activity associated with the area. Although the gates have long gone the names are still used to this day. On the map, it shows there was a gate on each one of the twelve roads coming into Norwic.

The Black Tower and part of the city wall are still there to this day. The tower has a morbid history attached to it, both past and comparatively recent 2nd World War stories, that we will relate as the story proceeds. The gates of Ber Street were on a high road above the river valley that commanded a splendid view of the area, with a typical cobbled Roman road, very wide which was later laid with wooden blocks. Our great grandfather in the Williment family, whose trade was a pavior, probably had a hand in the more modern paving with similar types of wooden blocks.

Westlegate Street [off from All Saints Green] was once very narrow almost a passageway that led into the city and had a gateway called Brazen Door. This street was there for many years without the actual door and only the top bar of the gate remained stretching across the road joining the two houses on both sides. Norma remembers walking through this door with her mother and grandmother. The bar was removed in the 1930's when the street was widened during redevelopment. Further along the wall was Saint Stephens Gate, which was the main gate for the road to London. One gate still existed at the junction of Grapes Hill, St. Benedicts and Barn Road until the air raids of world war two.

EDWARD 1ˢᵗ
King of England 1272----1307 AD

Henry 3ʳᵈ died when his son Edward 1ˢᵗ [called `Longshanks' because of his thin long profile] was on a crusade. He married Eleanor of Castile in 1254 and was enthroned in 1272. When she died 1290 he married Margaret of France. He had a troubled reign, continually in dispute with Scotland, Wales and France who were all hostile to English rule. He was however one of the greatest English kings and made many improvements, summoning Parliament frequently. The most famous meeting in 1295 of councillors, called the Model Parliament included the clergy and nobles.

He set efficient rules for maintenance of public order by statute and curbed the power of church courts. The Statute of Mortmain (1279) required anyone who wished to give land to the church first had to obtain royal permission and in 1290 he expelled the Jews. The Wigmore's took part in Llewellyn's claim for the sovereignty of Wales but when Llewellyn was killed 1282, Welsh independence ended and from then on it was under direct English rule.

EDWARD 2ⁿᵈ
1284 – 1327
And a family Scandal

In 1307 Constantine Mortimer, descendant of Rudolph [half brother of Richard 1ˢᵗ of Normandy] was one of the great men chosen to travel with King Edward to France for his interview and marriage to Isobel the daughter of the King of France, [Philip de Valois, Carolingian dynasty, see early charts]. Sir Roger de Mortimer meantime had gained more power and riches than the King himself and ingratiated himself, after a time, with King Edward's wife Queen Isobel. National matters were made worse with the legacy of his fathers' actions against the French, Scots, nobles and clergy. 1314 Edward led his army into Scotland and was crushed by Robert the Bruce at Bannockburn, which won Scotland's independence. Edward's troubles deepened; his personal ones overshadowed the national ones. His wife Queen Isobel had returned to France with their son and Sir Roger Mortimer who was now her lover.

Once established there she organised an army. In 1326 the Queen and Mortimer invaded England, seized and executed her enemies the de Spencer's and captured and imprisoned her husband King Edward 2ⁿᵈ. Later Parliament met and chose Prince Edward as king though Isobel and Mortimer still remained in control by keeping King Edward 2ⁿᵈ in prison. While they were still committing adultery they had King Edward murdered. At first there was nothing to prove against them and Sir Roger surrounded himself with Welshmen for protection.

EDWARD 3rd
(1327-77 AD.)

Edward 3rd came to the throne a very angry and bitter man; furiously jealous of **Sir Roger Mortimer** for flaunting his vast wealth and for the power he exercised because of it, which the king must have felt humiliating. The resentfulness aroused in him and others added to the anger over the murder of his father, and the further shame regarding his mother's obsession for this **Sir Roger Mortimer**. It drove the king to take action; he co-opted the help of powerful friends to secure **Sir Roger's** capture and bring to an end the situation between his mother the Queen and this man.

Parliament was summoned; plans were made to ensnare Mortimer, and they set a trap. Mortimer became suspicious when he took up quarters in Nottingham Castle and instructed Welsh mercenaries to keep strict watch, blocking every approach. But the castle custodian betrayed him and revealed the secret entrance. The trap was sprung and the king's men entered the castle killing two of the guards in the passageways approaching the rooms used by **Mortimer** and his mistress. They broke down the doors to the room; Sir Roger was caught with Isobel and they could do nothing to release themselves from this awkward situation.

Charges were brought against him: -

1) He had made trouble between King Edward 2nd and his wife
2) He had the King murdered.
3) Usurped the power of the Government with several other devious acts. He was condemned to death without a hearing and

transported to the Tower of London to serve four years severe imprisonment with his nephew but arrangements were made for his nephew to escape. On the 23rd November clad in black Sir **Roger Mortimer** was taken through the city of London and executed at Tyburn in the same way as he ordered the death of the youngest de Spencer. He was hung drawn and quartered, displayed in

Castle Rising Norfolk where the Queen was kept prisoner **Unknown source** Plate 43

public like a criminal, the King took pity and allowed his family to give him honourable burial in an obscure place.

Note ; - The term hung drawn and quartered does not apply in a normal hanging but more of a strangulation, then drawn [cut from neck to lower stomach also horizontally across the stomach] and the innards were removed while the victim was sometimes still alive. This fate was normally reserved for traitors.

Later permission was granted for his remains to be removed and taken to the family vaults at Austin Priory, Wigmore. Edward arranged for his mother Isobel to live at Castle Rising in Norfolk. The walls of the keep are 50ft high and of great strength, he often visited her but she was not allowed out without his permission; it is said that her screams can still be heard in the castle. In 1349 **Constantine Mortimer** and his son **Roger** were given the Kings licence to travel to Rome.

The French again threatened invasion in 1351 and King Edward commissioned Mortimer and John D' Engaine to arrange all able-bodied men that had sufficient estates in Cambridgeshire and Huntingdonshire to defend the realm. Constantine died leaving no heirs. Nothing more was mentioned of the account of this invasion. **Roger de Mortimer`s** own grandson, after loyally serving the King well became one of the original Knights of the Garter and all that had been taken from his grandfather was fully restored to him. In later years Edward 3rd was victimised by his own courtiers

*Typical and his mistress Alice Perrers and died ill and neglected by all

Knight Plate 44 except Alice who robbed him. His son, the Black Prince is

Artists Impression one of the great royal heroes of English history but unfortunately never became king as he died before his father.

THE PLAGUES DURING THE REIGN OF EDWARD 3rd
Son of the Black Prince

1337 saw the beginning of the 100 years war between England and France begun by Edward the 3rd to protect the wool trade. It was also the first outbreak of the 'Black Plague" that finally reduced the population of Europe by 40%. Also known as 'The Black Death' a disease carried by rats transferred by fleas that spread rapidly with the movement of birds, people and trade. The first and most famous outbreak and the most written about, occurred in 1348-50AD, which initiated the break-up of the medieval world and the beginning of modern times. Other epidemics took place in 1358-60, 1373-75 and occasionally between 1380-1400AD.

The first occurrence of the plague in England began in Bristol, which, to the people of Norfolk still seemed a long way off as they cheerfully celebrated the wedding of Edward to Philipa of Flanders. It was Queen Philipa [Edwards's wife] who encouraged the first of the Flemish weavers to cross the channel and teach English people the art of weaving. As people became skilled in this work it expanded into a textile industry that was to last for 500 years. Unfortunately the arrival of the Flemish weavers was possibly one of the many ways the Black Death gained a foothold in England and sowed the seeds for future rebellion.

All too soon the plague reached London and fear started to reach into the hearts of those living on the East Coast, stealthily it crept into Norfolk through the quiet country lanes and villages. Its chilly fingers were far reaching; soon it was stalking the rubbish-lined streets of Norwich, which stood like a tinderbox ready to ignite with the filthy stench and germs hoarded there for centuries. There was no running water or sewerage system, people were squalid, repulsive and vile smelling. It was one disaster piled upon another as weather patterns also started to change [sounds familiar?] bringing famine to people and animals; disaster was inevitable.

The disease Rindepest killed even more animals as they roamed at will through narrow streets that prevented the flow of fresh air. These lanes were awash with human and animal excrement mixed with domestic rubbish, these filthy conditions were exploited by the rats and the fleas they carried. The only wide road in Norwich of any consequence was the old Roman road called Ber Street. The harbour entrance at Caister became blocked in 1346 due to all the waste coming downstream from Norwich, at this time the chief settlement in Norfolk. The replacement harbour also became blocked ten years later so they diverted the river southwards to the harbour that is used today. The plague, a fearsome terrifying disease spread rapidly, death occurred within 24 hours. The most infectious type was when the virus entered the lungs and the resulting sputum contained bacteria infected blood that was extremely contagious to anyone who dared approach or enter the room.

It rapidly spread to every street house village town and city in the country, anywhere people gathered the plague followed. Whole areas were wiped out and the tumbrels (carts) of death were kept busy day and night carrying bodies to the plague pits. The disease cut across all national boundaries and all classes of people, bringing terror, and dismay and depressingly there was no medical answer to stop its progress.

Sir John Paston pleaded with his brother to protect his children, not allowing them to be taken anywhere near the sickness. He writes in a letter to his brother "And if any souls have died in Norwich for God's sake send the children to live with friends in the country". We have included above a paraphrase at this point, of a cutting from a local paper relating to this period. Out of a population of 6,000, 2,400 died in Norwich. Lists show that even ten years later market stalls and houses stood empty, bereft of life as the plague left very few people to tend to these things. The Black Plague was so called because it created black splodges or pustules under the skin and had several different forms.

1] Bubonic Plague was named from the Buboes or swelling in the groin and armpit that rapidly spread to the rest of the body. This disease affected both rich and poor alike, so you can understand how whole families; streets and villages were wiped out. Following the swellings there was vomiting, fever and frequently early death.

2] Pneumonic Plague affected the lungs.

3] Septicaemia Plague entered the bloodstream and killed within 24 hours.

MEDICAL CARE

There had been limited plague outbreaks before but from 1300 to 1600 the Black Death was the scourge of Europe; combined with famine and war it gave rise to apocalyptic visions such as Peter Bruegel's painting "Triumph of Death". While treating patients doctors wore protective clothing. In order to purify the air they breathed, they wore special beaks on their masks containing spices, carried fumigating torches and cauterising stick's, all of which had long handles that allowed them to cauterize the swellings without approaching the body too closely. If all treatment failed a Pomander filled with perfume was used in the area of the sick person. On death, a cross was buried with the corpse to ease the dead person's path to heaven. The bodies of the poor were cast into mass graves.

The old Black Tower in the city wall on Carrow Hill in Norwich was used to isolate those that were very badly infected and included a morgue to house the dead. Mass burial sites (plague pits) to accommodate them were dug around the city. This had to be done quickly so that bodies were not left to rot. There was also a very large extension made to St. Peter Mancroft churchyard in the City of Norwich so the market place was moved a few yards from its original position and still exists there today With little trade and almost nothing to sell, the wool and other industries had diminished, genealogical records were in chaos. What is left of the steps of St. Peter Mancroft church that were there before the extension of the graveyard can be seen today. Some of this space has been used to build shops, a public house etc. since that mass burial.

An Artists impression of protective clothing worn by doctors when treating patients of the plague Prayer book. Disinfecting stick scented smoke to cover smells and cauterizing the wounds   Plate. 45

These burial places in Norwich are revealed in such places as All Saints churchyard on All Saints Green where so many were buried the earth to this day is piled behind a wall 3ft higher than the road. We have a faint recollection that even in our early childhood behind the city wall there were desolate streets of houses, many of which stood empty and no one seemed to want.

Unattended churches slowly decayed, with no one left in the parish to repair them or to attend services. But these are only memories of our childhood; maybe some are recollected stories recounted by our mother.

These buildings were avoided for a long time with their empty faceless windows looking out on streets where only the grass grew. We have included all these facts to emphasize the importance of this period, that affected not only our relatives that lived then, but it also engineered a social change sowing the seeds for economic revolution.

Top: City Wall /Black Tower   Plate 46
mortuary Carrow Hill during Black Death
The narrow streets of the Cathedral Close

The chronic shortage of labour gave the surviving peasants the chance to escape from the Lord of the Manor and to demand a better standard of living from those who apparently owned them. These people began to realize the power of supply and demand plus how the mastery of money and resources by the collective masses can sway the ambitious control of Lords and Kings. After the ravages of the plague had died down labour was scarce, there was competition between both landowners and the new industries and crafts for the few able bodied people available.

Though the dead are silent they can still speak to us in a way, in 1517 AD the **Bulwer** chart 49 p.208 shows that in the same year a father and two sons died revealing a possible tragic link with the plague at this time. Tracing the family tree was difficult during periods of national disturbance or when disasters like the plagues struck. In general most victims were buried in mass graves, and there was not much time to record other individual events. However we found the various Manor Rolls very helpful during this phase of our research. The death of King Edward 3rd again started rival claims to the throne that eventually led to the war of the roses. [See Royal Line].

IRMINGLAND

*Osbert de Somerton owned this Manor and the Bacons held it after him until 1323 when it merged with Castle Acre. **John de Dalling** and John de Bintree held this in 1392 mentioned earlier in our story and were Lords there until **Thomas and Margaret** possessed Bintree Manor for life. In 1395 **Simon Bulwer** settled it on his wife with all its demesne lands, it then went by fine to John Foxley, who handed it back to **John** and **Maud Bulwer** for life, the remainder to William Shrimpling who married their daughter. After they died it was settled by fine to William Hastings of Aylsham.

We found that in 1327 AD Geoffrey Bulwer living at Langham sued **Robert Bulwer**; also there was another court action between **Robert Bulwer** and **Simon Bulwer**. Many of the court actions at that time stemmed from the in fighting between families. The first born son had all of the inheritance as the Barons refused to split the estates leaving the rest of the family sometimes without assets or even much to live on. In 1390 the Bintree's son Thomas released all his rights and in 1433 it went to a John Betts in total and became joined to the Manor of Whitefoot Hall owned by Warner de Irmingland [since 1196] and Godfrey held part share for the Honour of Clare. Later it again came into the hands of the **Bulwer** families of Buxton and also for Hainford, which was listed in the will of **Thomas Bulwer** of Saxthorpe.

The Peasants Revenge 1381
In the reign of Richard 2nd son of the Black Prince
Gissing Manor was used as Headquarters and William Bulwer of Pickering was involved.

The Black Death had swept through Europe killing almost one third of the population creating a shortage of labour which obliged those who survived to work harder and yet when they asked for more wages a law was passed to counter this. The disastrous effects of the plague, famine and appalling weather conditions combined with heartless behaviour from landowner's aroused intense hatred among the people. But the havoc created by the shortage of labour worked as a rare favour for them!…it gave them work. They felt a sense of freedom and a new feeling of power. No longer slaves to the Lords of the Manors, they felt they could demand a more reasonable wage, and something never experienced before, freedom of choice. This euphoria did not last long, but it was enough to enable them to see how much better life could be.

If you look at the Bulwer charts for this period of time you will see the descent listed was very sparse because whole families had died out because of the plague. The labour situation had a cumulative effect on everything, the economy, militia, and people, rich and poor alike.

*Information obtained from various documents.

Then there was the added misery of the poll tax, introduced in 1377-1381 resulting in a rebellion of exceptional ferocity by the Peasants. Evasion of taxes was widespread and the disadvantaged poor expressed violence towards those instigating and recording every petty offence in the Manor-rolls; people felt these officials had betrayed and deserted them miserably. The consequence of these ruthless actions ended in civil war.

On June 1381, Londoners and townsmen joined agricultural workers from all over the East and Southeast. The ebb and flow of supply and demand had turned full circle; the day of labour surplus had turned to a shortage and gave them a sense of power. The people took action! Wool and grain growing industries were the first to taste their fury and received the full impact of the unrest and vengeance.

Converging on London they were joined by a multitude from Kent and Essex led by Wat Tyler and John Ball, a priest. The local people assisted them. Prisons were thrown open, the homes of magistrates and ministers were wrecked and the Tower of London was ransacked. England feared a wave of attacks from France where the situation was even worse. A meeting was arranged with King Richard but cancelled over rumours that men from Blackheath had attacked the property of Royal advisors.

The Palace of Savoy, home of John of Gaunt, (the Kings uncle), was attacked and burned to the ground. The King commanded the crowds to disperse but to no avail, and he fled for his life to the Tower. On 14th June 1381 officials met rebels at Smithfield where King Richard aged only 14 years came face to face with Wat Tyler their leader. Even though Tyler was wounded they still presented their case to the King, who pretended to agree.

Another meeting was arranged after which the Lord Mayor of London, William of Walworth ran Wat Tyler through with his sword and beheaded him. The fearful crowd then dispersed although violence continued in East Anglia. The Prior of Bury St. Edmunds, St. John de Cambridge was mobbed, chased by the crowd and beheaded. His body left in the fields of Mildenhall, Norfolk for the birds; his head displayed with that of John Cavendish a Justice. Henry Rye and Robert de Salle (rebels) were seen running from the scene of the murders.

On the 15th June legal and local government officials suffered in Norfolk, Manor Rolls were destroyed and Manor Houses lay to waste. On 17th June in Norwich, lawyers were targeted. The Priories of Carrow and St. Benet were destroyed. Henry de Spencer, [probably ancestor of the late Princess Diana] opposed the rebels, rode around the county like a bounty hunter seeking them out.

Also on the 17th June **William Bulwer** [married to **Alice Pickering** who you will see in the family charts from about this time] spent the night at Rougham to meet William Ropere, then traveled from village to village gathering men endeavoring to create mayhem. Uprisings in the whole of the area of South Greenhoe resulted in John Palgrave fleeing for his life**.**

William Bulwer met the main body of rebels 18th-20th June overseeing their defeat in a battle near North Walsham. Much information was gathered in documents describing these events; four regions were involved in West Norfolk, and quickly spread across the county. Nothing more was heard of many taking part in the uprising at Palgrave on the 18th of June.

John Betts and Hugh Butcher turned up at Hartly threatening to behead John Wolterton unless he paid them twenty pounds, after this John Betts was arrested, but [later acquitted]. **Thomas Gissing/Malet** [you can read about him in the item on Gissing] was imprisoned in the Tower of London for a time, but no further records have been found about him.

The Black Death also caused a breakdown in order. **John Bulwer** was charged with trespass, for leading his farm animals backwards and forwards trampling over his neighbour John Palgrave's crops and also stealing farm animals and implements. Philip Drynal of Hopton in Little Cressingham was less fortunate, was arrested and beheaded, others were made fugitives.

Another group at Geldere and Metford, numbering about 200 men, led by **John Boys** of the Grimshaw Hundred, who on the dates of the 17th -18th June followed the track of what is now the B1109 Kimberly Hackford Road, Norfolk.

On the Saham Toney road they stole and pillaged. At Holme the monks received the distressing news of the beheading of John de Cambridge. After the rebels were defeated came the punishments, some tenants were then re-admitted to lands, though not if they had withheld their services or there were non-attendances in the court, all these people were punished and disinherited.

The hated Poll Tax where everyone over the age of 15 years had to pay one shilling, [a substantial amount in those times] was lifted. Wat Tyler had died without gaining better pay or conditions for the peasants who returned to their homes, back to a life of hard work and deprivation. King Richard temporally lost much of his power and any promises that were made to the peasants were broken. Those kings who seek to circumvent the system and rule alone more often than not paid dearly for it.

Sir John Falstaff
One of the notable men of Norwich

Sir John Falstaff was one of England's great military captains of the Middle Ages; a soldier of great fame who lived in the reign of Henry 5th but later was imprisoned in the Tower of London. On his release he built and owned Caister Castle near Yarmouth [now a motor museum]. He also lived in a great mansion in Norwich that is thought to have been demolished in 1657 and was replaced by the present building that we know today as the Samson and Hercules at Tombland; [in recent years a leisure complex] this will be mentioned again later in the book.

Samson and Hercules stands on the site of a Great Mansion owned by Sir John Falstaff
Plate 47

Caister Castle built by Sir John Falstaff
Plate 47[a]

The 100 years war with France had its roots in the conflict of 1066 but was formally established in 1328 with the death of Charles 4th [of France] who died without an heir and Edward 3[rd](of England) claimed the French Throne. In 1351 the French threatened to invade as Philip de Valoise wished to give England as a wedding present to his son. In England Henry 5th became king in 1409, he married Katherine de Valoise daughter of Charles 6th of France and later when Charles went insane, he claimed the throne of France and that started the war.

Falstaff commanded the archers at Agincourt in 1415 distinguishing himself by his military service. He won a remarkable victory [1429] in the battle of Herrings by forming a defensive barrier of Herring boats to beat off the French army, but was defeated at Potiers by *Joan of Arc. It was asserted in one of the books that we read that Sir John Falstaff, who was one of William Shakespeare's greatest characters in his plays, was portrayed as a braggart, rogue, drunkard and thief, whether in real life he was any of these we are not aware.

*Joan of Arc [1412 -31] was an illiterate French peasant girl who decisively turned the tide of her country's fortunes in the hundred years war. She was captured by the Burgundians, sold to the English and died at the stake 1431. Joan was made a saint and heroine of France 1920.

Chart of Kings and Queens from Henry the 7th 1485

This chart is to help explain the turmoil of the royal line at this time and is to be used with text

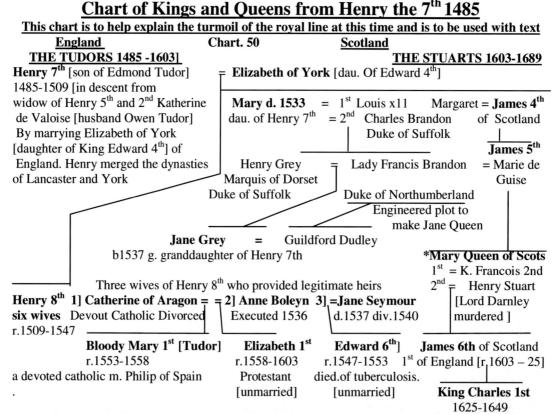

England   Chart. 50   Scotland

THE TUDORS 1485 -1603]   **THE STUARTS 1603-1689**

Henry 7th [son of Edmond Tudor] = **Elizabeth of York** [dau. Of Edward 4th]
1485-1509 [in descent from
widow of Henry 5th and 2nd Katherine
de Valoise [husband Owen Tudor]
By marrying Elizabeth of York
[daughter of King Edward 4th] of
England. Henry merged the dynasties
of Lancaster and York

Mary d. 1533 = 1st Louis x11   Margaret = **James 4th**
dau. of Henry 7th = 2nd Charles Brandon   of Scotland
       Duke of Suffolk

Henry Grey = Lady Francis Brandon   **James 5th**
Marquis of Dorset   = Marie de
Duke of Suffolk   Duke of Northumberland   Guise
       Engineered plot to
         make Jane Queen

Jane Grey = Guildford Dudley   ***Mary Queen of Scots**
b1537 g. granddaughter of Henry 7th   1st = K. Francois 2nd
       2nd = Henry Stuart

Three wives of Henry 8th who provided legitimate heirs   [Lord Darnley

Henry 8th 1] Catherine of Aragon = = **2] Anne Boleyn 3]** =**Jane Seymour**   murdered]
six wives Devout Catholic Divorced   Executed 1536   d.1537 div.1540
r.1509-1547

Bloody Mary 1st [Tudor]   **Elizabeth 1st**   **Edward 6th]**   **James 6th** of Scotland
r.1553-1558   r.1558-1603   r.1547-1553   1st of England [r. 1603 – 25]
a devoted catholic m. Philip of Spain   Protestant   died.of tuberculosis.
.   [unmarried]   [unmarried]   **King Charles 1st**
       1625-1649

Jane was great-grand daughter of Henry 7th; she took the crown four days after Edward 6th died by his will and was Queen for nine days. After a few months she was executed along with her husband by Queen Mary 1st. [Bloody Mary] of England. See page 229. Mary Queen of Scots 1542-1587 by marriage became Mary Queen of France] was a half French, Catholic and granddaughter of James 4th and Margaret Tudor [daughter of Henry 7th of England]. See Royal line page 502

THE TUDORS
HENRY 7th 1485-1509

We include a detailed description of this period so you can see how the selfish personal demands of those in power dictated a change from a Catholic to a Protestant country and which altered social and domestic arrangements in the land and changed everyone's way of life. Edward 5th was proclaimed king 1483, but was murdered before his coronation along with his brother Richard, in the Tower of London. When King Richard 3rd [r.1483-1485] was killed at the battle of Bosworth and his wife Ann and their son Edward had died, This ended the Plantagenet dynasty and the War of the Roses. Henry 7th [1485-1509] claimed the crown and was the first Tudor monarch. He was the son of Edward Tudor (Earl of Richmond) and Margaret Beaufort a descendant of Edward 3rd through John of Gaunt. Henry united the houses of York and Lancaster by marrying Elizabeth of York, which brought stability and by keeping strict control over a united nation and its purse strings. He was a devoted husband and father but lived a lonely unhappy life after the death of his wife.

Eldest son of Henry 7th Prince Arthur died 1509 should have married Catherine of Aragon [later she married his brother Henry 8th.]

HENRY THE EIGHTH
born 1491 – died 1547

Henry 8th succeeded to the throne following the death of his brother Arthur. His reign changed the course of the nation's history as his many marriages and divorce problems caused unrest and turmoil between Catholics and dissenters who were beginning to question the catholic faith in favour of new religious ideals. These revisionists led by a Swiss cleric named Calvin beganwhat was the start of the reformation. As a young man Henry 8th was self indulgent, pursuing his sports the same way as he did his ladies, his actions both strong willed and ruthless, in order to obtain his selfish desires. The antics of those in power also affected the lives of our ancestors. **Simon Bulwer** (married to **Jone Elwyn**) and **Thomas** of Hainford (married **Antonia Claxton**) were alive when Henry 8th became king in 1509 at the age of 18. At this time Henry's flagship 'The Mary Rose' was built, the first galleon to have cannons that fired a broadside. Unfortunately the crew was unruly and probably caused it to sink in calm water near Portsmouth c.1545 on its maiden voyage. It was raised from the seabed in recent years, and is seen on public display at Portsmouth.

Henry, determined to provide a male heir to succeed to the throne married six times, and in order to rid himself of a wife, person or any religious obstacle that stood in the way of his demands he used stories about misuse of property, rumours of corruption in the abbeys, priories and monasteries throughout the country as an excuse to destroy them. After being excommunicated from the Catholic faith, he dissolved and devastated the monk's habitations. The great cathedrals and abbeys across the land were plundered of their treasures, most ending up in Henry's coffers. Henry's six wives were; 1st wife Catherine of Aragon, [Spanish princess m.1509] a catholic largely responsible for events of the reformation; produced a daughter Mary [Bloody Mary, a catholic]. 2nd wife Anne Boleyn had a love affair with Henry, causing Catherine's downfall and foreshadows the historical events the fall of Cardinal Wolsey etc;

Anne had an temper that Henry had cause to regret and their marriage produced again only a daughter, Elizabeth [later Queen of England and a protestant] who continued the succession. His 3rd wife Jane Seymour died shortly after she gave birth to Henry's only son Edward [who died young]. His 4th wife was Catherine Howard, the second to be accused of infidelity and executed. 5th wife was Anne of Cleves. The 6th and last wife of Henry 8th was Katherine Parr who outlived him.

Many Priors disagreed with the Chief House of St. Albans and took advantage of the situation, becoming unscrupulous and irresponsible, selling what they could steal including the silver; a twelfth century seal was used to defraud when tenancies were granted on Ladies Day.

THE DISSOLUTION OF THE MONASTERIES
With Particular Attention to Bynham Priory

Henry came into conflict with the catholic churches over his several divorces. When his wife failed to provide an heir to the throne, he sought the help of Cardinal Wolsey who tried to persuade the Pope to annul this marriage on the advice of Thomas Cromwell [Earl of Essex].

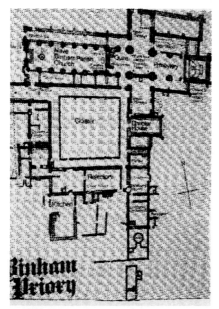

Ancient plan of Binham Priory Plate 48

The Pope refused, so the King prepared to rebel against the established order, broke with Rome and removed all the accumulative wealth of the monasteries, which, he claimed for the crown. This created a powerful class with a stake in a Protestant successor to the throne and he formed this new religion with himself as head of a Protestant state.

There were still conflicts as the Priory of Binham Norfolk was still rebelling against the mother church of St. Albans. Its construction was not completed until the middle of the 13th century, and was a copy of the Cathedral in Rheims, France.

The Ruins of Binham Priory   Plate 48 [a]

The Priory came under a battering from Henry's wrath; all its wealth and possessions were stripped out. Much of the monastery was pulled down and building materials taken for other uses, until only seven bays were left of the once huge monastery, but there is still enough left to visualise what it looked like.

It is part of **Bulwer** history [this priory was built by **Peter Valois** whose daughter married **Roger de Dalling**]; we visited this Priory and were overawed by the massive structure still being used as a parish church. Although greatly reduced to only one fifth of its original size the remains are still very imposing. On entering the site through arched ghettoises, you are confronted by the massive gable end of the building with what had once been an enormous and beautifully elaborate window, this was bricked up in 1809. The rest of the site contains some well-maintained ruins of the various room layouts, which are clearly marked as to their purpose.

The abbey was involved in the *reformation that had already divided Europe causing more unrest. Binham was given over to Thomas Paston, the details clearly outlined in the Paston letters written during the 33rd year of Henry 8th. In Blickling church [North Isle] on the gravestone of Geoffrey Boleyn, you can see portraits of himself and his wife, their five sons at his feet, and their four daughters at her feet. Over their heads is a text in Latin, which says 'this Geoffrey was father to Sir Geoffrey Boleyn, Lord Mayor of London, and great grandfather to Queen Elizabeth'.

Also from this family was John Boleyne of Salle, who lived in 1283, who was probably the son of Simon Boleyne who purchased these lands by fine, in the 37th year of Henry 3$^{rd.}$ In Bloomfield's History, under the town of Blickling it says that Simon Boleyne's mother was sister and heir of **Robert Malet**. She had lands in Walpole, Stalham, and Brumstead in Norfolk and the family is said to have had an interest in the Hawes and Morehall in this town. King Henry 8th died in 1547 AD. son Edward now nine years old succeeded him.

EDWARD 6th AND KETT'S REBELLION (1549 AD)
Kett and his men lost the battle but had stood their ground against greed and power

The introduction of a new sheep farming industry and its low manpower requirements needed more land; this progression answered the greed of land owning Barons and solved the labour problem. Barons cast their envious eyes on common land ripping out the existing fences and hedges, enclosing them within their own boundaries, this caused much stress to countryfolk.

These Landlords cast people from their small cottages and places where their homes once stood were leveled and returned to fields for sheep farming. Possessions were left to rot in the fields as the landowners grabbed all the territory they could. The sick were evicted and the small strips of common ground the poor once used were taken over. With this body of men and their families now without a home, work or money; the people furious and hungry started to react.

The Barons grew richer, religious leaders said nothing. This dispassionate view of the clerics, eager to ingratiate themselves with those with money and power, raised the anger of the people to such an extent it suddenly boiled over, leading to assaults on Abbots their Abbeys, Monasteries and the clergy in general.**From every village and homestead they came, carrying any weapon they could find, scythes, pitchforks, and home made weapons,

*See item on Huguenot's page 232 ** [similar in content as the army of Bodica and more recently through lack of arms, "the Home Guard" during the Second World War].

Soon they were twenty thousand strong marching to Cringleford, near Norwich, crossing the river at Eaton to camp in Bowthorpe Woods. Even more arrived as the news spread. The great uprising had started.

At the same time the soaring prices of wool for the manufacture of cloth increased the anxieties of the people even more. With all the inhuman acts that had gone before the Barons saw opportunities to exploit the new wool weaving and cloth trade, leaving the main industries in turmoil. The people living in the towns were furious, trying to find the extra cash they would need to cover new taxes.

A fair was held at Wymondham in Norfolk where many people attended a meeting to hear what could be done to win back the right to get fences removed from enclosures on their land. Complaints went unheeded so the men of Attleborough and nearby villages decided to remove these fences themselves. Sergeant Flowerdew's fences were first to go. Robert Kett and his brother angered him, so he sent them to Wymondham.

In 1549 AD Robert Kett and his brother held several Manors in the district and agreed to meet the people at the old oak tree near Wymondham [which is still in existence] to hear their grievances. They sympathized with the terrible injustices to the poor and decided to act for them by firstly tearing down their own fences. Both brothers agreed to become the leaders of their revolt that came to be known as Kett's Rebellion; they called on the people to stand firm, and they did.

The Kett's sent men armed with signed documents called 'The Rebels Complaints' to all the country houses of the Barons and landowners, requesting food provisions for the camp. Anyone who enclosed land was brought into the camp and tried, especially if they were among those who had ill-treated or turned out the poor, some were even hanged for their abuses.

The city dwellers of Norwich became frightened, and sent the kings' herald to offer pardons, though he suggested that rebels should leave quietly. "Leave quietly"! What an offer to give to starving men, who had been dispossessed of everything they owned, even in some cases their homes.

The rebels were enraged over this insensitive remark, and hearing of the order for the arrest of Robert Kett they became so aggressive that the Mayor, Aldermen and retinue had to leave quickly and return to Norwich. On their arrival the gates were shut, peace was at an end between the city and the rebels. Kett and his men attacked, captured the city and camped on the high land of Mousehold Heath overlooking Nowich.

They held Norwich for three weeks, hoping that the whole country would rise and free the nation from the greed and cruelty of the Lords. But these hopes were not to be realized so they fought on alone. Among all the tragedy there was a humorous side to events that must have caused a shout of delight and much laughter.

When the Earl of Warwick came with reinforcements to free the city they lost their way and marched straight through to Mousehold heath into the Kett's encampment where they were captured. The supplies and arms were very welcome but it left the Earl of Warwick very embarrassed over this mistake and the loss of these vital weapons and also a deep desire to take revenge.

He found the rebels not only still defying him, but he was probably the butt of jokes on both sides, which made him even more determined to change the situation. Warwick [related to the Mortimer's by marriage] was also part of the de Grey/Beauchamp family. He was a hard unscrupulous individual with no sympathy for the rebel cause.

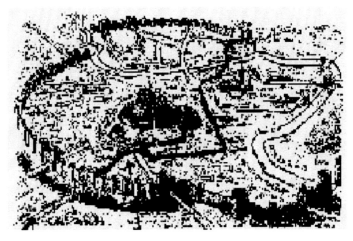

Possible route of Warwick's army

Artists Impression   Plate 49

Kett's encampment on Mousehold Heath, which overlooked the city of Norwich, where he had all the advantages but made the same fatal mistake as King Harold, by leaving an area of high ground he moved to the much lower land of Dussledale, which was between the river and the Cathedral. Everything then came to an end; the fields of Dussledale ran red with blood and were littered with the bodies of the honest men of Norfolk who had only requested a fair deal.

Using force Warwick entered the city by the Brazen Door in Westlegate Street, and quickly took possession. His first task was to hang sixty men without any trial or questions.

The poorly armed rebels were only a rag tag body of starving men, waging a fight against nobility and well-armed soldiers, some of whom were mercenaries from Germany, paid and trained to kill.

They made their point but there was a price to pay

The price was paid in the blood and tears of those who dared to defy the greed of those in power. The rebels had won a moral victory but had lost the power struggle. Men were hung by the hundred, some innocents were pardoned, others were caught running away, and all were poor wretches who could hardly afford to live, just wanting something better for their families.

Iron Bands supporting tree

Sign

Kett's Oak as it is now
Plate 50

Rhyme;   Ah! Robert Kett, Robert Kett
Lest We Forget. Lest We Forget

Kett and his brother were captured, taken prisoner, tried and condemned to death on 26th Nov. Robert was hanged from Norwich Castle 7th Dec.1549. His brother was hung from the church steeple at Wymondham for all to see. The men that were left sang a rhyme [as above] summing up what they felt.

Nobody did forget, for Kett is now part of our Norfolk heritage, a wealthy man who had no need to fight for the poor but both he and his brother did just that. The old oak tree is still living, so old it has steel bands round it to hold it together and cement poured into its hollow trunk to support it; classed as an ancient monument fenced off and maintained by 'The National Trust'.

It can be clearly seen by the side of the road that hundreds of motorists pass every day, mostly unaware of the important happening that took place there so many years ago and started a revolution that affects our lives today. Enclosures of land were still carried out, but there was no spirit left in the people to fight it or dare to protest. However people eventually reap what they sow. Warwick paid for his arrogant behavior when he tried to bully young King Edward aged nine, who succeeded his father Henry 8th in 1547.

During this period of time [from 1400 to 1600] our family ancestors were, **Roger** died1483 and **Catherine de Dalling, Simon** d.1504 alias **Bulwer** who married **Margaret,** and **Roger** d.1517 married to **Elizabeth.**

At the time of **Simon and Jone** the family split into two main factions. **Thomas** [will written 1607] took his young bride **Antonia** to live in Hainford Hall and **Roger** initiated the family branch of **Bulwer/Lytton/Cobbold** of Knebworth. There was no modern news media like today as we hear within a minute of any incident even thousands of miles away; it was days or weeks before news spread by kings messenger's or travelers was heard; fact was often mixed with gossip. **Roger de Dalling** and his son **Simon de Dalling** must have learned of the murder [1483] of the young princes Edward 5th and Richard, [sons of Edward 4th 1461-1483 and Elizabeth Woodville].

The Bulwer/ Dalling families of this period

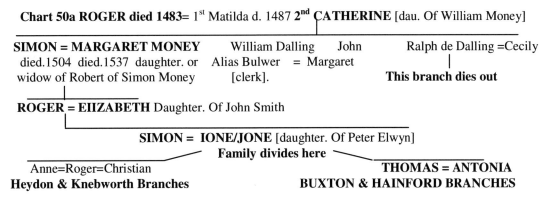

Chart 50a ROGER died 1483= 1st Matilda d. 1487 **2nd CATHERINE** [dau. Of William Money]

SIMON = MARGARET MONEY	William Dalling	John	Ralph de Dalling =Cecily
died.1504 died.1537 daughter. or	Alias Bulwer	= Margaret	
widow of Robert of Simon Money	[clerk].		**This branch dies out**

ROGER = EIIZABETH Daughter. Of John Smith

SIMON = IONE/JONE [daughter. Of Peter Elwyn]
Family divides here

Anne=Roger=Christian	THOMAS = ANTONIA
Heydon & Knebworth Branches	**BUXTON & HAINFORD BRANCHES**

NOTE; FAMILY MEMBERS IN CAPITAL LETTERS

THE ARUNDAL FAMILY AGAIN INVOLVED
In using Lady Jane Grey as a pawn in a bid for power

We have now come to the time when the two young princes had been murdered. Henry 8th [1509-1547 son of Henry 7th] married six times, had died, and his young son King Edward 6th was in poor health. This left Henry's 8th daughters, Princess Mary a devout catholic and Princess Elizabeth a protestant as prospective heirs but the Arundals and Warwick families still had ambitions to by-pass them both and insert their bloodline onto the throne of England. The Arundel families were elevated, mainly due to marriages into rich and well connected families, starting from a single Cornish manor to twenty-eight larger houses throughout the West of England.

They were involved with Ann Boleyn, Henry 8th the Reformation, and the cruel murder of the two young princes Edward and Richard in the tower. Like all families they had their hero's and some wayward members, such as James Tyrell who married into their family. He was knighted in 1471 and executed for treason in 1502. It is quite clear that the Arundel /Warwick families had a very strong influence over the succession of the English monarchy and manipulated events using the power of four earldoms and their money to make or destroy kings. Richard Neville [Earl of Warwick] was known as the kingmaker.

After Edward died the nation was fearful of Henry 8th daughter Mary [the next in lineage]. Her fanatical ambition was to make Britain a catholic state again if she succeeded King Edward. John Dudley Duke of Northumberland, a powerful Protestant, was Regent to young King Edward; he was also father-in-law to Lady Jane Grey whose husband was the Earl of Warwick, [see p.230].

Due to the controversial marriages of Henry 8th Northumberland plotted to persuade Edward to make Henry 8th daughters Mary and Elizabeth illegitimate, thereby leaving his daughter in law Jane (by this time the Lady Jane Grey a relative of Edward 6th see page 221] and great granddaughter to Henry 7th to succeed to the throne.

In 1553 at the age of 17 Jane Grey became a helpless pawn following Edward's death. A personal and religious power struggle began and Northumberland's plan was enacted. The Princesses were declared illegitimate and Jane seized the crown but the plot failed as she was not accepted and was Queen for only nine days.

Mary became Queen and imprisoned Jane and her supporters in the Tower of London. Mary, only daughter of Henry 8th and Catherine of Aragon provided a text book example of a ruined life caused by childhood trauma of a parents divorce resulting with fanatic indulgence to cling to her catholic upbringing. She came to the throne and against the will of the people prepared to marry a catholic, Phillip of Spain and create a catholic state which led to conspiracies to overthrow her but Queen Mary 1st 1553-58 [Bloody Mary] avoided the grasp of Warwick.

Anger against Mary's proposed marriage to Philip of Spain increased and a rebellion led by Sir Thomas Wyatt marched to London but were defeated. On the same day in 1554 Mary beheaded Jane and her husband Dudley. Thomas Wyatt was executed two months later. By now the Catholic Church was involved in the reformation that was already devouring Europe.

Mary was sincere, devout and kind to those of her own faith but became known as 'Bloody Mary' because of her vicious callous attitude toward all Protestants and lacked skills of administration. These events of personal and religious ideologies were of major importance to the nation. Mary died childless in 1558. Her half sister Elizabeth 1st Protestant daughter of Henry 8th and Anne Boleyn became Queen.

Some of the information their family history contained in this section were derived from an article in the Daily Mail March 21 1996. See item on Baconsthorpe page 148

FAMILY TREE SHOWING ROYAL MARRIAGE CONNECTIONS TO THE ARUNDALLS

Chart 51

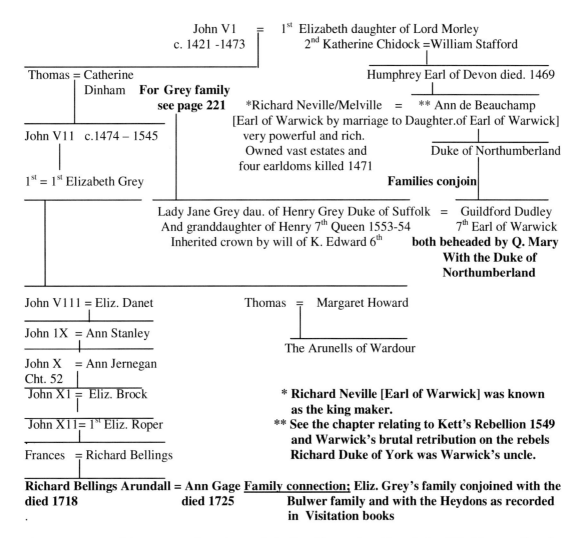

As a note of interest the Arundel family who lived in Waldour Castle Wiltshire had a unique history dating from the twelfth century. A priceless collection of 28,000 documents was found which had until 1975 been stored in an old pram in Arundel Castle.

The the combined efforts of Cornwall and Wiltshire Record Office's, jointly purchased, restored, indexed them were made available for a closer examination.

This historical collection from a single family details gives a record of the development of Britain from the 12th century. The family lived in Cornwall and Wiltshire and were closely involved with kings and princes.

Queen Elizabeth 1st
(GOOD QUEEN BESS)
1558 – 1603

When Queen Elizabeth 1st became Queen it was a time of conquest, a time to build an empire, Sir Francis Drake sailed the seven seas and piracy was rife. It was one of the most exciting times to live and a time of hope if you had the money! Having said that it must be noted that for the first time the needs of the poor were seriously considered. The Elizabethan Poor Law was introduced in 1601 as a consequence of the religious reformation some seventy years earlier and those in power realizing the link between poverty and diseases that spread among rich and poor alike.

Life was still bad for the poor, most of whom lived in filthy, unhygienic conditions, ripe for the spread of disease, so people were asked to clean the streets especially the area in front of their homes. This work was unsupervised but if the order to clean was not carried out, it was repeated and offenders given extra chores such as leveling the paths, cleaning the ducts and gutters.

As there was no sewage system townspeople discarded the contents of their chamber pots on to roadways, so Elizabethan houses were built with the first floors overhanging the ground floor level. This gave limited protection for those passing underneath, not leaving them smelling of roses or gaining decorations of any kind. Throwing rubbish into the river in Norwich was not allowed beyond the chain at Carrow. In 1558 water pipes were laid from the river to the market place and also to the houses of the rich.

James Bulwer and his son **John** must have appreciated these improvements. Guilds were set up for young boys in the different trades, but only the rich and powerful had the opportunities to acquire the knowledge and skills of the gold and silversmiths; others had to take what was left. Our ancestor **Thomas Bulwer** who lived in Saxthorpe was apprenticed to a shoemaker, later his son was a Glover [a keeper of records].

This age of adventure could also bring heartache to some, as we noted. **Alexander Bulwer's** son **Thomas** went off to seek his fortune abroad never to return. This must have brought sorrow to his father as we notice that in his will he left one hundred pounds to his son Thomas in case he returned after his own death. If he should stay six months, the money would be his, though he sadly concluded that his son was probably already dead.

Religious Trouble Starts To Brew In Europe
Circa. 1515 AD.

The Reformation caused many Huguenots, [strict French Protestants] to flee from France to England in 1572. Queen Elizabeth although a Protestant was not personally devoted to any religion so she tried to strike a balance between the different faiths. We will now explain how and why our Grandmothers Bulwer's family [the Williment line] arrived from Europe to settle in England. Throughout history the various forms of belief have created upheavals between families and nations, some peaceful others autocratic to the point of genocide and murder to protect that belief. It was at this time that various factions in Europe took positive stances particularly in France, Holland, Britain, and Spain. Queen Elizabeth took an active interest in government, her upbringing on the fringes of court made her cautious with diplomatic decisions, especially on religion, but her support of the Protestants began to upset Catholics at home and abroad, particularly in Spain.

All church denominations became involved in a reformation that was about to devour *Europe. Serious divisions of religious beliefs emerged when some Protestants sought to purify their faith removing Catholic philosophy; teaching people to lead a simple quiet life devoted to their creed. In Europe this sect was called Huguenot's, in England they were Puritans. Laws were made in England that declared Queen Elizabeth the supreme governor of the Church of England and all Englishmen were required to attend church services. No doubt she found that to control the church herself was a means to control her subjects and an excellent method of communication throughout her kingdom.

Queen Elizabeth's encouragement of the Protestants and her popularity from loyal subjects caused more awareness of class and creed. The ways of the affluent were disliked; different ideas began to emerge that showed in Puritan dress, almost like uniforms. It must have been strange to see these contrasts of style all mixing in the streets of Norwich where the Puritan movement began. The colourful dress of the wealthy contrasting with the grey/black/white attire of a new cult of people calling themselves Puritans and the dirty ragged appearance of the very poor. In France similar lines of reasoning was taking place; Catherine De Medici, an Italian catholic, niece of Pope Clement 7th daughter of Lorenzo de Medici, [Valois/Carolingian dynasty] became a pawn of Clement to further his alliance with King Francis 1st of France. He arranged her marriage to the future Henry 2nd of France where she was until the birth of her numerous children received with hostility.

*However in the end the Puritan situation of unrest in Europe spilled into Britain and Spain.

Katherine Valois of England

Katherine **Valois** daughter of Charles 6th of France, married Henry 5th King of England [r.1413-22 House of Lancaster], was determined to unify under a strong **Valois** rule, asking Huguenots and Catholics to debate. On his death she married Owen Tudor son of Edmund Tudor of Richmond England [Welsh origin] and deciding to set seals on peace negotiations by marrying her daughter, Margaret de **Valois** to Henry de Bourbon King of Navarre, one of the most powerful of the Huguenots.

This resulted in more arguments and violence but in the end her support of the Huguenot's resulted in civil war in France and open war between Catholic Spain and Protestant [Puritan] England. After a decade of civil war, peace was arranged in France. Soon after this the Huguenot General de Coligny started to try and manipulate the Valois Dynasty Kings in order to get help for the Huguenots in Holland [historians are very vague about the Kings of this time] where uncertain we have left names out.

Catherine de Medici, of France did not agree with her husband in supporting Holland as there was fighting in that country. She feared by withdrawing troops King Philip might attack France, as he was a Hapsburg. His family was a long-term rival of the **Valois** Kings of France, and Europe's wealthiest Monarch, a proclaimed guardian of the Catholic faith. An attempt was made on the Huguenot General Coligny's life in, which possibly Catherine was involved. The next evening the royal council met to discus the growing tension between the two religious groups; Catherine de Medici's son Charles, despite his own regard for de Coligny reluctantly decided to oppose him but this only stimulated an increase in the fighting.

After her husband's death in 1559 and during the reign of the next monarch France again started to divide along religious lines. She took great interest in the political life of France and sought earnestly to create unity and find suitable husbands for her daughters and thrones abroad for her sons. Unfortunately she had not grasped the division within France over religion that became more and more apparent when she blundered from one mistake into another. Queen Catherine did her best to try and unite the various religious factions, but the Huguenots were victimized and later many were driven out of Europe by force, some arriving in England. The Royal purse was empty, caused by the dynastic wars between **Valois** and the German royal dynasty of Hapsburgh.

Note; The frail 15-year old boy Francis Valois 2nd who became King of France was of the *Carolingian dynasty that snatched power from the Merovingian hereditary line in the time of Carloman resulted in the Valois families taking control over the thrones of France and Italy in 647 AD

English Royal Line.   **Scottish Royal Line**   **French Royal Line**

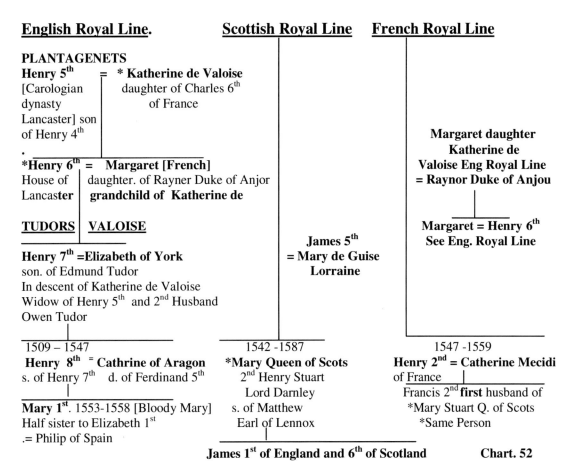

PLANTAGENETS
Henry 5th = * Katherine de Valoise
[Carologian   daughter of Charles 6th
dynasty   of France
Lancaster] son
of Henry 4th

Margaret daughter
Katherine de
Valoise Eng Royal Line
= Raynor Duke of Anjou

*Henry 6th = Margaret [French]
House of   daughter. of Rayner Duke of Anjor
Lancaster   **grandchild of Katherine de**

TUDORS | VALOISE

Margaret = Henry 6th
See Eng. Royal Line

James 5th
= Mary de Guise
Lorraine

Henry 7th =Elizabeth of York
son. of Edmund Tudor
In descent of Katherine de Valoise
Widow of Henry 5th and 2nd Husband
Owen Tudor

1509 – 1547	1542 -1587	1547 -1559
Henry 8th = Cathrine of Aragon	*Mary Queen of Scots	Henry 2nd = Catherine Mecidi
s. of Henry 7th d. of Ferdinand 5th	2nd Henry Stuart	of France
	Lord Darnley	Francis 2nd first husband of
Mary 1st. 1553-1558 [Bloody Mary]	s. of Matthew	*Mary Stuart Q. of Scots
Half sister to Elizabeth 1st	Earl of Lennox	*Same Person
.= Philip of Spain		

James 1st of England and 6th of Scotland   Chart. 52

In the forefront in the religious wars was the family of de Guise who were no friends of the *Valois dynasty [the kings of France at that time]. This proved quite a problem for the troops of Scotland whose loyalties were divided, because they provided a bodyguard for the Valois Kings and had previously led the army of Francois to retrieve Calais in 1558. They were also supporters of the senior house of Lorraine, which proved a dilemma but this was solved later when the Valois dynasty became extinct.

Also at this time Martin Luther started to spread the influence of the Huguenots; by 1559 their churches numbered 2000, one third of France was now Protestant and they began to enter politics. **The country began to divide along lines drawn over religious aspects making local nobles take sides, resulting in eight religious wars that affected the realm over the next half century. It presented a fascinating picture of world development and by looking at the charts you can see the trends of these interrelated families. From 1562-1570 however forging the national identity was still the main concern. The nobles formed a powerful pyramid, and the King of France would have been the apex.

*See item regarding the start of the Carolingians/ Italian and French Dynasties
** During this time due to assassination, lack of heirs and rivalry, the War of the Roses also occurred at the same time as the religious battles in France.

1572, Day of Death for Huguenots in Paris.

A great purge took place, many fled from France, some to England but for those who remained Sunday August 24th 1572, was a day of death. The Bells rang out over the quiet City of Paris, a signal for all Catholics of the city to rise against the Huguenots. Without warning a troop of soldiers led by the Duke of Anjou marched into the house of General Gaspard de Coligny the leader of the Huguenots.

One soldier ran his pike through the General another threw his lady out of a window down to the soldiers waiting in the street below, to be murdered; if people walking past did not have a white cross on their cap they were killed on the spot. Over 3000 Protestants were butchered on that day. This massacre was the result of religious and dynastic rivalry in France between the Huguenots and their Roman Catholic, Guise opponents. At the centre of the web of intrigue was Catherine de Medici of Italy's most powerful family the **Valois** dynasty, determined to preserve her adopted country and her families' royal power.

In spite of her attempts she did not obtain peace in her time as she had hoped, though it did come through King Henry 4th of France, the same Henry of Navarre who married her daughter Margaret de **Valois.** He persuaded the country to cease hostilities, giving freedom of worship to the Huguenots, conditions that remained until the time of Louis xiv.

The Flemish silk weavers started to move into England from the 27th August 1572 in larger numbers to escape the purge. Some settled in Norfolk and among these were probably ancestors on our grandmother's **Williment's** line.

The Willimott`s /Wiggett`s etc. were possibly of this exodus and those that came to Norwich brought prosperity as their skills in weaving made Norwich famous. At first they were called Strangers and were at a ratio of 8000 out of a total of 16000 [about 50% of the population] and reluctant to share their hard won knowledge with people who were for the most part hostile to them. Strangers Hall still exists in Norwich and was devoted to the Weavers.

The Puritans in England wished to lead a simple life and a return to the basic teachings of the bible and to correct the attitudes of pleasure loving uncaring people of the court and they were jeered at in the street. It was these contrasting attitudes that were again to sow seeds of discontent and conflict, soon to turn to a hatred, which our family was to be drawn into.

While the Puritans lived their somber life style and the poor struggled to live, the *Duke of Norfolk had built his Palace near the river in Norwich in the time of Henry 8th. Except for the Royal Palace there were none to equal it. No expense was spared for the great feasts where dishes that contained the most exquisite expensive cuisine were served on gold and silver platters. The guests, dressed in the finest of clothes, walked off their heavy meals through the grounds and along the riverbank, seen not only by the hungry populace but also by the Puritans, all of whom wanted this great extravagance and over indulgence stopped.

The building was demolished in 1662, rebuilt by the 6th Duke of Norfolk Lord Henry Howard and used by the family. After a disagreement with the Mayor, Thomas Havers the 8th Duke demolished part of it; the rest was used as a workhouse. Later in 1674 it became a Roman Catholic Chapel, which survived until 1950 but nothing now exists, although this place still retains the name of Duke Street, showing that names from the past still can still revive old memories.

Old Dukes Palace Norwich

Artist impression

Plate 53

David who worked as an electrician for the Eastern Electricity Board [1950] opposite the site of the Dukes Palace remembers that he walked across the road into this very old building, which had a marvelous vaulted ceiling, to view the articles put up for auction each week. After the last war a Public House called the Dukes Palace still stood there but has since disappeared possibly due to the bombing that Norwich received during Second World War, following which the a vast redevelopment program was instigated.

The Dukes Palace was situated in the parish of St. John Maddermarket and nearby is an Elizabethan building called the **Maddermarket, which as far as we know still performs Shakespearean plays. This building stands in Dove Street [opposite Duke Street], which was named after our relative John Dove son of William Dove, a Woolen draper of St. Peter Mancroft, Norwich. John was a brewer who in 1704 married Elizabeth Beevor, more on this family later.

*See Burke's Savilles Guide to Country Houses Vol.3
** Madder is a term used in the dyeing of cloth or sheepskins so we presume this area must have been a market for such a trade. Note; William Shakespeare who lived 1554-1616 married Anne Hathaway; many of his plays depicted life at this time and his works are performed somewhere in the world every day even now.

SPAIN ATTACKS ENGLAND

To recapitulate from previous pages, when Henry 8th died his son Edward ascended the throne in 1547 but he died in 1553. "Bloody Mary" Henry's devoted catholic daughter [from his marriage to Catherine and half- sister to Elizabeth] succeed to the throne. She mistakenly tried to destroy the Protestant Church and marry the Catholic, King Philip of Spain. Sir Thomas Wyatt was determined not to let this happen, he organised a rebellion in London, was defeated and on the same day Mary executed Lady **Jane** who was Queen for nine days in 1553. 1554 Mary married her Spanish king; but he did not return her love. She died one of the most feared English Queens holding a bible stained with tears; Elizabeth succeeded as Queen in 1558. Catholic Spain and Protestant England had long been at odds. Queen Elizabeth encouraged those trying to break the Spanish monopoly on the riches of the New World like Sir Francis Drake who robbed their treasure ships and challenged their sea power. This explains why the animosity built up between the nations.

Relations terminated when she sent soldiers to support the rebellious Dutch, seriously weakening Spain's position as the leading maritime power. These events plus the execution of Mary Queen of Scots [a Catholic], moved Philip of Spain [House of Hapsburgh] to send an Armada, with Duke of Median-Sidonia against England 1587/8. War was never declared King Philip 2nd of Spain but a war began, lasting throughout Elizabeth's reign. attacking first and sank most of the Spanish ships before leaving the port of Cadiz. Another one hundred and thirty Spanish galleons were assembled (68 fighting ships, others carrying 30,000 soldiers and supplies), As a storm dispersed them, they reassembled near Plymouth on July 31[st.]1588. The English, anchored near Plymouth were in two fleets, one under the command of Charles Howard, 1st Earl of Nottingham, with Captains Drake, Frobisher, and Hawkins;.

They attacked but could not break the Spanish formation so called upon the fleet under Lord Henry Seymour anchored in the Channel. The sea battle raged; Yarmouth fearing a landing strengthened the town walls. After losing most of their fleet, due to the weather, lack of supplies and the Duke of Median-Sidonia being desperately ill, the Spanish ran for home. More ships were wrecked by storms on their hasty retreat around Scotland and Ireland. This final smashing of the Spanish navy in 1588 left the English and the Dutch in an almost unchallenged position to colonize and expand trade not only to Europe but the New World and the east. This opened the door to improving the lives of English people, the country becoming richer.

Note; Having command of the high seas it gave Elizabeth and the future monarchs more freedom, and enabled people to be freed from catholic restrictions. It was recorded jokingly Drake "singed King Philip of Spain's beard";

SIR FRANCIS DRAKE AND THE GOLDEN HINDE

On one occasion Drake captured a Spanish galleon and seized a treasure of 26 tons of silver, 13 chests of jewels, coins with 80lbs of gold and had to reduce the weight of his ship by discarding its ballast. Despite Spanish protests over this robbery on the high seas he was knighted by Queen Elizabeth and became Sir Francis Drake.

Although Lord Howard of Ellingham was the Lord High Admiral because of his social rank it was Drake as Vice Admiral who exercised the real leadership, assisted by his kinsman Hawkins. Both

The Golden Hinde   Plate.54   Drake and Hawkins died off the coast of Nombre de Dios in the Caribbean Sea when raiding Spanish settlements, which were a failure due to their disagreeing with each other. The replica of the Golden Hinde visited Great Yarmouth in 1994 to celebrate the 800 years centenary of the Norwich Charter. It was a great attraction and we took the opportunity to see for ourselves what life was like for the crew onboard this famous ship. It was much smaller than we expected and the distance between decks reflected the average *short stature of the occupants of those times and they also kept the centre of gravity low to stop the ship capsizing in gales.

There were sleeping quarters for twenty officers and one hundred and sixty four men. Half the crew would sleep as the others worked; boys would do the lighter work. Food on board frequently went rotten because apart from salting and pickling there was no way to preserve it. An onboard brig was used to hold victims before judgment of misconduct and a great cabin used by the officers to plan the tactics of battle; decks were painted red to cover the bloodstains. The deck was also used for recreation. Another famous ship of these times and also involved in the battle was of the same type and called "The Ark Royal" she carried the Admiral and other important officers. During Elizabeth's' life, although marriage negotiations started with numerous suitors, none were completed and Elizabeth died in 1603 without a husband or an heir. The success of her reign was both national and local government unity with a monarchy that she conducted with firm yet benevolent management and involving a naval enterprise which has never been surpassed.

Note; we have included this information because historically it was the exploits that Drake undertook on this ship that paved the way to create an Empire and national wealth for many generations to come. The average height of an Elizabethan was 5ft. 4` [162. 56 cms.]. Norma [co-author] who is on the short side had difficulty standing upright in this ship.

THE DUEL
From the Visitations Book 1600 AD

As children we lived in Mansfield Lane, Lakenham, Norwich, and walked along streets where we believe a gruesome duel took place between Lord Mansfield [the defender] and Sir John Heidon/Heydon [the challenger] centuries earlier. In those days the sword settled many disputes.

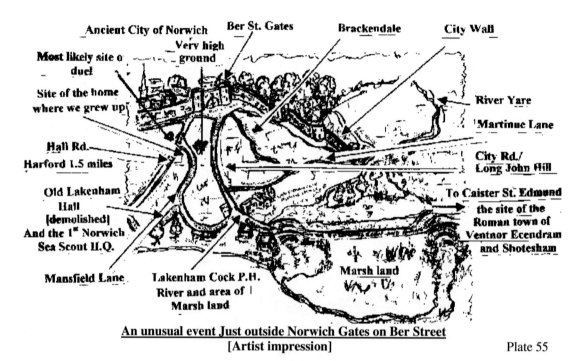

An unusual event Just outside Norwich Gates on Ber Street
[Artist impression]   Plate 55

You can see from our map, the river area that the Lords John Heidon/Heydon and Mansfield passed, could have been where the present Lakenham Cock Public House now stands near the river, which has grassland with a millpond. Traveling to the brow of the hill may have taken them to the junction of the two present highways of Mansfield Lane and Long John Hill where we believe this duel took place, which is approximately 1.5 miles from Harford.

It is not clearly described in the victor's vivid portrayal of the duel and route taken from Norwich but his reports clearly fit the scene, and the roads in the vicinity bear a marked relationship to their names. The land on the hill between the two roadways had many more grassed areas, where we spent many happy hours of our childhood, it is now a housing estate. It is interesting to note that the contour of this area of Norwich [unlike the east toward Yarmouth which is very flat] is very high and slopes off quite steeply into the river valleys; there once must have been large lakes in this district, unlike today as they are now ponds.

A Severed hand in a showcase

The abbreviated accounts of the duel described by Sir Robert Mansfield below.

*"Sir Elwyn Ryche carried me without Ber Street Gate where my dere nephew Kynvett brought Sir John Heidon thither. Whereupon we rid away towards Shotesham, Mr. Doyleys' place and close upon this side of the *water. I pleaded with Elwyn Ryche to go to my nephew Kynvet to the end that we might be dismissed. And he made me take a wai to the top of the hill between two great highways. Where he would, he nedes me leight, for he would ride no further, although he saw company riding on both sides.*

Another account states that the place of this duel was only one mile and a half from Harford, which would make our estimate of the position of the site, seem to be correct. A devious battle then took place, in which Robert Mansfield said,

"Three times I spared the life of Sir John Heidon, and three times he responded with treachery. After receiving severe wounds to his arm, he was forced to sign a document with his good hand."

Artist's impression

The hand of Sir John Heidon   Plate56

[Sir Johns' hand had been severed from one inch below the little finger down to the wrist]. It must have been a macabre sight when this occurred. According to later studies it has been suggested that the hand was not completely severed, but was finally amputated by a skilled person. Sir Robert Mansfield claimed the mutilated hand, had it dried and framed in a box to hang on the wall of his living quarters for years as a prized possession.

The mummified hand was finally lodged in the very old Canterbury Museum together with the full account of the event, where it can be seen today.

When the Romans attacked the small settlement [centuries earlier known as Norwich], they used the route of Long John Hill and the high ridge overlooking the town and river, building a great wide highway on it [Ber St.].

*From visitation book 1600.

The Sequel "The Beast With Five Fingers"
Scenes of the past brings nightmares to the present when Alan finds a cold clammy hand in bed

Over 300 years later someone had the idea of making a film that seemed to be based on this gruesome event, though somewhat changed in content, starring the actor Peter Lorrie. It was called 'The Beast With Five Fingers', which depicted a hand that had been nailed to a board. One night it came to life and escaped from its resting-place to crawl along the picture rail to his bed and strangled him. Our family, who liked a good story, were given permission by our parents to see the film at the cinema. It was a mistake! In the middle of the night piercing screams awakened everyone. "I've caught it; I've caught it, Arrrhh"!!! We all converged on the source of the disturbance, the shouting continued until the light was switched on, and the gentle voice of our mother could be heard.

''Hey! Hey! Calm down calm down. Its all right you've been laying on your arm, and its gone dead, let me rub it for you it will bring the circulation back''. By now everyone was in the room demanding to know what was happening, we were all ordered back to bed, satisfied that Alan had not caught the beast with five fingers after all. Though for future reference watching horror pictures was banned for the younger ones of the family. The chart below indicates the time period of this event [1600]

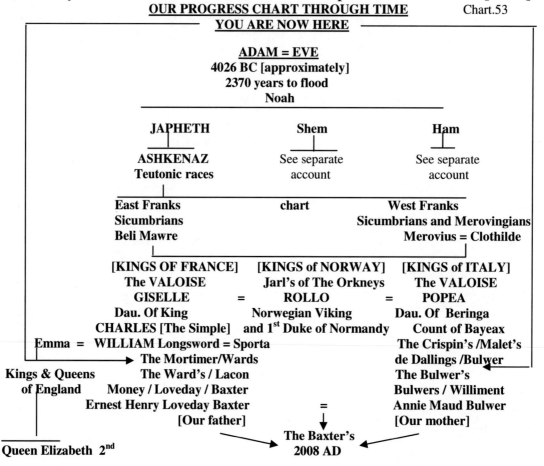

OUR PROGRESS CHART THROUGH TIME   Chart.53

YOU ARE NOW HERE

ADAM = EVE
4026 BC [approximately]
2370 years to flood
Noah

JAPHETH	Shem	Ham
ASHKENAZ	See separate	See separate
Teutonic races	account	account

East Franks	chart	West Franks
Sicumbrians		Sicumbrians and Merovingians
Beli Mawre		Merovius = Clothilde

[KINGS OF FRANCE]	[KINGS of NORWAY]	[KINGS of ITALY]
The VALOISE	Jarl's of The Orkneys	The VALOISE
GISELLE =	ROLLO =	POPEA
Dau. Of King	Norwegian Viking	Dau. Of Beringa
CHARLES [The Simple]	and 1st Duke of Normandy	Count of Bayeax
Emma = WILLIAM Longsword = Sporta		The Crispin's /Malet's
The Mortimer/Wards		de Dallings /Bulwer
Kings & Queens The Ward's / Lacon		The Bulwer's
of England Money / Loveday / Baxter		Bulwers / Williment
Ernest Henry Loveday Baxter	=	Annie Maud Bulwer
[Our father]		[Our mother]

The Baxter's
2008 AD

Queen Elizabeth 2nd

CHAPTER V1
THE MORTIMERS AND WARDS
In The Early Stuart Period.

The following pages will concentrate on our family ancestors in more detail, one lineage at a time so as to keep their stories flowing. You will note that the beginning of our book relates to national and family events that occurred during their life times, which they were involved in; and that affected their lives and ours even today. The early Stuart period was the start of innovations that eventually presented a challenge to the monarchy and began a better way of life for ordinary people.

King James and King Charles Create Turmoil

In 1603, church bells tolled in Woodalling as they did throughout the land to relay the sad news that the popular Queen Elizabeth 1st (also known as 'Good Queen Bess') had died. Her reign had seen much of the world explored, which initiated the start of the British Empire and made her people prosperous. She was the last of the Tudors and when the Scottish King James Stuart [starting the Stuart dynasty], came to the throne, memories were still full of the Scots' rebellion in the reign of Edward 1st.

Roger de Dalling lived at this time, he married twice producing a family of six girls and two boys. Like many other families they must have been fearful of the future, as serious issues would affect them and important decisions had to be made throughout James' reign. They would later find themselves involved in a Civil war, as the new monarch who claimed the crown of England would not be of English blood.

On his journey to London, James was welcomed almost everywhere with a great amount of celebration. That is until the loyal subjects actually viewed their new ruler and noted with astonishment that he looked anything but monarch! Short, overweight and with eyes bulging out of his head. King James 1st attire was padded making his body look even more corpulent and his legs spindly. He refused to ride on his horse in the normal way and instead, was carried around on a specially made chair strapped to the horses back.

His ancestors held the concept that they had the divine right of kings, which was now unacceptable for a monarch in England and a head-on clash with Parliament was going to be inevitable. At each stop on the Royal Progress he was made welcome by the local landowners, who invariably laid on a lavish banquet in his honour. He enjoyed his food, often over eating.

Note; - A new habit started in the form of tobacco smoked in pipes which became common practice probably brought from America by Drake/Hawkins and their crew in 1566 but in the present day is considered a health risk.

An interesting humorous point to note is that at one such banquet King James enjoyed the beefsteak so much he drew his sword. The room reputedly grew silent in anticipation of what was to occur. He stood up and prodded the loin of beef with his sword and said; "This loin of beef I honour and hence forth thou shalt be called Sir Loin [hence the name Sirloin Steak today].

After two years of consideration he was confirmed as king [[1603- 1625]; a few weeks later he was crowned in London as James 1st and seated upon King Edward's Coronation chair. Although born a Catholic, due to his Protestant views he promised that he would do nothing to harm the memory of Elizabeth.

During his reign he ruled as both King James 1st of England and King James 6th of Scotland. The two thrones were united; unfortunately the two kingdoms were not because of King James' 'strict obedience of his will', not only to his subjects but also on the very seat of power in Parliament that caused unrest in England.

He insisted that everyone should conform to his religious beliefs, and those who did not comply were harshly punished. Many loyal subjects could not tolerate the scenes of selfishness, greed, pomp and ceremony. Some decided that they could not handle his harshness and fled the kingdom to far reaches of the world [at least to that which was known at this time] for example, one group of people left Plymouth in 1620 aboard a vessel named "Mayflower" and their destination was 'The New World'.

They landed at Plymouth, New England in what is now the United States of America. This group of people is better known as the Pilgrim Fathers and Americans celebrate the date of their arrival (22nd Dec.) as Forefathers Day. Later a group moved further inland and named their area Norfolk and its capital Norwich, just as if they had dreamed of a city with a white castle high upon a hill in the centre of a town with narrow streets.

In England the Puritans still witnessing the same self-indulgence by the wealthy reacted to form their own cult, practicing self-denial. They believed all things should be plain and simple, and leisure time should be spent in quiet prayer as opposed to frivolous music, dancing and sports. They strongly disliked banquets and grand looking churches with stained glass windows and decorative interiors. Feelings amongst the Puritans ran high; they wanted to see the so-called pleasures of life removed and replaced by a life of simple penitence.

Note;- Shakespeare became a very popular play write at this time [d. 1616] producing historical plays such as Julius Caesar, Macbeth and Hamlet. Also James 1st ordered a new translation of the bible which was printed in 1611. [Known as the King James Bible]

Guy Fawkes Tries to Blow up Parliament.

5th November 1605

The unrest and distress of the nation grew and in 1604 a group of men who had suffered from the wrath of King James 1st, decided to take action. Led by Robert Catesbury, they elected to rid the nation of James by planting a large quantity of gunpowder below the very seat of power; Parliament! A brave soul named Guy Fawkes had volunteered to ignite the fuse and make his escape. However the plot had been exposed to the authorities by one of the conspirators Thomas Mortimer alias Percy who had taken fright. The rebels were all captured and executed. Guy Fawkes night is still celebrated each year on November 5th with bonfires and fireworks.

Guy Fawkes   Plate 57
Artist impression

Thomas Percy was from a branch of the **Mortimer** family, not a controversial figure, but a flattering dangerous knave exercising influence on events leading up to and beyond the gunpowder plot. He married Martha Wright whose mother spent years in prison for religious beliefs, her daughter Ursula, married into family of **Ward.**

Our relatives The Mortimer/Ward's involved in the conspiracy

The families we are concerned with were involved in the Gunpowder Plot conspiracy, they are the Wright's, Ward's and Percy/Mortimer's who are among our ancestors and interrelated as seen from the chart below.

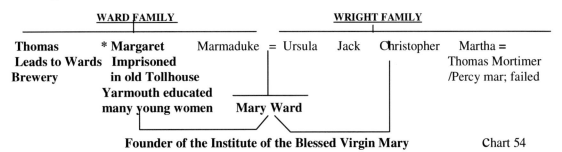

WARD FAMILY   **WRIGHT FAMILY**

Thomas   * Margaret   Marmaduke = Ursula   Jack   Christopher   Martha =
Leads to Wards Imprisoned   Thomas Mortimer
Brewery   in old Tollhouse   /Percy mar; failed
                Yarmouth educated
                many young women   **Mary Ward**

Founder of the Institute of the Blessed Virgin Mary   Chart 54

Robert Rookwood and his second wife who had considerable estates were imprisoned. After his father died Ambrose his son inherited Coldham Hall, Norfolk built a refuge for priests. The hall has been altered since Rookwood's day's but has priests hiding places, probably designed by Nicholas Owen; the Chapel still exists. Nicholas loved and stabled horses, quite a catch for the conspirators in setting up escape plans.

Note. Those emphasized in bold type were among the main conspirators related to our family; many more were involved from districts centered on the Coventry and Stratford Upon Avon areas. From the book "Guy Fawkes and the Gunpowder plot" by Lady Antonia Fraser. *Record still seen in this building. Ursula Wright Served many years in prison for refusing to attend Protestant services.

ENEMIES IN THE MAKING

During the reign of King James [Scotland 1567] and England [1603] James very often traveled to and from Scotland with his son Charles attending his two kingdoms and regularly rested at a large country house where the wealthy owner Sir Oliver Cromwell entertained him. Nearby, in the town of Huntingdon lived Sir Oliver's brother, Robert, whose son had also been christened Oliver [nicknamed Noll] who was later to be the dictator of all England. It was on these visits at the great banquet given by Sir Oliver in the Kings honour that his nephew the young Oliver and his friend **Erasmus Earle** almost certainly met and played with the king's son Charles [later King Charles 1st]

All the boys had totally different and opposed characters, which were revealed in their games. Charles was strong minded but refined, whilst both Oliver and **Erasmus** were strong robust lads in mind and body, fearing no one. They were often seen fighting, and on one occasion both King James and Sir Oliver had to separate them. It was the meeting of these boys that later changed the course of British national history. This progression began in childhood, with their natural contrasting personalities and rivalry that continued into adulthood, later making Oliver and Erasmus bitter enemies of Charles

Oliver Cromwell and **Erasmus Earle's** friendship in youth continued throughout adulthood and after these three boyhood friends' attained powerful positions the people eventually split into two factions Cavaliers and Roundheads which cumulated in a civil war. Two close friends were later to become the other ones executioners when Charles became king. Erasmus and Oliver both became anti royalist Roundheads with Erasmus taking the role of Oliver's advisor.

Oliver's temperament could not accept Charles autocratic ways, he had been taught to believe that royal demands were law and not to be questioned. Oliver and Erasmus engaged in a vindictive battle to overthrow the king who had once been their childhood playmate and it was this violent clash of personalities that led to Charles's downfall and execution.

An unforeseen tragic future awaited them all when Oliver became a General of the Army and dictator. His friend **Erasmus** became England's top lawyer [Sergeant at Law]. Later the niece of **Erasmus** married into the **Wiggett Bulwer** family and brought with her the wealth and prestige of her Uncle **Erasmus**. It is from this point in time that we found strong family history and detailed records of individual family members, where names and dates are linked to life stories and personalities.

ROUNDHEADS VERSUS CAVALIERS
Rebellion starts in Norfolk

When King James 1st [of England and 6th of Scotland] died in 1625, the young Prince Charles inherited his father's title and became King Charles 1st of England. His enthronement caused more unrest as those who supported his lifestyle became known as the Cavaliers; the way they dressed and lived angered the Puritans immensely.

The drab, plain, black and white clothing, short-cropped hair and reserved manner of the Puritans who were ridiculed with the name Roundheads contrasted starkly against the Cavaliers with their lavish silks, gaily coloured clothing, long hair and flamboyant manner. The attitudes of both parties became antagonistic; the Cavaliers did everything they could to enrage the Puritans and the Puritans in turn became so bitter that nothing would please them. They would preach at length against any pleasure, even their dress styles were extreme, eventually reaching the stage where conflict between the Cavaliers and the Puritans (now joined by the Roundheads) came to a crescendo.

Thomas Bulwer of Levisham Hall Buxton was alive at this time also his brother **Alexander** [our line, see item on Bintree] who married Elizabeth. We assume that they had leanings toward the Roundhead cause, as a tale written in the Bulwer histories, contend that Oliver Cromwell visited Heydon Hall, was chased by a bull and escaped by frantically climbing a tree until help was forthcoming.

The reign of King Charles 1st was one of continual discontent, he frequently summoned and banished Parliaments, firmly believing that his word was law, and when members dared to disagree, he dismissed them! He even spent long periods without a government at all. This embittered the Puritans and the Roundheads who were strong supporters of Parliament. The Cavaliers supported the king and the feud between the two factions grew.

The time was ripe for civil war between Government and Monarchy. In his struggle for power as King, Charles still insisted on the divine right of kings and Parliament regarded him as a tyrant. After one embarrassing encounter Charles left London to summon his Cavaliers to join him and at the same time the Roundheads also began recruiting. Preference for one side or the other became compulsory; you had to be either a Cavalier or a Roundhead, there was no middle ground. This rivalry turned county against county, family against family and brother against brother. Charles gathered his army in Nottingham, among them, his nephew Prince Rupert and sent his son, Prince Charles the future king abroad for safety.

OLIVER CROMWELL
1599 – 1658

Oliver Cromwell who was born in Huntingdon the son of a country Squire went into East Anglia at this time to recruit cavalry. Later he became an English General and dictator, a brilliant military leader, devout Puritan and a good politician. At the outbreak of the civil war 1642 he commanded a well-disciplined cavalry troop of ardent Puritans, who demonstrated their ability to overwhelm the Kings army, led by the kings nephew Prince Rupert, at the battle of Marston Moor in 1644. Cromwell was then second in command of what was called the New Model Army, which greatly helped in the victory at the Battle of Nasby in 1645.

Oliver Cromwell, now leading the Roundheads, massed his troops in East Anglia and urged every household in the region to fortify their homes. He trained some of his troops in Chapel-in-the- Field, Norwich, [an open area of ground] using the old Drill Hall as a base. The Drill Hall was part of the old city wall, which disappeared soon after the 2nd world war finished, [probably when the city was being developed]. He made the Guildhall [still standing in the center of Norwich] his armoury and **John Bulwer** was his armourer. By the end of the first civil war in 1645 Cromwell emerged as the most powerful leader on the parliamentary side and he tried to compel King Charles in to making concessions.

In late 1645 small groups of Jews had been living in England and a Rabbi from Amsterdam made a request to Cromwell that an official community be established. This appeal was granted because it was claimed that it would hasten the return of the Messiah and also because the new English Republic was regarded as illegitimate among the monarchies of Europe. The Jews with their international connections, financial and diplomatic expertise could be useful in overcoming this difficulty, but they were not welcomed by many and not allowed British citizenship until 1858. Owing to disputes regarding money King Charles had promised Scotland, Parliament declared the various ways he had used to raise these funds were illegal; this issue resulted in civil war.

Charles was defeated in 1648 and surrendered to the Scots who released him one year later on condition parliament paid the debt. This was done with a contract that Charles agreed to sign, but failed to honour so the monarchy was abolished and he was imprisoned. Oliver reorganized the parliament in the same year and then turned on the Scots, winning many battles against those who supported Charles.

Note: - some of this information was derived from the Encyclopaedia International

After the war with the Dutch, he dispersed parliament and although against absolutism he became a supporter and a dictator. Oliver Cromwell and his friend **Erasmus,** [who was then High Sheriff of Norfolk and Councilor to Cromwell] discussed with other high officials the fate of the king at a meeting in what is now the Elizabethan Museum in Yarmouth where the execution of King Charles was decided. *One room of this house is of historical importance as A. D. Bayne claims that:

"It was here that Oliver Cromwell met senior Officers to decide the fate of the king". There is a large wall plaque stating the names of those who attended that fateful meeting to decide the execution of King Charles 1st which confirms this.**A letter, written by a Mr. Hewling Kuston in 1773 was sent to a Dr. Brooke of Norwich that stated: -

*"When I was a boy, they used to show me a large chamber in the house of Nathaniel Carter that had been the house of his father in where the infamous murder of Charles 1st on the scaffold was finally determined. The principal officers of the army were held in this chamber. Including***Erasmus Earle** president of the high court of justice.*

A room above stairs was chosen. Others were strictly commanded not to come near with the exception of the man appointed to attend dinner. This was ordered at four o' clock, though it was put off from time to time, until past eleven at night, they then came down, and after a short repast, immediately set off for London". The result of this meeting in the room, on November 6th 1648, Parliament was purged of anyone who refused to put the king on trial.

Charles 1st was taken to Westminster Hall and brought to trial where he was charged with ruling as a tyrant and not obeying the laws of the land. He was not imprisoned for long, found guilty sentenced and beheaded on Jan. 30th 1649. After the death of King Charles 1st his son was proclaimed the king of Ireland and Scotland.The future King Charles 2nd of England tried to keep the war going by organizing attacks from the sea also creating a few battles inland to try to regain the English throne. Parliament tried to pass an exclusion bill to eliminate his succession to the throne. He recalled the government to retain his right and realize his ambition to be a Catholic King of England.

*A Royal illustrated History of Eastern England.
Letter published in Hughes letters, "Nobles memoirs" of the Pectorial house of Cromwell. Vol.iii page 168. * Cromwell's chief justice and connected to the Bulwer's by marriage.Note; - Samuel Pepys lived at this time in Seething Lane London close by the Tower and wrote profusely in his diary of the London scene. He worked as Secretary to the Navy Board that maintained the Royal Fleet and often visited Westminster and so obtained gossip to add to his diary.

Close by the Elizabethan House/Museum is the Star Hotel, [later bought by our great Uncle], which was also mentioned in connection with these events and had something to do with these meetings too. It was then called the Stone House [unless they had two meetings?] There is much more that we could tell you about this fascinating Elizabethan House/Museum but due to time and space we leave it to you to unravel its past and secrets, perhaps with a visit.

CROMWELL PURGES RELIGION.

Going back to 3rd June 1647, Oliver Cromwell and the Long Parliament, the celebration of Christmas was stopped as they considered it pagan; the people were getting too immoderate in behavior, especially the richer classes, Christmas puddings were banned for the same reason. But the wealthy obtained them from abroad, many ignored these new laws, others rioted, the worst being in Canterbury where church services still took place, but they were soon in trouble with the authorities.

Shopkeepers who remained open over Christmas to obey the law were attacked by their neighbour's and forced to ask for protection. **Erasmus Earle** being a close confidant of Cromwell probably went along with these ideas most likely including his family. The **Bulwer's** who were also closely associated with Cromwell were probably also in agreement with this ruling. These situations still existed until the Catholic King Charles 2nd later restored these celebrations during his reign.

Parliament resumed power, declared England "The Commonwealth" in 1649 and Oliver Cromwell was appointed its ruler, in real terms a dictator. He began his rule as a strong opponent of absolutism, but by the end of the power struggle, he wielded absolute power himself. Oliver gave the most trusted and important post in the land to **Erasmus Earl**, who became Parliamentary Lawyer, and Sergeant at Law, in today's terms equal to the Attorney General.

During the lifetime of **John Bulwer** his family was one of those that left Guestwick to settle in Norwich. We were unable to discover much more about him due to a serious fire in the Norwich Library where many of the historical documents for this period were destroyed or are still unavailable.

1658 was a bad year; Oliver Cromwell died and so did his Commonwealth and there was no one to replace him. On his deathbed he named his son Richard to succeed him as Lord Protector but under the threat of anarchy Richard abdicated in 1659 and the protectorate collapsed.

Although England had not been unhappy under Cromwell, they missed their king; by popular demand the monarchy was reinstalled and the son of Charles 1st was asked to return from France and claim the throne. He agreed and celebrations were held on the accession of King Charles 2nd. At the start of his reign he was a popular Monarch but failed to act out his role, neglecting his duties in favour of his own selfish pleasures. England was once again discontented with its Catholic king.

BRING OUT YOUR DEAD.
The Plague Returns 1665

In the densely populated areas, London and other cities like Norwich were like tinderboxes waiting for a spark. There was no sewage system, or piped water. What little water they used came straight from the river or local well and was mostly foul. Bedding was usually made of straw, often shared with rats and mice and other unmentionable vermin, which multiplied rapidly. Rubbish and excrement was thrown into the narrow streets where it was left to rot and wash down into the river.

In June of 1665, Samuel Pepys wrote in his diary that this was the hottest summer he had ever known, and that he had noticed two houses with red crosses painted on their doors, which told him that, the people inside had bubonic plague. This scourge had returned suddenly striking town and hamlet alike. It spread quickly from village to village, town to town, street to street across the whole country.

When a household became infected, its front doors were marked with large Red Cross to inform people to keep away. Large carts constantly rattled along those filthy cobbled streets to collect the bodies, loud voices shouted out; "Bring out your dead" and the hand bells rang emphasizing the emergency of the situation. This, it turned out was, the worst of all of the outbreaks and caused the greatest loss of life. In Cities like Norwich 300 people died in one week rising to a peak of 3000. Very few families escaped the contagion.

One village near Northampton still stands as a desolate reminder of those days, empty houses in fields still and quiet. There is no doubt that the City of London would have been completely wiped out by the plague but for a twist of fate on the 1st September 1666. A fire possibly originating in a baker's premises in Pudding Lane, which started after the baker had stoked his ovens ready for the early morning bread and retired to bed.
A spark from the ovens probably set the bakery alight and then quickly spread along the congested streets with their thatched roofs until most of London was burning. Some people were too ill to move and those bodies not yet buried all burned in the flames, but the ferocious fire did stop the

plague. St. James Palace [where the House of Parliament now stands] vanished in the flames together with all the valuable historical records that it contained. Records from this period were scarce although some were still kept, few people had the energy or the time to keep them up to date and as the plague burned out in the flames there began a new awareness of cleanliness and public health.

Cromwell's ideals had brought a permanent change in the relationship between the people and monarchy during these turbulent times of civil war when most of the **Bulwer's** took the side of Parliament [Cromwell]. When Charles 2nd died in 1685 his brother James, the Duke of York, another devout Catholic became King James 2nd of England; although great efforts were made to keep him from succeeding to the throne. We list below some of our family that lived in this century.

Thomas Bulwer Senior and **Anthonia [d 1607]** our branch of the Bulwer family, had a son **Peter** d 1634 who married **Elizabeth [White]**. One of their sons Thomas [of Buxton d 1694] [married 1st **Elizabeth Ferrier** 2nd **Anne Marsham**] his brother **Alexander** [d1687] married **Elizabeth** and when Thomas junior aged only one year died, with no other male heir, **Alexander** son of [**Alexander**] inherited the **Bulwer** titles for this branch.

STEPPING OUT OF THE DARK
Organized official improvements for the quality of life starts.

In circa. 1700 the city of Norwich slowly developed and changed into the modern city we know today, but still had a long way to go. By the early 1700's Norwich was a thriving trade centre and the second largest city. **Thomas Bulwer** of Saxthorpe and his family witnessed these events that improved the quality of life. His son Thomas Fearnly Bulwer moved into Wood Dalling Hall with his family at this time.

As anyone could now move to another area and marry this caused many abuses of the marriage vows, and runaway heiresses and wives caused much concern to their rich fathers or husbands. Lord Hardwick in 1753 introduced the Act of Parliament that helped to prevent this. In 1754 printed registers appeared and marriages were only legal if the nuptials took place after the Banns in the parish church were called. In 1812 printed formats had to be used and in 1837 national registration began.

One big step forward came at the end of the eighteenth century when an order was issued that Norwich was to be lighted at night. All households that could afford it were to hang lanterns at the side of their houses each evening to provide candlelight for those that passed by and a paving committee was appointed to provide a form of rough paving along streets.

Road names began to appear on walls in 1771 AD, and were written as they were spoken, some have lost their meaning, but street names in the main thoroughfares are still understood and used. Mail coaches were being employed for national distribution of letters and parcels. The populace began to think they were generally well provided for as far as transport was concerned, except that when it rained coach wheels became so clogged with mud in the rutted streets that the horses had great difficulty in dragging the loaded carriages through the mess.

The impact of this service was fully appreciated when at last there was some form of planned communication, which was the forerunner of faster organized movement of goods and other commerce. There were very few bridges, so most of the trade in this century was by river as the roads in winter were usually impassable. It was not until 1800 that street cleaning was initiated, filth on streets disappeared removing that which was the main cause of disease and deaths though the ages.

Yarmouth, which was in competition with Norwich for trade, tried blocking the river, and taking over as the main port. The filth and rubbish floating from Norwich to Yarmouth did not help but business people in Norwich have always been tenacious; this was true in that century especially when competition developed into a serious trade war between the two communities. Unfortunately all goods transported by sea destined for Norwich had to come through Great Yarmouth and had to use the River Yare, which only the smallest craft could navigate.

All goods in and out of Norwich were transferred on to the smaller Wherries at the port of Great Yarmouth where officials were able to make some very easy money by levying tolls on all imports passing through.
An engineer called William Cubitt drew up a plan for creating a new waterway link between Norwich and Lowestoft to bypass Yarmouth, who was taking advantage of the stranglehold that they had on the Norwich trade. At first Parliament rejected the proposal but later agreed to allow a new channel to be cut linking the river Waveny to the Yare at Reedham and Haddiscoe.

A SUMMARY OF THE EVENTS.

As far as we know none of our family in any lineage were involved with government or the crown at this time. Thomas Bulwer [d 1759] who married Mary [d1756] John [b1773] who married Susannah [m 1836] lived to see three Monarchs and the turmoil that surrounded them. When Fredrick, Prince of Wales son of King George 2nd quarreled with his father he accepted the political position in government as leader of the opposition and set up a rival court against the King at Leicester House, which included Lord Cobham, George Littleton and William Pitt.

His father had made Robert Walpole head of government but after Queen Caroline died Walpole lost his most staunch supporter though the king remained loyal to him. During the kings last years he was obliged to leave all affairs to William Pitt. George 3rd the son of Fredrick 2nd Prince of Wales and the grandson of George 2$^{nd;}$ was regarded as insane, with manic depression for certain periods of his life. The American rebellion took place during his lifetime. These were the times of Handel [the great musician/ composer], riots in Scotland and Spain began causing havoc on the high seas by robbing merchant ships, brutalizing and murdering their crews.

In 1739 the nation went to war, Walpole resigned after it finished. In 1742 his principal ministers were Henry Pelham 1743 –54 and the Duke of Newcastle 1754 –56. France declared war on Britain and in 1789 saw the beginning of the French revolution. Scotland thought this a good opportunity to regain their kingdom, but Bonny Prince Charlie lost the battle at Culloden where even the wounded were shamefully slaughtered. The Duke of Cumberland pursued Charles's followers, slaying without mercy, burning and destroying their homes. He captured many Clansmen and took hundreds of suspects who he executed or imprisoned. Prince Charles went into exile, which ended all Stuart hopes for their return to the British throne.

Only faint traces remain in their songs with a few legends of their national heroes remain. Many Scots emigrated and settled in British colonies abroad making a success of their lives. We discovered many Scottish names connected to our own ancient family lines as well as the continental ones, even though there was a lack of transport in those days people from England and Scotland travelled far and wide, and spread over the earth's surface.

CHRONOLOGY FROM 1603 TO 1789
1603 James 1st becomes King of England
1625 King James dies and Charles 1st becomes king.
1640 Erasmus Earle b1590 [father of John and grandfather to Erasmus b.1658] served in the court of Charles 1st became Sergeant-at-Law. and M.P. for Norwich during the Long Parliament. Changed his allegiance from the king to Oliver Cromwell his close friend.
1642 Oliver Cromwell fought in the civil war and his army won a great victory at the battle of Nasby [1645].
1643 Erasmus purchased Heydon Hall from Sir Robert Kemp.
1647 Cromwell and the Long Parliament stop celebration of Christmas.
1649 King Charles 1st beheaded.
1649 Abolition of the House of Lords.
Some Notes from Encyclopedia Internationals and The Squires of Heydon Hall [p.xv]

1649   England declared a Commonwealth

1650   **Erasmus** Earl [born 1590] moves into Heydon Hall.

1658   Oliver Cromwell dies, his son Richard holds power for a few months. Grandson of Erasmus born in this year.

1662   Recognition in the development of sign language. John Wallace in competition with **John Bulwer.**

1667   We find a **Harold Bulwer** listed but have no details on his life or family so we cannot include him in family records yet.

1674   **John Bulwer** instigates sign language in England.

1721   Grandson of **Erasmus** b1658 was not so fortunate in his choice of bride, she was cheated of her inheritance by her cousin, creating bad feelings. **Erasmus** died of a broken heart in 1721. Following his death his wife handed over the administration of the Earl Estates to Augustine third of his four sons [b.1692 d.1762] who inherited Heydon Hall.

1740   Norwich gains fame for its cloth making at this time, also in 1760 and 1795.

1748   Norwich Library formed in rooms joining St. Andrews Hall.

1754   Norwich Assembly Rooms are built and still used today.

1756   Charles Weston starts first bank in Norwich.

1756   Augustine Earle's daughter Mary married William Wiggett who in 1757 built Norwich Theatre in Theatre Street. They bought out her sister's share of Heydon and took possession, this sister moved to America.

1762   Augustine son of Erasmus died.

1765   In Probate Mary Earle and William Wiggett inherited the titles and deeds of the Bulwer estate provided they changed their name to Wiggett Bulwer.

1771   *Norwich Castle ditches filled, and a Cattle Market established.

1772   Norfolk And Norwich Hospital built. Now a new hospital has been built on the outskirts of the city.

1785   First Stagecoach and mail service from Norwich to London.

1789   Act passed for a bridge, on the site where King Street Gates stood. It was not appreciated until the coming of the railway in 1884 [Toll Bridge made free on August 10th 1881]. Lake Lothian became a Harbour in Norwich and a channel was cut from Norwich to Lowestoft but Norwich as a Port did not quite live up to its name and the Dock at Carrow Road was abandoned.

Note; - *In the course of our research we realized that the ditches associated with the Norwich Castle were situated in an elevated position well above the river level. The ditches as stated above were filled in many years ago and must have been on a very much lower level than we see today possibly filled by the same spring that fed the castle well and the river.

THE LACON/MORTIMER WARD BEEVOR CONNECTION
From Gissele = Rollo and William Longsword = Sporta
A Preview of five families   Chart 55

RUDOLPH [son of WILLIAM LONGSWORD and SPORTA] = GUNNER
HUGH MORTIMER = Emma, dau. Of Osbern Grandson of WILLIAM LONGSWORD
WILLIAM MORTIMER/WARRENNA 1st = twice 1st Gundred 2nd sister of the Earl of Chester.
All these below are cousins linked by marriage which also includes the the Crispin / de Dalling / Bulwer / Valoise families

William Mortima/Warrenna 2nd = Isobel Beaumont + 2   Adeline = Robert
Willian Warrenna 3rd = Margaret   Henry = Margaret Dau. Of Conte de Montago
William Warrenna 4th   Roger = dau. Earl of Warwick
                                    William Beaumont = Arnice dau. Of Raph de Geuarda
                    Beumont's   Thomas Beaumont = Agnes, dau. Of Amauri Comte of Mortain.
                    Lineage   Robert = Isobel
__The Beevor FamilyConnection__   Robert le Bossu Armice ;   Thomas = Isobel
          Rev. Beevor   dau of Ralph de Geal
                                     MARGARET MORTIMER = SIMON WARD 1391
Martha died 1764   Carolina [Will 1755]   JOHN WARD Lord of Kirby Bedon
=Edmond Lacon   = Robert Ward   JOHN WARD / Attwood d.c. 1445
                                            ROBERT WARD = Alice dau. Of Robert Kemp
     __Lacon's__   /   __Ward's__   ROBERT WARD = dau. Of Cobbledyke Esq.
* John Lacon   [cousins] = **Elizabeth Ward   ROBERT WARD = dau. Of Sir Giles Cappel
  __Lacon / Beevor Family Connection__
C 1700 Edmond Lacon of Otley Shropshire   __Lacon / Ward/ Beevor Family Connection__
= Martha [Dau. Of Rev. Beevor] --- sisters -- CAROLINA BEEVOR = ROBERT WARD
= 2nd wife Sarah Mortlock
Edmond Knowles Lacon   ** ELIZABETH WARD = *JOHN LACON
John Mortlock Lacon   Cont. on page.264. chart.62.

SUMMARY OF THE LACON FAMILY LINEAGE Chart 56
Up to the time of John Lacon = Elizabeth Ward

**The Lacon family is reputed to be the oldest family lineage existing today in England and using various charts, ancient writings and other information our research pieced together an amazing trail that led us to a Roman senator that walked the earth during the time of the Roman occupation of this country who linked up to what we consider not only [POSSIBLY] our fathers ancestors but to many other families living today. Unfortunately some positive information is not complete but the facts that we have gathered indicates a fair judgment that a lineage can be formed using our text from p.258 to this page. this is not proved due to lost records and only can be related from our grandmother's statements.

***Laco [Roman Senator Procurator of Gaul sent to Britain by Claudius Caesar.
John Lord of Lacon 1293 = Ellen heir to Nicholas Corton.
Alan Lacon = Agnes Dau. of Walter Pembridge, William = Margaret dau. of Sir Ralph Buckingham.
Richard =Elizabeth Pashshell, a very wealthy heiress to Sir Hammond Pashshell of Wiley.
William   = ??? Sheriff of Shropshire 1452
Richard   =   Alice dau. Of Thomas Hoord of Salop.
Thomas   =   Mary dau. Of Richard Corbett
Edward   =   ???
Dorothy   =   William Loughton
Edmond Lacon   =   Martha Beevor [dau. Of Rev Beevor of Otley]
Robert Ward   =   Carolina Beevor
*John Lacon [of Shropshire – cousins]   = **Elizabeth Ward [of Yarmouth]
* +**Same persons
***Came with Claudius c. 40.AD. settled in Wem, Shropshire and his descendants became Lords of Lacon].

FAMILY AND NATIONAL STRUCTURE
Chart Showing Links Between The Lacon / Ward / Beevor Families

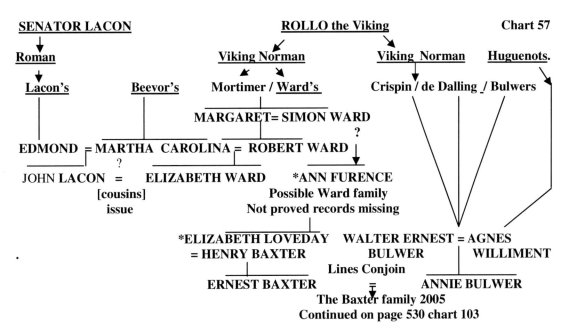

*OUR LINEAGE FOR LACON/ WARD NOT YET PROVED. MOTHER OF ANN DIED IN CHILBIRTH AT SEA.
. FATHER AND HIS SON DIED IN SHIPWRECK. ANN WAS MADE AN ORPHAN AND THE. RECORDS LOST.

THE LACON WARD BEEVOR MORTIMER FAMILIES
From 1475.

We bring to your attention the structure plan below of inter-marriages between these three families at this point, not only because it linked in marriage to the **Wards and Lacon's**, they are important to our own family, as can be seen by the family chart. This union created the success of Lacon's Breweries in Great Yarmouth. It also it portrays the close ties between those with money and their marriage partners.

The Beevor family was the central link joining Lacon and Ward   Chart. 58
Our father's lineage ?

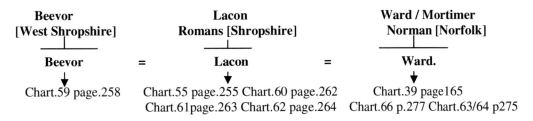

Continuing our father's possible lineage we include the Beevor family, as the two Beevor sisters formed the central link between three families of Beevor Lacon and Ward. Carolina Beevor married Robert Ward, Martha Beevor married Edmund Lacon and their offspring [cousins] intermarry when John Lacon married Elizabeth Ward linking all three families.

Note. We can be reasonably sure that our fathers lineage though his mother [our grandmother] comes via the Wards and absolutely certain our mothers lineage through her father [our grandfather] comes from the Bulwer/Mortimer's once more linking the families. *See page 396 chart 91.

THE BEEVOR FAMILY
A most contented nation in the time of Queen Anne circa 1700

The Rev. William Beevor

The reign of Queen Anne started with a feeling of well being throughout the land because:-.

1. Gibraltar had been captured, in 1704
2. England and Scotland were successfully united.
3. In the war with the French, Britain was victorious.
4. The Beevor family [which originated in West Yorkshire] recorded four fashionable weddings.

The Rev. Beevor saw four of his five daughters married in his lifetime and gave enormous settlements to each, ensuring a marriage into what was and still are called 'Good Families'. The first to marry was Elizabeth the eldest aged 22 years, to John Dove a brewer from an adjoining parish, on 29th May 1704 in South Walsham St. Lawrence Norfolk. John leased considerable amounts of land to his father-in-law the Rev. Beevor. Elizabeth and John produced a son they named John. John's father was William Dove a Woolen draper of St. Peter Mancroft, Norwich (Dove Street is still named after him).

When Elizabeth's husband died in 1739 there was a fascinating account of his inventory and will carried out by his wife's brother Thomas Beevor of Norwich, and Robin Ward of Yarmouth. It became known that in his will he could not make up his mind who to leave his property to, his son or his married sister so he left it to his widow to decide.

There must have been some unsettled times in this family because when Elizabeth died eleven years later, she had certainly made up her mind and left everything to her brothers and sisters by name, instructing the executors to carry out her will as though her son John were dead! The **Rev. Beevor's** second and fifth daughters **Martha** and **Carolina** are the ones that we are interested in. See cht.59 p.258 and Item on the Lacon's for continuation of the Beevor story.

Note of interest; - At this time Tea was an expensive novelty imported from China and those that could afford it held regular social gatherings called tea parties. It cost ten pounds a pound and was pronounced 'Tay'. It was stored in a caddy with a stopper as in a bottle or a locked casket. At first the pots were made of dark red stoneware but as these were expensive and easily broken the British made their own from silver [now known as Queen Anne's teapots]. Tea was served in cups that were like and termed as dishes usually with blue patterns, wide and shallow with no handles, [ouch] so British importers asked the Chinese to make saucers [which the Chinese never had]. All Porcelain china had to be imported from China as they alone had the secret of making it. Also a special design of Queen Anne furniture was created at this time that took in consideration the humane form and designed furniture for comfort.

Chart of the Beevor family
Chart 59

Abraham Beevor c1628-1703 = Elizabeth Savile1630-1695 lived during the time of Cromwell, King Charles 1st, Charles 2nd, King James 1st, Queen Mary = William Duke of Orange [Prince of Holland] founded the Bank of England to finance his war against France] and Queen Anne.

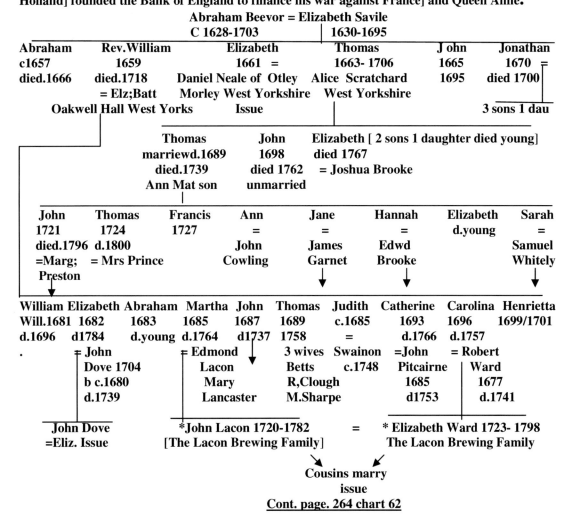

Cont. page. 264 chart 62

KINGS, QUEENS AND RULERS OF GREAT BRITAIN FROM 1600 AND OTHERS WHO LIVED IN THEIR TIME

Stuarts	James 1st 1603 -25 King. of England 6th of Scotland; son of Mary Queen of Scots. Charles 1st 1625 -1649 [beheaded] boyhood friend of Erasmus Earle and Oliver
.	Cromwell [later Dictator] and Guy Fawkes [of the gun powder plot]
Dictator	Oliver Cromwell [Lord Protector] 1653 – 1658 and his son Richard 1658 -1659
Stuart.	Charles 2nd 1660 – 1685 son of Charles 1st Plague and the Fire of London [1666] James 2nd [7th of Scotland brother of Charles 1st] 1685 -1688 Deposed by Whig Revolution
Orange/	William refused to be Regent [for the exiled King James 2nd] and would not allow his
Stuart	wife to succeed to the throne as her right so William and Mary agreed to jointly share King and Queen William 3rd [Duke of Orange Dutch] 1689 -1702 and Mary 1689-1694
Stuart	Anne 1702 – 1714
Hanover	George 1st 1714 – 1727 A German who could not speak English so Robert Walpole officiated for him and became the 1st Prime Minister. George 2nd 1727 – 1760. Opposed his father and saw the 1st World War 1756 – 63 George 3rd 1760 – 1820 Captain Cook led a voyage of discovery to Australia and New. Zealand On 4th July 1776 was The American Declaration of Independence. George 3rd purchased a country house on the outskirts of London [Buckingham Palace] in 1761.

THE LACON DYNASTY.
From 1293

There are several factors why we feel certain that the accounts of the ancient Lacon descent links historically with the modern Lacon family.

1] We know Senator Lacon arrived on these shores and settled in Shropshire.
2] He established a small hamlet of Lacon near Wem in Shropshire.
3] The earliest written record that we could find was from 1293 onwards when the Lacon's were Lords in that area in the reign of Edward 1st.
4] Three ancient writers and other modern authorities substantiate these claims.

In spite of the huge time gap between Senator Lacon and Ranulph Lacon we strongly believe that Ranulph is his descendant. Historians do not make any positive claims regarding Anglo / Roman histories as these are in a difficult time period due to the ravages of Viking marauders and are not very well recorded as to family histories. So we leave the Lacon account as stated, not proven. You will find it very difficult to trace lineage's and marriages before the above dates, so we will only relate the important issues in our writings and by following the charts provided; you will find charts of a later date regarding these families.

This is the last of Ranulf Peveral's Manors worth mentioning he held them under Roger; Elnoth held it in Saxon times though it had a very different designation than any of his other manors. We have not yet found any information to substantiate this but we still believe these facts are more than coincidental. It did not go to Cressage [Cressingham] to repair the shattered fief of the de-Lacey [Lucias family], nor like Western and Whixall to reward the services of Guy le Strange.

Whenever Lacon escheated to the Crown the king added it to the endowment of the Chapel of St Michael at Shrewsbury Castle. Some incumbents of St. Michael's enfeoffed a Toret or Corbet of Moreton both in Lacon and Scoulton. Corbet again in the 13th century had his tenants in both manors, each tenant being named after the name of the place of his enfeoffment.

A suit starting in 1271-72 tells the status of Lacon and Scoulton as far as Corbett was concerned. Richard de Sarr Parson in 1271, of the church of St. Michael in Shrewsbury Castle, impleaded Robert Corbett at Westminster for the purpose of obliging him to render right and Customary Services for the free tenement.

This he held under the said Parson in Soleton and Lach; to which the Parson complained that whereas his predecessor had been seized at the time of Henry 3rd at a rent of five shillings, of which Corbet did keep two. The suit had been adjourned until Oct. 1272, then went to Grand Assize, Corbet won by default. The next piece of Corbet's mesne-tenure at Lacon has some influence on the early genealogy of the Lacon's, and shows the advantage gained by a closer inspection of the original document.

The Feodary of the Bradford Hundred of 1284 and commonly known as Kirby's Quest says…"William de Laken holds the vill of Laken and upper and Lower Lacon" and the map shows they are spread over one and a half miles of low lying wet country.

The Pedigree comes from the Carwin Newlings Ms. and even more elaborately described by the learned Glover. The earliest record we could find was 1216 and the continuous line started from the family of John Lacon in 1273 seated in Lacon near Wem in Shropshire.

This family held many important national roles; we will mention only those that have a bearing on this narrative. We noted that Richard de Sarr's first added title occurred about 1271 when he was made a knight, and became Sir Richard [sixth on Chart] and became King Henry 4th Council Lawyer.

He married the heiress of Sir Hammond Peshall of Wiley, Shropshire that greatly enhanced the family to the Barony of Corbet, which was inherited from the Brampton family. Sir Richard also gained the great wealth of the Hartley's, but when they supported King Charles their lands were confiscated.

Some migrated to Yorkshire and settled in Otley in 1726. This was probably when Martha Beevor went to visit her Aunt Elizabeth Neale, who lived there, and where she met Edmund Lacon, Aunt Elizabeth's favorite nephew. It was the connection with the Lacon's in Yarmouth, and the advent of the two cousins marrying that drew us to do further research on them.

The Lacon family, which is reputed to be the oldest recorded family in Britain, married into the House of Wiley, whose ancient seat was near Wem in Shropshire. Those old pedigrees have a lot of interesting information to offer and are well worth more detailed research. We have a copy some of these ancient documents but alas due to copyright restrictions are not able to publish them here, which is sad, but from information we gained from them we have created a text from the original. [See section 'Lacon Pedigree' page 262].

The following text is a continuation of the Beevor family where it conjoins with the Lacon's of Norfolk. **Martha** the second daughter must have visited her relatives in Otley West Yorkshire as we have said; she met and married **Edmund Lacon** of Otley. They raised two sons Thomas (who changed his name to Barker) and John, who introduced **Lacon's** name into the **Wards** brewery business.

The third daughter Judith married Lawrence Swainson about 1715 and nothing more was heard of them except that she was widowed before 1748. His fourth daughter Catherine, at the age of 24 pleased her father by marrying the Rev. John Pitcairne 1717, they made their home at Burgh Castle, Norfolk near the Roman walls; one year later her father died.

The Rev. Beevor's fifth daughter **Carolina** married **Robert Ward** of the brewing family, at Great Yarmouth in 1719 in the soaring grandeur of Ranworth Church. She was twenty and he twenty years her senior. They produced four or perhaps five children, **Elizabeth**, Catherine, Caroline, and **Robert** who inherited the old family house on Church Plain Yarmouth and in due course took over the office of Mayor in 1729. It was his corporation that sent fifty pounds for the relief of British Captives at Merquinez and admitted a freeman by birth in 1740.

Robert owned several ships that were used for the brewery business and died at the age of sixty-four; there is a slab in St. Nicholas Church Great Yarmouth to his memory. His only son **Robert** married Susanna Sophia and produced three sons between 1745 and 1749, **George, Robert** and **Gabriel** but unfortunately their father died when only 33 years old, leaving his mother and others as guardians to his young children.

His share of the brewery was to be carried on by his executors until his son was 21 years but this apparently never happened; his mother lived on for many years. She saw the brewery enlarged and saved by the marriage of cousins Elizabeth [her daughter] to John Lacon, son of her sister Martha, a union that made their fortune.

And so the marriage triangle of the Lacunas, Ward's and Beevor's was completed when John Lacon (son of Edmund Lacon and Martha nee Beevor) asked for the hand of his cousin Elizabeth Ward in marriage, a union which also concludes the story of the Beevor family. We will now concentrate on the Lacon/Ward family.

Note of interest; The Bulwer families living at this time were Thomas [d.1750] and his wife Mary, whose son Thomas [married 1st Anne Paul 2nd Mary Billing]. As they were landowners and farmers living quite near to the Lacon's they likely grew grain for the Lacon beers and probably met socially and on business.

PEDIGREE OF THE HOUSE OF LACON

Saxon / Roman Descent mostly obtained from the Carwin Newlings M.S.S.
And compared with the more elaborate pedigree of the learned Glover
Earliest chart after the account on Senator Lacon

The senior branch of the family became extinct, perhaps there were too many daughters or not enough natural/illegitimate sons, or it could be they had displeased the monarchy, the family moved to Yorkshire leaving their estate to Childs.   **Chart 60**

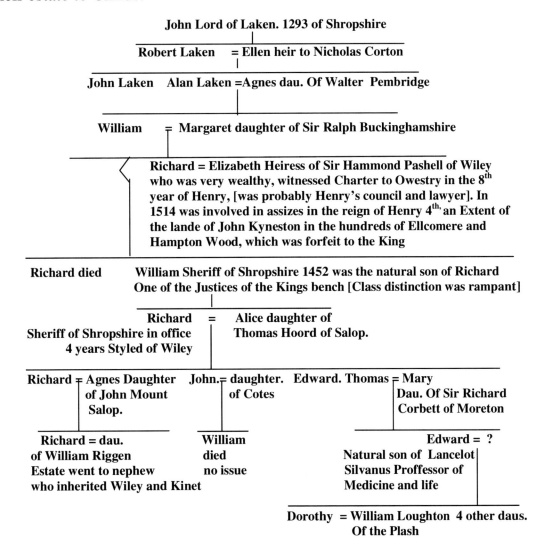

See the account in C. J. Palmers Perlustrations page reference 257 vol.1. and Burkes Peerage under Lacon. We also hold photocopies of some ancient family trees.

Also living at this time in the Bulwer lineage were Simon and Isobel [who purchased Gissing Hall Norfolk], their son John de Dalling and his wife Maud de Bintree, also their son Roger [who married twice]. The Beevor/ Lacons [North of England] and the Bulwer [East Anglia] families though living many miles apart were destined to meet and link again later by what we believe to be our parents marriage.

DESCENDANTS OF EDMUND LACON AND MARTHA BEEVOR
LINE OF INHERITANCE

Break in lineage

Chart 61

<u>**FROM 1741**</u>

Edmond Lacon = Martha   Whose sister   Carolina Beevor = Robert Ward
Of Otley | daughter of Rev Beevor

John Lacon 1740   =   Elizabeth Warde of Yarmouth. [cousins
John and Hubert Lacon owned property at Weeting All Saints [Will dated 1702]
When John Lacon and Elizabeth Ward married it was said to have made their fortune.

Edmund Lacon = Eleanor co-heir to Thomas Knowles D.D. [Thomas assumed the name of
.   Barker.
        Female issue only. Passed to next in line.

Edmund Knowles Lacon = 2nd wife Sarah Mortlocke
Baronette,

John Mortlocke Lacon   =   Jane Stirling Grahame from a large family one of Johns daughters
b.1786   married C.J.PALMER F.S.A.
Captain Highlanders.

Henry Lacon = no Issue
H.E.I.C.S.
                            Passed to next in line
Sir Edmund Knowles Lacon = Eliza Dixon daughter and co-heir Thomas Beacroft Saxthorpe.
B1780 Baronette

Henry James Lacon   = Louisa Roberts

Capt. Henry Edmund Lacon son and Heir

Capt., Sir Edmund Broughten Knowles Lacon [4th child died without issue] Passed to next in line

Thomas Beacroft Lacon = Florence Banks of Toronto Canada 1911

Sir Geo., Haiworth Usher Lacon = Vere Lacon daughter of his cousin

Sir George Vere Lacon1910 =

The story in respect of the Ward's of Broke and Yarmouth is continued in the following Great Yarmouth Section. Edmund Lacon married Martha Beevor and Robert Ward married her sister Caroline Beevor. [See Yarmouth Ward families].

We have charts of descent from this family going back to 1209. Headed Pedigree of the House of Lacon [Saxon Roman descent.] mostly obtained from the Carwin Newlings MSS and compared with the more Elaborate Pedigree of the learned Glover showing earlier descent.

DESCENDANTS OF JOHN LACON AND ELIZABETH WARD
Chart 62

JOHN LACON of Otley = Elizabeth daughter and co-heir of Robert Ward of Great Yarmouth
County of YORK   1745, d 3rd April 1798 act 73 buried in Yarmouth Chancel
Settled in
Norfolk
about 1740
died at
Bristol
Died 1782 at 72. Buried in Ciften church near Bristol. His will in which he is described of
Yarmouth County of Norfolk Merchant dated 8th of July 1782 and proved 17th October 1782

1st Eleanor youngest daughter =	Sir Edmund Lacon	= 2nd Sarah dau of	others
co-heir of Thomas	Bart; b.22. 10.1750	John Mortlock.	John
Knowles of Bury	Knt at St James	of Cambs	Judith
County of Suffolk	19.12.1792		Elizabeth
pc pre bentory	Mayor of Yarmouth 1792		Carolina
of Ely; married 1770	1795-1798 -1812		Martha
d.November 1781; buried at	Bart; 1818 d 1820.		
South Walsham and	buried. t Ormsby		
afterwards removed to Ormsby			

Sir Edmund Knowles Lacon
= Eliza?Dixon eldest daughter
  and co-heir of Thomas; Bancroft
  of Saxthorpe Norfolk
  Sir Edmund was
  High Sheriff of Norfolk 1823
  Bart; Of Great Yarmouth and
  Ormsby Norfolk bart; M.A
  of Emanuel Col., Cambs; M.P
  for Yarmouth 1812-1813.

John Mortlocke Lacon
= Jane dau of Patrick
Stirling of ttendriech.,
Esq.,Merchant in Dundee.
John was from Yarmouth
born 9 2.1786 Mayor of
Yarmouth 1827.

Georgina	Thomas	Eliza	Henry Sidney
Lacon	Beacroft	Walpole	Hammet
	Lacon Esq,	Lacon	Lacon Esq

[1] Amelia Grahame   [2] John Edmund Lacon [3] Henry Lacon [4]   Louise= Captain Spankle
= Charles John Palmer Collector of Customs   Will,. S .Lacon   eldest son
Author of 'Palmers.   of Yarmouth.
Perlustrations
5] Jane Lacon
6] Mortlocke Lacon   son of = daughter of
7]Grahame Lacon   Mr Searjeant Captain Spankle
[8]Charles Lacon
[9]Clementia   Edward Sherwell Esquire
[10]Richard Lacon   one died at sea 1847?
[11]Harriete Lacon
12]Frank Lacon

<u>Note</u> of interest; John Lacon of Otley [c1710 d. 1782] was the fore-runner of the Lacon's of Norfolk and lived during the reigns of Queen Anne, King George 1^{st,} George 2nd and George 3rd. He witnessed the seeds of democracy being sown and the power that once considered the exclusive right of monarchs eroded. On the night of 16th December 1773 a group of colonists in America threw 342 chests of tea into Boston Harbour. This was a signal for revolution and this act became known as the Boston Tea Party. For line of inheritance see page 263

The Town Walls of Great Yarmouth

Before we attempt to discuss the Ward and Lacon family further we would like to tell you something about Great Yarmouth where the branch of the Mortimer/Wards later made their home. Yarmouth was an important and wealthy town during the 13th century, due to its fishing industry. King Henry 3rd who granted a licence to the people living there to enclose the town with a wall and moat.

This licence was not taken advantage of for at least twenty years, eventually they started building it in 1281. It took one hundred years to complete the 2238-yard enclosure with a twenty-foot high defence wall. It was interrupted by the terrible consequences of the Black Death epidemic in 1348, which killed two thirds of the population of Yarmouth when almost 7,000 people died.

The walls were constructed of brick and rubble faced with flint and brick dressings. The Northwest tower was `D` shaped and constructed in the same manner as the walls. It was flat topped with a wooden floor, which was used as an observation post, originally part of the defense wall and possibly the last of the towers to be built. In 1334 only another eleven yards of walling was required to complete the town's defences to the river waters edge.

The threat of invasion from the Spanish Armada in the sixteenth century brought the need to strengthen the defences. In consideration of the new type of warfare that was being introduced; from bows and arrows to the use of artillery, we can see a similarity to the same concerns that were expressed when we first heard of the hydrogen bomb.

So it was with relief when new artillery pieces were placed along the length of the wall and also along the shoreline for defence, these cannons made the wall more or less obsolete.

Much of the wall has gone, but the parts that remain are maintained, and a plaque high on the wall in St. Peters Plain commemorates the Spanish Armada. In the civil war of 1642 the town took the side of the Roundheads [Parliamentary army] and guardhouses were set up in the towers. People who were known royalist sympathisers were locked up in them.

This situation continued for 18 years until the death of Oliver Cromwell, after this the walls served no purpose, were neglected and so decayed. The Black Tower had a conical roof added, this is still there today, it was used for domestic purposes for a time. A number of small industries also used these walls as secure boundaries and still do today.

THE ROWS OF GREAT YARMOUTH

Them there long bars of the gridiron,
That Dickens he wrote on so square,
Them `ere rows is a great institution,
In the town at the mouth of the Yare.

Plate.58

By Charles Dickens

Artist impression

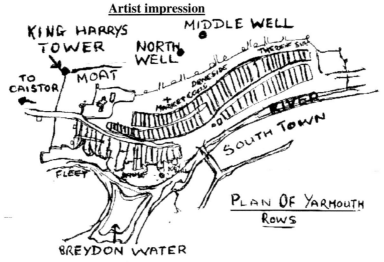

One Hundred and Fifty narrow Rows running east to west; some still survive

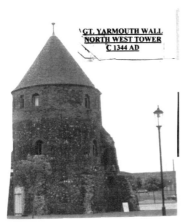

Yarmouth town walls and tower   Plate 59 / 59 [a]   **A typical Yarmouth row**

For 900 years the town buildings were constructed in Rows within its medieval walls, amounting to around 150 of them. This arrangement as far as we are aware is not found in any other town. The word Row derives from the medieval word Ranga and the Latin word Rengetta were both used in documents in 1198 to describe a basic land holding within a borough. Ranga is a range or row. A Row was the passage separating two Rengettas (or two rows of houses or bits of land). There are only few of these rows still to be seen in Yarmouth as Yarmouth today has much wider streets as main thoroughfares.

*Troll Carts or Harry Carrys were twelve foot long and three foot wide with two wheels made from solid ash or popular, five inches thick and two foot in diameter specially constructed under the cart so it could be loaded to its maximum width and still negotiate the narrow walls of the Rows. The driver stood across the staves controlling the horse with his reins. Later, laws were introduced to control reckless behaviour by those who made it a sporting event, by racing their troll carts down these Rows often colliding with people and houses in the process.

Panelled rooms and ornate ceilings can still be seen in the old merchant's houses of Rows 11 to 17 which are presently in the care of English Heritage. Some were destroyed or badly damaged during the Second World War and 1995 saw further loss when a large fire in the rows destroyed more of them.

The old fourteenth century museum still stands in what used to be Castle Row (the row itself was demolished in 1621] some of this building dates from the thirteenth century. It was originally part of the town fortifications then a private house and is one of the oldest buildings in the country, first recorded in 1362; became a tollhouse then a town **jail for many years. Later from 1500, it became a civic building and was used for the receipt of dues and taxes.

The site of the first settlement is on the south side of the town by Sir Thomas Meadowe's house, Fullers Hill, Yarmouth, which is the oldest East/West row and the highest point. Later the Lacon Brewery was built on the site and was a landmark for many years.

Of the many cottage industries that began in these famous rows; one was the Wards Brewery that incorporated quite a few of them. It began as a collective endeavour by some enterprising people who lived in the rows who started a brewery business under the direction of George Ward that grew; absorbing row 18 in 1691. When Robert Ward's daughter married John Lacon in 1743 it was renamed Lacon's Brewery. Being developed by local employers it has an interesting history, which connects to our family, as you will read.

Over a period of time due to fire, redevelopment, and possible neglect these unique Yarmouth rows will all gradually disappear into history unless strictly protected. Row 18, which the brewery absorbed, contained the Wrestlers Inn Hostelry; dated 1691, which was associated with Admiral Lord Nelson.

*See; -Palmers Perlustrations by Graham Palmer**Margaret Ward was jailed here, her cell is still there with a description of what she achieved during her imprisonment for her part in the Gunpowder Plot conspiracy, and she taught the children to read.

In the nineteenth century Charles Dickens often stayed in Yarmouth where he wrote his own favourite novel, "David Copperfield" and used the old Star Hotel by Yarmouth Quay as a backdrop to his book. It held the hearts of many East Anglians, as the scenes he portrayed were so vividly descriptive of the town and its local environment, it seemed that he had taken this little town to heart. Life for young Dickens was hard, his father was jailed for debt and Dickens himself was sent to work at twelve years of age in a blacking warehouse. This affected him deeply, but gave valuable experience of life to his writings in many ways, including his unhappy romance with Maria Beadnell, an experience that he used in his book "Little Dorrit". In 1836 he married Catherine Hogarth and they raised ten children, but they became disenchanted with each other and the marriage broke up, due to his affair with a young actress who became his mistress.

The setting for the book "David Copperfield" in Yarmouth seems to have been accidental, as he originally had planned to base it in Yarmouth, Isle of Wight. However really bad weather and a morbid curiosity over the brutal murders by James Rush at Stansfield Hall, near Norwich, was mentioned to him by his friend **Edward Bulwer-Lytton** of Knebworth who was also an author. This must have changed his mind as Dickens, accompanied by friends visited Norfolk instead. Edward added his mother's name Lytton after his own surname of Bulwer and had this legally confirmed although the rest of his family retained the original appellation of Bulwer.

These added topics of conversation may have fostered the budding friendship between them and drew Dickens attention to these brutal murders, so he decided to research and relate them in his story. No doubt he was able to obtain first hand accounts of these happenings from **Edward** and his cousins in Heydon as the father of the murderer lived on one of their Estate farms at the time these ghastly events took place. [Details of this are related in another story in this book p.308]. Dickens and his friends stayed at the Royal Hotel on Marine Parade Yarmouth, which has since been rebuilt, and there is a plaque to commemorate this. Dickens wrote to a friend that he had visited Norwich and considered it a dull place; moving on to Yarmouth he stated: -

"The success of the trip for me was to come to Yarmouth where we went afterwards, is the strangest place in the wide world, with many miles of barren marshes between it and London"

This statement is reiterated in the novel by David Copperfield as he first catches sight of Yarmouth from Barkis's cart, when he says to Barkis that a mound or two might have improved it.

A remark, which is true for this is an area that is rather flat and marshy along this stretch of coast, yet beautiful in its own right. Jack Sharman aged sixty-six, custodian of the Monument to Nelson at that time, had at the age of nineteen served on Nelsons Flagship "Victory" during the battle of Trafalgar. It was from him Dickens learned all about the townspeople and also the storms and shipwrecks, which are so vividly described in the pages of "David Copperfield".

We remember in our own childhood there was an old upturned boat on the beach called Peggoty's Cottage on the North Denes, whether this was the original one is hard to say, but we children loved to believe that it was, and wove our own tales around it. Much of this old Yarmouth has since gone, what the second world war left, the planners finished off, but those who read "David Copperfield" would know that it lives on through Dickens and his book.

Artist impression of Peggoty's Hut as used in the film "David Copperfield" by Charles Dickens in 1971 starring Sir Laurence Oliver, Sir Michael Redgrave, Sir Ralph Richardson and Dame Edith Evans on location at Benacre Beach, Norfolk Plate. 60

Dickens wrote fourteen novels, some of these were published in serial form in periodicals, they include 'Pickwick Papers', 'Oliver Twist', 'Nicholas Nickelby', and 'The Old Curiosity Shop', not forgetting 'A Christmas Carol' and many more. These stories were written in incredible and rapid succession from 1836; all are still read or used as the basis for stage and TV productions and films to this day.

The difference between these two contemporary authors **Edward Bulwer-Lytton** and Charles Dickens [who became firm friends] was that one wrote everyday personal stories about the wealthy, the other more strongly about the everyday existance and injustices in the lives of the poor. These stories reflecting their own life styles and character during the time in which they lived. **Edward Bulwer-Lyttons'** writings seem to have been forgotten though his friend Charles Dickens books still live on. Dickens died of a stroke in 1870, and **Edward died** in 1873 when an ear infection caused inflammation of the brain. They were both honoured with burial in Poets corner in Westminster Abbey. But to revert back to the famous Rows of Yarmouth, Rampant Row, Cramp Row, or Common Ramp Row were in a district of dilapidated housing, built against the

Ramparts [town walls]. A great many of these buildings were described as hovels. Regent Street was the first wide thoroughfare constructed in 1813. Red Herring formed part of the staple diet of the poor in Yarmouth, these fish were known locally as Ramp Row Goose, showing the poor quality of people's lives. Many rows were demolished in 1902 to accommodate Lacon's Brewery. The site of the Maltings was on the south side of the row now known as Rampant Road.

The oldest row was probably Row 10 built in the 11th century, and contained fisherman's cottages which were let on a seasonal basis. Again because of the needs of the expanding brewery other rows were demolished such as Row 17 in 1890. Lacon's absorbed Rows 15-16 in 1899, these are shown on the plan as being covered over and a part of Lacon's bottle store. In Row 32 was the Kings Public House where Joshiah Cutts the last town crier lived; he wore the ancient costume of blue coat and knee breeches with long white stockings.

Admiral Lord Nelson also visited this public house; Central Arcade now occupies this spot. The large mansion on the south east corner was owned by Mathew Gunthorpe who campaigned against the local smugglers in 1790`s, and on the North East corner there lived a Dr. Girdlestone of Castle Row in 1792 seen daily, dressed in black clothing, powdered hair and pigtail, white silk stockings, half garters white frilly shirt and carried a gold tipped cane; truly `a doctor of distinction`.

Some Rows were infamous, such as Row six, the former Body Snatchers Row, receiving its name from former inhabitants whose activities were to dig up bodies from the local cemetery, hide them in their houses, then transferring them to London to sell to Hospitals for teaching and research until their dark deeds were discovered. One culprit named Vaughan was imprisoned in the Old Tolhouse [still in existence] and sentenced to transportation. Row 95 Kitty-witches Row was traditionally used for witchcraft and Mathew Hopkins the 17th century self styled witch-finder made it his job to seek out some sixteen Yarmouth women who indulged in this practice and arrange for their execution

Other rows such as Broad Row, Market Row, [which still survive as major thoroughfares]. Gurney Bank Row, Fighting Cock Row, Sarah Martin's Row, Old Hannah's Row, [murdered by her husband John, the last man hanged for this crime in the borough]. Row number two took its name from an unsavoury hostelry; formerly Black Horse Row, this has a story of one fateful Christmas Eve of 1853, which strikes fear into the hearts of listeners; all these rows have interesting stories to tell.*

*Read "Norfolk remembered" by Robert Bagshaw. ISBN 0 900616 30 X

St NICHOLAS CHURCH
Great Yarmouth

Where Thomas Bulwer was married in 1861
Artists impression   Plate .61

You may recall we spoke of the lovely church of St. Nicholas Great Yarmouth, which is said to be the largest parish church in England and many of our ancestors were associated with it. It was built on the sandbank, which later became the town of Great Yarmouth. The present structure was founded in 1101 AD on the site of an earlier chapel used by fishermen and was built by the same Bishop Losinga who erected the beautiful Norwich Cathedral we see today.

The base of the tower shows the "long and the short" work in stone that describes the type of construction carried out by Saxon craftsmen. These first few rows of brickwork are all that is left of the earlier church. Like most churches much of the town's local history can be found on the tombstones within the church and churchyard. It was part of a priory like Norwich, but in the same way was brought to an abrupt end in the reign of Henry 8th, together with many other churches. Another extension was planned but the ravages of the Black Death stopped this for a time.

One event of the town's history we found inscribed on a gravestone in this churchyard details of a disaster in 1845 when the Haven suspension bridge collapsed and many people died. A description on a headstone with the eye of God looking down on this happening. The famous soldier Sir John Falstaff has a memorial which is located inside of the church. If you ever visit Yarmouth, which is a very popular holiday resort that has long golden beaches and is steeped in history, we recommend you consider all the historical events and places we have mentioned.

In 1942 this church was completely gutted by the firebombs dropped from enemy Luftwaffe bombers but was restored once more in 1957 but without its spire. Some of our ancestors were christened, married and buried there, including **Sir George** and **Lady England's** son with his wife **Anne** (nee **Bulwer**) who lived at 26 South Quay, which at that time had a Tudor appearance, but now looks like a Georgian type of house. Rachael the daughter of **Thomas** and **Anne Bulwer** lived there.

*The Mortimer's of Norfolk
Continued from p.242/244

Robert Mortimer came into possession of Harlexton in the County of Lincoln 1192 AD. This property or the charts appertaining to this Manor are considered a guiding light through the complexities of genealogical records during the reigns of King's Richard 1st and John.

The Wigmore part of the family grew rich and powerful; [more on this later] but it is the Norfolk family who developed from them we are interested in at the moment. They moved from Attleborough to **Kirby Bedon 1189 AD in the time of Richard 1st.

*TheMortimer's Hotel Norwich still exists and is used

Photo by Derek Edwards Copyright Norfolk Museums

.   and Archaeology Service.   Plate **62**

In the year 1286 **William Mortimer** had the Letters of the Kings Protection during his absence beyond the seas. His Manor of Chanticleers still stands on the north side of the church at Woodbridge Suffolk. This picture is of William de Mortimer's house on St. Giles Street in Norwich, later used as a hotel. below a note of interest. [Though this is probably not the William Mortimer of Norwich] in Somners antiquities of Canterbury:-

Robert Mortimer raised a son William who, for not obeying the law was excommunicated. He committed a wrong against the church by stealing from the Manor of Deopham a parcel of land belonging to the monks. He then had the audacity to intrude into their company. The Archbishop was informed and when the whole congregation came into the church, SirWilliam Mortimer was with them. Mass had just begun when the Prior stopped it and the excommunicated man was thrown out heavy-handedly.

*See chart of William Warrenna / Ward cht.39 p.165 + several others for other name changes.
**See item on Kirby House and Manor [page 273] '

William Ward had all the lands of his father released to him in the Manor of Scoulton on the 8 June 1294 and with sixty others he was summoned to the king to advise on affairs of state. In 1295 **William Mortimer** was appointed Commissioner to levy 800 men in the counties of Norfolk, Suffolk and Huntingdonshire and in the same year he was made Warden for the Norfolk coast.

After William died his son **Constantine** was seized by the King in a fight over property with William's' late wife. **Constantin**e held Manors in Attleborough from where he was summoned to Parliament in 1341. He was asked to travel to Rome with the Kings license with one valet two horses and two servants and on his return Sir John D'Egaine commissioned Constantine to array all able-bodied men and sufficient estates in two counties for the defense of the realm.

On his death in 1334, leaving a wife but no issue, **Sir Robert Mortimer** who married twice became sole heir. Marjorie his first wife, the sister of the great Sir John Falstaff of Caister Castle died in 1341. **Sir Robert** died in 1382 and according to his will requested to be buried in the Collegiate church of the Chapel in the fields Norwich.

His second wife outlived him. There were two sons **Constantine** the younger and **Thomas** who died after him. **Constantine** left a widow Mary [died 2nd May 1406] the daughter of Elizabeth Park; the daughter of John Cailey was given the custody of Bukenham Castle in 1295.

THE ESTATE OF KIRBY BEDON.
One mystery solved.

We found this quite by accident when looking at the Manor of Kirby Bedon in Bloomfield's Norfolk and discovered the link between the **Mortimer's** and the **Wards;** great excitement followed as we had found one of the missing links. The reasons why their names were changed so frequently as we said before, was usually because they had offended the King and in fact when we read the account of Kirby Bedon we found their names mentioned in the rebellion instigated by William Bainard who was disinherited.[See item on William Rufus]

Looking at the chart for **William Warrenna** 1st [page 165] the line of the daughter Adeline [married to Robert Beaumont] leads down to Robert who was a twin; this **Robert** changed his name to **Fitz-Roberts**, then to **Boscoe**. His son **Thomas** changed his name once more to **Ward,** now comes the clincher; **Simon Ward** was also of this line and it was Simon who married **Margaret Mortimer** bringing it into line with the charts in the visitation book. [See chart 39 page 165].

he Wodehouse Manor in Kirby was originally part of the Kirby Bedon/Saham Manors. Thomas Fitz-Roberts son of Maud Bedon having purchased several parts obtained a division, made it into a separate Manor and came to live by the wood there, calling it Woodhouse Manor.

The King repossessed this, probably in the time of the *rebellion but re-let it to Bosco/Ward in fee-farm for 6 pence per year, payable to the Hundred at Henstead; the Manor extends into Apton, Bramerton, and Arminghall. This was the time of many changes in name due to various rebellions, the **Mortimer** and **Ward** families included in this were ****de Bosco/de Bois** [related to King Stephen] of Kirby.

It was by that name in 1280 he obtained the lete with all its liberties, which at one time belonged to **Hereward the Wake**; *****Lakenham,** [where we lived as children], Rockland, Yelverton, Wicklinham /Whitlingham, Framingham, Trowse, Bixley, Castor /Caistor, Porland /Poringland. It continued with this family until 1580 when it was conveyed to ****William Godsalve. Later it was purchased by the Lord of Sahams Manor and rejoined to it. The family line continues through **Thomas Ward,** who goes to live at Yarmouth, which is where we will pick up this story again later.

A church service among the ruined walls Plate 63
These ruins are opposite the church of St Andrew.
Photo by Derek Edwards Copyright Norfolk Museums and Archaeology Service

Some of the walls and the Norman tower remain of St Mary's Church Kirby Bedon. A service was held amid these ruins in the late nineteen nineties for the first time since Queen Ann ruled in England. The church started to decay during the reign of James 2nd who was Catholic and a more so during the civil war under Cromwell.

Note; if you refer to the Ward family tree, it can be seen that Simon Ward was living at this time at Kirby Bedon Norfolk. He was a descendant of Roger de Mortimer [Count of Mortain who was banished from France and his father Hugh Mortain, whose father was half –brother to Duke Richard 1st of Normandy. See chart].
*When studying the line culminating in the Wards. (See Patent Rolls 1321). (See Woodhouse Manor Kirby **See chart for William Warrenna and also charts for Wards of Brook.
*** Lakenham was the area where as children we were brought up not knowing our distant relative Hereward the Wake [once owned this district]. Hereward was the son of Godvia and nephew to Turold.
****See Bloomfield's Norfolk [Bec Manor of Kirby Bedon].

WARDE'S OF BROKE

Arms a cross vert-between four martlets, gules
Crest on a mount vert. an eagle displayed ermine
Continued from chart 39 page165   Chart 63

Edward Wright	=	Margaret dau; of Edward Singleton

Geoffrey Warde died at Broke 13. October at 1.am 1568	=	Jane dau. And Heyre

Thomas Warde of Broke 28th October 1584 Will proved 22.9.1585	=	Mary dau of Richard Spencer of Seething Norfolk living 25th April 1583	Mary= Robert Obit Turner

THE WARDS OF GREAT YARMOUTH   Chart 64

[1]? sonne	Nicolas 3 sonnes	Edward Ward [Bixly]	**TOBIAS** = Yarmouth	**THOMASINE** dau. of Edward. Fisher	Thomas	Stephen	Alice

Text and chtart.66.cont. on p277
Names in capitals are family members

Continuing on Great Yarmouth, the scene of the old local families that we will later fit into our tapestry of life, the Mortimer/Wards. There are several breaks in this family line, names are changed and inheritance seem to be switched from one side of the family to the other; the reason is not clear and we must accept that it is almost certainly lost in time because of the plagues.

If you follow the family trees down to Duke Richard 1st of Normandy you will find the Mortimer family line on various charts in this book; [for example see page 165 Beaumont to de-Bossco. Some of the Mortimer families settled in England after the Norman Conquest and developed into three main branches with several name changes. Turning to the item on Kirkby Manor at Kirby Bedon p. 273, which once belonged to **Hereward the Wake,** you will see that there are two lines of the family. One family line from **Giselle** the daughter of **Charles the Simple of France** descending through the **Mortimer** lines and interestingly for us also into the family tree of **Earl of Warrenna/Mortimer.**

The Manor of Kirkby at Kirby Bedon resolves the matter of name changes for the **Mortimer/Ward** families. **Margaret Mortimer** came from the family that lived at Brooke (see chart of **William Warren** and the Manor of Kirkby). It is stated in the visitation accounts of the Manor rolls of Kirkby/Kirby Bedon and other books, that the **Mortimer's** were kinsmen of King William 1st.

The Puzzle of the Mortimer's and the Wards Resolved.
When Margaret Mortimer married Simon Ward on 20th June 1301.

This chart is for explanation only as to how we found the Ward and Mortimer connection.

THOMAS = ISOBEL issue leads down to WARDS*when   Chart 65

SIMON WARD = MARGARET MORTIMER in 1391

JOHN WARDE Lord of Kirby Bedon = Heir of John and Thomas de Bosco of Kirby Bedon

JOHN WARDE [Gent] son and Heir = KATHERINE dau; of William Appleyard of Braconash and Dunston Norfolk. Will proved 27th Oct. 1445 ordered his body to be buried in Church of Kirby Bedon often called John Attwood. John de Bosco. He fought at the siege of Calais

| SIR THOMAS WARDE Rector of Morley 1480 | John Warde | Robert Ward [Gent] Elder son | = Alice dau. Of Robert Kemp |

Continuing this line of the Ward's of Broke [as it was spelt then], Norfolk, Thomas Warde and his wife Mary lived there from 1558 – 1585 in the time of Elizabeth 1st and the Puritans. The fourth son Tobias [Toby] Ward of Brooke married Tomassine, the daughter of Edward Fisher of Great Witchingham. They produced one son [no name given] who in turn produced three sons, Augustine, [the first born], Joseph, and Edward.

During the civil war of 1642 (King Charles 1st v Cromwell) the Ward family supported Oliver Cromwell and brought money and plate for the use of Parliament and in 1648 Jeffrey Ward signed the solemn league and covenant to prove he was a Parliamentarian. The next year he held the office of bailiff and remained in favour until 1661 when he refused to sign an act of Parliament. He was also required to swear certain oaths, which he declined to do. He was dismissed and George Tillyard was appointed in his place. This however was no problem to Jeffrey Ward as the breweries that he had started in the famous Rows of Yarmouth were established and prospering.

After Jeffrey died in 1664 aged 74 years his nephew Gabriel inherited his properties under the will and married Mary Mackye a merchant's daughter. Gabriel also became a merchant and a bailiff in 1689. He died leaving a son Robert. It is interesting to note that **Robert** voted for **Erasmus Earle** [who was a relative of the Bulwer family] in the Norfolk elections of 1714. If you remember **Erasmus** was mentioned earlier as the Chief Justice and Confident to Cromwell.

Robert took over the job as bailiff with Sir Thomas Medowe; together they entertained King Charles 2nd and his servants and in the following May he and his brother James accompanied the king to Great Yarmouth to see the Dutch fleet under Admiral de Ruyter defeated off Southwold. The sound of the gunfire from the ships could be heard in Yarmouth.

*see chart 39. page 165

THE WARDS OF YARMOUTH FAMILY TREE
Following on from the Wards of Kirby Bedon page 275.chart 63/64.   Chart 66

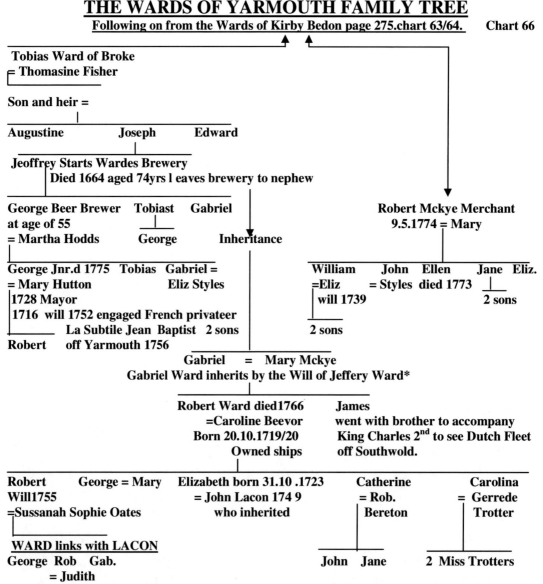

Tobias Ward of Broke
= Thomasine Fisher

Son and heir =

Augustine   Joseph   Edward

Jeoffrey Starts Wardes Brewery
     Died 1664 aged 74yrs l eaves brewery to nephew

George Beer Brewer   Tobiast   Gabriel   Robert Mckye Merchant
at age of 55   9.5.1774 = Mary
= Martha Hodds   George   Inheritance

George Jnr.d 1775 Tobias Gabriel =   William   John   Ellen   Jane Eliz.
= Mary Hutton   Eliz Styles   =Eliz   = Styles died 1773
1728 Mayor   will 1739   2 sons
1716 will 1752 engaged French privateer
            La Subtile Jean Baptist 2 sons   2 sons
Robert   off Yarmouth 1756

                    Gabriel   =   Mary Mckye
           Gabriel Ward inherits by the Will of Jeffery Ward*

           Robert Ward died1766   James
              =Caroline Beevor   went with brother to accompany
              Born 20.10.1719/20   King Charles 2nd to see Dutch Fleet
              Owned ships   off Southwold.

Robert   George = Mary   Elizabeth born 31.10 .1723   Catherine   Carolina
Will1755   = John Lacon 174 9   = Rob.   = Gerrede
=Sussanah Sophie Oates   who inherited   Bereton   Trotter

WARD links with LACON
George Rob Gab.   John Jane   2 Miss Trotters
       = Judith
Last of Wards of Yarmouth See charts of Wards of Yarmouth; John Lacon Cont.p. 278 chts. 67
                                And Lacon section, descendents of John and Eliz. p264 cht. 62]

BEEVOR links with WARD

Eliz.	Caroline	Martha	Catherine	Judith	Thomas	Caroline=Robert Ward
26.10. 1744	= James	17. 10. 1745	20.1.1747	15.6.1748	Barker	28.6.1750

*Jeffrey Ward's son **George** [who married Martha Hodds] was a Beer Brewer and elected as the first Mayor of Yarmouth in 1671 also in 1684 and again 1690. At his first mayor's banquet, the town gained a charter that gave consent to this office and he contributed ten pounds for the Golden Chains of the Mayor regalia. A great feast was prepared in celebration and no doubt much of the local Ward ale was quaffed. He died in 1690 aged fifty-five years leaving three sons, **Tobias, Gabriel** and **George** [junior] who married Mary Hutton and raised a son **Robert.**

Above information taken from visitation books

George took over as mayor in 1728. Historians recorded that on September 1st 1756 HMS Hazard engaged a French privateer "La Subtile" Jean Baptiste de la Harpe commanded the French ship, which had twelve guns and 86 men. The battle raged 6 hours, Frenchmen tried to board the Hazard, which went aground off Winterton. Some of the French crew were captured taken to Yarmouth and imprisoned.

They engineered an escape by undermining a wall until the last one became stuck in the aperture. Alas his shrieks alerted the guards and he was recaptured, [perhaps he had too much of Lacon's ales] the rest escaped. Sad to say money could not be found for the brave shipwrecked British seamen who were ignored. Their wounded were quartered with the poorer classes that had to collect money to feed them.

Top pictures
Robert & Caroline Ward

Lower
Daughter Elizabeth
Plate 64

Now we have outlined the families of the Wards and Beevor's we can also integrate these two families with the third by the marriage of Elizabeth Ward and John Lacon in 1749. He inherited the Ward's brewery in Great Yarmouth and began to carry on the family business.

<u>WARD FAMILY OF GREAT YARMOUTH</u>
[Continued; from page. 277 chart 66]

ROBERT WARD 1719-20 Owned ships died. aged 64	=	CAROLINA BEEVOR Rev. Beevor's 5th daughter. did bookwork		Chart. 67

Robert died aged 33 Will1755 = Sussanah on death Elizabeth inherits business	George = Mary = Sussanah Sophie Oates	ELIZABETH b. 31.10 .1723* = JOHN LACON 174 9* son of EDMOND and MARTHA See cht.62 p.264 descendants of above ↓	Catherine =Rob. Bereton ____ John Jane	Caroline = Gerrede Trotter ____ 2 issue
George Robert	George Robert Gabriel			

+ Cousins
Note.   Above Information taken from visitation books

There were three Robert Wards all living at this time; by following the family tree you can see one was Elizabeth's' father, another was her brother who had a son named Robert. All rather complicated [see chart on page 278] but we can now establish that all the main characters are now in place of the Lacon/Ward families.

*Robert Ward senior and his son Robert (Elizabeth's brother) ran the brewery between them and transported much of their products by sea from that Brewery. They owned several ships that were used for the brewery business and were thought to be the last Wards of Yarmouth. Robert Ward senior died in 1766, and Robert his son intended to run the business with his mother Carolina doing the bookwork, but this was destined never to happen, as he died aged 33 years. This now leads us to describe a sequence of events that created the Lacon brewery from the three main families.

Before Robert's young family came of age his mother Carolina died, Elizabeth, [Robert's sister] inherited the business; she and John Lacon [cousins through the two Beevor sisters] decided to marry each other and it is these two cousins we will concentrate on. John Lacon and Elizabeth Ward had completed the family triangle joining the Beevor's, Wards and Lacon's; the Brewery became known as Lacon's.

They bought their house, Quay House, Great Yarmouth from her grandfather Edmund Lacon, that stood on Hall Quay. This building fronted south extending nearly as far as George Street and was probably on the site of the town dwelling of **Sir John Falstaff K.G. spoken of in previous pages. One of the appointments this knight held was that of the governor of the Bastille.

It was said that the marriage of John and Elizabeth made their fortune as founders of the Lacon/Ward Brewing family in Norfolk, acquiring considerable lands and property in Great Yarmouth,

Bulwers living at this time

We noted that in the year 1880 **Harry Bulwer** aged 13 years, the son of **Thomas Henry Bulwer** [deceased] was brought up initially by his grandfather, who unfortunately died one year after, and it was his aunt Jane the widow of William Adams [late foreman of Lacon's brewery in Yarmouth] who continued to look after him. For more information see entry under family of **Thomas Henry.** When **Harry** moved to Eastbourne he worked as a cabman and brought up his family there.

---

* Some of this is repeated on p. 261 that deals with the Beevor family.
**He built Caistor Castle and a Mansion in Norwich where the Samson and Hercules now stand.

RULINGS ON ALEHOUSES
The Official Papers of Nathaniel Bacon *(In Part)*
1580 – 1620

We have included an extract of his papers because they not only affect the control of the brewers, but also touched the community life of the ordinary people.

[3]. Item….Any Innkeeper, Aylehouse Keeper or canyker (canner)? Shall utter or sell less than one quart of best ale or beer for less than a penny or less than two quarts of small beer for a penny. And be informed here to view the potts weither they be of the assize or not.

[4]. Item … Whether the beer or ale sold in the said house do not exceed the assize enjoyed to the brewers which is strong beer at the vj s. the barrel and small beer at iiij' s the barrel.

[5]. Item … Wether any person dwelling in any other towns ajoinynge do resort to the sid houses and continue tippling and drinking there. And wether any of the town shall send for beer there. And wether any of the towne shall send for beer and ale houses. To tipple and continue drinking. Thereby to defeat ye intent the good meaning of the law.

[6] Item … To certifie the name of some persons that mai testifye ye offenses committed against some of these articles. Endorsed copy of these articles to be dl. (delivered) to the Const. [Constable].

Touching the Kings service about the alehouses there has been a proceeding in most parts of the county And wee have admitted a great number at the rent prescribed. And yet in general conference among ourselves, before anie alehouse keeper, did receive his licence, wee thought it good to agree that no suritees. But subsidy men should be admitted for the better government of their alehouses.

This was performed in some parts of the Contrey and broke in others. In my opinion yt it were more for the Kings hono r. yf. Yo. R. Lo (Honour if you look)? And the rest might think so that such a direction might well be given generally, for liberty be given to take sureties at tha discretion of thee justices of the peace without betraying them to subsidy men. Then men of no value (as unseason yt was used) will be taken. And so no care had for breaking of their bonds in admitting disorder in their houses. Wich will cause ye service to be ye worse spoken of. As yf ye rent did embolden to do so if any fears should be conceived. That this course fr unseason of such value should hinder the unseas of alehouses.

There will not prove anie such cause as I see already by experience. For rather they would lose their victualing.

They will by some means or other get those governed and then it will be more for the hone r of the King to have it so governed. I thought it fit for me to aquaint yo r Lo (your lordship) herewith and so leave it to yo r wisdom to judge thereof. Thus beseecging God to give yo Lo: much increase of Hon r to his Glory, I take my leave from Stewky this 2nd June 1608.Yo. Ho at Commaundment.

Endorsed copy of a letter to my Lo Northt.

ALE BEFORE BREAD
The Authorities Get Tough with the Malsters
Requiring Particulars of Malsters.
From the Official papers of Nathanial Bacon 1550-1620

After our hearty commendations. Whereas of late tymu a great inconvenience and damage has risen to this kingdom, by the excessive number of Maulsters now growne throughout the realme wereof much waste and consumption of grayne hath been occasioned.

Alehouses The sprinnge of evil greatly increased scarcitie of bread corne hath happened, the husbandman chosing to rather to sow Barley then wheat or rye, by reason of his ready vent thereof., besies sundry abuses are found to bee practiced by Maulsters, as well in buying Barley on the ground before it bee reaped. Whereby the markets are unseasonabl and unreserved, as by malting it at unseasonable tymes of the yeare whereby it becometh unwholesome and deceitful in the use: with abuses and inconveniences having at severall tymes been represented to his Ma ste [Majesty] and the board and at he present tymes requiring a reformation by more due execution of the law in that behalfe, wee therefore by his M ste speciall direction doe rquire you, or any two or more of you in yo r severall and resptive divisions to send us a true particular of the names and quantities of all the Maulsters within that county, and what number you shal think fit to bee allowed.

Whereupon his Ma ste is resolved to take such futher course for reformation of the abuses as shall bee meete and so allowed, wee bid you & etc.

W. Cant.	Thomas Coventry.	H.Manchester
Bridgewater	Fra: Cottington	Dorset.
Wimbaldon	H. Vane. J. Coke.	Frs: Windebanke.

Note all written matter in these letters as written in original text

NORFOLK MALTINGS

There are only a few of the old malting's left in Norfolk sad to say, yet most of the larger towns in this country had one at some time in their history. From the small back streets of the Yarmouth Rows, the Wards home made brew developed into a large industry employing many people but after the company finished the malting's could not easily be converted into any practical use so they were demolished. Many other buildings also connected to this industry were destroyed in the concentrated bombing of the last war. Those still standing can be found as examples of their bygone history. Lots of the fine tools of their trade can be seen in various museums around the county.

A network of inland waterways were used to transport goods such as Malt and Barley that were conveyed mainly by river in horse drawn barges and where practicable by sea, by the breweries own Keels, Wherries and Sloops. This particular aspect was of great interest to us as we are still earnestly researching a reputed past family tragedy concerning our great-great-grandmother **Anne Furrence** who we believe was related to the Wards.

The story of these tragic events is told on page 308. Anne's father, a Captain was drowned at sea in a storm off the Norfolk Coast possibly navigating one of the ships for Lacons; as yet we cannot find any record of this as proof. Most of the really old records kept by the brewery on shipping are no longer available as the brewery itself was bombed during the war and most records were destroyed.

To navigate the bridges and shallows, the Norfolk Wherries could raise or lower the sails and keels as necessary and carry up to forty tons of cargo a day. The malting's were usually built near to landing places where the larger sea going Wherries or sloops could load up with beer and other goods for London and other ports.

Wells-on-Sea was the most important port in Norfolk where the out loading gantry on the quay side was built for shipping malt direct to Guinness in Dublin and to several Thames-side breweries. The channel was difficult to navigate so the harbour tug Marie, owned by Smiths towed these sailing barges up to three miles out to sea to ensure a safe course. The North Norfolk coastline is well known for its sand-banks, which shift with the tides. Its golden sand and shallow waters are mostly very safe for children to paddle in. However there are some dangers on some parts of this coastline where the tide can change very quickly and move fast to trap the unwary as it did when King John and his party tried to escape across the Wash.

THE WARD AND LACONS BREWERY

With the modern plant and techniques used for the production of ales, the smaller breweries could not compete. The national breweries took note of the great demand for local ales and other popular local brews as the taste of the old provincial beers was rarely excelled and bought them up.

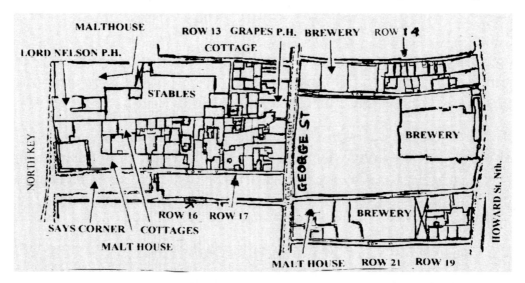

PLAN OF LACONS BREWERY 1883   Plate. 65

Local people protested but their objections fell on deaf ears; most of the small breweries have sadly gone and the old pyramid shapes of the malting's have been replaced by a square barrack block design. The Norfolk based brewery of Lacon's has now disappeared, along with many other local ales and small beers into the control of brewery giants that have taken all the small breweries out of circulation in their efforts to control the market.

The brewing industry is currently in for more change as new processes are much faster and fewer breweries are required. Also the new strict laws on drink driving and government taxes are forcing sales of beer to decline; instead of a night out having a drink with friends consuming several rounds of beer it has become popular to go for a meal instead and have a glass of wine. Many public houses are being forced to close, the owners taking advantage of the high land values to knock the pub down and build houses and flats on these large sites.

Whitbread's Brewery who bought out Lacon's, kindly provided us with an inventory of repairs carried out on one of Lacon's sloops 'The Eagle' We found this document very interesting and have printed it out for you to read. We thank Whitbread's this and other information that they kindly supplied.

Interesting Itemized Bill for Repairs Regarding the Sloop Eagle for Comparison with today's Prices

*Copy of a Bill for repairs for the Eagle Supplied by Whitbread's Brewery.

Plate 66   *Kindly supplied by Whitbread's Brewery

Note; This Bill of Reairs shows clearly the amazing differences of todats prices

Lacon's Ales, Favoured by The Gentry

In 1671 Charles 2nd and the Duke of York landed at Yarmouth with many other nobles and were elegantly entertained with Lacon's Ale. Sir Henry Shears a skillful engineer landed there in 1685 to survey the haven and piers. He was entertained at the Three Feathers Inn, [which still exists], paid them one hundred shillings for their trouble and also enjoyed the local Lacon Brew. As also did Prince George of Denmark who sailed into Yarmouth and before leaving for London, ordered a stock of his favourite beer. He left the same day for Windsor taking this local brew with him. There were many admirers of this ale and if royalty demanded it, so did London.

Five years later King William 3rd disembarked at Yarmouth and was elegantly entertained by the Civic leaders. Another Royal visit, this time to Lowestoft, was again noted in the Yarmouth records, so it would not be surprising to suppose that Lacon's beers were called for in the celebrations. Lord Nelson landed at Yarmouth with Lady Hamilton after the victory at Aboukir following the Battle of the Nile.

Sir Edmund Knowles Lacon headed the Yeomen Cavalry, escorting the distinguished visitors. Our ancestors **John Bulwer** and **General William Wiggett Bulwer** were alive at this time. **John** [from our direct line] was a Yeoman so he was probably there on this auspicious occasion. It seems a very small world to us at times and must have seemed an even smaller one then.

THE SWAN SONG OF THE NORFOLK BREWERIES

After John and Elizabeth Lacon took over the business they expanded it and renamed it Lacon's Brewery. The firm prospered in the time of Napoleon; and when Napoleon was thrown out of France in 1814 it was Lacon's who supplied 70 barrels of ale to celebrate at the festival, these cost ninety-five pounds six shillings. John and Elizabeth's son also became a maltster and ran the business, including a coal merchant's yard, which was known as Lacon & Coeval & Co.

John Lacon, Elizabeth's husband died 1782 and conveyed Hall Quay to his son John who had married Catherine Evans of Bury St. Edmunds. They owned much property in Norfolk and Suffolk but lived at Ormsby Hall. In the 1850's Lacon's made a successful assault on the mild ale market in London and this became a celebrated drink, having the considerable trade of two or three thousand barrels a week, at first transported by sea and then by rail. One of the ships previously mentioned was the sloop Eagle that traded their beer round the coastal ports.

The business only lasted a few more years, after which, it was leased to E.H. Lacon for twenty pounds per annum. In the middle 1800`s the next generation produced two more brothers, one of whom wasted his fortune by building Shadingfield Lodge. This building still exists opposite the Wellington Pier Great Yarmouth and was in use as a hotel but now operates as a Casino with a new name. It has an interesting past, which involved royalty, as you will read.

Yarmouth Shadingfield Lodge Yarmouth

on the sea front, now a Casino   Plate. 67

E. H. Lacon spent vast resources on this hotel to entertain Edward the Prince of Wales and his beautiful mistress [the actress Lilly Langtree] who were regular visitors

His efforts to gain access to royal circles failed, made him bankrupt and the business went to his brother who had no sons, the inheritance then went to a daughter with two sons.

The eldest son took his mother's maiden name of Lacon, and moved to Ormesby Hall receiving the title Baronet. He left the house to his son James and the family now lives at Somerton. The other son retained the family name of his father and remained on the Kevil Davis side of the family. He enclosed the road south of the hall retaining 300 acres of common land in Ormsby St. Michael that was used for the cutting of fuel [peat] for the villages.

When we last visited Great Yarmouth there was an information board explaining the story of Lilly Langtree and her association with Edward the Prince of Wales [later King Edward 6th] on the wall outside this hotel; we understand [at this time of writing] that this memorial has been removed.

While researching this story we found to our excitement that this Norfolk family line also contained the Viking Rollo of Normandy in 938 who you will find in the charts of both families and see that the two lines of France and Italy conjoin with Rollo's two wives. The Lacon's connected by marriage to the Mortimer/Wards and Bulwer's whose lines we previously researched are all kinsman of William the Conqueror.

MR. C KEVIL-DAVIES JP

Mr. Davies was the grandson of Ernest Lacon and in 1945 he was appointed vice chairman of the Lacon Brewery after he returned from war service in the army.

He retired as chairman shortly before the brewery was taken over by Whitbread. For the portraits of Robert Ward and his family we must offer our grateful thanks to Mr.Kevil Davies and for his encouragement and interest in our research, which was most helpful in promoting the success of our inquiries. Due to the fire at the Norwich record office our research at this time was again brought to a sudden halt but we continued to search elsewhere.

Enemy bombs during the Second World War destroyed the old malting's and cask store [built in1912] and when this was later rebuilt with a modern plant, it attracted the attention of Whitbread's the multi national brewers. They bought Lacon's out in 1966 and traded and brewed under the name of Lacon's for two years, after which supplies of beer for the area came from London.

Sadly Lacon's finally closed in 1968 and its well-known logo the Lacon Falcon was gone forever although many a pub sign still displays it, especially in Norwich and Yarmouth. A Falcon is still shown on some of the Whitbread beers as a reminder of the past.

There was great public outcry against this closure as it was not the only preferred local brewery to go. Many others were bought or closed by the larger breweries such as Pockthorpe Brewery, which started brewing in 1793, merged with Morgan's and Bullard's and later sold to Watney Mann. Morgan's Brewery of King St. Norwich was established in 1720 closed in 1985. Bullard's Anchor Brewery started 1837 by Richard Bullard. Young's and Crawshay bought out James Watts. Most of these names have now been forgotten, superseded by the multi national giants of the industry however several small breweries have recently made a comeback proving customers preference for 'Real Ale' brewed by the old methods.

Many brewers now use modern technology with the aid of chemicals in the form of prefabricated beers to quicken the process of manufacture and even some so called wines have very little natural ingredients using chemicals to create a false taste.

In general the day of the small family brewery was over
But a few have been able to survive.

WE START OUR RESEARCH INTO THE FURRENCE FAMILY

We have now covered the main historical facts of the Lacon story and will continue this intriguing family lineage which we believe to be our connection to the Lacon/Ward/Furence/Loveday families. Ironically we found our own grandfather Baxter was a foundling! There was no record of his father but we did research his mother to find that she spent most of her life in The Norwich Workhouse or worked as a maid in a large house on Earlham Road.

There were more positive results regarding our grandmother Elizabeth Baxter's lineage in regard to the Lacon's but it was the story she told us of her great grandmother Ann Furence that made us try and research her background but each time we had unbelievable blocks put in our way.

1] There were no living persons, as far as we know, who could answer our questions on the life of Ann Furence [daughter of a sea captain]. She was born at sea, her mother died in childbirth and her father and brother were later drowned in a shipwreck off the Norfolk coast.

2] The story our grandmother told was of the torn out page from the baptismal register, which was the only record of her birth. The church gave no help to our enquiry and seemed quite indignant regarding our request.

3] There had definitely been records of the Furence / Ward family held by the Norfolk Archives Department but these had been borrowed in 1975 and never returned [or mislaid] there must have been a story to tell.

4] A book which was held in Bedford Central Library with information on notable Naval Officers that we found helpful, was unfortunately missing on our next visit.

5] And to complete our frustration, during our enquiries the New Norwich Library burnt down and many books and local records were lost forever, it seemed any possible chance of locating other evidence was dashed. Our efforts that have so been tantalisingly close to locating firm evidence which was needed to prove Grandmothers story has eluded us.

Uncanny events in the lives of the Baxter side of the family brought such frustration to our research that we followed a clue to prove their lineage and hit a brick wall with no possible way to resolve it. Perhaps one day we may find clues to the origins of Anne and our grandfather **Henry Baxter** but it is almost certain that great grandmother **Abigail** has taken both these secrets to her grave.

Note;.maybe others may find these missing books and documents and trace facts on Anne Furrence and her family. See text of our research page 394/5 and cht 92 page 396

Her grandparents and parents name was **Baxter** and traded as [butchers] though we took **Abigail's** maiden name of Baxter we have not researched her ancestry very far back in time, which we should have done. We found records to showing **Henry** was born in a Norwich workhouse.

YOUR PROGRESS CHART THROUGH TIME

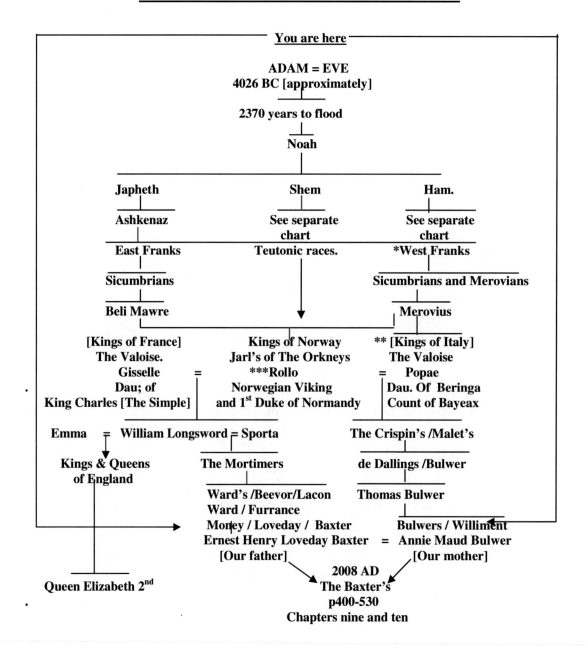

Chart 68

CHAPTER V11
HOLKHAM HALL
During the reigns of Edward 1st to the 3rd.

HOLKHAM HALL   Plate 68
Lordship and Landscape in Norfolk.

While continuing the histories of the **Dalling/Bulwer** families we found that the **Bulwer's** were in residence at Holkham sometime after the plagues during King Edward 1st reign but no clear evidence that they were Lords there. Holkham was also involved in the disturbances of the reformation; there were secret rooms for the priests [priest holes], which are still in existence, [see item on the Huguenots]. **John Dalling** [23.5.1284] witness on a grant of land. 1293-4. **John Bulwer** owned one acre, formerly property of Ralph Marriot.

Bulwer general notes
*__John Bulwer__ of Holkham Hall, **Richard** and **Walter** do not appear as grantors or recipients in these deeds, perhaps the crisis in farming in 1315 had forced them to sell their lands. But later they appear many times as witnesses.   **John Bulwer** was immensely active between 1377/83. **Laurence Bulwer** was sworn into tithing 22/7/1356. **Walter Bulwer** Chaplin surrendered land to his brother **John** 1364. 1322-9 Richard Neal's court rolls. **Thomas de Dallyng** who acts as a witness many times appear to be a court official.14.12.1329. **John Bulwer** is witness to a grant.

13.7.1332 Manor Court.
Rose Bulwer in dispute with John Smith is also mentioned. Richard Blakeman and **Agnes Bulwe**r reach agreement with Alicia Otes, **Rose Bulwer** is fined for various misdemeanours. Three entries for **Richard** son of **John Bulwer** [in lieu of Debt].

* The break in family records occurred about this time [1300's] during the Plagues and the records became slightly confusing though we did find the names of first born children in the Thurning Manor Rolls. In respect of Agnes Rattlesden there seems to be some confusion as to the name of her 2nd husband there is no doubt that he was a de Dalling but whether he was John or Roger as the records only list Roger.

22.7.13. 23. Leet court **Richard** son of **John Bulwer is** mentioned as married. Thomas Lamming of Gaywood collector's accounts. **Rose Bulwer** versus John Smith. Trespass of Simon Mous agreement reached. **Walter Bulwer** Chaplain tenant by grant of **Richard Bulwer** [if he pays the rent of 14pence] **Agnes Bulwer** v Alicia Otes suit. **Richard Bulwer**, v Robert Fish, **Thomas de Dallyng** is a witness.

Public Record Office Document

28.12.1332. James Becces sold land to **Simon** and **Helewise Bulwer**, but was ordered later to retain this land.

1332.   Tax return of Holkham lists **Agnes Bulwer** paying 12d [Old Currency]

6.5.1333.   **Agnes Bulwer** will pay back Robert Andrew 36 shillings next Martinmas.

28.12.1342   Richard Bakehouse has died, no heir came forth.

8.12.1334   Lord of the Manor granted lands to **John** and **Margaret Bulwer. Margaret** daughter of **John Bulwer** marries without licence. **John Bulwer** of Holkham, **Richard** and **Walter** do not appear as recipients in these deeds, but appear many times as witnesses.

1377   **Lawrence Bulwer** was sworn into tithing,

27.7.1356.   **Walter Bulwer** Chaplin surrendered land to his brother **John**.25.6.1361.

18.6.1333,   Grant of land to **Roger de Dalling**.

18.6.1333.   Grant of land **Walter Bulwer** Chaplain land adjacent.

17.4.1331   **Richard** son of **John Bulwer**, releases land to John Richard Neale, which he acquired from Edmund Otes.

13.10.1332   List of land acquired by Neil Family. **Agnes Bulwer's** land near Bondescroft

4.11.1323   **John Bulwer's** land 1 acre **Walter Bulwer's** land

25.3.1334.   **Agnes Dallyng** widow of John married Richard Blakeman. Of Holkham paying a dowry of half a mark. **Agnes** involved in legal battle with former-in-laws, after a suit that involved the assize of Novel diseissin she established that her dower should be confirmed to her by **Richard Bulwer**, a relative of her former husband [28.3.1335]. This meant half a message and twenty acres of land which should remain the property of her new husband if **Agnes** should die first instead of reverting back to the *Bulwers.

*This follows on from the legal wrangling over Field Dalling

Inquisition, Post Mortem, and Close Rolls May 1319

Whereas Thomas Earl of Lancaster brought before him there a writ of covenant against **John de Warrenna** Earl of Surrey, who came and acknowledged that the aforesaid Manors were the right of the Earl of Lancaster, and granted him in this court. This is inserted here as it pre-empted the statement made below.

12.7.42.1348 Edward 3rd. **John de Warrenna** Earl of Surrey. Lands in Wood Dalling to revert back to The Earl of Lancaster [John of Gaunt].

22.4.14. Henry VII Robert Dyne referred to a time when **Thomas Bulwer** was seized of the land of Thirning. More proof of **Thomas'** existence is as stated in the Doomsday Transcript for Norfolk.

Doomsday Transcript by Mundford [Norfolk only]

We have not been able to check these, but think they may apply to the separate Manor of Dalling built by **Rogers's** son **John,** on lands owned by Sir John Hobart. More confusion here as **William Warrenna** seems to be involved, giving a much earlier date than these court cases? But if the reader has time, the following Chancery Proceedings might throw some light of this. There seems to be more that one Dalling concerned here.

Chancery Proceedings

Richard Dalling……… …p.181 Suite 60	
Nicholas Dalling…………p.343 Suite 159	
William Dalling………… p.39 Suite 9	
William Dalling………….p.46 Suite 170	
William Dalling……….. p. 276 Suite 370.	
Roger Bulware………… p.114 Suite 49	
John *Bulware ………… p.248 Suite 49.	

7.4.1331 **Richard Bulwer's** lands. 1.11.1323. In Addition to above 1 rod of **John Bulwer's** land. Same in Domsday transcript by Mundford

The Bulwer's of Norwich 1291-1392 From the Norwich Deeds

1291. **Peter de Dalling** Chaplain, deceased, late Master of Magdalen Norwich selling lands to Adam de Saham, linen Draper in Lek Market 1299 Richard de Aula selling to **John de Dalling** and **Katherine** his wife, land in St. James

1305. Henry le Cranworth. Le Coner and Letitia his wife, selling lands to **Andrew de Dalling** in St Andrews. Andrew Frenoble selling to **Andrew de Dalling and Beatrix** his wife, land in St. Peter Hungate.

1306 **Andrew and Beatrix de Dalling** selling to William de Verney of Crostwick, land in St. Andrews.

Note-: *as spelt in Manor Rolls.

1309 **Andrew de Dalling** and **Beatrix**, land sold to William Wade a cutler in St Peter Hungate. **William Dalling** and **Alice Bridget** his wife of Billingford land in St. Peter Hungate.

1317 John **Dalling** and **Katherine** sold land to Robert son of Lawrence Tanner in St James.

1322 **Andrew de Dalling** and **Beatrix** sold land to the Friars and Preachers in St. Peter Hungate. Also William Sheppirde and Joan land in St. Katerine **Andrew de Dalling** to Aveline a daughter of John Bates of Billingford lands in St. Peter Hungate.

1323 Henry Sything Coupere living in Norwich, and Matilda to **Andrew de Dalling** and **Beatrix**, Land in St Andrew.

1330 **Beatrix** widow of **Andrew de Dalling** to John Weston and Joan land in St. Andrews.

1331 **John de Dalling,** [tailor] and Helwysia selling through their attorney William de Dalling land to John Meche' and Christian, Land in St. James
William Hemstead Mayor of Norwich, planned insurrection to force an issue against the king. He believed the City was too important to be punished. Arrangements were made for John Gladman Merchant to ride through the city with a crown and sceptre, with three unknown men. [Including **Richard Dalling** Cutler, of St. Andrews Hill; shop still there] acting as if they were three valets to the King. They urged the people to riot and were punished by being excommunicated. The Mayor was imprisoned for three weeks, and the city was fined.

Close Rolls 1380-1443

1283 **Simon de Dalling** receiving a pension of thirteen shillings and four pence

1388 **Thomas Bulwer** involved with a captured ship the le Clement at Holkham.

1430 **William Dalling** indicted for bribery.

Norwich Cathedral Charters.

1121-35 At Bacton witnesses includes Roger Valonuis/Valoise and Ralph, son of Toraldi/Turold of Dalling

1150-97 Turold is witness again [son of Odo]

1145 Turold chaplain to Bishop William Turke.

1174. Turold Chaplain mentioned

1240 Witness to quit claim.

1294. Simon de Dalling witness

1298. Simon to quit claim.

1303. Same.

1347 Grant to William de Dallyng late of Fulk Bindulf in Calais.

1352. Commission of Oyer and terminer to Richard de Kettleshall, on complaint by Ralph Earl of Stafford, that John Bullock, John Bulwer, and others carried away their goods at Wells Warham and Styvekye [Stiffkey] 20s. fine.

1357 August commission Oyer terminer to John Bardolph on complaint of John, Earl of Richmond. That Matthew Bulwer of Castle Acre and others stole goods at Castle Acre and South Acre and assaulted his men and servants.

1361 Manors of Wood Dalling and many others given over to William and Maud Count of Henland and Earl of Leicester.

1392 May. John Dalyng was the master of a ship, lately wrecked off Seland, which goods come ashore on the island of Thanet, Walmere and Sandwich. Orders for the arrest of those involved all the crew was saved. The goods belong to John de Odebereshuasen and Arnold Speryng, and they have been granted restitution.

From the Close Rolls;

1319 John de Dalling was Sheriff of London. William de Cawston was listed as being there too.

1320 Edmond de Acre acknowledges he owes a debt to John de Dalling the younger and Nicholas de Cawston [401].

1324 Enrolment of a deed of Edmund de Baconsthorpe witness John de William and John de Cawston citizens of London.

1331 At Norwich to the Sheriff of Norfolk. John one of several asking for the release of Thomas Bintree to answer a writ.

1283 Simon de Dalling is mentioned as receiving a pension.

1316 Manorial lists Field Dalling. Peter son of Philip de Dalling.

1330 William de Dalling indicted Judge Paston for bribery, early in the 14th century Eustice de Dalling mentioned.

1388 Thomas Bulwer one of several involved with a captured ship 'le Clement' at Holkham.

1466. Obit of Mag. Simon de Dalling referred too.

1349 Edward 3rd part one Membrane 22. + [Continued on next page].

**A break in family records occurred about this time, due to the plagues raging, but records at Thurning and some Manor Rolls and other sources have proved very productive
Note; -From 1319 to 1324 these roll's repeated the same information, some of which we have omitted. We have transcribed the above information from Manorial Books held by The Norfolk Cultural Services Department Norwich.**

To the Bishop of Norwich, order to admit a person to the third part of the church of St. Mary Itteringham. Further to what pertains to his office in this matter, though the king lately forbade him to admit a parson thereto until it had been discussed as to whom the advowson pertains, and afterwards at the suit of Edward, after that to Maud, late wife of John de Dalling. Showing it had been agreed that Edward should present his clerk and Maud hers at the next voidance and that they had sued before the Bishop to admit Edward's clerk.

Asserting that his hands were bound by the prohibition aforesaid and they beseeching the king to provide a remedy that the coalition of the third part should not fall into the hands of the Bishop by the lapse of time, which, will soon happen, it is said that the king ordered Robert de Morlee to ascertain whether the said agreements were made between Edward and Maud. And to certify the King thereupon in chancery, Robert returned that agreements were made between Edward and Maude in the form as said that they should present alternately by deeds made between them.

Deeds 1406-1446.
1401 –Bulwer deed Henry Bulwer, Chaplain of Cawston. Roger Bulwer, shown as accepting lands in Salle.

1471   John Bulwer of Sedgeford land to Thomas Denys and others in South Creak, from John Bulwer to others Land in Croxton.

1337 Thurning Manor deeds and Bulwer deeds confirm this, Deeds Thurning Manor 1476-1557.

1316 Manorial Lists.
. Field Dalling. **Peter de-Dalling** son of **Philip de-Dalling,** Swainsthorpe. **Simon de Dalling** Wood Dalling, **Earl Warren**, Simon de Rattlesden, John Newman, Ralph de Stinton.

Offenses
The Official Papers of Nathaniel Bacon, Commission to John Sturmy, Thomas Hindringham and John Claver, with Walter de Norwico, Robert Baynard, and John Ingham, to make inquisition of the Counties of Norfolk and Suffolk, regarding diver trespasses, felonies, oppressions, crimes of violence.

Note

These too have been transcribed, the above information from Manorial Books held by The Norfolk Cultural Services Department, Norwich.

.

Master **Simon de Dalling** and Thomas Jernmuth undertook to sue his business before them under his protection. But he now understands that the said **Simon** and Thomas maliciously detained his commission therein. Showing it in divers parts of the counties and by threat exhorted money from some men that they should not be disturbed in the premises, and have not yet sued anything in the said business.

They have counterfeited the seal of the Mayoralty, and done other evils of the like nature. Assignment to find out how long **Simon** and Thomas detained his commission? What sums they obtained by exhorting? Whether they did not sue his business as aforesaid? And the whole truth as to the counterfeiting of the seals, and the sealing.

28.2.1320 Complaint by Aline late wife of Edward Bernel. That **John** son of **Simon** de Wode Dalling and others broke her close at Thirnyng fished in her stews and took her fish. Protection granted to **Thomas de Dalling** and for his ships, [of the then Bishops Lenne]. So called because they once belonged to Bishop Odo half brother of William 1st, who displeased the king by rebelling, later it came into the hands of King John brother of King Richard of England. [So it was renamed Kings Lenne/Lynn].

Ancient Petition 1420 Thomas Bulwer
Ref. SC8 / 96 / 4793, [transcript]

In 1420 A **Thomas Bulwer** lived in Cromer but we have not been able obtain his actual place of residence. Cromer has a place in the lives of several of the Bulwer family. Though family members [including our parents], felt strongly about the fact that the **de Dallings or Bulwer's** lived at Gunton Hall at one time, we have found no written evidence to prove this, though there are one or two indications it could have happened.

*Thomas sent a petition in Norman/ French [not easy to translate] to the then Duke of Gloucester [a rough synopsis as well as it was possible to do is inserted]. It went as follows; - A petition for the return of, or compensation for, goods taken from places of residences round the Cromer area, and compensation was also required for damage done and expenses incurred.

*See, copy of official document from Central Library London, translation made from Norman/French. See P. Rutlege in acknowledgements.

The original document was damaged and faded by age, the dialect was a type of Norman French, which was very confusing to the *translator. This document went, together with several other letters from the same area, regarding the breaking of the truce between England and Flanders, to make it easier to understand we have rendered the translation as closely as possible.

C.A Harris, translator states: *It was difficult to translate the various symbols used but conclude: - 'the letter seems to be asking for either to have their goods returned, to be allowed to sell or possibly to be reimbursed.*

Comments by P. Rutledge, Archivist on the letter above.
As addressed to the Duke of Gloucester regarding the breaking of Truces between England and Flanders. Another notable member of the **Bulwer** family from the Heydon branch is **Edward Lord of Dalling** Hargreys and Holwood who was born in 1649 the son of **Edward Bulwer** and **Ann** [nee Young]. He was one of the gentlemen of his majesty's privy chamber, married Hannah Penyer/ Perrier who had one daughter from a previous marriage, which resulted in a court case over inheritance when he died on 4th October 1725. This was an ancient manor with many previous names. It held the manors of Dalling Hargreys, Moncleuax, Halwood, Noijois, and Hargraffe. With house and estate at Churchgate also another estate at Thurning.

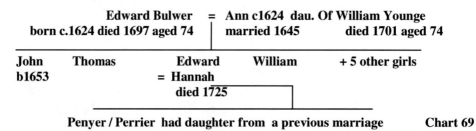

Edward Bulwer			=	Ann c1624 dau. Of William Younge	
born c.1624 died 1697 aged 74				married 1645	died 1701 aged 74
John	Thomas	Edward	William		+ 5 other girls
b1653		= Hannah			
		died 1725			

Penyer / Perrier had daughter from a previous marriage   Chart 69

In Edward Bulwer's time, Charles 1st [1625 -1649] was King and Edward was a gentleman of the king's privy chamber. He must have been a royalist who saw the bad relationship between the king and parliament at first hand, which resulted in *civil war [1642]. Charles 1st was executed and the House of Lords was abolished. Cromwell in 1653 became Lord Protector over a republic that lasted until he died [1658]. His son took his place but failed to govern as his father did. The constitution was revived and Charles 2nd [son of Charles 1st] returned to be crowned on 23rd April 1661. In 1665 there was the great plague and at least 110,000 people died in that year.

*We noted that there was a John Bulwer who was Armourer to Oliver Cromwell. This armoury used to be in Chapel in the Field Gardens [now demolished]

THE WIGGETTS OF GUIST
NORFOLK

The name Geust (Geggset) means as set by the river or waters then corrupted to Guest (in dell or vale). To be clear on the **Wiggett / Bulwer** family history you should study the chart 72 page 304 where you will find that the Wiggett's married into the **Bulwer** family in the1500's, after which it can be seen that several marriages took place between these two families. Geoffrey de Save held this manor at the beginning of Henry 3rd reign, rent of assize 101 in Guestwick Bintree, it then came to John de Save, and from him to the crown.

Guestwick Hall   Plate 69

When King Henry 8th granted it to Alice de Luton, the nurse to his son Prince Edward in his 28th year, for her life. To be clear on the family history, study the family tree and follow the lineage. Later the Wiggett family owned the manor in 1580 when John Wiggett seized the lands. His son and heir **Peter** married **Alice** the daughter of **Simon Bulwer** and **Joan Allyne** of Woodalling. **Ann**, daughter of **Peter Alleyne** succeeded then **a Henry Wiggett** followed them; in succession **William Wiggett** [who married **Anne Sheringham**] produced seven sons. One of whom, John we found was buried at Whitwell Church Reepham in 1692.

Register of Gresham School.

Edward Bulwer b.1771, an eccentric mender of pots and pans was the most badly dressed member of the Bulwer family; became the rector of Salle 1818. He married twice [see p. 302] 1st Amy Grover [died] then to the family disgust married his daughter's maid who he had sent to jail for debt. Later you will read, a visiting Reverend described his dress and manners, and concluded that he was the most unlikely parson anyone could meet.

Augustine Bulwer Clergyman left 1774, ordained 1784 at Norwich, Rector of Heydon 1786-1831 and Salle 1706-1818, vicar at Corpusty 1790-1831. **Thomas Bulwer** left Gresham School and became a Farmer in Heydon 1774.

Pedigree of the Alleyne/Elwyn Family and the inter-marriages with the Bulwer's.

Chart. 70

From the Book 'Norfolk Families' by P.P.Moore

JOHN ELWYNE =   CATHERINE de DALLING
b. c. 1450   [Bulwer]
of Wood Dalling   **[Main line]**
died 1502 / 1532

PETER ELWYNE   =   LUCY
Of Wood Dalling   died before 1556
Bought Thirning Hall
From William Wiggett.
Will 1557

Sir John Elwyne   JOANE   William   dau.   Alice
              b. c. 1515/16   died before 1557/68
              = SIMON BULWER
              of Wood Dalling
              [born 1510 died 1568 / 69]   [See the rest of the Bulwer families most of who
                [Main family]   lived in Heigham Hall Norwich. This area was
                Beginning of our line   devastated during the Blitzkriegs of the 2nd
Peter = Eliz. Kett d. 1603   World War
of Thurning   THOMAS BULWER = ANTONIA
chief steward to   [Our line]
the Earl of   See charts for Buxton Hainford and Elsing families page 361& 348
Sussex died.1595 will

Peter of Thurning   =   1ST JANE BULWER 2nd Katherine Lynge
Son and heir under   daughter of Roger
21 in 1565 died.1607   of Wood Dalling
                 and Christine daughter
                 of John Wroute
                 married m Guistwick
                 [Main family]

        Peter   = PALGRAVE FOUNTAIN
        born 1598   [Our line]

        Peter   = ANN ROLFE
        born 1623   [Our line]

     *ANN ELWYNE= WILLIAM BULWER
      born 1662/3 [Main line]
      of Dalling see chart for Bulwers
      [Our line] had son Edward a priest died.1724

1687 LINK WITH THE MAIN FAMILY [WILLIAM OF DALLING]
See chart 82 p.361 cht. 84 p.362 cht 85 p. 367 for Heydon and Buxton Hainford Elsing families
To correspond with associated text this chart is repeated for Buxton Hainford and Elsing families

NOTE; NAMES IN CAPITAL LETTERS ARE MEMBERS OF OUR FAMILY.

HEYDON AND THE EARL FAMILY

The town of Heydon is five miles from Aylsham Norfolk (name signifies the high down or plain on the hill). It was not known by that name in the Domsday Book but as Stinetuna or Stinton later Salle. King Harold Godwin originally owned the manors of Heydon and Cawston. Whither, a Saxon was lord here at the time of the Domsday survey. King William deprived him of the Lordship and gave it to William de **Mortimer/Warrenna** or **Warren**, of whom Ralph of this name held it at the Conqueror's survey. It continued in the **Warrenna's** ownership till they enfeoffed William Caineto [or Cheyney]; he founded the Priory of Regular Cannon's at East Rudham, Norfolk about 1143 then moved out.

As a matter of interest the Domsday survey of Stinton (Heydon) listed:
3 carucates of land in demean, and 8 in tenants hands, 9 villeins, 39 boarders and 3 servants. Woods that maintained a 100 swine, 1 mill, 2 working horses, 40 swine in the yards, 120 sheep, 27 goats, 3 beehives the advowson of the church, which had 14 acre's of glebe. 14 socmen that held 80 acres of land, and had 4 carucates of ploughed land among them.
A wood that maintained 10 hogs, 1 acre of meadow, and 1 border, 2 of the socmen Earl Ralf held, (when he forfeited his estate, and they had 12 acres of 20 pence yearly value. The whole manor was then worth 5l pence and rose to 7l; the town was above a mile long and half as much wide and paid [xi.d] 11pence to the king's tax towards every 20s raised in the hundred.

The hundreds of South Erpingham belonged to the crown until it was granted to John de Burgh, Earl of Kent who released it to Edward 1st. Having passed through several hands it came finally to the Kings son John of Gaunt and became part of the Duchy of Lancaster with the manor of Aylsham, the Hundreds of Erpingham, Gallows and Brothercross.

If you visit the church at Heydon you will notice two Roundhead Helmets, rusty and coated with dust on the sill of a window that has been bricked at the back of the tomb of Erasmus Earl. Could they possibly have belonged to **Erasmus** and Oliver Cromwell? In 1648 **Erasmu**s the close friend of Oliver Cromwell succeeded William Denny Esquire as Steward of Norwich and was chosen as recorder there in the room of Samuel Smith Esquire until 1653.

Erasmus Earle purchased the Manors of Heydon and Cawston from Sir Robert Kemp. Oliver Cromwell used to visit his friend **Erasmus** at Heydon regularly. On one such visit he ran for his life to escape the wrath of a bull and survived only by beating a hasty retreat up an oak tree.

Little is recorded on the life of Reverend Augustine Earle, brother of Erasmus, but we do know he was married with at least one daughter, Mary who later married William Wiggett Bulwer. He was one of the non-Commissioners of Excise and a member of the Society of Antiquaries. Heydon was not enfeoffed to the Dalling or Bulwer families but they acquired the property in the time of Oliver Cromwell.

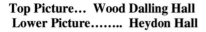

Top Picture... Wood Dalling Hall		**Top picture Heydon village street**
Lower Picture........ Heydon Hall	Plate 70	**Lower picture Heydon village green**

The village of Heydon has many interesting features and has retained its old world charms which are all centered on the Hall. The old smithy where the blacksmith created a life-size model of a mare and foal out of horseshoes still exists; he unfortunately was the last blacksmith working on this estate and has since retired.

On one visit this man informed us that he was intending to retire and as there was no one to take his place and he was concerned as to the future of all the ancient tools of his trade in the smithy. We made enquiries as to this and other matters and were assured by the Heydon estate manager that the old workshop and contents would certainly be retained for posterity. Heydon Hall has delighted film and television crews alike as it generates an air of mystery and history; over thirty films have been made there and it is said that the ghost of old General Bulwer still haunts the Hall. Perhaps he is still searching for something and would have dearly liked to acquire the title of Lord Erpingham.

Chart 71   **SIMON AND JONE DALLING / BULWER**
COMMON ANCESTOR TO AL BRANCHES BELOW

***HEYDON LEADING TO KNEBWORTH/HAINFORD BRANCHES** [see also chart 85
page 367]   Continued from chart 49 page 208

SIMON = JONE	Roger	William	Anne = Thomas	Audrey = William		Maud
Dughter of	died 1517/18		Smythe	Smythe		
Peter Elwyn						

ANN = ROGER	= **Christian**	John William Christopher	**THOMAS = ANTONIA** + Others		
DAU. OF	daughter. of				
WILLIAM	John		Our family line of Hainford Elsing and Buxton		
BULWER	Wrowte		**See page 349 Chart 79.**		
See page 362	**See visitation Book [Guistwick]**				
Chart.84	**amd Manor Rolls 1513 1569 & 1613**		**Hanford Man.Rolls**		
Aylesham Branch	**See.page 348 chart 79**		**See page 349 chart 79**		
			Vis; Bk. 1604 – 1810		

Anne dau.of William Beck = **Edward = Margaret**   + nine others
         Issue

Edward   **Roger = E.liz.** daughter of Robert Cock   William   Thomas   + 6 others

Edward = Anne   William = Elizabeth   + 5 others
   Daughter of William Younge   daughter of Thomas Self

3 issue + Edward = Hannah Perrier/Penyer   William = 1st **ANNE** = 3rd wife **Francis Lee**
.   died   daughter of Edward Lee **Main line**

       Rev ; EDWARD BULWER [Aylesham branch]

JAMES BULWER [Will 1783]   THOMAS [Aylesham Branch]
= Mary [lived at Sutton [Will 1799]   **Butcher = Eliz. Gottesham**

JOHN [well known councilor]   MARY =   SARAH = John Gedge
                       Joseph Decker   of Sutton
                       Swannton Abbott [See will]   **Sarah = Rice Wiggot + 4**

             MARY = James Bulwer   **William Wiggot = Mary Earl**   + 4
               m 1799   daughter of Augustus Earl
                           changed name to Wiggot Bulwer
       Cont. on page 362 chart 84   Guistwick/Heydon Branches

General Earl =	**Eliz. Barbara** **Augustine**	**Edward**	+others
Wigget Bulwer /	**Warburton** **= Bridget Lloyd**	**born 1771** = 1st **Amy Grover**	
Heydon branch		**Rector of Salle** 2nd **=Ann Warterick**	
	Augustine	**See p.298**	
		Edward Mary Blanche **Marian**	

William Lytton Bulwer	Henry Lord Dalling	**Edward Lytton Bulwer** + 3 others
= Emily Gascoyne	= Georgina Charlotte	**= Rosina Wheeler**
	Wellesley	**Start of Knebworth branch**
Col. William	Edward Earle + 4 others	**Robert** **Emily**
Earl Gascoyne	Gasgcoyn Bulwer	**Knebworth** [Little Boots]
Lytton Bulwer		** More details on those below see footnote
= Marion Dearing		* Anne Bulwer descendant of sister of Alexander [died 1687]
dau. Of William Wilson Lee Warner		= Henry Marsham [3rd generation down
		Anne Elwyn = William Bulwer [Heydon died 1735]

Cont. page 348. chart 79 Heydon and page.362 Aylesham. The Aylesham branch is shown in
**black capitals and chart is repeated p362 Buxton Hainford families to correspond with
associated text**

CHART FOR THE EARLE / WIGGOTT / BULWER FAMILY

The earliest records we researched were the ancient families of Fountain/ Briggs and Earle. In 1350 it appears the family divided and one branch was established in Suffolk and another [Thomas Earle] had settled in Salle near Heydon close to the Fountains estate. There seemed to be a William de Earle in 1361 then a succession of John Earle's acquiring land in this area taking, advantage of those who perished during the Black Death.

Chart 72

Thomas Earle=Ann Fountaine late 1500

3 dau's one of whom [Anne] became ancestor to William Darwin	*Erasmus Earl 1590 –1667[Sergeant at law to Oliver Cromwell] bought Heydon Hall. 1650	=	Francis Fontaine [Cousin]

John Earle, Sheriff of Norfolk 1622-1667 = Sarah dau. Of Sir John Hare d 1667

Ralph Earle Buried near his Grandfather at Heydon born.1655.	Mary = John Bassett of Irmingland	Erasmus heir on fathers death. born.1658 -172	= Eleanor Castle d.1736 of Raveningham Hall
	Three sons all died young	Augustine Earl 1692-1762 Heydon Salle and Cawston [inherited after the death of Erasmus] = Frances Blacklock of Seascale Hall] Dau. Of Robert Blacklock died 1762	

Erasmus [Lunatic disinherited] 1717 = Hannah Maria Grey] died 1768	Elizabeth 1739 = Sir Henry Calder	**Mary Earle = William Wiggett/ Bulwer 1737 -1798 1730 -1793

CONTINUATION OF THE HEYDON LINE FROM p. 208. Cht. 49.

General William Earle Wiggett Bulwer b1757 -1807 =Eliz.Barb. .Warburtom Lytton b.1773 d.1843	John b.1766 = Mary Thomas Issue b 1759 d 1821	***Edward b 1771 d 1846 Rector of Salle 1818 = 1st Amy Grover 2nd Ann Waterwick	Augustine = Bridgett Rector of Newton	Mary b1759 d.1821	Francis b1758 d 1796	Sarah b 1763 John Godfrey Leading to* Marshams

Will. Lytt:Bulwer b.1799 d.1877 = Emily Gascoyne b.1808 d.1836 dau; Earl Gascoyne d.1872]	One Child	Henry Lord Dalling born.1801 d.1878 =Georgina Charlotte Wellesley m.1848	[2 Daughters]	Ewd; Lytton = Rosina Wheeler born. 25.5.1803 d.1865
			Robert Emily[Little Boots] [See chart for Knebworth Hall families]	

Col: William Earl Gascoyne b.1829 m.1855.d.1910 =Marion Dearing dau; of William Wilson Lee Warner died.1906 Continued on page.321	Henry = Isobell Buxton born.1820 m1863 d.1934 Issue	Rose = soldier d.1914 . Issue	Mary Issue married. 1858	Elizabeth died.1916

See Squires of Heydon Hall By Mrs. Jane Preston

***Rev. Edward Bulwer reputed to be a complete misfit as a cleric. See text on page 298 and charts page 302/303 ***Six children Following this chart you will find a Rice Wiggett married Sarah, eldest d. of William and Francis Bulwer of Wood Dalling they had five sons and two daughters. All died young except William Wiggett who married Mary Earle was made heir to the Bulwer titles and Halls, providing he changed name to Bulwer. Bulwer family moved from their ancient family seat of Wood Dalling to Heydon Hall. See next chart 84 page 362

Note; Members of Aylesham families in capitals

GENERAL SIR WILLIAM EARLE BULWER 1757-1807
AND HIS WIFE ELIZABETH BARBARA (NEE WARBURTON LYTTON) BULWER (1773-1843).

The Main Stream of the Bulwer Family in the Reign of King George 3rd

William E. Bulwer [cousin to the Buxton/Hainford Bulwer's] was born on 1st January 1757 the eldest son of William Wiggett Bulwer and Mary Earle the daughter of Augustine Earle and niece to Erasmus Earle. He rode on horseback to attend Paston Grammar School school with his friend Horatio later the famous Lord Nelson and admitted to Cambrige in 1748 at the age of seventeen. Straight from college he entered the army and quickly reached the rank of Captain.

As a young officer he fell in love with a beautiful young girl from boarding school and due to the strict conventions of that time his family would not agree to a marriage below his class so she became his mistress and he vowed that he would marry no one else. One sad morning she was kicked by her horse and killed, this event possibly altered his personality. He became ill tempered, land hungry, engrossed in reckless heavy borrowing on the estate, making extensive alterations to the house.

It was by chance that William met a friend **Mrs. Elizabeth Warburton Lytton,** who although separated from her husband Richard, shared the responsibility of their only child, a daughter **Elizabeth** born to them June 1st 1773. No doubt **William** had noted she was heiress to the family estate of Warburton Lytton's.

Elizabeth was a woman of intelligence, as she later proved. His sudden proposal of marriage to his friends' daughter, a girl half his age, probably even surprised himself and his financial problems seemed to be eased at their wedding on her birthday, the 1st of June 1798. **William** [who at this time was **Col. Bulwer**] found that the Lytton's had survived more than one break in family blood descent by being grafted on to other family names.

His wife's grandfather was a Warburton and had acquired a second name with its fortune by marriage with a Miss **Elizabeth** Lytton whose family name was originally Robinson; there is no genuine Lytton blood.

William's hope of financial security was dashed when he discovered that his wife had very little money, and was depending on her father for both cash and land, but her father who was very much alive had extraordinary powers of spending.

THE EMOTIONAL TRAUMAS OF MARRIAGE

The marriage seems to have been the decision of her mother rather than hers. It was a very bitter match; no doubt caused by fate and the tragic demise of his first love, denying him a life that he had desired, had bearing on this.

Elizabeth too found that the true romance that she had known with her merchant lover had been crushed by the will of her father, so you can see how **William** and **Elizabeth** though joined in marriage, lived their lives on remembrance of past pleasures which eventually tore them apart. Bitterness grew between them because of the extreme jealousy of his one-time friend now his mother-in-law and his gout, plus a heartache he could no longer bear.

According to the diaries of Miss Green the two grew apart. Now this is rather strange to understand, as they seemed to put all cares to one side at times, and found enough incentive to create passion for the arrival of five children. First born was **William** 1799. **William Henry** was born in 1801 [the William was not used for obvious reasons]

The arrival of a third child that died at birth sparked off the inevitable volcano waiting to erupt between **General William** and his interfering mother-in-law who after his violent rage against her, never visited his home again, ever. His wife by now endured these rages with an indifference that made them appear even more extreme.

Sometime between rows they found time to conceive their third and most gifted child **Edward**, born in 1803. He was to become his mother's sole cherished property, disliked and ignored by his father. In spite of this **Edward** became the most talented man of his age, which gained him a resting-place amongst kings at Westminster Abbey, London.

As he was a forceful and enterprising type of person at an early age William was regarded so highly as an officer he was appointed in 1804 as one of four Generals whom the defense of the nation was entrusted. His command head quarters were based at Preston Lancs; popular with his men, also the rich and the poor of the district; money was no problem.

Events that occurred during his lifetime were the Napoleonic Wars, Wellington, and Waterloo. Enclosures were still made, bringing poverty; landless redundant workers drifted into towns for work. The urgent need of cash for Heydon repairs was out of reach.

The Generals famous sons overshadowed his achievements, which was unjust as he was considered to be a fine soldier and businessman.

His frequent absence from the family, due to his army duties caused them both to be ill tempered; her aloof mocking attitude to the Bulwer's Heydon life style that she compared to the elegance of her mother's home in London caused resentment of each others families.

General William's eldest and favourite son **William** was of course groomed to be the heir of Heydon and received his father's special attention. He completely took over the raising of his first born not allowing any interference or influences whatsoever from his wife.

Henry their second son was under the control of his grandmother who had been banned from the family home, which broke her heart. When Henry became a man he would also become a very public figure in his own right. **Edward**, the third son with a share of his mothers' property, would in adult life be like his father and find fulfillment in his chosen work. However he found terrible unhappiness, disappointment and bitterness in his domestic life just as his father had before him.

In later years William [the General] suffered great pain due to gout and had to have his bedclothes hooked up as not to touch him. Fate again struck a harsh blow as just before he could obtain the chance of acquiring the wealth of his rich father-in-laws estates he died suddenly aged fifty in his sleep on the 7th July 1807 leaving the estate in chaos as his military interests cost more than he gained owing over £63,000 [roughly £10 million today] plus his fathers debts.

Most of the estate had to be mortgaged and his wife and three young sons were left to cope. The closest thing to him on this earth, his pet spaniel dog, lay under his master's coffin refusing to move or eat and subsequently died. **General William Earle Bulwer** so proud of his lineage never did gain the prize he most longed and worked for, that of the peerage as Lord South Erpingham, the name of the district in which his property was situated and which was once the home of Kings and Lords.

Later the titles of Wood Dalling, and Irmingland were committed in 1841, for £307 pounds by **Mary Johnson** wife of **Thomas Fearnly Bulwer** of Wood Dalling Hall, those of Irmingland were at the same time sold to William Earle by the same **Mary Johnson** for £170 pounds. This money was used for legacies in the will after the death of her husband; John Ireland was steward for these transactions.

An Unfair Judgment
The following stories are from the notes of the General. Robert de Grey v Mrs. Elizabeth Mynne (nee Heidon)

*Comments on the Notes Made by General W. E G. Bulwer

Among the Parkhurst Correspondence at Cambridge Ec 11 34 The Lord Bishop of Norwich received many letters of cause (complaints for him to give fair judgment). According to the Visitation Books, one that he dealt with, in the writer's opinion, [**General W. E. G. Bulwer**] was adjudicated upon unfairly as the Bishop was the friend of a benefactor. The reason for this interest, is one of their descendants Hannah Maria of the Grey family married **Erasmus Earle** in 1717. [See chart 72 p.303]

To return to our story, Thomas de Grey of Merton married Ann, the daughter of Henry Everade of Linstead Suffolk. They produced a daughter Hannah and a son they also named Thomas de Grey. Ann, the mother died and the father remarried Temperance, daughter of Sir Wymonde Carew of Anthony Co. Cornwall, but Thomas (senior) also died in 1502 AD when his son was only seven years old and left him as heir to his fortune.

Thomas junior was made ward of Temperance his stepmother; the lad was very frail and unhealthy. His stepmother remarried Sir Christopher Heidon of Baconsthorpe who we wrote about earlier and as she feared the family fortune would slip from her grasp promptly married Thomas to a relation (probably the daughter of her new husband) Elizabeth Heidon of Saxlingham Hall. (1506 AD)

The bride was about sixteen and the groom about ten years old. The boy died at Baconsthorpe, the place where he was married. The young widow re-married Nicholas Mynne Esq. evidently a great favourite of the Bishop who thereupon sued for the widow's dower. Robert de Grey, the young lad's uncle pleaded the marriage was null and void, resisted him. The Bishop then wrote discreditable letters to his chancellor and others on the subject, that they for the most part might give them their opinion of the marriage as lawful and the answer was Mynne had not a chance of winning the dispute.

Nicholas and Elizabeth Mynne lived at Little Walsingham, produced several sons and named them all Nicholas. Did they have a sense of humour or did they do it to confuse genealogists and people like us? What the sequel to this case was we do not know as the report ceased at this point.

*These notes are taken from an abbreviated copy of the Parkhurst Correspondence at Cambridge Ec.ii. During the reign of Elizabeth 1st 1502 AD.

MURDER AT STANFIELD HALL

This crime happened over 150 years ago in 1849, and is of special interest to our family as James Rush, the murderer, was brought up on land leased to his father by **William E. L. Bulwer**. James Rush was the last murderer to be hanged at Norwich Castle. The notes on this crime come mostly from the account of Edward Bulwer written in Ledgers held in the Norwich library Record Office. James Rush senior had leased this land from the Bulwer's for twenty-one years.

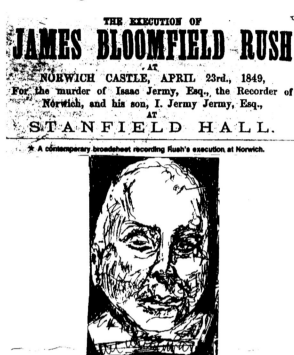

THE EXECUTION OF
JAMES BLOOMFIELD RUSH
. AT
NORWICH CASTLE, APRIL 23rd., 1849,
For the murder of Isaac Jermy, Esq., the Recorder of
Norwich, and his son, I. Jermy Jermy, Esq.,
AT
STANFIELD HALL.

★ A contemporary broadsheet recording Rush's execution at Norwich.

Plate.72   **James Rush Death Mask**
[artists'impression]

When his son grew up, James junior became an auctioneer and surveyor. He accumulated some money and leased a farm belonging to Isaac Jermy the City Recorder for Norwich. He was soon in trouble over money and had arguments with Isaac; he added to his many problems by taking the family governess Emily Stansfield as his mistress Even worse she became pregnant.

He also had to borrow a very large sum of money from Isaac, who had no other alternative but to sue for it. James, a heavily built and violent man decided to use violence to solve this sad situation reasoning Isaac was the source of his troubles so he would have to pay.

Picking up a shotgun, and with rage in his heart, he left for Stanfield Hall, Wymondham. Soon this tragic Jermy family was left dying in pools of their own blood with the exception of their maid Eliza Chestny, who was badly wounded and left for dead. Unfortunately for James she recovered enough to witness the crime and the trial took place in Norwich in 1849. Eliza was so badly crippled she was brought to court in a litter that was specially designed for her, to give evidence. James Rush's bullying and intimidation of the witness did not help him or affect her bravery; she stood her ground as he roared out his innocence. It took only six minutes for the jury to find him guilty.

Note: Edward Bulwer who was commenting wrote this account in the Bulwer Ledgers and notations in the visitation book. The Bulwer's went to live at Baconsthorpe briefly; this is probably the reason that interest was taken in the site.

The iron nerve he previously displayed now deserted him when faced with the scaffold rubbing his hand across his eyes; his body trembled at the prospects now confronting him.

Soon it was over, his death mask is now on display at the Castle Museum Norwich. In those days a hanging was not only a punishment but also a popular entertainment. A raised stand was made so that the huge crowd of people could get a better view of the event. What tales this old Norwich Castle could tell if its stones could only talk, but maybe they do as the old place has its ghosts in the dungeons! [It is well worth a visit] We also wonder about the cryptic remark of Edward Bulwer about James the father of the murderer, holding the lease on Bulwer land.

Were there any more repercussions in this direction? For in those days it reflected on the whole family even more than today. Punishment for often minor crimes was dealt out very harshly, even in the 1800's when in Boston Lincolnshire a young lad was sentenced to death for stealing a sheep. Many crimes in towns were committed after dark but the introduction of public lighting greatly reduced this.

Another interesting item from the book 'Boston' by the writer Herbert Porter was that in 1827 illuminating was mainly in the form of tallow candle's, oil lamps or gas [c.1810 lit by Tinder Boxes]. In respect of candle's and oil lamps, Snuffer's were employed in courts, churches and other public buildings whose job was to snuff [trim] the *candles at regular intervals to ensure they kept alight. This practice was still being performed even up to the 1930's. We expect there are many Snuffers tools and trays in the old buildings that people see, but are not aware of their purpose.

Also in 1827 John Walker a druggist of Stockton-on-tees invented what he called friction lights; Priced 100 for ½ d with a free sheet of sandpaper, that were the first form of matches. The old Lamplighter would be a familiar sight in towns with his long handled torch walking the streets and alleys, an impossible job on windy evenings. In the domestic situation the housewife had a scissors-like tool with a box attached to one blade in which the snuff [burnt wick] of the candle was caught after she cut it off.

When **David** and his brother-in-law **Edward** [**Norma's** husband] were employed as electricians much of their work involved wiring up rural houses and churches that up to that time were still using candles or oil for illumination.

Note; *the snuff was the burnt part of the wick that if left would restrict the flame or put the flame out.

LIFE AFTER THE DEATH OF THE GENERAL
Barbara takes over her life and the life of her son Edward

On the surface, past life problems first drew William and Elizabeth together and distorted their true personalities as underneath they might have had lovable characters but through fate their true loves were denied them. After his early death Elizabeth obtained a court order assigning her the guardianship of her children. She then left Heydon and bought a house at Nottingham Place, London.

When Squire William came of age in 1820 he took over the reigns of Heydon Hall; the inhabitants assembled on the Green at noon, and were sorted into equal divisions and 2,000 people cheered as they neared the hall getting more exited as the aroma of the roasting ox and the sight of all the laden tables caught their eyes.

Henry lived with Elizabeth's mother (Mrs. Warburton) and Edward stayed as always tied to his mother at Montague Square (later at Nottingham Place). Edward's grandfather Richard sent him to a famous school, which assisted his education.

Elizabeth's father became a friend and benefactor and they became much closer to one another, spending much of the year together. Owing to the illustrious careers of their sons and husbands, whose positions and actions in both public and private life was, and will always be an influential part of this nation's history, so it is only right that we devote some time on what they achieved.

SONS OF THE GENERAL

William Earle Lytton Bulwer [1799 – 1877]
The Eldest Son of General Sir William Bulwer Married Emily Gascoigne 1827

William inherited Heydon estates and all the debts that his father had made upon it. His mother was aware even before his birth, that once he was born as the first child, he would be removed from her care and groomed ready for the future Lordship of Heydon. Being considered the special property of General Bulwer, who decreed that his wife could administer the nursery but not rule over it. The grief of losing her first child was too much to bear and her nerves were so shattered she was fortunate to survive mentally.

William Henry Earle Lytton Bulwer (1801-1872)
Baron Dalling and Bulwer Married Georgina Charlotte Wellesley 1848

Better known as Sir Henry Bulwer, he was born at 31 Baker Street, Portman Square, London on the 13th Feb. 1801. The second born of the three sons of the General (Colonel of the 106th regiment at the time of

Henrys birth) Henry was said to be a kind, considerate man, and a natural diplomat. He studied with the Rev. Mark Drury under a Dr. Curtis at Sunbury, Middlesex; after leaving there went to Harrow, his first schooling was by tutors. He entered Trinity College Cambridge in 1819 and shortly after went to Downing College, but never completed the honours. It was here that he met his friend Alexander (later Chief Justice) Cockburn.

He published a volume of poems in 1822 and left Cambridge in 1842 to join the Greek committee in London who authorised him to go straight away to the Morea with a large sum of money for Prince Mavrocordato. Hamilton Brown accompanied him and it was during this period abroad he was gazetted on 19th Oct. 1825 as a cornet in the 2nd lifeguards.

On 2nd June 1826 he joined the 58th regiment, 27th June 1826 obtained an unattached ensign, and on the 1st January commuted his half pay and became a diplomatist. Henry liked gambling and on his journey to his new appointment as attaché at Berlin he stopped in Paris for a game of whist and won a large sum of money, which enabled him to join a very select group of people. April 1829 he was attaché' in Vienna, by 1830 was transferred to The Hague.

Lord Aberdeen, the foreign secretary on the 25th of August dispatched him on a special mission into Belgium, because of a revolution in Brussels. As he arrived at Ghent conflict began and on entering his hotel a shot rang out. The commissioner standing next to him was hit. Henry quickly left for Brussels where he found Dutch troops had established themselves on the hills.

Summoned back to London, the cabinet congratulated him on the thoroughness of his dispatches. He returned to Belgium several times then became the Liberal MP for Wilson (1830) Coventry, (1831-33) Marylebone (1835) before returning to Brussels in [1835-36] as charge de'affairs.

He received his nomination as secretary of the embassy at Constantinople while visiting Paris on the 14th August 1837 and distinguished himself by negotiating a commercial treaty with the Port. Palmerston the British Prime minister pronounced the treaty as a masterpiece and appointed him as secretary of the embassy at St. Petersburg but was delayed due to ill health but instead of this appointment he was dispatched to Paris (1839).

International worries mounted and as there was a possibility of war with France he was made charge-d'-affair's and ambassador at the court of Isabella 2nd and became arbitrator between Spain and Morocco where he negotiated an agreement between both powers, and the peace treaty was signed in 1844. The Spanish marriages and intrigues of Louis-Philippe created problems, and without doubt if Lord Palmerston had not interfered Henry would have prevented those fateful marriages resulting in the French revolution of 1848. One month later there was a serious uprising in Madrid. Marshal Narvaez proceeded to suppress the constitutional guarantees.

Henry formally protested in the name of England and Narvaez accused him of being an accomplice of the Protagonists and required him to quit Madrid within forty-eight hours. With no time to inform London, the first the ministers knew of the dismissed British ambassador was when he walked into the Downing Street Foreign Office to report it. Of course the Spanish ambassador M. Isturitz was at once told to make his departure from England back to Spain.

On 27th April 1848 Henry was gazetted as a Knight Commander of the Bath and three years later to the Grand Cross. He was now Sir Henry Bulwer. On 9th December 1848 he married the Hon. Georgina Charlotte Mary Wellesley, youngest daughter of the first baron Cowley, and niece to the first Duke of Wellington.

On 27th April 1849 Sir Henry became ambassador in Washington and brought a satisfactory conclusion of the Bulwer/Clayton treaty. He was an extremely popular speaker commanding large audiences on his every appearance. Soon after a brief spell at the court of the Grand Duke of Tuscany in Florence he retired on 26th January 1855. Although officially retired he still remained in the diplomatic service as there was a great demand for his talents in diplomacy. He took on many more assignments adding much more to his high reputation.

Retiring altogether from the diplomatic service in 1865 he still continued working and was elected as an MP the member for Tamworth, on 17th November 1868 again as a Liberal until his peerage on March 21st 1871 as Baron Dalling and Bulwer.

Sir Henry Bulwer was an outstanding man of his day as was his brother Edward with his sweetness of disposition and highbred manner. He sauntered through high or lower classes with the same easygoing nature that made him a favourite with all and his were the keenest observations achieved by feigning apparent indifference, yet arriving at the correct conclusion every time. He wrote many books on his experiences and the people he associated with. He died suddenly on the 23rd of May 1872 in Naples without leaving any children so the title became extinct. He was sadly missed.

Edward Lytton Bulwer [1803 –1865]
Later the 1st Lord Lytton married Rosinna Wheeler 1827

After his father died Henry, the youngest son of General Bulwer stayed with his grandmother in London. **Edward** was with his mother and grandfather at Knebworth, where he was eager to learn from his grandfathers' inexhaustible supply of books, and that for the first time in his life he had a close relationship with a male relative.

Sadly he and his grandfather did not always see eye to eye so it was decided to give him an academic education, his grandfather died soon after of an apoplectic fit in 1810.

Edward was sent to a preparatory school at Fulham in London and his first introduction to life without his family, as he put it "a place in which minds are to be broken and hearts initiated into terror". The two boys that were to look after him were much older and talked in such obscene language he was ignorant as to its meaning.

At the age of twelve he was sent to school at Rottingdean where academically he excelled. His tutor Dr. Hook claimed that he was remarkably brilliant and talented boy, but his wild uncontrollable nature and his love of pleasure could lead to his ruin. This observation was proved correct in 1818 when he hit a teacher, became arrogant, uncooperative and conceited.

This attitude was due to the jealousy of his school peers of his outstanding abilities resulting in him being bullied. His mother had to remove him from the school suggesting he attend Eaton instead, Edward flatly refused. After many family debates they reached a compromise that he should have a private tutor. Most of his life he suffered with an infection to his ear that interfered with his early education and as you will read, this was to become fatal in later life

Edward grew up far too quickly, became aristocratic and overbearing, knowing that he had been born into higher class and status and had superior abilities, which created in him a holier than thou attitude. This disposition made him a loner who enjoyed the time spent on his own, but having said that he loved a party.

His brother William was now in sole charge of Heydon; he was eighteen years old and Henry lived with his grandmother.

We have to leave out much of the detail of Edwards's young life, as it would take up too much space and time. However we felt that we could not avoid telling you the story of the time when he was wandering in the countryside and met a Gypsy girl.

<u>A Gypsy sweetheart and a jealous threat to his life</u>
<u>[A paraphrased version of Edwards account]</u>

Taking a break from his studies the young Edward decided to travel. He was tired after a long day of walking. The sun was setting, sending out its long beams of light, and casting eerie shadows through the trees, and he was considering the beauty all around him, when he was startled by a silvery young voice speaking over his shoulder. A beautiful gypsy girl was standing close by. "Mai I tell you fortune, me pretty young gentleman"? She said.

"Pray do!" he replied crossing her palm with silver. "Only give me a sweetheart as beautiful as yourself" She blushed and studied his hand. "Chut Chut" paused and continued "You lost your father when you were young and have brothers but no sisters" "Ah! You did have a sweetheart when you were a mere boy and will never see her again. Never! The line is completely broken; it cut you to the heart, nearly dying of it you will never be as gay again." he snatched his hand away amazed.

"You are a witch!" he stuttered as she continued. It would take more time and space than we can afford to tell you all the story of that evening. As they talked of gypsy life, she constantly gazed at her own palm lines that said that sorrow for her was very near. He never knew her real name, so decided to call her Mimi, he asked if he could stay with her family for a few days so he could learn the gypsy way of life; her eyes sparkled at the prospect, and then saddened again. Yes, he could stay with her and her grandmother but something she saw in her hand and the sign of the star-crossed lines worried her.

They walked on through the woods to a clearing, and before him was the encampment, silhouetted against the setting sun. She took his hand after passing a group of men and boys who glared at the stranger. As they entered the large tent an old woman was stirring a large pot that was hanging above the log fire. Mimi stood talking to her in a low voice, the old lady shaking her head. The pleadings of her beautiful granddaughter had won her over. She turned round beaming with happiness. "Yes you may stay, but what money have you"? "Money"! Was this a trick?

Her eyes flashed angrily, "You mistake me, it is dangerous to carry money, it is best for grandmother to care for it, and return it when you go". He handed fourteen pounds to the old lady and she called the family into the tent to speak to them. They agreed he could stay so they all sat round the log fire to share the contents of the pot, which consisted of potatoes, bread, and meat with herbs; everyone being hungry, anything that resembled food was eaten.

Each day after the men went tinkering and the women fortune-telling around the neighbourhood. **Edward** and the girl would each slip away to meet at a prearranged spot where they talked for hours. At one of these secret meetings she sat very quiet. "What's wrong? He inquired; on impulse she kissed his forehead. "Do you love me"? She asked.

The question caught him unawares and he could only blurt out the truth and say that he did. "If you really love me, will you marry me"? "Marry you?" he said aghast. "That would be impossible!" Well I don't mean as you marry, but as we marry" "How is that"? "You break a piece of baked earth with me, like a tile for instance, into two halves" "Well in grandmother's presence, it lasts only five years, not long" she pleaded, "If you wanted to leave before, how could I make you stay".

 Edward declined, although in love with her, his station and lineage would not permit it. From then on he observed rudeness and insolence from the three young gypsy men indicating he had stayed too long. They followed him and sat near if he sat next to her, there was a terrible argument amongst them but she did not divulge what it was about, and became worried and sad looking.

That night he lay in his corner of the encampment. Everyone was asleep except the old woman, who sat on her stool, gazing into the embers. A shadowy form stole across the tent, laid her head on her grandmothers' lap and wept bitterly. It was Mimi. They both rose and crept out of the tent; all was quiet so Edward slowly made his way from the tent to find Mimi and the old crone seated near the wood. The old woman put her finger to her lips and bade him follow her through a gap in the hedge. Mimi remained her head buried in her hands.

"You must leave us, you are in grave danger, the young men are jealous of you and the girl, their blood is up and I can do nothing to keep it down. I can do what I like with all except in love and jealousy. You must go" "I cannot leave"! "You must, you must" said Mimi who had crept silently up and put her arms around him.

"It's not for your sake that I speak; you had no right to touch her heart. You deserve the gripe and the stab, but if they do hurt you, what will the law do to them? I once saw a gypsy hanged, it brought woe on us all! You will break her heart and ruin us all. Go''! Said the old woman .

They both looked very worried and **Edward** turned to Mimi.

"Mimi will you come too?" he said. "No! She cannot leave her people; she is a true born gypsy", said the old woman. "Let her speak for herself". "No I cannot" she whispered, "I will see you again Let me know where to find you". "Don't fret; you will have crosses enough to bear without me. I will come to you later".

She took him aside, kissing his hands and pledged to find him before winter. They both urged him to go at once, but he could not in pride skulk away at night, but promised to go openly the next day. They all went back to the tent, the fire was nearly out, and he fell into an uneasy sleep. When he awoke all were assembled around the tent; the three young men came in and shook his hand. Had they changed their minds? "You leave us?" said the tallest of the three. "We shall accompany you a part of the way and wish you luck".

Mimi was nowhere to be seen, only the old woman. She got him some breakfast but he could not eat and so remained silent. **Edward** went to her and whispered, "Shall I not see her again?" "Hush leave her to take care of that!" He took up his knapsack for his journey, and the old lady drew him to one side and slipped him his money." But you must take some" he said. "Not a penny, Mimi would not forgive me. Off and away! There will be a storm before noon. Go with a light heart, success is on your forehead!" The gypsies all gathered round and escorted him to the edge of their domain.

There they formally took leave of him; Edward traveled some three miles with the woods on one side of him. Then he saw Mimis' dark eyes peering at him through the dense foliage, and she was soon by his side. She was only with him for a moment holding him tightly in her arms. Kissing him she then sprang back, pointing to her open palm at the lines. She said, "Look this is the sorrow, it goes on and on to the end of my life"! "No you promised that we shall meet again" "Ha! A gypsy promise!" she cried and was gone, he tried in vain to catch her without success.

*For many years he tried to find her, but never did. Forlornly he carried on with his travels living recklessly, and while in Paris in 1825 he tried everything including gambling for very high stakes. Unfortunately luck was not on his side and one-day he looked in the mirror and did not like the reflection he saw, he vowed never to gamble again, and he never did.

*There are many books on the life of Edward Bulwer some that relate of this part of his life. For more information on this story see 'The life of Edward Bulwer 1st Lord Lytton' by his grandson the Earl Of Lytton published by Macmillan & Co. London 1913 vol. 1

GRAND CHILDREN OF THE GENERAL

Arms Gules on a chevron argent, between two eaglets reguardent or as many cinquefoils sable. Mantling gules and argent. Crest on a wreath of the colours, a horned wolfs head erased ermine crined and armed or. Motto – "Adversis Major par secundis"

William Earle Lytton Bulwer [Squire William] son of the general married 1st Emily Gascgoigne 2nd Elizabeth Green. William and Emilyraised six children;-
Col. William Earle Gascoigne Lytton Bulwer [W.E.G.L.]
Edward [Teddy] b1829 d.1910 m Isabella Anne Buxton b1838 d.1883.
Rose Emily b1833d.1905 m 1856 the Rev. Charles Jenynnings
Mary Eleanor b.1835 d 1926 m 1858 Henry Caldwell, b1815 d1868
Elizabeth Maud b. 1836 d1916.
[William] Henry b.1836 d1914 was educated at Winchester, joined the Scots Guards and served in the Crimea. He was severely wounded in the battle of Alma where nearly all his regiment was killed. The army made many bad mistakes and they left in disgrace.

Col. William Earle Gascoigne Lytton Bulwer [W.E.G.L.] b1829 – d1910] was the first-born son of **William and Emily** and eldest grandson of the General. He married **Mary-Anne Dering Lee Warner** only daughter of **William Wilson Lee Warner** of Quebec House Dereham 5th May1855 took up residence at Heydon Hall and produced four children. **William** [W.E.G.L.] was promoted to Colonel commanding the third battalion of the Norfolk regiment, then to Brigadier General commanding the Norfolk Voluntary Infantry Brigade gaining a CBE. and Jubilee Medal later appointed High Sheriff and J.P. for Norfolk.

CHILDREN OF WILLIAM [W.E.L.G.] BULWER

William's [Manny.] married Lillian Mary Petrie
Sybil was W.E.G.L.B'S 2nd child b.1860 d.1867 died early.
Marion was his 3rd child b.1863 d. 1863 [one month old].
Edward Augustine Earle Bulwer [Ed] b1864 d.1934 second son of the of Colonel William E.G.L.Bulwer; b.1864, married 1st cousin Henrica Eleanor Coldwell b1868 d.1963 It was **Edward** the son of **William** and Mary-Anne who inherited Heydon Hall when his brother **William** [Manny] died on 8th July 1915. The maintenance required on the Halls of Quebec and Wood Dalling were beyond the financial resources of **Edward** so to his great distress Quebec had to be sold.

William Dering Earle Bulwer [Manny] b.1857, d 1915 [married Lillian Mary Petrie b.1885 died 1948]. William died when his children were quite young.

One year later [1914] with all its emotional and attached family history **Wood Dalling** too came under the hammer. This hall had been owned by the Bulwer's since **William Warrenna** exchanged Dalling for land that Turold Crispin/de Dalling held in Lewes, where William Warrenna built his Cathedral during the time of King William. We understand from a lady living in the area of Wood Dalling that in her generation a Colonel Duff lived in Dalling Hall until his death when it was sold, and then passed out of the family ownership!

Though it had for many generations before, been held by both the Thomas's [father and son of our line. See Manor Rolls and visitation books also a story further on in this book]. When **Edward** died in 1934, there was a family discussion and our grandfather and his brothers were involved in a legal claim on the estate, **William** [our grandfather's brother and his son **Reginald**] had returned from Australia for this event.

Much to their disappointment their claim on the estate failed; the reason was, as we now know that they seemed unable to trace their relationship to Thomas Bulwer our ancestor. As children were not included in adult matters in those days and this information was only discovered by us during this research. The title and Heydon Hall went to **Mary [Molly Elizabeth]** b.1911 daughter of **William Dering Earl** [**Manny**] and her husband **Hetherington Long** as you will read later.

CHILDREN OF MARY ELIZABETH [MOLLY] EARL BULWER
Capt. William Hanslip Bulwer-Long, to whom the Hall descended. b.1937 d.1996. Married Sarah Rawlingson 1962.
Mary-Ann Hetherington Long b1935.
Timothy Hetherington. b1942.
Elizabeth Tessa. b.1944.
David Earl b1948 [divorced).
Sarah Jane b.1951.

CHILDREN OF CAPT. WILLIAM HANSLIP BULWER-LONG.
Timothy.
Edward b.27/11/1966.
Benjamin b22/2/1970 married Rhona Brindley b1969.
Rosamund.

CHIDREN OF BENJAMIN.
Lettia b.27/1/1999.
Rose Earle b. 27/2/2001.

It was during the war period of rationing that the names of Duff and Long were still their official used surname on their Ration Books and it was not until 1964 that Molly's family name of Bulwer was added.

Note; some details taken from the book Squires of Heydon Hall by Jane Preston

CAPTAIN WILLIAM BULWER -LONG
SON OF MARY ELIZABETH HETHERINGTON-LONG
HEYDON HALL NORFOLK.
1937-1996

The sudden death of **Captain Bulwer-Long of Heydon Hall** in 1996, following a heart attack, was reported in the Eastern Daily Press. **Captain Bulwer-Long** [b. 1937] belonged to the Wiggett-Bulwer family that dates from early history as this book shows. [See chart]

Captain Bulwer-Long   Plate **73**

He went to school at Wellington then to the Royal Military Academy at Sandhurst before being given a commission into the Cavalry regiment 9th Queen's Royal Lancers in 1957 serving in Germany, Northern Ireland, and Aden, between 1957 and 1966 being the aide de-camp to the G.C.O. Northern Command, 1961-62. When a member of the Army Cresta team 1963, he won the Grand Military Hunters Chase, one of the many accolades gained in his long equestrian association. He left the army in 1966.

In 1962 he married Sarah the only daughter of Sir Frederick Rawlinson and they made their home in Heydon, with 160 acres and ten pounds in the bank, having to live in the farmhouse for a while as the Hall was derelict and uninhabitable.

After selling the farmhouse they started the long process of restoring the Hall, which took 30 months of skilled craftsmanship and a reduction in size. With due respect they must be congratulated in transforming a very run down old Hall into the magnificent looking building we see today.

In 1988 Captain **William Bulwer-Long** became High Sheriff of Norfolk and a well-known Norfolk landowner. He had many accolades that included 35-point to-point victories, chairman of Norfolk County Landowners Association, Vice-Chairman of Norfolk Farming and Wildlife Advisory Group, former Steward of the Jockey Club, and a steward of Fakenham, Yarmouth, Newmarket and Aintree and a director of Newmarket and Fakenham Race Courses.

Captain Bulwer-Long cared deeply about conservation, farming and village life; reputed to be a great man of Norfolk. He left a widow, two sons and a daughter, **Timothy, Edward** and **Rosamund.**

OTHER BULWER DESCENDANTS OF NORFOLK

With reference to Mrs. Jane Preston's book "Squires of Heydon Hall", recently published [ISBN 1899163 751], providing excellent historical background on the Earle, Wiggett, Bulwer families we hope that our book will fill in some gaps she left, particularly in the Appendix, "I think we might be related". With regard to our families we refer to p367 and 368 of our book, Simon and Margaret Money, and Thomas and Antonia of Hainford. [Will 1607].

While researching our family history, the families below were found in the registry files on births deaths and marriages, they seemed unconnected to the main Bulwer family chart, although this does not necessarily mean that there is none, but we had no spare time to devote to this research at this juncture.

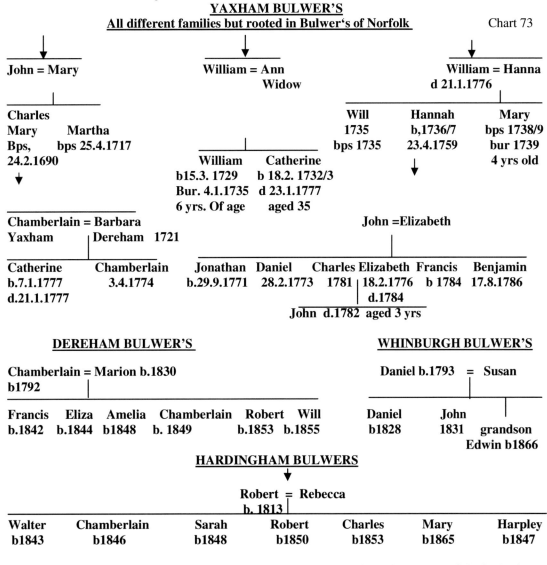

YAXHAM BULWER'S
All different families but rooted in Bulwer's of Norfolk   Chart 73

John = Mary   William = Ann   William = Hanna
                                        Widow   d 21.1.1776

Charles   Will   Hannah   Mary
Mary   Martha   1735   b,1736/7   bps 1738/9
Bps,   bps 25.4.1717   bps 1735 23.4.1759   bur 1739
24.2.1690   William   Catherine   4 yrs old
                            b15.3. 1729 b 18.2. 1732/3
                            Bur. 4.1.1735 d 23.1.1777
                            6 yrs. Of age aged 35

Chamberlain = Barbara   John =Elizabeth
Yaxham   Dereham   1721

Catherine   Chamberlain   Jonathan Daniel   Charles Elizabeth Francis Benjamin
b.7.1.1777   3.4.1774   b.29.9.1771 28.2.1773 1781 18.2.1776 b 1784 17.8.1786
d.21.1.1777   d.1784
                                              John d.1782 aged 3 yrs

DEREHAM BULWER'S   **WHINBURGH BULWER'S**

Chamberlain = Marion b.1830   Daniel b.1793 = Susan
b1792

Francis Eliza Amelia Chamberlain Robert Will   Daniel   John
b.1842 b.1844 b1848   b. 1849   b.1853 b.1855 b1828   1831   grandson
                                                                        Edwin b1866

HARDINGHAM BULWERS

Robert = Rebecca
b. 1813

Walter   Chamberlain   Sarah   Robert   Charles   Mary   Harpley
b1843   b1846   b1848   b1850   b1853   b1865   b1847

There are many other Bulwer families we have not been able to include because of the lack of space and no time to research them all. But maybe others will find the opportunity to carry this work on, and to conclude this task. We extend our apologies to those who have been missed out as we know there must be many more according to the census.

THE HEYDON LINE OF GENERAL BULWER

Cont. from page 362   From 1757   Chart 74

General William Earle Wiggett Bulwer b1757 -1807 m =Eliz.Barb Warboton Lytton b 1773. d.1843	John b.1766 = Mary Thomas Issue d 1846	Edward b 1771 Rector of Newton	Augustine = Bridgett d 1821 6 Issue	Mary b175 9 d 1796 3 Issue	Francis b1758 =John Godfrey b 1762 d 1831 2 Issue	Sarah b 1762 ↓ Leading to the Marshams

Will. Earle Lytt:Bulwer = 1st Emily Gascoyne dau;] Earl Gascoyne b. 25.5.1808 d.1836 2nd Elizabeth Green	Child Rose b.1801	Henry Lord Dalling d.1872 =GeorginaCharlotte Wellesley m.1848	[2 Daughters]	Ewd; Lytton1803 -.1865 = Rosina Wheeler	

Robert   Emily[Little Boots 1829]
= [See chart for Knebworth Hall families] 1802 / 1885

Col:William Earl Gascoyne [W.E.G.L] b.1829 m.1855.d1910 =Mary Anne Dearing 1829-1906 dau; of William Wilson Lee Warner	Edward [Teddy] = Isobell Buxton	Rose =1856 Rev Charles Jennings	Mary =1858 Henry Caldwell	Elizabeth 1836 / 1916	Henry d.1914

William [Manny] Bulwer b1857 -1915 =Lilian Mary Petrie 1885-1948 Heydon	Sybil 1860 /1867	Marion Dearing Bulwer 1863 – 1863	Edward [Ed.] = Eleanor Cauldwell Bulwer [1st cousin] b 1864-1934

Mary [Molly] Elizabeth Bulwer/ Dearing /Bulwer b.Aug.1911-1998 =Hetherington Long b.1905-1989 Heydon	Marjorie Dearing/Bulwer b.Aug 1912	Rosemary	Jane

Captain William Hanslip Bulwer Long b.1937 d 1996 = b.1939 1962 Sarah Rawlingson Heydon	Mary Ann b 1942	Timothy Hetherington b1942	David Earl divorced	Elizabeth Tessa b 1944	Sarah Jane Wiggett b.1951

Timothy	Edward born 27.11. 1966	Benjamin born.22.2.1970 Heydon Hall = Rhona Brindley born.1969	Rosamund

Lettia   Rose Earl
born 27.1 1999   27.2. 2001

HEYDON FAMILY CHART TO YEAR 2001

The family of the late Col. Bulwer Long presently resides in Heydon Hall; Benjamin and his wife Rhona have now taken over the estate.

THE LYTTON BULWERS
OF KNEBWORTH HOUSE HERTFORDSHIRE

Originally this was a Saxon settlement. The Domsday Book spelt the name Chenepeworde, which means a village on the hill. Another rendering Ceebas' Camp suggests it could have been the home of a fifth century Saxon Prince. The building dates back to Tudor times has had several owners, one was Sir John Hotoft whose daughter married Sir Robert Lytton.

The Lytton's were from Derbyshire; Sir Robert Lytton was the governor of Bolsover Castle, and Grand Adjuster of the Forests of the Peakland. His wife Agnes Hotoft whose father Sir John was treasurer of the household of Henry 6th owned Knebworth and died there.

Knebworth Hall   Plate.74

Sir Robert Lytton was founder of this large family's fortune at Knebworth, a trusted friend, courtier, and Privy Councilor of Henry 7th who also fought by his side in the battle of Bosworth and whose son was Governor of the Castle of Boulogne.

Even though there was a break in the bloodline since Sir Robert Lytton bought Knebworth in 1492 the estates had been passed on to close relatives by marriage into the Robinson families; [**Barbara Lytton's** real name was **Robinson**].

When **Barbara Lytton** married **General William Earl Bulwer** of Heydon in 1798 it started the **Bulwer** connection with Knebworth. After the General died, his wife left their son **William** in Heydon Hall as heir. **Henry** was already living with his grandmother, so she took the young **Edward** to London where they all lived for some time.

Later they went to stay with her father at Knebworth and were there when he died. Being the natural heir she was the first **Bulwer** adopting the surname Lytton to live there, although this branch of the **Bulwer** family was based in Hertfordshire it had its roots in Norfolk. When her son Edward succeeded his grandfather in 1878 the inheritance came down through these families as outlined in the next few chapters of this book.

See Knebworth chart 75 page 323 [next page].

Chart 75   <u>**The Knebworth Families**</u>   [cont. from page 362 chart 84]

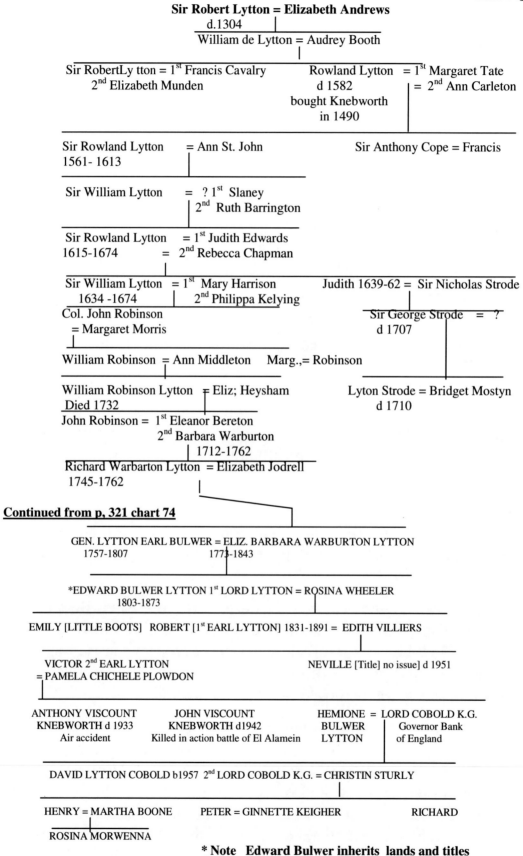

Sir Robert Lytton = Elizabeth Andrews
d.1304

William de Lytton = Audrey Booth

Sir RobertLytton = 1ˢᵗ Francis Cavalry   Rowland Lytton = 1ˢᵗ Margaret Tate
2ⁿᵈ Elizabeth Munden   d 1582   = 2ⁿᵈ Ann Carleton
bought Knebworth
in 1490

Sir Rowland Lytton   = Ann St. John   Sir Anthony Cope = Francis
1561- 1613

Sir William Lytton   = ? 1ˢᵗ Slaney
        2ⁿᵈ Ruth Barrington

Sir Rowland Lytton   = 1ˢᵗ Judith Edwards
1615-1674   = 2ⁿᵈ Rebecca Chapman

Sir William Lytton   = 1ˢᵗ Mary Harrison   Judith 1639-62 = Sir Nicholas Strode
1634 -1674   2ⁿᵈ Philippa Kelying
Col. John Robinson   Sir George Strode   = ?
= Margaret Morris   d 1707

William Robinson = Ann Middleton   Marg.,= Robinson

William Robinson Lytton = Eliz; Heysham   Lyton Strode = Bridget Mostyn
Died 1732   d 1710
John Robinson = 1ˢᵗ Eleanor Bereton
      2ⁿᵈ Barbara Warburton
       1712-1762
Richard Warbarton Lytton = Elizabeth Jodrell
1745-1762

<u>**Continued from p, 321 chart 74**</u>

GEN. LYTTON EARL BULWER = ELIZ. BARBARA WARBURTON LYTTON
1757-1807   1773-1843

*EDWARD BULWER LYTTON 1ˢᵗ LORD LYTTON = ROSINA WHEELER
1803-1873

EMILY [LITTLE BOOTS]   ROBERT [1ˢᵗ EARL LYTTON] 1831-1891 = EDITH VILLIERS

VICTOR 2ⁿᵈ EARL LYTTON   NEVILLE [Title] no issue] d 1951
= PAMELA CHICHELE PLOWDON

ANTHONY VISCOUNT   JOHN VISCOUNT   HEMIONE = LORD COBOLD K.G.
KNEBWORTH d 1933   KNEBWORTH d1942   BULWER   Governor Bank
Air accident   Killed in action battle of El Alamein   LYTTON   of England

DAVID LYTTON COBOLD b1957 2ⁿᵈ LORD COBOLD K.G. = CHRISTIN STURLY

HENRY = MARTHA BOONE   PETER = GINNETTE KEIGHER   RICHARD

ROSINA MORWENNA

* Note   Edward Bulwer inherits lands and titles
Present known living family up to 2007
KNEBWORTH FAMILY MEMBERS IN CAPITAL LETTERS

THE WHEELER/DOYLE/BULWER FAMILY CONNECTIONS
1756 AD

To understand the charts in this chapter we have included the history of various characters from these three families and how the upbringing of their children affected the lives of the next generation bringing sadness and tragic consequences.

You will read how the child hood experiences of Rosina Wheeler created a personality that clashed with Edward [the youngest son of the General] the man she married, and caused so many violent disagreements, finally resulting in their separation and divorce. Their self-indulgence in turn particularly affected their only daughter Emily [Little Boot's] to who's needs they were both heedless until it was too late.

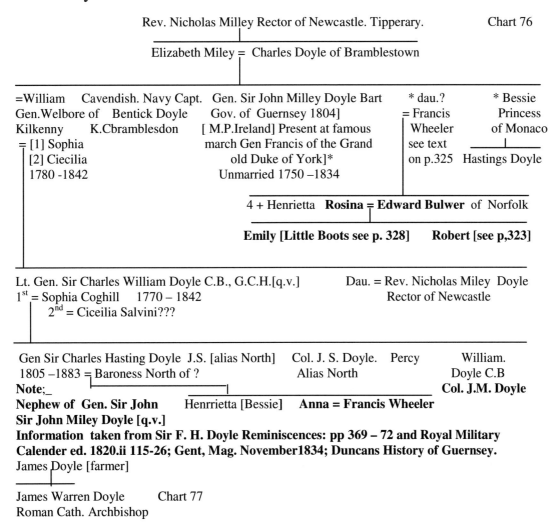

Rev. Nicholas Milley Rector of Newcastle. Tipperary.   Chart 76

Elizabeth Miley = Charles Doyle of Bramblestown

| =William Gen.Welbore of Kilkenny = [1] Sophia [2] Ciecilia 1780 -1842 | Cavendish. Navy Capt. Bentick Doyle K.Cbramblesdon | Gen. Sir John Milley Doyle Bart Gov. of Guernsey 1804] [M.P.Ireland] Present at famous march Gen Francis of the Grand old Duke of York]* Unmarried 1750 –1834 | * dau.? = Francis Wheeler see text on p.325 | * Bessie Princess of Monaco Hastings Doyle |

4 + Henrietta **Rosina = Edward Bulwer** of Norfolk

Emily [Little Boots see p. 328]   Robert [see p,323]

Lt. Gen. Sir Charles William Doyle C.B., G.C.H.[q.v.]   Dau. = Rev. Nicholas Miley Doyle
1st = Sophia Coghill   1770 – 1842   Rector of Newcastle
      2nd = Ciceilia Salvini???

Gen Sir Charles Hasting Doyle J.S. [alias North]   Col. J. S. Doyle.   Percy   William.
1805 –1883 = Baroness North of ?   Alias North   Doyle C.B
Note;_   **Col. J.M. Doyle**
Nephew of Gen. Sir John   Henrrietta [Bessie]   Anna = Francis Wheeler
Sir John Miley Doyle [q.v.]
Information taken from Sir F. H. Doyle Reminiscences: pp 369 – 72 and Royal Military Calender ed. 1820.ii 115-26; Gent, Mag. November1834; Duncans History of Guernsey.
James Doyle [farmer]

James Warren Doyle   Chart 77
Roman Cath. Archbishop

Note. As can be seen from the chart the historical background of this family helped to shape the history of our nation, boasting of at least four generals but as they are only associated by marriage to our family we have not enlarged fully on their illustrious careers due to space and time. More facts on their military and family history can be found in Duncan's History of Guernsey. The daughter of Sir Charles Doyle [Anna] married Francis Wheeler, and were parents of Rosina Wheeler who married Edward Bulwer of Knebworth.*Francis Wheelers wife and her sister Bessie, left for France with the children [see page 325]

FANCIS MASSEY WHEELER MARRIES ANNA DOYLE
IN THE EARLY 1800's

Francis Wheeler at the age of seventeen married a beautiful young girl of fifteen, a **Miss Anna Doyle** who came from a high-ranking military family. She agreed to the arrangement mainly to free herself from her mother. As she was the reigning beauty in the area it made her the subject of men's cravings in the other houses. This and her tantrums drove poor Francis to alcohol and when his wife's sister Henrietta (Bessie) came to live with them it pushed him into isolation.

He and his family lived in the region of Lizard Connell, Tipperary in old decaying Ballywire house, near the sea a few miles from Limerick in Ireland during the early eighteen hundreds. Francis later became a drunkard who had neither energy nor the money to do the repairs necessary to the leaking roof and crumbling walls. He spent half the day hunting on horseback or lazing in the stables recovering from his drunken stupor of the night before and to avoid his wife and her sister Bessie.

One unusual thing we noticed, no where could we find a mention of Mrs. Wheeler's Christian name in any book or document and she was always refered to as Mrs Wheeler but after much research we now known it to be Anna. Of their six children only two survived, Henrietta and **Rosina**. What with the drunkenness of their father and the irresponsibility of their mother, their childhood was not a happy one.

When **Rosina** was only three years of age the marriage came to an end due to the provocative sarcastic nagging of her mother and aunt, which drove Francis to cling even tighter to the bottle. With the constant reminders of the splendor that they were used too and the squalor that they now lived in, bitterness spilled over onto the children.

 No doubt the cruelty that Rosina received from her mother created in her the inability to control her temper and affections. **Rosina** escaped her sad environment by indulging in reading advanced political philosophy.

In 1812 Francis' wife and her sister Bessie, [he could not separate or keep them apart] decided they could no longer stay. Tempers raged. Bessie changed sides taking the husbands part. Screaming at one another they left the house in a rage of abuse with the two girls in haste to live with their kind rich uncle Sir John **Doyle,** Lieutenant Governor of Guernsey.

Francis never saw his family again apart from his favourite daughter **Rosina** on just one occasion, which left him unhappy and depressed, as you will read later.

Sir John Doyle, Lieutenant Governor of Guernsey
And Miss Rosina Wheeler
1817-1825.

The **Doyle's** were an important military family who had six Generals serving this nation between 1756/1856 AD. **Sir John Doyle** had been a soldier of distinction, well respected and popular. Rather vain and too easy going, especially, to the wiles of a pretty face which later brought his downfall at the hands of his new guests. **Sir John** was overjoyed at the arrival in Guernsey of his two beautiful nieces and the two children who suddenly presented themselves, brightening up his rather dull life. The two women soon settled into a hectic round of parties. They reveled in the glamour of the official receptions and their presence enhanced these events where extravagance seemed to have no limits, which they soon noted and used.

Mrs. Anna Wheeler took full advantage of her beauty, flattered by the Duke of Brunswick, toasted by the officers of the German Legion, Dukes, gifts of diamonds and proposals entranced her, but because of all this self-indulgence the two children were neglected. Kind old Uncle John spoilt them by employing a French Governess, Irish nursemaid and even made a nursery for them and Mrs. Johnson [who provided the leisure moments for **Sir John**] took them on outings. The extravagant parties continued for years, even the little girls were sometimes brought down from their beds to entertain the guests with recitations or poems etc.

Money seemed no object until Sir John suddenly became aware that people were questioning his credit. He began to show his feelings over it. The two women saw their games were over and the good times were at an end. Their real personalities started to emerge, tearing each other apart with their violent tempers and creating an intolerable situation for **Sir John.** The children had by this time grown into very beautiful young ladies which provoked the jealousy of their mother.

Sir John had to find a way to escape not only from the women but also from the £20,000 debt that they had built up for him. He sought early retirement, fled to London, leaving the women and the young ladies to find their own fortunes outside the government mansion. **Anna Wheeler** fled to Caen in France with her sister and offspring, joining some cranks to found a new religious sect that was known as the Goddess of Reason. The **Bulwer's** involvement with the Doyle family began when Francis Massey Wheelers' daughter **Rosina** unable to tolerate her mother's moods left her to the cult of being Goddess of *Reason in Caen to spend

*Extracts from; - **Miss Greene's diary.**

a short time with her great uncle, Sir John Doyle in London. Rosina must have met her first real love at this time, he was an officer in the army, but was suddenly posted to Ireland. **Rosina** carried his letters in her bosom and swore she would never part with them. So deep were her feelings that she thanked her great uncle, bade him goodbye and set out to track down her lost love with the excuse of visiting her father in Limerick, but instead went to her mother's brother in Kilsallaghan, eight miles from Dublin.

It was here that she met Miss Mary Greene who was to become her lifelong friend and confidant and the mother that she never really had. They both found a kind of mother and daughter relationship, and someone with whom **Rosina** could confide. Miss Greene's biographical notes on her life with Rosina were an invaluable record of the **Bulwer** family history. **Rosina** must have changed her mind and eventually visited her father as stated in the diary.

In Miss Green's many descriptions about her life with **Rosina,** and her future family she recalled the excitement felt when **Rosina** for the first time since she was three years old was about to meet her father. As she was his favourite daughter you can imagine his sadness and how disappointed he must have been when the only emotion **Rosina** showed was her sarcasm and contempt of him. Her reaction was so hostile he never forgot and it was reflected in his will. After a bitter row they parted never to meet again as he died a few years later.

A family gathering took place after the funeral when Rosina was chided for her absence from the family in Caen and even more eruptions ensued when it was learned that Henrietta had been left most of her father's estate. The outcome resulted in her mother and sister leaving to live in Paris. **Rosina** detached herself from them and returned to great uncle Sir John Doyle in London who spoiled her.

Her beauty attracted many invitations and new friendships in literary circles, which included Thomas Campbell, *Lady Caroline Lamb, Miss Langton and others. No doubt she had heard them talk of a young man of great ability having just won the Chancellors Medal at Cambridge and this aroused her interest. This man was **Edward Bulwer**.

They met and fell in love.

* Lady Caroline Lamb after the shock of hearing the death of her ex lover Lord Byron invited Edward Bulwer to her house which started their association which ended in May 1824.

SIR EDWARD GEORGE LYTTON BULWER
First Baron Lytton
1803-1873
AND ROSINA BULWER LYTTON.

In this part of the story, the Bulwer's reclaimed some of the past glories of leadership. After a troubled courtship, with the engagement on and off **Edward Bulwer** and **Rosina Wheeler** were finally married on the 29th August 1827 strongly against the wishes of his mother, who resented it so much that she immediately stopped his allowance, refusing to co-operate or recognize the marriage.

This above all destroyed happiness in his new family, and turned him into a workaholic, which ruined his health. After his mother realized what she had done she tried to repair the damage, but it was too late. Ironically this situation gave him courage and determination to succeed in his own right. At last he gained independence from his mother, and lived life rather too much to the full. **Rosina's** upbringing was much to blame for this attitude and bad qualities. She was bad tempered, lacking in refinement, obscene in manner, combined with a willful nature which sometimes led to violence and certainly lacking in dignity, but still a very beautiful woman.

EMILY LYTTON BULWER
Little Boots 1829

Edward and **Rosina** were expecting their first child and he did not want his wife or himself to lose their social independence or miss social gatherings for the sake of the baby. Miss Green, Rosina's lifelong friend helped with the birth. Unfortunately the child became ill, its mouth covered in white blisters.

Later Miss Green could see the helplessness of the children that stemmed from the attitude of both parents, that could not be condoned but in some way could be understood. Because in **Sketch of Emily Bulwer** Plate 75 those times this attitude was fashionable, some parents sought to distance themselves from their children yet wanting to appear to be genteel.

Edward and **Rosina's** domestic arrangements in 1829/31 became distraught; he was determined to purchase a house in London. After much searching he decided on 36, Hertford Street, which at that at the time cost two thousand five hundred and seventy pounds. Though it absorbed much of their capital they bought it, and spent another eight hundred and twenty pounds on its re-decoration.
Above are Extracts from Miss Green's diary

Emily was baptized the Sunday before they left Woodcot [September 8th 1829] to live at Vineyard Cottage, Fulham while they waited for their house in London to be decorated. It was to be the last home that **Edward** and **Rosina** shared together, the family was doomed to separate because of both parents' selfish interests. Three years of domestic arguments had irreversibly disrupted the marriage so much that Rosina went to Weymouth for an eye cure. Sometimes she stayed at Tonbridge Wells with **Edward**, but lived mainly in London.

Miss Greene did make a point of seeing the child if she could as there did not appear to be any family attachment. Even meals were disjointed as they acted as individuals, Edward in the library, Rosina in her dressing room, and Emily kept in the nursery.

It was Miss Greene's compassionate desire to mother Emily through most of her short life and she was like the good fairy godmother to the family, totally taken for granted by the parents. It is the diary of this good lady that tells us so much about them. It is a great pity there is no room or time to tell you more of this.

Her mother continually remarked on the child's ugliness and the other imperfections she could see mainly based on reports from the servants, whether true or not. Miss Greene remarked in her diary that she had never seen a child so neglected, with all true feelings repressed. The child's father was always very busy and spent so little time with his family that he seemed to forget Emily's existence.

After much arguing and tears it was arranged that **Emily** was to be taken from the house and fostered. It fell to Miss Green to try to limit the pain and sorrow at the departure of the child into the care of others that Edward would later regret for the rest of his life. Within a week she was taken out of the house later to meet a tragic end.

Edward in coping with the realities of life and the whirlwind of entertaining distinguished guests in luxurious surroundings, living a strenuous life as an M.P. and author, [writing ten novels at this time] took such a toll on his health that in 1833 his health broke down altogether. They both decided that he needed a complete rest and change of scene, so they embarked on a holiday through France, Switzerland and Italy. This was to no avail as their close company only spread the seeds of discontent in their marriage, the damage done was irreparable. A friend described his moods as "a man flayed and sore all over".

LITTLE BOOTS, DIES
The following is a paraphrased version from Miss Greene's Diary. b.1829

Miss Green seemed to be the only one who cared for the children in their younger days. On November 8th 1831, their second child **Edward Robert** was born. Miss Green reminded Edward of his callous treatment of **Emily;** he relented; Emily living with her aunt at Woodcott was brought back. **Edward** tried to get **Rosina** to

Rosina and Robert Plt **76**   mother the children, but it was too late; she had lost all maternal instincts, she now only required the social life he had encouraged.

The disagreements worsened, all the family had a last try to make it work. **Edward** and **Rosina** separated in 1836 when **Emily** was seven years old. And it was a bitter blow for the little girl, from that day forward she did not have a permanent home. Miss Green filled the gap by giving love and attention to the two children, which they sadly did not receive from their parents. **Edward** finally removed **Emily** from the family circle and the rest of her sad little life was spent in Germany being ill-treated by the lady who was supposed to be caring for her, she found some happiness when she fell in love with her friend's brother, but love was not returned, so she felt betrayed and alone.

Because of this neglect and isolation from the family, her health deteriorated, the stress was too much to bear, it brought on an old spinal complaint which was not treated and got worse. **Edward** refused to have her home, and for two years left her in Germany, before realizing that he had left her illness too long. After being advised that it was serious and too advanced for any cure. **Edward** brought his daughter back to England but again failed to give her the attention she was crying out for.

He spent much of his time away making a good living as a full time accomplished writer and an MP. **Rosina** devoted more and more time to her dog, shocking people on every occasion she could with extravagances, which combined with her mocking sense of humour she sadly began to lose her friends. Edward became very disappointed and filled with despair, immersing himself with achievements and work. **Robert** her brother was at boarding school. Miss Green was banned from the house, which left **Emily** lost and lonely. On April 29th 1848 at the age of twenty **Emily** died of typhus fever, **Edward** was deeply shocked when this happened and for the first time came face to face with himself, realising what he had done to his own daughter. But it was too late!

RIVALS OF THE PAST

Charles Dickens   *Edward Bulwer*   *William Thackery*

Edward provoked a rivalry with many of the leading men and women of his day, especially Thackery a fellow author, who gave **Edward** insolent criticism of his style of writing, and a personal caricature that was so stinging it almost led to a duel.

Edward Bulwer and Charles Dickens   Plate 77

At first Charles Dickens joined with Thackery in this, but as neither of their joint efforts succeeded, they could not stop **Bulwer's** hold on the mass of public interest. Later **Edward Bu**lwer formed a very firm friendship with Charles Dickens, and they started the Guild of Literature and Art for destitute Authors and Artists by working together.

Edward wrote many books and these two men were to become among the most well known authors of their time. Both became famous as a writers and dramatists, Edward working with and assisting Charles Dickens. It is said he did not like the finale of Dickens's novel Great Expectations, and said so; he then suggested a new one, creating a happy ending.

Edward Lytton Bulwer Plate 78

It was not until 1856 that Thackery tried to amend his past actions and insults by retracting them. But **Edward**, who was perfectly happy with his friendship with Dickens, did not want to know. His friendships also extended to Lady Caroline Lamb, Harrison Ainsworth, Disraeli and Lords Palmerston, and Tennyson.

Edward was also an astute politician, whose career culminated in the post of Colonel in Lord Derby's ministry 1858/9. He had a part in the Bill that established British Columbia as a colony and supervised the formation of Queensland Australia as a separate state. In New Zealand, Lytton Sound is named after him. He also played a major part in the political reformation of England.

His health deteriorated from working long hours, and in 1833 the couple took a holiday in Europe, but instead of resting and concentrating on winning back the affection of his wife, he wrote two more novels, refueling **Rosina's** smoldering anger and fiery nature that exploded once more. This left her isolated and dejected causing more rows. **Edward** like many men in these circumstances took revenge on his wife by being unfaithful.

He told **Rosina** he had found someone who he considered much more of a wife. **Rosina** never forgave him for this; her hatred of him and all the male gender, including her son, lasted to the end of her life. They formally separated on the 19th April 1836. It was a great pity **Edward** had so little time for his family, an attitude that caused so much grief for him and others.

Later in life **Robert** and his father **Edward** put the past to one side and became friends **Robert** rose in stature to become Viceroy of India in the reign of Queen Victoria [r.1837-1901]. Edward was the writer of numerous popular novels, one of the leading men of his generation and can only be fairly judged by reading his full biography.

*Some of the honours and achievements conferred on Lord Edward Lytton Bulwer [which were numerous]

1830 Elected MP for St Ives, Cornwall as a Reform member
1832 another general election selected as MP for Lincoln as a Radical.
1834 another general election Re–elected for Lincoln and retired 1841
1838 Baronet of the United Kingdom.
1858 Colonial Secretary of State and Knight of the Grand Cross-of
St. Michael and St. George and made a Peer, Baron Lytton of Knebworth.

Edward died at 2 pm. On Saturday January 18th 1873 after the happiest weeks of his life in Torquay, Devon, with his son and daughter in law at his side. He had an ear infection that caused inflammation to the membrane of his brain. We will leave him here and although there are many documents devoted to this brilliant man we felt we had to include some background to his sad life story. Tempestuous and unpredictable, he became a leading Member of Parliament, playwright, author, living for a time with gypsies. His request to be buried at Knebworth was not carried out, as instead they honoured him with a state funeral, and was buried in Poets Corner Westminster Abbey London.

*Source 'Edward and Rosina 1803 –1836 by Michael Sadleir also vol.1 and 2 Life of Edward Bulwer 1st Lord Lytton by his grandson the Earl of Lytton. Note Louisa/Lorina Bulwer lived during this time, mentioned here because Christies auctioned a Sampler, which they thought had been embroidered by Rosina but we informed them that it was done by her relative Louisa. [See Item on Louisa/Lorina Bulwer].

ROBERT BULWER-LYTTON
1st Earl of Lytton and son of Sir Edward
1876-1891

Robert Bulwer and family   Plate **79**

Robert married Edith Villiars; they had several children one of whom, Betty married Gerald Balfour, **Constance** became a dedicated suffragette, **Emily** married Sir Edward Lukins a distinguished architect, **Robert's** son **Victor** became acting Viceroy of India and a very influential Member of Parliament. **Robert Bulwer-Lytton** served in Vienna and Portugal before going to India as Viceroy. They were a very close family and found it hurtful when, through the nature of his national duties and tragic fate they were often kept apart.

His last post was an ambassador to Paris where he died in 1891. **Robert's** wife Edith was well respected for her tireless work assisting in hospitals. He was more successful as a diplomat than a poet, a life which he would have enjoyed; one of his well-known poems is included below.

We may live without poetry, music or art,
We may live without conscience, and live without art
We may live without friends, and live without books,
But civilised man cannot live without cooks

Robert Bulwer-Lytton

VICTOR BULWER-LYTTON.
2nd Earl Lytton and son of Robert

STATESMEN AND AUTHOR

Victor, son of **Robert Bulwer-Lytton** was born in India, and returned as governor of Bengal in 1922 to 1927, becoming acting Viceroy in 1925 for four months and was a strong supporter of the League of Nations, leading a delegation 1927/28. He was the British delegate in 1931, chairman of the Leagues Commission on Manchuria in 1932.

He fought hard in Parliament for women's rights on behalf of his **sister Constance** and supported her in the struggle. He married Pamela Plowdon [who was admired by Winston Churchill] and had two sons and two daughters. His sons **Anthony** and **John** both died in separate tragedies neither married, so Victor's **brother, Neville Lytton Bulwer** succeeded to the title as the third Earl Lytton.

As there was no living male heir **Victor** left Knebworth House to his daughter The **Lady Hermione** who had married Cameron

Victor Lytton Viceroy to India Plate.80 Fromanteel Cobbold [later Lord Cobbold and Governor of the Bank of England]. His second daughter Lady Davinia married Lord Erne and lives in Northern Ireland.

The family shortly before leaving for India   Plate 81

LADY CONSTANCE LYTTON BULWER
DAUGHTER OF ROBERT.
A suffragette who assumed the name of Jane Wharton

Lady Constance Lytton Bulwer was born in Vienna and when forty years old became champion of women's' rights passionately involved with the suffragette movement [much against her mothers wishes].

Under the assumed name of Jane Wharton she was arrested at a demonstration in Liverpool and imprisoned in hospital cells. She began a hunger strike, as did the others imprisoned with her for the cause. Needless to say to ensure that none of the women prisoners gained public sympathy by a possible death, the authorities gave them punishments that in no way related to the crime.

They were force fed, and in the case of **Constance** this was so horrific, she never fully recovered her health and it affected her to such an extent she suffered a serious heart condition that partially paralyzed her for the rest of her life.

Lady Constance [Suffragette]   Plate. 82

Constance hated moral blindness with a vengeance, and this gave her motivation to keep protesting the suffragette cause, even after two terms of imprisonment. Later she wrote a book called "Prisons and Prisoners" which did much to improve the lot of women in British prisons.

Her brother **Victor,** also a supporter had a Bill of rights put through Parliament, sponsoring women's rights. But it was not until the First World War, [when women were enlisted and expected to give their lives for their country],that the motion got under way in Parliament.

Lady Constance Lytton Bulwer
Disguised as Jane Wharton   Plate.82 [a]

EDWARD ANTHONY JAMES LYTTON BUWER
VISCOUNT KNEBWORTH

Born 13th May 1903, Died in Air crash 30th April 1933

Anthony, son of Victor was very close to his parents and when away from home he wrote letters constantly, giving a wealth of information on his short and full life. Born on thirteenth of May 1903, he was named **Edward** after his royal godfather Edward the 7th but was always known as **Anthony**, his second name after his other godfather, Viscount Cranborne, the Marquis of Salisbury, a name that his parents had chosen.

Being the first-born son of the family, he received much attention and was a very active happy child that loved the life of adventure having an interest in everything and lived his life to the full enjoying every moment.

Family connections enabled them to have a close association with royalty; and this brought him his first public engagement, when he was chosen to be pageboy at the wedding of Prince Arthur in the summer of 1911. A very dignified eight-year-old arrived at Buckingham Palace Gate in the royal coach. When the royal footman opened the coach door, he stepped out beaming broadly, obviously very proud of himself, dressed in scarlet livery with plumed hat and sword.

War with Germany was declared August third 1914, and the family was glad when the Grand Duke [who had been renting Knebworth in their absence] had to return to Russia. **Anthony** was being educated at West Downs near Winchester at this time. The war made a great difference to normal activities with most of the men on active duty there was a huge deficiency in many of the essential everyday services; women and the youth of the country were called upon to help out.

As in other areas the whole scout movement was assisting the war effort. Instead of the usual scouting games they went on route marches, or war exercises, such as message carriers on cycles, and other tasks. **Anthony** was an active Scout with the school group, which was divided into six patrols. Anthony became a patrol leader and must have found these activities very exciting not knowing the full implications of war.

His headmaster paid tribute to his many sporting achievements. Writing to his parents he said. "I don't know of any old boy whose life has brought so much honour to the school". An unfortunate illness affected his examination results, so he was unable to do himself justice in the entrance examination for Eaton.

In 1916 he entered Eaton and loved the whole of his stay of six years except for the deprivation that came with the war, such as the restriction of heating and scarcity of food. In one letter home he stated that his bath had come with his ration of one half inch of hot water.

News had arrived stating that the fate of their last Knebworth tenant was unknown. The Russian armistice was signed and fighting had ceased. **Anthony** seemed to take less interest in many sports except his boxing and won the lightweight boxing championship.

He started to consider his future, becoming very despondent. This mood seemed to increase his determination, and he did very well in his last year at Eaton. For the first time the family were separated as his father had been given an overseas appointment as Governor of Bengal and they left for India on March 9th 1922.

He left Eaton in the same year with glowing reports, to join the officers training corps at Tedworth, became an officer, and was received in Trinity, Cambridge University but could not settle as he missed his Eaton colleagues who were now at Oxford. He finally moved and went to Magdalene College Oxford in October 1922, staying at 108, Abingdon Road Oxford but he missed his family even more after three years of separation.

Anthony took his degree at Oxford before sailing to India to rejoin them once more. The last time they were together was at their home in the Manor house at Knebworth and **Anthony** was at Eaton. Though it was only a few years, they had all grown up. It must have been a joyous occasion when they all met at Darjeeling India. **Anthony's** stay so enthralled him that he did not want to leave. The family returned home without him, arriving back in England from India on the 21st April 1927 and went back to the Manor House Knebworth.

In one of his letters to **Hermione** [on May 25th from Government house Darjeeling] he was obviously very homesick. He enjoyed the time he spent with his father when there were no official engagements but was torn apart by the spell India had cast over him, and the love for his family at home in England. His father finally persuaded him to return home in June but he was back in India again in September to stay until the spring. On his return to England **Anthony** found employment with a firm of Stockbrokers in London on a commission basis but this way of earning a livelihood was not for him. He left the company for a salaried occupation in the Central Education Department Conservative Central Office, which included traveling.

The more he saw of political life, the more he saw the evils of class war. In his letter to his father [Earl of Lytton] wrote; "I'm afraid that I have not started too well and horrified my Chief's Private Secretary on the day of my arrival when I told him in no uncertain terms that the University apathy to politics seemed a really healthy sign. I disagreed with all his fanatical views and told him to take a long holiday before the labour party won over the electorate". Also the labour people are bound to win but it has got to happen and in my lifetime and there will be great changes, the aristocracy will be destroyed and it does not matter whether we give way to wealth or socialism.

His letters home revealed he was still taking a long look at his position in society, and the social class of which he was a part.

He and his sister **Hermione,** engaged in verbal politics, she often gave him friendly advice. He considered that the aristocracy of this country was inevitably doomed because the changes that were already taking place in attitudes were creating social changes that would force the upper classes to engage in the commercial world.

His break came when invited to enter politics to contest the labour stronghold of Shoreditch. It seemed an impossible task but his constant campaigning in the district won the hearts of the electorate if not the seat, after the announcement he was hoisted up on to their shoulders. Lord Edbury the chairman offered him a seat on the board of the Army and Navy Stores and hoped he would become an executive of the company.

Fate took a hand when **Anthony** applied for selection to be the new member for North Herts. The choice fell to Harold MacMillan, later to become Prime Minister. This decision prompted the current Prime Minister Stanley Baldwin to write and apologize. After one year MacMillan decided to retire from this candidature of the Hitchin Division and stand again for his old constituency of Stockton.

Anthony was asked to stand, and it was a proud moment for the family when he was elected as the member for his home constituency. It was 1931 and he found himself sitting in the House of Parliament with many new young faces, bewildered at being unexpectedly elected for the first time. It was not very long before Mr. Duff Cooper [who we will meet again later on in our book] the Under Secretary at the War Office made **Anthony** his Parliamentary Private Secretary. This gave him a definite status in the House, which was a significant launch into a political career.

Youthful ambitions took a serious turn, which sealed his fate when he joined the auxiliary Air Force to be trained as a pilot.

The love of flying was his only recreation. This soon became an absorbing passion and he quickly became a Squadron Officer for 601 squadron at Hendon.

His mother became worried about his possible overwork, particularly the dangers of his flying duties. Parliamentary responsibilities, the job at the Army and Navy Stores, plus his love of flying, boxing, and authorship, he was certainly over occupied and loved every minute of it.

Anthony and his Tiger Moth   Plate.84

After a while flying became his overriding obsessive pastime. He was bored with politics and business, considered the world existed on slavery, with the have and have nots, the latter being ruled and manipulated by the rich few. On his many visits to Knebworth, local people used to listen for his tiger moth airplane arriving, and he entertained them with his antics, executing loops and other aerial displays, it was the best year of his life

It was 1933, when he confided to his sister **Davina** about his love for his childhood sweetheart, and how he was yearning to get married, though sadly his life was soon to end. He went with a fellow officer Roger Bushell to spend a happy day with his mother and father. As he left home no one, least of all Anthony, knew that tragically it was the last time they would wave him goodbye as his plane disappeared into the sunset of a lovely spring evening.

The next day he took a practice run with the squadron to prepare for a display for the Prince of Wales. The maneuver they carried out was one that dipped over the airfield and the leader for this run was a stand-in for their own leader, who was not available. **Anthony** obeyed the strict instruction to watch the leader plane in front of him, which he did but it dived so steeply and for so long that the first three planes following actually hit the ground. **Anthony** flying to the left of these aircraft struck a slight rise that turned his plane over violently. **Anthony** and his passengers were killed instantly, it was a sad ending to several promising lives, and especially for those left behind.

The subsequent inquiry found no blame attached to him or the machine as the cause of the accident was entirely due to following the rigid rule of obeying the lead aircraft and the rise in the ground came at that point. What a pity he could not have lived to formulate the ideas and judgments of his young mind as he settled down. Although violently snatched away, he died as he lived doing the thing he loved most, flying. We had heard much about him from our grandfather so we were saddened by the news of his death

JOHN VISCOUNT KNEBWORTH
Born 10th March 1910 London

John Bulwer   Plate. 85
killed on active service

Moving on a few years tragedy struck again in the family history. War created heroes who stuck to their post to defend a strategic position, knowing full well that they themselves almost certainly would be killed. Those at El Alamein in Egypt were such heroes and it was in the hands of the great armies to be able to turn the tide in our favour sadly some had to be expendable to win an objective for the sake of all those at home. We as children were avid listeners to the news, that even now we find it a must, to hear the 10 o' clock news before going to bed.

Though we had never met our distant cousin's, we were saddened when we heard of the tragedy that struck the family again in 1942, when **John,** the youngest son of **Victor** and **Pamela** was killed fighting for his country in the battle for El Alamein, a famous battle in the Second World War that was won on sheer guts and determination.

The German Commander, General Erwin Rommel was a very skilful war veteran who was called the Desert Fox with good reason. Like Saladin of old he often extracted praise even from his enemies. In fact Churchill was moved to speak of his skills in warfare that gave the Germans the advantage. On the 20th June 1942 news came that Tobruk had fallen; 30.000 British and South African troops were taken prisoner. Nothing the Allies could do to match the brilliance of this man until they appointed a new General named Bernard Montgomery, known to his troops as Monty. He not only put fighting spirit back into the men; his tactics outwitted the Desert Fox.

Initially all the factors were against our desert armies, and the nation was holding its breath; the Navy too did not have an easy run to the North African coast and many of our ships were lost trying to bring supplies to the army.

But General Montgomery, [Monty] had realized that the Germans had only one route open to them across the Mediterranean Sea and took advantage of this fact. The German intelligence failed, as unknown to them their Enigma code had been cracked by an ingenious device made by our intelligence service, and were being outwitted by the code breakers at Bletchly Park, Bedfordshire who could break their cipher and read every secret message on a daily basis. This of course baffled the Germans who could not understand how our side knew their every move in advance.

Also Italian radio signals were intercepted, which gave advance warning to our submarines, aircraft, and other ships and false aircraft signals were sent out to cover the wireless code breaks. The German movements were known beforehand, which cost them at least one third of their troops and replacement supplies.

By November the Germans lost sixty two percent of all their shipping starving them of vital equipment, so the land battle for North Africa became a major sea battle instead.

The axis powers sent submarines into various harbours in order to locate and sink our ships. Due to their success the British suffered heavy losses of shipping and Rommel gained the advantage with replenishment of supplies and fuel. The British suffered heavy casualties in land battles as Rommel built up his depleted army and stores. Malta received a heavy bombing and was under siege, the British succeeded in the sea battle and eventually starved the German army of vital supplies.

Rommel was now in serious trouble with only twenty serviceable tanks remaining and the Italians fifteen. The Allies were outclassed in the air until the new aircraft arrived, including a new fighter plane, the Spitfire. Rommel made his first big mistake when he decided to attack the Russian front.

To Rommel's dismay his troops were now overstretched and resources were dangerously low; instead of an attack he had to decide; retreat or fight to the last man. Monty now with superior sea power had amassed an overwhelming fighting force. It was again a battle of wits between the two Generals but in a final desperate tank battle with restrictions on his fuel Rommel decided to make one last stand at El Alamein and lost.

On the 23rd October 1942 Monty attacked Rommel's position, forcing him to retreat and Monty chased him for 1,500 miles across the desert. Rommel was at last defeated and the sacrifice of our young men to overcome evil it seemed was not in vain.

Sadly it was at this last great battle at El Alamein, that the second heir to Knebworth was killed among all those other brave men not able to savor the sweet taste of victory. The news must have brought more sorrow to his family and many others too. The flower of manhood in many countries was creamed off before it could achieve anything. For those at Knebworth it was double bitterness as their second son was now deceased.

LORD CAMMERON AND LADY LYTTON COBBOLD

The earliest record of a John Cobbold that we could find was in Suffolk 1274. Since the early eighteenth century, the Cobold's were brewers and bankers in Ipswich; they were probably of Saxon origin as the Old Saxon word Kobold meaning Goblin is associated with mines. [Cobalt Blue].

In the nineteenth century the Cobbold's were exceptionally prolific. John Cobbold who died in 1835 married twice and produced twenty-two children. His eldest son and grandson also produced respectively fourteen and thirteen offspring. One of the thirteen children, the ninth, was Nathaniel Fromanteel grandfather of the first **Lord Cobbold**.

Lady Hermione Lytton Bulwer became engaged to her future husband during the Christmas holidays and was married on 5th April 1933 at Knebworth. After the honeymoon they settled in Milan in a country villa above Lake Como in Italy. After her brothers were killed they probably moved back and occupied Knebworth Hall where they raised their family, and until the time of his death, Hermione's brother Neville held the titles.

Lady Hermione now lives in one of the houses on the estate, as her husband died in1987. Her son David inherited the titles and resided in Knebworth Hall with his family. He has now passed the house over to his son who has dropped the name of Bulwer and taken the family name of Cobbold.

LADY DAVINA BULWER-LYTTON

Davina, last child of **Victor,** and sister to Hermione, married **Lord Erne** in Westminster Abbey on St. Swithins day July 15th 1934. They lived at Crom Castle, Loch Erne, Northern Ireland. Looking at the map of Scotland where we had planned to spend our holiday we saw a Loch Erne very near to the location where we were staying and concluded [wrongly] that this must be the one.

Through our research we found a second cousin living near there and decided to kill two birds with one stone and pay a visit.

After much searching we found a castle there but no local memory of the **Bulwer-Lytton's** or **Lord Erne** so we conclude our information must have been incorrect as to location.

But life is strange, on returning home after our holiday in Scotland we received an excited telephone message from **Barbara** our second cousin to say that for some unknown reason she happened to turn on the radio, something she rarely does and to her amazement she heard **Lord Erne** giving a talk, and by a weird chance she had located the family at Loch Erne in Ireland.

LORD DAVID LYTTON COBOLD

Lord David with his family Xmas 1989   Plate.86

Lord David Lytton Cobbold succeeded to the title on the death of his father in 1987 and changed the family name from **Bulwer to Lytton Cobbold. David** was the only child of **Lord and Lady Cobbold**. He lived [at the time we started writing this book] in Knebworth Hall with his wife **Christine** and their family of four children **Henry, Peter, Richard, and Rosina.**

Sadly the ancient family name '**Bulwer**' is no longer used by the Knebworth family branch which is now known by the name of **Lytton Cobbold,** but that's life. We have completed up to the time writing most of the story on the branches of the Heydon and Knebworth families.

Note: - The following pages will show that our family line develops as one of the 3 main branches Heydon Knebworth, and Buxton/Hainford/Elsing. We have dealt with two [Heydon and Knebworth] and will now concentrate on our own family line starting from the reign of Queen Elizabeth 1st.

CHAPTER VIII
WE RETURN TO THE MAIN FAMILY LINEAGE c. 1500
*The de Dalling/Bulwer Conundrum

JOHN DALLING AND DESCENDANTS

[BROTHER OF SIMON = MARGARET MOUNEY OF OUR LINEAGE]

Pedigree from visitations of 1563, 1568, 1613,
Other names listed from wills and Manorial Rolls etc.

Chart. 78

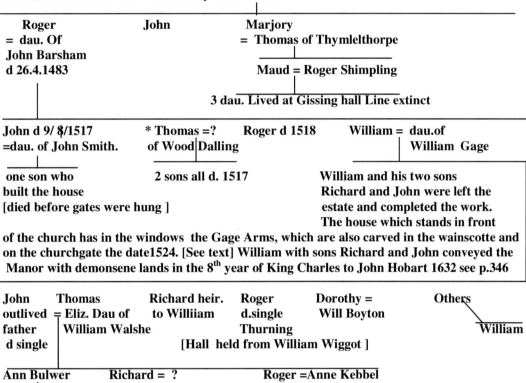

John de Dalling = Margaret daughter of John Smith Horsham London, Merchant [brother to Simon de Dalling = Margaret Mouney] appointed to collect all arrears for Farm rents, pensions and demand service due to the Priory of St Faiths

Roger	John	Marjory
= dau. Of		= Thomas of Thymlelthorpe
John Barsham		
d 26.4.1483		Maud = Roger Shimpling
		3 dau. Lived at Gissing hall Line extinct

John d 9/ 8/1517	* Thomas =?	Roger d 1518	William = dau.of
=dau. of John Smith.	of Wood Dalling		William Gage
one son who built the house [died before gates were hung]	2 sons all d. 1517		William and his two sons Richard and John were left the estate and completed the work. The house which stands in front

of the church has in the windows the Gage Arms, which are also carved in the wainscotte and on the churchgate the date1524. [See text] William with sons Richard and John conveyed the Manor with demonsene lands in the 8th year of King Charles to John Hobart 1632 see p.346

John	Thomas	Richard heir.	Roger	Dorothy =	Others
outlived	= Eliz. Dau of	to Williiam	d.single	Will Boyton	
father	William Walshe		Thurning		William
d single		[Hall held from William Wiggot]			

Ann Bulwer	Richard = ?	Roger =Anne Kebbel

Richard bps 1692 minor

*This line descends from John d.1487 when family split so names are not on full chart of Bulwer families. See separate history information taken from visitation book of this period. John and Thomas of Wood Dalling and most of their families died in c. 1517 probably due to the plague. Caroline Pratt appointed guardian, tenant in Manor, which was transferred to Gaywood Manorial books, and succeeded to Eliz Newson on the conditional surrender of this Manor. Richard son of John admitted as tenant on death of father, family heirs not forthcoming all daughters who married into the Lammas family.

THIS BRANCH OF BULWER FAMILIES NOW EXTINCT
While writing histories of the Dalling/Bulwer families, we have often wondered why the families split at this time. After reading the escapades of these two families we got a general feeling that family honour was at stake. Although John [married to Margaret Smith] was not of our lineage he had strong ties and involvement in the lives of his relations and had an interesting life. He was the son of Roger and Catherine and brother of Simon and Margaret Mouney he became a London Merchant and was appointed to collect all arrears of farm rents, pensions and demand service due to the priory of St. Faiths, Norwich.

Name changes.

Name changes began to be noticed more after the invasion of William the Conqueror. The Crispin's [female line down from **Rollo**] first changed their name from Crispin to de Dalling in the time of Turold who lived at Wood Dalling. The second name change came in 1530 when Simon de Dalling changed his name from de Dalling to Bulver. This change was expressed as TOUT COURT [without argument]

The reasons behind these changes were mainly to avoid being caught and punished over some misdemeanour, bringing shame on the family name even to losing their home and all their possessions and worse arousing the wrath of the king. This is why some names are so difficult to trace. To really understand all of this, you would have to have lived in those troubled times when punishment was harsh.

But we do find some help in The Manor and Pipe rolls, Charters Deeds and other documents. The invasions and rebellions that took place in those times destroyed many of these papers and we have noted some of the information we have found with the aid of our researcher.

Some of the examples of these are listed below.

1478 –Bulwer deeds enfeoffment from Nicholas Harman and others to **John and Simon Bulwer**, one acre in Cawston. William Dalling clerk and Simon Bulwer executors. Witnesses to the will of Thomas Brygge, where **Roger Bulwer** was named as son and heir to **William Dalling** deceased, married to **Alice** daughter of John Barsham in [**Bulwer** deeds] 6.5.1500.

Enfeoffment to William Crane clerk, John Capps, and [**John Dey**, who married into the **Bulwer** family], and to **Roger,** son and heir of **William Bulwer** of Wood Dalling [deceased] and to **William Dalling** son and heir to the late **William Bulwer** proving **John Dalling** was the son of William Bulwer.

Several members of this family, and others related to them died around this time, so we conclude the plagues may have been around that area. This John Dalling (grandson of John brother of Simon) started to build another Dalling Hall opposite the church but died in 1517 just before the gates were hung. Several members of this family, and others related to them died around this time..

*See chart on previous page.

They did leave traces of their occupation in the windows of the house with the arms of Bulwer and Gage and a date of 1584. The same arms are carved in the wainscoting of the house at Church Gate. The brother of John senior, *[William] inherited but also died in 1517, his sons Richard and John succeeded

Roger Bulwer senior was grandfather to **Richard**, and **William**, and their defender in a court case. In 1337 Thurning and **Bulwe**r deeds confirm this, as do the deeds of Thurning Manor 1476-1557. In the 2nd year of the reign of Charles 1st a contention arose when the sons of **William Bulwer, (Richard** and **John Bulwer)** were in dispute with John Hobart 1632 [Chief Justice of Common Pleas] over the Manor of Verly/Dalling, who sometimes took matters into his own hands.

Richard and **John** died and Hobart claimed ownership of the lands of Dalling Kerdiston and Thurning together with their demesne lands. The **Bulwer's** must have borne in mind that a duel that took place between Sir Thomas and one of his neighbours Oliver Neve of Great Witchingham Hall. The details are sketchy, but since there are a great many Hobarts and no Neves in the records after this, gives some indication of how this duel went.

In Cawston there was a dueling stone (a ball on a plinth), commemorating this duel. By the nature of the man you can understand why the **Dalling's** never argued and felt obliged to convey these lands by fine, rather than engage in combat with such a forceful family in the 8th year of the reign of Charles 1st [1632] and the family still holds them as far as we know.

Eventually **John Dalling's** family died out through lack of male heirs and the last of the line of **Bulwer's** in this area was **Augustine Bulwer** 1726. The family survived for a time and transferred their seat to Gaywood where they only had issue of daughters who married into the Lammas families.

It must be noted during the above period, the turmoil of Roundheads and Cavaliers [civil war of state v. monarchy existed 1642 John Bulwer was war armourer] when England had a dictator in the form of Oliver Cromwell after King Charles 1st was executed in 1649.

* See Chart. p.78 and a note written in margin of his will states that this proves that Roger was son and heir to the late William Dalling [Clerk] .

Added information in the Manor Rolls the Gaywood Families.

1686   **Richard and Ann Bulwer** admitted on the surrender of Isaac Abraham. **Richard** son and heir of the above, admitted tenant on death of father, he being a minor Caroline appointed Guardian.

1704   **Augustine** admitted tenant on surrender of sister. **Augustine** admitted tenant on surrender of Everett. **Richard Bulwer** died. **Augustine** admitted to his lands. **Augustine** junior, Guestwick mentioned [almost unreadable].

1723   **Augustine Bulwer** junior admitted on surrender of **Augustine** Senior

1724   **Augustine** Junior admitted Timothy Fish.

1725   **Augustine** and **Ann** admitted on surrender of William Scarffe.

1726   **Augustine Bulwer** has died. **Ann** admitted to lands held 1704.
        1726-1743 **Ann Bulwer** died without issue surrendered land to Thomas Lamming. But Jeffrey Lamming son and heir of Thomas Lamming inherited, she having named him heir of Augustine. Bulwer. During this period of time Queen Anne 1702-1714 [daughter of King James 7th] had a deep friendship from the age. of thirteen with Sarah Churchill [later 1st Duchess of Marlborough] a domineering woman of strong personality, devoted to her husband John; This friendship became so strong Queen Mary, Anne's mother tried to keep them apart.

After Queen Mary's death Queen Anne bestowed financial rewards and titles to the Churchill families. Sarah had a big influence on Anne's state decisions that brought terror to her son-in-laws, and the Prime Minister Robert Walpole. No doubt the Bulwer's enjoyed the music of Handel and the inspiration of Isaac Newton who found the physics of science and discovered the secrets of the universe. In the end Anne and Sarah argued over religion, politics and bullying.

THE MANOR OF CLEYTHORPE/CLEITHORP/CLEY

Ralph Duke of Norfolk held lands here during Edward the Confessors reign and for a time under William the 1st. But these were forfeit after his rebellion in 1075 when he was deprived these lands that were then held by William Fitz Richard. In the Domsday Book it states the name of Cley /Cleitorpa comes from the stream or river that rises above the head and flows through the centre of the town, then along the coast until it falls into the river Wissey. *Some of this land was inherited or gained by **Turold** from **William de Warrenna.**

*[See list under Turold William of Warrenna's man pages.161, 167, 169

BUXTON HAINFORD BRANCH

Continued from page 208 chart 49 Thomas and Antonia   Chart 79.

SIMON de DALLING d.1504 =MARGARET MONEY/MOUNEY d.1537
[break see Dalling chart for John Dalling. p.344.cht.78]
Main family .Daughter of Robert Mouney/Money
descendants associated with St.Peter Mancroft Church Norwich]
Name change Alias Bulwer 1530 TOUT COURT   [See item on Simon Dalling]

ROGER = ELIZABETHh
d.1517 or 18 | Daughter of John Sowth

SIMON=JONE Descendant of Alleyn An ancient House[p.361]
[See page 32 of Book Holy Grail by Laurence Gardner]

[1]ANNEe = ROGER [2]CHRISTIAN	THOMAS BULWER=ANTHONY/ANTONIA CLAXTION
Heydon /Knebworth	of Guistwick and Hainford	of Leverna Suffolk.
↓ Lines	his is the grandfather that	In the reign of King James
Cont. on cht.71.p302		initiated our book
Cousins to Buxton /		
Hainford / Elsing families		[break I] others

PETER d 1634 = ELIZABETH   Elizabeth   Robert = Margaret // John   William
Entered in the Manorial Roll 1575-1633   1634   _____
Owned Chequers P.H. Binham   issue
With his brother Robert   Not all children are included [break 2]

William	Thomas =1st Ann Marshham	ALEXANDER=ELIZABETH	*Ann=HenryMarsham
bur.1643	of Buxton 2nd =Elizabeth	Will 1693 d1687	
.	1694 Ferrer	Cordwinder	Issue
	Aged 82	[Shoemaker]	
		Stratton Strawless and Elsing	

Thomas died   Ann = Captain Thomas   Hainford Manor Rolls for
   as infant | England son of   sequence of inheritence
                | Sir Geo; England   p355/357

         Five sons   three daughters   Not all children are included
                                                            // [break 3]

ALEXANDER = ELIZABETH Thomas Eliz. Ann = Sarah   Palgrave Sussanah Peter d 1710
East Bilney | Goodred   went to | Levik =Daynes = Newby _____ = Mary
   . | Australia 3 Issue 3 Issue Rachael Alexander. 1680
            | Father distressed   Hainford

Mary	Sussanah	Ann	THOMAS b 1693 d1712 = MARY.d1756 aged 60
d1714	d 1712	c.1690 d. 1765	Lived at Stratton Strawless, Elsing Hainford
			Saxthorpe and Woodalling [Leased Bul. 11/37
.			31.12.1799 From William Earl Bulwer to Thomas
.			Bulwer farmer of Woodalling Also lived at Cley
			Trade Glover
			LINE CON.; on page 361 chart 82 page 367/8 charts.85/86

Pedigree two taken from Visitation Books of 1563 – 1863 /1613 and deduced from wills 1694, 1687, 1704, 1770 and P.R.O.   * Start of Marsham / Bulwer Hainford families. For earlier generations see Vis; of Norfolk. Harl. Soc.Pub. 32.p. 92. Simon Bulwer and Jone Elwyn raised several children; one Roger [married twice] started the Heydon/Knebworth families, and Thomas [married to Antonia] who started the Hainford families [our line]. We were unable to include all the children from the different families on this chart so have inserted break lines to show that the family lines extend and made other charts to development of other family lines. See chts. on p.348. cht.79 p.362.cht.84.p368.cht.86.

SIMON DALLING AND HIS WIFE MARGARET MOUNEY AND THEIR DESCENDENTS

Simon.born.1504 .died.1537- Margaret widowed 1537.
Bishop of Norwich

OUR FAMILY FOUND AT LAST IN 1530 THE NAME CHANGED TO BULWER

COAT OF ARMS
Arms: - Gules On A Chevron, Between Three Eagles
Close Regardent Or As Many Clinque Foils, Sable, A mullet for difference.
Crest: - A horned wolfes' head erased ermine, crined and armed or,
[Which can be are borne by the descendants].

The objective and main reason for this part of our book is not only to prove our own lineage but for the sake of our grandfather and his brothers who knew their ancestry [which was refuted by others] but could not prove it. It was this fact that drove us to positively prove without a shadow of doubt that their claim was correct to link us to the main **Bulwer** family by using stories passed down through the family, modern research aids, manor rolls etc. and an able researcher.

We will now relate some of the story that our mother had sewn and woven into our hearts and minds that fitted into place with other facts we found to further our research and confirm with the help of official documents to state that Thomas who married Antonia was without doubt the link that connected our family to the Bulwer lineage. We have found as stated below, some of the answers to our questions as to descendant's names, births, marriages and deaths, which were listed and recorded.

The dates we found were not always specific and often did not make much sense but in general we felt that we were on the right track, so we kept going. It was around the time of the worst of the plagues in the fifteenth century that we had most trouble fitting names to the lineage.

In our research so far we found the following statements that later tied up with the official documents: **Margaret** and **Simon Dalling**, [who changed their name to **Bulwer** in 1530] were the forerunners of our branch of the **Bulwer** family who lived at Hainford Hall. **Simon** has an interesting history being Chaplain and late Master of Magdalene Church, Magdalene Road. Norwich [See Norwich deeds] when **Andrew de Dalling** a relative was preacher at St. Peter Hungate, Norwich, which we believe is now a Bible Museum.

Simon and his descendents were born during the time of great religious upheaval that changed the course of English history and must have been bewildered by the obsession of Henry 8th to produce a son and heir. The turmoil started when Henry, who had married Catherine of Aragon and wanted a divorce [see Royal line and Henry 8th] because she did not produce a son. The Pope in Rome would not agree to this.

In order to achieve his aims King Henry formed his own church in 1533 [more details in later pages] and appointed himself as its head, which started the Reformation and caused violent division between creeds. Thousands were put to death, both Catholic and Protestants; churches and abbey's were ransacked and destroyed; so you can imagine the concern of **Simon Dalling** and other **Bulwer** relatives who at this time held high positions within the church.

Some odd things happened at this time for instance, why did **Simon [married** to **Margaret]** change his name to Bulwer, "Tout Court" [With out argument]. Did he offend those in power and make himself scarce? From the Visitation Books 1513, 1569, 1613 and added information from wills, there was a notation to say that this Simon became bishop of Norwich. He led a battle during the Peoples Crusade and was killed, [the latter we cannot confirm as it was loosely referred to in a book]. These Visitation books and other documents clearly show the lineage from Simon Bulwer [married to Jone Elwyn] to Thomas Bulwer of Buxton [married to 1st Elizabeth Ferrer then to Ann Marsham].

It was during Henry 8th reign in 1530 that the families of **Roger, Simon, and John** separated. Although Thomas is mentioned in Visitation Books and the Manor Rolls we had a difficult task in proving that he was the son of Roger. [See following pages]. After King Henry died in 1547 his son Edward became king and treated Catholics more harshly than his father. Ketts rebellion in Norfolk took place shortly after this in 1549.

We have ascertained the family lineage as follows.

<u>**Simon [d 1504]** and **Margaret**</u> as featured on the previous paragraphs raised seven children; we have not named of all of them on the chart. Simon's descendants were associated with Saint Peter Mancroft church Norwich. Changed family name 1530 and their eldest son was:-
<u>**Roger [d1517]**</u> the first born of Simon and Margaret; married **Elizabeth** the daughter of John **Sowth or Smith]**
<u>**Simon Bulwer**</u> [married **Jone Alleyn from** an ancient house, forerunners of the Knebworth Heydon and Hainford families.
<u>*****Thomas Bulwer**</u> [married to **Antonia**] brother of Roger, lived at Hainford Hall. **Thomas** had a serious dispute with his father Simon, which caused a family division and was possibly cast out in disgrace, so we had great difficulty in tracing him. There seems to be little reference to his existence in the **Bulwer** charts though he is definitely listed in the Visitation Books, the wills of the Guestwick families and his own will of 1607. His oldest son was Peter.

* **Our family line**.

Admons: 1633 and 1634

Peter Bulwer [d.1634] married **Elizabeth White** daughter of John White of Wisbeach; deed contracted between **Anthony/Antonia Bulwer,** mother] now a widow, and Peter Bulwer [Son]; another dated 1598 is between Robert Green of Catton and **Thomas Bulwer** of Hainford. We have copies of these two lovely old documents, which are in English listed in the Index. Unfortunately all [as far we are aware] admons: 1629/1639 did not survive due to the library fire in Norwich, but are mentioned on our chart.

On **Peter's** marriage he inherited two public houses in Bynham [now known as Binham] one called the Chequers the other the White Hart which has since been demolished. Later the Chequers was sold to Charles Weston [who started the first bank in Norwich] by **Thomas Bulwer** of Buxton, with a proviso that some of the profits of the public house went to the poor of Hainford. This public house descended through the family line for several generations; **Peter** the son of **Thomas** and Antonia inherited the hall, then it passed [confirmed by the Manor Rolls] to **Peter's** son **Thomas** of Buxton [married to 1st Elizabeth Ferrer 2nd Ann Marsham].

YOUR PROGRESS CHART THROUGH TIME

Chart 80

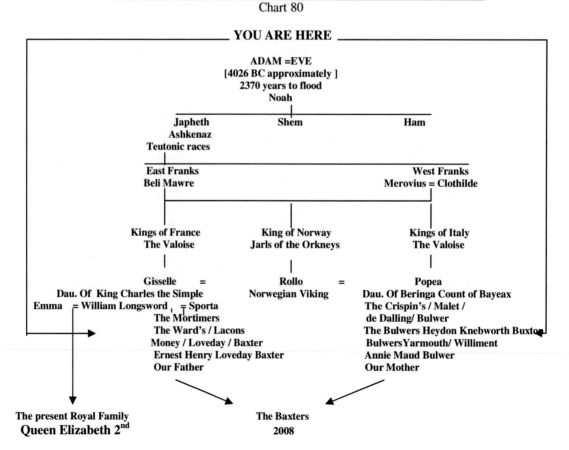

BUXTON, ELSING, STRATTON, SAXTHORPE, HAINFORD FAMILIES
From The Visitation Books 1563 1589 1615 With Added Information Extracted From Various Wills
The search for the mysterious Thomas Bulwer

Throughout history the past has been conveyed from older to younger generations and although in 1882 our great grandfather Thomas Henry died when his family was still young [our own grandfather was then only 10 years of age]. Someone must have made them aware of their family background because after the death of Edward Bulwer in 1934 a claim was made on the estate by our grandfather and his brothers at a family meeting in Heydon Hall. Although they had memories of what they had been told of past family history they could not verify the lineage of **Thomas** vicar of Buxton nor **Alexander** his brother. Their connection to the main Bulwer family at this time could not be proven at the meeting and the claim failed, much to their disappointment.

Stories discussed round the fire during our childhood all those years ago now seemed to be falling into place. The first time we knew we were on the right track of our **Thomas** was that during our research we found that a **Thomas Bulwer** was buried at Saxthorpe and whose memorial stone is in the church behind the font. Was this him? We now had to prove it. At this point we came to a dead end (excuse the expression) with no further leads; we failed to find a positive link with **Thomas** though knowing he had existed we soon realized there was more than one Thomas. We asked Gill McKenna of Family Research, to help us find which one fitted our lineage.

The Thomas we had heard of was supposedly cast out of the family because he was a compulsive gambler, and an embarrassment to them. The mystery was to which family did this Thomas belong? What had he done to deserve such treatment? Was this the same Thomas whose father wrote despairingly in his will, that this son had gone over the seas, and he feared he would see him no more, but left some money's for him should he return, Did he come back? Was he the Thomas who had disputed with his father the Bishop of Norwich over a gambling debt? Or was there a dispute over religious/political issues of that time?

After much time and effort she finally gathered the clues together. Little snippets of stories we remembered from our childhood as told by our mother slotted into place with the collected facts. From Bloomfield's History of Norwich to the Visitation books and Hainford Manor Rolls, there they all were. We found that he **[Thomas]** was mentioned there and proved it in the clues that both our Grandfather and the rest of us had missed. From that time on things really began to move forward.

With these accumulated facts we can now put the record straight, and say our lineage from **Thomas** did exist and is proved by the Manor Rolls recorded during their lifetimes. **Thomas** has been definitely put in his rightful place, which confirmed that our family line hailed from Buxton, Hainford, Elsing and Saxthorpe. These documents led us to the **Thomas** whom we had already discovered buried at Saxthorpe Norfolk. Having obtained all this information on our family line it was a proven fact!

If you look at the chart, you will see **Roger** was the first born son of **Simon** and **Margaret.** Follow the line down and you will see Roger's first born was another **Simon** [b.1510] who married **Jone** the descendant of the ancient family of **Alleyn.** They had a son **Thomas** who married **Anthony/Antonia Claxton** daughter of John Laverne Suffolk establishing the **Bulwer's** of Hainford, Buxton, Elsing, and Saxthorpe through their son * Peter.

Pedigree of the Alleyn/Elwyn Family and the inter-marriages with the Bulwer's. [From the Book Norfolk Families.by P.P.Moore]

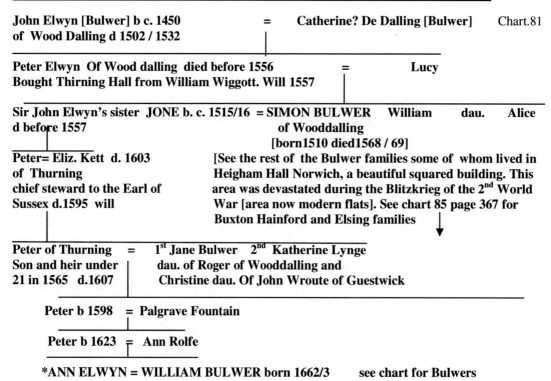

| John Elwyn [Bulwer] b c. 1450 | = | Catherine? De Dalling [Bulwer] | Chart.81 |
| of Wood Dalling d 1502 / 1532 | | | |

Peter Elwyn Of Wood dalling died before 1556   =   Lucy
Bought Thirning Hall from William Wiggott. Will 1557

Sir John Elwyn's sister JONE b. c. 1515/16 = SIMON BULWER   William   dau.   Alice
d before 1557   of Wooddalling
                                  [born1510 died1568 / 69]

Peter= Eliz. Kett d. 1603   [See the rest of the Bulwer families some of whom lived in
of Thurning   Heigham Hall Norwich, a beautiful squared building. This
chief steward to the Earl of   area was devastated during the Blitzkrieg of the 2nd World
Sussex d.1595 will   War [area now modern flats]. See chart 85 page 367 for
                             Buxton Hainford and Elsing families

Peter of Thurning   =   1st Jane Bulwer   2nd Katherine Lynge
Son and heir under   dau. of Roger of Wooddalling and
21 in 1565 d.1607   Christine dau. Of John Wroute of Guestwick

      Peter b 1598   = Palgrave Fountain

        Peter b 1623 = Ann Rolfe

    *ANN ELWYN = WILLIAM BULWER born 1662/3   see chart for Bulwers

*THESE ALSO LINK [1687] WITH THE MAIN FAMILY [EDWARD] GUESTWICK [See wills of William and Edward Bulwer] *See chart page 361 Chart 82.for Heydon and Buxton Hainford Elsing families to correspond with associated text of Buxton Hainford and Elsing families. *Many of these lands were either sold or transferred by fine to others, some were kept as inheritance such as these ones which passed on by Thomas brother to Alexander of Elsing G/G/Grandfather to Thomas of Hainford =Antonia. See chart 84.page 362 and chart 85.page 367. Note;-From 1319 to 1324 these roll's repeated the same information some of which we have omitted because of lack of space. We have transcribed the important information above from Manorial Books held by the Norfolk Cultural Services Department Norwich.

BULWERS OF BUXTON [COUSINS]

Rev. Thomas Bulwer son of **Peter** lived at Buxton 1600-1603, a well-loved and charitable man. Many of the town streets and closes are still named after him and the church at Buxton combines monumental and Bulwer Arms . There is also a memorial in the church: which says;

The family shield Sir George England
Artist impression of   Plate. 87

Here lies a case of soul, whose mind
Was born to benefit mankind
A charity not out of breath
By length of life, nor yet by death
Thou Buxton hath the greatest dole.
To Church, Priest, Poor both body and soul,
If thou a pillar dost not rear,
Let other six Towner's twitch thine ear.
If thou forget, this stone shall be
A monitor to posterity.

Thomas [married 1ˢᵗ Elizabeth Ferrer] 2ⁿᵈ Ann Marsham; their son Thomas died as an infant] but their daughter Anne married Thomas, the son of Sir George and Sarah [nee Wallenger] England and had five sons and three daughters all alive in 1762. She died aged forty. There is a memorial in St. Nicholas Church Great Yarmouth to the England's. The Hall where Thomas Bulwer of Buxton lived was Levisham Hall of which nothing remains above the ground. This building had been surrounded by a moat and belonged to Bishop Jeggins of Norwich [whose son built it]

On the death of Rev: Thomas Bulwer of Buxton [will 1687 d. 1694] this line becomes extinct and the inheritance of first-born was transferred to his brother Alexander. Cross-references prove the link to the main family by the wills of cousins Thomas Bulwer of Buxton and William Bulwer of Guestwick who married Ann Elwyn. They are both mentioned as benefactors in each of their wills as stated in the Visitation books 1664. See item 'Case Proved'.

In the next section we begin to see our own branch of the family start to form with the families of Hainford, Elsing, Saxthorpe, Beccles, and Yarmouth.

This to us was the most exciting part of our book, and at first, the most frustrating. At last we had found our roots, if only our parents and especially our grandfather Bulwer were alive to see the results of our research, it would have delighted them as at last we have found answers, beyond all of our, and their expectations.

FAMILY ESTATES PASSED ON

<u>Alexander</u> [d.1687 married to **Elizabeth White**] inherited the estate from Rev; Thomas Bulwer of Buxton, [his brother] whose male child died early, **Alexander** lived in **S**tratton Strawless and Elsing. He was a Cordwainer [shoemaker]. On his death the estate should have passed to his son **Peter** who married Mary but **Peter** died with no heirs so the estate passed to Peter's brother Alexander.

<u>Alexander </u>[d.1698 married **Elizabeth Goodred**] lived at East Bilney. Was a Juror 1647, 1658 and 1673. When he died his estate passed to his only remaining son **Thomas** [who married Mary].

<u>Thomas,</u> [our Thomas was a glove maker of Hainford b1674 d1759 aged 75 who married **Mary**], We had a difficult time tracing this Thomas, although we knew he existed but like our grandfather had to prove it. This was achieved when we found that he had baptized his children at Hainford circa. 1721-31 this proved that the family line continued. See Manor Rolls 1736 for court case over inheritance. See also Inquisition and Post Mortem Rolls Close Rolls May 1319. His son Thomas inherited.

<u>Thomas</u> married 1st Ann Paul [nee Fernley] continued on page 358.

<u>Hainford Manorial Books.1604-1675.</u>

These are in Latin, not indexed and difficult to read. **Thomas Bulward** is a Juror **Thomas Bulward** is to marry **Ann Marsham**, daughter of **Robert** whom the court is being asked to accept as a joint tenant with **Thomas. Richard** and **Alexander** are Jurors.1673 **Alexander** is a juror. The next information we found for 1673 was that his grandson **Thomas** was admitted as tenant. These manor rolls are further proof of the relationship with **Simon Bulwer** of the Main family; this information is as follows.

<u>Hainford Manorial Books.1604 -1675.</u>

These are also in Latin, not indexed and difficult to read. [Our researcher Mrs. McKenna flicked through these documents and noticed some Bulwer's mentioned and now realized there were some specific dates of 1687 when the Alexander's died which ought to have been looked at more carefully. **Thomas Bulward** is a Juror [of Buxton]

1649 **Thomas Bulward** is to marry Ann Marsham daughter Of Robert whom the court is been asked to accept as joint tenant with Thomas;

1649 **Richard** and **Alexander** Bulwer are Jurors.

1654 **Alexander** Bulwer is a Juror.

1673 **Alexander** is a Juror.

<u>Hainford Manorial Books.1675-1733.</u> With a rough Index in time scale] <u>mentioned</u> **Alexander Bulwer** surrendering some lands and is a Juror **Alexander Bulwer** is a juror. **Thomas Bulwer** admitted as tenant

Note; - We have transcribed information from Manorial Books held by Norfolk Cultural Services Department Norwich.

Here is a gap here of a few years.

1713   **Thomas Bulwer** is a juror.

1714   Special court called by **Thomas Bulwer d. 1759 Bulwer 4/331 Genealogy notes]** Saxthorpe register and manor rolls confirm these dates] he is claiming land left by his grandfather Alexander Bulwer who died in 1687. William left it for his wife's use, and then to his son Peter and to Peter's male heir. In the event of Peter having no male heirs the land goes to his brother Peter then Alexander and to his male heir i.e. Thomas [1681] must have been when Alexander originally acquired this land.

1723   **Thomas** Bulwer admitted to more land, on the surrender of Clements Ives of Coltishall.

1731   Entry concerning **Thomas** and **Mary Bulwer.** Thomas Marsham and **Alexander Bulwer** mentioned.

1733   **Thomas Bulwer** is a juror. We found two indentures one is between **Peter Bulwer** and **Anthony/Antonia Bulwer** [widow] the other is dated 1678 and is between Robert Green of Cotton and **Thomas Bulwer** of Hainford.

Grants appointments and Offenses from Patent Rolls.

        Alleyn, [name changed later to **Elwyn**] received the lands of **Edwin** [Earl of Mercia descendant of **Offa**] son of **Leofric** and the **Lady Godiva**.

        Hainford Manorial Books 1736-1810. Indexed.

1736   **Thomas and Mary Bulwer** arranges a mortgage with Thomas Marsham

4.6.1737 Last August **Thomas Bulwer Gent o**btained a mortgage of £84 pounds on the land inherited from **Alexander Bulwer** with Clement Ives. This has not been repaid and now comes John Ives, the son of Clement to court and is admitted to this land.

10.1750. This entry is a "Common recovery". This was a way to convey land which was the land inherited from Alexander with him being admitted as a tenant again by using a fictitious third party always called Hugh Hunt! **Thomas Bulwer** appears to be disputing the above event concerning the land that he inherited in 1714 and then being admitted tenant again on the surrender of Isaiah Seely.

1752   **Thomas Bulwer** and **Mary** surrendering one parcel of land. that he inherited from **Alexander** to John Caston.

Note; - We have transcribed the above information from Manorial Books held by the Norfolk Cultural Services Department Norwich. Also 1714 is an entry date 1754 when Thomas Senior was born. 1733 entry when he became a juror aged 41. 1759 when he died aged 75 all other entries on this page except those for 1677 and 1678 apply to Thomas Senior.

1757   **Thomas Bulwer** admitted tenant to land on the surrender of John Ives. This is land that **Thomas Bulwer** surrendered on the 4.6.1737 Now **Thomas Bulwer** the son is readmitted and arranges Mortgage of one hundred and sixty pounds with Thomas Marsham 1760 Thomas Bulwer has died since the last court. 1st proclamation.

1761   Second proclamation asking for heirs to come forward.

1762   Third proclamation no heirs have claimed the land so the bailiff is instructed to find a tenant.

1763   **Thomas Bulwer** of Saxthorpe a Glover the only son of **Thomas** comes to court and claims land of his father [see Bulwer; Genealogy 4/331 Notes. B1728 d.1801 14th April [from slab in Church at Saxthorpe] Four parcels of land described that **Thomas** senior had inherited from **Alexander Bulwer** of Elsing.
And also a parcel of land that **Thomas** senior had been admitted to in 1771. Robert Marsham acknowledges the repayment of the mortgage of 1757 by **Thomas Bulwer** late of Saxthorpe and Elmondale House, Yeoman.

1771   **Thomas Bulwer** surrenders land called Kirby's [Chequers Pub] he had since 1757 from Ives to Charles Weston on condition he pays an amount yearly to the poor of Haynford. According to to the will of **Thomas Bulwer** 1693 We assume from the above statements in the Manor Rolls that **Thomas Bulwer** [the father] married to **Mary** got into debt. His son **Thomas** came forward with a mortgage of one hundred and sixty pounds to settle this account. In 1759 his father died and after three proclamations a bailiff was appointed to find a new tenant. After the third proclamation **Thomas Bulwer** [married to Ann] the son comes to court to claim lands of his father. In 1771 **Thomas** surrenders the land called Kirby's (Chequers Pub] that he bought from Ives with the condition as stated in the will of **Thomas** of Buxton.

1772   **Thomas Bulwer** surrenders lands at Mill Hill and Brooks Park that he had from his father in 1763 to Robert Marsham.

1772   **Thomas Bulwer** surrendering lands that he had from his father to John Seely

1798   Robert Marsham son of Robert Marsham is being admitted to five acres of land formerly of **Peter Bulwer.**

1803   Robert Marsham [cousin] only surviving trustee of Bulwer's. Trust for Hainford allotted land to John [Richard Dashwood]. Esq. and Charlotte and also James Nash.

<u>Thomas</u> [b1728 d.1801 son of **Thomas and Mary**] lived first at Hainford where he was baptized. Later he was a farmer in Heydon, and then moved to Saxthorpe and from there to Wood Dalling. His 1ˢᵗ wife Ann Paul [nee Fearnly] was a widow who had been married to Richard Paul who died after ten years of marriage. **Thomas** and Ann produced Thomas [Fearnly Bulwer]. Sadly Ann died when Thomas Fearnly was ten years old, the only surviving child.

His 2ⁿᵈ marriage 1773 to **Mary Billing** at Cromer where they lived producing a son **John** and six other children they then moved to Saxthorpe Manor. Thomas Fearnly took Saxthorpe over while **Thomas** [Senior] leased out Wood Dalling Hall for 21 years from 31ˢᵗ December 1799 Bulwer Genealogy 11/317 states "from William Earl Bulwer to **Thomas** Bulwer farmer of Dalling", who died [1801] two years after lease was taken out.

Thomas Fearnly Bulwer his son, a farmer took over Wood Dalling Hall two years after his father died on a 2ⁿᵈ lease for twenty-one years [10ᵗʰ October 1809] for one year of promises to the poor of Dalling 5/1 paid [Bulwer. 4/313]. He married Mary Johnson and had two children who both died young; Rachel Jane b.1795 d.1816 and a son Thomas who died in infancy. When Thomas Fearnly died aged 67 in 1827 his widow Mary Johnson sold the Manor with other properties to **William Wiggot Bulwer** of the main family to pay legacies through John Ireland the solicitor, when **Mary** died this particular line also became extinct. Thomas Fearnly Bulwer of Wood Dalling half brother to **John Bulwer**, took over the lineage for our family [see p.367. chart.85]

<u>Summary</u>

3] Thomas Fearnly Bulwer lived at Wood Dalling Hall with his family, when he died [1827 aged 67] his widow [Mary Johnson], to obtain money to pay out legacies, sold it back to **William Wiggot Bulwer** (main family]. Thomas Fearnly Bulwer of Hainford *John Bulwer of our line was buried in Wood Dalling Church which has a slab with his inscription. This added to information obtained from official records like the Manor Rolls, Visitation Books and other sources researched by a professional researcher, Mrs. G. McKenna, prove the relationship of **Thomas and Alexander Bulwer**, to the **Bulwer** family lineage.

*see page 362 chart 84 page 348 chart 79 page 367 chart 85 [and write up on Thomas] * The facts above were taken from The Bulwer Genealogy Notes See 'we might be related compare <u>Inquisition and Post Mortem Rolls Close Rolls entry 22.4.14</u> Henry V11 Robert Dyne referred to a time when Thomas Bulwer was seized of the land of Thurning. More proof of Thomas existence is as stated in the Domsday Transcript p.169. Norfolk *See copy of Hainford Manor Book Rolls 1604 1675 our book. Broomfield states there was a break probably when the family went to Thurning.

<h2 style="text-align:center"><u>CASE PROVED SUMMARY
THOMAS WHO MARRIED MARY IS PART OF THE MAIN
BULWER LINEAGE</u></h2>
<u>From official documents</u>

1] The Norfolk Visitation Book 1664 clearly shows the lineage from **Simon Bulwer** of Guestwick, who married **Jone Elwyn** down to **Thomas Bulwer,** rector of Buxton, [wife Ann former wife Elizabeth] See cht.79.p.348.

[2] Wills

Thomas of Hainford married to **Anthonia** was previously missed in our search as it is just listed as **Buliver** of Hainford Gent. According to the will they had an eldest son **Peter,** and also a son **Richard** [less than 26 years of age] and daughters **Elizabeth**, **Margaret** and **Cle**? Brother-in-law was a Mr. Owen Claxton of Great Hautbois.

Edward of Guestwick.

On the death of **Thomas** of Buxton his brother **Alexander** is mentioned in his will 1694 [written in 1693] and names his cousin **William of Guestwick** as another benefactor. Confirming the link to the main family is the will of this **William Bulwer [1685]** that mentions **Thomas Bulwer** of Buxton. When Thomas died inheritance passed to his brother **Alexander** whose descendant **Thomas** [married to Mary] mentioned in next paragraph, inherited titles. Also for other proof to link our family to the main branch see page 531.

3] **P.R.O**. Describes* **Thomas [married to Mary]** b 1728 baptizing his children at Hainford. He was buried in 1759; his surviving son **Thomas** married 1st Ann Paul widow of Richard Paul. Sadly Ann died leaving one son Thomas Fearnly Bulwer aged 10 years. Soon after Ann died **Thomas** married Mary Billings [d.1810]. **Thomas** the father died 1801.

Domsday Transcript by Mundford [Norfolk Only]. **

Wood Dalling was re-enfeoffed [to the de Dalling's again in 1530, when the name officially changed to Bulwer and was affected by **Simon Dalling** ["Tout Court"]. Wood Dalling was the main **Bulwer** family's seat until **William Wiggett Bulwer** married **Mary Earl** daughter of **Augustus Earle**, niece of the famous **Erasmus Earle** Chief Lawman to Oliver Cromwell. The main line of the **Wiggett Bulwer** family then transferred their seat to Heydon which was previously the family home of the Earle family.

*P.R.O. Public Record Office.
**See chart for Thomas. Inquisition and Post Mortem Rolls Close Rolls entry 22.4.14.

*Thomas [senior married 1st Ann Paul] leased out Wood-Dalling for twenty-one years, from 31st December 1799. Bulwer genealogy 11/317 states "From **William Earl Bulwer** to **Thomas Bulwer"** [senior] farmer of Dalling who died after two years of the lease in 1801.

The 2nd lease for this property [on 10th October 1809] for one year of promises to the poor of Wood Dalling from **Thomas Fearnly Bulwer** [son b.1761 died 1827 farmer 5/1 paid [Bulwer. 4/313]. **Thomas Fearnly** lived at Wood Dalling Hall with his family, and when he died in 1827 aged 67] his widow [Mary Johnson], to obtain more money to pay out legacies, sold it back to **William Bulwer** in the main family.

John c 1771 first born of **Thomas** [senior's second marriage to **Mary Billing**] married **Susannah Rook** of Cromer in 1801 raising six children William-John, mentioned in sampler of Louisa Bulwer.

Thomas, 1802-1885 [our great-great-grandfather married to Maria], brothers William Robert, Henry James Sister Charlotte, most mentioned in 'The Squires of Heydon Hall' by Mrs. Jane Preston

Interestingly Edward, **[John's** brother] was born c1774 and married Mary Miller and raised a son John. James born c1776 [also John's brother believed to have moved to London, working as harness maker]. Charlotte born c1806, William [died young]. Mary Anna married Edward Kenny 1801 and after her husband died she lived in Yarmouth. Sarah was born c1783 at the farm in Heydon.

In the time of John Bulwer [married to Susanna Rook] King George 3rd bought Buckingham Palace 1761 for his wife Queen Charlotte [who he married the same year and raised 15 children]; he had it enlarged but never lived there; Queen Victoria was the first monarch to move in.

The Boston Tea party 1773, American Declaration of Independence 1776 and the movement to eliminate slavery [1787] took place. John Wilkes, a rogue politician provided hilarious incidents both inside and outside parliament and was a constant thorn in the side of authority. By marrying a rich heiress to The Manor of Aylesbury he used his newly found wealth to antagonize the establishment and was regarded as the people's timely choice for liberty and free speech.

---

*This fact from the Domsday Transcript is repeated and confirmed by Norfolk Visitation Book 1664. which confirms statements taken from other sources including 'The Bulwer Genealogy' [see above]. These facts have been repeated for added proof.

Our family line of Hainford Elsing and Buxton

These are the family members mentioned in text above

Chart 82

See visitation Book [Guestwick] and Manor Rolls 1513, 1569
& 1613 Hainford Man. Bk. 1604 – 1810

[SIMON and JONE]
See chart 84 page 362
See chart 79 page 348

THOMAS = ANTONIA + 5 Others

PETER = ELIZABETH

Thomas = 1ˢᵗ Elizabeth Ferrer   ALEXANDER = ELIZABETH   Ann = Henry Marsham
= 2ⁿᵈ Ann Marsham
Buxton Family   ALEXANDER = ELIZABETH   Thomas=Dorothy
Son and dau died no male heirs   GOODRED

THOMAS = MARY

Ann   Mary   Robert   Leonard

1ˢᵗ Ann Paul =   THOMAS=2ⁿᵈ MARY BILLINGS   = Peter
    Elwyn [see chart 70 page 299]

Thomas Fearnly=Mary Johnson   JOHN=SUSANAH ROOK   Peter   Thomas   Ann=Will Bulwer
Line became extinct family   married 1801   Guistwick
inheritance went to John
and Susanah   THOMAS = MARIA DICKERSON

Our great great   our great great
grandfather   grand mother page 368

Thomas our great-great-grandfather's story and his descendents is continued later in the book

YOUR PROGRESS CHART THROUGH TIME

Chart. 83

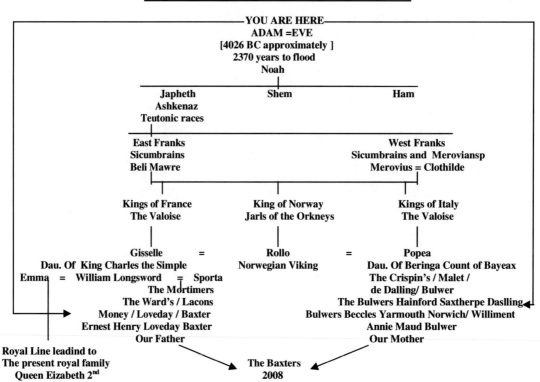

Families on the next page could not be included in chart 82 due to lack of space. Some names we have included again as a reference. These records also tie in with the Bulwer of Buxton pedigree in the visitations of 1664 which give the connection of the Buxton Hainford and Elsing families to the Simon who married Joan Elwyn.

SIMON AND JONE DALLING/BULWER **Chart 84**
COMMON ANCESTOR TO ALL BRANCHES BELOW

DALLING/HEYDON/GUISTWICK/AYLESHAM LEADING TO <u>KNEBWORTH</u> BUXTON
| Cont from p.302.cht.71   / HAINFORD/ ELSING
| This chart deals mainly with the Heydon/ Aylsham Branches   Cont.from p.348 cht.79

SIMON=**JONE**	Roger	William	Anne = Thomas	Audrey = William	Maud
Wood	Dau. Of	d 1517/18		Smythe	Smythe	
Dalling	Peter Elwyn the		//		

Anne	= **Roger** = **Christian**	John	William	Christopher	//THOMAS=ANTONIA+ 5 Others
Dau. Of	dau. Of				
William	John			**Our family line of Hainford Elsing and Buxton**
Bulwer	Wrowte			**See p.348and 367 Chts.79and85**
Issue			**See visitation Book [Guistwick]** amd Manor Rolls
		1513 1569 & 1613	**Hanford Man. Bk. 1604 – 1810**

Anne dau.of William Beck   = **Edward** = **Margarete**   + nine   others see other chart
       Issue |

Edward   **Roger** = E.liz.   William   Thomas   + 6 others   see other chart
          | dau of Robert Cock

Edward = **Anne**   William = Elizabeth   + 5 others see other chart
     | Dau; of William Younge   dau of Thomas Self

---

3 issue died 3 more + Edward = Hannah Perrier/Penyer   **[1]Anne** = **William** = 2 other wives
.   Aylsham Branch   main family
                    _____   **Heydon**   linescome from
                              Edward Bulwer[Priest]   **Branch**   Francis dau of
                                   | Edward Lee
_____   See note on page298

James Bulwer [Will 1783]   Thomas [lived at Aylesham]
= Mary [lived at Sutton [Will 1799]   Butcher = Eliz. Gottesham mentioned in Jane Prestons book
     | | Squires of Heydon Hall p235
_____   _____
John [well known councilor]   Mary =   Sarah = John Gedge
     | Joseph Decker   of Sutton
_____   Swannton Abbott   [See will]   **Sarah** = **Rice Wiggot**+ 4 issue
                   | |
            Mary = James Bulwer   **William Wiggot = Mary Earl** + 4 issue
                m 1799   Changed name to Wiggot Bulwer   dau; of Austus Earl

---

General Earl = **Eliz. Barbara /Warburton** * Edward = 1st Anne Groover   **Augustine** + Others
Wigget Bulwer | **Lytton**   Priest   2nd = Anne Waterrick

William Lytton Bulwer **Henry Lord Dalling** **Edward Lytton Bulwer**   + 3   others
= Emily Gascoyne   = Georgina   = **Rosina Wheeler**
. see other chart **For**   Charlotte Wellesley   **start of Knebworth branch see page 323**
Heydon

Col. William   **Edward Earle** + 4 others   **Robert**   **Emily** see other chart
Earl Gascoyne   Gasgcoyn Bulwer   **Knebworth page 323**
= Marion Dearing   More detail on Edward see write up below page 297/ 69
dau. Of William Wilson Lee Warner   Anne Bulwer descendant of sister of Alexander [died 1687]
Continued on page321 Chart.74   = Henry Marsham 3rd[generation down]
↓   Anne Elwyn = William Bulwer [Heydon died 1735]
   Owing to lack of space our family line is not included on this chart see chart 79 page 348

Variation of fonts denote different family branches.

Note; for family connection to the Earle family see page. 303 chart. 72

This chart is dealing with the Dalling, Heydon, Guestwick and Aylesham families. For Buxton,
Hainford and Elsing families see pages 348 chart 79 and 361 chart 82 367 chart.85& 368 chart 86
To correspond with associated text this chart is repeated on p302 for Buxton Hainford and Elsing
families.

WE VISIT THE HOMES OF OUR FOREBEARS

HAINFORD AND SAXTHORPE HALLS

HAINFORD HALL

A once elegant home now a deteriorating empty building surrounded by mud and heaps of wrecked cars each with of course their own a sad story to tell   Plate 88

As you can see from the photograph taken in 1997, the house was totally eloquent in its despair, falling apart, old and dilapidated, crying out in its tatty misery to be totally renovated and cared for. Bricks and mortar really are silent, but they can tell a lot and like seeing a beloved parent growing old; it made us sad. A car breaker was now in possession of it; his business was not really suited to this rural area but we are influenced by the past.The unsightly array of 360 old rusty and decaying cars scattered individually or stacked in heaps between what used to be a very stately old Hall which had trees and grassed lawns within its grounds. These wrecks that once had proud owners, obviously had been involved in tragedy with their own story to tell, as did the hall behind them. In their various stages of decay that did not add anything to the scene around them.

We obtained permission from the owners to visit the Hall, and to wander around its rooms which later **David** took advantage of while in Norfolk. He found it quite a shock to see the very poor state of the grounds and structure of the building The owner was very helpful and willingly unlocked the large padlock that secured the old solid wood entrance door and temporary woodwork. It was quite an experience to hear the creaking hinges as the door slowly opened to reveal the dust-laden interior.
David almost felt that he should not enter and intrude on the tranquility of a bygone age of his ancestors.

He stepped over the threshold to find some of the original wall paneling still there and wandered from room to room stopping every now and then to ponder. Although it was a bright day, the cobwebbed dirty windows restricted the light. There was a huge open fireplace in the main living room where no doubt family evenings were enjoyed round a blazing log fire with children playing laughing and singing. He listened to hear the whispers of a bygone age, and imagined what the curtains and furnishings had looked like. He investigated the empty dusty cupboards, and other rooms, trying to imagine what his forebears might have looked like, the clothes they wore, and would have enjoyed bringing the old hall to life again with the family around that blazing log fire and catch a glimpse of its former glories. But there the building stands, friendless and neglected for all to witness, just a decaying old Hall crumbling back to dust.

David's son **Jason** could be heard quietly moving about in various rooms but he really wanted to get out, as he too felt uncomfortable as if he was intruding. After climbing the rickety staircase **David** was to find to his great delight, in what was probably the old nursery; there was an old fashioned child's rocking horse once the pride and joy of a young family member who had grown to an adult and was now long gone. In another corner was a very ancient child's pram with four large iron wheels supporting a box like carriage that was covered with black leather material. The handle was vertical with a horizontal bar for pushing, it was covered in a thick layer of dust that buried most things.

Looking through a gap in the window shuttering a good view of what must have been the main tree lined driveway could be observed. He tried to visualize the scene with the servants probably standing in that same position as they waited to see the arrival of the new master of the Hall. As happened when Simon Bulwer brought his new bride Antonia back in a horse drawn carriage all those years ago.

It was at this point that his daydream was shattered by the sound of breaking wood; this was followed by a shout from the next room where he found that his son had put his foot through a rotten floorboard. This confirmed the owner's suggestion that they take great care where they walked and on seeing the gaping hole in the far wall where the west wing used to be, they decided to make a quick careful exit.

On leaving the grounds **David** and his family looked back knowing that next time they visited the building could be gone for ever. Hainford Hall was empty, the windows boarded up, eyeless and forlorn and ready to say goodbye, and there was nothing, nothing; we could do about it.

SAXTHORPE HALL

The information we have provided on previous pages have proved beyond doubt and given the answers to what our grandfather and his brothers so earnestly sought. Yet for a long time we could not trace **Thomas.** This is where the Manor Rolls Visitation Books and Wills came into their own and here our researcher found an incident that almost completed the whole ancient Bulwer family story. We finally found the mysterious **Thomas** had lived in Saxthorpe. So like the good people we are, we went visiting the home of our grandfathers;

Saxthorpe Hall   Plate 89
This was the home of Thomas Bulwer

After his father died **Thomas** was the only son left of his own family that came in line for the inheritance, the family had moved from Hainford to live at Saxthorpe. After we had searched for every clue and fact from documents to prove our lineage we felt we had to visit their homes to substantiate our findings. Saxthorpe Hall did not look like a hall at all, but resembled, a large and comfortable old farmhouse. It was very well cared for by the residents, unlike Hainford and had been updated and divided into separate abodes.

Though it has kept its original name we doubt if the ancient Bulwer's would have recognized it as such and wondered what they would have made of this modernized dwelling. They would be amazed at all the gadgets that we consider part of every day life; compared to ours today their lifetimes were hard and comfortless. We were pleased to see that someone had cared for and restored another of these ancient old houses.

This manor had been in the possession of **Thomas,** who had married twice, 1st to Ann Paul 2nd to Mary Billing's. The objective and main reason for this part of our book is not only to prove our own lineage but to look into the past to see where and how our blood relations lived their lives in those harsh times. It's a great pity that our grandfather and his brothers never had this opportunity.

Norwich Freemen [early book].

A **Thomas** Bulwer of Norwich and his son **John** [we are at this moment uncertain of his position in the family] lived in Guestwick during the time of Oliver Cromwell and decided to leave for some reason to settle in Norwich 1654 and practice as physicians. We suspect they moved to assist Cromwell's army who trained in Chapel Field Garden's Norwich and presume that it could have been this **John Bulwer** who became armourer for Cromwell and using the Guildhall as a base was probably involved in the turmoil of State versus Monarchy.

Language for the Deaf and Dumb

We were restricted in our research due to the recent fire at Norwich Record Office but found that **John,** during latter part of his life, gave his attention to a new type of language, and helped to develop a method to communicating knowledge to the deaf and dumb. History seems to have repeated itself as one of the modern day families is carrying on this same tradition by using sign language that was developed in the time by her ancestor to help the handicapped.

Right through the ages there always have been caring people who strive to improve the quality of life for those less fortunate. **John Bulwer** was also one of these and although he did not invent sign language, he did introduce it into this country and trained others in the art of using and teaching it; a Dr. Wallis was involved in this at a later date.

1553   **John Bulwer** son of **Simon** late of Wood Dalling apprenticed for eight years to John Baker, Grocer.
1723   **Thomas** admitted to more land, on the surrender of Robert Ives of Coltishall. **Thomas Bulwer** is a juror.

We have taken information from two different Hainford Manorial Books one from 1675-1773 the other from 1736-1810. Some of this information may overlap in time scale and contain duplications of the issues of that time but together they give a wider picture of events. All these records tie in with the Bulwer of Buxton pedigree in the visitations of 1664, [see next page] and there we have our link with **Simon Bulwer** [of Guestwick].

We found that in 1772 **Thomas** had a farm in Heydon. It has been a strange feeling researching family histories, for all these months we have been placing them into the rightful place in the jigsaw of their times. Seeing where they lived, walked, died and finally buried. Finding the issues in these records that brought to them both sadness and pleasure feeling their presence and almost drawing their portraits.

WE THINK WE MIGHT BE RELATED!   Chart 85

Chart below defines the Hainford and Buxton Branches and their connections Cont; from page 348 [showing several branches of this family] also page 361 from Simon and Margarete Mouney

For antecedents and descendants and links to main family line see visitation books for Buxton, Hainford 1664 and 1694 1675 –1733, 1737 -1810. Bulwer pedigree 4112, 41323 also Bulwer pedigree 4/323/2 1818. Burks Peerage. Public Record Office London S.C.8/96/4793.685 and Manor Rolls.

SIMON BULWER = JONE ELWYN   Roger   William   Ann   Audreye   Maud
Link | dau. Of Peter Elwyn

Roger **THOMAS BULWER = ANTONIA CLAXTON** William Alice   Thomasine Dorothy Eliz
↓ of Hainford | dau. of Hammond   = Mary   1st = William
Heydon will 1607 | Claxton   2nd = Robert
Families died 1671
page 362   **PETER = ELIZ.WHITE**   Thomas [died]   Richard Eliz. Magararet   Ele
died..1634 Entry in Manor of Briston
Admons 1633 & 1634   Roll [1675 – 1733
Listed but all of the admons 1629 –39 did not survive the Norwich Libary fire.

William Thomas of b 1612 d 1693.aged 82 will **ALEXANDER = ELIZABETH**   Ann = Henry
Buxton   = 1st Eliz Ferrer d1643 aged 29   died 1687 died | before Thomas   d1714 | Marsham
= 2nd Ann Marsham d 1690 / 91   of * Stratton | Strawles and Elsing
Thomas Ann d. 1682 = Thomas England **/issue** ◄ was born See | Hainford Manorial   Thomas =
died – Inheritance passed to ──────────►   Books 1736 –1818 and will 1693   Dorothy
brother Alexander

ALEXANDER   Thomas   Anne   Sarah   Palgrave Peter will 1710
b1678   [Went abroad   = Levick   =Dayne   = Newby 1680=Mary   Ann = ? Elwyn 1748
= **ELIZABETH**   Never heard
GOODRED   from again]   3 issue   2 issue   Peter   Ann Elwyn = W. Bbulwer
Dau = Mayes   = Palgrave | Guestwick
Fountain

Peter = Amy Peachman   Robert 1753   Dau born 1680   Edward died. 1724 [Priest] = ?

John b. 1732 = Eliz born. Lyng   James   Thomas = Eliz.Gottersham
1734/4   = Mary   **of Aylesham**
Amy   Eliz   of Sutton   [See page. 362, chart 84

Ann   Susanah   *THOMAS = MARY [OUR GREAT GREAT GREAT GREAT GREAT
d.1690   d.1712   died.1759 | died1756   **GRAND PARENTS OF ELSING HAINFORD**
Lived at Elsing   aged 75 | aged 60   **SAXTHORPE AND BUXTON FAMILIES**
See Saxthorpe and Hainford Manor Rolls and
Visitation Books See also Bul. 11/ 317 Lease 31.12 .1799

Alexander   **Ann**   **Mary**   1st Ann Paul = *THOMAS = 2nd **MARY BILLING**
bpts Oct.1731   **bp.Sept**   **bps 1721**   married.1761 | died 1801 /   **married 1773**
bur.7.12.1731   **c 1723**   will   **died aged 73**
c1823

Thomas Fearnsly = Mary Johnson   [Hainford manorial books
c1761 m 1792 | b c 1761 m1792   1736 –1765 and 1736 1818]
d. 1827 will   Lease 10/10/1809

────────► **JOHN = SUSANNA ROOK**
cont; on chart 86

Rachel c1794 died 1816 aged 22 yrs   Thomas [died in infancy]   **page 368**
This Line now extinct estate passed to half brother John 2nd marriage   **see text**
Family of Thomas Fearnsly extinct some
────► **Denotes line of inheritance**
NAMES IN CAPITAL LETTERS ARE OUR FAMILY LINE.

Decendants of the Hainford Branch
and children of the 2ⁿᵈ marriage of Thomas Bulwer to Mary Billing 1728
to our great grandfather Thomas Henry of Yarmouth
cont. from cht.85. p.367

THOMAS = MARY BILLINGS   Chart 86
| Farmer at Heydon, 1772 moved to Hainford- and Saxthorpe after death of
. | Anne Paul [nee Fearnsly 1ˢᵗ first wife]. Leased Dalling Hall see page 356 until death in 1801

JOHN = SUSANNA 1801 Edward Mary James Charlotte William Mary= Edward Sarah
| ROOK of Cromer   died young   Kenny b.Heydon

*William John =ANNA THOMAS = MARIA * Robert=Susan Charlotte Janes *Henry.=Mary
b.23.11.1801 DICKERSON | Norwich| died Young |
| 5 Issue some in America | m.1836 5 Issue Norwich   4 Issue
| See tapestry byhis
| dau; Louisa   THOMAS HENRY = SARAH SMITH This chart is cont; on chart 87page 374

Edgar Turner Walter Turner Louisa /Lorina Amelia   Anna Maria Bulwer =George Young
. Bulwer   Bulwer   Bulwer   Bulwer   mentioned on Louisa's tapestry
               America   Embroidered Tapestry died.aged 7   and EdgarTurners's will

NOTE; OUR FAMILY MEMBERS ARE IN CAPITAL LETTERS.

The family of William John and his wife Anna Turner

William John [baptised 20ᵗʰ November 1801 married Anna Turner of Chakens Isle of Ely, Chippenham Cambridge] they owned a shop in Cromer and raised five children which was confirmed by **Louisa** in her tapestry sold by auction at Christies of London. Later they moved to Beccles then to Great Yarmouth. In Jane Preston's book 'The Squires of Heydon Hall' [p.230] in 1903, a lady Mrs. William Bell claimed she was a sister of William John c1801 [see chart for John Bulwer c1771] called upon Sir Henry Ernest Bulwer and explained that William John was sick, paralysed and in need, but she had limited resources'.

Much like our grandfather and his brothers experienced at the hands of their family members, Sir Henry stated "he did not know of him". She replied "I know you don't but he is one of the poor Bulwer's and the rich Bulwer's of course don't know them"! Sir Henry said he did not know any rich Bulwer's either; but she made her point adding she could see the likeness to her father in him, bandy legs and bald head, which he did not appreciate, so she came away empty handed! [Where was Anna his wife, was she heartless too?]. After William died in 1886 Louisa's mother [Anna] kept the house on in Crown Road Great Yarmouth where they took in lodgers. Her mother cooked and Louisa became a housemaid. This must have influenced the bitterness, which she displayed in her Tapestry. After her mother died she lived in 22 Audley Street; sadly Louisa became mentally ill and died in Great Yarmouth Infirmary "Belleview Workhouse" on Caistor Road.

*William John, and Robert both lived in Beccles for a while, [again substantiating Mrs. Preston's book]. Then Robert moved to Norwich where he ran a taxicab business and John to Cromer to own a Grocers shop. Thomas could also be the uncle that Robert referred in her book.

Edgar Turner Bulwer son of William John [see will] married Ann Angood and owned a woolen drapers shop in Market Row Great Yarmouth. We traced him to various addresses in the town.
Walter Turner Bulwer became a hotel waiter and lived in Hungate Lane Great Yarmouth. Walter later went to America with relatives.
Amelia Bulwer died aged seven years
Anna Maria Bulwer [see item on Louisa's tapestry below] married twice, first to George Young and produced one son Arthur, named in the Will of **Edgar Turner Bulwer**. Her second marriage to Arthur Edgar Pinching produced one son George, also named in **Edgar Turner's** will.
Louisa/Lorina Bulwer mentioned above was the daughter of William John Bulwer and Anna Turner [born 1849 she was brought up in Beccles Norfolk and moved with her family to 23 Market Row, then 7 Geneve Terrace, later to Crown Road all in Great Yarmouth and other addresses).
It was stated in the will of her brother Edgar that she was unable to conduct her own affairs in the latter part of her life. [See profile]. During her adult life Lorina embroidered a script on *a long band sampler tapestry and after reading these needleworked statements we considered she was certainly able to speak her mind on family issues. By studying the tapestry of her description of family members, their politics, morals and their right to the name of Bulwer; they all came in for a lashing from her humorous vitriolic tongue; [humorous to us at least].

Her stinging comments were made up of some truthful facts, half-truths and some fantasies. She had a malicious sense of humour and obviously enjoyed embroidering every comment that she made on her sampler, just as we did in reading them, though not with such spiteful delight, as the persons she referred to must have been very upset. She certainly had all the correct names of her family and others with whom she was acquainted. However we cannot comment as to how she came to acquire the details of this very personal history of the Bulwers and whether all the comments were fact or fiction.

Lorina loathed socialist views and those who supported them, as can be seen by comments she made regarding Edgar Turner Bulwer her brother E. Bulwer, and William John her father; [all can be seen on our family charts] and her thoughts as to her relationship with Queen Victoria. Louisa referred to her mother [Anna Turner Bulwer] as 'Ancy Nancy tickled my Fancy' William John her father was much discussed on the tapestry so was his brother Thomas [our great-great grandfather] married to Maria [Plowright] Dickerson whose uncle she named the Tin Man.

*This was recently featured in the Asian and Fine European Costume, Textiles and Fans Catalogue, at Christie's London 19th November 2002 Lot No 341 page 49 and described as 'An extraordinary long band sampler, chaotically worked in coloured wools on a pierced cotton ground etc. It sold for £1,500 pounds at auction.

Other parts were hilarious, addressed to the Maharajah who lived in a palatial mansion in Kelvedon, [Suffolk] The Maharajah mentioned in a television documentary, no doubt had connections with Robert Bulwer of Knebworth [Lorina's relative], who was Viceroy of India at that time. We suspect Lorina in her confused state thought the wonderful diamond, the 'Star of Africa' was a gift to Queen Victoria by the East Iindian Co; when in fact it was sold by the Transvaal Government, which presented it to King Edward 7th.

It was split up and each piece named Cullinan.
*Cullinan 1 [The Star of Africa] King Edward placed in the royal Scepter. Cullinan 2 is mounted in the Imperial state crown. 3 in Queen Mary's Crown and several others cut from the same stone [and numbered] are among the British crown jewels.

Louisa's tapestry stated that there were supposedly many land ownership transfers from India, but her family said she was off her trolley, which is easy to understand as she claimed to be the daughter of Queen Victoria. Her allegation was that she had been abducted as an infant and given to *William John Bulwer to bring up. She scandalized most of her family with a malicious delight, which resulted in her being put into the institute mentioned on her tapestry, [Belview], a mental home in Yarmouth. To give you an idea of her state of mind we have included below some extracts of the comments she so vividly expressed regarding family members and others. We managed to get a complete text of this extraordinary long band sampler, some of which is unprintable

Extracts from her tapestry roughly 176 in. long x14in.wide
This is an aggravation regarding the socialist's, within families and friends. **Lorina** referred to John Mann the sexton as; - *"the one who agreed [to it]. He should take the three rotten putrid carcasses out of the grave, put the old bugaboos in a tent on the beach and turn them into old Aunt Sally three-sticks –a –penny. E. Bulwer can play the violin and **Mrs. Anna Maria Young the Tambourine John Mann the Sexton can carry the three sticks a penny. A socialist bank holiday next Monday, they could make a good payday as a rush of visitors is expected. After that have them cremated no one would buy the ground after their putrid socialist carcasses unless the ground is reconsecrated.*

*****E. Bulwer Esq**. must have this notorious party cremated smash their coffins take a pitchfork and throw their rotten carcasses into the furnace. Old mad Molly Hawes a single woman a vile old faggot from Colney Hatch Asylum call Plowright a tin man Norfolk Street Lynn Norfolk*

*[see internet for more information]**Anna Maria Bulwer/Young was a sister of Louisa Bulwer
***Edgar [Louisa's brother] owned a drapers shop in Yarmouth. See will on page.372.

her Uncle,she was buried In Great Yarmouth first cemetery in the name of Marian wife of Thomas Bulwer were on the gravestone Her son Harry Christian **Bulwer** *is buried perhaps in the same grave. E.Bulwer Esq; must have this notorious party cremated smash their coffins, take a pitchfork and throw the rotten carcasses into the farness.*

This fellow Harry makes vowel servant a light-eyed woman the fellow Harry has light eyes all the children are born and pass by the name of Bulwer. The only name they can claim is their mothers maiden name of **Smith. E. Bulwer Esq. must prosecute them for using the name Bulwer. Mary Jane Emily, the fellows Hawes are all married in the name of Bulwer.

Wonder people have not thrown all the slops of this notorious bug lice and flea tribe Cambridgshire Socialist den and pelted him with rotten eggs and after that have them cremated. No one would buy it after their putrid socialist carcasses, unless the ground was again re-consecrated'.

Another note states *Anna Maria married when we lived Seymour Place the house is the property of Mr. Hotblack shoe manufacturer of Norwich. Thetford delivery stables St Georges Road supplied the wedding carriages that sent the postillions I do not know her eldest son living is forty years of age. Mr. Young wore a false nose false teeth false hair enameled nails false feet or stump legs.*

E. Bulwer Esquire must have seen through the art of Basted mongrel False nose chest expander sears and hermaphrodite or eunuch both these women are well known to Madam Rachael London, also the Langhams Bookmakers the Rookery Newmarket Cambridgeshire.

My mother Ancy Nancy tickle my fancy was married to Mr.W.J. Bulwer at Chippenham Church Cambridgeshire by license from the Bishop of Norwich Cathedral Norfolk. Her plate was sent to Molinari Halesworth. [Jeweller] Suffolk for Mr.W.J.'s monogram. E.Bulwer Esquire is semi royal.

I am Princess Victoria's the late Queen Victoria's daughter, Lorina Bulwer was taken to the royal nursery Queen Victoria in her infancy passing as Miss Lorina Bulwer and living with Mr. and Mrs. W.I. Bulwer grocer Beccles, Suffolk, and his wife Ancy Nancy tickle my Fancy.

Who sent me the so-called Miss Lorina Bulwer to a Belgian School at Beccles Suffolk who sent me all my French Books. E. Bulwer was told my genuine name, he should have told me.

I would have found my way to the English government and informed of the notorious three sisters Taylor passing in the name of Victoria the next one Adelaide, the third one called Sarah Ann. These three women have defrauded the revenue of thousands by passing in the name of Victoria, and Adelaide poor people with absurd ideas these imposters and pretenders are the sisters of Charles Taylor Chippenham.

And so it goes on; Lorina must have had had much fun and self-satisfaction in making her tapestry.

From the *Will of Edgar Turner Bulwer [read 1917] Of Crown Road Yarmouth Gent. (Written 1907)

The House at 20 Nelson Street, Central was left to housekeeper Annie Starling. The three cousins mentioned were Mary Elizabeth Farman wife of Robert Farman of Gorleston, **Rachel Jane** [nee **Bulwer**/Adams] widow who fostered **Harry Henry Bulwer** [son of **Thomas Henry** our great grandfather], Emily Plowright George, [wife of Mark Patrick of Great Yarmouth].

Photograph of a Typical engine of that time   Plate.90
[This engine stood on Norwich Castle mound several years ago]

Two godchildren were also mentioned, Winifred Bulwer Self, and Ronald Self. Nephew's Herbert Young Pinching, of Province Arizona USA. [Son of the late **Anna-Maria** Pinching by her first husband George Young], Arthur Edgar Pinching [employed by the South Pacific Railway] and Niece Lily Hamel [formally Lily McAfee] wife of Dr. Hamel of San Fran Cisco also sister **Louisa Bulwer** [who made the tapestry] stated in will as being incapable of running her own affairs.

*From the Norfolk Will Index 1871-1941
**Many of the family members mentioned above and future pages are vividly described in the tapestry created by Lorina.
Note; some of this information is repeated due to descriptive text and facts from wills.

THOMAS AND MARIA [nee DICKERSON] OUR GREAT – GREAT GRAND PARENTS c 1800

Thomas, the second son of **John** and **Susannah** was our ancestor born in 1802 and married **Maria Plowright Dickerson** in 1836. **Thomas** lived in Cromer, and moved around quite a bit before settling in Yarmouth. He became a master butcher having a shop in Market Row and later one on Caister Road near Geneve Terrace [on Crown Road Great Yarmouth]. They raised **Thomas Henry, Mary Elizabeth**, **Rachael Jane**, **Emily Elizabeth**, and **Christopher Hawes Bulwer**. Several of his relatives went to America prospecting for gold.

*Geneva Terrace on Crown Road Great Yarmouth [still exists]　　　Plate 91

*His sister **Mary** married Dr. Herbert Young and had one son Arthur by her first husband George Young who died, later she married Arthur Edgar Pinching; Arthur was employed by the South Pacific Railway of America [See Will of **Edgar Turner Bulwer**]. These people are also mentioned on the tapestry embroidered by **Louisa/Lorina Bulwer**. The other brothers and sisters of **Thomas** were: **William** the eldest, **Robert** who married **Susan Sophia and** came to Norwich to start a Taxi business and had five children. Charlotte and James [both died young] also **Henry** who married **Mary.**

The family of our great-grandfather **Thomas Henry** including our own grandfather. **Walter** did not live in this particular Geneva Terrace as we first thought, but found that for a time it was the home of **William John Bulwer,** his wife and daughter **Louisa**. This was rather confusing as we discovered that **Thomas Henry** and his family lived in another place of similar name, Geneve Terrace situated on Caister road Great Yarmouth now demolished due to redevelopment, so we had a lot more research to do.

Note; *some of these names are mentioned in Mrs. Preston's book 'Squires of Heydon Hall and also on the tapestry embroidered by Louisa Bulwer.

FAMILY CHART OF THOMAS HENRY AND SARAH BULWER
Line con.from page 368 chart.86

Chart. 87

* THOMAS HENRY BULWER = SARAH SMITH
[our great grandparents] born 1838-died 1882   married.1861

Fredrik	William	Louisa	Anna	Henry / Harry	WALTER
					[our grandfather]

Family Lines from the Thomas Henry and Sarah [above]

Oldest son of THOMAS HENRY   Fredrik born1860 =

William=Rose Bone   Louisa = Alexander Burton Chapman
           Died aged 93

John   Mary   Barbara = John Palmer

David = 1st Moiré   Mary = James Kennedy
         Anderson   Beauchannan

Paul   Jonathan   Stephen   Andrew

Second son of   THOMAS HENRY   William Hawes Bulwer = Rachael Rice 1888

Reginald [maybe others
immigrated to Australia with parents c.1904

Oldest daughter of THOMAS HENRY   Louisa Jane Bulwer = L.Goate
                                          the Proprietors Star Hotel Yarmouth

Christopher   [maybe more]

Second daughter of THOMAS HENRY   Anna   =   Daniel Lund
                                          Born 1868   married 1893.

Donald   Reginald
Born 1894   born 1895

Third son of THOMAS HENRY   Henry/Harry = Ada Wickham
              brought up by his grandfather and Aunt Jane after his Father died
                            moved from Yarmouth to Bournmouth

Ada	Louisa	Harry	Edward	May	Annie Elsie	Cecil Earl born 1909 =1935
	born1900	born 1902		born1904	born 1905	Dulcie May Wellington

Michael   Joyce   Graham moved to Suffolk   John
= Elizabeth Reuardy
Born 1965   Karen born 1966   Mark born 1969

Our Grandfather The Youngest Son of Thomas Henry

Chart. 88   WALTER ERNEST BULWER = AGNES SOPHIA WILLIMENT
                   born 1870   died1942 | born 1870 died1942
                             married | 10.6.1897

* ANNIE MAUD = ERNEST BAXTER

Our Present Family   Continued on page 531 chart 103
NOTE; OUR FAMILY MEMBERS ARE IN CAPITAL LETTERS.
*We have now arrived at the point in time when all the families mentioned in previous chapters
were to be finally joined by the marriage of our parents.

OUR GREAT GRANDPARENTS
Profile of Thomas Henry and Sarah [nee Smith] Bulwer's Family and their descendants

As we are now approaching more modern times, due to lack of time and space it is only fair to respect the privacy of those still living so we have not included all the details we have found during our research.

Thomas Henry [our great grandfather, the first son of **Thomas** and **Maria** nee **Dickerson Bulwer**] was born in Chichester 1838.

We were unable to identify the exact area or why they happened to be here at this time. **Thomas Henry's** first courtship ended when **Sarah Smith** came on the scene, she lived with her parents by the quayside at Great Yarmouth Norfolk.

Her father was a mariner and her mothers' name was **Jemima**. Thomas married **Sarah** in 1861 in St Nicolas Church Yarmouth and we particularly noticed the unusual name of the witness on the wedding certificate, which was William Jealous Fulcher. **Thomas** and **Sarah** lived at 39 South Market Street where **Thomas,** a master butcher owned and ran his own butchers shop.

This shop was still in business at that site until a few years ago. [**Norma** remembers visiting relatives there with her grandfather as a child]. This establishment together with an old public house, the Prince of Wales' Feathers, and one or two dilapidated houses that linked it with the past, survived right up to the time of writing this book.

Soon after their marriage, **Thomas Henry** was made bankrupt due to the compulsive gambling habit he had developed. **Sarah** was later to regret coming between him and his previous girl friend, as she and the family were constantly living on the breadline because of his wagering. This situation often reduced her to tears of despair. Because of these constant cash-flow problems they were forced to sell the butcher's shop [though later other relatives regained the business].

Mrs. McKenna [our researcher] tracked **William John** and his family to number 7, Geneva Terrace, Crown Road, Great Yarmouth; but we did not find our Grandfather and his family in this street and we had great difficulty in locating their address. For a while all traces of the family we were looking for was lost, and what added to our confusion were the changes that had been made over the years, as we discovered

We visited London Record Office to research this and found an old map which showed there had been a Geneve Terrace off Caister Road where **Thomas Henry** and family had lived; Great Yarmouth Library also verified all this information.

The family had been forced to move here following the bankruptcy, this is where our Grandfather was born in a house opposite the old Hospital [which is now closed] and just behind his father's butcher's shop, which is still there at 357, Caister Road. The shop now sells electrical goods and the area around Geneve Terrace has been re-developed. The family soon moved from here and we lost track of them again, eventually finding that they had moved to Banham, Norfolk, and later to Beccles in Suffolk where we discovered other Bulwer relations lived.

Thomas and Sarah had six children but very little information could be found on the early lives of these youngsters. Before **Thomas** died the family was in an impoverished state. He worked at the Old Cromwell Hotel as a barman, which was then owned by his daughter and her husband **Mr. Goat**. At sometime, probably just before his death in 1882 he must have changed his occupation to a Commercial Traveller, as this was marked as his profession on the death certificate.

The Cromwell and Temperance Hotel   Plate 92

showing what used to be the Star Hotel next door

*Young children today are treated with care according their age, but for the working class children then childhood as we know it never really existed and the only games they played was the one of survival. They worked from the age of four embroidering shawls etc. The very first train steamed into Yarmouth during this early period of our grandfathers life, which must have been a great wonder and speculation to him, also other children and adults [and what a blessing to the commercial world too].

The family of Thomas Henry and Sarah Smith.
Fredrik born 1860. Again we became a bit confused as our mother told us it was Fredrik, son of **Thomas** who went to Australia during the Gold rush. But this was not correct, as he never left England. Our second cousin Barbara Palmer living in Bishopbrigg near Glasgow told us **Fredrik** was her grandfather and had always lived at 36, Harford Street Norwich. He had two children, William [b 1892] and Louisa [our grandfather' nephew and niece]. William worked as an electrician for Norwich Corporation [later the Eastern Electricity Board] in the same department as David and Norma's husband Edward.

*Life for the working class was exceptionally hard during Victoria's reign and no mercy was given in order to make money. Even pregnant women were chained to the coal trucks, which they dragged along rails in the pit. Exploitation of Children Act was enforced in 1833

William was a very private person, [gruff], with very little to say. He was married to **Rose Bone** who died at the age of 93. They had 2 Children **John**, and **Mary** [deceased].

Louisa [William's sister] married Alexander Burton Chapman, and set up home in Carshalton Road off City Road, Norwich. Although we knew Louisa and Alexander were both deceased, we had no idea where **Barbara** their daughter was located. In order to find her we went to The Eastern Evening News, Norfolk [a Local Newspaper], and inserted an appeal for information including a photograph we had of her.

To our great surprise we received a phone call from her son **John** in Scotland, saying that an old neighbour of hers had sent a cutting from the Eastern Evening News. We started to correspond with her and would like to thank **Barbara** for supplying all the information about her father, mother, grandparents and their families.

Barbara is the only child of Alexander and **Louisa**, Chapman. The family was interested in amateur dramatics and when Barbara was a young girl she belonged to a group called the Avenue Players, trained by a Mrs. Elsie Burrows [Drama]. Mr. J. W. Gaze [Builder of Hall Road] who arranged the music and Mrs. Gaze who wrote the plays. **Barbara** was courted by John Palmer who was a pilot in the R.A.F. during the war. He was sent to America in 1943 to learn the art of gliding and it was there that he obtained his wings. He flew many daring raids over enemy territory training airmen on how to pilot gliders

Barbara Palmer   Plate 93

for D. Day, ready for the time when planes would tow the gliders full of the men of the invasion force into France [which you will read about later].

He married **Barbara** in April 1945 after being demobbed from the R.A.F. and started working for Norwich Union Insurance, in Surrey Street Norwich, he was promoted in 1946/7 and sent to Kings Lynn. Later he was transferred to the Glasgow office. **Barbar*a and John raised two children **David** and **Mary**. **David** married Moira Anderson and has four sons **Paul, Jonathan, Stephen** and **Andrew** and **Barbara** is their proud grandma. **David** has since remarried, and is a director of his own Fuel Efficiency Advisory business in the Glasgow area. Barbara's daughter **Mary Elizabeth Palmer** married James Kennedy Beauchannan and lives in the North of Scotland with her family.

*Norma and her husband Eddie David and Heather visited Barbara in Glasgow while on holiday, for a family reunion.

William Hawes Bulwer 2nd Son of **Thomas Henry,** was at 17 years old a footman to John Harcon J.P. Lieutenant Colonel of Walington Hall, Great Cressingham. When the Colonel died the Hall was taken over by another family and we suppose William moved away. He married Rachael Rice in 1888 had one child named Reginald; there may be others.

We found him recorded as living at several different addresses in Norwich. Eventually he was made secretary to the Norfolk Club, Upper King Street frequented by the Bulwer Clan. He immigrated to Australia in 1904 but we could not find any further information except that he visited Norfolk in 1934 with his son on the death of Edward Bulwer [main family at Heydon].

Annie Bulwer   William Hawes Bulwer   Lady Holmes Walter [our grandfather]

Louisa Bulwer's wedding to Stephen Goate
Picture taken in The Star Courtyard   Plate.94

Louisa married Stephen Goate who owned The Cromwell and Temperance Hotel, which is now the Star Hotel, Great Yarmouth. Louisa was our Grandfather's sister and we have inserted her wedding photograph as many of those in it are known to us; it was taken in the Hotel courtyard that has now been integrated into the Star Hotel as part of the dining area.

Our grandfather is the handsome young man leaning sideways on to the wall. His brother William is the one standing with his back against the wall of the hotel looking across at the beautiful young girl, who we think, is Lady Holmes. What ever was involved in that look we can only guess at? Perhaps the young lady had something to do with it we wonder? Directly in front of William is Annie the youngest sister, she is standing behind and between our grandmother Sophia, and her sister Louie. The bride is our grandfather's sister, directly behind her is our great grandmother and behind her to the right is our grandmother.

Our great grandmother **Sarah** Bulwer [in centre of picture] is standing in front of **Louie**; her husband our great grandfather as we said previously, had already died. More of the Bulwer's are in the picture but we have no way of confirming their identities. When visiting Wellesley Park Hotel Yarmouth, **David** noticed a large framed plaque on the wall inside the entrance setting out the rules and regulations of the Temperance Society signed by **William Goate** who was a founder member of this group in Yarmouth. **Louisa,** grandfather's sister comes into our story again briefly following the account of when **Norma** went to Heydon Hall.

Anna was born the 19th July 1868, she was the second daughter of **Thomas** [a butcher] and **Sarah Bulwer** of 25 Nelson Road Yarmouth. She married Daniel Lund a bookseller's assistant in 1883. Witnesses were **Fredrik T. Bulwer** and Elizabeth Goate, **Anna's** sister in law. **Anna's** father **Thomas** died in 1882, and apparently Daniel's father who was a clerk in holy orders had also died, Elizabeth Goate took his place. **Anna** and Daniel Lund had two sons **Donald** and **Reginald**.

Their first born, son **Donald** was born 19th July

Anna Bulwer Plate. 95 1894 when they were living at Deneside Yarmouth and the second son was born one year later. They must have moved as Donald's Grammar school report shows **Donald** as living at 62 North Quay. Both sons did very well in their education; **Donald Lund** as Cambridge Junior gained 2nd class honours with a distinction in Chemistry and later found employment in banking. **Reginald** also became a Cambridge Junior in 1911 and gained local 3rd full honours 1912, and exempt from London Matriculation. He was made Bursar in August 1912. One of these boys in later life worked as executive in the Norwich Union Fire and Accident department on Palace Plain, Norwich.

Anna was a charming woman loved by all, when she died at 50 years of age in 1918 with breast cancer she was sadly missed. We have included a photograph of her; we think she was rather beautiful.

Harry b.1867 5th child of Thomas Henry and Sarah Bulwer.
After his father died, **Henry** [called Harry], at the age of thirteen moved in with his grandfather and Aunt **Jane** Adams [nee **Bulwer**] widow of William Adams who had been foreman of Lacon's Brewery. Unfortunately within one year his grandfather also died.

Harry's Aunt Jane continued to look after him, and moved to Eastbourne taking the young Harry with her. Sarah his mother and our great grandmother moved to Norwich. On leaving school Harry became a cabman and lived in Silverdale Mews, Eastbourne, marrying Anna Wickham a widow in 1898. They raised five children [1885 Cert].

Thomas Henry b.11 March [quarter 19.GRO.] at the next census after this date no more Bulwer's were registered at 134 Caister Road [butchers shop or in Geneve Terrace.
Harry Edward Bulwer b.1902. Dec [Quarter, 2b.66]. married **Ada Louisa Wickham/Bulwer** at Christchurch Silverdale Mews [Eastbourne] born1900 September [quarter 2n 75.] [Cabman].
Cecil Earl born1909 Dec [quarter. 2b.65] married **Dulcie May Wellington,** on the 6th April 1935. **Cecil** had five children **Elsie May Michael Joyce Graham** and **John.**
Elsie May born 1904 Joyce born 1905 no more information.
John and Michael, no more information.
Graham married **Elizabeth Ruardy** in 1965 and raised two children. **Karen** b. 1966 and **Mark** b.1969. We have not managed to identify all of this line, but this is all we know of their descendants living and dead at this present time. **Mark** who is in the Navy did contact us briefly in 1997 when he discovered we were both researching the same families. But we have not heard from him since, which is a great pity, as we would have taken great delight in sharing this information with him.

Our Grandfather Walter Bulwer
b. 1871 d. 1941

Walter was the youngest son of **Thomas Henry** and **Sarah Smith;** this young family must have had hard lives as their father was addicted to gambling, which probably contributed to his death, but **Sarah** his wife stayed with him and struggled to raise her family. **Walter,** our future grandfather was just ten years old when his father **Thomas** died after having an epileptic stroke. Thomas was an addictive gambler and when he died only possessed twenty pounds, which was found in his pocket. It must have been a difficult existence for his family and even worse after he died. We could not find any more information on their young lives.

At the age of twenty-two Walter began working for the Post Office, he was single at the time. We took the opportunity when in London to visit the Royal Mail Post office [Records Office], to gather information of our grandfather's occupation, and found documents explaining much about his working life. He started work as a postman / temporary sorting clerk and telegraphist on the 2nd day of October 1893 at a wage of seventeen shillings per week rising to twenty-eight shillings per week.

On the 19th April 1928 he was promoted to an overseer; his wages rose on a graduated scheme to thirty-nine shillings per week and he was issued a uniform to the value of two pounds seven shillings and six pence. His record shows that in the last six years of service he had only 114 days off sick and he discharged his duties with diligence and fidelity, to the satisfaction of his superior officers. **Walter** was awarded the Imperial Service Medal after working for the Post Office for 37 years and 6 months retiring at sixty-one years of age with a pension of thirty-two shillings per week. He was apparently very happy in his work and popular with the people on his post round.

WALTER ERNEST AND AGNES SOPHIA BULWER
Our Grandparents
Sophia born 1870 died 1941   Walter born 1871 died 1941

Walter and Sophia [We will call her Sophia, as she hated being called Agnes and we never dared mention her age] were married at Holy Trinity Church Heigham Street, Norwich on July 10th 1897 when he was 26 and Sophia was 27. His family were not recorded as witnesses, we wonder why?

Right
Walter and Sophia
Bulwer
Our Grandparents
Plate.96
Left
Our Mother
Annie Maud
Bulwer
As a child

Plate 97

Sophia was a good woman and a devout Salvationist which gave her a happy outlook and a social life. Her lifelong friend Sarah Cook, also a Salvationist who had her home in Potters Bar, London, used to visit Sophia for long periods, and was easy prey to our boyhood pranks. By nature Sophia was judgmental, quick tempered and over sensitive, an attitude that was sometimes exploited by her grandchildren.

If the children wanted to subvert her authority in a subtle way they sang a song about a "Little old lady dressed in blue, sweet and shy," which she took as a description of herself. They knew that she hated them singing it and became very annoyed. Our mother had to put a stop to it, but Sophia was really loved by them all and had many fine qualities.

OUR MOTHER ANNIE MAUD BULWER
Born 10th February 1900 ----- Died 1st July 1975

Our mother **Annie Maud Bulwer** was born on the 10th February 1900 at home in 322,Unthank Road Norwich. Later her parents Walter and Sophia moved to Southwell Road, Norwich and when older rented a flat in Helena Road. Their family social life was very much revolved round the activities of the Salvation Army, local concert parties and amateur playhouse groups that provided them with friends who often visited. Both **Annie** and her future husband **Ernest** Baxter attended Crooks Place School where we believe they first met and were childhood sweethearts.

Our mother was an only child, desperately lonely, longing for brothers and sisters. She was brought up in a very strict household where manners and her piano tuition were the priority. This was in order to satisfy the ambitions of her proud father who wanted his talented daughter to be an accomplished concert pianist. She certainly deserved the role, but this was not to be. As happens in most cases of strict upbringing she rebelled against the rigid discipline of her parents and much to her father's dismay decided to throw fame and ambition to the wind. She did not follow the path of being a concert pianist as her father hoped and planned for her but instead decided to marry the man she loved.

Annie married her childhood sweetheart Ernest against her parents wishes to gain what she had always wanted, a large family to made up for the loneliness of her childhood. Her father in turn made his own protest for her defying him and refused to sign the marriage certificate, a decision he never openly regretted but made them both sorry. Annie and Ernest were as most parents and grandparents who had been brought up in Victorian ways, were very strict with children.

 Our Mother was a kind loving person with great empathy for others and she sacrificed a lot for the benefit of her family in those exceptionally hard times. She certainly gave enjoyment beyond words both to family and neighbours and friends with her highly skilled art as a pianist. In those days the piano was an important part of social life and on many occasions the loud singing of our family brought neighbours to our house. Even those standing outside our open windows often joined in the chorus of war time songs that could be heard all over the neighborhood.

Sorrow and deprivation for our family through a disappointing deathbed action from our grandmother, health problems, one crisis followed another, as you will read, and was certainly not deserved. Father was very sincere and did his very best to provide for his family, but his life was a struggle as it was for most other working dads, to keep a job and survive on the very low wages of that time.

BACK TO FAMILY STRUCTURES
Kidd, Thirkettle, Rix, Wilkinson Families
And Their Connection to the Webster's, Williments and Bulwer's

Now we would like to concentrate on the ancestors of our grandmother's nee Williment lineage, and have managed to get as far back as 1570. As there are not many historic or general details of these families we believe they must have come with the Flemish weavers from Europe with Wiggetts Willimott's etc. and were possibly involved with the reformation that started on the continent.

We have previously included some of these events such as the reformation to give the general causes and histories of these times that provide a reason to why people moved away from persecution. We thank our cousin Peter Green, an archivist who formulated a mass of information from a database and much of the lineage that we have used in this part of the book. We have many more lineages available but we have endeavored to simplify these charts rather than confuse you with too many lines of these families.

We will now concentrate on these four major lines that lead to the present time and living family.

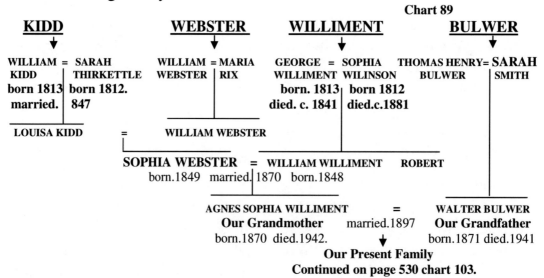

Chart 89

Kidd/Thirkettle Families. William Kidd was a bricklayer who married **Sarah Thirkettle** in 1821 they produced a daughter **Louisa Kidd.**
Webster/Rix Families; William Webster married **Maria Rix** and produced a son **William Webster** who later married **Louisa Kidd.**
Webster/Kidd Families; William Webster and **Louisa Kidd** produced a daughter **Sophia Elizabeth Webster.**
Williment/Wilkinson Family; George Williment married **Sophia Wilkinson** 1847 produced a son **William** who married **Sophia Elizabeth Webster,** our great grandmother.

WILLIMENT/ FAMILIES

We continue to outline the main families connected to our own that we can relate to and who are important to us. We have gathered all we could find on the immediate family, others are included in the family trees.

George and Sophia Williment our great great grandparents. **George was** born in 1813 and lived in Coburgh Street Norwich. He was a wood paviour and bricklayer by trade who probably helped to lay the wooden blocks in Ber Street Norwich. In 1847 he married **Sophia Wilkinson** [b.1812 Gorleston, near Yarmouth] who was a mangle worker, which we assume to be either a vegetable worker or clothes wringer. They raised three children. She died in d1881 and George 1841.

Francis George the first-born c.1847 married **Ellen Fox** in 1868 and produced three children.

William second son [born 1.8.1848] French polisher by trade married **Sophia Elizabeth Webster** [born 29.11.1849 married at Great Yarmouth 25.7.1870] was a tailoress. They produced **Agnes Sophia Willment** [conceived before marriage] and four others [and William]

Sophia married our grandfather **Walter Bulwer**

Robert born 1850 [our grandmothers uncle] married **Maria Quantrill** in the grandeur of St Peter Mancroft Church, Norwich on the 3rd March 1873. Later Maria lived with one of her daughter's in the row of old cottages near to the working windmill [at that time] on Helena Road Norwich, which was opposite our grandparents flat. The windmills sails were later discarded and the machinery was driven by a powerful engine to grind the corn into flour.

It was a fascinating experience for us children to stare from our grandparents' window at the whiteness of the whole area that surrounded the mill and the white shadows that moved about inside it. **David,** when aged around six sneaked out from his grandparents flat to explore the Mill and was brought back looking like a white ghost to his distraught grandparents for a stern talking to. The history to this Windmill as our grandparents told us, during the First World War a German spy was caught beaming out messages from the glass canopy that covered the top of the tower.

It was not until researching this part of our story, we remembered that both mother and grandmother often used to stop to chat with an old lady and her daughter who lived in the cottages mentioned above, not realizing they were relatives. We vividly remember them sitting by their front door and their long garden that was always a riot of colour. They both wore long black voluminous dresses that were covered with black lace and little black bonnets similar to the Dutch style of dress, which never seemed to come off no matter what the weather.

In fact the bonnets were designed to accommodate the tightly woven hair buns of the early 1900's. The older lady used to sit quietly rocking herself in a wooden rocking chair smoking a clay pipe, which fascinated us, as women of that time would not dare to smoke, and a pipe was definitely masculine. We also remember that the mother had a very large hairy mole on her nose that looked enormous to us children. We refused to kiss her, claiming that her mole was only safe to be viewed at a distance, which was unkind. However the mole on the end of her very large nose caused so much mirth among us children, which we dare not reveal to our mother and tried to look anywhere other than her face. We now realise that this woman was Maria Quantrill the wife of **Robert Williment** and the old cottages where these two ladies lived were destroyed in raids during the Second World War.

Writing this book has brought back memories and relationships that we had forgotten, some names meant nothing to us, but linking these families together has given us a much wider vision. Now they are not just individuals in association but are real family characters [see chart below] that give us a clear picture on how our family came about. It has also brought together families that have lost touch over the years. The old lady and her daughter have been dead many years now but their memory never fades.

WILLIMENT PEDIGREE [No 1].

Chart. 90

GEORGE WILLIMENT b [c1813 Norwich] = m c 1847 **SOPHIA WILKINSON** b [c1812
. Bricklayer ,Wooden paviour d before 1891 | Gorlesdon] Mangle worker died After 1881

Francis = Ellen Fox **WILLIAM = SOPHIA ELIZABETH** **Robert = Maria Quantrill**
b1847 Norwich born.1.8.1848 **WEBSTER** born 1850 b.1850 [both Nch]
married 1868 a printer born 29.11.1849 m 3.3.1873 St Peter Mancroft.
1885 ▼ Norwich Thorpe Nch.
Pedigree No.2 25.7.1870 married. Gt Yarmouth 1929
 | d.1917 See pedigree No 3
 | |

AGNES SOPHIA Emily Elizabeth b.1871 *Eliza Maud Louisa Ann Eva = Wlliam
c18.1.1870 = Henry Jacob Green d.1878 b.1880 = Edwd.[Ted] [Bob] Henry =
d.1941. m 11.6.1917 d1951 spinster d.1947 Hutchins Inman Miriam
WALTER Peter Green **Peggy Doreen Vera William**
See chart adp.= Monica =Tom =Reg = George = Daphne Thelma
for Baxter | Philpot Anderson Legget ?
p. 530 and Caroline Robert | | |
p. 396 Marsdon Mark Pam Ann Glenis Janice Robert

Maria Eliz. Robert Mary Sarah Charles Lily George
Martha 1874 b.c. 1876 Ann Isobella Herbert Mary b. c.1890
b.1873 | b1878 b 1881 b.1885 b.c.1888 ▼
=Rbt.Allen 1900 | |
 | Robert
Elizabeth

THE WEBSTERS AND WILLIMENTS JOIN IN MARRIAGE
WILLIAM WILLIMENT MARRIES SOPHIA ELIZABETH WEBSTER
OUR GREAT GRANDPARENTS

Sophia Webster, our great grandmother went to live with her grandmother in Yarmouth before she was married. **Sophia** her daughter [our grandmother] was born at Thorpe Blofield near Norwich on 29th November 1849. We found out that she was born out of wedlock and think this was the main reason she would not reveal her age.

These women used to speak of someone they called 'Old Sam Webster', who old Sam was, we as children never did get to find out as he was a taboo subject, but and it seems Old Sam was a disgrace to the Williment's, not to be discussed under any circumstances. Nor did we find a Sam in any of the Webster Charts.

Sophia was tailoress when she met **William Williment.** The wedding banns were read at her Parish church in Norwich and married there July 20/25th 1849. Our great-grandfather **Williment** we found had several different jobs and varying occupations during his life. They must have moved frequently to be near each job because in 1851 they were living in Thorpe St. Andrew Norwich, in 1870 Row 134 Great Yarmouth after Sophia and Williment's marriage and then 25 Coburgh Street Norwich in 1881.

In 1870 he was a French Polisher, 1881 a general labourer 1910 a boiler cleaner, and in 1917 they moved to Cantley [Norfolk] where he worked in Sugar Beet factory. During 1917 he moved from there to Silver Road, Norwich, then finally in 1928 to 179 Colman Road, Norwich where later their daughter Bessie lived. The family were all girls apart from one boy William, [by hearsay, he was adopted] but again there was some mystery attached to this one too. These were hard times and money was short; we never did meet our Great Grandma Sophia as she had died before we were born.

PROFILE OF THE WILLIMENTS OF CANTLEY NEAR NORWICH
Family of William and Sophia Williment.

From the stories passed down to us by our mother we felt we knew her quite well as they often spoke about her. **Sophia Williment** was a petite clean hardworking little lady very fiery in character, someone who kept her girls clean, well fed and firmly in hand. Their bare pine board table was so well scrubbed it looked white through so many years of hard cleaning. All the cracks were "fied" out, to remove the last crumb; no trace of food was allowed to desecrate it.

Hands had to be well scrubbed, and nails cleaned before they were allowed at the table. Great-grandmother had trained her daughters well in setting high standards of hygiene and housewifery, and all were successful in the running of their own homes.

Left to right Mother Great Grandmother and Aunt Maud Plate.98

Her four daughters when young were inseparable, but in later years **Sophia** became aloof from her sisters, who did not seem too keen on her either. We must admit though our grandma was a bit of an oddball. She could have begun entertaining ideas of grandeur when she discovered our grandfathers' background. We were not allowed to discuss her attitude to find the reasons, but we found that she was very fickle with her friends and neighbours.

Our Great Grandmother with some of her daughter's

Sophia [front left], Eva [holding Vera the granddaughter Bessie and Laura [top left Maud's companion Plate. 99

Agnes Sophia b. 18th January 1870 our grandmother, who was the eldest daughter, married **Walter Bulwer**. She obviously loved her parents as she was always talking about them.

Emily Elizabeth [far right] b. December 1871 also known as Bessie married **Jacob Green** and adopted one son **Peter Marston Garner Green.**

Eliza-Alice was born in September 1878 not much known about her, as she died very young.

<u>**Maude**</u> **Louisa** who took the photo, [b. Sept. 1890; unmarried] was a companion and friend to Laura [left top row] who was a quiet kindly lady in total contrast to **Maud** who was a bully by nature, aggressive and forceful but could also be generous and kind. They lived at 33 Paragon Hill, Norwich in a small terrace house with dark wood panelled walls. German bombs flattened most of this area during the war years but it has now been redeveloped. **Maud** was the dominant character of the family and also had an eye for business. **Maud** and Laura kept a sweet shop on the corner of what was Rigby Court, St Giles Street, Norwich and often gave us children lovely presents before the war years, but we had to be on our best behavior to obtain sweets.

<u>**Louisa Ann**</u> [not in photo, b. 1885] lived with her family in Norwich then moved to Cantley in 1910. She married **Edward [Ted] Hutchinson in** 1914 and they moved from Norfolk when Ted obtained a job at Wolverton railway depot. From there they went to Stratford, in East London where they made their home near the docks. Ted became a docker and they raised two daughters **Peggy** and **Doreen. Both Ted** and **Louisa** died, **Louisa** with diabetes while on holiday in Norfolk and was cremated in Norwich. We had lost touch with **Peggy** and **Doreen,** their daughters until recently. Again while researching for this book we located Doreen, who lives at Maulden Bedfordshire, which is only ten miles from **David who lives in** Bedford. **Peggy** lived in Cornwall at first but has since moved. Doreen is presently moveing to be with her daughter Pam.

<u>**Eva**</u> [b.1890 married **Bob [Robert] Inman]** is on the photograph holding her daughter **Vera**], full of character, full of fun, the tomboy of the family. We remember that she liked to tell tales about the past and the older she became all these stories somehow got mixed in together; Kaiser William and Hitler were muddled up with antics during the two wars. She was good fun to be with, a real old style Norfolk countrywoman. Bob came from the Lake District area, possibly Sedbergh or Jedburgh and had two children, Vera and William. They used to antagonise each other; Bob always annoyed her by refusing to go to the toilet without his hat on; a habit acquired in the days when they had an outside lavatory.

David Heather and his parents took them **on** holiday to visit Bob's relatives to stay with **Bob's** relation's **Constance** and **Bill** who had a teenage son and daughter. Pity we never kept in touch. **Bobs'** sister was a tiny, dominant woman, who played whist all day and liked to win. Woe betides the other players if she did not. Bob's sister married **Tom** a very placid man who worked very hard; from what we remember he looked after a farm. He was a true giant of a man who she dominated. His hands were so large that he could wrap his fingers around a football, easily picking it up with one hand.

<u>William Williment</u> was born the same year as our mother [1900] and the only boy in our great grandmother's family; we think that maybe he was adopted. The sisters never spoke of his origins, but thought a great deal of him. He fought in the First World War and lost an arm. As a boy **William** was a great practical joker, and sometimes his jokes would go too far with his sisters, but he was greatly loved anyway.

After his return home from war service, the loss of one arm was no deterrent to his practical joking. It was his favourite trick to take a deep breath, which then caused his false hand to take a firmer grip on anything he wished to pick up. Unfortunately it was also used to pinch any young ladies' bottom that happened to be near to hand especially his sisters. The more they squealed the more he laughed and the more firmly it gripped. He then had to make a quick exit when he released the mechanism. When

William as a young man Plate 100 his arm was not required, he took it off and hung it over the mantelpiece.

We know that **William** married a girl called Miriam and they had a daughter called **Thelma** and after his marriage he sadly left the family circle and moved away but was never forgotten as they always spoke of him. He did come to Norwich once for a visit; our mum was so disappointed not to see him, but as he later explained, by the time he had visited all his sisters he was emotionally drained. According to the family in Norwich it seems that his wife considered **William's** relatives beneath

William after his return from the 1st world war. Plate 100[a]

their station in life. Following that visit they never saw or heard from him again. Ah well that's' life for you!

Lincolnshire and parts of Norfolk have very much the same landscape as Holland, flat and wet, in fact from the time of Hereward the Wake, Lincolnshire was called Holland, so it is not surprising that when the Dutch came to help drain the Fens, some stayed and bought farms. The family moved to Cantley where many nationalities had made their homes and were working in the Sugar Beet factory, including the Dutch. Perhaps that is where **Robert** Williment met Maria Quantrill. [See chart].

Our great-grandmother **Sophia** used to take some as lodgers; mother told us it was a fascinating experience watching the various customs and ways of living and eating, and many wore their national costumes during that period of time. Also the Dutch would eat their fish raw taking turns from a dish in the centre of the table, never using a knife or fork. They all regarded our great grandmother with great respect, calling her mother. Although **Sophia** was small and petite, she was strong willed and loyal to her friends, standing for no nonsense from anyone, a great character.

Our questions about Old Sam Webster and answers to the mysterious origins of a son and brother, **William**, and aloofness of our grandmother in later years to her sisters is a part of life that's lost in time to us, as all this particular generation have long since died, so sadly this is another part of our record must rest with them. William affectionately known as Willy, the only boy with five girls in the family, generated much interest and from what we hear of his character, created quite a bit of fun too.

Life in the time of our grandparents
1800 – 1900s

King William 4th reign was short and following his death his neice Victoria became queen. This was the exciting time of the birth of steam engines. In London the most thrilling sight was the steam coach built to carry passengers on the roadways. William Murdock lived in Cornwell where he experimented and dicovered how to make coal gas and used it to light his home. Another venture was to build a coach/locomotive driven by a steam engine at the back and the local villagers all agreed it went like a little demon. Unfortunately the vehicle lived up to its name when on one dark night whilst being prepared for a trial run it built up a head of steam, away went the coach with Murdock racing after it. Then after cries for help and a tremendous crash he traced the sound of moaning to the spot where the local parson lay flat on his back in the road, more frighted than hurt and checking if all body parts were present. After regaining his speech he had a lot to say about a monster spitting out fire and steam that had knocked him down.

In those days most houses had no sewage and were visited by the night cart sometimes called the honeycart or the Humdinger [The hum was the smell and dinger was his bell]. Billy Blazer of Long Stratton Norfolk collected the effluent from the bottom of the garden and if there was no back entrance it would have be brought through the house. Being renowned for his love of a tipple he sometimes it spilt on the floor or over him. One shopkeeper sought to tell Billy about losing customers through his smelly clothes to which Billy replied, "If you had as many customers as me you'd have something to grumble about". One thing for certain was that wherever he went he was sure to leave his hum behind.

Before the advent of modern technology life was very hard for families with little time for relaxation in the struggle to live decently. Even in our childhood there were few if any household aids. Washing clothes for example was done by hand and was hard toil. Many a time there were howls of pain when we caught our fingers in the rollers of the mangle when trying to help mother wring the water from our clothes.

Wash day in the courtyards   Plate.101   **The families of the Courtyards**
Photos from Derek Edwards Copyright Norfolk Museums and Archaeology Service

The pictures above show the living conditions in the slums of Norwich 1800's possibly Rigby Court near where our aunt's Maud and Laura had their sweet shop, which was on the corner of Bethel Street and St. Giles. The shop is still there but there are no courtyards now.

CHRONOLOGY DURING THE LIVES OF OUR GRANDPARENTS

1812   Britain was at war with the United States of America. This really started when Britain tried to stop trade between USA and France. After many years of heated bickering, war was declared on June 18th 1812 resulting in the British being defeated at Lake Champlain. A peace treaty was signed on June 6th 1815.

1815   A new department store called Chamberlains opened in the centre of Norwich. By 1900 it was the most elegant of shops situated on the corner of Dove Street. It was destroyed by fire in the Second World War [then replaced later by a Tesco store].

1833   The Factories Act was introduced to stop exploitation of children who often started work from the age of four years. There was very little schooling especially for the children of the Weavers who were very poor.

1839   Children were still expected to earn their keep in food and buy their clothing from the age of twelve and thirteen.

1840   There were several schools started from 1830/40 most children only attended Sunday school and about 50% were able to read and write or do basic mathematics.

1850	John Jarrold started a printing business in Suffolk. He moved to Norwich and became a major employer useing the old Silk Mill that has now been sold by Jarrold's; it is still an attractive building by the river, providing a home for many birds, which flit in and out of its vine covered walls.
1852	A Parson who was riding through Longham perceived some wires stretching from pole to pole and inquired the reason from an elderly local resident. The man pointed and replied incredulously "There's a young man who lives there, and a young lady who lives there, and they tells me, that they make love by means of them there wires. On further inquiries the Reverend gentleman ascertained that this was true. Snow so deep the father of Horatio Nelson records that where it drifted it had to be tunneled out for carriages and pedestrians to pass underneath its surface. Roads were impassable, there was a rail crash in Attleborough killing four people. 6th January, the same year, papers full of murder, shipwrecks and cholera. Transport was by a dicky [donkey/horse] cart or even dogcarts. Water was still dangerous to drink.
12.9.1852	Ships sail for Eastern Europe in active preparation for Crimean war. September 12$^{th.}$ Plague of cholera was so bad in London that bodies had to be removed by carts. Police were stationed at each end of some streets to stop people entering. In Norwich also, fresh meat was flown from a kite for two hours and when brought down it was black and putrid indicating something was wrong with the air. The heat was oppressive and spreading the disease, which subsided as the weather cooled. Mr. Lee Warner died June 16th.
1853 AD	Battle of Waterloo. Napoleon defeated by Wellington
1855AD	Another bad winter with mass unemployment and food riots. A Dereham man weighing 60 stone was buried in the local church. They had great difficulty in getting him through the church doors. News from our war fronts: - Sebastopol, a victory, but a witness stated that nothing would have saved the British had the Russian's been sober. The Son of General William Earl Bulwer, William Lytton Bulwer was badly injured in the battle for Balaclava. We claimed victory, but our army in the Crimea was destroyed in a day of humiliation! On July 5th there was a gathering of **Bulwer** family for the marriage of Miss Lee Warner to **Captain William Bulwer** July 8th. The father of Lord Nelson said his son would approve the use of steam driven ships, as they would reduce time spent in battle.

At Trafalgar half the ships not in action because of lack of wind. 14th July Marine Parade opened at Yarmouth.

1857 AD   A.J. Caley makes Mineral Waters in a cellar at the back of a shop in London Street, Norwich later moving to larger premises in Chapel field Road producing Mineral Waters, Cocoa and Chocolate. This company which grew into a very large local employer was recently taken over by Nestles and closed down.

1857 AD   Last of wooden ships launched, but soon became obsolete.

1861AD   Insurrection in Poland. Civil war USA. Prince Albert dies.

1862AD   Disaster when sluice gates in Fens of North Norfolk, [Near Kings Lynn] broke letting the sea in covering 50,000 acres. Steamers travelled over roads, farms, and crops.

1863AD   January 15th. The Prince of Wales bought his Norfolk royal home at Sandringham. March 10th Prince of Wales married Princess Alexandra. President Lincoln of USA assassinated. General Lee Wilson surrenders with 25,000 men. A young parent in Dereham named his child Nahershallalashboz. Someone at the christening objected, so he decided that if he could not have the longest name he would have the shortest and named him Uz.

1868AD.   Our Grandfather **Henry Baxter** was born.

1872AD   Smallpox in Norwich 14 cases and two deaths.

1873AD   January, Napoleon dies of a heart complaint.

1874AD   7th August. Highwayman captured in Norwich; sentenced to six months in prison. 11th September train crashed at Thorpe, on the London to Yarmouth line 24 killed, 60 injured.

1878AD   Week of torrential rain day and night flooding river valleys, tearing up trees and destroying bridges at Hoe. On roads that were still in use the water came up to horses knees.

1879 AD   Largest departmental store outside London, Bonds opened in Norwich, it is essentially a family business. During the 1939- 45 war, the old Bond's building was destroyed when a firebomb hit the thatched roof. [It had been turned into a Cinema]. The heat and flames were so horrendous that they set fire to store next door. True to the stubbornness of Norfolk people within three days the shop re-opened and any stock left useable and smelling of smoke was on sale among the rubble. Fashionable clothing could not be wasted, due to the scarcity of materials in those days. Soon a new store rose from the ashes and still trades today, though sadly under a different name

PROFILE OF THE LOVEDAY FAMILY

It was not until we started researching the families referred to in this book that we realized that very little was known of our relatives on grandmother's (**Loveday**) side of the family. It became a fascinating experience to gather all the dormant stories of the past and fit them one by one like the pieces of a jigsaw to create a picture of their lives. There were many stories but all were fragmented. It was by chance that we stumbled across the **Ward /Lacon** branch but very little was actually spoken about them as our mother did of the **Bulwer's** and **Williment's.** The families on our grandmother **Loveday's** side seem to originate from the Blofield / Acle area of Norfolk. We could not, as we said before in the **Mortimer** account, find any record of the birth of **Anne Furrence.**

ANNE FURENCE
THE KEY IS LOST; ONE MYSTERY BRINGS ANOTHER

When our grandmother **Elizabeth Baxter** came to live with us at West Earlham, Norwich, while sitting round the coal fire she mentioned that her relations had a coal delivery service, **Lacon Yovil and Co**. that had connections with **Wards** brewery of Great Yarmouth, which in her time became Lacon's brewery. This company also at one time delivered coal to our house at Mansfield lane Norwich and our mother used to mention about them being related to us, which prompted us to research the **Lacon** families.

As you may recall, earlier chapters it took us on an incredible journey back in time to the Roman Senator **Laco** then coming forward in time to the **Lacon/Ward** dynasty, but we could not find the key evidence needed to unlock the family records we needed to link **Ann Furrence** [our grandmother's grandmother] with the Wards of Yarmouth. This turns about to be understandable considering the story that is about to unfold.

From memories of long ago related by our grandmother, we remember clearly her story of an unfortunate family. This aroused our interest in the tale of a shipwrecked captain and his family and raised our curiosity to research our own father's family line. According to one story about a sea captain called **Money/Marriot or Ward?** who went to sea and as was usual in those days he took his family with him. Where

impression of a shipwreck Plate 102   did this man fit in the family tree? His wife gave birth to a daughter while at sea but sadly died during the birth. The child survived and it was said the father brought her back to be fostered by a relative in Blofield near Norwich.

He returned to sea taking his son with him; both were shipwrecked and drowned leaving the baby Anne orphaned, all their family records which had been on the ship were lost with them. From birth, marriage and death certificates we pieced together a family tree but could not obtain any certificates of an **Ann.** There seemed to be no record of her baptism in Blofield or any other official records that we searched, though we did trace girl named Ann who appeared to be the daughter of **Thomas Furrence** [a Farmer of Upton. c.1804) but again no official records of her birth. Our researcher found there was an article relating to this family, using official records in a local magazine in 1975. Regrettably these have not been traced since and are listed as missing from Kirby house.

According to our grandmother, **Ann Furrence** was our Great Great Grandmother; it seems that when Ann reached adult years she went to reclaim her inheritance but the records were lost and from what was said, the only available proof she had was in the church baptism records. Unfortunately the relevant pages had disappeared, and as there was no birth recorded her inheritance money still lies in chancery. Our Grandmother **Baxter** was very positive about this matter but there was neither proof as to **Ann's** ancestry or any clear account as to what really happened. We still remain fascinated by this story and our research has been limited because of time and the complexity of these events.

One Explanation of Grandmothers Story
We did discover a **Samuel Ward** of Stokesby near Gt. Yarmouth who married Judith Furrance daughter of **William Furrence** and according to the chart she was a cousin to **Ann Furrence** our great, great, grandmother. **Ann** was by repute the daughter of **Thomas Furrence** and **Ann [nee Carter]** but no official record of her birth can be found. **Ann Furrence** married **John Money** a basket maker of Acle who later had to obtain poor relief. They had several children, the oldest was **Charlotte** our great grandmother. We know that the Furrance family records were available in Kirby House in 1976 as they were referred to in a magazine article that described the family but unfortunately these records are missing from the Norfolk archives and no others can be found so we are still not able to prove a family connection as yet.

We have made a chart of the Loveday family, which includes our grandmother Loveday/Baxter, these were real Norfolk characters, down to earth and very amusing personalities as you will see when you read the story of our grandmother and her husband Henry Baxter. Grandmothers sisters too, were very outspoken, and were not very patient even with their own families. They also had an inbuilt suspicion of strangers, a trait that you still can find in this area.

CHART FOR FURENCE AND LOVEDAY FAMILIES.
Our Grandmother Baxter's Lineage

Thomas Furrence = ?   Chart 91
Farmer of Upton
Will 1760 d1789

THOMAS FURENCE=ANN CARTER Mary William Harrison= Lydia   Judith = Samuel Ward
b 1804   1793   d 1844 aged 82   d 1836   1753   m. 30/5/1768 in Stokesby
Aged 70

*ANN   = JOHN MONEY   William   Samuel Eliz. *Mary   John   James   William
FURRENCE Basket maker   b 1825   bts.1771 1713   1776 Twins   1780
of Tharston   =Sarah Jermy = Eliz. shared cottage
At Stokesby Alexander with Daniel
William CHARLOTT John   Mary   James   William 24/4/1797 20/3/1787 Binns £3-10s
= Rob. Loveday 1829   1833   1885

Charlotte Maria = Edward ** Leonard * Mary-Ann John *Jean *ELIZABETH LOVEDAY
= Richard   Dawson [Farmer] Sea Captain   = HENRY BAXTER
= Sarah   Our
grandparents

Ivy   Earnest Lesley * May   Sidney Thomas George
= ? Mealham America Livpl. Amca.   [Farmers]   America
[Blofield]

Kathy =|George Ellis   ERNEST ≠ ANNIE   Molly /Nelly = Ernest
BAXTER BULWER   [nee Baxter] Barber

Catherine Christopher
↓   ↓   DEREK Norma Alan   Raymond David Brian Ann John
.   died. 1/12/30   died.25/12/07   =
Issue↓   ?Woodrow
*Mary Ward = John Miller 22/2/1791[Stokesby].   See chart for Baxters [chart 103] Issue

Due to the fact we know little about the above families we can only assume the true relationship of Ann Furrence to the Ward family is as on the chart above which has been derived from information supplied by our researcher. Whether or not Ann was adopted as our grandparents told us is not proved but one clue we found was that her Aunt Judith married a Samuel Ward.

Catain Marriot/Ward?   =   Wife
Drowned at sea   died in Childbirth at sea
with son

ANN orphaned and placed with relatives   Son drowned at sea
as on above chart
No official documents confirming birth found

* Family records mislaid for Furrence family but 1841 census list Samuel Ward as agricultural labourer. William a carpenter and Mary Ward his wife both 60. The 1851 census only list William Ward at the time of the sale of the estate 1802 John Ward lived in a cottage on The Green jointly rented with Eliz. Crane £4-2s
** Our great Uncle Leonard was a sea captain who fought in the battle of Jutland in the old sailing ships. During the fight a mast was shot down and struck him [See story].
* +*-+-* +*Three sisters and their niece had a serious disagreement, and even when by chance in their old age they had the opportunity to put aside their past differences. Whatever the cause, Elizabeth stood firm and would not meet them.

Robert Loveday married **Charlotte Money** and they were our great grandparents. They produced eight children. **Maria** married **Edward Dawson** one of the twins who with his brother Sidney ran the Dawson's Farms at Blofield. **Edward** and **Maria** had seven children, some of whom we never met. Our grandparents used to walk to their house every Sunday, stay for a meal and were returned home in the pony and trap complete with farm produce, including fresh milk in a jug from the cow.

Using your imagination you can assume their having had great difficulty considering the bad roads with the ruts and lumps they would encounter to get home without spilling it but it seems they never lost a drop. **Maria and Edward** had a child **Ivy** who married a **Mr. Mealham** and they had one child Kathy.

Kathy and **Norma** used to go about together until **Kathy** married **George Ellis** and had two children, **Catherine**

Kathleen Mealham   Plate.103   **and Christophe**r. Her husband retired **George** from British Rail and they still continued to live in their lovely cottage at Blofield. Sadly we heard that he has since died.

Granny's brother Leslie Loveday went to Liverpool and nothing more was established about his life. **Ernest** and **Thomas** went to America and **George** also left for America after the First World War and became a train driver on the locomotive "Syracuse" in New York. May also went to America and stayed for many years. In the seventies she decided to return to England once more to settle here, but as we all know things never stay the same, if you do return conditions are always different as life has moved on.

Following a disagreement with her sister *Elizabeth [our Grandmother] she returned to America once more, leaving several members of the family not on speaking terms. There were two other sisters that we remember **Jean** and **Polly.** As they were involved in the families' dispute with Granny there had been little communication. **David** met these sisters while working as an electrician in Blofield quite by accident, noticed the family resemblance, checked the name on the work sheet and introduced himself, having heard about the dispute he tried to rectify the gulf between all the sisters.

- **3 three sisters involved family dispute**

They were agreeable and wanted to reunite the family once more. **David** broached the subject with his grandmother, but to no avail, she remained unforgiving. They were never reconciled, and so the situation remained until they all died.

The next brother of that family was **Leonard; Oh Leonard!** Our Great **Uncle Leonard** and his wife **Sarah** were real characters. He, as a young man joined the Royal Navy and rose to the rank of Captain. **Leonard** was an "old sea dog" and had "Sailed the Seven Seas Me Heartys" on one of the old warships; he had a great sense of humour. He was involved in the only major sea battle of the "First World War" that took place on May 31st 1916 at Jutland near the Danish coast. British Navy warships had confined the German Navy in the port with a blockade and the Germans pulled out all stops to make a dash for it.

The sea battle raged from the afternoon of the 31st until darkness when the Germans, although having the better armour, shells, and communications, were hopelessly out-numbered so withdrew leaving the British in control of the seas. It was during this battle that a mast was shot away on Leonard's ship, which fell catching him a glancing blow to the side of the head that rendered him stone deaf for the rest of his life. It also sent his voice several octaves up the scale causing much secret mirth to us as children. We dared not reveal our amusement too much, as it would have caused our mother to award very swift retribution.

This disability did not deter him although **Captain Leonard Loveday** was forced to retire; nevertheless his sense of humour came to his aid, and he used his situation to make others laugh. One instance came about through the family buying one of "them thar' new fangled gramyphones m'dearies''.

They all wanted **Leonard** to hear this new fangled contraption, as he called it. This was an HMV (His Masters Voice) gramophone; with a picture of a little dog looking with his ears pricked up, and turned towards the great horn on the gramophone. **Leonard,** with his head submerged in the trumpet of the machine listened like the picture of the dog.

He emerged with his face lit up and his eyes widened. Everyone waited with baited breath. He could hear it!! With a huge smile on his face, and in his high pitched voice he exclaimed. "I cun ear um...I cun ear um. The'er a fartin''. For several hilarious moments of time, the room just rocked with laughter. After he died his wife Sarah suffered with high blood pressure and complained frequently that all she could see was "baskets of flowers, baskets of flowers". The condition caused her to trip and fall breaking her leg, she refused all treatment and died.

CHAPTER 1X
THE BAXTER FAMILIES

The earliest ancestor of the Baxter family found so far are our great-great-great-grandfathers, **Samuel Baxter** and **John Cooper** both butchers; their wives names we have not been able to find yet. Samuel's son **John Baxter** married **Caroline** daughter of **John Cooper** 4th October 1840. He followed his father's trade and lived in Chapel Street, Crook's Place, Norwich, raising a child who they named **Abigail Sarah** born 6th November 1843. The childhood that we have known did not exist for the working families in the 1800's their children's wages, though poor relieved parents of some of the cost of food and lodging. Most youngsters were certainly expected to earn their keep by the age of 12-14 years.

Abigail Sarah Baxter [our great grandmother] became a domestic servant to a wealthy family who owned horse-racing stables in Ireland. From the facts that we have managed to gather, it seems at the age of 26 years she was made pregnant, probably by a member of this family and paid off as the maid. For any girl this was a disaster as generally it was regarded as a shameful sin. **Abigail** was disowned by her family and had no choice but to be admitted into the Norwich Workhouse at West Wilmer where our grandfather was born on 21st November 1868. She named him **Henry** with no fathers' name shown on the certificate. As there was no provision for babies in a workhouse Abigail had to make the terrible decision to abandon her child. to be done for ancestors

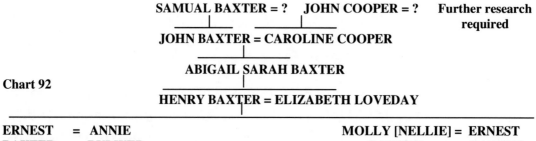

SAMUAL BAXTER = ?   JOHN COOPER = ?   **Further research required**

JOHN BAXTER = CAROLINE COOPER

ABIGAIL SARAH BAXTER

Chart 92

HENRY BAXTER = ELIZABETH LOVEDAY

| ERNEST BAXTER [our father] | = ANNIE BULWER [our mother] | MOLLY [NELLIE] BAXTER | = ERNEST BARBER |

She made **Henry** a foundling, leaving him on a doorstep to be found hopefully by some caring family. **Henry** was found with a very large sum of money in those times, (said to be £100 pounds) on the doorstep of a Mr. and Mrs. Clarke of Ber Street and was given to Mr and Mrs. Strivens, also of Ber Street, Norwich, to bring up. The hundred pounds was from Henry's father for his sons education, we have learned fairly recently that the Strivens family is related to our sister **Ann** through her husband **Tony.** Abigail obtained work and lived in as a domestic servant at 19 Earlham Road, Norwich. It was a very attractive detached house fronting on to the street with a steep embankment behind it.

This area was destroyed with bombs during the 1939/45 war and has since been rebuilt. Due to the large volume of traffic, roads have collapsed into tunnels that were dug centuries ago for mining purposes. It became so bad that even a bus dropped into a large hole that appeared on Earlham Road.

As far as we know Henry never had any emotional bond with his mother, only a duty type of relationship. Abigail spent all of her life as a domestic servant until she became ill and returned to the workhouse, where she died as she lived, unwanted, and unloved on the 8th March 1914 aged 71 years. Her next of kin, Henry her son was not present at her death, we wondered why? We suppose that as they lived harsh times, peoples' attitudes toward one another were often hardhearted and they had to be to survive. There is not much that we know or can record of Henry's young life. He met his mother from time to time but life was difficult for them both, neither had much money, or time together for love to grow.

CHRONOLOGY OF EVENTS FROM 1880
Down to the time of our Parents

1880AD   17th to 23rd January, intense cold 26 degrees of frost; A train was embedded in snowdrifts between Hardingham and Kimberly; traffic movement between Norwich and London suspended. Snow 12 feet deep all the way from Millfield to Quebec House Dereham and 50 lives lost in snowdrift in Yarmouth. March 14th Revolution in Russia the Czar and his family assassinated. March 14th Boar war ends.

1882AD   An elephant broke lose in Dereham, went to nearest house, smashed the larder window and ate the entire contents.

1887AD   October Cyclone in the Bay of Biscay, Cleopatra's Needle in transit to London by barge breaks free from towing ship and had moved ninety miles from its station.

1894 AD   **9th November our father was born**

1900 AD   **10th February our mother was born.** Labour party formed by trade unions and the Bulwer's obviously had an interest in politics, as you will note from Lorina's tapestry.

1914 AD   August; Germany declares war; our father joins the army.

1918 AD.   Women over 30 years granted the right to vote [see item on Constance Lytton Bulwer [suffragette jailed for the cause].

1922 AD.   October; B.B.C. is formed causing revolution in Radio

1923 AD   Carrow Bridge, Norwich opened by Edward Prince of Wales built in the shadow of the *boom towers of the 12th Century Along the banks of the river to Foundry Bridge, beautiful gardens once reached down to the rivers edge.

*The boom Towers were used in the same way as road toll barriers but these barriers dropped across the river to stop ships, enabling tolls to be collected

OUR GRANDPARENTS
HENRY AND ELIZABETH BAXTER
Married 1892

Life for **Henry** changed when he married **Elizabeth Loveday** on the 26th December 1892 at St. Michael at Plea, Norwich. Both were in their late twenties. They saved hard to buy a house in *Newmarket Street Norwich. Being a craftsman he took pride in his home, making many improvements and raising two children, **Ernest Henry Loveday,** (our father) born on the 9th November 1894 and **Mollie** who insisted we call her **Auntie Nellie.**

Around the same time our mothers' family, the **Bulwer's** moved into nearby Hill Street when the offspring of the **Bulwer** and **Baxter** families [our future parents] were of school age. It was at this point in time when they were living near each other, they met at their school, Crooks Place and became childhood sweethearts. After the Great War they married to create later the **Bulwer/Baxter** families and once again unknowingly linking up the lineage to Rollo the Norman Viking. [See chart next page]

After the children married our grandparents moved to Lothian Street and rented out the other property. Aunt **Nellie/Mollie** married Ernest Barber who at one time assisted our father in business and later became a successful director of in a large Norwich shoe factory. He was pompous, extremely class conscious, and considered himself superior. Once attaining his position within this company he did not want to associate with what he considered to be the lower levels of the family, which meant us, as you will read later. Their one son John, became a well-known Norfolk farmer who owned Croggham farm near Wymondham Norfolk introduced the first French Carollas [a cattle breed] into this country. John had four sons. We never had any contact with this family, although they were close relations [cousins]. Later in life John went to live in France and one of his sons, as far as we know still has a farm here in England.

Henry had to mind his 'P's and 'Q's as Grandmother Baxter would stand no nonsense. She was strong willed, thrifty and in Norfolk terms, a bit of a spitfire, life was never dull. As children we loved running through Granny Baxter's house in Lothian Street, down the long narrow kitchen into the scullery, passing the last room, [later a bathroom] and out into the garden. Here there was a small cobblestone section with a bench seat under a tree, a quiet peaceful area. We ran round again and again until we were eventually stopped by a grown up.

* After the grand parents died, Alan lived in the house in Lothian Street when he first married Joy Thompson and David and Heather Baxter rented a house in Newmarket Street shortly after they were married [1963] nearly opposite to where their grand parents had previously lived and where our grandfather died in 1939 but David's previous employers in Bedford requested him to return as they required a refrigeration engineer. This move was to be permanent!

Henry had an infectious laugh much like the old record of the "laughing policeman" and when in company every one joined in with him even if they did not get the joke because his laugh was so contagious. Both grandparents had a great sense of humour and there was always a battle of wits going on between them that made us laugh. Unfortunately we have not the space to expand on this side of their characters. After they moved they kept the original Lothian Street house and retained it as an investment.

<u>Our two families conjoin again after approximately 1200 years</u>

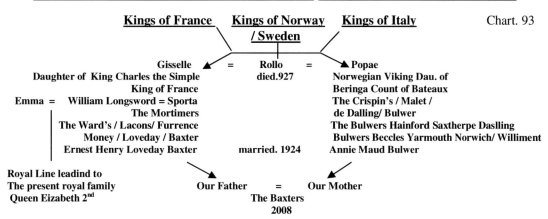

Chart. 93

It is sad that we really never had the chance to learn more about their lives as they were the last generation to experience what hard times really were. But no doubt they enjoyed their children, as we do ours, not realizing that when they married they would join together the two families of Valoise again after many hundreds of years.

*Entertainment of this time period was more boisterous, often combined with audience participation. The most renowned theatrical venue in Norwich was the Connaught Varieties in Goat Lane, where entertainment was of a kind that has passed away forever. This included a chairman with his hammer who was master of ceremonies and who introduced the acts. On the backs of the seats there were shelves for various beverages. For the more sophisticated members of the audience partitions were devised to screen off the more luxurious areas.

The Empire in Oak Street [unofficially known as the FleaPit] was a cinema that accepted jam jars as payment for entrance and was one of the last theatres to do so, and the audience was often shocked by being drenched with disinfectant sprays from the trigger happy usherettes. There was also music in the streets in our grandparents Norwich; Victorian days were rather more rowdy, sometimes it was the music of the Hurdy Gurdy or Barrel Organ but it was mostly the organ grinder with his little monkey clad in a red coat that drew the biggest crowds.

**We have depicted Norwich in this text but this was typical of most cities and towns.*

ERNEST HENRY LOVEDAY BAXTER

Born 9th November 1894 – Died 1st August 1980
Our father's young life and The Great War
1914 – 1918

Ernest Henry Loveday Baxter was born on the 9th November 1894, and in those day's great importance was made for young people to learn to play a musical instrument and his parents were no exception. From an early age he was taught the piano, becoming talented in classical music. In retrospect it seems strange that with all the family history down to our day, we cannot recall our parents telling us much about their own young lives.

But Dad did tell us of some of the lighter moments of his early life such as the time he worked in a chemist shop, making, under supervision, various medicines, herbal remedies, ladies beauty powders and creams that often contained finely ground metal. Needless to say something went wrong and he had to contend with an extremely furious lady whose complexion was not what was intended, a positive raw red, instead of a glowing pink that took weeks to get back to normal.

Whether it was to escape the wrath of that woman or the call to arms, that we shall never know, he just volunteered and went to fight in the 1914 – 18 war. All his previous efforts were wasted; his ambition for music vanished when he was enlisted into the Cavalry in 1914 and sent to the front line in France. This was to be a terrible war for those men, battles fought from trenches; a life of mud, deprivation, hunger, indignity and danger, they lived and died by bullet or gas.

The killing went on endlessly in those water and mud filled rat-infested trenches in all conditions, hail rain snow or sun. Their were living in conditions worse than animals; rats running uncontrolled would try to eat anything, alive or dead; the army being what it is gave Dad [one of the shortest men] the largest horse. He told us of many exploits he had with the horse named 'Big Ben' for whom he obviously had great affection, it was his closest companion during many daring missions near enemy lines.

During a lull in the fighting, exhausted, he managed to snatch some sleep in a trench and while asleep a rat bit his hand causing damage to his little finger. Later, after the war had ended, when at work, a bristle from the brush he was making pierced the very same finger which became infected this combined injury made this finger permanently rigid. Unable bend it, he was never to play the piano properly again.

His piano playing sounded terrible to us children and it must have been a great disappointment to him when we all cried, "Get off dad and let mother play."

He often spoke of the funny side of his army life but went quiet when we enquired about the horror of this terrible war. He was reluctant to discuss it, even with mother. There was only one particular story of terror that he told, which must have had a special meaning for him as he often mentioned it and seemed he was awe-inspired even when telling what he had witnessed; the troops named the incident the: -

<u>The Angels of Mons.</u>

A great decisive battle was raging between the two armies that continued into the night. Father's task was to help to supply the front line with ammunition, food and water, a dangerous job out of the trenches, always in sight of the enemy, who knew if they could stop the supply they would win the battle. Shells and bullets saturated the area combined with the screams of wounded men and horses, some horses bolted, killing the rider, the job had to be done irrespective of the human cost. Whether it was a trick of light or something supernatural he could never explain, he said it was a sight he could never forget or even understand. Amid all the horror of all the human carnage he experienced, a great bow of light suddenly appeared between the English and the German lines, made up of what the men later described as a host of angels. Shelling stopped and there was a deathly silence.

It was strange that after this incident the Germans retreated, probably in fright and the battle went in favour of the British. Dad did not escape unscathed as later in the war he was caught in a cloud of mustard gas, which affected his breathing for the rest of his life. The constant explosion of shells deafened him permanently although mother used to say that if you offered him money he would hear you.

The enemy was on the run and the roads had to be repaired for the British troop transport to follow. Father was sent with two other soldiers with Big Ben, his horse, towing a cart containing a tar barrel to fill in the shell holes. They were to report any hostile movements and return if they found trouble, as the enemy was only ten miles up the road.

It was a scorching hot day and after some miles, they came upon a farmhouse, made a search and questioned the farmer who was very frightened. Getting no information from him they stole his eggs and made a meal taking the remaining eggs with them; further along the road they entered some farm cottages.

Again after a search they found a frightened family who gladly exchanged a barrel of wine for some precious eggs; the wine proved a stronger temptation than the men and also the horse's will to resist drinking it. This later resulted in them all leaving the road and falling headlong into the dry ditch together with the barrel on the cart that spilled its load of hot tar everywhere.

Neither the soldiers nor the horse seemed to care when they and the horse fell into the ditch. How long they all slept is not known, nor how the patrolling Germans failed to discover them [they were probably so drunk they were mistaken for dead]. They somehow managed to get back to their unit and scrub down the horse in an attempt to get rid of the tar, ready for the final inspection by the G.O.C. and in preparation for the next major push forward.

Unfortunately the harder they tried to remove the tar from the horse the more hair came off leaving a large bald shiny area of skin. Panicking the unit officer ordered father to keep the hairless side of the horse to the wall when the General came round. When he did arrive to inspect with all the pomp and ceremony required by the army, the inevitable happened just as he passed, Big Ben decided to turn round inviting the astonished General to stop and confirm what he had seen. He raised his cane to the horses' nostrils and shouted to the Sergeant **"Get this horse out of the lines and into quarantine, it has the mange, blast it!"**

The horse was led away with our father, its rider and put into quarantine well back from the front lines. Through Big Ben's apparent condition fathers' life was probably saved and our family is now in existence. When the battle recommenced his whole unit was declared either killed or missing by being caught up in an ambush.

The horrors of the First World War gradually filtered through to the British public despite the government's attempt to restrict this terrible news. A hate campaign against anything German began, which brought embarrassment to the royal family whose ancestry was German, so they decided to change their image. On 19th June 1917 it was announced that the royal surname of Sax-Coburg-Gotha was to be changed to Windsor.

When the war ended 11th November 1918 **Ernest** returned home and started to plan his future with his childhood sweetheart **Annie Bulwer.** It was this association and future marriage and the true life stories of our ancestors as told by our mother that inspired us to research and discover the amazing link that we believe brought these two major family lines that descended from Rollo the Norwegian Viking down to our own living families as outlined in the following pages.

CHART DETAILING THE ROLLO /GISSELLE / FURRENCE LINEAGE
Incredibly the marriage of our parents in 1924 probably linked our families once again after several hundred years,

We continue with this very incredible connection between the old Mortimer/Crispin families [See chart below] with Rollo the Norman Viking as their common ancestor. We feel it's amazing and ironic that our parents marriage in 1924 possibly linked these families once again [*according to our belief] two major lines conjoin after several hundred years.

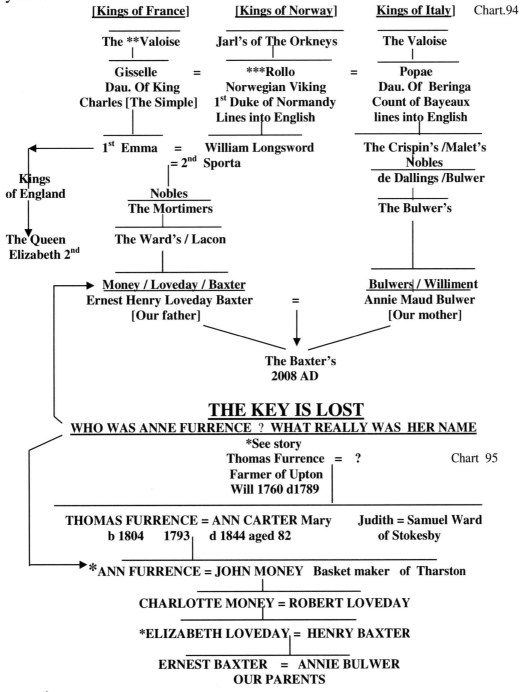

[Kings of France]   [Kings of Norway]   Kings of Italy]   Chart.94

The **Valoise   Jarl's of The Orkneys   The Valoise

Gisselle = ***Rollo = Popae
Dau. Of King   Norwegian Viking   Dau. Of Beringa
Charles [The Simple]   1st Duke of Normandy   Count of Bayeaux
     Lines into English   lines into English

1st Emma = William Longsword   The Crispin's /Malet's
= 2nd Sporta   Nobles
Kings   de Dallings /Bulwer
of England   Nobles
     The Mortimers   The Bulwer's

The Queen   The Ward's / Lacon
Elizabeth 2nd

Money / Loveday / Baxter   Bulwers / Williment
Ernest Henry Loveday Baxter = Annie Maud Bulwer
[Our father]   [Our mother]

The Baxter's
2008 AD

THE KEY IS LOST
WHO WAS ANNE FURRENCE ? WHAT REALLY WAS HER NAME

*See story
Thomas Furrence = ?   Chart 95
Farmer of Upton
Will 1760 d1789

THOMAS FURRENCE = ANN CARTER Mary   Judith = Samuel Ward
b 1804   1793 d 1844 aged 82   of Stokesby

*ANN FURRENCE = JOHN MONEY Basket maker of Tharston

CHARLOTTE MONEY = ROBERT LOVEDAY

*ELIZABETH LOVEDAY = HENRY BAXTER

ERNEST BAXTER = ANNIE BULWER
OUR PARENTS

*No documents found for the birth of Ann Furrence

PROGRESS CHART
Chart 96

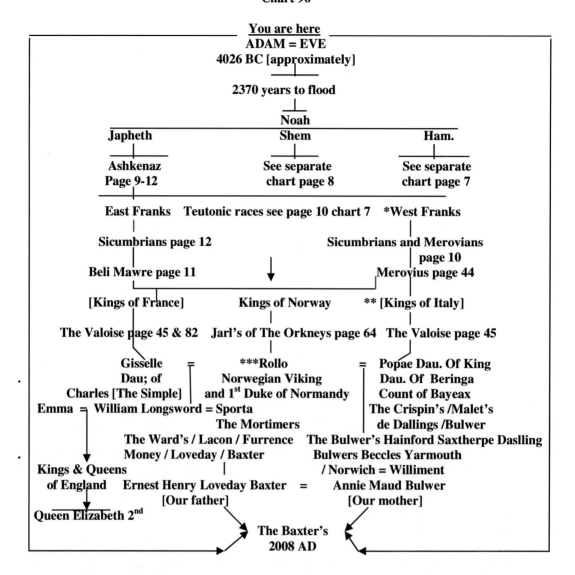

The above progress chart has now finally reached our present living Baxter and associated families and has covered the years from 4026 B.C. until the year 2007 AD and their histories as far as we could ascertain them. There are still the histories of the modern Baxter families to follow and the friends and relations associated with them.

We sometime found names we could not readily trace and these did take some time to find, but with the aid of the charts in Laurence Gardner's book 'Blood Line of the Holy Grail' and other historical documents it was fairly easy to follow through. We are very grateful to him for his permission to refer to his work and for this reason can recommend his book for your further studies.

PROFILE OF THE MODERN BAXTER FAMILIES
ERNEST HENRY LOVEDAY AND ANNIE MAUD BAXTER
OUR PARENTS

Our father Ernest Baxter		**Our mother Annie Baxter**
Born 9th Nov. 1893 died 1st .Sept.1980	Plate 104	born 10 Feb 1900 died 22nd Aug. 1975

They were married on the 24th July 1924 at the Chapel-in-Field Church, Norwich later to buy the bungalow in Lower Hellesdon where their son **Derek** and daughter **Norma** were born. Father started working for his uncle who owned Potters Brush Works in Bethel Street Norwich and taught him the trade; on his death our father inherited the factory.

The family moved into one of a row of houses in Bethel Street, Norwich which at some time in the past belonged to the Flemish weavers. These houses were three-stories high with huge airy rooms, and several flights of stairs; Norma remembers living there although she was only two years and six months old. The factory was at the rear of the house and fortunately the business thrived, the home was always full of happiness and love, making the bond between our parents even greater. There seemed to be a great future before them, but alas this was not to be.

Times were difficult for business just after the war; though his small factory began to thrive with about fifty employees; later **Norma** was often taken there and talked to the ladies who made the brushes. She remembers how they sat in small groups around a central stand that held a pot of very hot pitch.

Each woman grasped the required amount of bristles, bound the ends with twine, dipped them into the hot pitch and quickly inserted them into the holes in the head of the brush. Little did father know then, the total disaster that was about to befall him! Later followed a great grief over a loss of his firstborn son Derek, bankruptcy and eviction, and the poverty that would take firm hold on this little family.

THE YOUNG BAXTER FAMILY

Father with Derek
18 months old plate 105

Norma aged 2yrs
plate.106

Derek was born on the 5th July 1925 but died five years later, in tragic circumstances on the 31st. December 1930, as you will read. **Norma** was born on the 6th May 1927 and married **Edward Hart** at Old Lakenham Parish Church on 23rd September. 1950 They had two children Susan and Michael. and three grandchildren Edward died 1st December 1998 and is sadly missed.

Alan and Raymond plate 107.

Alan Henry was born on the 23rd September 1928, and married Joy Thompson on the 12th September 1953 at Norwich and had three children David, Bryan, and Allison. Sadly we lost our brother Alan on 25th December 2008.

Raymond Walter was born 5th June 1931, he married **Brenda Moore** on the 21st March 1958 at the Norwich Registry Office, and had two girls Denise and Dawn.

David Cedric was born on the 1st January 1934. He married **Heather Willimott** at the Great Cressingham Methodist Chapel, Norfolk on the 26th October 1963, moved to Bedford to work; they had two children Jason and Carie. Jason his son married Nicole Clarke and has three children Charlie, Abigail and Freya. Carie married Richard Robinson they now have four children Jessica, Mason, Finley, and Verity.

plate.108 **David 1944 aged 10**

Mother, Ann and Brian [Bill] 1951. Plate. 109

Brian William [Bill] was born on the 4th April 1937 and married Gloria Hill on the 5th August 1961. They had four sons Paul and Mark (twins), Ian and Neil. Sadly Paul died at 18 months of age when a sudden pneumonia type virus infection struck him and to our grief he died within 24hrs. in Dec. 1963.

Our sister **Ann,** [the baby of the family] was born on the 20th February 1941 and married **Tony Carter** on the 30th of March 1963 at the Old Lakenham Church. They had three children Sharon, Rachel and Sean.

THE EARLY YEARS

Everything looked rosy for **Ernest and Annie**, a secure future, a nice bungalow on Low Road, Hellesdon Norwich, their own business and the beginnings of the large family that she had always longed for. But fate was lurking in the wings ready to strike some rapid savage blows that would tear most families apart. Being the first-born, **Derek** received the expected attention and love that was poured on to him by all. [The birth of a daughter.

Norma, made the home even more contented]. Derek was forever full of mischief as he grew up, and wanting to help his mum gave **Norma** her medicine [half a bottle of syrup of figs and always the artist, painted the walls with sunshine). The arrival of their second son **Alan** completed the picture of proud parents with a home that even boasted of an Adam Bede fireplace in the living room. It had a black lead grate with a brightly burning fire, which was never out and with hobs used for cooking and boiling kettles; gas and oil lamps were still widely used for lighting, the house had several quaint stairways and a cellar where the coal was stored.

Interestingly, Penny-Farthing Bikes and the lorry pictured are typical of their day with their solid rubber tyres, which must have been a source of many medical problems for the rider or driver. These conveyances were still being used in the early days and up to 1930. We can remember seeing prams, push chairs invalid chairs and a type of invalid bed all made of wickerwork before the use of wood or cloth sides, they all had large iron wheels. Mother had a cradle made of wickerwork it became brittle; care was taken that the baby was not injured when put in it. .

Penny farthing and other bikes
Plate 110

Woodbine cigarettes at two pence for a packet of ten; a local newspaper would cost two pence and children's frocks were six pence each. Commercial aviation was in its infancy and strong competition began between air and sea travel. The new method of traveling by airship, although they could easily outrun the ocean liners was *abandoned following the crash of the R101 October 1930 and the Hindenburg explosion in 1937for safety reasons.The future was already in the making when the prototype super-marine Spitfire took off and safely landed at Eastleigh Hampshire [Mar. 1936].

.*Airship manufacture later resumed in the same hangers in Bedford that the R101 was made in 1929.

It is worth mentioning that during our youth, bread rolls could be bought for a halfpenny each! More important to us was that we could buy one farthings worth of sweets in huge cone shaped bags; the lady at the sweet shop would cram the bag full and top it up. We could get into the cinema for six pence;

A typical delivery van of 1930's   Plate 111

buy ice cream for two pence [wrapped in brown paper ugh!] at the Theatre de Luxe [known locally as the flea pit] picture house.

Derek started school and made a friend called Pauline Pod who lived in Rigby Court. The sweet shop that belonged to our Aunt Maude and Laura was on the right-hand corner of this court facing the road in St. Giles Street, which is still there today. Our family visited Paulines parents until their house was pulled down, roughly at the same time as ours to make way for the new City Hall and fire station. **Norma** remembers it had steps down into a large dark room that faced into a courtyard.

Aunt Eva   Aunt Bessie   Sophia our grandmother

Pauline Podd

The great aunt's and our grandmother with the children
Vera Robert Pauline Pod and Derek   Plt 112

Our parents never allowed themselves to swear in front of us but Pauline was not averse to using the odd swear word. Derik usually would reply "God will not have you in his Heaven". She answered with as many swear words she could think of at the time. One aspect of life that caused Norma some distress were the mice that lived in the house; whenever father caught one he threw it on the fire alive; **Norma** never forgave him for that.

A TRIBUTE TO OUR PARENTS
1930 – A YEAR TO FORGET
Events which altered the course of our family life, and made it stronger

The Black Hole

The first near tragedy occurred one evening at bedtime, mother bathed her young family as usual and clothed in pyjamas, all sweet and clean she took the three children and climbed the stairs, not prepared for the sight that met their eyes when opening the bedroom door.

Instead of the pretty room and those inviting white sheets they found a huge black hole, with oily black cobwebs hanging from ceiling to floor in great festoons hiding what used to be the fireplace. The bed and the carpet glistened black in the light, with oil and smoke, a dark and oily cavern. Our mother with her little brood stood in stunned silence. When she recovered her voice, she shouted for dad, the children started to scream frightened by the sight of their once neat clean bedroom.

Family in happier times Derek, Mother, Alan and Norma Plate.113

Father employed a lad whose job was to trim the wicks and light the lamps and oil heaters, he had failed to maintain them. His inattention caused such drastic results that he was sacked and we never saw him again; we expect he learnt not to be so lazy, Norma though young, felt sorry for him

After the First World War for ten years there was a glut of work needed in catching up with things neglected during the war years, and money flowed. Then followed the great slump, far worse than the modern boom bust recessions of today. The whole nation was in turmoil with hunger marches and strikes; wealthy stockbrokers, businessmen, and others had become too greedy, making overconfident decisions that later caused bankruptcies, dragging innocent hard working small firms with them in a downward spiral, our father among them.

From Landed Gentry to the lowest paid worker, few escaped; there was mass unemployment with no hope of support as we have today; when there was no income you had to rely on the charity of others. Trading became difficult but fathers brush works was doing well considering the situation. His brother in law Ernest Barber asked to come into the business to assist him and father agreed.

Before going away on a business trip to negotiate the purchase of materials father passed the management over to Ernest, emphasizing the need for caution and to check the solvency of any company placing an order. While he was away Ernest received a very large order from what he thought was a reputable company and being over enthusiastic supplied them, failing to check their credibility.

This company went into liquidation overnight and dragged Potters Brush Works into bankruptcy with them. Fearing what was to about to happen, father had some of the valuable furniture removed to his mothers' house for safekeeping, [or so he thought] at least there would be something saved of our old home while awaiting the bankruptcy hearing.

Another event loomed in the form of an eviction notice from the local council advising that other accommodation must be sought due to the proposed demolition of our house, making way for the New City Hall and Fire Station, an occurrence that was welcomed by all accept us. This meant that we would not only have lost all our savings, the business, and most of our furniture, but now also the house that father was so desperately trying to hold on to

Except for those with good memories, this picture taken in the 1930s could be a bit of puzzle. The church tower is the clue. This is another picture of Bethel Street as it was before the coming of the City Hall, police station and fire station on the left.

I think you can just see the sign hanging there Potters Brush Works. The workshop was at the rear of the house

. **Photo by Derek Edwards. Copyright Norfolk Museum**
and Archaeology Service Plate.114

He sent us this old news paper cutting from The Eastern Evening News many years ago of the old Bethel Street before it was cleared to make way for what is now the Norfolk police and fire station H.Q. It is our father's own writing below the picture. Our house is the one in the fore-ground fitted with a bracket that held the sign Potters Brush Works that once had been our home, and our father's work place.

"What else could go wrong?

TRAGIC LOSS OF A SON AND BROTHER
1930

While waiting for alternative accommodation we were still at this time living at Bethel Street. **Norma** was sitting in the baby chair in front of the guarded fire. **Alan,** the baby was asleep, when mother decided to collect some coal from the cellar to build up the fire; she was gone for several minutes. **Derek** was at a mischievous age and wanted to investigate everything and it was concluded later that he somehow gained entry into the pantry helping himself to a bag of dried peas [probably thinking he had found some marbles], and was playing with them.

Hearing his mother coming he picked some up and ran to the cellar door, laughing and shouting '' Look what I have found mummy!'' The door opened and caught the boy's hand knocking it upwards into his face shooting a pea into his mouth, where it dropped neatly into his windpipe like a cork into a bottle. The excited laughter of a child suddenly stilled to a shuddering gasp for air.

Mother dropped the coal, repeatedly hitting him on the back, but not succeeding in the desperate attempt to dislodge the obstruction. She grabbed his feet, and with his head near the floor continued with the hopeless task of banging his back to release the pea from his windpipe while the child continued with horrible gasping noises desperately struggling for breath trying to cling on to life.

There was no other help at hand nor anyone to notice the terrible effect it had on the other little pair of eyes that were watching seeing this tragic and desperate drama unfold in front of her. Though still too young to talk well, **Norma** instinctively knew that there was something terribly wrong and started to scream. The piercing screams of both mother and child brought the milkman running in from the street and he frantically tried to remove the obstruction.

Unable to do so he rushed the whole family to the Hospital on his milk cart, but it was too late. Derek was pronounced dead on arrival. How we all hate those words, and know just what it means for all those tragic people who have heard them.

As you will read later, history repeated itself again within the family and the terrible effect it had on our parents when the news reached them of their grandson meeting a similar fate thirty four years later and nearly on the same date. Following the trauma of their son's death, fate dealt another blow, as only three days later the order came to enact the bankruptcy order and the bailiffs arrived.

Even those usually hard hearted men of the law saw reason to take pity but they had a job to do and reluctantly removed every piece of value from our home, furniture, the lot, leaving the bare necessities to live. The tears of our parents were to no avail; debts had to be paid. An incident our mother never forgot was when a friend left her five shillings to pay for one week's meals. There were no social services in those days, and neighbours and friends often used to try and give each other support in those hard times. Mother placed the money on the mantleshelf while going to the door to let the bailiffs in; on her return to the room she passed an official who was there to enact the law coming hurriedly out of the room and decided to check the mantleshelf for the money. It had gone too! No money, no food!

The agonising events worsened at the inquest and post mortem. Every one, including the coroner was saddened having to deal with the death of a child. What mother and father had to go through at this time was more than could be imagined, as they listened to the proceedings of the gruesome autopsy to verify the cause of death of her first born. The sympathetic Judge apportioned no blame to the family and extended his deepest sympathy.

The scene and feelings of the whole community on the day of **Derek's** funeral cannot be fully put into words, kindly relatives, friends and neighbours brought in chairs, tables, and lit a cheery fire to brighten up that sad day; the memory is still with **Norma** to this day.

To her the ladies all dressed in black looked like witches sitting around the fire crying into their pure white handkerchiefs, never speaking. But as our parents used to say, sad endings were a time of new beginnings and we suppose it was because of using this philosophy they always managed a smile, even during times of heartbreak giving the family new strength.

Mother was resilient, father even more determined to succeed, they both realised it would never be the same again. Though the worst was over, the events caused psychological problems to those that were left. For years after, **Norma** had nightmares, trying to play with her older brother who would stay just out of reach; unable to touch or get close to him and she would awake crying.

One day after they had moved, **Norma** re-enacted the traumatic events of that tragic day with her brother Alan, in the greatest detail; mother silently listening. It must have torn her apart but she did not try and stop it, which say's a lot for her love and patience. She was amazed that one so young had understood and absorbed so much detail.

This enactment was a blessing in disguise as it helped to heal the wounds though the dreams stayed with **Norma,** gradually fading completely by the time she was eleven. No more dried peas were ever allowed into the house, boiled sweets were always broken up and marbles were banned.

Gone was our dear brother, gone was the family livelihood.
And then
EVICTION!

Gone was our home and furniture,
all in one year,

It was truly a time of new beginnings.

THE DEMOLITION OF OUR HOME AND THE FAMILY BUSINESS

AND WE ARE FORCED TO MOVE
To 6 MANSFIELD LANE, LAKENHAM NORWICH
THE HOME OF OUR YOUTH

Our life goes on in endless song.
In spite of earth's lamentations
We hear a real though far off hymn,
That tells of a new creation.
Through all the trouble and the strife.
We hear its music ringing,
It finds an echo in our soul.
How can we keep from singing.

The day the family moved house it was raining, well not just raining it was coming down in buckets, probably resembling the feelings of our parents. The new baby **Raymond** was put into the pram with **Alan** and **Norma** sitting on each side under the hood. Friends and relatives rallied round to help the family make a fresh start.

The End of Potters Brushwork's
Dad's workshop [Potters brushworks]   Plate. 115

Photo by Derek Edwards. Copyright Norfolk Museums and Archaeology Service

GONE! OUR HOME! OUR LIVELYHOOD! OUR BROTHER!

But the city gained a new fire station

The country's economy was going through a very difficult period at this time; father, like many others could not find work and the attitude of those in authority was callous. In those days those people who held power were determined that any charitable money given had to be earned in what they called a means test. How mother hated this inquisition and loss of dignity. Those desperate for cash had to present themselves for a humiliating intensive investigation into their money and possessions and if considered destitute were given stupid and futile jobs, making sure that every penny given had to be worked for. Father had the indignity of the ridiculous task with others to dig holes in the ground for no purpose and then fill them in again for the wage of one shilling. Feelings were running high, so the government had to stem the tide of anger in the unemployed.

Thousands were still out of work and in the same situation of trying to feed their families, most of those that had fought for their country had come home to nothing. The family struggled through, mother having the most worry trying to find ways of feeding the growing healthy youngsters with no income and no help from the state. As the new son and brother started to make his presence felt, Raymond, like Derek, grew to be full of mischief. Being the youngest he was blamed by the others who took full advantage of his mischief, and so he was considered the main culprit, to receive the retribution for things that he did and did not do, from his frustrated parents.

Father had no job or money to refurnish the home and so decided to get back some of the valuable furniture that he had removed to his mothers. 'It had gone!' together with his hope of getting a reasonably furnished home once more. Without consulting him, his parents had sold it all to make more room in their house. This hurt him deeply and caused a family split that lasted for several years The events and tragedies of those past few years changed the well being, status and attitude of the whole family for ever, bringing worry and despair to our parents, but the situation was controlled somewhat with young children's laughter and devoted parents.

Our family had now regained its composure and father with the help of others, managed to rebuild our home with second hand furniture. Its appearance and structure was not always improved by the kamikaze antics of the children, who when mothers back was turned, jumped from great heights hoping to be assisted by the springs in the sofa to touch the ceiling. Unfortunately the springs often gave way, and visitors received a nasty shock if a spring came off the retaining webbing as they sat down. This was not always by accident but sometimes pre-arranged though we as youngsters did not really mind about the state of the home, it was liveable in and we were happy.

After a while we had a visit from a Mr. Corn who owned a small brush factory. No doubt he had noticed the family had regained its dignity and thought it prudent to pay a visit. Not for a friendly business chat but to see if he could extract any repayment of moneys owed to him by father for materials supplied before bankruptcy and he was very belligerent about it.

A hard foul-mouthed man who had no respect for the presence of women and children. He was brought to his senses though when he confronted our Mum, who still could show that she was his equal when it came to straight talking, without the foul descriptive. Though we found it fascinating to sit and listen too [especially as swearing was unacceptable in those days] we were always told, "God was; listening", at the time we wondered how many black marks were put in Gods book against Mr.Corn's name.

Mother gathered her children like a mother hen with chicks, and told him in no uncertain terms, that if he wanted to discus these matters, to request it decently from her husband and in a civil manner. Would he please not call at her door using foul language in front of her children, and to go home and scrub his filthy mouth out! Then in a more conciliatory tone, she said that she was sorry, but we had lost everything we had through no fault of our own but would eventually repay every penny we owed if we ever got back on our feet again, but her first responsibility was to her very young family.

We never ever truly recovered from our financial trap as mother was always expecting another baby. Mr. Corn was so impressed by mother's straight talk he offered father a job straight away as foreman in his brush works. This was the first ray of hope in that terrible year of trouble and sadness. Father had a job! Gradually the family settled down but it was a hard upward struggle even to live, as the whole country was slowly coming out of recession, but somehow father managed to scrape enough money to pay living expenses, plus various items for the home.

These were days of hardship and worry, but the leisure times were very happy times for all, singing round the piano [which we always seemed to have], with mum, a community spirit was the order of the day at that time; a more natural way of life with relatives and neighbours. Boys were encouraged to join the Scouts and to go on camping holidays for the outdoor life and girls encouraged to join the Guides and Brownies with the same privileges.

Note of interest; at this period of time although business was bad, exports were enhanced by the new freight service when trucks could be shunted directly onto boats to be ferried to France. On June 5th 1930 the Government rejected plans for a Channel Tunnel.

The first one of many instruments father brought home from the various auctions he attended was a Harmonium, a musical instrument that was a cross between a piano and an organ. It had to be pumped with the feet and gave an unusual sound that we liked. Mother spent many happy hours playing it.

It was two years after Derek Died in 1932 when **Norma** started school and it was usual for infants to rest on camp beds before doing anything active. Every year pupils moved up a class with a new teacher but this did not fit into **Norma's** way of thinking, as she liked the camp beds and toys in her old classroom so she decided to return. Being small she was not noticed when one pupil was missing from her class and that there was one extra in another until the next day when register was read. A search party was sent out; when found, **Norma** had to explain to both teachers; she never tried that trick again, particularly as she came to be under the teacher's watchful eyes; having made her mark, the teachers kept a wary watch on her movements.

At first she found learning was difficult but having a lively outlook on life and a very enquiring mind she soon found that life had other things to offer, and it could be rewarding to listen and learn, [well, some things anyway], on other subjects she was not too sure. Mother would never tolerate lies deceit, or stealing; woe betide any of us breaking these rules and we relate this story as an example. One day **Norma** succumbed to the temptation provoked by the sight of a bright new ball, and was soon brought into line by mother. Her teacher held up a lost ball for someone to claim, and as no one did, that brand new, shiny, brightly coloured ball was something she just had to have. **Norma** could not resist as we had very few toys and no one seemed to want the ball. ...so she claimed it. Mother's keen eye soon spotted the brightly coloured object when she brought it home ''Where did you get this from?''

''The teacher gave it to me''. ''Oh! Why did she do that?''

We could never lie convincingly to our parents, as they always seemed to know. Their eye's seemed to go right through you to read your thoughts, so **Norma** sheepishly owned up. Mother's instant reaction was ''Well'' pause, "my little lady, you can just take it back, and explain to the teacher just why you told a lie'. You can also expect a word from your father about this". As they say it was Tout Court.

The little girl feeling very humiliated did what she was told, head hanging down with shame, she delivered the ball back to the teacher who accepted it without comment which made her shame seem worse, but when it was done, she never repeated the situation again ever!

ANOTHER ADDITION TO THE FAMILY NEW YEARS DAY
Then there were four!

David was born on the 1st January 1934 and nearly won the award for the first baby of the year, which was a new pram, but he arrived one minute too late and another family claimed it. He had missed the time of family tragedy but like many more children, the unknown future was to be a war that would leave vivid memories of childhood deprivation and fear.

Mother was very ill before **David** was born; the strain of the past years and the hard economic times took its toll on her health and she almost had a miscarriage. **Norma** was at an age to understand and help. She was able to cope with the family and the chores by also assisting to reduce mother's high temperature with cloths dipped in cold water, laying them on her forehead, making many cups of tea for visitors and cooking family meals until mother was well again.

We all had our own jobs to do at home; even father did his part after a long day at work and there were no five-day weeks in those days.
These were happy times in spite of the poverty trap we were in; we all sang songs as we toiled at our tasks. Music and singing was an important part of our family life and so it continued through the years. After **David** was born there was even more work for our poor Mum, with none of the modern aids that we take for granted today. Automatic washing machines, microwave ovens, and dishwashers were not available. All clothes were either scrubbed by hand or boiled in a boiler heated by coal or in an electric copper boiler and dried in front of a blazing fire in the wintertime when and if there was enough fuel.

We liked the smell of the clean linen when it was almost dry, though it probably caused all the colds we used to suffer during those early days. To help to dry wet clothes we were taught to use the mangle or wringer, which was basically two large wooden rollers in a metal frame, pressed together by massive springs the tension of which could be adjusted according to the clothing that went through the machine. On one end there was a large cogged wheel with a handle that was turned to advance the machinery and force the item through the rollers.

These mangles are almost extinct today, owing to the arrival of modern technology in the form of the washing machine/spin dryers that are now on the market. The main concern then was to not let your fingers get caught in the rollers or your hand would soon be turned into a webbed foot. Dad and the four growing children somehow took the pressure off mother, and she soon regained her strength. **David** had a mass of blonde tightly curled hair just like the boy in the picture called "Bubbles" by Millais and found his place at the family table with the rest of us.

NORMA GOES TO HEYDON HALL.

Grandfather often spoke with **Colonel Edward Bulwer** at Heydon Hall when they met at the many garden parties or fetes held there in those pre-war days and always asked him to attend to demonstrate his skills in Phrenology. Grandfather had studied and practised the art, which was a skill where fingers are run over the scalp to find the raised areas on the skull that has adjusted itself to accommodate the growing brain.

The theory behind this that the more knowledge people take in for certain subjects stimulates an area of the brain that develops in this place and enlarges the skull to accommodate it, this enables the person to have more ability in certain fields. These areas indicate the special abilities each individual develops during their active lives. Grandfather used this information to inform children and adults what subjects they would excel in. [These garden parties were discontinued before the Second World War]. According to **Captain William Bulwer Long's** letter to us 26 August 1993, **Colonel Edward Bulwer** died in 1934. His death ended grandfathers' association with the Hall. It was also at this time some questions regarding entitlements to inheritance were raised. Grandfather and his brothers considered they had a claim on the estate.

As children we never really understood what the issue was, but the adults were excited so it filtered through to us, as Mother did an unusual thing. She had always treated us alike but on this occasion **Norma** received special treatment and she was fitted out in expensive clothes, cut from Harris Tweed that grandmother ordered and paid for in blue to match her eyes. What was afoot? No one said! There was a lot of whispering and quiet confidential talk. Something important was about to happen, mother gave **Norma** a brief account but she was instructed not to tell even her brothers, it was a secret, so she refused to think about it. But all this was to no avail as somehow the boys got to know anyway.

Soon after, **Norma,** dressed like a princess went in the taxi that drew up in front of our house, and with her grandfather, was whisked away to Heydon Hall. It stopped outside the gates of this huge imposing building with its massive neatly manicured lawns each side of a long driveway. All grandfathers' brothers had arrived and after the usual family greetings their attention was drawn to the little girl, but instead of making a fuss of their little relation there were cold looks in her direction and enquiries made to why she was there.

It was not until years later that she understood fully why her uncles had behaved in such a manner.

Children are sensitive to atmosphere; their cold attitude towards her was hurtful, though quickly forgotten in the development of events. A discussion took place in low voices and it was decided that **Norma** would have to wait in the great entrance hall. She looked around and stood there terrified, but when grandfather said to stay, then stay you did and no arguments. One look at his eyes was enough to deter most people; they were dark brown and sharp as razors.

The brothers were conducted away into the depths of a dim corridor that led off from the right hand side of the great hall, their voices getting fainter and fainter as they disappeared into the half-darkness of the main part of this great house. Doors opened and shut and an eerie silence wrapped around the child. To a seven-year old being left in this vast strange place surrounded by swords and shields with long dead and stuffed animal heads hanging from the walls, not to mention the fearsome looking knight in a suit of armour, holding a great Saxon axe that seemed about to descend on her head [towering above the very seat on which she was told to sit] was very frightening.

So there she sat, not daring to disobey her grandfather, but too nervous to sit there either. She gazed round the hall that had a red and cream carpet surrounded by dark highly polished wide wooden floorboards. There at her feet was the reflection on the polished boards of the man in armour. She removed herself quickly from the seat and ventured to the carpet near the door to gaze at the man in armour at a safe distance, then turned to investigate the interesting array of pictures on the wall. It seemed ages before a door opened, there was a sound of voices so she sped back to the seat and waited. The brothers advanced into the hallway looking disappointed and quietly concentrating on their own thoughts.

Once outside the hall they all had quiet discussion at the gates for a few moments, shook hands and went their different ways, we were to see them together only once more and that was only more by accident than design. William returned to Australia. The others went to their homes and again these relatives went out of our lives forever.

Our parents never talked about what transpired at that meeting but strange events continued to happen, that we remember in detail, even though we had no explanation for them. It is a great pity that in those days children were not allowed to ask questions on what was considered to be the adult world and it was more than we would dare to enter a discussion with a reasonable question on family matters, this was an area strictly for adults. Children were to be seen and not heard and could only surmise answers by discreetly listening at a distance.

Mr. DUFF-COOPER SECRETARY OF STATE VISITS OUR COUNCIL HOUSE

Mr. Alfred Duff-Cooper; a high profile member of his majesty's government visited our home! In this part of our story the words are carefully chosen and thoughtfully written so as not to give undue offence. We are not sure but we think he had a claim on the ancestral home of Woodalling Hall, Norfolk as we discovered later that a Colonel Duff had lived there at this time. Duff Cooper held the important office of Under–Secretary of State at the War Office. A man you will read about in Anthony Bulwer's description.

A black and gleaming limousine driven by a chauffeur that only the very rich could possibly own drew up outside our home; there was a authoritative sharp knock on our front door and mother answered it, and in, (for better use of the word)... SWEPT ... this elegant individual.'' UPPER CLASS '' written through every fibre of his expensively cut dark suit. Even to our young and inexperienced eyes, we could see this was an individual who thought he was very special and in hindsight we now know he was. He was from a different environment; a man of means entering a world that he obviously did not want to associate himself with.

It was an environment that Duff Cooper wanted to depart from as soon as possible. It must have been a new experience, a shock to his ego and general air of superiority. In some ways we could sympathise with his attitude, as we had seen better times, and we must have seemed to him to be, [and were] very down at heel. Our council house was shabby but clean, there were large holes in the lino [Vinyl today] and loose springs in the upholstery. We were the victims of a situation like many others, over which we had no control, sad to say we were still fighting life's battle to survive after bankruptcy.

Children were rarely allowed into adult conversation as in those days as we previously mentioned "Children were to be seen and not heard." and were usually told to go into another room while adults talked. Though we generally found a way of knowing what was in the air. We had a shrewd guess as to the reason for this mans visit after listening at the door to his icy, curt and reluctant conversation, a facade of cold politeness from a man who just wanted to bring this situation to a close. Children pick up vibrations that emanate from the environment that they are in, far more quickly than adults do, usually assessing a situation and to generally draw accurate conclusions about people, though not always understanding the underlying purpose of the conversations.This call was obviously about the Heydon Hall visit and the place where grandfather had taken Norma, and the people mother used to speak about in those stories.

A meeting had been held there but the content of their discussions was never fully explained to us, which was a pity as we could have included this knowledge in our book today. The occasion of a Rolls Royce outside No 6 created much interest with the neighbours whose noses were compressed against the glass in their windows, with curtains flapping at such goings on, wondering what on earth was happening at number 6.

It was fortunate that there was no frost on that day as with all those noses pressed hard against the glazing they would have made a permanent feature to each house, though it was highly entertaining to us. This discussion was soon concluded and he again. "SWEPT" back to the gleaming limousine that stood outside our house with the uniformed chauffeur waiting at the car door to assist him, it then sped off, out of our lives, taking him back to his elevated position, much to his relief and ours!

Our front door was slammed shut and we saw a different attitude in our mother, one she rarely revealed. Instead of her normal calm, she exploded and we stood amazed at the torrent of angry words, which conveyed to us that in no way did she like the visitor and did not care who knew it. We have related this incident in our life as it happened and you can judge for yourselves the manner of the man. You will have read **Anthony Bulwer Lytton** of Knebworth views when he was later made Alfred Duff-Coopers Parliamentary Private Secretary and compare the incident at our house with the comments made by Anthony when worked with him.

This sums up what Anthony Bulwer, our mother and we as children saw in this mans attitude to life, and unfortunately this includes some of our rich relatives too. You can find the relationship of our grandfather to the Heydon/Hainford families by studying the **Bulwer** family tree from Thomas Bulwer of Hainford, though there was no recognition of this relationship at the time, and never would be at any time in the future.

Mechanised petrol driven methods of transport were slowly replacing the horse and with more use of the motor car, ships, aeroplanes and trains the world was becoming ever smaller. Yet the attitudes of the class system were still in place. However this would change even if it took a war to do it; when the men returned from the war they began to fight the systems of the past and demand a fair deal for the working classes. The years ahead would dramatically change most of the class system for the better in this respect, as predicted by Anthony Bulwer, when everyone would have the opportunity to compete for a fair education, job advancement and living environment. Though class distinctions do still exist even to this day as we recently found out.

MOTHER GOES TO WORK

Mother was expecting her fifth child; money was short and even though food was relatively cheap there was still not enough to feed her still growing family. So she obtained a job in a shop called Henry Jarvis, in St Benedict's Street to help out in providing for the new infant. Soon after we had another visitor to our house very much to the amazement of all of our neighbours

Mother

Once more a gleaming long yellow and black chauffeured Rolls Royce stopped outside and an old lady dressed in a rusty black satin dress covered in frills adorned with jet black beads, alighted and came to our door. Mother invited her in and they both went into the kitchen to talk and we were sent into the garden to play. This was our great *Aunt Louisa Goate a widow, and sister to our grandfather Walter Bulwer.

Mother on Henry Jarvis staff outing

[photo of the shop in St Benedicts)

Plate.116

Great Aunt Louisa   Plt. 117.

Louie had married Mr. Stephen Goate a sea Captain who bought what was then known as the Stone House and renamed it "The Cromwell Temperance and Commercial Hotel". It later changed its name to the Star Tavern, Great Yarmouth, as described on p.429 and still exists today as the Star Hotel.

We have included a summary of events connected to this hotel over the years as a matter of interest, it was sent to us by the present management to whom we are very grateful.

We understand that Louie moved to London after her husband died then moved back to Norfolk in 1934, and very kindly invited us all to visit her at her new home near Great Yarmouth. Before she died she gave our second cousin Barbara Palmer two oyster shells complete with small pearls attached and Barbara passed one on to Norma later in life, something that she still treasures.

*Not to be confused with Louisa Bulwer daughter of William Bulwer

Our family eagerly took up her offer for the seaside outing. She lived in a long white thatched house, which as far as we can remember was very near to some water, probably on the riverbank at Gorleston. As you approached the house, there were two or three stone steps with a handrail that turned to the left down to a small paving block before the door where she stood to welcome us. We stared in with spellbound fascination at the gold nugget displayed on her sideboard. One would not dare to have such valuables in the house these days.

STAR TAVERN GREAT YARMOUTH AND LORD NELSON
Built in the early 17th century

The Black Death, which had killed 7,000 local people, had almost been forgotten. New invasions of Dutch settlers arrived; fine new dwellings were built along the waters edge on Hall Quay. They traded in wool, fish and grain, and made full use of the seventh haven.

The following text might be confusing in respect of the houses that were built along Yarmouth Quay as they involve family and national interest. They changed their names, position and use but basically we are discussing the history of two houses, built for rich Dutch merchants. Originally both were flint faced and looked out onto Hall Quay for four hundred years. One was originally called the Stone House and the other the Star Hotel said to have been built in 1694 by Anthony Ellys and later owned by a certain William Crowe who was also mentioned as being a successful businessman and bailiff.

A book published in 1878 gives a description of one of these fine houses The Stone House which states; *"At the Northwest corner of Row 62 is an old house with a squared and smooth cut flint front having stone dressing to the windows". It has but one storey, with dormer windows in the roof; the rooms are low, with panelled wainscot".*

This presents a good specimen of a style prevalent in the later part of the seventeenth century and passed into the possession of the Bradshaw family as a private house. It was in the time of the Bradshaw's that the house was changed to the Star Hotel. A member of the Earle family had been president of the High Court of Justice and held court in both this and the Elizabethan House further up the road, now a museum. One very large room is where they held a meeting to sentence King Charles 1st, sending him to the scaffold in 1649.

The terminus for the Stagecoach left from one of these houses to start their dangerous journeys from there to London, via Lowestoft at 2pm daily, later a new service the 4.40pm to Birmingham was added. They were often accosted by highwaymen, the equivalent of todays muggers.

Great Yarmouth was prosperous during the early 17th century; the fishing industry began to flourish, and with the new harbour completed this encouraged all types of shipping and merchants to visit Yarmouth. The settlers coming from Flanders [see item on the Huguenot's] probably brought in the **Williment's/Willimott's,** relatives on our mothers' side; we have included part of their family tree's earlier in this book.

Admiral Lord Nelson was a Norfolk man, born at the old rectory at Burnham Thorpe on the 29th September 1758, he attended Paston Grammar School and rode on horseback to this school with General William Earle Bulwer b. 1757.

Napoleon in 1800 had created a vast empire and intended to add Britain to it; a sea war between Britain and France began. Lord Nelson later landed at Yarmouth on November 6th 1800 after winning the Battle of the Nile and the enthusiastic crowd removed his carriage horses and pulled the carriage to the Wrestlers Hotel for him to receive the freedom of the borough.

It was during this ceremony that Lord Nelson laid his right hand on the book and the local dignitary insisted that Nelson place his left hand on the book instead "please my Lord", to which Nelson replied "That Sir   is most definitely in Tenerife"

It was here that a local artist named Keymer painted Nelson's portrait and where Nelson personally recruited young men to sail with him in his ship `The Gameness' and to encourage them he gave a dinner for the entire village. The portrait was presented to the Friendly Society, who later gave it to the Star Hotel and as it was a prized possession it was placed in a position of honour over the fireplace in the main room known as the Nelson Room. This gallery has grandly decorated ceiling and finely carved wall panelling. On another occasion he visited the Star Hotel; it is said that he slept in a room on the upper floor.

Nelson defeated Napoleon at Trafalgar on the 27th of September 1805, with the help of his recruited men of Norfolk but was killed in the battle. His body was returned home in a cask containing Spirits of Wine to prevent decomposing. The local public house was renamed the Nelson in 1807.

In the nineteenth century the Star Hotel was the local H.Q. for the Tory Party and they used the balcony to address the crowds below on the Quay. No doubt everyone had fun when their opponents the Whigs who had their HQ nearby also met along the Quay. Great Yarmouth was prosperous in the early seventeenth century.

The Stone House was bought in July 1890 at an Auction by our great uncle **Mr Stephen Goate,** [as stated in a previous page] who renamed the old house, "The Cromwell Commercial and Temperance Hotel". It had nine bedrooms and a bathroom. He engaged the services of a local architect Arthur Hewitt, who drew up plans for a larger building with additional upper floors amounting to a further twenty-five bedrooms.

The OldCromwell and Temperance Hotel   Plate.118

The exterior was also altered at this time to the pleasing design it has today and was completed in 1891. The Old and original Star Hotel next door was a well liked stay for author Charles Dickens where he gathered material for what was his favourite book *David Copperfield.

Many of the towns buildings are mentioned in this book and also have their place in our family history.

The old hotel closed on Sunday 21st September 1930 just before 10-pm and the site was sold to the Postmaster General for £18,500 pounds and then demolished. Everything except the panelling of the Nelson Room was removed, sold by auction and bought by the Metropolitan Museum of Art in New York. This was not the end of the old Star as the licence was transferred with all the panelling and ceilings which were removed and taken to the hotel next door which then adopted the name of the Star Hotel.

We often pass the Star Hotel but only once had enough time to stop and look it over. We will have to make a point to revisit it again in the near future on our next visit to Yarmouth as it has a place of fond affection in our hearts.

Yarmouth has many associations with well known men and women of history and literature such as Admiral Perebrowne, Sir John Falstaff, Anna Sewell [creator of Black Beauty], Daniel Defoe [who created the character Robinson Crusoe after watching a storm just off the Yarmouth port] and not forgetting Charles Dickens' book "David Copperfield".

Note; - *for more detail see Item on Yarmouth
Some information is included twice because it is important to both time periods.

RARE EVENT
A DAY AT THE SEA SIDE

Although the sea and beaches were only twenty-two miles away we seldom went anywhere that was not in of walking distance of Norwich as money in those days was needed for food and clothes. So an outing to the seaside was always an exciting prospect, but even this childish dream was soon to dashed when the beaches were mined to prevent enemy landings.

We were never told in advance of these excursions, as we would get euphoric with excitement. These were also the romantic days of steam locomotive trains that gave us such thrills when as children we boarded a carriage. Slipping away from the watchful eyes of our parents as soon as possible so that we could lean out of the trains windows to sniff the smoke, steam and soot produced by those monster machines, and gazing at them in awe as we rounded a bend in the track.

What happened when mother saw her black-faced offspring we will leave you to guess, we would all be walking home again if she had her way! For her all the romance had gone, it was now the children's dream, the tears and grit from our eyes had been wiped away; it was worth the temporary wrath of our parents with all the extra work it entailed. But the excitement for us soon returned when the shrill whistle blast from the engine told us we were near the station and a clean up. Buckets and spades at the ready, windmills spinning so fast that all the colours merged giving a rainbow of coloured lights in a circle round the centre.

Once on the beach our imaginations ran riot, sandcastles with real moats knights and royal ladies, tunnels and smugglers. **Alan** was not impressed and watched amused at his brother and sister's very vivid imaginations and their clumsy efforts.

Alan Norma and Raymond playing sandcastles   Plate.119   Perhaps they were thinking about the stories mother used to tell and not about the realities of life [Oh! The sweet, dreams of youth]. The day went so quickly it was soon time to go back to the excitement of the train and all that lovely black smoke.

THE LAST OF THE OLD SAILING BOATS

We can remember father telling us to put on our best clothes, as he wanted to show us something we might never see again. He took us to Yarmouth harbour mouth; his timing was perfect. Looking out to sea we saw just off shore, one of the most beautiful ships we had ever seen.

Plate 120

It was the last of the Windjammers looking so grand on that clear day with the morning sun giving a rosy hue to her sails that were being filled by a gentle breeze. We caught our breath watching spellbound captured in a moment of time taking in the graceful lines of her hull, and noting how she was standing in the water just off Yarmouth harbour.

All too soon she was gone, over the blue horizon of the calm sea lost from our view. The silence was broken by father saying 'I hope you took that in, as it will never be back this way again, it's an end to an era"; and so it was. Modern reproductions of sailing ships can still be seen but are only built and used for educational purposes.

Much has disappeared of the old ways to make way for new ideas in economics and technology, we expect every generation feels the same. Unfortunately some things that are irreplaceable have gone too, such as good manners and respect for other people. In spite of these lost standards, life has still much to offer, as each generation gives something for the next one to build on, but much is abandoned too because of greed and in the name of progress.

Many of the great industries that were household names in towns and cities have been bought merged or liquidated. In Norfolk Lacon's, Bullard's, Barnes and Pye, Bonds, Jarvis, Prices, Colman's, Bolton & Paul, Caley McIntosh to name but a few.

But none of these things gives us such an unforgettable recollection, which was to stay with us, as on that sunny morning when we witnessed the end of sailing ships as a means of commercial transportation. When the sails disappeared over the horizon it was truly a time of new beginnings once more, as mother always said.

REAPING THE RICH HARVEST OF THE SEA
A way of life with scenes of yester –year never to return

We cannot leave Yarmouth without mentioning its other source of prosperity, the fishing industry, and particularly the herring Drifters that brought in their catches and created a wealth of hustle and bustle combined with local colour. This section is not only an important part of Yarmouth history but also essentially the environment of our great grandfather, his brothers and sisters and all of their families who lived there.

.**Catching the Silver Darlings** Plate.121

Yarmouth became rich by exploiting the harvest of the sea. The season lasted from October to December; the drifters left port each day to reach the well stocked fishing grounds of Smith's Knoll. Drifters usually carried a crew of ten men with sleeping quarters in the aft of the wheelhouse and cabin.

In the early 1900's there were about 2,000 fishing vessels moored alongside the river bank, so tightly packed you could walk from one side of the harbour to the other over their decks. As the ships began to arrive people gathered to watch as they passed the Harbour bar and even more would come to see the fisher girls' sort and clean the fish.

The catch   Plate 122   **Fishing fleet in harbour**   Plate.123

Each vessel carried a large number of nets. The old salts used to insist that there must always be an odd number, the reasons behind this contention is not clear. It was said that if a drifter's nets were joined from end to end they would probably stretch for two miles forming a barrier below the surface that was supported by buoys and weighted by heavy ropes. Nets were thrown over the starboard side of the ship and the vessels were allowed to drift with the tide, the mizzen sail was set to keep her in line with the nets.

The engine's would be switched off and the Herring swimming into the nets were caught by their gills. During the night, each Skipper would check to decide if there was enough fish caught for them to be hauled in. As nets were dragged in over the side they were shaken, and the writhing mass of silver herring would fall to the deck and were quickly shovelled into the hold.

Sorting the fish   Plate.124

This work might take up to four hours even with a bad catch; sometimes a larger catch could take ten hours or more of very hard work and they would often stay another night if their catch was small. It seemed to us that hundreds of Scotswomen descended on Yarmouth to work during the the herring season.

Our grandfather would take us to visit his brother's butchers shop in Geneva terrace during the Herring season. We then all went to the fish market where the activity amazed us, the overpowering smell of those beautiful silver fish, and the deft fingers of the girls as they sorted through them cleaning, cutting and tossing the fish into baskets.

Happy Scotch Lasses.   Plate.124[a]

This all seemed to be done with one quick movement of the hands, which were darting in and out of the mountains of fish, working with such speed it really was a sight to witness. Their hands darting so swiftly that it was almost impossible to see individual movements in what seemed to be a never ending long stream of the silver darlings that cascaded into the wicker baskets in all their different sizes.

If their rapid methods of working were ever to be studied and recorded it would make a time study technician's pencil give off steam! Somehow they managed to converse with each other in their raw accents, and sometimes even stranger words that we dare not repeat, these were banned from our young ears by our mother.   Thousands of barrels were stacked on the South Denes awaiting the catch; this was also the place where the fishermen spread their nets to dry. Most of the fish went to curing yards to be gutted, some went to smoke houses to be cured as kippers, bloaters or red herring and were packed with ice and salt to be exported to Northern Europe.

In another area we all listened to the amusing chanting patter of the Auctioneers, as they offered and bargained prices for the fish with the buyers. The herring had been sorted according to size and quality of the catch, which buyers inspected before buying. Young boys were there in droves stringing up the silver darlings for their mothers, as herrings were a staple diet of the poorer folk in South Town, Yarmouth. One of the towns Rows was nicknamed Red Goose Row as the Red Herring was their main food. After the season had finished the local people had common grazing rights on this land.

The demand for herring declined and as the catches were still large this led to low prices. When herring numbers fell the smaller boats could not earn their keep and were laid up, as they were unable to compete with the larger vessels that had expensive gear. The romance with the sea has gone with a few boats just scraping a living; the silver darlings have

Crossing the Harbour Bar   Plate 125

almost disappeared from our coasts it seems forever.

Home at last   Plt 126

No more do those raw Scots voices ring out their cry. "Come buy my Collar Herring" across the waters. No more do the fishing smacks fill the rivers and the harbours of Norfolk and Suffolk, nor do the people come to watch as all the boats cross the harbour bar.

Our generation was possibly the very last to witness those extremely exciting experiences, or to have the same emotions we did then. We remember it as a great Norfolk event with all the foreign boats that came and with the Scots lassies bringing life and wealth to Great Yarmouth around the port area. The large merchant's houses were built here and the ordinary people were confined to the narrow streets of the Rows but all these things are now part of history.

Unfortunately [in the year Nov. 2002] due to overfishing in our traditional fishing grounds the E.E.C. banned all fishing for Cod in this area, an action which has bankrupted and brought an end to most of the fishing industry in Norfolk. This decision not only affected the boat owners and crews but many associated businesses connected to the fishing industry

THE LYDIA EVA
YH 89

PROBABLY THE LAST OF HER KIND

The last steam drifter docked at Yarmouth   Plate. 127

The Lydia Eva is the last surviving steam herring drifter and is preserved as closely as possible to her original design as a working ship of the age.

It was the last one built in 1930 for Mr. Harry Eastick of Pavilion Road Gorleston who died many years ago aged 85. His family was long connected to the fishing industry and he also owned the Berryhead, H.E. (Harry Eastick), Harry and Leonard Young, Ernie, and Herring Seashore.

When the Lydia Eva came up for disposal in May 1971 an appeal for funds was made and the Port and Haven Commissioners received a large donation from the Kleinwort Trust, which along with other public support ensured its future as an exhibition ship and she was given a berth, kindly provided free of charge.

She did leave Yarmouth for eight years for exhibition in London but was so neglected that the Norfolk Local Authorities and others decided to bring the old lady home to Yarmouth and restore her where she still lays at anchor on the river. The Lydia Eva is a major attraction for the tourists that visit Yarmouth and the East Coast.

ALL CHANGE
Food for thought/the case of supply and demand.

After King George 5th died his son Edward became the reluctant Monarch, who from early age showed his contempt for the Victorian straight-jacket that he found himself in and wanted freedom, which caused great problems for the monarchy. This story is included with more detail in the item on the 'Royal line'.

When Norwich extended its council house estates the trams in the city centre became too restrictive to their plans, so in 1936, three years before the outbreak of the Second World War it was decided to phase them out and put buses into service instead; as children we were sad to see them go.

It was exciting to ride on a tram as their highly polished wooden seats offered a lot of fun when going round corners, sliding from one end to the other, often landing on the floor. But seen from the point of view of the many cyclists, whose wheels became trapped in the sunken iron trackways and which often caused them to fall off, it must have been a relief to them when the whole system was removed.

The first buses like the trams were noisy and uncomfortable as they had solid tyres and their suspension was almost non-existent, which earned them the name of boneshakers. The one that served our area of Lakenham, Norwich belonged to Fitts Buses, and was driven by Cliffy Blyth. He comes easily to mind as he had ash blonde curly hair, and he also delivered our newspapers.

As the economy improved at this time more money became available for investments, which meant extra jobs. It was still considered a good idea for young girls to go into service as housemaids or servants of some kind, which helped them to improve their skills as future housewives and mothers leaving their husbands free to earn the wages.

Everything has changed since then, and we can see the deep thinking of Anthony Bulwer on these issues when he said women would never again be forced into domestic service but be allowed to choose and prove their worth, but the pendulum can and has in our opinion, swung a bit too far.

Lots of jobs done by people have been taken over by machines and many women earn more money than their men folk, some of whom stay at home taking the wife's former role. Family structures are now at breaking point their genealogy and books like this will become almost impossible in the future, with children unable to identify their fathers, let alone their grandfathers.

BRIAN WILLIAM [BILL] MAKES IT FIVE

On the 4th April 1937 we welcomed the new addition to our family when our brother **Brian [Bill]** arrived; the smallest baby to be born into our family yet who grew to be the tallest.

CHARLIES HOUSE
[CHILD CONTROL WITHOUT TEARS]

Every night of the week except Friday, we prepared for bed at six with a bath and story time to enable father to have his meal in peace. Then it was bedtime, which to us, especially in the summer was the start of fun. Most times during the lighter nights, one of us would think of something exciting like leaping off the headboard on to the mattress in an effort to reach the ceiling. Then followed hide and seek under beds, until fathers' patience snapped, he would run up the stairs to find us apparently asleep.

From then on he started to creep silently upstairs often catching us leaning out of windows, an ideal situation, with bare bums all in a row; there was a good slap for each one, which hurt our pride more than anything else. We had the last laugh for a time, stuffing pillows under bedclothes and listen for him creeping up the stairs, then disappear under beds, behind doors or anywhere else. Thinking we were pretending to be asleep to dodge the issue he went to give us each a whack and found himself slapping the pillows, we rolled about laughing, in our hidey-holes

After the first whack he cottoned on; by ordering us to come out from under the bed we emerged laughing, but he had some tricks up his sleeve. One had us fooled for a long time, 'Charlie's House' that he invented. In our parents bedroom was a cupboard about four feet high, which he called Charlie's House, when Charlie was angry he would make gurgling, swishing or banging noises. When extremely annoyed, he might come out and settle the score; we did not know it was a water tank with a ball valve under the control of father.

These noises caused us concern, and so not to disturb Charlie we tiptoed past his house and talked in whispers until we forgot him and our exuberant playing made Charlie start gurgling again. Finally there would be a bang when we pushed our luck sending us scurrying back to bed putting as much space as possible between Charlie's house and us. To discuss in whispers under the sheets the brave acts we would do if Charlie came out. This pleased father, now he could read his paper and enjoy his meal without interruption and did not have to raise his voice; a twist of the tap or a knock on the water pipes did the trick. If we were extra noisy a good bang on the pipe-work with a short brush was enough give him the peace he wanted.

CHAPTER X
THE DRUMS OF WAR!
<u>THE WORLD IN TURMOIL</u>

Adolph Hitler

The peace conference following the 1914-1918 war inflicted a vindictive peace on Germany and failed to gratify the territorial ambitions of Italy and Japan so these sores continued to fester through the years. The reasons that started the Second World War would require a book by itself, but basically it arose out of the inability of the League of Plate 128Nations to resist the spread of international anarchy by appeasement. The fanatical German Chancellor's [Adolph Hitler] and his Nazi Party's ambition to control all Europe at any cost followed a mad philosophy to create a German master race. To achieve this they had to first build up a massive war machine to take over other states and exterminate all the non-Aryan males in Europe by selection.

In March 1938 Germany annexed Austria and in April Britain and France pledged to defend Czechoslovakia against Germanys territorial ambitions.Prime Minister Neville Chamberlain after a conference on the 30th September 1938 with Adolph Hitler in Munich and flew home delighted with a draft agreement signed by Hitler stating that he had "achieved peace with honour and Peace in Our Time". Germany broke the pledge and Britain agreed to allow them to annex Czechoslovakia but in October German forces invaded, and started crushing Jewish establishments. In May 1939 Germany formed a 'Pact of Steel' with Italy and Germany.

Russia seeing the massive buildup of war machinery Germany had stocked tried desperately to join forces with Britain and France to attack and stop the German's, but was rebuked and a line of appeasement was adopted. Russia recognized what was to come took the attitude of if you cannot beat them, join them, and promptly signed a secret pact of non-aggression with Germany but on September 1st 1939 shockwaves traveled round the world when Germany invaded Poland. People could not believe that a secret pact existed between Russia and Germany. The two countries then carved up and shared Poland between them and Hitler started to attack the Jews in their Warsaw Ghettos. Neville Chamberlain, the British Prime Minister, called on Germany to withdraw from Poland; an appeal, went unanswered, and at 11am on 3rd September 1939 Britain declared war on Germany.

BRITAIN AND FRANCE DECLARE WAR ON GERMANY
11am September 3rd 1939

In the autumn of 1939 our family was a close one, relatives visiting one another regularly, and the young Baxter family was nearly complete. All the grandparents were still living at this time. Most people were enjoying the luxury of having a radio, which was their main connection with the outside world; it also promised to be a long hot summer.

The winter was over and no one paid much attention to the rumbles of war, our Grandfather and Grandmother Baxter were visiting again after being almost strangers to us due to the serious family dispute that had occurred several years before. We spent many happy hours together with them but his year was to be very eventful and like all children we soon adjusted, not knowing we were soon to lose both of our grandfathers in this period of time, face hunger and many terrifying nights of bombing.

Our Country Prepares to Fight

Thousands of soldiers were sent to Europe merely as a gesture of national solidarity against Germany. America was inward looking and decided not to join us and to leave Europe to sort out its own problems, but we still sent our army. Our contingent was called the British Expeditionary Force (B.E. F.). It was a lost cause as they were ill equipped and no match for the German army that had preparing for years.

Any male under the age of forty-five had to register and a whole generation quickly disappeared out of our lives leaving big gaps in industry and commerce. Our neighbour's the Ramsey's son's and daughter, had been close friends of ours for many years, donned their uniforms and left to fight. People did not move very far in those days marrying and making their home in the same area, every one knew each other. Women were called upon to work in the armament factories to aid the production of airplanes and weapons and even young ladies took on the job of lumberjacks [Jill's]. Britain was unprepared for war, and frantic efforts were made to arm the forces. The first part of the war was comparatively quiet with both sides reinforcing their defenses and preparing for attack.

Those that were not eligible for conscription being considered too old or unfit enlisted in the Home Guard called "Dads Army". They were given no weapons to use and told if we are attacked use anything to hand like pitchforks, hammers and the like; looking back this was laughable but it was all we had. Apart from missing those we knew who had left home to join the forces, all seemed quiet,and life carried on in the same way.

OUR GRANDPARENT'S [BAXTER]
FROM 1938

We have not said much about this particular Grandfather because due to a serious family dispute there was no communication following our father's bankruptcy; when we were looking for support it was sadly lacking.

When we did all get together again around 1938, we learned to love these relatives as well as our other two grandparents; they all had a great sense of fun and Grandfather mispronounced words or got them completely wrong which always made us curl up with laughter.

We spent many happy hours with them and when they died we had lost not only both of our much loved grandparents during that time, but we missed all the family stories they could have told us of their lives; time is our enemy but it is also a healer. There were two photographs of our grandparents

Grandfather Baxter. Plate.129 but it was rather unfortunate that we could only find the one of our Grandfather when he was young; the matching one of Grandmother could not be traced.

Grandfather Baxter was a clever handyman, something his daughter greatly appreciated. One very hot summer's day in 1939 he was working in her garden and became so hot he decided to go inside to cool off. Unfortunately he made a stupid mistake and chose to stand in front of the open refrigerator that resulted in his death from double pneumonia.
grandmother could not settle after his death, and after a while she moved into her daughter's house, which did not and could not last, as the daughter and son–in-law were both class conscious. Her mother was a very down to earth Norfolk lady, in fact very ribald, so much so she was about to disrupt their well-ordered, sedate and prosperous way of life.

It would be an understatement to say that she heartily disliked her class-conscious son-in-law Mr. Ernest Barber and real venom flowed between the two, inspiring her vitriolic tongue. Her blunt mannerisms and rude comments brought out the antagonism in him. In fact she became a real embarrassment while living in his house, and was totally banned from his company, which did not deter her very mischievous antics [which we found hilarious] to bring them both down to earth. Our Grandmothers son inlaw, **Mr. Barber** was a director of a large local shoe factory and would often entertain fellow directors for dinner. Grandmother would take fiendish delight in making a detour through the lounge,

carrying her used chamber pot on her way to the toilet in order to empty
it, while the guests were still enjoying their evening meal. There was an
angry response and outrage from her son in law, while howls of laughter
erupted from his guests. In fact they enjoyed her company so much they
insisted that she join them at the table on their next visit, reluctantly
Ernest Barber agreed; it was a bad mistake!

Grandmother seemed to be able to expel wind at will and when someone
asked her how she was, she looked at her son in law and said in her
broadest Norfolk dialect "Fartin full and fit to go a jarney" or "Farting
full and ready to fight" whilst grinning at her son in law. The whole room
would explode, in more ways than one and with the words "disgusting
old woman" ringing in her ears from the embarrassed son-in-law she was
ordered out of the room, leaving a split among the directors, some of
whom wanted her to remain. But **Ernest Barber** was definitely
determined to transfer her to another place out of his sight.

She later told us with a hint of a smile that she could often hear Ernest
shouting at her daughter after the guests had gone "That woman has to
go!" Needless to say Grandmother Baxter and **MR.BARBER** as she
called him would never live in the same house ever again. No one could
talk down to her without receiving a cutting humorous verbal riposte.
Granny left her daughter's home to stay with us, as you will read later.

WAR! THROUGH THE EYES OF THE CHILDREN
David was only five years old when war was declared. Like us all he
remembers more good times than bad, this is a fact of life. But what are
bad times? Looking back he concluded there are many levels of good
times, depending on how we view things. This was also the attitude of
our parents, and it created so much happiness in our family.

Like most of this generation his childhood memories were dominated by
the war years, and will stay with him forever. Although childhood
memories are intermittent, some are very clear, yet others flit in and out
of the mind like some half-forgotten old movie. **David** could sense that
the adults were very worried as he listened intently to adult talk of war,
he wondered." Who was this bad man they called Hitler"? His
involvement with war was confined to his tin/lead soldiers. Some were
Red Indians with bows and arrows, facing toy soldiers in uniform with
guns, others had horse drawn carts with big guns on them, he and his
brothers played war games for hours. But when would our war begin?
He tried to interpret the adult talk, imagining he saw lots of soldiers in
various uniforms, fighting each other on the bridge near where we lived,
what would be their weapons? What if the enemy crossed our bridge and
took the City? For a small child it was all too confusing so he was content

to leave it for his dad to sort out, and he went back to his toy soldiers and his brothers. Suddenly his play games became reality with real soldiers, sailors and airmen all around, some were men he knew, but where was the fighting that seemed to surround him; where were the baddies hiding? He asked many questions, listened with the adults to the radio news and he was more confused than ever.

Oh! It was all too much for a little boy to puzzle out so he lost interest, as children have a more sensitive attitude; he detected the urgency and worried excitement of the adults as each news item on the preparations for war was listened to with baited breath. It is a strange fact that even now after all those years there is a strong urge not to miss the 10pm. news before going to bed.

Our Living Environment

Overnight it seemed that unemployment was a thing of the past as most of the young men and women in the country were being either conscripted into the armed forces or put to work in munitions or other related war efforts. We were at war, and from then on our social structure, our way of life and attitudes toward life itself, would never be the same again. This was a dangerous time to be alive and Hitler had promised us a blitzkrieg! Our grandfather Baxter had died and it was then that we started to ask ourselves. "What was life all about? The past and the future; what did it all mean?"

How we enjoyed those magic moments of discussion round the fire; the air raids would later disrupt those loving Friday family nights, when after our baths, the table was set for father; *blackout curtains drawn tightly across windows. Air Raid Wardens patrolled the area to check for any chinks of light that escaped in case they might be seen by enemy aircraft.

In the early days of the war our chairs were placed around the fireplace in anticipation of mother's stories. This was a time of love and happiness, what tales she told, often about families from the past; Father who was late had done the shopping and proceeded to cook dinner, which to us in those days of real food shortages was wonderful.

He used his love of cooking plus a lot of ingenuity to make it worthwhile, but it was still made with meager rations. Sometimes we would finish with a singsong. When the fight to pay attention was lost, and the eyes of the younger ones closed in sleep. We later would remember these good times and find the strength, to face the horror of what the future nights would bring!

*Curtains made of thick black material to stop light showing on the outside of the house.

This book has brought back oh so clearly the memory of the reality of those bygone days. It was at this time **Alan, Raymond** and later **David** joined St. Albans church choir and felt the impact of many a hymn book thrown by the bad tempered Mr. Benson the choir master. When our minds go back to search our innermost thoughts, as to what was said during those loving hours we all spent together; the stories told by our parents remained in our minds as do the questions…Oh! If only they were here to reveal answers to those things we would dearly like to know, or even just to talk; but it is all too late, very sad words.

At first, the war was not taken seriously, as it seemed to us and everyone else to be a phony war and very far away. Everything settled down, quiet and an uneventful and remained so for a while, but soon it was to become a fight for survival; to us as children it was all a great adventure. Later, life was to become very different; our once blazing coal fire would become a dim shadow of its former glory.

Due to the shortage of fuel, wood, paper [that we screwed up into tight balls to make it last longer], old shoes with card or paper stuffed in the holes until of no more use together with any other rubbish not required was used as fuel. As long as it would burn and give off heat we were very grateful to use to cook our meals and provide warmth on those cold winter nights.

Country folk fared better than those living in towns, wood and food supplies were nearer to hand and more easily assimilated without authorities knowing. Although we did have electricity for cooking and tap water, to save electricity we used the Triplex open fire [as far as the coal or other fuel rations allowed], this cast iron fireplace not only heated the room but had the option of moving a lever to direct the heat to a back boiler for heating water or alternately to the cooking oven. It also had a hob that swiveled over the fire that was normally used for heating kettles etc. We often took turns to sit on this warm hob until one day **David** found that he had acquired painful rosy cheeks.

As time went on there was now little food to set on the table, rationing was the order of the day, many new government rulings came out, water was regulated, a brick was to be placed in water cisterns to limit the supply to flush the toilet and a maximum of five inches was allowed for bath water. Later all drinking water had to be boiled due to possible contamination when the water and sewage pipes were broken during enemy bombing and became mixed with the main drinking water supply.

Victoria Railway Station was near the centre of Norwich where Sainsbury's supermarket now stands], about 200 yards from our house which was used during the war as a coal storage and troop transit/ marshalling yard. Those called up for service reported here, were issued with uniforms and other kit then put on trains to report for active service. These troop movements were definitely on *'Jerry's' priority 'destroy' list and of course the station and the bridges were prime targets for enemy bombers. This railway line was at the bottom of our garden at the base of an embankment spanned by a road bridge which made our home a very dangerous place to live, as the German pathfinder airplanes followed this railway line as a guide into the city for their bombing runs.

One interesting fact comes to mind is that the area under the bridge was of fine sand and was an attraction to us children to play with. We used to uncover numerous clay pipes under the sand that were used many years earlier by older women who used to sit and smoke, or perhaps someone in the past must have manufactured them there.

The air raids were frightening, some even terrifying but they taught us about life and death, people, relationships, of hardship, also sadness when people we knew were killed. Neighbours really were neighbours in those days, bound together by war and necessity. It was in those dark days that mother's piano talents were greatly appreciated by us, and the local community even through the most difficult times there was always a singsong around the piano. You will read later that father was a member of the F.A.P [First Aid Party] on duty at all hours during this time.

Our excitement began when we heard trains approaching the station. "What would it be carrying this time, soldiers, guns, army lorries?" Rushing to the fence, we waited. Suddenly the locomotive would explode from the arch of the bridge, belching smoke and steam from its nostrils like some prehistoric monster. Many other engines that had worked that line years before having been brought out of mothballs, each one had its own name proudly displayed on each side or sometimes on the front. Even the very old engines were used, one golden oldie snorted smoke out of a great tall funnel that seemed out of proportion to the rest of it.

How did those soldiers fare in those cattle trucks in hot sun, rain or snow? **David** often wondered why we were so popular! They all used to shout and wave as they went by; disappearing round the bend in the track we could still hear them loudly singing all the old First World War songs. Happily it seemed to us, [but more likely it was to drown out their own anxious and disturbed thoughts], until their voices faded into silence. We did not realize then that we might have been the last contact that they had of their home city, probably reminding them also why they were fighting.

* **Slang word for Germans**

As we watched this unfolding drama, not knowing it was the start of their journey into a disastrous battle in France and the defeat at Dunkirk, many of these men would never return.

Large and weird looking enclosed electric motors with fans on each end of the shafts, were placed high up on poles or on buildings in every area of the city and tested regularly at prearranged times as a rehearsal for the real thing. These were the air raid sirens, which afterwards we all came to know only too well. They were designed to make a loud wailing noise to warn people that enemy planes were heading their way. Portable sirens were available too in case of a power failure, these had to be cranked by hand. They sounded a long series of intermittent urgent sounding notes, which we called "the crash warning", that meant there was imminent danger from planes overhead. A loud single note was the relief we waited for, as it described the enemy leaving and was called "the All Clear "; we were told in advance if they were testing the machines.

The first time the sirens had sounded for real **David** was out shopping with his mother and grandmother Bulwer and as they walked by the curved church wall on All Saints Green, a deafening wail suddenly rent the air. All traffic stopped, drivers got out of their cars to look skywards. David's mother and grandmother dropped to their knees, hands clasped in prayer. As if by clockwork things changed halfway through the Lords Prayer, when they both jumped to their feet realizing everyone else had disappeared. Both women grasped the hands of the bewildered little boy, whisked him off his feet, and raced across the road through the doors of the Tuns Public House, [later called the Wig and Whistle]. The sight of two women with a small child and no male present in his pub was a new experience for the landlord it was just not done in those times.

Air raid or not, business, was business, he gladly took their money for double whiskies, which were downed much more quickly than the women intended. Before the last drop had entered their mouths, the "All Clear" sounded. The two women being Salvationists realized they had succumbed to the demon alcohol; made for the door and left the public house dragging the bewildered child behind them onto the street even more quickly than they came in, hoping their Salvationist friends had not spotted their misdemeanor.

They now seemed extremely happy doing their shopping. When **David** asked them if the war was now over, whether it was the whiskey or not it took them quite a few moments to stop laughing. If this was war at least it was fun thought David. This story was told on many occasions as in those times if women were even seen near a public house, or smoking a cigarette, it was frowned upon.

Any women who did was thought to be of low moral standard and them of all people being strong Salvationists. Our mother and grandmother getting high in a pub was the highlight of their lives. Especially if you knew the character of our grandmother! She had prudish ways and always dressed very primly, a bit snobbish and very conscious of other people's opinions. After the scare of the morning on All Saints Green the adults talked and concluded that the raid was a rehearsal for a possible air attack on us that night. Our parents decided it would be a good idea, to have our grandparents (mothers side) come and share our already overcrowded house at Mansfield Lane until the war was over although no one realized at the time it would last six years.

The first night they stayed with us to the shock of everyone the siren sounded! 'Panic stations,' everyone frantically struggled with their gas mask with the added problem of poor Bill still a baby who had to be totally enclosed in his gas mask. After the all clear sounded we were exhausted, no one went to bed that night and we sat huddled round the fireplace. To our surprise nothing happened. For all of us children our first school was St. Marks infants, **David** well remembers the school party, for the coronation of King George 6th, where they served the luxury dessert chocolate Semolina. No persuasion of any sort could persuade young **David** to eat it. Not even by Miss Rowlands the head mistress. The family found afterwards that **David** thought it was what we as young ones describe as Ka Ka; and no way would he have it near his mouth.

Another amusing incident at this school worth mentioning was when our family among others, was invited to form a guard of honour for a local dignitary when he visited the school on Empire Day. Unfortunately Miss Rowlands who was the Headmistress chose to take a position alongside our brother Raymond. While holding the children's hands on each side to stop them surging, she leant forward to peer round the corner to check the dignitary's arrival. With his free hand Raymond tipped her very large black hat forward with his flag on a stick and for her everything went black. She was unable to see and could not to release her grip on the children, began shouting through her hat "Everyone stand still", with the dignitary surprised to see her appearance; she was furious; Raymond was never her favourite pupil.

Nobody would confess or tell so retribution was bestowed on everyone! It was the last party at St Mark's infant school as it was bombed shortly after. [It still exists as a commercial unit]. Soon after this the adjoining St. Marks Junior School was totally destroyed by incendiary bombs. David was sent to the modern *Cavel Road Infants School Lakenham

*The old Cavel School building was demolished and a new modern school replaced it in 2005

THE CHILDREN ARE EVACUATED
The words on everyone's lips as evacuation fever took hold and Norma loses her best friend

A disturbing event happened in 1939 when the government asked parents if they would like to evacuate their children to Canada or Australia. The government considered Britain was liable to be invaded and decided to get them to a safer environment. It was planned to move the children from London first into rural areas, then later gave the parents a choice either to have them remain in England and face the obvious dangers or evacuate to Canada and other colonies. Mother would not let us go, saying that we all should face the dangers together as a family

Due to an incident when a bomb fell in the field near **Norma's** friend Ivy Aldhams house, it slightly deafened her and gave a reason for a family discussion on the children's future and evacuation. The children excitedly agreed to emigrate but they understood it could be the last time they saw their parents. Another bomb fell at the top of Queens Road, near what used to be a butchers shop. Ivy's sister Joan found the butcher lying dead over some sacks when she was sent to buy some meat for the family.

Class 3a of Lakenham Norwich

Senior Girls School City Road

Norma Baxter, June Gibbs

Pearl Thompson,

Betty Hood, Muriel Moore,

Marvelyn Pye,

Ivy Aldham, Beryl Carr,

Beryl Dickerson   Plate 130

In view of these incidents they decided it was best to send their family away, as they had relatives in Canada. Great secrecy was maintained; the children were kept at home and not seen for months before they sailed. Although the war was tragic it brought some memorable occasions such as when dad was dozing in front of the fire after a hectic night with no sleep. Without warning there was a terrific bang which rudely awakened him.

Everyone was in a panic and made one dive to get under the small table, resulting in the last one pushing the first one out the other end. We finally controlled ourselves and rolled about on the floor laughing, until the guns began to fire and it all began again. We later learned that a strangely shaped canister had fallen from the sky, which had landed 50 yards away and went to investigate, much against our parent's wishes. Daylight air raids brought their own horrors and also some amusement as **Norma** vividly remembers, still reminiscing over her school days.

One day before her best friend Ivy embarked for Canada she sat at her desk at school and stole a glance out of the window. The sky was perfect and looked so inviting but to her horror she noticed the silvery streak of a plane flying very low and banking towards the school as it opened fire on targets below; we all disappeared under the desks including the teacher Miss Chapel who was rather large. Her dress covered her shoulders as she threw herself down; with some parts higher than she intended revealing a large backside covered with a vast expanse of pink drawers. A titter went round the classroom but we no longer laughed when we later heard what happened during the attack. The factory girls had left their shift at Carrow works and began to climb up the steep hill and as they reached the black tower the German plane swooped; there was no time or place for them to hide. They presented a perfect target on the steep hillside and the Hill ran red with their blood.

Many died there on that lovely summer afternoon; others were so shocked that they later had to have treatment. The ambulance crews were summoned, to take away the dead the wounded and the dying. On another occasion a group from Norwich after spending the night sleeping on the golf course to escape the bombing realised they had to get a heavily pregnant young woman home very quickly and seeing a slowly moving army vehicle flagged it down. Refusing to listen to the soldier's protest they climbed in the back demanding help. After the truck moved they were shocked to find themselves sitting beside an unexploded bomb.

Almost 1,500, 000 children were evacuated from Britain from 1939-1941 onwards; among them was our friends the Aldham family who disappeared from our lives. Sadly their father died shortly after they left. It was dangerous journey they embarked on, ships were attacked en-route, one ship full of children was sunk and all were lost.

Norma kept in contact with her friend through those war years until she married and then lost Ivy's address, it was not until 1988 that they resumed contact through the efforts of Ivy's cousin who must have phoned all the Harts in Norfolk and we extend our thanks to him. Norma called Ivy in Canada; they exchanged addresses once more, there was so much to catch up on; it was arranged that Ivy and a friend should come and meet Norma in London for the first time in fifty years. Norma was grateful to have met her friend. Ivy and her companion, made plans to return again but Ivy died from a heart attack two years before this could happen. 200 people attended her funeral and she was as greatly missed.

Note; of the four sisters who went to Canada one died leaving a young family, one suffered a stroke and bad nerves due to being parted from her mother at the young age of seven. Some time later a thug murdered another sister.

ENGLAND EXPECTS!!!

Our tranquil way of life was turned upside down, fathers, brothers, sisters, aunts, neighbours all disappeared in a tide of uniforms. Father was exempt from the armed forces as he was of the older generation but was expected to defend the homeland and to provide emergency services.

When the Anderson shelter was delivered the job of bolting together the sheets of galvanized steel was a major task and a large hole was dug to accommodate it; the shelter, chicken house and run took up much of our back garden. Every large family had a one, usually shared with another couple from nearby; ours was shared with Mr. and Mrs. Cole next door. It stood three feet high above the ground and was covered with earth on which we grew marrow's cucumbers and flowers.

Elsie Cole

Woolworth's Fire Team [Elsie is middle row]   Plate. 131
Photo by Derek Edwards. Copyright Norfolk Museums and Archaeology Service

Elsie Cole our neighbour's daughter joined Woolworth's Fire Prevention Team who on a rota basis had to patrol their place of work day and night reporting any possible danger and fighting the fires caused by incendiary bombs. A frightening experience for any woman especially when there were no lights allowed; not even a torch. The Ramsey family, our other neighbours had their own shelter. Those with no gardens shared a communal shelter specially built usually above ground, near their homes that held many people.

In May 1940 Winston Churchill was elected Prime Minister, he proved to be a strong leader during a time of great danger. All agreed this was the war to end wars, a blitzkrieg, a war at lightning speed that would use air power with bombing from modern planes to flatten the enemy [or drop deadly gas canisters that could knock out a city in one raid], thankfully this never happened here. The latest German tanks could advance at such speed and overrun any army using conventional weapons. Our army was ill prepared and badly equipped.

Everyone said the war would all be over quickly but were unaware there were to be many sleepless nights in store. Father had finished working at Corns Brush Works and joined the rescue and ambulance patrols, known as the First Aid Party (F.A.P.). Of course the extra adults in the very overcrowded house, with five growing children full of mischief did not work out and the grandparents soon moved back to their own home.

DUNKIRK OUR FINEST HOUR
The battle of the little boats

It was termed the Battle of Britain, but in reality it was the battle for Britain and began when Hitler commanded that a Blitzkrieg would start on Holland Belgium and France. In May 1940 Allied forces were taken completely by surprise; outnumbered outgunned, and fighting against a well equipped fully trained modern German army, our troops did not have a chance to make a stand against them.

They were forced to retreat to the beaches of Dunkirk where they were trapped with their backs against the sea to be shot to pieces on the sands. These brave men stubbornly continued, and refused to surrender; A massive effort was then

Volunteers waiting for the call to sail   Plate 132   very hastily engineered to rescue them from the French coast. This was attempted by ordinary people no matter what age or state of health who were not a part of the fighting forces and who owned a craft some as small as a rowing boat. They volunteered to take their boats from England across the Channel to bring home our troops who were frustrated, tired and exhausted from out of the death trap they were in. This they did, sailing right through the bombs and bullets to return them temporally to their families; this endeavour is remembered as the battle of the little boats for all time to come.

Amazingly of the 338,000 French and British soldiers that were originally sent to fight, 335,000 had been snatched off the shores of Dunkirk and brought home in operation Dynamo. They lost the battle but they did not lose the war. Army and seafarers alike were all extremely brave people; it was quite an outstanding achievement, a tribute to our Royal Navy, all those little civilian boats, the Merchant Navy and our brave soldiers who refused to surrender. By the morning of June 4th 1940 the evacuation was ended.

Note; Facts derived from the book 'Our finest hour' by Martin Gilbert

In 1940 life changed dramatically and it was a very different Britain; beaches were barbwired and mined and trips to the sea were banned. Seafaring villages were emptied, troops took them over, their occupants moved inland placing the villages out of bounds to the public and classed as military zones. Beaches continued to be mined and the slogan 'Careless talk costs lives' came into being. Factories were reorganised to make munitions and war equipment. Boulton and Paul of Norwich turned from making wire netting to barbed wire and aeroplanes. Laurence Scott also diverted, from generators to winches for shipping, and other war efforts. Both these factories were situated near railways for ease of movements and were the targets for the German bombers. The main task was to destroy German air power [the Luftwaffe] if we had failed we would have undoubtedly lost the war.

We were still young children, but even now find it hard to imagine the Britain of our youth. Each man woman and child was issued with a National Identity Card, which was always carried and had to be produced when asked for by those in authority. Food, clothes, sweets, coal and all other types of fuel were rationed. Most intriguing of all was the radio personality William Joyce, known to all as Lord Haw Haw who was reputed to have kept a paper shop before the war on the corner of Grove Road, Norwich. He moved to Germany to take charge of the German Radio propaganda.

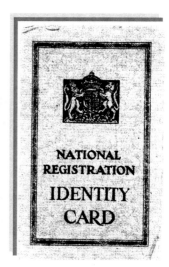

Plate.133

He uncannily knew when the Norwich City Hall clock was slow, and he took pleasure in informing us of these facts in his daily propaganda programme and also warned of various air raids; his catch phrase was "Jarmuny Calling, Jarmuny Calling" ["Germany Calling, Germany Calling"] spoken in an upper class English accent on the German radio. There were active German spies in all areas. After the war Joyce (Lord Haw Haw) was caught, and although an American citizen, tried and hung as a English traitor for his efforts. We were totally defenceless, out numbered, and out gunned with very few aircraft at the beginning of the war. But with courage and determination knowing the odds were against us, the people and the British forces put on a brave front. Churchill inspired the people to be courageous in the face of the enemy. His slogan was;

"We will fight on the beaches we will fight on the shores..
We will never surrender"
and we never did!

THE BATTLE OF BRITAIN

*"Never before in the field on human conflict
was so much owed by so many to so few"*
Winston Churchill

In the summer of 1940 for ten long weeks Britain stood alone, while the RAF fought their battles in the skies to gain control of the airspace overhead. Whilst Hitler prepared to invade England under project "Sea Lion" we found ourselves vulnerable and open to attack until material help arrived from U.S.A. Hitler started his Blitzkrieg to soften us up. In Britain anyone who could fly a plane, young and old were enlisted, trained to fly anything that could be armed and get off the ground.

German Bombers attack   Plate.134

These pilots with their back up teams kept the planes in the air sometimes twenty-four hours a day. We watched as they attacked the German intruders zooming round and round high above our heads, often looking like small silver dots dancing in the arch of the brilliant blue skies above, until one side or the other either fled or were shot down in flames.

There were no defences ready to ward off an invasion, unbelievable but true; in place of guns we gathered up our pitchforks, pickaxes, and anything we could throw or use as a weapon. Hitler promised us a blitzkrieg, and he kept his word as some of the most terrifying moments of our lives were spent in air raid shelters during 1941/2 listening to the high pitched shriek of the Stukas and the whistle of the bombs descending. We only found comfort when the night sky was dark cloudy and overcast. But it was those oh so beautiful brilliant moonlit nights, with their sparkling stars, [you could really see them then] that brought fresh terror. There was a popular descriptive film about the war in Poland called **Everwatching eyes**   Plate 135 "Dangerous Moonlight that portrayed the terror of those times.

Local units called 'The Home Guard" were recruited, composed of older men and laughingly referred to as Dads' Army that had uniforms but no weapons. Several crashed enemy pilots who parachuted to safety were held prisoner with a British pitchfork pressed firmly against their ribs until help arrived, it was all we had for home defence.

STARVATION
The Menace of the U. Boat

Having survived Dunkirk, and become masters of the skies, we now to protect our merchant fleet. They were a brave section of the unarmed forces in the forefront of the battle of the seas. They had no protection, and were very vulnerable to attacks from merciless U-boats. Hitler decided to stave us into submission and as the blockade of Britain became serious the government had brought in ration books from 1940, as transporting food was the Achilles heel for this country.

The Germans noted this fact and were determined to starve us into submission so 'Dig for Victory' became the slogan and we did just that. Pig Clubs started, vacant cages were used in London Zoos to create extra space and gardens were made into vegetable plots. All kinds of food was grown and nothing was wasted. It was mother's daily problem to find some sort of meal and how to get enough to feed her growing family, as food was always scarce and meagre. Our family was scraping their plates clean and like majority of the country began to seek out anything that was edible; we were at this time really on the breadline. Dad obtained an allotment to provide us with sufficient vegetables and had constructed a hen house and run in our back garden.

If our artillery fire or fighters became too ferocious for the German bombers they unloaded their surplus bombs anywhere and made a dash for home. It was while helping his dad on our allotment, **David,** [aged about six years] excitably ran to his father with a finned object saying, "Look what I found Dad". Father almost took root; he gently removed the incendiary bomb from the childs hands placed it on the ground and both ran to safety. We will not go into the resulting discussion but it was the last weeding David did on the allotment. The authorities introduced a wonder chicken food additive called Karswood, a brightly coloured brown powder that smelt vile. It was mixed with scraps of food such as potato peelings and old cooked vegetables etc. We still remember that!

Father instructed us in the job of feeding the chickens; often we got the mixture wrong, but this additive had a tremendous effect on the egg laying power of the hens. The poor hens often laid eggs as big as tennis balls, sometimes with no shells. Whether they died of fright or the exertion we don't know, but father was not pleased when another of his precious egg-laying hens passed away even if he was given an egg so large it was too big for his egg cup. We never gave a thought to the poor old cockerel that also had to eat this powder! And come to think of it, so did we when we ate the chicken.

RATIONING FOR THE NATION

Until food became scarce, people were not aware of the contribution made by the brave merchant seamen to keep food lines open; there was very little commendation either during the war or after it for them. Many were torpedoed and sunk, many died in order to feed the nation.

Enthusiasm for the all-too-common queues which rationing enforced was not widely shared in wartime Britain.

Ration Books   Plate. 136

The ration book and clothing card etc. issued by the government contained several pages of coupons marked with the day week and year. At times it was a case of first come first served and of course queues formed even before the shops opened. Every time a ship was sunk we lost vital supplies of food, oil or equipment and rations were reduced. Norma once complained about lack of food so father handed her a ration book, and told her to get on with it. She realised her mistake and returned the Ration Book into the family pool.

Soap was in short supply and as there were few stockings of the nylon variety, girls would use leg tan to darken their legs, even putting a dark line with eyebrow pencil down the centre of the back of the leg to imitate a back seam, which they found extremely difficult to do.

The average weekly amounts of food per adult were as follows.	
*Bacon and Ham	4 ozs. A week [100 grams]
*Butter	2 ozs a week. [50 grams]
*Margarine	4 ozs a week [100 grams]
Meat	To the value of one shilling
Cheese	2 ozs a week [50 grams]
Sometimes doubled to	4 ozs a week [100 grams]
Cooking fats	4 ozs a week [100 grams]
Tea	2 ozs a week [50 grams]
Coffee	often made from dried .
	Dandelion leaves and blanched acorns.
*Sugar	8 ozs. A week [225 grams]
Milk	Often falling to two pints.
Dried Milk	One tin/packet every four weeks.
Preserves	lb [450 grams every two months.
Eggs	lb [450grams]
Fish	Un-rationed and cheap .
Sweets	2ozs./350 grams every four weeks
Bread	Unrationed and cheap.

We registered our ration books with the butchers and grocers where we collected and paid for food. Our choice was the local shopkeeper. Mr. Scott of St. Johns Close for groceries and the meat from Mr. Stockings of St. Stephens Street in the City who would order stock

Note: - January 1940 * sugar, butter and bacon were rationed. Shop eggs were always stamped with a little crown, and Bill the youngest boy could not understand why our hens always forgot to stamp ours.

accordingly. Our chickens were a great source of food and one cooked chicken could feed the family for three days; first oven cooked, then cold and finally the bones and scraps were used with vegetables in a hot pot or soup. The amounts supplied from the shop varied according to what shipping had arrived and the allocation for each person was controlled by the Government. At intervals the government announced the quantity that would be supplied for each coupon depending on availability of stock, which as we said depended totally on the brave merchant fleet getting supplies past the U boats. Later in the war it often fell to **David** to get the meat and also try and get any un-rationed meat products from Malcolm's market stall, such as a penny worth of cattle bones or animal intestines [chitterlings and tripe] to add to the family rations.

AMERICA ENTERS THE WAR

In March 1941 America agreed to sign a pledge that they would give material support to Britain's war effort on a Lend Lease arrangement.
On the 17th of October 1941 Tojo became head of the Japanese State and by then the Americans were expecting some form of aggression to start somewhere in the East. However they were caught by surprise when in December 1941 escaping detection and without any opposition Japanese aircraft swept in from the sea and hurled themselves at the American base at Pearl Harbour in Hawaii.

The first attack began about 7.55am on 7th December 1941 lasting about half an hour; there were four separate torpedo bomber attacks. America's introduction to total war came with the greatest naval defeat since the battle of Trafalgar, which was made possible on the Japanese side by a combination of superb training, and remarkable duplicity and American total negligence. The first two attacks were directed at the main targets the battle ships, lined up in battleship row, on the Southeast shore of Ford Island. The third attack was by a single plane on the cruiser Helena and the fourth assault struck ships on the North of the island.

Japan also began attacking the British forces in such as places as Malaya, Singapore, [where sadly we heard that our neighbour Cyril Ramsey was listed as missing] and other places in the Far East. They drove the allied forces down the West Coast of Malaya, led by Lieutenant General Yamashita's XXV army. The British retreated into Singapore totally demoralised without the command of sea or air on the 31st January 1942. At 7am on 15th February Lieutenant General Arthur Percival GOC Malaya surrendered to Japanese Commander Lieutenant General Yamashita. This was a bitter blow, as we had lost many men following a brave stand. A dismal fate awaited these prisoners who received callous treatment by the Japanese and many died.

AIR RAID PROTECTION

Because all of the national effort was concentrated on weapon production the self-protection element was neglected and it was some time after the war started large public shelters were built. **David** remembers that a big area of the Lakenham Cavel school playing field was roped off and children were warned by Mr. King [the Headmaster] that there would be severe punishment for anyone found on the wrong side of the rope. Two massive monster diggers arrived and started clawing three large holes in the ground, so deep they went out of sight. Three underground shelters were built, with 30 steps leading down into them at each end. They were six-foot wide, eight-foot high, thirty foot in length, with slatted seats on each side. The only one allowed to carry a torch was the teacher, for obvious reasons.

On arriving at school, the first thing **David** had to do was place a cloth band over one shoulder. These were bands of different colours according to the class you were in. In the event of an air raid, the teacher in charge of the class had a flag with the corresponding colour to the band we wore and had to follow this into the shelters. Once inside the teachers would then call the register; not that it made any difference, trying to control two classes in semi-darkness was almost impossible though some order was maintained. Everyone used to join in a singsong, or recite the numerical (times) tables to pass the time.

The children practised this procedure regularly and so did not panic when this became a reality, as one morning with no pre-crash signal the crash warning siren sounded. Leaving the classroom they walked in single file to the shelter, and started to descend the steep steps. A lone German bomber roared overhead on a trial run to bomb Hartford Bridges, a railway viaduct carrying passenger and freight trains to London from the East Coast. The children froze! Then pushed forward, those on the steps trampling those that had fallen, luckily no one was hurt but as everyone laughed; the plane roared back again and there was a terrific explosion.

The teacher eventually calmed things down, and encouraged everyone to sing songs until the all clear sounded; the bomb had missed its target and landed in adjoining fields. We sometimes stayed out in the open to watch, fascinated by the planes, caught up in the excitement of the chase going on far above our heads. This was stupid, as there were plenty of nasty things in the way of shrapnel, falling out of the skies. Enemy planes were not averse to machine gunning anything that moved even small children or animals. It was on one of those bad nights of three air raids and father was still out on duty; during the third and worst raid of the night Raymond went missing.

He was there when we once again all pulled our clothes on during the siren but not when mother did her head count in the shelter so Alan being the oldest boy was despatched to find him. Going into the blacked out house with the noise of war all around outside, he found Raymond swaying gently at the top of the stairs fast asleep. He had only got as far as putting on his shirt. Alan gently led him to the shelter where Ray collected his thoughts, embarrassed but no doubt pleased it was pitch dark. No matter what the weather, we had to make it to the shelter and it was an added blessing for Raymond that this was a night when there was no frost!

CHRONOLOGY 1938 - 1942

1938 **September** Prime Minister Neville Chamberlain signs deal with Chancellor Adolph Hitler which allowed Germany to annex parts of Czechoslovakia but in **October** German forces attack it.

1939 **September** 1st; Germany invades Poland and Chamberlain announces at 11am 3rd **September** that Britain was at war with Germany and World War 2 starts. **October** American President Franklin D. Roosevelt's first warning of the production of an atomic bomb. **December** the last un-rationed *Christmas dinner.

1940 **February,** Hitler orders a full blockade of shipping to Britain and 'U' boats cause disruption of our food supplies **May**; Churchill forms a government. **June** defeat at Dunkirk and the last British troops are evacuated. Italy declares war on Britain. An invasion from Europe is expected. **August;** the Battle of Britain. **September;** the blitz of British cities

1941 Our sister **Ann** was born on 20th **February** in the middle of an air raid. **May;** German battleship Bismark sunk. **December**; Japan bombs American ships in an unprovoked attack. Many ships are sunk while at anchor in Pearl Harbour. America declares war on Japan and their ally Germany and joins with the British

1942 **January**; Japan takes Philippines, Malaya, Indonesia and Singapore; [our neighbour Cyril Ramsey taken prisoner] **April,** U.S. aircraft bomb Tokyo. **August**; Germans make mistake in laying siege to Stalingrad [and in 1943 pay the penalty of the Russian winter]. **October**; General Bernard Montgomery attacks General Irwin Rommel at El Alamein, **John Bulwer** was killed there. We won this battle, sadly Knebworth lost a son and heir.

As a note of interest even before the war Christmas dinners were not only a special event but probably the only time we would have a chicken for dinner and these were a luxury until dad reared his own. Turkey was certainly not on the menu for ordinary people. Fruit and vegetables were seasonal foods as they were not imported or stored as they are today.

George Swein was a photographer travelled around the bomb torn streets of Norwich on his bicycle to capture the horror of those times. On one occasion he arrived at the bombed out Hippodrome Theatre in the smoke and rubble heard a strange and terrible wailing noise. Searching through the wreckage he found a sea lion that had escaped and was looking for his master who unfortunately had been killed along with the manager and other staff. The Hipperdrome was rebuilt and became a popular venue for Norwich people and was typical of the entertainment of that time catering for general audiences with comedian's, singers and a host of international variety acts.

Amoung the stars of the early fifties and sixties who appeared there were; Laurel and Hardy, Marie Lloyd, Charlie Chaplin, Flanigan and Allen, Sandy Powell, Max Miller, Elsie and Doris Waters, Anne Shelton, Hutch, and Phyllis Dixie the stripper. Prices ranged from two shillings and nine pence for the stalls, ten to fifteen shillings for a box. To sit in the cheapest seats which were high up [termed in the Gods] and furthest away from the stage, you suffered from a hot stuffy and smoke filled atmosphere. For this privilege you queued for tickets at the tradesman's' entrance.

In those days there was more audience participation, and boo's and yells could be heard for quite a distance. The competition between the Old Hippo [as it was called then] and the Theatre Royal nearby caused the old Hippodrome to close for a few months. It was during the sixties, in David's teenage years, he took great interest in the art forms at Norwich Hippodrome, which provided exotic tableaux scenes in the form of nudes. In those days the show was only legal providing the young ladies kept perfectly still and did not make the slightest movement.

There was a constant battle amongst the lads to obtain the front stalls and armed with peashooters and a load of peas [dried ones!] they tried their hardest to get their aim straight with the frantic manager trying to keep the situation under control. Unfortunately the nude performers were forced to retreat under a hail of hard peas so the manager had to terminate the performance and close the safety curtain or lose his licence. These shows continued but the fun was over, as the manager had to provide netting to protect the artists and his licence.

The Hipperdrome remained open until the spring of 1960 then it was closed and left empty. It was sold in 1966 to the great disappointment of the people of Norwich.

This has prompted our memory to a joke we played on our parents as a surprise when we booked a box at the Theatre Royal, Norwich, normally used by dignitaries. Mother did not consider this as a joke and we had a hard job trying to get her to take a seat with the main audience staring up wondering who this family was.

Now returning to the war era it was reported that in York a hardworking Reverend heard noises coming from a heap of rubble that was once a house, he took off his jacket, laid it on the ground and franticly dug a space for an old codger to climb out and then went to get him a cup of tea. When he returned the old codger had gone and so had his wallet along with the coat. Oh well, blessed are the poor! Often the people of Norwich when out shopping would suddenly hear the loud roar of aircraft engines as a low flying Dornier, Heinkel or Stuka bomber streaked above them on its way to pick a target. This would cause mass panic and as Norwich was often undefended they had the freedom of the skies [for a time!].

There are many stories of the war that could be told such as a hit and run air raid on July 9th 1940 when a sudden attack on Norwich left twenty six dead. By the end of the war 330 had died and 1100 were wounded. With all the terror around us as children we accepted what the days and nights would bring and the public in general made life as happy as possible. Life went on and it is amazing how people will adapt to the most serious situations. In one newspaper it was reported that during a wedding there was no warning of an air raid until the service was interrupted by a roar of planes, a loud explosion and part of the church roof caved in. It did not deter their enthusiasm to complete the ceremony they just moved into the other side of the church and continued singing, except for the organist who had decided to leave in a hurry.

1941 OUR FAMILY COMPLETE
But without Derek whom we all still missed

Mother was now having her seventh and last child and could not use the outside shelter. The boys had joined the 1st Norwich Sea Scouts and organised a team of older scouts to erect an indoor Morrison shelter so she did not have to go outside to the Anderson shelter. It was big enough for us all to crawl inside and looked rather like a large chicken coop, with its top and bottom made of strong sheets of steel. The sides were heavy wire mesh, one side of which was removable. We soon made use of it as our stage complete with curtains [when our parents were out].

The boys enticed their Scout leader to inspect the bolts on the inside and once there they promptly hooked the side on. He was trapped, like a chicken in a run with his tormentors on the outside flapping their arms and clucking like chickens, from then on he was known as Chicken Davis. He was often seen walking his two huge St. Bernard dogs, which the locals eyed with suspicion, as it was said they ate two bucketful's of meat every day, the question was where did he get the meat, and how?

Chicken Davies was quite a well-known local character and his charisma enabled him to mix easily with leading Norwich citizens. He had a full and active life but his interests unfortunately led to him becoming the focus of local gossip bringing him to the attention of the law, which led to his early death.

Our sister Ann arrives in the middle of an air raid.

Ann started to announce her arrival when dad was out coping with one of the worst air raids of the war. The screeching noise of the Stuka planes, the explosions and then crashing sound of brickwork collapsing was too much for our mum as we all crouched with hands clasped around our heads. It was the only time we ever saw her cry. She cried for dad, who was out there with death happening all around him, pulling men women and children from the rubble. Mother asked us to pray with her for his safety as we huddled together in the Morrison shelter.

The baby was coming and **Norma** was the only one able to help at this time, she was just thirteen. Mother said to her. If I can't hold out will you be brave and fetch the midwife for me. **Norma** agreed, but prayed heavily that Dad would return before she had to honour that promise and face the unknown dangers that were everywhere out there on the streets. Her prayers were answered as father arrived home in the early hours of the morning, tired, white faced and exhausted, his eyes were red rimmed with smoke and tears. Had she been older, she would have spared him the trip and fetched the midwife herself; when questioned about that terrifying night all he would say was, "It was beyond belief. "We made him a cup of tea before he went for the Midwife and our sister **Ann** arrived on the 20th February 1941, completely unaware of the trauma of the night.

Grandmother [mothers mother] early in her marriage had been through a very hard time with grandfather, who seemed to have inherited the Bulwer addiction to gambling. However she was strong willed and won the fight by taking his wages, debiting the money owed for housekeeping and returning the surplus, but considering the past she was heartbroken when he died. For us too the year 1942 started badly,

Grandfather Bulwer's health had been failing for some years. We used to sit on his knee while he told us stories and he always found time to play games with us. But gradually he became short of breath and could no longer cope with our boisterousness, we knew he was ill and were also very distressed but understood. He became really ill and we lost our second grandfather the on the 26th January 1942 Grandmother became very depressed, very lonely and demanding more and more of her daughter's limited time.

She was inconsolable, the shock of her husband's death developed into pneumonia; our mother was obviously torn apart between her duty to her mother and her own children. Father was kept busy with the dead and the dying from the air raids, there being so many, the city mortuaries were unable to cope.

Front row Mother Ann as a baby] Raymond aged 10 years David 8, Bill [Bryan aged 6 years Grandmother   Plate.137 Back row. Norma aged 14 years Alan aged 12 years

Mother through the extra work with **Ann,** who demanded her mother's constant attention; the nightly raids and lack of sleep, was exhausted by all the constant hard work with her new baby but our Grandmother's pneumonia became worse, and so **Raymond** and **David** were now appointed to stay and care for granny untill mother could get there.

Two of her friends helped at night. The two boys who were still quite young sometimes became very bored with minding their **Grandmother,** so during the day they developed games to help pass the time, which sorry to say became, to put it mildly very noisy, as they did not fully appreciate how ill she really was. **Grandmother** died in her sleep on April 27th 1942 during one of the worst air raids in the war. The doctor said she died of a broken heart in her flat, amid the falling bombs and diving planes.

It was a great pity that just before our grandmother Bulwer died, she, in a delirious state changed her will. She must have had the assistance of others to take this action but whatever reason they had for doing this we never found out. Sadly she left her entire financial resources to the local hospital and nothing to her only daughter. This was a bitter blow, which our mother did not deserve. Although the will could not now be altered; after the intervention and help from a relative we received a token amount from the hospital, out of pity more than anything to our impoverished family. This money would have put us back on our feet, but that's life for you, which at this time was proving to be very difficult for us all

We checked her flat each day to see if the explosions all around had disturbed the coffin. A daunting task for us as our parents had no time to do this in the struggle to survive. Imagine the effect on us when we found the coffin had moved off the trestles during an air raid.

As her burial took place, we remember the soldiers standing to attention and saluting as her coffin passed en route to Old Lakenham Church; how she would have loved that had she known. Death through warfare did not touch our family then, but it almost did later in the war, as you will see. **Norma** had taken the scholarship exams the day after the bomb killed her classmate. She passed the scholarship but never knew whether this was on merit or compassion for the days and nights were bad in the extreme.

Norma was a quiet home loving girl, who liked nothing better than to curl up with a book in front of the fire [when coal rationing allowed]. But dad was concerned for her future and encouraged her to go out and make friends, and if possible find a boyfriend. This notion was not to her liking, she had four brothers, and that was enough for anyone wasn't it? But he persisted and finally she agreed; she liked dancing, though she did not find it easy to make friends, so dad used to meet her and take her home as American servicemen always hung around the entrances to these places.

This was a terrible part of the war with constant night air raids sometimes three times in one night. Yet despite lack of sleep the war also had its funny moments such as when father was off duty, catching up [if he could] with some well-earned sleep when the crash warning siren went off, we all tumbled out of bed grabbing our clothes and dressing as we went to make a dash for the shelter

The Boars Head Surrey Street   Plate. 138

Photo by Derek Edwards Copyright Norfolk

Museums and Archaeology Service

Our minds became half deadened with weariness. Everyone was present except father, who half-a sleep, in the dark was having difficulty with his clothes. In her hurry mother had abandoned modesty, and left her long bloomers lying on the bed. Father, somehow in the urgency mistook them for his trousers. We all met in the shelter where the loud shouts and of laughter made all the close neighbours enquire the reason for our hilarity. The news of father's attire was relayed from shelter to shelter, much to his embarrassment.

The noise of the bombers had been drowned out for a moment or two of light relief. Somehow we still managed to communicate with our neighbours across the gardens with another moment of fun in the heat of an air raid, defying those intent on our destruction. Our period of fun ended when there was a piercing scream from the Ramsey side of the fence.

 In the darkness their mother had sat on a hedgehog and had no idea what it was, but she certainly felt it, thinking it was perhaps some practical joke by her family. This was enough to bring out the whole neighbourhood to enquire who was being attacked. But this time it appeared it was the son being attacked by his mother. The next four nights were the worst of the war, we had no sleep, and rows of houses disappeared into piles of rubble. During these raids the city centre was unrecognisable. We have inserted some pictures of well-known local Norwich buildings, places that were damaged and have since been rebuilt.

The old thatched theatre All Saints Green   Plate.139
Photo by Derek Edwards. Copyright Norfolk Museums
and Archaeology Service

What was once the heart of the city was gone leaving a pile of twisted and burnt buildings, from Orford Place to Theatre Royal was just an open wasteland. Brigg Street had vanished, just flattened. The stores of Woolworth's and Curl Brother's [now Marks and Spencer], were now only just burnt out shells open to all weather's.

After the rubble was cleared a huge hole in Theatre Street stretching right over to Orford Place was all that was left of the burnt out shops caused by incendiary bombs dropped on Orford Place and Brigg St. This pit was put to good use by constructing a large water reservoir for fighting the fires, but a great deal of Norwich had vanished. This reservoir was also the centre for ending a good late night out with an illicit swim by those that had over indulged after leaving the New American Club which rose out of the ashes of bombed out shops. We looked with awe at this new brash and glittery entertainment centre for American troops, which attracted the girls.

This also provoked the envy of local lads and British troops causing many a fight outside. The very old Thatched Cinema [All Saints Green] had gone forever and was unrecognisable and as the rubble was cleared they found a large unexploded bomb that had dropped in Theatre Street and people were not allowed near the crater until it could be carefully made accessible and defused. Though deeply shocked Norwich braced itself and its spirit returned with people even selling goods amidst the blackened ruins of shops, businesses carried on as normal.

We include a real life paraphrased account of our neighbour Cyril Ramsey traumatic story.

As a tribute to the men and women that suffered in inhumane conditions as Japanese prisoners of war

Cyril Ramsey and a Picture of some of his Regiment.
Many sadly never survived the harsh treatment.   Plate 140

The capture of Singapore February 15th 1942 and the consequent collapse of European control in South East Asia had created a vacuum that communism tried to fill, which enabled Japan to conquer the Dutch East Indies and the Philippines. Most of our soldiers transported to support troops under General Percival in that zone were met by

Cyril Ramsey Plate 141

the Japanese who were prepared for their arrival. They were taken prisoner together with all arms and equipment.

Cyril Ramsey was our neighbour when we lived in Mansfield Lane, Norwich. He enlisted into what was then the 5th Royal Norfolk Regiment and was sent to Singapore. After being taken prisoner he worked on the Burma/Thailand Railway being used as slave labour, the conditions and environment being so bad thousands died, but his will to live kept him alive, though he spent many years in the living hell of the cruel Japanese prisoner of war camps.

Cyril was one of many prisoners with whom there was no contact during the war except a card sent by the Japanese Red Cross link in the later period of war, to state he was alive and in good health, when in fact he was seriously ill.

He did survive, Cyril's story continues later in our book.

DANGEROUS MOONLIGHT

Our father was in one of the many small teams of brave ambulance men and women that had the gruesome work searching blazing bombed buildings for the injured or dead during and after an enemy attack.

Father ➜

The Surrey Street First Aid Party   Plate. 142
Later moved to the Ambulance Depot in Hall Road.
Father is first on the left, the man on the far right Mr. Larwood who was in charge of this unit. [In civilian life he was a cook, later he made Norma's wedding cake] next to Mr. Larwood is Mr. Miller who married a Mary Catchpole. Her father at that time, owned the hardware shop in St Johns Close. Hall Road, Norwich.

Snatching sleep between raids they waited at their H.Q. for the phone call that informed them that Gerry [the German planes] was on his way again. Following the siren and the crash warning, the thrum of the German pathfinder planes would be heard, following the railway lines and river, until they found the spire of Norwich Cathedral. They dropped brilliant flares on parachutes that lit up the whole city to aid the bomber's path to identify targets. They then fanned out to drop incendiary and cluster bombs that created fires to brighten up the area even more causing so much damage.

As we crouched in the air raid shelter we listened to the throbbing drone of the heavy bombers laden with their cargo of death then the ensuing thunderous bang of high explosives that flattened what was left. The crash of falling brickwork following those horrendous explosions left an eerie silence and a strange feeling of relief as the drones became fainter and we snatched some sleep. Life went on it was school as usual for us the next morning. It is strange that with all the dangerous disruption and lack of sleep the routines of life still carried on and was accepted.

the next morning. It is strange that with all the dangerous disruption and lack of sleep the routines of life still carried on and was accepted.

While all this was going on those courageous men and women of the fire and rescue services were busy with their hosepipe's, stretchers and the British bulldog spirit to carry on irrespective of the screeching dive-bombers, thunderous explosions, smoke and fire that was all round them.

One member of the team in father's branch of the First Aid Party, a large man who was constantly tormenting others with what he saw as a joke.

Due to the nature of their work the resulting fatigue and shocks they were always receiving, his attitude was not always appreciated; perhaps it was his way to relieve his own tensions. It only needed a spark, to cause bad feeling and they all warned him of this. One day, after the whole unit had been through a terrible night's work we heard that this man had tampered with father's lunch, a precious commodity during wartime.

Rescue teams in action

Plate 143

The result of his action made father act out of character. His fist caught the tormentor, a beefy character, squarely on the jaw and it needed two buckets of water to revive him. He learned his lesson; his jokes were never repeated and he respected father and others from that time on. Despite lack of sleep, emotional and physical effort; life went on. People still went to work and school if these buildings were still there. Later teachers were sent round to people's homes to teach the younger ones if their schools had been destroyed. **David** travelled by bus to get meat from the city, sometimes taking a detour round the bombed buildings, then it was on to school for him.

Plate 144	**Living through Hell**	Plate 145

The support services for-ever listening, searching salvaging and comforting less fortunate

A family celebrate their survival after their Anderson shelter balances on the edge of the crater

Going back to 1941 when the battle for Britain was in full swing; in old antiquated planes they flew, soaring into the heights, zooming out of sight into the clouds dancing climbing and streaking down after the enemy. Many enemy bombers were destroyed, though we didn't hear much about our own planes. We did not have very many at the start of the war so they must have been successful in their missions.

As Britain slowly strengthened home defences the skies were never empty, especially at night they were filled with noise of zooming engines of the planes. Guns from the ground sometimes boomed out, but not always if our planes were in the skies, with the light from the searchlights picking out the enemy during the night raids. The daylight battle for Britain started in early August, these were lone attackers on a quick sortie of hit and miss runs risking the fire of ground guns, and the skill of the spitfire fighters, which continued until the middle of October. Then the day battles died down only to restart again at night also the noise of our own bombers on their missions to Germany all through the winter of 1940/41.

Hitler realising he could not control the skies gave up the thought of conquering Britain and turned his attention to Russia, making the same mistake as Napoleon, and he was defeated in exactly the same way. It was by the limitless frozen space of winter bound Russia and the Russian people who used the tried and tested burned earth policy, thousands of German soldiers froze or starved to death. There is no doubt that the invasion of Britain would have succeeded if it had been carried out instead of attacking Russia. At that particular time we lived with death all around us, but amazingly we survived, and still found pleasure in living, though we grieved with and shared the sorrow of those less fortunate

The Germans had designed a warplane that instilled a nightmare of terror into our hearts, the Junkers Ju.87 [The Stuka bomber]. Its wings were cranked back for extra strength, enabling the plane to dive at 85% giving pinpoint accuracy. The undercarriage was fixed in the down position, to reduce drag; spats were fitted over wheels with sirens attached that produced an ear splitting scream which rose to a crescendo

German Stuka Bomber Plate 146 increasing speed as it hurtled in a steep dive earthwards. You can only imagine the psychological effect this had on the people below, as planes dived one after the other screeching down to their targets. The extremely loud cruuummmp of the bombs as they hit and exploded sending tons of bricks and metal into the air that then crashed to the ground. We heard even while in a crouched position with our hands clasped tightly over our ears to try and shut out the deafening noise of planes, and explosions. Not forgetting the sound of the falling bricks and mortar as each building hit crashed to the ground, to form a useless burning heap. Also the boom of our guns [if there were any?] trying to shoot down the enemy planes. Then in contrast, moments of silence apart from the soft drone as the bombers banked round for another run. This stupid situation of planes passing one another, they, to drop bombs on us and us travelling the other way to drop bombs on them, continued throughout the war. Life went on, it was school the next morning, the adults searching through the rubble, clearing up the mess or going to work. The raids, yes they were terrifying but they taught us about compassion, caring and sharing, about life, and death too.

Although the Stukas were brilliantly designed they were no match for the daring little Spitfires that would run rings round them in a dogfight. One night in 1941 in a really bad air raid, the Germans dropped what they called Bread Baskets that contained incendiary bombs loosely held in containers and designed to cause maximum conflagration. The containers opened at high altitude and the bombs   scattered over a large area of the city exploding in all directions setting the centre ablaze.

This assisted German bombers to identify targets and drop the high explosive bombs on selected buildings. On one occasion we watched from our our back garden until the wrath of our mother forced us to retreat to the shelter. As we entered we heard the terrifying screech of a dive-bomber followed by terrific explosion, shrapnel and dust showered everywhere, some landing on the roof of our shelter. We learnt later a high explosive bomb aimed at Thorpe Railway Station, off target, **Brilliantly designed Spitfires** fell on the then congested area of Ber Street about **on patrol that outmatched** five hundred yards from our house. In a similar **the German** p**lanes** Plate. 147 raid no warning sounded, one of **Norma's** classmates Doris Johnson lived in Peggs opening and had just passed the scholarship for the Blyth Jex School. As a reward her parents bought her a gold watch.

That night her father hearing the droning of heavily-laden planes, shut off the lights and looked out of the window just as the bomb exploded with almost a direct hit on their house. It was probably a land mine and it devastated the whole area. Our Father, who was with the ambulance team attending to search the rubble, found the mother sitting among the ruins of what had once been her home rocking backwards and forward, moaning, clutching what looked like a football tightly in her hands. It was her husband's head; it took three men of the team to free her fingers holding on to the grisly object. It was rumoured her hair, turned grey overnight, she had been driven to the limits of endurance. Everyone in that house except her was killed with many more in the area. All they found of the young girl was her arm with the watch still strapped to it. How the mother escaped or what happened to her afterwards we never knew. After a visit to the mortuary and the hospital father's First Aid Crew proceeded on to Carrow Works [Colman's Mustard and other foods] that had again suffered terribly. The situation in the city was grave; the circling dive-bombers continued a relentless rain of bombs.

On the way there a bomb fell close to the front of father's ambulance, some of the team were blown out of the back. Father found himself at the bottom of a crater that was rapidly, filling with sewage water. After a few minutes the others started searching for him. Looking up, and in the glow of the surrounding fires he saw white anxious faces peering over the rim of the crater, and voices shouted down "Ernie! Ernie! Where the hells are you, come out of there you silly bugger!" His voice went back. "I can't find me falshe teeff!" Their response was unprintable, when they arrived at Carrow Works in another vehicle the situation was shocking but they did what they could for the dead and dying people. When father eventually arrived home he was visibly shaken and exhausted refusing to talk about it until much later. Not many days passed without incident, some get imprinted on the mind never to be forgotten as **Norma** recalls.

It was one of those very dangerous beautiful, sparkling and romantic evenings with a clear velvety sky and full moon. Norma had been to the pictures with a friend. As they walked home a dogfight started up overhead. No sirens had sounded, and it was hardly noticeable at first. Those long fingers of the search-lights that probed the night skies seemed to grasp at the stars searching for those elusive bombers. They suddenly converged to pick out two tiny specks weaving in and out of their beams then darted out of view for a few seconds, until red streaks of the tracer bullets were seen against the gold of the rays and the blackness of the skies around and above.

The family at home stayed outside to watch fascinated by the events above, but darted for cover as things started to hit the ground around them. This could have been an appealing picture but there was a life and death battle going on above. One of the planes was hit, and fell out of the sky! Was it theirs, or ours? There was no way of telling. **Norma** froze and could not move, as she watched with horror, it seemed to be heading straight towards her home; she started to run, and then stopped again rooted to the ground as the plane disappeared with a deafening bang and brilliant flash! Her one thought was her family. Flames and smoke leapt into the brightness of the night, dimming the bright stars. She ran even faster than before with the air battle still going on high above her head. Silhouetted in that bright moonlit sky there were some parachutes coming down too, were they Germans? She, by now didn't care. As she got nearer home she realised the smoke from the crashed aircraft was obviously coming some distance away from the back of the house her house which eased her thoughts. She found out later it had come down on open ground then was Hipperson's farm and now the Hewett school grounds; we have enclosed a photo of the wreck.

Trembling in relief and gasping for breath, subconsciously aware that the battle was still taking place above, she continued her walk home. Just as quickly as it started they were gone, only the exploding shells and the burning plane, reminders of what had been happening. By this time police and other emergency services were organised, the older members of family and neighbours at the scene formed a line across the field to search for survivors helped by the light shed by the burning wreck, everyone acted as a team in those times. Next day a tragic story unfolded, the Americans came to collect the remains of the plane [a wing had fallen on the railway line at the back of our house and another part of the plane that had fallen

Stricken American Bomber   Plate 148
Photo by Derek Edwards copyright Norfolk Museum
and Archaeology Service'

on our roof], showing how close death had come to our family that night. The airman told us of the young eighteen-year-old American navigator who had jumped from the plane only to find his parachute would not open. Of course the poor young man mercifully was dead before he hit the ground and buried himself up to the armpits. Every bone in his body was broken. **Norma** had not been aware that one of those men who she had seen was that young American boy plunging to his death who at the time she believed to be a German parachutist.

Due to the serious situation that was building up in our devastated city father was now on permanent F.A.P. duties, only coming home for short breaks. Mother had a hard time coping with her now large family through all those extremely bad nights and days. But father, as fathers often do, took some punishment from us and in one incident that we have never forgotten was at the later end of the war when he came home from a long torturous night desperately wanting sleep and slumped into his chair.

A plan was hatched to get him out of our play area and into bed, and knowing our sister **Ann** was only three years old and too young to understand or receive any punishment. She was persuaded to gently tap her slumbering dad on the head with the small but weighty brush while we hid under the table.

Unfortunately things did not go as we planned; she raised the brush above her head and brought it down like a professional golfer, shouting WHAM! It nearly laid poor father out for the count. Although he was obviously dazed it did not take him long to access the situation and made straight for Raymond and started to chase him round the table. We won't go into the painful aftermath but father lived to try and explain the reason for that large lump on his head and what had happened to his First Aid work colleagues. He said it was more dangerous to stay at home than risk Hitler's bombing at work.

CHRONOLOGY 1943-1944

1943 September; we attack Italy and it surrenders. Great concern in our War Cabinet when the photo reconnaissance planes sent to North West France confirmed the fears of the military that some form of new German weapon was being installed. Soon to be revealed as a pilot-less Flying Bomb that would travel at 400 m.p.h. carrying 1 ton of high explosive in the nose cone. By **November;** more of these sites had been observed. Miss Constance Babington-Smith daughter of the director of the Bank of England and a senior intelligence officer was given the task of ascertaining their purpose and reported to her chief that she suspected that they were being used for pilot-less aircraft, later proved correct. One of the main radar stations for tracking these rockets, [code named Big Ben] at Darsham Norfolk Nicknamed "The Pylons" was being used to great effect, the first in the world, reaching up to 340ft.

May; an exciting time for us as we see large troop movements along the railway at the back of our house. A massive exodus; train after train taking men and machines to secret locations. **June;** we watch in amazement as the sky was black as far as could be seen with a never ending flow of planes and gliders all going one way. The roads filled with military vehicles all moving south. At last we were going to chase Jerry right into his front room. It was D-Day at last! Hitler refused to submit and in June he bombards Britain with V1 rockets then in September the dreaded V2's started to arrive.

Continuation [from previous item] Cyril Ramsey's ordeal and a Summary of his account of the journey from Chungkai.
[If you recall Cyril Ramsey was our neighbour who was taken prisoner by the Japanese and used as slave labour].

In 1944 the Japanese decided to move a large number of their prisoners away from the railway at Chungkai, to begin a nightmare journey to Japan. Seven hundred and fifty were taken aboard a small cargo vessel of about 5000 tons that had been built on the Clyde. Its' old name the Glasgow Belle could still be seen written on the bridge, the Japanese renamed her 'The Osaka Maru'.

The men were herded down steep steps into a dark hold fitted with shelves, which were spaced with about four feet between them. They endured this journey with barely enough room to sit, squashed together with their knees up to their chins. Needless to say some were seriously ill before they even left port in that terrible heat and lack of air they were fighting to breath in a hell hole devoid of space or light. British doctors [who were also prisoners] protested, saying over half would be dead within twelve hours but the Japanese were determined to get these prisoners away to Japan dead or alive. A large convoy left port, soon most were ill with malaria, dysentery and other related illnesses. After eight weeks the stench was unbearable, sweaty unwashed bodies mixed with excreta and vomit combined with the steam from the cooking of their daily meal of dried seaweed and rice was to remain with the survivors of that hell ship forever.

To make matters worse they ran into a typhoon, and the boat was taking in water making it difficult to control. Those that could glimpse the outside reported an American submarine had torpedoed one of the convoy, and set it alight. Its crew and prisoners had to choose the sea or the blazing ship. By the third day of the storm, the Osaka Maru was in serious trouble and had lost its steering. There was terrible crash and a grinding noise, as they struck a rock, those who had the strength staggered to the deck. The Japanese were not interested in stopping them; it was every man for him self in the confusion. The next day all the crew had gone and the prisoners were left to their fate; there was an island in the distance but being too weak to swim they stayed on the stricken ship with plenty of fresh air but no food, water or means of escape.

Three Japanese destroyers arrived, and for some unknown reason fixed a line to their ship though other ships in the same convoy were left to their fate. Reaching Formosa they were herded on to another ship the Hakusan Maru and back again to a dark airless hold and the old conditions only worse, as this time the Japanese battened down the hatches. The old sicknesses returned and the death rate soared.

American submarines attacked again and after eight days quiet there followed twelve hours of terror with no means of escape. Eventually they reached Japan where the populace treated them with hostility, with no restraint from the authorities. Cyril did survive though there is no doubt, had the war continued he probably would have succumbed. He was very ill with a hole in his side you could put your fist in. When the war finished he was not allowed home for six months in order to repair his health; after returning to England he set up a retail business in Lakenham near his old home. Now retired the last we heard he still lived in Lakenham fighting for compensation for the ex Japanese prisoners of war. This long battle resulted in the recognition by Japan that they did owe these men something and we believe this matter has been resolved, though for many it was too late. We extend our thanks to Cyril for his kind permission to use his story for which we were very grateful.

The Terror of the V1's and V2's

Towards the end of the war, the Germans were facing a series of defeats, grasping at straws and franticly searching for a weapon of mass destruction. These were known as Vergeltungswaffens [vengeance weapons]. During our research we found an interesting story of how the allies became aware of this, and were able to slow their manufacture and eventually destroy them through the efforts of a young man and his friends. Pierre Ginter who lived in Goetheschule [Luxemburg] refused to join the Hitler Youth and was removed from his home to work as forced labour in Pennemunde [Germany]. He

The V2 Rocket

Plate.149

realized it was a research establishment to develop and manufacture an ariel torpedo [flying bomb] that would bring England to its knees.

One bright sunny day he watched, along with Reichsmarshall Hermann Goering [one of Hitler's right hand men] and other prisoners and spectators the first launch of this terrible destructive weapon the V1. Pierre concealed his mirth as the first rocket exploded on take off, but his demeanor turned to horror as the second one made a perfect launch. Realizing its implication Pierre knew someone had to alert others to what he had learned and took the risk of writing to his friend in Goetheschule outlining the situation. He volunteered to work a late shift in the office and to cut a long story short, during one of his shifts stole the keys to the Commandants office and began a search of the files. To his astonishment a German officer entered to demand what he was doing in the filing cabinet. "I am stealing some paper to write to my mother" he spluttered. His cheek paid off and the officer strode out leaving him to locate and copy those precious documents.

When he was allowed to return home he passed them on and they were safely delivered to the British who using this information promptly targeted and destroyed the V1 plants and launch pads which gave us time to win the war. These pilotless rocket planes named the V1 packed with high explosive nearly turned this war game in their favour. The German's bombarded Britain from June 1944 with these weapons and a desperate effort to destroy them and their launch pads was made by the Allies. The V1's flew in a straight line governed by a guidance system at a constant speed; at pre-determined time the engine cut out usually over a populated area and dived to the ground. They were easy prey for our gunners and the RAF who were able to shoot them down or adjust the V1's planned course by flying alongside and tipping their stubby wings. The British public came to call these missiles "doodlebugs".

In September 1944 German scientists designed a new rocket, the V2 that went much higher, faster, flew further, was portable and virtually noiseless. Because of their speed they were impossible to shoot down. The British could find no answer to this and urgently sought a way to destroy them at source. One terrifying thing, you were never sure where they might land. Two thousand Londoner's died as they demolished the city. One evening about half past six, **David** arrived at the Scout hut for the cub pack night and was leaning against a very high flint and brick wall, near to the entrance of Old Lakenham Hall [Now Lakenham Hall Housing Estate]. He and his friend were waiting for Neville Coe [Boson] the cub leader to unlock the door of the cub room. Without any pre warning the crash siren sounded, immediately followed by the now familiar sound of the throbbing engines of a V1 Flying Bomb.

Grabbing **David's** collar in one hand and his pal Brian Moore in the other, Boson threw them down to the ground at the base of the wall. The engines stopped, there was an eerie silence. **David** was laying face up at the bottom of the heap under Brian and Neville who was using his body to protect them. Looking up at the sky, he noticed this sausage shape with wings passing above them. It went out of his sight then an almighty explosion. **David** said if he was a cat that would have been one of his nine lives gone. It had missed the city and landed in the fields. **David** grew up with the war and he took most of it in his stride; they all just got up from the ground brushed themselves down and went on with their cub pack night. There are many things he remembers even today such as where he laid on that night.

Note; A documentary on T.V. released an unknown fact that Germany had developed an underground factory built by slave labour to manufacture these rocket bombs. Professor Barnes Wallis a brilliant British engineer had invented a bouncing bomb that was previously dropped from an aircraft onto the dams was used to roll into the cave entrance and successfully blew the place up.

THE FINAL PUSH INTO EUROPE

David and **Norma** remember how the grown ups were getting excited over something that was about to happen; for days there had been great debates over where it would take place, and what the Generals were planning. But what was it? Suddenly in the early hours the air was full of noise, no one had much sleep that night because of the noise of throbbing plane engines and the movement of heavy military transport carrying troops and army equipment, the noise never stopped but at last we slept. When **David** awoke full of excitement, it had happened, **Norma** told him they had been going over to Europe all night non-stop. The adults too were exclaiming; it's started! It's started!

We all ran outside to look; the skies were black with planes, in every direction you looked, stretching back as far as we could see. The plane engines were labouring under their heavy loads, towing gliders full of troops behind them. Our cousin **Barbara's** husband **John Palmer** had been specially trained for this type of work, so we expect that he was up there amongst all the noise and trauma of the night. We noticed day after day long trains with open trucks passing the end of our garden one after another packed with soldiers their equipment and supplies; then leaving the old Victoria Station empty returning to reload. The roads out of Norwich were filled with military vehicles all heading one way.

After a bloody battle on the North coast of France the landing was successful and Germany eventually surrendered May 8th 1945 and Victory in Europe day [V.E. day] was declared. As there are many books on this war period we will move on.

THE WAR IN EUROPE IS OVER AND JAPAN IS TARGETED

Now the people celebrated, street parties were on every corner. **David** had spent the day with his friends, returning home he found the house empty and everyone gone. Hearing loud music and singing he made his way towards it. Someone told him there were big parties in the City streets so headed that way hoping to find his family there. Making his way up Hall Road/Ber Street he passed singing and dancing groups.

David by this time was a tired bewildered young boy; he arrived at the market place where it seemed they had all gone mad. His big sister was there too just as bewildered as he was, watching the same people. Men were hugging each other, [unusual then], all the kissing and hugging of the women was beyond belief. Everyone seemed to be falling about with bottles of drink in their hands; **Norma** was more interested in the ones climbing up the lampposts to hang up Union Jacks or had stitched them into their clothes, others had made bloomers from the flags.

David did not find his family there, how could he hope to among those thousands of delirious folks; **Norma** did not dance about or act the fool but she felt happy inside to know the war was finished. The hours flew by and not realising the time **David** wearily struggled home. Luckily they had all been out except the parents who were celebrating with the neighbours and knew the younger children were in bed but concerned as to where the rest of the family had gone, thinking **David** was with them.

They were astonished when he walked in on his own at one o clock in the morning and he explained what he had seen but to him they too seemed more than just happy. Once again the piano came into use. But **David** had switched off and gone to sleep. **Norma** was not so lucky; it was nearer two when she eventually came back.

She had met a boy she knew who brought her home, which was like a red rag to a bull, father over reacted worried sick for her safety, he was waiting at the door when she arrived home and she got his belt. She had never seen him like this before; he caught her across the face with the buckle, it was no use saying she forgot the time watching people's antics that night, she knew she should have been home long before. Next morning Dad realised he had made a bad mistake and brought her a cuppa in bed but she refused to speak to him and had a real nasty bruise on her eye. She wouldn't accept his apology either, remembering he did not give her a chance to tell him anything. Fortunately this situation did not last very long, soon all was forgotten.

Thousands of men began returning home to their families but for some there was to be no family to return to as many civilians had died in the bombing. War has no respect for people. Death had claimed many victims, and the increase in immorality had disrupted other lives. Time had moved on so fast for some that they found they were unable to cope with the hard and bitter pill of life in the raw; it nearly choked them. People's lives and attitudes changed so dramatically during the war period, it would never be the same again.

One sad case we knew as a cheerful and handsome man engaged to a pretty girl before the war became a RAF rear gunner and was badly burned when his plane crashed and caught alight. His appearance was so mutilated and scarred; he found life very difficult, he tried hard to cope. A happy joking personality; and a very brave man. Tribute must be given to those many men and women who suffered terrible disfigurement some had to remain in the confines of special homes and were given every assistance to have some sort of existence to lead happy lives as far as possible under their circumstances.

THE ATOMIC BOMB
Japan Surrenders

The war with Europe was over but the war with Japan was still in progress. With the development of the Atom bomb the allies realized they had the ultimate weapon to win the war. The very nature of the Japanese and their culture would never have allowed them to give in lightly preferring to die rather than surrender. But the allies rather than losing any more men gave the Japanese an ultimatum. President Trueman said, "If they do not accept our terms they may expect a rain of ruin from the air the likes of which has never been seen on this earth".

The consequences of this warning were spelled out to the Emperor of Japan Hirohito but went unheeded. The Americans took the initiative and dropped the first uranium derived Atom bomb named "Little Boy" on the city of Hiroshima, on 6th August 1945 with horrendous consequences. The second bomb, a plutonium device named "Fat Man" was dropped on the city of Nagasaki on 9th August 1945 and proved decisive, this one bomb totally demolished half the city, with seventy thousand casualties, some survivors were still dying from the effects of radiation years later. The Japanese Emperor throwing all national traditions to one side surrendered on August 15th 1945.

COUSIN PEGGY`S WEDDING
LONDON

The reception July 31st 1948   Plate.150

We have included this particular wedding, as it is memorable not because it was one of the few occasions when most this family line was represented. (We guess you might call it a gathering of the clan) but it portrays the image of some of the family not often seen. After the honeymoon, Peggy went to live with her new husband in Cornwall. We do not have any other photographs to record those that have died. On our visits to London there always seemed to be some hilarious incident that usually pivoted around our aunt Maud who was by nature rather domineering.

On one visit to London there was a heated discussion as to which of the four corners of a road junction they had arranged to catch the coach for the trip home to Norwich. Maud decided on which corner it had to be and they waited and waited. As the coach approached everyone kissed goodbye and then watched in horror as it sailed by on another road and disappeared into the blue yonder. Father was the only one that had sufficient cash to pay the rail fare home for all [including Aunt Maud much to his disgust] out of the money he had saved for a new Macintosh [raincoat]. He was re-paid in kind namely from Aunt Maud with a pair of very old-fashioned Chemise [clean but used knickers] for our mother although clothes were scarce he was speechless with rage!

On another visit Maude while marshalling her troops [our family and others] on to a tube train, the doors closed with her on the outside trapping and crunching her umbrella and left her holding the handle in shocked surprise still on the platform. She eventually retrieved it when the doors opened again and she rejoined the family, when we went down the escalator she dropped her flowers at the bottom. Unfortunately everyone that stepped off the moving stairway had no alternative but to step on them. She managed to make a grab for them and stood leaning [clutching a bunch of stalks] against the wall fighting back tears.

WE LOOK TO THE FUTURE
A Time of New Beginnings

The war was over, or was it? The physical side of war was over, then the war of politics and national greed started. Russia was still a communist nation with ideals, which were not in our interests. Each nation grabbed what they could of the spoils of war from a defeated Germany. Winston Churchill, our wartime prime minister could see the dangers lurking in the shadows knowing what was about to happen and wanted the non-communist nations to now move against Russia to avoid a long drawn out conflict with them. He contended that an "Iron Curtain" was about to be drawn across Europe by Stalin's Russia. He was a man of foresight who knew that trouble lay ahead and wanted to contain it and to prevent further hostilities. His warnings went unheeded, everyone was grasping the hand of peace and friendship the mood was against more war.

People had had enough of military action and like Chamberlain in 1938 wanted to appease; Churchill was branded as a warmonger, defeated at the ballot box and Labour swept into power in July 1945. Mr. Clement Attlee was elected the new Prime Minister with promises of wealth and more power for the people. Churchill's foresight was later proven right; a cold war resulted with the Anglo /American world powers making a stand against Russian Communism which caused many serious problems and tensions. A full-blown war was only prevented by the fear of new weapons that if used no one could contemplate the terrible outcome a time of brinkmanship, between leading politicians. Bluff and counter bluff in a cold war that continued for many years. Russia seized German territory then put a circle of strangulation round Berlin that left other international countries [mainly American and British forces] behind the Russian lines.

The Russians greed for more power and territory tried to starve those trapped within their ring by refusing any road or rail movement through. The allies refused to give in to them and organized a massive airlift of food and other essential goods that was the only way the population of Berlin could survive. The Russians also built a high wall across Berlin, with a "no mans land" that divided their sector from the others, which also divided the German families who lived on each side of the wall.

Many brave souls attempted to escape to the other side, cheered on by loved ones and the Allied soldiers. Only a few made it, others were shot as they tried to dodge the hail of Russian bullets. Often they were left to die where they fell as no one dared to help the victims. This wall remained for many years until Russia was forced into economic isolation the old style communist leaders and their ideals lost out in time. But the political struggle in Russia continued until recent times.

Those British troops returning from war did not want to remain in the old type class system. In war they all had to pull together and in peace wanted to create a fair and just future for the next generation. Out would go the poor man's health service where mothers saw their children die when there was no money to pay the doctor. Up to this time our parents paid sixpence or a shilling each week into a medical club hoping it would cover the doctor's fee when anyone was ill. With six children there were many times that a shilling was not available, our doctors understood but there were probably many that did not.

Then the most cherished document in the history of our nation was created by the incoming Labour Government, a coveted scheme devised for the luckless of society. The weakest to the wall practice was to stop and the new government announced that, every worker had to pay into a government scheme (deducted directly from his or her wages) that would provide free Medicine, Doctors and Hospital care for all. A policy people would have the right to rely on when in need. It was called the National Health Service. If out of work there would be no means test that our father had to endure in the stingy years before, with the indignity of digging a hole and filling it again for no practical reason for one shilling while an official watched to make sure the shilling was earned.

The Baxter family listened with excitement to the radio as the government gave the ordinary family an opportunity of improving their lot and started to take interest in politics, having long discussions about each party, just as Hermione and her brother did at Knebworth. With most of the adults having been involved in the war there was much work to do to rebuild Britain. A mammoth task awaited those in power to accommodate all those looking for work and a home including father as the First Aid Party was disbanded. The family was approaching their teenage years. **Norma** had started her Scholarship course at the Norwich School for Art and shortly after, **Alan** gained a scholarship to the Norwich Commercial College.

Long after the war had ended rationing continued and living was very basic with long working hours and poor wages. With six children it was a constant worry for our parents. Incomes still had to be carefully managed to ensure that there was a roof over our heads and food to eat. Our coal was still delivered by Lacons' lorry, bread and milk at first was brought by men on bicycles or barrows and then by vans. Tradesman's visits to our house were for them a trip into the unknown, full of hazards for the unwary, unless they were aware of childhood pranks. **Norma** knocked out the bakers' roundsman's, who was not expecting to meet a budding cheer-leader swinging her hockey stick. The breadbasket on his shoulder went one way and the roundsman the other in a heap on the floor. He said he encountered more dangers visiting us than he did during an air raid!

Raymond's friend Billy Bird lived nearby whose older brother worked in a chemist shop and made his own fireworks. Chemist's shops would stock numerous and dangerous chemicals on their shelves for people to buy; there were no restrictions in those days. **Raymond** and **David** were soon experimenting with ingredients to make explosive concoctions. Initial trials were promising so to prove their effect they decided to put some in the enclosed space of the porch with a string soaked in turpentine that led to the back of the air raid shelter.

They lit the string fuse and waited but had many failures. They then made one last effort and put the remains of what was left in one pile, lit the fuse and waited. This time the result was devastating not only for them and the resulting wrath of their father and the poor baker's roundsman, who again arrived on the scene at the wrong moment. As he puzzled at this pile of material that had a piece of lighted string, there was a great flash a bang, and billows of smoke that sent him [after discarding his basket] running onto the road. He was found by mother, leaning on the gatepost; she thought he was the culprit, which did not help matters. After the turmoil had died down and suitable punishment had been administered, we all settled down leaving the baker and our parents with a few more grey hairs. Soon after the Bird family immigrated to Australia so we lost our friend. We then resorted to making bows and arrows, a more primitive occupation, trying to shoot an apple off our brother Bill's head. Unfortunately he rose up from behind the air raid shelter far too quickly and received an arrow straight through his cheek!

Another favorite occupation was our jaunts to Norwich Castle without parental knowledge, to wander round the museum and gaze at the many stuffed animals and mummified bodies of long dead Egyptians. After the guided tour of the dungeons, our sister Ann, then aged four, was deposited in the arms of an attendant after refusing to continue up the long winding stairway to the battlements. She happily sang to him much to the amusement of the people behind but not to the poor man carrying her. Our parents were promptly informed; these exciting expeditions were abruptly ended and we were grounded for several weeks.

Lenny Goodings, our fruit and vegetable man delivered his wares piled high on a cart pulled by his faithful horse. Many people bought from him, as the local shops were too costly. He had a large brass hand bell that would awaken the dead and shouted out his amusing sales cry "Ripe Strawbeenies" even during winter. Whilst attending to his customers needs he constantly supplied his horse with a carrot, but it was clear to the other housewives that there was an ulterior motive to his being stationary for what seemed an unnecessary wait to his other customers and the horse. The reason for this was that each day one particular housewife developed a habit of collecting her vegetables dressed in very, very low cut tops. Being well proportioned with very little underclothing she was more than eager to pick up the many carrots that Lenny dropped at her feet on to the road that were not charged for.

Unfortunately being cross-eyed, this practice did not help his sight as one morning while gazing at her finer points he made the unfortunate mistake of not holding the carrots near enough to the horse. His carthorse then made a sudden lunge taking the carrot and also Lenny's finger. The horse did not appreciate the gift of this finger and promptly spat it out leaving others to scrabble about in the gutter to reclaim it. Poor Lenny was rushed to hospital on his cart minus one finger of his left hand and clutching an extra finger in his right. The lady was left standing in embarrassed silence among tittering and tutting women. The use of the horse and cart for everyday transport has long gone. The need for speed and efficiency has given us the motor car and the supermarket. The mode of life has changed so dramatically since our great grandfather's time makes one wonder what's in store for our grandchildren.

EMILY AND LOUIE BARNS
Local Characters of The Past

Every era has its characters and sisters Emily and Louie Barnes were certainly two of them. The photograph at **Norma's** wedding from left to right of [I'm in charge, Louie Barnes, extreme left] truthfully shows her character. Then Mrs. Ramsey, **David, Alan, Father, Granny Baxter,** Tony Asker [best man], **Mr Hart,** our **Mother, and Mrs Hart** [the two short ones peeping over shoulders], **Alfred Hart**, Mrs Rose Cole. [She and Mrs Ramsey were our next-door neighbours]. Bridesmaids left to right **Joy Thompson**. The young pageboy is **John Hart,** Norma's sister **Ann, Norma, Eddie**; next to him Jean Woods and the small bridesmaids, **Margaret** and **Barbara Hart** with our younger brother **Brian [Bill].** Far right, with our brother Raymond standing directly behind him.

The reason we have inserted this photograph here is mainly for Louie Barnes.
Though we also have Mrs Ramsey and Mrs. Rose Cole
Our next-door neighbours and all the family together in one spot   Plate.151

Norma's Wedding 23 September 1950

Emily Barns was deceased just before this marriage, she and Louie lived together as sisters and companions in Hall Road, Norwich and were frequent social (also conveyors of complaints) visitors to our home. Their many visits to the local Saint Marks School to air their protests to the head master, Mr. Bush, to state, in no uncertain terms, of the latest torment they had suffered from so called local ruffians, often accusing the wrong lads. He did his best to satisfy their forceful demands but woe betides him if retribution was not promised. The more the two sisters complained the more the schoolboys tried to think of the next trick to play on them.

Once the women ordered the whole school out to try and find the villain who had forced a huge hard carrot into their letterbox, where it had become solidly wedged. Using knives and a host of other weapons including foul language they wrestled with this monster, Emily inside pulling and Louie pushing. It took two hours of their valuable time to get it out! They then marched to the school with the offending vegetable.

Mr. Bush, with much annoyance succumbed to Louie's strong demand to assemble the whole school in class lines in the playground, solely for them to single out the culprit. He watched as they enjoyed their role as investigators and the implied importance of their visit. Later only for him to realise that he had assembled the whole school for them to identify someone they already knew very well, our brother. Raymond pleaded innocence and Mr. Bush still angry with the women, believed he was not guilty of their charge. We think that the two old ladies enjoyed their moments in the limelight and **Ray** of course relished watching the antics of these two old women trying to find ways of removing the monster carrot that he had hammered through their letterbox while they were visiting our mother!

Both had more than a casual crush on their local doctor and both insisted that he would benefit if they kept him in a plentiful supply of knitted woollen socks. But unfortunately they never did ask or care what size was required. Some he could not possibly get on his feet, others were so big he could put both feet into one sock. But there was we believe a strategy to his tolerance, as he constantly admired their valuable antiques.

Louie worked in the mustard and tea departments of Colman's, lining tea chests and barrels before they rolled down the ramp to be filled. She had to actually get into them when they were on their sides to do her job. Louie loved a joke, but of course factory hands sometimes took them too far. Why she should have been found asleep inside a large empty mustard barrel no one found out. For whatever reason she was inside one large barrel while it lay on its side, when someone gave it a kick that sent it on its long journey of over thirty feet down a sloping ramp.

Gathering speed with Louie inside being spun like a top, it came to an abrupt halt against the others, luckily they were not filling or Louie would have been on her head and buried in mustard. When they pulled her out of the barrel it was two weeks before she could stand upright. The culprit insisted that he did not know she was inside. Emily was as quiet and serious; Louie was loud with an eccentric sense of humour, slightly simple in some ways, but sharp as a needle when it came to having an answer and putting others down it they took too many liberties or tried mocking her in any way. She cut straight though their criticisms with a tongue lashing enough to let them know not to try again. These sisters were great colourful local characters the likes of which are not seen today. Our family was still poor, but rich in the support and love from our parents and of course the music provided by the piano. Out went the indoor Morrison shelter and the Anderson shelter in the garden was dismantled. The hole it left provided the opportunity to discard all the unwanted items of war and old furniture that was replaced by more partly worn furniture from the sale yard. The enthusiasm to dispose of the old furniture was over estimated for the size of hole and the final item; the double mattress although covered with soil was still too near the surface. Of course the springs in it did not rot, and this fact did not escape the notice of the council official when we later moved house. He wrote with a wry sense of humour that our garden had been left with a permanent sense of spring so would we kindly remove the buried rubbish.

An unforeseen statistic occurred that affects us even today, when all the men returned from the war there were numerous marriages. This of course gave way to a baby boom and this can be seen from statistic charts that when those babies grew up to be adults another baby boom occurred. Today the government is concerned with the question of finding the money to pay for all these extra pensions. This increase in the birth rate was called the bulge and of course brought problems for the service industries i.e. more education, housing, jobs and also wages.

As National Service was still compulsory all males reaching the age of eighteen had to spend at least two years in the armed forces, this also helped to reduce the number of unemployed. In earlier years Norma wanted to join the Women's Land Army but her mother had strongly objected as she did not want anyone to leave home before marriage so Norma settled into a normal work routine with the Eastern Electricity Board where she met her future husband Edward Hart.

The war changed the previous way of life in this country and women became more liberated. With their menfolk away for long periods there was a new freedom and love was the only commodity left unrationed. There were many marriages that were performed during a 48-hour pass and the awful reality that the bride could become a widow before she could settle down to being a wife. The servicemen knew their wives were at home but due to security the women could only imagine their husbands situation and any news could be bad. With the added problem of GIs [American Servicemen.] in transit many hearts were broken and 70, 000 British war babies had American fathers. The mothers of these children. were often treated with hostility; as no one wanted to support these offspring.

David passed the scholarship to enter the Norwich City Technical College in 1946 and **Raymond** started work at Colman's of Norwich. When **Alan** our brother reached the age of eighteen, he was conscripted for National Service and joined the Fleet Air Arm. **Raymond** later enlisted in The Royal Medical Corps and was posted to Hong Kong. **Bill** and **Ann** were still at school. **Alan** and **Raymond** returned home after their two years service to be demobbed. Although **Ray** never returned to his previous employment at Colman's of Norwich but made a career as a skilled guillotine operator until moving to Luton with **David** to work in the car industry.

<h2 style="text-align:center">WAR TIME LOVERS</h2>
<u>Pat and Giovanni</u>

This was an epic love story that hit the headlines, both in Norwich and the National press. Pats [Normas friend] parents had both died; her father from a heart attack and her mother with cancer soon after, leaving Pat on her own

She fell in love with an Italian prisoner of war Sianno Giovanni. Local Authorities had noted their meetings during the war period and as he was still classed as an enemy soldier he was moved away from the area.

They still managed to contact each other; after the war a great effort was made to keep Giovanni in Britain but the local authorities refused and he was deported.

Again Pat was alone, but she was a fighter, decided to find some way to get him back to England. She learned if she could find him a job here he would be allowed to come back. She got in touch with The Evening News in Norwich.

GOLDEN MEMORIES: above, Pat and Giovanni today and, left, pictured on their wedding day.

Stars that have pride of place
LIKE many Italian prisoners of war Giovanni Siano fashioned replicas of the Italian army star from threepenny bits.
He made two of the metal stars and wore them on his uniform.
When he left, Giovanni gave one to Pat and said: "One day they will be together again."
Now the stars sit side-by-side in a special box in Pat's jewellery box.

*Wartime love story that hit the headlines Norma is in the centre. of the photo behind the bride

Plate.152

The very next day a farmer offered him a job Giovanni who just had one day left on his travel permit. Haste was a priority but he arrived back in Britain on Christmas day 1947 and and the couple were married the following March.

Sadly soon after they celebrated their Golden Wedding. Giovanni died.

DAVID CALLED TO ARMS
1955-1957

It was now **David's** turn to do his National Service in the Royal Engineers and he received orders to report to Malvern on the 9th May 1955. This to **David** was a boring waste of time, and he enjoyed taking retribution on the somewhat over enthusiastic Sergeant Major who seemed to excel in voice and deed and held a powerful influence over his subordinates. After initial basic army training, David being a refrigeration engineer was instructed to maintain the air conditioning on some portable radar trailers. It was obvious that these vehicles had been in store for quite a long time but did not realize that he and others were being prepared for war in the Suez Canal and after a few weeks he was suddenly posted for service abroad.

Unfortunately someone must have forgotten to stamp this on his papers as he was unexpectedly placed on permanent staff at an embarkation camp and saw preparations for war being enacted. Thousands of troops passed through with all their vehicles and equipment, including his portable radar, staying for one night; then speeding off to ships and planes to invade Egypt as they had just nationalized the Suez Canal.

The Sergeant Major became more of a pain to all in his charge and it became a battle of wits between him, those in transit and the permanent staff, who did their best to encourage the men and women passing through the camp by distracting his attention away from them. Each time he left his office the door opened sharply, he then took two paces back and in true military fashion, arms swinging shoulder high, marched off to his chosen destination.

Unfortunately unknown to him on the very occasion he wanted to impress, his feet got entangled in a thin piece of wire that somehow had been placed across his office doorway and he fell headlong at the feet of the visiting officer. Another brilliant plan was enacted when the Sergeant Major could no longer stand the terrible stench that forced him to vacate his office opposite the stores each time his orderly lit his free standing coke heater. He had enough, every morning smelly smoke [and steam] belched from his office chimneystack and heater.

Red faced he strode from his unwelcome place of work and quick marched to those that supplied the coke. New coke did not stop the stench. He never caught the night hawkers who in the cover of darkness climbed on the roof above his office to give a plentiful supply of fresh urine straight down his chimney. There was always a demand for a window view from the stores opposite his office and it's a wonder that the roars of laughter from these observers were never detected.

The Sergeant Major's over enthusiastic sense of discipline was always his best weapon and he had his own sly smile when playing the game of "O' Grady Says" on those bitterly cold winter mornings on a wind swept square. If your concentration slipped and you made a mistake your punishment was a quick run round the square with a rifle above your head knowing that he stood warming his hands on a portable coke brazier which he previously arranged for the occasion. Those who fell foul of his commands or who he considered slow in running joined others to white-wash each piece of coke with a paint brush and he later noted every stain on the coke.

After these grueling tasks, **David** from his place of work used to watch out for the sergeant Major going for his breakfast. Because he had missed his, he used to creep into the cookhouse and obtain a very large plate of egg bacon tomatoes fried bread etc. from a cook friend. One morning he and his pal Byrne got caught by "you know who". Not answering to the Sergeant Majors demands as to what he were doing there, it was not appreciated when Byrne explained that he should know it was rude to talk with a mouth full of food. Two cooks one in front and one behind marched them both at a quick march straight into the guardhouse.

David was not charged with leaving his place of duty but for reasons he could not understand was charged with having dust in the welts of his boots and confined to barracks. Byrne was confined to cookhouse chores. **David** thinking the charge was a joke laughed and a further punishment was given, he was to assist the Sergeant Major in preparing for the Officers Ball. This was a mistake as **David** spread the whole box of French chalk he was to use over the floor when only a small amount was necessary. Both he and the Sergeant Major frantically swept it up and tried to make the floor less slippery.

When the officers and their wives arrived for the ball **David** was detailed to be ladies cloak attendant and promptly placed a saucer in a conspicuous position that contained one or two of his own coins. While he was happily scooping the money into his pocket from the saucer that the officer's wives had kindly tipped for their coats, the master of ceremonies (the Sergeant Major) was busy trying to pacify the dancers. The dance hall resembled a battlefield so much so they found it easier to drink and fall over, rather than try and dance. Everyone had a good time.

We will now leave the rest of the story of **David's** army life as with his sense of humour he was lucky to escape without more problems. Except to say that one of the most interesting aspects of his duties involved the invasion of the British army into Egypt to reclaim the Suez Canal 1956.

KENNY DUGDALE

As you can see this photograph clearly shows his strong character   Plate. 153

We feel that although not a blood relation Kenny adopted our family! On moving from Lakenham to West Earlham we suddenly found an addition to our family unit in the form of Kenny Dugdale. Much to our parents surprise they had obtained another son and we a brother; from that day on he spent much of his leisure hours with us and was included in all family events. Ken had good but elderly parents but owing to his brother being older it was understandable that he would look for others of his own age group and so our lives became much livelier, more than we really wanted. There were numerous [we say incidents] that at the time created mayhem but looking back provide hilarious talking points even now, but unfortunately we do not have the space to include them all here

For instance in our youth we all arrived on motor cycles at an exclusive holiday hotel and on seeing us arrive the rather large elderly, refined grey haired receptionist exclaimed in a loud refined voice "Good lord the tramps have arrived!" On hearing this, Kenny with a cigarette hanging from his lower lip produced and directed the largest cloud of smoke that he could muster straight at her. She was lost from view to only to emerge across the other side of her small office spluttering and choking with others in attendance. Our presence there was not appreciated especially when we invented a new form of croquet and were banned from the hotel lawn areas for the rest of our stay by the owner Captain Dingle!

In 1956 when **David** was in the Royal Engineers and Kenny was in the Royal Signals they were both stationed near Aldershot. Ken arrived on **David's** camp and said he was on a few days leave and had no money to get home, asking if he could stay in **David**'s billet. With the permission of the corporal [given unofficially] Ken used **David**'s Royal Engineers jacket and beret to obtain illicit meals from the cook house. However there was one thing that Kenny had forgotten to tell **David** which was the small item that he had deserted and the military police were searching for him.

He had reasoned that the last place they would think to look for him was on an army camp not considering that if caught he would get a few months in military prison with **David** as his innocent cellmate! **David** realized there was something wrong when an officer found that there was an extra bed made up in the billet and wanted a head count to know who occupied it; Ken quickly disappeared. A few days later **David** received a very worried letter from his mother stating that she thought that Kenny had dug a hole under the shed and was sleeping in it. **David** phoned and told her to report it to the police or she might get involved in aiding him. This she did and an army truck with redcaps and police arrived but before they could get near Kenny he scaled the six-foot fence and was gone, over the park and onto a bus.

Our sister **Ann** arrived home and could hardly speak for laughing as she told of how she had seen Ken in her workplace [a large departmental store] attentively watching a cooking demonstration. Then much to the annoyance of the demonstrator was eating the food before she could put it on show and she spent most of her time slapping the hand of the culprit, a soldier with an overfilled mouth, much to the amusement of the onlookers. He was eventually caught asleep on the carpet at his own home much to the shock his family who were unaware of his presence.

Following army life Ken turned up in Bedford to ask **David** to obtain employment at his works. Not having learnt by past experiences David did get Ken a job but Ken was soon overspending his wages by hiring cars, unable to pay his last hire he offered to repay the elderly owner in kind by replacing her old damaged toilet with a new one. After demolishing the old one he asked for the cash for the new toilet and materials which she had no alternative but to give. Unfortunately he then returned to work in Norwich and the elderly lady was left with only a bucket and spade while the policeman with a smirk on his face cross-questioned **David** as to the possible location of the villain.

Eventually Ken met Rose, and settled down and between them they bought a cottage and smallholding at Rotten Row, East Tuddenham, Norfolk but sadly Rose died not many years after they were married, which left him desolate. He never remarried but found many outlets for his numerous talents and was very popular in his own and other villages. He was a character who had an inbuilt personality that would not accept discipline of any kind; full of determination and a stubbornness that caused his downfall as he was overweight, hard drinking and could not abide medical warnings, he died of a heart attack in May 2005. A personality helping others and hard to replace.

WE SAY A SAD FAREWELL TO LAKENHAM HOME OF OUR YOUTH.

It was a nostalgic day when the family uprooted and moved from the home of their childhood, but not as sad as the last move which was in more tragic circumstance. This time it was in youthful enthusiasm to a grand modern four bed roomed house on a new estate in West Earlham.

All that was left were memories of our childhood, lots of deprivation, of cold and hunger, of the terrifying hours of the Blitz; the Baedeker raids on Norwich when Hitler promised to destroy us as we lay in the Morrison shelter. He might have destroyed our buildings and infrastructure but certainly not our spirit as we still had our parents and those piano sing songs, true neighbourly help, many laughs and a few tears. Having said that the most important of all, the house in Mansfield Lane was a place full of love and children's laughter despite the odds stacked against us.

Gone were the shabby old rooms, "L" shaped poky little kitchen, [where Duff Cooper stood in heated debate with mother] with its old cooker that had cast iron Queen Anne legs. Gone were the draughts and misshapen bedrooms, the lounge with its triplex stove, and draughty doors each side of the fireplace, the old electric copper kettle that stood on a little shelf in the kitchen, dangerous for us as children. **Alan** when much younger had one day pulled the plug out and tried to take it off the shelf. Its contents of boiling hot water spilled over his head, when bandaged made him look like an Indian Raja; this pleased him once he got over the shock and pain.

Looking back, the war almost forgotten, and the time of schooldays at Mansfield Lane. The move to our new home at West Earlham was a sudden dramatic change, a move into the adult world, a time to work for a living, dance halls, late nights and courting and those mad last minute sprints to catch the bus to work. Not forgetting **Mother** with five sandwich boxes to fill. On one occasion it was one of her bad mornings and unfortunately **David picked** up the wrong sandwich box at work.

He fully appreciated the effort mother had made with those delicious sandwiches only to later hear what his mate was going to do to his wife as his sandwiches were only held together with marmite and butter! We won't go into the rest of this story. We were moving to a house with central heating and a separate dinning room. We now had wage packets, motorcycles etc; sadly the nostalgic memories of the home of our youth, where we clung together as a family remembering Charlie's house and wartime Britain is now family history. Again it was a time of new beginnings. We were emerging from the poverty trap and our parents were beginning to see some comfort in their lives at last. But time goes so quickly and the stay at West Earlham soon passed.

LEAVING THE NEST
Sad but proud parents prepare for their children to make it on their own

Norma married **Edward Hart** on 23ʳᵈ September 1950, just before we left Lakenham for West Earlham. There were four bedrooms in the new house so for a short time **Norma** and **Edward** came to live with the family and were given the large bedroom; soon they were offered a private flat that some work mates had vacated. **Norma** happily married moved into her new home. **Alan** married **Joy Thompson** and lived in Granny Baxter's old house in Lothian Street. After leaving her daughters house where she and son-in-law could no longer tolerate each other Grandmother Baxter moved into the room that **Norma** and **Eddie** vacated, and we believe she really enjoyed her confrontations with the family and realized we were as mischievous as she was.

Granny Baxter with Rex [our dog] while she was staying with us at at West Earlham   plate.154

She stayed for sometime but the house was so full of noise and teenage pranks that she decided to live with her niece **Ivy Dawson** where she contracted an ear infection and died on the 21ˢᵗ June 1957. On that date we lost the last of our grandparents and that generation disappeared from our lives.

It was during this time that **David** [still in the Army] had some leave and was shocked to arrive home at West Earlham to find his family had gone and the house empty with no forwarding address! **David** knew that his parents were trying to get back to live in Lakenham, but where? With near neighbours all out it was some time later that at last he found neighbour who said they had moved near their old house. Bewildered he inquired from the council and was told they had moved to 5 Mendham Close Lakenham and did not have time to let him know.

He finally located his family at the new address almost opposite his old address in Mansfield Lane. What a relief, they still wanted his company. **David** was demobbed from National Service on 9ᵗʰ May 1957 and returned to his old occupation as a refrigeration engineer with the Eastern Electricity Board. **Bill** was called up for National Service in the Royal Air Force and left home.   As **Ray** and **David** felt unsatisfied in their work, a friend told them of the fabulous wages he was paid at the booming car plant at Luton; they decided leave home to join him and earn the big money "Just for a short time"; but this was not to be.

Little did they know that it would be for a very long time. In fact it was for the rest of the life of their parents and they both still reside in Bedford. Due to the high earnings in the area many men flocked to the factories of the booming car industry. This meant of course that accommodation was hard to find, and initially they obtained lodgings in at a place called 'Comfort Café. Both agree that it was the most uncomfortable place they had ever slept in, and were served the same menu each nigh; [toad in the hole]. When David put on a false Yorkshire accent the café owner took offence, so they left and bought a caravan at Wilstead near Bedford

With only **Ann** the youngest daughter remaining at home of a once large family there must all have been a terrible quietness in the once vibrant house. The boys of course with all their new surroundings and challenges did not seem to have let the situation at home register and did not realise the heartache they left behind. To add to this our sister **Ann** met **Tony Carter** who she married. Due to his employer transferring his position to Oxford they also had to move away. Mother was desolated, but soon she and father were gadding around having the time of their lives, travelling and going out, things they never had time or money to do before.

The children were now all adults preparing to settle down and have their own families. **Norma** had married **Edward** Hart, **Alan** to **Joy** Thompson **Ray soon to** marry **Brenda** Moore, **David** to **Heather** Willimott and **Bill** to **Gloria** Hill. The house in Mansfield Lane has since been demolished with many others due to subsidence, probably caused by the rumble of the trains affecting the railway banks, the holes dug for air raid shelters probably did not help. A local government estate office and car park is now on the site of our old house. The old railway line at the bottom of our garden that led to Victoria railway station has been taken up and replaced by a pleasant walkway leading to a supermarket and car parks.

David on a recent visit walked into the local fish and chip shop in St. Johns Close where his family used to collect the weekly war time rations. He could still picture the scene just before the war of Mr. Scott the grocer surrounded by sacks of dried pea's sugar, prunes etc. all loose to be put in brown bags that he weighed for you. Due to rationing the sacks of food became non-existent and those massive jars of sweets that lined the shelves were empty! This was sixty-five plus years ago. Not much is left along what was the railway side of our road where we used to live, except memories. The old bridge is still there [where we waved to the troops and also knocked off some unfortunate mans hat with a stone]. The shops in St. Johns Close where we used to queue for our wartime rations still exist to prove it was not just a dream, but our friends and neighbours have all gone.

BRIAN AND GLORIA BAXTER
The Tragic Loss of a Son, Brother and nephew
1963

We were not certain whether to include this traumatic family story as the family concerned might still be affected by their loss and it might bring back the painful memories of the sad death of a child. So we asked if we could include their story. We felt it wrong to leave it out due to the ironic fact of history repeating itself once again in our family in this way; **Brian (Bill)** and **Gloria** both agreed. It was many years since this event took place, though the memory will always be there the pain has faded. **Gloria** was our sister **Ann's** best friend, she and **Bill** our brother fell in love and married.

Their first two boys were twins named **Mark** and **Paul**, strong, healthy lads the pride of the family. They almost reached their first year when disaster struck. Both had colds bad enough to request a visit from the doctor who prescribed medicine. After he left, the children were fed. **Paul** started to cough and went blue in the face. The doctor was called back and he summoned an ambulance. Unfortunately in Norwich there were two roads of similar name at opposite sides of the city and the ambulance went to the wrong one. By this time things were desperate so **Bill** dared not wait longer for the ambulance and took the boy himself by car to the Jenny Lind Hospital that was very near, but it was too late, **Paul** died in his arms on the hospital steps aged 18 months.

It was a year when a 24-hour killer virus was rampant and sadly Paul was one of its victims. **Bill** was too distraught to be able to break the news to the grandparents of the child, so **Norma** volunteered but knew it was one of those very, very difficult times in life that every one has to face and it had to be bravely done. She knew that it was a case of history repeating itself with memories of her brother **Derik** and would open old and very deep wounds in her parent's hearts as it already had done to hers.

At first the parents could not comprehend what had happened as Norma found it too difficult to explain, and it was as well that she had her brother **Alan** with her, as they could not grasp what she was telling them. He had to tell them that the boy had died in a way that **Norma** found she could not do, with all her brave attempts at it. After the awful truth was finally understood the effect was terrible, as **Norma** knew it would be, for in that moment they relived for the second time their own trauma with their son **Derik** who also died very suddenly. She too shared this grief with them, old and painful memories do not die nor ever fade away. On the day of the funeral **Norma** and **Eddie** stayed behind with **Mark** who refused to be comforted, although just a baby he was aware of tragedy in the air.

Mark sensed something terrible had happened and declined any consoling. **Norma** also remembered that at the same age she too knew that a terrible thing had happened to her brother **Derik,** all those years before, and for **Mark** being a twin it must have been more of an agony. Slowly he became exhausted and with the tears still wet on his cheeks he went to sleep in his cot drained of energy, while **Norma** tiptoed quietly back downstairs. The day over, the painful night began. **David** stopped with **Bill**, **Gloria** and her parents to share in their grief. He admits this was one of the most difficult, traumatic nights of his life, trying to talk about anything and everything to distract them from the awful shock, and memories of that week.

Though at these times it is difficult to know under these circumstances whether it best to leave others to their own quiet thoughts, he did his best although hiding the need to share in their tears. In spite of this unfortunate event the family bond was strengthened and they moved home, their family expanded once more with the birth of another son Ian. To quote our mother once more, it was a time of new beginnings. [Bless her Heart]. This event caused unrest within the family, each person taking stock on life determined to make changes.

Edward [still working at the Electricity Board] and **Norma** now had two children, **Alan** [a director of a large motor company] and his wife **Joy** had two sons and a daughter, **Ray** [still at Vauxhall's Luton] and **Brenda had** two daughters. **David** [at this time was working as a refrigeration/air conditioning engineer at a well known confectionery company Meltis of Bedford], returned with **Heather** to work in Norfolk. However could not settle and when after a few months his old firm asked him back they returned to Bedford where he had enjoyed his employment and running many social events in his spare time.

Later **David** worked at the new County Hall as a maintenance engineer. [**Bill** became a supervisor at a large chemical factory in Norwich] and **Gloria** at this time again had two sons. **Ann** and **Tony** [Manager of a transport company] were expanding their family in Oxford later moving to Northampton. It was a happy period of family life but time moves on and the tide of life sweeps all before it; no one can so far control the life cycle and we were about to experience more of life's bitter pills with the loss of both our parents, and father and mother-in law's.

The older generation was gradually being taken from us and we had to accept this fact as we all do, that life passes on, then passes away. So we decided to write this book about our ancestors so that the future members of our families will remember them and us in the years to come.

MAD HATTERS TEA PARTY

When any dignitary attends an official function, although the organizers meticulously research and plan every move so that the event goes off smoothly, no one can plan for the unexpected and sods law takes over. No matter how much care and effort is taken there is usually the unplanned embarrassing occurrence that the public never hears about. One such event that **David** was involved in happened when the Duchess of Kent officially opened the New County Hall [at this time **David's** new employment] in Bedford and attended a buffet.

The planning complete, with all *those involved given instruction on procedure; on arrival the Duchess would be greeted by the officials of the County and would declare the new County Hall open, then proceed along the first floor corridor to the waiting number 3 and 4 lifts that would take her to the 6th floor. The management was advised to use number 1 and 2 lifts as 3 and 4 were prone to malfunction but this advice was ignored.

Security in the form of Claude would be responsible in seeing that no one came in the side entrance unless wearing an official lapel nametag. **David,** normally employed as an Engineer, had the job of taking the Duchess, County Council Chairman, her security man and 3 others by lift to the 6th floor where she would be introduced to the County Architect and other senior management. Mean-while Bert using number 3 lift would take the remainder of the party to the 6th floor with strict instruction to wait until number 4 lift had gone up and count ten before moving his lift to make sure that the Duchess arrived first.

The big day arrived and everything was in place but from the moment John, David's supervisor arrived, disaster struck. John had decided to appoint himself unofficial lookout and would be in the office opposite the lifts to inform **David** when the Duchess would be in the corridor and as there was still several minutes to spare, test out the lift. There was no need for this as **David** had already tested the lift and did not want to aggravate any problem but was told to do it.

To his horror the old fault occurred on the down run when the lift did its own thing and insisted on stopping on every floor giving a violent jerk on moving off; valuable minutes were wasted. Knowing that he could do nothing about it and would have to let it finish the down run to the basement then bring it up to the 1st floor, knowing it would perform correctly on the up run; it was only the down run that the fault occurred and there was no way to control it.

* **False names have been used for obvious reasons.**

Coming up from the ground floor he arrived on the 1st floor; thankfully the Duchess was running late but who should appear but his boss the County Architect who was late and wanted **David** to collect his wife who was in a wheelchair on the ground floor and take her to the 6th. Oh no! He would be on that down run again! No amount of explaining would alter the Architects mind, **David** was told in no uncertain terms to do it. So he did.

Arriving on the ground there was a large crowd including the wheelchair crammed against the lift door waiting for the Duchess to walk down the stairs after visiting the 6th floor. David started his journey up with the lady in the wheelchair while John came from the office to announce that "the Duchess" ....what! No lift and demanded from Bert "Where the F.... is he" wondering what to do, he virtually left this world.

Suddenly the lift arrived at the 1st and John gave a sigh of relief ...But it did not stop and shot past with the wheelchair inside to the 6th floor. John's description of **David** could not be repeated and he retreated to hide in the office. After another painful journey down David's feared the worst but thankfully after stopping at every floor it finally reached the 1st and was just in time to see the Duchess come round the corner. Unfortunately John, emerging from the office did not and in a loud voice bellowed "Where the F... have you been. It's a gooooo".

Seeing the look on **David**'s face, turned round to face the Duchess and the crowd of officials that were looking at each other in bewildered embarrassment except the Duchess who no doubt having heard the expression before somewhere had lost her composure and was unable to hide her amusement.

John made a quick exit down the stairs. **David** knowing there was more to come ushered his charge into the lift which had stopped about 5 inches below floor level and tried to explain to the chairman who was in a daze that he could not get into the lift as he was standing in front of the lift controls.

 The chairman while talking to the Duchess appeared to understand and decided to move himself to one side but unfortunately moved back just as **David** stepped down into the lift neatly running his new shoes down the shin of the Chairman and on to his foot. With a muffled groan the chairman hobbled to the other side and pushing his glasses back, glared at **David** who apologized but could no longer hide his smile and kept his face as close to the lift control panel as possible.

After a while the lift decided to move just as the chairman stuttered "We will now take you up… and the lift gave a violent jerk downwards catching him on one leg, off balance and into the arms of another space traveler. It was a situation that could not fully be described as by this time **David** was openly laughing with the Duchess, trying to explain what was happening and what was going to happen and there was nothing he could do about it; the lift had developed a fault!

The lift arrived at the ground floor and the doors opened to the amazement of the crowds outside to unexpectedly see the Duchess inside the lift and stood staring in as if the passengers were goldfish. Then someone started clapping. The detective probably thinking it was some form of ambush, spread eagled himself across the lift doors until they closed and number 4 lift happily jerked again to proceed to the basement.

In the meantime Bert had been counting to ten and took his charges to the 6th floor to the surprise of the receiving party. But where was the Duchess! Where was the Duchess? The management waiting could not understand as they watched the lift indicator lights; **David** had taken her to the basement. After a brief visit to the basement the lift behaved and with no further problems number 4 lift took them to the 6th floor with no stops. No doubt someone in management must have uttered 'chop off his head'!

The Duchess, still in the lift who while concealing her laughter behind her hand asked **David,** "and what is your job here" "I'm not a lift Engineer" replied David they all laughed which broke the embarrassed silence.

 Another amusing incident occurred when Claude, who you may recall, was given the task to watch for and stop gatecrashers who might try to enter the buffet area. He was keeping a watchful eye on the crowd outside when saw a tall shifty eyed man lingering about with what appeared to be a lump under his jacket; sometimes leaning over to talk to two others who were shorter than himself and appeared to be smooching around.

The taller suddenly swung round and took long strides toward the side entrance. Claude sprang into action. Noting that the stranger never had any lapel identification barred the way. "Sorry Sir you are not allowed in here". "I am the Chief Constable" was the reply, "Oh yeah! And I'm the Duke of Clarence" retorted Claude and started frisking him. The stranger tried to hide his anger and the embarrassment of being frisked, pulled his identification from a side pocket. He was the Chief Constable! Apart from these hiccups the day went well.

MAKING A SPLASH.
We Spend a Day on the River with Raymond

One day shortly after their two children had grown up and married, **Eddie** and **Norma** decided to visit **Raymond** and **Brenda** in Bedford. They took **Eddies'** mother with them. This was to be their last holiday with her as sadly she died shortly after. On arrival **Raymond** suggested taking them all out on the river in his boat. It was a pleasant day and all approved it. Having noticed the rest of the folks at the Marina always dressed up for their boat trips; **Ray** decided he too for appearance sake, had better follow their example.

This was a mistake…when pushing off from the bank the pole stuck. We heard a dull thump; the pole slowly leaned over and a splash; rushing to the side, all we could see was a balding head slowly rising up from the water. He stood up with his chin just above the water, and the air was a bit blue and sounded remarkably like words that our mother definitely would not have approved of. He climbed aboard covered in mud, reeds and dirty river water, from which mud oozed from every fiber of those beautiful clothes he had debated so long over. He scrambled up the bank, and we must confess we are a terrible family for laughing at others misfortunes.

Raymond found his old working clothes and finished up in a pair of trousers where one leg was split up the seam to the knee, and covered with paint splashes very unlike the well dressed fellow mariners that he wanted to emulate. Poor **Ray! Eddies'** mother just could not stop laughing for days after.

Later against all advice he decided to go to St. Neots for a boat trip during the floods but unfortunately he lost control of the boat in the fast currents and after a hectic few miles he finally made an unintended stop on an island at an angle of forty five degrees.

Life is never dull when **Raymond** is around, as all the grandchildren will testify. Norma's grandson **Nathan** could never get over the fact that a grown up would allow him to paint a face in water-colour on his baldhead [WOW!]

This was not always an advantage as when he was a young lad he often found that he was taking the blame because of his reputation for mischief. There were many things he did not do, as his sister and brothers were very well aware of how to avoid nasty situations laying blame elsewhere. Only now in shame we can say we are really sorry and mean it. This situation we are sure can be found in countless families throughout the ages.

1994 DISASTER STRIKES AND WE FACE A CHALLENGE

It was with shock and dismay when the inhabitants of Norwich and Norfolk heard that the modern Record Office was severely damaged by fire it was feared that many of the priceless and irreplaceable historical documents had been destroyed by fire and water.

We were currently researching the **Ward** family using the visitation book held by the Norwich Record Office, when our efforts were brought to a sudden halt as the book we were using was unavailable due to an over night fire. It seems ironic that while we attempted to research the tragedy of the **Captain [Marriott/Money?]** story and the little orphan girl who we wanted give a rightful place in family history may have gone forever.

The information that we had managed to record prior to the fire proved to be invaluable to us and we continued our research using the documents and books at the Yarmouth record office where the staff were very helpful, but still unable to solve the mystery as you will read. What information we had gathered proved an exciting break though. We found that the Ward /Lacon family tree reached far back in time but the missing documents restricted our search.

But again on Tuesday September 3rd 1995 we heard the news that yet another serious fire has destroyed an important area mentioned in this book, this time in Great Yarmouth. Many of the most ancient buildings in one of the remaining old rows of Great Yarmouth had been guttered by fire. We are amazed that so many priceless buildings or documents that are held in trust for the nation can be subjected fire or flood. How is it that even modern purposely built buildings are so vulnerable?

The public library has been rebuilt and contains the latest technology to aid educational studies. The Archive department has been refurbished with new material and the original documents that they managed to save after having them professionally cleaned and dried out from the fire and water damage.

The public also responded by giving many copies of books and replacing some documents lost in the fire. Of course there were a great number of valuable family, local, national and international records completely destroyed and cannot be replaced!

This was a great set back and disappointment to us personally as it stopped our research for a while until what remained of the ancient documents were once more available to the public.

CELEBRATION
The Sand the Sea and the Marsh.

1994 in Norwich was an important date, being the 800th centenary of the Freedom of Norwich. We visited the many demonstrations of industry and way of life from past generations that we have tried to portray to you in this book. Some emphasizing the time when Norwich was a port, and the rivers, which were the main source used to keep produce flowing in and out of the city. The way of life that our ancestors had then eventually improved to give us the benefits of their endeavors and ingenuity which gives us the comforts we enjoy today.

As the last of the Wherries made their final trip along the river, dropping anchor to line up along the riverbank from Pulls/Phuls/Pilsbury ferry, you could not help remembering all those people of the past who took a share in forming its history. A new bridge had been built that would completely isolate Norwich from the sea, as far as the larger shipping was concerned.

Eric Edwards   Plate.155

The turning basin has been neglected, it has silted up and is in a dangerous condition. Among all the boats there was the Lydia Eva, one of the small brave vessels that in the war of 1939-45 defied the raging of both sea and enemy to rescue many soldiers that were stranded on the beaches of France, to bring them home from Dunkirk. One man we particularly noticed was Eric Edwards the Norfolk Marshman whose picture is often shown in the local papers.

His array of old agricultural tools and other instruments were certainly a sight to behold as you can see by some on the photographs that we have taken. The traps and snares looked cruel but used to be the only means of subsistence for some in those days of long ago. There were some ingenious shovels used in ditching, also a pair of thigh boots over 200 years old soaked in goose grease, so highly polished they looked new.

As well as his local knowledge of nature and the marsh, he is a skilled Thatcher. We have mentioned this because soon like some of the people in this book such as the blacksmith at Heydon, he will soon retire. These old professions and skills will vanish with them and another section of the 'old ways' that will disappear and would be lost to us forever. We have taken a long journey through TIME and learned much about history and our past family that has astounded even us.

CHRONOLOGY
1945 – 1975

1945 **January:** Red army liberates Warsaw and enters German territory. **February:** Allies bomb Dresden possibly a 100,000 people killed. **March:** Allies cross the Rhine into Germany. **April:** American and Soviet troops meet on the Elbe. Mussolini taken prisoner by his own people and shot. Hitler commits suicide in his underground bunker President F. Roosevelt dies. **May;** Germany surrenders May 8th declared V.E. day and as we write [May 8th 2005] it is exactly sixty years ago to the day when we as children got ourselves involved with the celebration. **June:** 26th United Nations Charter signed. **July:** Labour under Clement Attlee wins election. British forces take charge of their sector of Berlin. U.S.A. tests atomic bomb. Big three Churchill [Britain] Truman [U.S.A]. Stalin [Russia] met at Potsdam and gave an ultimatum to Japan, which was ignored. **August** USSR Declares war on Japan. And the U.S.A. drops Atomic bomb on Hiroshima with horrendous consequence; no response so another is dropped on Nagasaki. To avoid further mass death and heart breaking injuries, Japan surrenders and the 2nd World War is over. Blackout ended. August 15th is declared V.J. day. **October:** United Nations comes into existence with 29 nations **November:** Trial of war criminals start.

1946 **January:** U. N. Assembly meets for the 1st time under one flag. **April:** Public morality council objects to artificial insemination on grounds that it is a form of adultery. One of our family was in later years threatened to be sued by others]. **August:** Negotiation's between Mountbatten and Gandhi in respect of Independence of India. **September:** Winston Churchill urges Germany and France to reconcile proposing a United States of Europe.

1947 **January:** British coal industry is nationalized. **March**: America starts international resistance to the spread of communism. **April:** School-leaving age increased to 15. **August;** The cessation of British rule in the Indian sub continent; two new states are born India and Pakistan partition. See item on **Lord Lytton**, Viceroy of India. **October:** the sound barrier is broken in a jet Bell–X–1. November: Princess Elizabeth marries Philip Mountbatten.

1948 **January:** Gandhi assassinated. **May:** Jews in Palestine proclaim the state of Israel. British Troops withdraw and Arab neighbours attack. **June:** Soviet's impose a blockade encircling Western sectors of Berlin putting a stranglehold on the allies hoping they would withdraw or submit to starvation. A massive airlift of food and supplies is instigated. **July:** National Health Service is operational.

1949   **February:** End of clothes rationing. **March:** Temporary end of sweet rationing. **April;** N.A.T.O formed by 12 countries. **May;** Soviet blockade of Berlin ends. **June:** South Africa introduces. Apartheid and passes law to ban interracial-marriage. **August:** Rare event, Big Ben was slowed by 4.5 minutes due to starlings perching on minute hand. **September:** Sir Stafford Cripps devalues the pound.

1950   **September:** Norma marries Edward Hart 23rdSeptember. Nationa Service increased to 2years which later affected David's length of
.   conscription.

1951   **May:** Festival of Britain starts. **June:** Dangerous spies Guy Burgess and Donald MacLean exposed. They escape to Russia, their espionage for the Soviet Union presented a major threat to world peace for many future generations. **October:** Winston Churchill elected as Prime Minister

1952   **February:** King George 6th dies. Churchill announces Britain has developed an atomic bomb. **November:** U.S.A. detonates 1st Hydrogen bomb in Pacific. **December:** The dreaded smog descends on cities in Britain. **January:** 31st most disastrous sea floods hit East Anglia. **David** while at a dance at Gorlesdon Floral Hall was advised to join with others from Norwich and immediately get the coach home as flooding had closed the main road to Norwich, the only way home was south via. Lowestoft. The sea, driven by a severe north-westerly gale had breached the sea defenses at Kings Lynn, Hunstanton and Horsey, flooding large areas of Norfolk, and was only 9 miles from Norwich. Those unfortunates living in low-lying terrain that was filling up like millponds were at risk. Many homes and businesses were submerged or collapsed. Water, electricity, telephone and other services were disrupted; large areas were completely cut off and impassable to the emergency services. At least 47,500 households lost electricity supply. All service personnel at the Electricity Board were called in to get supplies going again and repair the industrial machinery that had been submerged and filled with mud etc. David and his brother-in-law Eddie were called to help, working 18 hours a day. One village that David was sent to, the butcher asked him to get his large 8 ft. x 8 ft. commercial walk-in- freezer. When he asked where it was, the butcher pointed to it. Being made of cork it had floated into the middle of a neighboring field, still full of meat! Many people died including the family of our brother **Bill's** friend who were all swept away at Sea Palling; he was the only survivor. **May:** Edmund Hillary and Sherpa Tenzing Norgay reach the peak of Everest.

June: Elizabeth 2nd crowned. Scientists James Watson and Francis Crick discover the double Helix structure of DNA. East Germans rise up against Soviet rule .

1954 April. Col. Jamal Abdul Nassar comes to power in Egypt. **July** all U.K rationing comes to an end.

1955 **May: David** reported to Malvern Royal Engineers for 2 years National Service **April:** Winston Churchill resigns succeeded by Anthony Eden who defeats Clement Attlee in general election.

1956 **July:** Egypt Nationalises the Suez Canal and in **October** British and French troops attack. Further unrest in Israel and Hungary. **November**: United Nations imposes cease-fire in Suez. Soviet forces invade Hungary.

1957 **January:** Anthony Eden resigns. Harold Macmillan becomes Prime Minister. **March:** Common Market set up. **August:** Last of British colonies [Asia] declares independence. **October;** Soviet Union launch Sputnik 1 the 1st artificial satellite of the earth. November: Russia sends first living creature [a dog] into Space.

1958 **February**: Plane carrying Manchester United football team crashed in Munich: team decimated. **December**: First stretch of Britain's Motorway M1 is opened.

1959 **September:** Soviet Union reaches the moon with Lunik 2. **October:** First use of post codes for sorting mail

1960 **February:** Elizabeth 2nd gives birth to a 2nd son Andrew. **July: Theodore** Maiman [American scientist] invents the laser ***December:** Last National Service man gets called up.

1961 **January:** Conovid a contraceptive pill goes on sale. **March:** The Beatles make their debut in Liverpool. **April:** Yuri Gagarin becomes first man in space orbiting the world twice in Vostok 1. **Bill** marries **Gloria Hill** 5th June. **August:** East German authorities build wall dividing Berlin bringing hardship on themselves and the West Germans **September 1st M.O.T** tests.

1962 **May**: Last London trolley buses retired: **July:** Commonwealth immigration restrictions come into effect, later to provide a tide of illegal immigration. First live television communication across the Atlantic by Telstar satellite. **October:** World on brink of nuclear war when U.S.A. discovers the Soviet's have installed missile bases in communist Cuba. Russia backed down and removed them.

*Note; It was noticed that it was about this time the climate seemed to change; the winter frost and snow became less apparent. We can recall that it was not unusual for snow-drifts sometimes 12 feet high blocking roads and traveling was sometimes impossible. The winter trips from Bedford to Norwich were hazardous as you could not determine the road from the fields or snow piled high each side. One night the Baxter's had to take refuge in the Caxton Gibet Hotel as the road was blocked and so cold our sister Ann had slight frost bite in her legs. This year 2007 it has been the warmest January ever.

1963 **January:** French President Charles de Gaulle vetoed Britain joining the Common Market. **Ann marries Tony Carter** 30th. **July:** Spy Kim Philby a high-ranking officer of M16 absconds to Russia. **August:** Martin Luther King speaking for black civil rights addressed a meeting of over 250,000 in Washington. **October**; 26th **David marries Heather Willimott** at Great Cressingham Methodist church, Norfolk. **November** U.S. President John F. Kennedy assassinated in Dallas.

1964 **June:** Nelson Mandela leader of the African National Congress sentenced to life imprisonment for treason by a South African Court. **November:** Britain in financial trouble borrows to save pound **December:** History repeats when **Bill** and **Gloria's** twin. son **Paul** dies tragic death. Capital punishment abolished.

1965 **January:** Winston Churchill Britain's Great War leader dies

1966 **June:** Barclaycard, Britain's first credit card. **November:** First man made object crashes onto the moon.

1967 **May:** Britain's first satellite goes into orbit. **June:** World unrest, still more problems in Ireland, Middle East, and Vietnam **November:** Britain devalues pound by 14%. **Dec;** First human heart transplant.

1968 **April:** Martin Luther King is murdered in Memphis.

1969 Our family involved in creating the world's first test tube foetus. **June:** Oil discovered in North Sea. **July:** American Neil Armstrong is the first man to step and walk on the moon.

1970 **January:** Britain's voting age lowered from 21 years to 18. **April**: Beetles split up. **June:** Edward Heath becomes Conservative Prime Minister makes momentous changes for Britain. **November** Charles De Gaulle dies.

1971 **February**: New decimal currency is introduced in Britain. **December;** first Liquid Crystal digital watch on sale

1972 **January**: Bloody Sunday in Ireland. **February:** Major power cuts due to miners strike. **May:** Duke of Windsor dies.

1973 **January:** Britain joins Common Market. October: Egypt and Syria attacks Israel. **April:** Britain institutes VAT

1974 **July:** IRA bomb Tower of London. Harold Wilson Prime Minister

1975 **June:** Britain votes to stay in EEC. Suez Canal re-opens after 18 years. **July:** Our mother **Annie died 01 /07/75** Inflation in Britain hits 25%. Russian and American spacecraft link up in space. **November**: First oil is pumped into Britain from North Sea. **December:** Parliament passes equal pay and sex discrimination acts.

DAVID AND HEATHER MAKE HISTORY
1969 -1971

On a personal note and in great secrecy in 1969/71, a married couple, part of our family were as far as we are aware, the first to create human life outside the womb and for the first time they have agreed to tell their story. This couple were invited by Mr. Jason Hassard, Genetic consultant Bedford General Hospital to take part in controversial experiments assisting the eminent genetic consultant Mr. Patrick Steptoe of Oldham Hospital, provided they signed a statement that no contact or communication by other means would be made to the media or even their family on the subject without the strict permission of himself.

Of course there were many that would have done their utmost to stop it, as no one knew the out-come of these experiments or what would be created. They had to sign another declaration in effect to consent to the destruction of the creation if in fact it was necessary. It was this clause that later caused problems. Due to the many trips they had to make to Oldham General Hospital, special leave of absence at short notice had to be granted from their employers by top management and councillors.

This obviously created much speculation over what was going on, from those who noticed their frequent absence, which was quite funny at times. Their involvement was only known by a handful of people. Even their own doctor was unaware until for some medical reason Mr. Steptoe decided that an injection was necessary that had to be given exactly at 5am and wanted them in Oldham for an operation seven hours later. An awkward moment came when they had to request their family doctor of Goldington Road Bedford to give the necessary injection.

When the situation was explained to him he was furious. How dare this man Steptoe interfere with one of his patients? The doctor who was highly respected did not realize that he was confronting one of the top consultants of the age and decided to tell this Steptoe person to get off his patch! He requested his patients to leave the room while he did it, when he recalled them, he profusely apologized and had a good laugh at his own ignorance on the matter. We suppose that he often laughs about it now but is proud to think that he was involved.

The doctor willingly arose at 5am the next morning and in his dressing gown administered the necessary injection so that they could leave for Oldham. When they arrived the medical team under Dr. Edwards was already waiting. After all the months of tests and operations the day had come which they will never forget. The elation on Patrick Steptoe's face when he bounded into the ward saying, "We have done it; we have done it and have obtained some beautiful results"

Then it was in every national newspaper with the accolades and sadly of course those with strong views against. The Daily Express and many other papers depicted on the front page a hand holding a test tube with a baby in it and the first picture of the "miracle of a life in the making", and the hunt was on to find those involved, but they never did.

Then threats came from abroad to sue for infanticide if in fact the creation had to be destroyed, so the tests were temporally halted and much hostility arose from others. This fact and the circumstance of not knowing what they were creating made them give it deep thought. More confusion erupted when a letter arrived, which gave them the opportunity to adopt a baby. It was an agonizing decision; should they take the risk of possible prosecution for infanticide, turn their back on having a possible child of their own or refusing the precious offer of adopting that might not be repeated because their ages would exempt them.

They sadly informed Mr. Patrick Steptoe that they would have to withdraw from the experiments. We must add our admiration for the lady and all those others who later continued and took the pain and risks in this pioneering work and brought it to a successful conclusion. Although they never produced a child of their own they know the heartache others feel in the same position and are happy that their efforts have given others the chance. They adopted a boy and a girl who have both grown to lead happy and successful lives.

CHRONOLOGY FROM 1976 -2005

1976. **January:** Two Concords take to the air. Turmoil in politics April Harold Wilson resigns and James Callaghan becomes Prime Minister. **September:** Serious drought hits Britain, drinking water threatened and rivers dry up.

1977 **Apri**l; Alpha Bravo oil rig blows up, **Augus**t; Elvis Presley the pop idol dies. **September**; Freddie Laker's budget Sky Train Airline introduced. **October;** Serial killer known as The Yorkshire Ripper still at large. The last case of smallpox is reported.

1978 **Augus**t; Pope Paul 6th dies and his successor John Paul 1[st]also dies. The third Pope in one year Pope John Paul 2nd [a Pole] is the first Non-Italian Pontiff for four centuries.

1979 **January;** Shah of Iran deposed by Moslem's **March** IRA bomb kills well-respected Second World War hero Airey Neave MP **May;** Margaret Thatcher becomes Britain's first women Prime Minister. August; Earl Mountbatten killed by IRA bomb.

1981 **July;** Prince Charles marries Lady Diana Spencer.

1982 We go to war in Falklands, Argentina sought sovereignty of the Islands and occupied these territories by force. Britain invaded to reclaim under Premiership of Margaret Thatcher and our troops arrive in Port Stanley 21st May. Argentine surrendered.14th June.

1986 Toil and trouble; We commenced researching and writing this book

1987 Stock Market crash

1989 Berlin Wall removed uniting both halves of Germany

1997 **2nd May** Labour won resounding victory to form government humiliating Margaret Thatcher and John Major's years in power from 1979 – 1997. Labour still in power. **August;** Princess Diana killed in car crash in Paris world wide mourning.

2000 Millennium celebrations worldwide **April;** Lydia Eva Cox [namesake legacy] dies. The Drifter was sold in 1990 for one pound, last surviving steam drifter ranked with Nations heritage Cutty Sark and Nelsons flagship Victory. A debate as to who should own her. Eva's father Henry Eastick named the ship after daughter [aged 19], but she was never allowed aboard due to superstition.

2001 **11^{h} September** terrorists strike at the heart of American National Economic Centre. Hi-jacked planes deliberately crash into twin towers in New York, thousands of multi-nationals died in the inferno and collapse of the buildings.

2004 A Sunami, occurred Boxing Day; massive earthquake under the sea. Tidal wave 30 metres high hit coasts of countries round Indian Ocean and islands leaving a flattened landscape crowded with holiday makers; reports of 200,000 people drowned, thousands missing, dragged out to sea by the undertow over hundreds of miles of coast-line stretching all around Indian Ocean; acts of heroism; 2nd worst world natural disaster known.

2005 200 years since the death of Admiral Nelson. October 1805 on board his ship in height of battle off Cape Trafalgar; international celebrations [including the French fleet] in recognition of his resolution moral physical courage, and qualities of leadership. Many of the important issues under international discussion include eradicating poverty in Africa, global warming, and a European constitution that will effect many generations to come. **7th July** Terrorism was brought home to the British people with Suicide bombers attacking three underground London trains and a bus killing many people. On the **21st July** a similar attack involving four different situations within minutes of each other failed due to faulty equipment and resulting in the biggest man-hunt Britain has ever seen. Most terrorists killed or captured.

CHAPTER X1
THE ROYAL LINE
TRIBES NATIONS MONARCHY AND PARLIMENTS FROM NORMAN TIMES

You will note from previous chapters that we have mentioned the ancient tribes that inhabited Britain and invaders such as the Romans, Saxons/Jutes Saxon/Danes and others, each having their own leader or king. These royal lineage's can be traced back by many different paths. Using the progress chart you will see our family has a common lineage with the royal line, which made it easier to trace from Adam through to Rollo on our mother's lineage and from Adam to William Longsword on our father's lineage. The Bulwer line evolves though Rollo and his wife Popae [Italian Kings] but the Royal line follows through his other wife Giselle [French Kings] to William Longsword who also marries twice 1st Emma and 2nd Sporta. Their descendant William the Conqueror invaded England in 1066 to take the crown of England by force from the Saxon King Harold Godwin. The royal line is a confusing one due to assassination, lack of heirs or other reasons; but since the Normans there have been only six true dynasties providing Monarchs of England.

We have separated in the following text the lineage into their respective houses, Normans, Plantagenet's, Tudors, Stuarts, Orange /Stuart and Hanoverian /Windsor. Chart 100 p.525 shows the royal houses from William 1st to Queen Elizabeth 2nd and Kings and Queens from William, though you will note from the following text some of the monarchs are not from true blood lines as the crown was sometimes seized or obtained by others. This situation has continued from the beginning of time.

We cannot cover all of the many happenings that occurred over the large time span we have used due to time and space. However we have mentioned many of the events our ancestors must have witnessed, were involved in or were affected by. These things often had an impact on their lives as well as ours too. Most British monarch's almost never used absolute power and have always wanted or were forced to consult others i.e. the Witan during Anglo Saxon rule then the Nobles and later Parliament. They sometimes tried to enforce their will as in the case of Bloody Mary England's first Queen and Charles 1st who lost his head; most of the trouble caused through the fact that religion and the state do not mix. Each change of ruler has an interesting story caused by a modification, replacement or removal of sovereignty some directly involving our own family who descended from Scandinavian, French, Italian kings or nobles. We have listed the various royal houses and the reasons they changed; the reader may wish to research the subjects we have mentioned in more specialised books.

ANCIENT BRITISH TRIBES with their own kings 54BC The Celts, Iceni, Brigantes, Atrebates, Belgae, Cantiaci, Trinovantes etc jealously guarded their area and homesteads around Britain.

THE ROMANS. Julius Caesar invaded Britannia twice, in 55BC and 54BC to steal the wealth of the tribes, as funds were low at home. Emperor Claudius invaded Britain in 43AD and the Roman occupation lasted until insurrection in Rome forced their departure for good in 430 AD. It was early in this period that Joseph **of Aramithea** arrived in Britain.

THE SAXONS. Following the Romans, Saxons in the majority ruling over other tribes. Becoming Kings of Kent, Essex, Sussex, East Anglia, Mercia, Northumbria and Wessex

THE SAXONS, DANES and NORWEGIAN'S. Hengest and Horsa c.449 AD [1st Norwegian, Anglo-Saxon, Jutes, and Danish settlers] A struggle ensued between the Anglo Saxons and the Vikings [mainly from Denmark and Norway] leading to Alfred the Great, 871 AD to Harold 2nd [1066]. The majority of these early kings are not listed in our story. **Rollo** the Norwegian Viking through his two marriages was the common ancestor to our family lineage. Royal inter-marriages resulted in several children of different nationalities each claiming to be heir to the throne.

THE NORMANS 1066–1154. [NORMANS]

William 1st the Conqueror 1066-1087 [married to Matilda] invaded England to take the crown by force in 1066. **Turold Bulver** arrived in England to assist him. The Norman invasion ended the Saxon kingship. William initiated the Domsday Book and a Feudal system. He died in Normandy in 1087 leaving a son William Rufus and a daughter Adela.

William 2nd Rufus r.1087-1100 the Conqueror's son inherited the kingdom. He created many enemies and died with an arrow to the heart in the New Forest. Henry his brother rushed to Winchester to be made king.

King Henry 1st [Beauclerk] 1100-1135 brother of William 2nt [Rufus]. Unfortunately his children were drowned in the White Ship in 1120 leaving his daughter Matilda as heir but this was not to be. Matilda's 2nd husband Geoffrey Plantagenet was hostile to the Normans. When King Henry died 1135 her 1st cousin Stephen Count of Bloise married to Adela daughter of William 1st invaded. [See p.197-cht.47]

Stephen 1135-1154 Count of Blois, [Matilda's cousin] persuaded his powerful friends in England to accept him as king; this led to civil war. Matilda never became Queen, but when Stephen's son Eustace was killed in 1153 [while plundering Bury St. Edmunds Abbey] and Stephen died shortly after; with no heir, it ended this line of Norman kings; Matilda had lived to see her son Henry 2nd [Plantagenet] take the crown 1154 AD

THE PLANTAGENET'S 1154 -1485 Houses of Lancaster [1439 – 1413] and York [1461-1470 also 1471 -1483]. For many years the monarchs fought died or were murdered in pursuit of the English crown.

Henry 2nd [Curtmantle] 1154-1189] was grandson of Henry 1st and a Norman who spent much of his time abroad; he had four sons Henry, Geoffrey, Richard [Lionheart] and John who tore their family apart though most of it was Henry's own fault. He was a popular monarch who restored the legal system of his grandfather of trial by jury instead of the barbaric trial by combat or ordeal that was used at this time.

Richard 1st [Lionheart] 1189-1199] 3rd son of Henry 2nd a Yorkist succeeded spending most of his time abroad fighting crusades and left his brother John to sort out problems at home. Richard died in battle 1199.

John [Lackland] 1199-1216 brother of Richard 1st.. After many disputes with the Barons, in 1215 John was forced to sign the Magna Carta one of the most important national documents produced. His greed for money and the cruelty he imposed on his subjects drove the Barons into revolt. They drew up a charter to address their complaints that outlined his entitlements in respect of money and service he could demand, how his judges should administer common law and much more. This charter gave us many rights today and it is ironic that in March 2005 there was a heated debate between the Houses of Parliament and the Lords that raged all night. The government was accused of abusing the Magna Carta in respect of locking up [indefinitely] accused terrorists without trial, which again emphasise the past is always a part of the present.

Henry 3rd 1216-1272 [eldest son of King John] known as Henry the Simple attained the throne at the age of nine on his father's death. He was a weak king who decided to rule without advice promising to keep to the Magna Carta but never did. He relinquished his power to the government to concentrate on the arts and ordered the rebuilding of Westminster Abbey [more suited to him than kingship]. He died in 1272.

Edward 1st [Longshanks] 1272-1307 Eldest surviving son of King Henry 3rd was regarded as one of the greatest kings and statesman. He towered over others, was devoted to his wife Eleanor of Castile and they produced sixteen children. When she died 1220 he built a memorial in central London at Charing Cross which marks the official centre of London from which all distances are calculated. He remarried to Margaret of France and produced three more children.

Edward 2nd [Caernarvon] 1307-1327 son of Edward 1st married twelve year old Isabella daughter of King Philip of France. She discovered that he was homosexual and after doing her duty in providing four children took a lover Roger Mortimer and escaped to France. See our story 'The Feast at Norwich Castle'. King Edward 2nd struggled with Thomas Earl of Lancaster who had many royal connections, and was uncle to Edwards's wife the richest landowner next to the king. He was a self-important brutal man who the king was afraid of. When Thomas tried to seize complete power and an alliance with the Scots king, Robert the Bruce, Edward captured Thomas and executed him, but was later deposed and murdered.

Edward 3rd [Windsor] 1327-1377 the son of Edward 2nd. When he became king his first act was to have Roger Mortimer executed and Isabella [his mother] put in a nunnery. The origins of the Hundred Years War lay in the Norman Conquest but actually did not rage for a 100 years it was instead a series of English/French conflicts. Although Edward had rights to the French crown, claimant King Philip 6th Count of Valois was proclaimed King of France. The dispute with France was about possession of French crown land. In later years this war involved people such as the Black Prince, Joan of Arc, Henry 5th. and not forgetting Sir John Falstaff at the battle of Agincourt. The Black Prince was involved in many daring exploits but died 1376 a year before his father Edward 3rd so was never made king.

Richard 2nd [Bordeaux] Plantagenet 1377-1399 son of the Black Prince and grandson of Edward 3rd. was arrogant, unjust, disregarding the law of the land and peoples rights. John of Gaunt his uncle ruled as his Regent. The Peasants revolt in 1381 was started by the imposition of the poll tax. Though only fourteen years old Richard 2nd rode to Smithfield to confront the rebel leader Wat Tyler and a mob of angry men, calmed them down and granted them amnesty, but the Lord Mayor of London had Tyler murdered. Richard exiled his cousin Henry Bolingbroke 1398 and after his uncle John of Gaunt died, confiscated the Gaunt estates. Bolingbroke was later released, returned to claim the patrimony of Lancaster and deposed Richard 2nd who had no heirs. Richard was imprisoned and murdered by Henry Bolingbroke who claimed the crown in 1400. The main trouble-makers for Richard were the influential Percy family who played a major part in his downfall and Henry's rise to power.

Henry 4th [Bolingbroke] 1399-1413 Duke of Lancaster, son of John of Gaunt [Duke of Lancaster] and grandson of Edward 3rd became king with only a distant right of succession. The rightful heir was Edmund Mortimer Earl of March. Rival claims to the throne from others later led to civil war, Yorkist against the Lancastrians known historically as the War of the Roses.

Henry 5th [Monmouth [1413-1422 House of Lancaster son of Henry 4th married to Katherine de Valois] claimed the throne of England and France. The efforts to try and regain the lost territories in France by diplomacy failed starting an all out war. The battle of Agincourt 1415 remains one of the famous battles of English history where the English army defeated a much larger French force.

Henry 6th 1422-1461Windsor; [House of Lancaster] son of Henry 5th married Margaret of Anjou. He became king of England 1422 aged nine months and soon after crowned King of France. Not suited for kingship being weak and timid it was left to his outspoken wife to fight his battles, as her husband was often insane. They had a son Edward who was such a surprise to him he insisted that the Holy Ghost conceived the baby. The rivalry to claim the throne cumulated in the War of the Roses 1455. Henry was taken prisoner but released two months later He was deposed in 1461 and escaped to Scotland, restored to the throne in 1470 and deposed again in 1471 Edward was killed [1470 battle of Tewkesbury] meanwhile in between the years the House of York reigned in Henry's place. Henry 6th the last Lancastrian king was murdered in the Tower of London

Edward 4th 1461-1483 [House of York] son of Sir Richard Plantagenet [in decent from John of Gaunt's brother Lionel Duke of Clarence] secretly married Elizabeth Woodville a beautiful widow and commoner 1464. She made the mistake of using her position to improve the wealth of her relatives with title's and cash that stirred up a hornet's nest. Edwards's brother Richard took revenge after Edwards's sudden death. One of Elizabeth's brother's was arrested for plotting to assassinate the king and beheaded with Thomas Grey [Elizabeth's son by 1st marriage] her other brother escaped to Calais to join the Lancastrians.

Edward 5th Prince Edward and Prince Richard 1483 were sons of Edward 4th. Richard their uncle [later King Richard 3rd] was the so called Protector of the two princes. The boy's fate is unknown but they were probably murdered in the Tower of London before coronation.

Richard 3rd 1483-1485 [House of York] youngest son of Sir Richard Plantagenet brother of Edward 4th was born at Fotheringhay Castle Norfolk 1452. Richard's son died and shortly after his wife Queen Anne died. A battle ensued at Bosworth between the Yorkist and Lancastrians's led by Henry Tudor against Richard 3rd last Yorkist king who was killed and so ended The War of the Roses; Henry Tudor became king.

THE TUDORS 1485 -1603]

Henry 7th 1485-1509 The first Tudor monarch was the son of Edmond Tudor Earl of Richmond [in descent from Katherine de Valois widow of Henry 5th and 2nd husband Owen Tudor]. By marrying Elizabeth of York [daughter of King Edward 7th] Henry merged the dynasties of Lancaster and York and this was sealed by the fact that to this day the badge of England consist of a large red rose of Lancaster surrounding the White of York. The Tudor's formed the elite Yeomen of the Guard to protect Henry from the envious eyes of the Plantagenet's that the house of Tudor knew had a better right to claim the throne. However he considered that he had won the title at the battle of Bosworth.

Henry 7th daughter Margaret Tudor married James 4th of Scotland and Henry, [son of Henry 7th] became King Henry 8th of England.

Henry 8th 1509-1547. When the Pope refused to agree to Henry's divorce from Catherine of Aragon in 1535 Henry assumed the title of 'Supreme Head of the Church of England' and appointed his chancellor Thomas Cromwell as 'Vicar-General' [whom he later beheaded]. The main aim was to sell the priories, convents and abbeys who owned two thirds of the land in England so that he could raise money and also free him of marital problems. He married six times to produce a male heir. Henry died 1547. [See main story]. Three of his children became monarchs.

Edward 6th 1547-1553 unmarried son of Henry 8th and Jane Seymour who after inheriting his fathers throne 1547 aged nine years died at the age of 15 years of tuberculosis. A plot was laid to by-pass his sisters Mary and Elizabeth by the Duke of Northumberland Earl of Warwick to place his own daughter-in-law Lady Jane Grey on the throne four days after Edwards's death, which succeeded for a few months.

Jane Grey 1553-1554 daughter of Henry Grey, Duke of Suffolk and grand daughter of Henry 7th inherited the crown according to the will of Edward 6th Jane was Queen for nine days and after a few months was executed.

Mary 1st 1553-1558 'Bloody Mary' a devout Catholic [daughter of Henry 8th and his first wife Catherine of Argon) was half- sister to Elizabeth succeeded to the throne but made the mistake of trying to destroy the Protestant Church and marry King Philip of Spain. Sir Thomas Wyatt determined not to let this happen, organised a rebellion in London and was defeated. The same day Queen Mary executed Jane Grey then married her Spanish king two months later. But he did not return her love and she died a most feared queen holding a bible stained with tears.

Elizabeth 1st Tudor 1558-1603 the daughter of Henry 8th and Anne Boleyn succeeded her half sister Queen Mary 1st 1542-1587. Elizabeth never married and died childless [see chart p.514]. Both Elizabeth and her rival Mary [Queen of Scots] had a common ancestor in King Henry 7th [who was married to Elizabeth of York] had a daughter by Margaret Tudor who married Scots King James 4th of the house of Stuart. Their great grandson was James 6th of Scotland. Elizabeth on her death-bed acknowledged him as her successor, so he became the first Stuart king of England and Scotland. To explain more fully how this came about, James 5th and his second wife Mary de Guise of Lorraine [whose daughter Mary Queen of Scots was half French] was sent to France for her own safety in 1548. She married Francois the heir to the French throne and so became Queen of France. When he died Mary returned home to marry her cousin Henry Stuart [Lord Darnley] a catholic.

This infuriated the Protestants in Scotland who were in the majority. Her son was later James 6th Stuart of Scotland and 1st of England. Mary's husband was murdered and she married the Earl of Bothwell three months later, again upsetting Scotland. Her people turned against her, she fled to escape her problems but was caught and forced to abdicate. She escaped to England and sanctuary with Queen Elizabeth but rivalry between them led to Mary plotting against Elizabeth who locked her up. She continued to conduct treasonable offences and was beheaded. Elizabeth 1st reign was one of great achievements; Sir Francis Drake, battles with Spain. Music, the theatre, Shakespeare's plays were all appreciated at this time. Queen Elizabeth died without issue so a search was made for an heir to the English throne and they found him in the family of Mary 1st Queen of Scotland and her son King James.

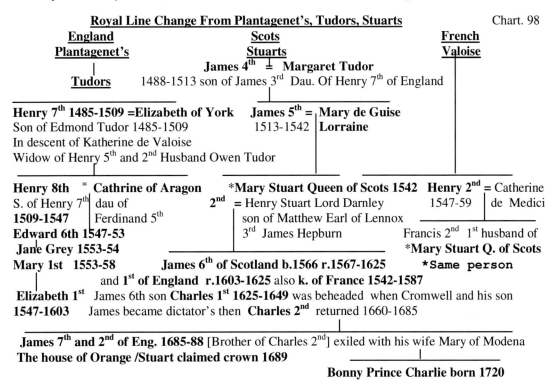

Royal Line Change From Plantagenet's, Tudors, Stuarts   Chart. 98

England	Scots	French
Plantagenet's	**Stuarts**	**Valoise**

James 4th = Margaret Tudor
1488-1513 son of James 3rd Dau. Of Henry 7th of England

Tudors

Henry 7th 1485-1509 =Elizabeth of York   **James 5th = Mary de Guise**
Son of Edmond Tudor 1485-1509   1513-1542   **Lorraine**
In descent of Katherine de Valoise
Widow of Henry 5th and 2nd Husband Owen Tudor

Henry 8th = Cathrine of Aragon   *Mary Stuart Queen of Scots 1542   Henry 2nd = Catherine
S. of Henry 7th dau of   2nd = Henry Stuart Lord Darnley   1547-59   de Medici
1509-1547 Ferdinand 5th   son of Matthew Earl of Lennox
Edward 6th 1547-53   3rd James Hepburn   Francis 2nd 1st husband of
Jane Grey 1553-54   ***Mary Stuart Q. of Scots**
Mary 1st   1553-58   **James 6th of Scotland b.1566 r.1567-1625   *Same person**
                and 1st of England r.1603-1625 also k. of France 1542-1587
Elizabeth 1st James 6th son **Charles 1st 1625-1649** was beheaded when Cromwell and his son
1547-1603   James became dictator's then **Charles 2nd** returned 1660-1685

James 7th and 2nd of Eng. 1685-88 [Brother of Charles 2nd] exiled with his wife Mary of Modena
The house of Orange /Stuart claimed crown 1689
                              Bonny Prince Charlie born 1720

STUART KINGS OF BRITAIN

James 1st of England and 6th of Scotland was the son of Catholic Mary Queen of Scots [daughter of James 5th Stuart] the first Stuart king of England who originated from Brittany later marrying into the Scots royal family. James harshness to Catholics and Protestants caused the Catholics to plan the Gunpowder plot. Protestants fled to distant lands some to America on the Mayflower others to Holland; during his reign the scale of poverty increased, which made those in power take decisions to help the poor. They strengthened the statute of 1576 that required the local communities to create work so that the poor had a chance to earn a living. Those refusing work were sent to workhouses and harshly treated to change their minds. Some sent to sea. This law was adjusted in 1601 and 1834 and lasted until it was reformed in 1946. James died 1625.

Charles 1st 1625-1649 son of James 1st a boyhood friend of **Erasmus Earle** and Oliver Cromwell [later both became bitter enemies of Charles 1st creating civil war]. When Charles was executed, the house of Stuarts' reign temporally ended and England became a republic. The all powerful and dictatorial power of the reigning monarch seems to have been brought to a head with the emergence of Oliver Cromwell as Lord Protector.

COMMONWEALTH 1649 1659 [Republic]

Oliver Cromwell the Lord Protector was in effect a Protestant dictator and when he died his son Richard became head of state.

Richard Cromwell 1658-1659 Oliver's son became Lord Protector but due to quarrelling among his army commanders and others the state was returned to the constitution of King, Lords and Commons.

THE STUARTS Return 1660

Charles 2nd 1660-1685 son of Charles 1st returned from exile and the Stuart's reclaimed the throne in 1660. The first incidence of the plague was recorded; the song ring-a-ring of roses originated from the description of spots, a pocket full of posies refers to strong smelling bouquets carried to ward off the stench. We suspect several our family members died of plague at this time, records show many early deaths. The great fire of London took place in 1666. King Charles 2nd having no issue made his brother James his heir. He being a devout catholic made no secret of his intention to return England back to Rome. Because of fear of him becoming king and his son continuing the catholic line, Parliament created the Test Act [1673]. This would have prevented any Catholics attaining public office, but failed to keep James 2nd from becoming king. The term of Whigs [horse thieves] versus Tories [Irish outlaws] came in to being, a slang expression describing political opponents. Possibly a joke, meaning they were both as bad as each other.

James 2nd of England [1685-1688] and 7th of Scots. Due to his strong catholic leanings his reign only lasted three years. William of Orange [a Dutch Protestant prince] was invited and he invaded in Nov. 1688. James was driven into exile.

ORANGE /STUART Queen Mary 2nd and King William 3rd. James' daughter Mary [a Protestant] and King William 3rd of Orange were first cousins [although a 15 year old reluctant bride] were married. Parliament had fought Stuart monarchs over its rights for many years and they intended to settle these disputes so a 'Bill of Rights' was presented in 1659, if the couple refused to sign it would have prevented them from ascending the throne. They signed and became joint monarchs, which ended Roman Catholic sovereigns. William refused to let Mary be the sole ruler and wanted to be equal in power so England had in effect two monarchs at the same time. From then on England became a Constitutional Monarchy [a monarch could reign but not rule]. William being a Dutchman was not a popular choice; the English did not welcome foreigners in seats of power especially as his interests still lay in Holland, which was under threat from France.

Queen Mary 2nd Stuart 1689-1694 a Protestant joint monarch with Cousin William died of smallpox in 1694. **William 3rd** 1689-1702 Duke of Orange son of William of Nassau and Mary Stuart [daughter of Charles 2nd]. William ruled a further eight years until he had an accident and died of pleurisy 1702. With no heirs Mary's sister Anne succeeded.

Queen Ann the last Stuart 1702-1714 was daughter of James 2nd brother of Charles 2nd of England. In Queen Anne's reign Scotland had no choice but to dissolve their parliament on 16th January 1707. An Act of Union was signed and England and Scotland became one country, the English flag of St. George joined the Scottish flag of St. Andrew and was called the Union Flag. Later in another Act of Union in 1801 the Irish flag of St. Patrick was added and this combination was called the Union Jack. During her reign regulations abounded, even air and light became taxable, every house with more than six windows was taxed so to avoid this people bricked them up and in some very old houses these blocked over windows can be seen today.   Catholic King James 2nd and Mary of Modina were exiled in 1689 but when their son Charles [Bonnie Prince Charles] was born in 1720 they considered that the throne was theirs by right and intended to retrieve it. However before Ann died without heirs she nominated Sophia of Hanover [a distant cousin] as her successor but Sophia died and her son George of Hanover was chosen as monarch in preference to the Stuart's. Sir Isaac Newton also lived at this time.

THE HANOVERIANS

The English system of government was totally different to what George 1st was used to. In Hanover he was absolute ruler, but was now under the thumb of the English parliament. This institution is different today in its function as then there were no formal political parties but instead groups of members that would gather together to push their own ideals and bribery was an acceptable situation. It seems to us that in this era there was much concealment of facts on royal lineage, and more emphasis on manipulation of half-truths provided to parliament and the public, but we leave it for you to research.

King George 1st 1714-1727 House of Guelph, Duke of Brunswick-Luneburg son of the elector of Hanover [German] the first Hanoverian monarch and a shock both in appearance and attitude He could not speak English, so appointed first Prime Minister Sir Robert Walpole to act for him. George's main interest was women, horses and food. His one son

George [later George 2nd] was aged eleven when his father abandoned his wife [in a prison] to claim the throne of England. They became a national joke; divorcing his wife for adultery! He arrived with two mistresses, one large and the other tall and skinny known as the Elephant and the Maypole both very ugly as he was. George Fredrick Handel [1685-1759] lived at this time and was duty bound to produce music on demand for George 1st. A Stock Market crash [1720] called 'The South Sea Bubble' occurred with charges of corruption pointed at King George. His wife died still in prison and he died one year later 1727.

George 2nd 1727 -1760 Duke elector of Hanover son of George 1st. When Frederick his son quarreled with his father, he accepted the political position in government as head of the opposition and set up a rival court against him at Leicester House, which included Lord Cobham, George Littleton and William Pitt. His father had made Walpole head of government but after Queen Caroline died Walpole lost his staunch supporter though the king remained loyal to him. During this time Scotland's Bonny Prince Charles thought it was a good opportunity to regain the throne, but lost the battle at Culloden where even the wounded were shamefully slaughtered. The Duke of Cumberland pursued the Scots without mercy burning and destroying. He captured Clansmen and took hundreds of suspects who he executed or imprisoned. Prince Charles went into exile, which ended all Stuart hopes for the British throne. In Scotland, only faint echoes and recollections remain in their songs a few legends and stories of their national heroes. Many emigrated and settled in British colonies becoming successful for themselves and their families. We discovered Scottish names connected to our ancient family lines as well as the continental ones. There was a general lack of transport but people still travelled long distances. In his last years George left all his affairs to William Pitt: The seven years war [1756-1763 in reality the First World War fought in Europe], but also in India and America involving Britain, Prussia and Hanover against France Austria, Saxony, Sweden and Russia. Bonnie Prince Charles made another attempt on the Throne but failed.

George 3rd 1760 -1820 the son of Fredrick 2nd Prince of Wales and the grandson of George 2nd; It was his son [later George 4th] that ruled in his father's frequent absence who although insane for periods of life with manic-depression. There were many important historical incidents that took place during his reign that changed the course of history in respect of the world and national environment. Thomas Newcomen in 1712 developed the steam engine from Thomas Savory's invention of 1698. The use of efficient steam power developed by Savory, Newcomen and Watt [1765] almost overnight increased production in every industry and created wealth for the whole country. In 1739 the nation went to war and

Walpole resigned after it finished. In 1742 his principal ministers were Henry Pelham 1743-54 and the Duke of Newcastle 1754-56. In the meantime France declared war on Britain and the explorations of Captain James Cook started from 1759/1779. George 3rd bought Buckingham Palace 1761 for his wife Queen Charlotte [who he married the same year and then raised 15 children]; he had it enlarged but never lived there; Queen Victoria was the first monarch to move in. The Boston Tea party 1773 American Declaration of Independence 1776 and the elimination of slavery [1787] took place. It was John Wilkes, a rogue politician who provided the hilarious incidents both inside and outside parliament and was a constant thorn in the side of authority. By marrying a rich heiress to The Manor of Aylesbury he used his newly found wealth to antagonize the establishment; he was regarded as the people's greatest chance for liberty and free speech. In 1779 saw the start of the French Revolution, replacing King Louis XV1 with a republic. After 1792 Austria, Prussia and later Britain tried to restore the French monarchy; this did not happen until Napoleon was defeated at the battle of Waterloo1815. The French revolution had ended Napoleon had conquered a vast empire across Europe but had failed to take Britain. After five years of trying to force Britain into submission he gathered a vast army to invade and sent the order to destroy the British Fleet. He underestimated the brilliant British Admiral Horatio Nelson a Norfolk man who outwitted him and won the decisive battle of Trafalgar but unfortunately lost his life in doing so. Nelson was the childhood friend of **William Bulwer**. Spain was causing havoc with pirates on the high seas robbing merchant ships, brutalizing and murdering their crews.

George 4th 1820-1830 King of Hanover and Prince of Wales was made Prince Regent due to his father's madness. George 4th married a widow but this marriage was made void and was forced to marry his cousin to clear his debts. He took great interest in the arts, one being the beautiful Brighton Royal Pavilion but again built up a huge dept which was passed on to parliament to find the funds. Queen Victoria later sold the building to the Brighton Town Council and it became a tourist attraction. During his reign George Stephenson created a railway system using the famous 'Rocket' steam engine carrying both passengers and freight, and James Watt used a steam engine in 1765 for pumping water. Richard Trevithick developed one that ran on rails for the miners. This was an exciting time for the young **Bulwer's** in Heydon and Dalling. As there was no male heir, William 4th succeeded his brother at the age of 50.

William 4th 1830-1837 King of Hanover [nicknamed 'Silly Billy] 5th Hanoverian King and brother to George 4th. His father was mad but still alive. He joined the Royal Navy; set up home with a married woman and raised ten illegitimate children, fought in the American War of

Independence and in 1818 married Princess Adelaide of Sax-Meiningen and becam king in 1830. The South African Colonies erupted in the Boer War. Calls were made to abolish slavery but there was so much opposition to this that agreement was only made to improve their conditions and the flogging of women slaves on plantations was stopped. Britain was the first nation to abolish the slave trade [1807] and slavery [1833-34]. Some owners refused to comply; serious action was taken driving it underground. Planters were angry thinking the slaves might get ideas above their station. 1834 six farm workers [The Tolpuddle Martyrs] were sent to Australia for administering illegal oaths and attempting to form a trades union to get better wages. The over privileged had no intention of sharing assets with what they termed the lower orders. 1836 the Martyrs were pardoned and returned to England but were harassed so much most emigrated. The rich remained as callous and selfish as before. The Great Reform act [opposed by William] was passed [1852] to redress imbalance and corruption in Parliament of regional M.P's. The morals of Royalty were extreme; William died childless [1837]

Queen Victoria [b.1819, r.1837-1901 Hanoverian House] niece to William 4th [daughter of his brother Edward, 1st, Prince Regent]. Her mother was Princess Victoria Mary the daughter of Francis Duke of Sax-Saalfield-Coburg. Edward died when she was only eight months old and left the family very poor, her uncle Leopold helped them survive, this affected her and she became very affectionate and sincere. The government realised the Duke of Clarence had no children and his past quarrels with relatives put his niece Victoria on the throne. Things changed and they received an annuity of £6,000 pounds to replace the £300 that they existed on. Victoria married Prince Albert [1840] Sax-Coburg-Gotha. The media was not kind, regarding him as a prude which is unlikely as reports state he had to satisfy Victoria's well known sexuality. Raising nine children during the years 1840-77 they presented to the nation a respectable family life. He died aged 42 with the appearance of someone much older. The inherited disease of Hemophilia caused the death of Leopold their son. Victoria became Empress of India [1877] involving **Robert of Knebworth** and by 1890 the British Empire [the largest in the world] owned one quarter of the globe. This was the age of Engineer Brunei, playwrights, artist's and dramatists like Charles Dickens, **Edward Bulwer,** Politicians Disraeli and Gladstone. Numerous Achievements must have caused wonderment to our Great Great Grandfather **Thomas Henry,** who probably read of the tunnel under the Thames, the ships SS Great Western and SS Great Britain, [the first, iron ocean going steam ships to be built and driven by screw propellers]. The the Irish famine of 1845-49 and the Indian Mutiny, which took place 1857. Victoria died in 1901.Her son Edward 7th succeeded to the throne.

GRANDFATHER'S DEAREST WISH HAS BEEN R EALISED
WE HAVE PROVED WE ARE RELATED

Sax- Coburg – Gotha / The Windsor's If you consider the fact that our present Queen is a descendant of William the Conqueror and he in turn was grandson of Rollo, it must make Rollo a common ancestor to the royal family and the Bulwer's, Lovedays and of course Baxter families!

Royal, Noble and Commoner Descent of England

[We have included this chart again to show how these individuals play a part in Williams's life]
The Sax Coburgh Line originated with The Sicambrians who by devious means subjugated the Merovians but intermarried with their Princesses and Queens in order to usurp their ancient rights and authority. See ancient charts. A.p.20.cht.11 B.p.45.cht.13. C.p.63.ct.17. text follows on surrounding pages to these charts. As you will read SaxGotha in the time of the usurpers was in complete rivalry with the Valois Families of France and Italy, though they stem from the same source, as you will see when referring to the charts.

Chart 99

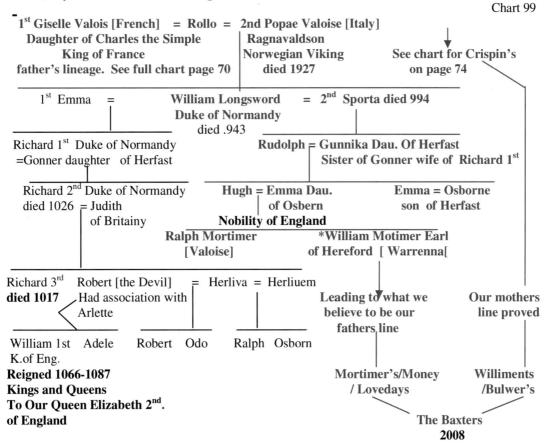

1st Giselle Valois [French] = Rollo = 2nd Popae Valoise [Italy]
Daughter of Charles the Simple / Ragnavaldson
King of France / Norwegian Viking — See chart for Crispin's
father's lineage. See full chart page 70 / died 1927 — on page 74

1st Emma = William Longsword = 2nd Sporta died 994
Duke of Normandy
died .943

Richard 1st Duke of Normandy / Rudolph = Gunnika Dau. Of Herfast
=Gonner daughter of Herfast / Sister of Gonner wife of Richard 1st

Richard 2nd Duke of Normandy / Hugh = Emma Dau. / Emma = Osborne
died 1026 = Judith / of Osbern / son of Herfast
of Britainy / **Nobility of England**
Ralph Mortimer / *William Motimer Earl
[Valoise] / of Hereford [Warrenna[

Richard 3rd / Robert [the Devil] = Herliva = Herliuem
died 1017 / Had association with / Leading to what we / Our mothers
Arlette / believe to be our / line proved
/ fathers line

William 1st Adele Robert Odo Ralph Osborn
K.of Eng.
Reigned 1066-1087 / Mortimer's/Money / Williments
Kings and Queens / / Lovedays / /Bulwer's
To Our Queen Elizabeth 2nd.
of England / The Baxters
2008

Edward 7th 1901-1910 real name Albert Edward was the son of Queen Victoria. As a child and youth he was wild and one child they could not control. He eventually married Princess Alexandra of Denmark. His exploits both in and out of bed involved legal battles. Most well known of his mistresses was Lilly Langtree the renowned Jersey Lily. He was one of the most popular and positive kings and is considered as the first and only monarch of the house of Sax-Coberg-Gotha named in honour of his late father Prince Albert who came from Sax-Gotha [Germany] though the family was and still is Hanoverian.

When as Prince of Wales he requested to be taken in disguise to see for himself how the poor of London lived, he must have been shocked at what he saw. Things improved slightly due to the efforts of the suffragettes; votes for women commenced in 1903 and a member of the Knebworth family played a leading role in this. The changes that took place during Edwards short reign that brought joy and dignity to the deprived are many. In 1906 a Liberal government was elected which started the first steps to form the Welfare State and a Peoples Budget [passed during King George 5th reign1911] where the State itself would take care of the poor, such as the miners act to stop exploitation and long hours underground. The old age pension act [1908], Trade Boards to inspect premises and to monitor the working environment and hours of work. Labour Exchanges for those that were searching for work and the National Insurance Bill for the incapacitated. Last but not least was the Super Tax on the wealthy to pay for all this, which provoked a savage verbal attack from the rich. Following Edward 7ths death his son King George the 5th succeeded.

George 5th [1910-1936] in 1916 he married Princess Mary of Tec [Denmark]. The bloodiest insurrection by the Irish Republican Brotherhood took place in Ireland with the intention of winning independence from British rule but they failed to take Dublin after five days of fighting, which left five northern counties in British control. Prince Edward son of George 5th was a youthful rogue but his experience of life with the underprivileged rubbed off in his efforts, with the help of his Liberal Government to get the poor out of their hell. He also helped to promote peace in Europe and made alliance with France to challenge the threat of the increasingly militant Germany which in itself was an embarrassing issue as he was nephew to the Kaiser. During the 1st World War anything with a German connection was a target for the people's anger which put the royal family in danger so in 1917 they decided to change their image and changed their r**oyal family name from the German Saxcoburg-Gotha to Windsor. Also the name Battenburg was changed to Mountbatten.** The war with Germany ended on 11th November 1918. In 1926 due to serious unemployment in a land promised to be fit for heroes, workers decided that they had had enough and caused a general strike.

Edward 8th [Jan.1936-Dec.1936] Prince of Wales 1st son of George 5th His parents expected him to marry into the aristocracy but he shocked his parents by mixing with shady characters and social climbers or insisting in going to the mud and rat infested trenches with the soldiers during the war [1914-18].

Note; Prince Louis Battenberg and Prince Philip [husband of Elizabeth 2nd] assumed the name of Mountbatten 1957].

He preferred married women and fell in love with an American social climber Mrs. Wallis Simpson in 1931. She was not accepted by his relatives and thought of as not fit to mix with royalty. He was nominated king on the death of his father but it was indicated to him in no uncertain terms by the Church, relatives and the commonwealth that it was either Wallis Simpson or the Crown. He choose Wallis Simpson, abdicated on the 10th December 1936, and married her in 1937. The couple moved to France into exile after he had reigned for only eleven months.

George 6th 1936 -1952 [Prince Albert] the 2nd son of George 5th 1923 his marriage to Lady Elizabeth Bowes-Lyon was a great success and they raised two daughters, Elizabeth [b.1926] and Margaret [b1930]. George served as a midshipman in the 1st world war. When his brother Edward abdicated George was shocked and unprepared. He had a speech defect, which made public speaking difficult. After Hitler's invasion of Poland in 1939 we were at war with Germany. The royal family refused to leave London and frequently visited the bombed areas of many cities, often going abroad to visit troops, and joined in with everyone else to celebrate the end of the war. On 15 August 1947 India was given its independence, which was   the end of an era. King George's health started to deteriorate in 1948 and the strain of war together with his exhausting public duties took its toll and he died of lung cancer in his sleep February 1952. He had seen his eldest daughter Elizabeth [married to Philip Mountbatten in 1947] she came to the throne in dramatic circumstance while on a tour of Africa, which brings us to our present monarch. We lived through this period of war and there were many issues that had an impact on our lives but due to time and space we can only mention a few.

Elizabeth 2nd was crowned 1952, succeeding her father having all the qualities for a monarch and has made a good queen. Queen Elizabeth 2nd is the thirty-fifth monarch from King Alfred, but the direct line to Alfred ends at Edward the Confessor when the Norman's succeeded to the crown. Queen Elizabeth and Philip Duke of Edinburgh raised four children Charles, Anne, Andrew and Edward; three of their marriages have sadly ended in divorce. Elizabeth's sister Princess Margaret had an entirely different personality. Margaret was one for the limelight and very talented with a natural ability to entertain, which the press noted was far too exuberant. She fell in love with Peter Townsend a pilot and war hero but as he was divorced, was not accepted by her family or the church. For the sake of her family and country she renounced him in 1955 but was never happy after this. At the age of 29 Margaret married Anthony Armstrong Jones in 1960 and raised two children, but the marriage was not to last and they divorced in 1978, which was to be the first of several royal marriage problems in the years to come. Princess Margaret sacrificed her personal life because of duty to her sister and the nation.

Egypt was never a British colony but was under its control as Britain was a major shareholder of the Suez Canal which was an important trade route to India and the Far East and it was in her interest to hold it. Colonel Gamel Abdel Nasser seeking to free his country from imperialist control seized the canal in 1956 and nationalised it. Israeli forces invaded the Sinai desert attacking Egyptian forces, which gave the French and British a pretext for their troops to get involved, arriving a few days later. **David** was at this time serving in the Royal Engineers and was a participant [see page 486/7]. Parliament in uproar as P.M. Anthony Eden had gone to war without consultation. America and Russia were in a cold war, which meant a probable world war if Russia took Egypt's side so the operation ceased; Britain and France were humiliated, Eden was forced to resign and Nassar became a great Egyptian hero. Irish Republicans resorted to extreme violence and our nation lost a most respected member, Lord Louis Mountbatten [the Queens uncle] when the IRA blew up his boat Shadow V in 1979 near his holiday home at Classiebawn Castle, Ireland. Technology and communication leapt forward with the latest electronics such as Television, Microwave's and other labour saving devices. There was excitement and change. The older generation were disgusted at the sexual freedom and a breakdown in moral values. A time for the Baxter family to become more individualistic and start their own adult lives.

David bought the first family car, a 1934 Morris 10 H.P. that was being used as a greenhouse to grow tomatoes. He restored it and proudly drove from Bedford to Norwich. How it reached there without mishap was a miracle, as the inner tubes were showing through worn rubber tyres and the steering was in need of some expert attention. The sprung seats had sunk so low a policeman stopped him and asked if he was driving by remote control. There was no MOT in those days. On one occasion the tyre blew out and the car finished up in a hedge, **David** changed the wheel, pushed the vehicle back onto the road and carried on to complete the one hundred mile journey to Norwich.

There are many important issues during Queen Elizabeth's reign that affected us, which we will mention but not enlarge upon, such as strikes, terrorism, blackouts and a three-day working week; the country struggled with near bankruptcy. In 1963 Britain was embarrassed by the fact that General Charles de Gaulle of France vetoed our entry to the European Economic Community [the Common Market]. In February 1971Britain changed over to a decimal currency. 1973 January Britain joins The Common Market and Margaret Thatcher was voted the first women Prime Minister [1979]. We go to war with Argentina [1982] over the Falkland Islands and recover these in fourteen weeks.

Prince Charles, eldest son of Queen Elizabeth 2nd and the Duke of Edinburgh and is heir to the throne. He married the beautiful 19 year old Lady Diana Spencer on 29th July 1981 and raised two children William b.1982 and Harry born 1985. Unfortunately Charles was it seemed still in love with a former girlfriend; unable to untie his emotions, all the dreams of that fairytale romance came crashing down!

DIANA PRINCESS of WALES
b 1961 d 1997

The story of Diana, which we felt we had to include as it was no doubt the most emotional national occurrence in our lifetime. The whole British nation and a great many people abroad involved themselves in her distressing story. Born into an aristocratic family that was torn apart by her parents divorce when she was only a child. She grew up to become a beautiful shy girl working in a children's kindergarten. After attracting the attention of Prince Charles, she was continually in the spotlight; every move was recorded by the media. This was every reporter's dream of a fairy tale romance and wedding. Due to space and time we will only highlight the important issues as there are specialised books written about this subject. Alas this dream romance was not such a fairytale after all; it was not to last, as Diana put it "from the start there were three people in her marriage her husband, his lover and herself".

After their divorce Diana involved herself totally in her charity work here and abroad and became even more popular than her in-laws making herself an equal to those that she tried to help such as Aids victims, the elderly, the terminally ill and the children caught up in the minefields of war. She caught the mood of the nation though her private life was often questioned by those in power. Her sudden death in Paris raised many puzzling queries. Was the car crash caused by the driver's error, pursuit by the media or his over indulgence of alcohol? Was she too popular for some? Or was she keeping company with those that were not appreciated by "the firm" as the Royals are known?

Whatever the cause of the motor crash in that Paris underpass on August 31st 1997 it still remains a very controversial subject to this day. The whole nation mourned her death in a way that the living generations who witnessed these events could ever forget. Thousands lined the streets to pay their respects at her funeral. Floral tributes were piled outside her home at Kensington Palace along with accolades from home and aboard. In her emotional interview before her death detailing her married life, ironically almost in tears, she stated she would wish that she would be remembered as the Princess of Hearts.

This she certainly was.

Prince Charles and Lady Camilla TIME passes and we have arrived at the present. After the death of Diana the heir to the British throne Prince Charles gradually introduced Lady Camilla Parker Bowles [a divorcee] to the media and the public for approval and finally married her. There are many books specialising in this interesting period of time.

PROGRESS CHART TO 2008

Chart 100

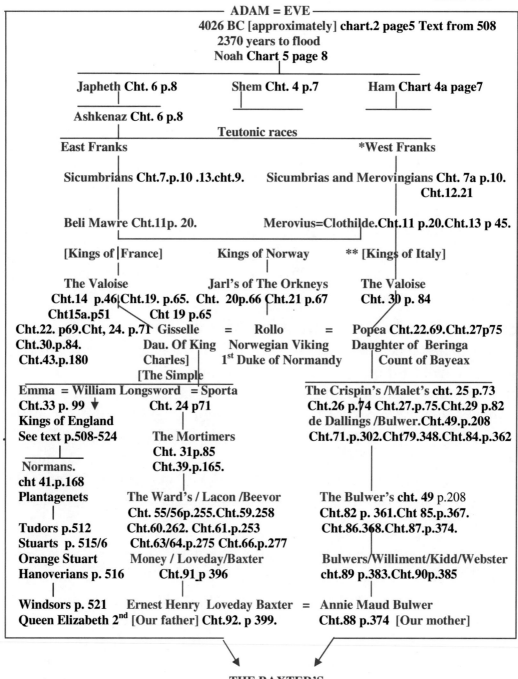

— ADAM = EVE —
4026 BC [approximately] chart.2 page5 Text from 508
2370 years to flood
Noah Chart 5 page 8

| Japheth Cht. 6 p.8 | Shem Cht. 4 p.7 | Ham Chart 4a page7 |

Ashkenaz Cht. 6 p.8

Teutonic races

East Franks   *West Franks

Sicumbrians Cht.7.p.10 .13.cht.9.   Sicumbrias and Merovingians Cht. 7a p.10.
Cht.12.21

Beli Mawre Cht.11p. 20.   Merovius=Clothilde.Cht.11 p.20.Cht.13 p 45.

[Kings of France]   Kings of Norway   ** [Kings of Italy]

The Valoise   Jarl's of The Orkneys   The Valoise
Cht.14 p.46 Cht.19. p.65. Cht. 20p.66 Cht.21 p.67   Cht. 30 p. 84
Cht15a.p51   Cht 19 p.65
Cht.22. p69.Cht, 24. p.71 Gisselle   =   Rollo   =   Popea Cht.22.69.Cht.27p75
Cht.30.p.84.   Dau. Of King   Norwegian Viking   Daughter of Beringa
Cht.43.p.180   Charles]   1st Duke of Normandy   Count of Bayeax
[The Simple

Emma = William Longsword = Sporta   The Crispin's /Malet's cht. 25 p.73
Cht.33 p. 99   Cht. 24 p71   Cht.26 p.74 Cht.27.p.75.Cht.29 p.82
Kings of England   de Dallings /Bulwer.Cht.49.p.208
See text p.508-524   Cht.71.p.302.Cht79.348.Cht.84.p.362

Normans.
cht 41.p.168
Plantagenets   The Ward's / Lacon /Beevor   The Bulwer's cht. 49 p.208
| Cht. 55/56p.255.Cht.59.258   Cht.82 p. 361.Cht 85.p.367.
Tudors p.512   Cht.60.262. Cht.61.p.253   Cht.86.368.Cht.87.p.374.
Stuarts p. 515/6   Cht.63/64.p.275 Cht.66.p.277
Orange Stuart   Money / Loveday/Baxter   Bulwers/Williment/Kidd/Webster
Hanoverians p. 516   Cht.91 p 396   cht.89 p.383.Cht.90p.385

Windsors p. 521   Ernest Henry Loveday Baxter = Annie Maud Bulwer
Queen Elizabeth 2nd [Our father] Cht.92. p 399.   Cht.88 p.374 [Our mother]

THE BAXTER'S
2008 AD
See chart 103 page 531

There are numerous paths of our family lines that we could follow but it would be too confusing to include them all. Rollo Ragnavaldsson is the common ancestor to both our parents, when they married both lines conjoined.

CONCLUSION

From kings and queens, nobles and knights to the poorest of the poor we have all shared life on this earth; we each came in with nothing and go out in the same way. Every person has left their mark in some way whether international, national, local or just within their own family group. No matter how small or large, that token has affected others and maybe those yet to come. Our generation has created the most progressive astounding achievements than was ever made by any previous generation and we have seen our environment progress in communications i.e. radio television and telephone. Power i.e. horse and cart to steam engines, from steam engines to, petrol, diesel, electricity; and rockets. The splitting of the atom and nuclear power are perhaps a step too far, often being used for the wrong purpose. Man never seems to learn when to draw the line. Now the time has come to reflect maybe on our own destruction.

The most astonishing feat was to overcome the force of gravity, and leave this planet and to land on another, which gives an indication of what could be in store for those yet to come as long as this civilization lasts. The newest innovations of course are the Internet, mobile phones and digital cameras, which are only in their infancy but will certainly shrink the world even further and change our way of life. There were few cars or radios and no form of television in our youth. Looking back in respect of creating life by artificial means, **David** and **Heather** can only say some of the risks they took resulted in the creation of life and joy for many couples that otherwise would have been childless has been well worth it.

It was great to research this book, to relive the lives of our ancestors and for a brief moment in time, share their experiences, from their beginnings in 4026 BC to the year 2007 AD. This comment can only bring us up to the present time and review the world as it is now and ask ourselves what we have left for the future generations if this way of life survives. So we bring into perspective the present living and future family generation as we, now being the oldies, begin to prepare to take our bow and retire to the wings as all those we mention here have done before us.

Yes! The western world has in terms of technology, provided an easier life, more time to spend with our families instead of the toil and sweat of our ancestors who found it a struggle to exist. But we often forget that much of the world still lives a dire existence that we think of as the past. Going back to the start of our book and the section TIME you may note as we have done, that the same disputes were and still are raging. One tribe in conflict with another tribe. Up to the present we can see some things never seem to change.

The present situation in the Middle East has certainly not changed, those countries at war are in the main the same nations and tribes and the same factions that existed well before Christ such as the Jews, Persians, etc. who split to form many different nations to spread across the world providing all the different languages, cultures and religions, some hate one another and still do. At this moment thousands are dying of starvation across the world and still the rich nations turn a blind eye. At this present moment there are seventy different wars taking place on the earth, mainly civil wars where the struggle for power is creating mass extermination, poverty and starvation, even forcing children to be soldiers just to exist or for a leader's personal power.

In the Far East people are still trying to come to terms with the 2nd worst world natural disaster man has ever known that occurred on Boxing Day 2004. A massive earthquake caused a tidal wave 30metres high to hit the coasts of several countries and islands leaving a flattened landscape. The coast was crowded with holidaymakers; reports of 200,000 people drowned and thousands more missing probably dragged out to sea by the undertow over hundreds of miles of coastline stretching all around the Indian Ocean. Now we appear to be subject to climate change and ice cap melt down happening in our own lifetime.

 Our generation has witnessed the terrible hurt mankind can inflict through callous ideologies of organizations, political ambitions, greed and stealth. With the aid of modern technology the world is now a very dangerous place to live and it is possible to even destroy our own existence. We feel sad and sorry the legacy secular sources seem to be leaving for generations to come and can only pass on to our families through word of mouth or text to learn from our experience of life.

We hope the future generations involved with our families may update this book with his or her own life story and expand on what we have provided. Having achieved our obsessive objective to find that elusive grandfather who our own grandfather tried so hard to place; we have at last put him in our family tree where he rightly belongs and give you the family chart as proof. But this still leaves us with the dilemma of that other grandfather on our father's side which we have yet to prove.

Considering we have covered such a large historical time span which affected the lives of our ancestors and ourselves there are bound to be some mistakes. We would welcome any factual correction though of course much of our family history like yours has been swallowed up in time never to be reclaimed. No doubt we will continue in our spare time to search in the hope that we can prove our fathers lineage through Ann Furrence but it seems that TIME has beaten us on this occasion.

THEN AND NOW

It is in keeping with the theme of this book "What is Time", to mention the preparation for the centenary of the 1st Norwich Sea Scout Group. This is one of the original groups started in this country in 1908 where members of our family spent many happy hours in their youth, also as a tribute to present and past scout leaders who have devoted time and effort for the benefit of many young lads living in the area.

All living members were contacted and a meeting was arranged at the 1st Norwich Sea Scout H.Q. on the 9th June 2007 to discuss collate and record all existing documents, artifacts and memories, and produce a book to celebrate the occasion. Of our family Alan and Raymond could not attend due to ill heath so only two of our brothers David and Bill [Brian] were present.

On arrival the external road walls looked the same, but looking through the original entrance we find what was the sweeping driveway is gone but the beautiful old Lakenham Hall is still standing and now used as the Norfolk Scout camping headquarters. Now there is a modern road and a large housing estate built within those lovely grounds with the wooded area's where we used to camp, have training sessions and organized games among the trees. We even made our own boats or used the sea-going cabin yacht with no supervision. Unfortunately those days are gone and what with rules and regulations and safety requirements, which perhaps go a bit too far, these restrictions, have destroyed the sense of adventure.

The old H.Q. in which there were serious competitions between the patrols had almost disappeared being replaced by a modern concrete utility building and the river banks where Sea Scouts used to swim and launch their canoes are now encompassed by modern housing.

To emphasize the theme of this book in regards to " TIME. On entering the moment came as David and Bill watched as their once youthful companions with eager faces came in. Instead there was a procession of old men complete with false teeth and bald heads, some stooped and leaning heavily on their walking sticks.

There they were after sixty plus years, Crusty Pie, Broody Hatch, Nuncky Folkhard and Squashy Lemmon. "TIME" had taken its toll on us all. Memories and experiences were exchanged. These men were once young lads who had once rushed through the door eager for life and like us will walk out with mission accomplished.

FINAL MAIN CHART "D" OF OUR FAMILY LINEAGE
FROM 4023 B.C. TO 2008 A.D.

Due to space constrictions we cannot place all the names to correspond to the same time period of co-existing families and our father's line of **Laco [Lacon] William Longsword/Mortimer/Warrenna/Ward/Loveday.** We have yet to prove our father's probable lineage but our mother's line is now definitely proved as per official documents. To find detailed family charts and text for individual names below please see index.

```
*   Adam & Eve                                    -                         Cht. 101
        Seth - Noah
              For full chart to time Jesus and of Joseph of Arimathea ▲
              see chart 2 page 5.        For chart of Viking ancestors from c.214  See p. 66& 67
                                         Norwegian Vikings who settled in the Orkney Islands

JUDEAN  Joseph of Arimathia1- 82 BC cht. 3 p. 6
S       Anna = Bran /Bron                 Ingald [The Wicked, King of Uppsal Sweden]
A       Ben [Heli]                        Olav d. c.710[The Tree Hewer King of Vermaland, Norway]
X       Dagobert d 389                     Halfdan [white Leg]Norway]
O       Fromund c400 =    see cht A.p.20.  K.Eystein [The Fart]
N                                          Halfdan [The Old and Stingy]
M       Farmund 419 = Princess Argotta     Jarl Ivar
E       Clodian d446 Lord of the West Franks = Queen Basina   Jarl Eytein Glumra
R       King Merovius 456                  Ranald [The Wise]
O       Childeric = Basina 2nd d481        [1st Jarl of Orkney]
V       Clovis 1st d 511= Clotilde 0f Burgundy   and father to Rollo
I       Lothar 1st = sisters [1] Ingun 2] Arrgund [Merovian power base taken over by the
A                                          Sicambrians see cht A.p.20]
N
S       Blitildis = Ansbert d. 570
I       Arnoald d 601Princess Dua of Swabia  Carloman of Brabant d. 814 [Valoise] See cht B.p45.
C       Bishop Arnulf of Metz = Dubo [Saxon]      for Sax Coburgh Gotha Pepin 1st
A       Ansegis Lord of Brabant Margrave of Scheldt  = Begga
M       Pepin the Fat  Mayor of Palaces of Austrasia Neustria & Burgundy d 714
B       Charles Martel [Illig.] Mayor of Palaces of Austrrasia Neustria & Burgundy d 741
R       Princess Bertha = Pepin 3rd [The Short] d 768.Alda [sister of Princess Bertha]=Theuderic 4th
I                       Holy Roman Emp. created by the catholic church [Sicambrian]
N                       and kings of Italy Kings crowned by devine right by Catholic priests.

        K. & Emp.Charlemagne [The Great]of France. D 814 = 4th wife Hildegarde  [Valoise]
F       Sax-Coburgh Gotha [Franks]  cht. 15a.p.51.        Cht.15a.p.51 [Franks]
R
A       K. and Emp Louis 1st [The Pious] d 840=2nd wife Judith of Bavaria  Pepin K. of Italy d 810
N       K. and Emp Charles 2nd [The Bald] of France 877    Bernard Emp. and K.of Italy d 818
K       K..Louis 2nd [ The Stammerer] d 879                Pepin Quintin d. 818
S       K.of France Charles 3rd [The Simple]d 922 Cht.C17.p.63.   Pepin Valiose de Senlis

                    NORMANS  dau.Name Unknown = Beringa See cht B.P.
                                               Conte. De Baayeaux
     Pricess Gissel [France]  =  Rollo Ragnavaldsson   = Popae [Italy] Valoise
     see cht.17C.p.63 Valoise   1st Duke of Normandy       see cht.17C.p.63
     Continued on next page      [Scandinavian]        Continued next page
```

*Rollo was common ancestor to the Italian, Norman/French and German lines that originated from the Valois families. The German line developed into the Hapsburg's [See chart C page 63 and item on Huguenots. You may note that that there were several intermarriages between these
*The brackets on left of page denote different national tribes or kingdoms whose families conjoined with our line Note; from Rollo's two marriages the family split into two distinct lines. From Gisele [Kings of England], and Popae [English Dukes, Lords and nobility].

CONTINUED FROM PREVIOUS PAGE   Chart 102

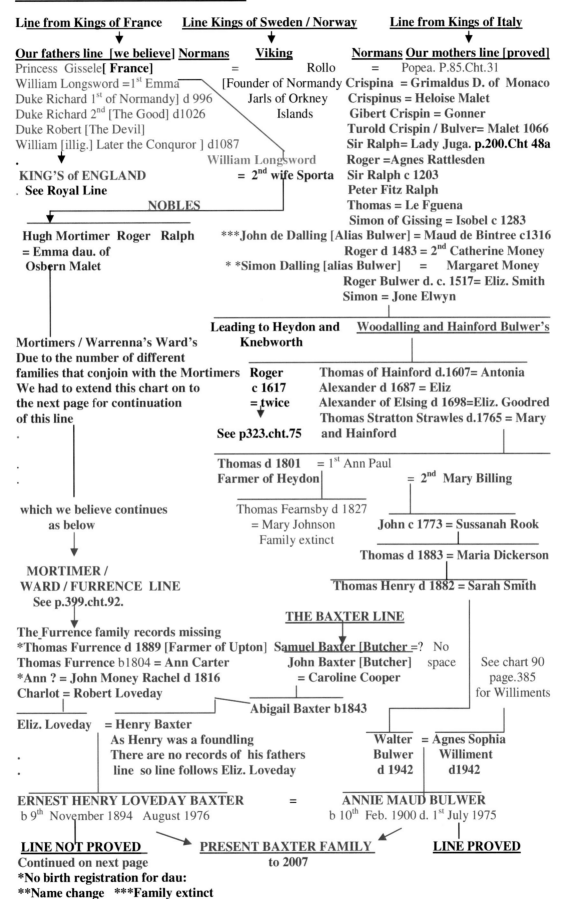

Line from Kings of France   **Line Kings of Sweden / Norway**   **Line from Kings of Italy**

Our fathers line [we believe] Normans   **Viking**   **Normans** **Our mothers line [proved]**

Princess Gissele[France]   =   Rollo   =   Popea. P.85.Cht.31
William Longsword =1st Emma   [Founder of Normandy Crispina = Grimaldus D. of Monaco
Duke Richard 1st of Normandy] d 996   Jarls of Orkney   Crispinus = Heloise Malet
Duke Richard 2nd [The Good] d1026   Islands   Gibert Crispin = Gonner
Duke Robert [The Devil]   Turold Crispin / Bulver= Malet 1066
William [illig.] Later the Conquror] d1087   Sir Ralph= Lady Juga. p.200.Cht 48a
.   William Longsword   Roger =Agnes Rattlesden
  KING'S of ENGLAND   = 2nd wife Sporta   Sir Ralph c 1203
. **See Royal Line**   Peter Fitz Ralph
            NOBLES   Thomas = Le Fguena
                        Simon of Gissing = Isobel c 1283
  Hugh Mortimer Roger   Ralph   ***John de Dalling [Alias Bulwer] = Maud de Bintree c1316
  = Emma dau. of   Roger d 1483 = 2nd Catherine Money
    Osbern Malet   * *Simon Dalling [alias Bulwer]   =   Margaret Money
                        Roger Bulwer d. c. 1517= Eliz. Smith
                        Simon = Jone Elwyn

                    Leading to Heydon and   **Woodalling and Hainford Bulwer's**
                      Knebworth

Mortimers / Warrenna's Ward's
Due to the number of different
families that conjoin with the Mortimers   **Roger**   Thomas of Hainford d.1607= Antonia
We had to extend this chart on to   **c 1617**   Alexander d 1687 = Eliz
the next page for continuation   **= twice**   Alexander of Elsing d 1698=Eliz. Goodred
of this line   Thomas Stratton Strawles d.1765 = Mary
.   **See p323.cht.75**   and Hainford

                    Thomas d 1801   = 1st Ann Paul
.   **Farmer of Heydon**
.   = 2nd Mary Billing

     which we believe continues   Thomas Fearnsby d 1827
          as below   = Mary Johnson   John c 1773 = Sussanah Rook
                        Family extinct
                                Thomas d 1883 = Maria Dickerson
     MORTIMER /
     WARD / FURRENCE LINE   Thomas Henry d 1882 = Sarah Smith
       See p.399.cht.92.

                        THE BAXTER LINE
The Furrence family records missing
*Thomas Furrence d 1889 [Farmer of Upton] Samuel Baxter [Butcher =? No
Thomas Furrence b1804 = Ann Carter   John Baxter [Butcher]   space   See chart 90
*Ann ? = John Money Rachel d 1816   = Caroline Cooper   page.385
Charlot = Robert Loveday   for Williments
                     Abigail Baxter b1843
Eliz. Loveday   = Henry Baxter
       As Henry was a foundling   Walter = Agnes Sophia
.   There are no records of his fathers   Bulwer Williment
.   line so line follows Eliz. Loveday   d 1942   d1942

ERNEST HENRY LOVEDAY BAXTER   =   **ANNIE MAUD BULWER**
b 9th November 1894 August 1976   b 10th Feb. 1900 d. 1st July 1975

LINE NOT PROVED   **PRESENT BAXTER FAMILY**   **LINE PROVED**
Continued on next page   to 2007
*No birth registration for dau:
**Name change   ***Family extinct

BAXTER FAMILY TREE

Con. From previous page and also page 374 chart 87   Chart 103

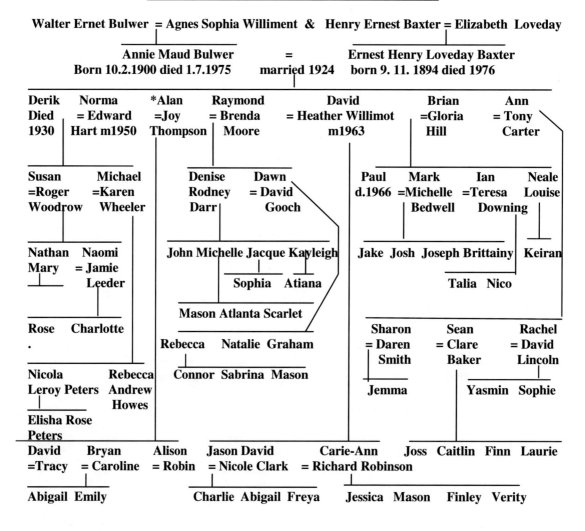

Walter Ernet Bulwer = Agnes Sophia Williment & Henry Ernest Baxter = Elizabeth Loveday

Annie Maud Bulwer   =   Ernest Henry Loveday Baxter
Born 10.2.1900 died 1.7.1975   married 1924   born 9. 11. 1894 died 1976

Derik	Norma	*Alan	Raymond	David	Brian	Ann
Died 1930	= Edward Hart m1950	=Joy Thompson	= Brenda Moore	= Heather Willimot m1963	=Gloria Hill	= Tony Carter

Susan =Roger Woodrow   Michael =Karen Wheeler

Denise Rodney Darr   Dawn = David Gooch

Paul d.1966   Mark =Michelle Bedwell   Ian =Teresa Downing   Neale Louise

Nathan Mary   Naomi = Jamie Leeder

John Michelle Jacque Kayleigh

Sophia Atiana

Jake Josh Joseph Brittainy   Keiran

Talia Nico

Rose   Charlotte
.

Mason Atlanta Scarlet

Rebecca   Natalie Graham

Sharon = Daren Smith   Sean = Clare Baker   Rachel = David Lincoln

Nicola Leroy Peters   Rebecca Andrew Howes

Connor Sabrina Mason

Jemma   Yasmin Sophie

Elisha Rose Peters

David =Tracy	Bryan = Caroline	Alison = Robin	Jason David = Nicole Clark	Carie-Ann = Richard Robinson	Joss Caitlin Finn Laurie
Abigail Emily			Charlie Abigail Freya	Jessica Mason	Finley Verity

During our research we have described many ancestors with their names and family homes that link together with our own families, and it is our sincere hope that many other families living today will be able to link in with some of these names.

You will find charts that we have formulated which will take you way back into history; perhaps you also will find great enjoyment in doing your own family tree. Maybe one day all these will be linked together into one great chart. You will also feel, as we do, very close to these ancestors as you discover things about their lives their hopes their despair and their joys. Almost as if they were looking over your shoulder and enjoying this task with you.

There are some new arrivals up to the time of writing that are listed on page 533 together with their photographs.

*Sadly we have to report that our brother Alan died 25th December 2007 a great loss and shock to the family.

MISSION ACOMPLISHED
NOW OUR GRAND FATHERS CAN REST IN PEACE   Chart 104

The chart below defines the Hainford Buxton and Aylesham branches and their connectionsTo each other and the main Bulwer families. Cont; from p.348. p.367 [showing several branches of these families] also p 361. From Simon and Margaret [Mouney] Bulwer.

For antecedents and descendants and links to main family line see visitation books for Buxton, Hainford 1664 and 1694 1675 –1733, 1737 -1810. Bulwer pedigree 4112, 41323 also Bulwer pedigree 4/323/2 1818. Burks Peerage. Public Record Office London S.C.8/96/4793.685 and Manor Rolls.

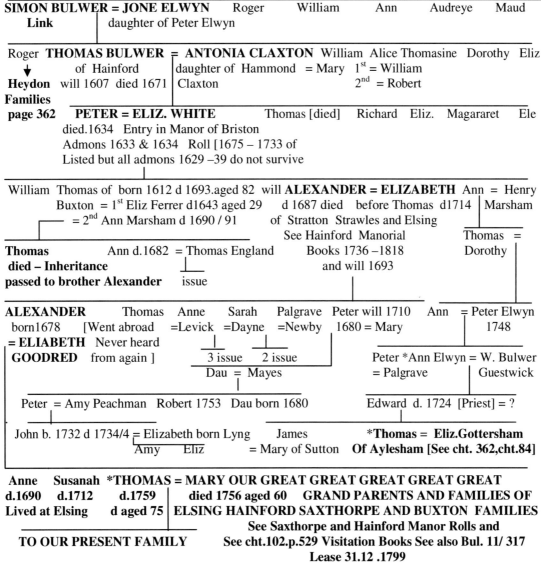

*When Ann Elwyn married William Bulwer of Guistwick it gave us another link to the main family line, also see further proof of wills and documents which firmly establish all the main factors of our research. We have also failed to find the family connection to Joslin Bulwer [probably a son of one of the other brothers] but certainly not William John Bulwer of Yarmouth but it was quoted by Mrs. Preston in her book that he was the nephew of *Thomas Bulwer of Hainford.

T I M E

Bulwer / Williment   Baxter / Lovedays

Our parents in later life
Ernest Baxter = Annie Bulwer   Plate. 156

OF NEW BEGINNINGS

Charlie and Rose Leeder	**Elisha Peters**	**Charlie, Abigail and Freyer Baxter**	**Jessica, Finley, Mason and Verity Robinson**
Plate. 157	Plate.158	Plate.159	Plate. 160

These are among the last children born to the Baxter Clan, up to this juncture so it is truly a time of new beginnings once more. As we are now 74 and 80 years of age on completion of this book, we think it is time to fold up our manuscripts, discard the computer and crash out!

We hope you our readers have enjoyed this journey through time with us, because we really felt we had begun to know our ancestors and felt close, as we followed them through the times they lived in. Now our job is done, and at long last we have found all our Grandfathers. May they rest in peace; we must admit though some of them made us feel like the poem we have expressed below.

We used to think, we knew, we knew, but now we must confess,
The more we know, we know, we know, we know we know the less.

THERE IS NO END TO THIS STORY
OR
OUR FAMILY

TWO MYSTERIES REMAIN UNSOLVED

We have obtained our objective in providing the facts that our mother's father earnestly sought to prove his relationship with the main family of Bulwer's of Heydon and Woodalling. Information in his time was not so readily available as it is today and we have proved beyond doubt we are related and have been amazed of our own achievement.

But sadly we cannot complete our research into the Furrence families and although the answer seems to be tantalizingly so near to the true facts yet so far away in finding their relationship to the Wards of Yarmouth. Our research did show Judith Furrence, was married to Samuel Ward of Stokesby.

Judith was the aunt of Anne Furrence whose registration of birth was stored with family records in Kirby House Norfolk and cannot be found. We know these records existed in 1975 and were used in a magazine article written about the Furrence family but the papers now are missing.

The other issue we are not able to resolve and probably never will is who our great grandfather was in our father's lineage? Our grandfather Baxter was a foundling born out of wedlock, so sadly his father's origins are now lost in time. We have found the registration of our grandfather Baxter in the books at the Norwich Workhouse, which does not show a fathers name.

When he was seven months old his mother had to leave the Workhouse with her child, and had to be escorted from the premises by two hefty police officers. She no doubt being very fearful of what life had to offer in the world outside their doors, the rest of what we know of her tragic story has been told earlier in this book.

This is just one of the many tragedies, which remained unspoken and unresolved. Here was a young girl, seventeen years old destitute and homeless, that came into the Workhouses at this time and received the cold comfort which was all that they had to offer in these hard years with little work and hardly any money. We hope that others will continue our research and hopefully find the answers.

BIBLIOGRAPHY CREDITS

We thought it only courteous to offer our grateful thanks to the numerous authors of books we have read, companies, individuals and other sources that have helped us in our research over twenty years. They have enabled us to finally collate all these valuable facts which we have added to our own, to trace our ancestors through the ages and the environment in which they lived. In respect of the lineage's of our many charts, we have included as many names as we could in succession but there are many that have been omitted due to space and availability. Listed below are many of the sources of our research and suggest that where possible the reader could also at sometime use them in their own research and enlarge upon their knowledge or visit the sites we have written about.

PERSONAL CREDITS

Mrs.G.McKenna of Family Research

Mrs. Jane Preston, author of The Squires of Heydon Hall [I.S.B.N.1 899163 75 I] and others.

Mrs. Val Miller, Manuscript Research. www.manuscriptresearch.co.uk

Mr. John Mathews for the excellent professional chart he drew on the Dalling/Bulwer lineage.

Mr. Kevil Davies London [for Ward family portraits].

Mr. Peter Green for his research of the Williment family

Mr. Derek Edwards of Norfolk Archaeology Service. For his Permission to use photographs inserted in Eastern Daily Press and Sam Emanuel of the Eastern Evening News.

Knebworth House for Photographs and information on the Bulwer families.

Mr. Jerry Bloom. Author and Publisher, @wymerpublishing.co.uk for valued advice.

Mr. Neil John Director European Print Group, Barry for his help and advice.

SOURCES

Complete Peerage by Henry Ellis "Introduction to Doomsday, pre-conquest of personal names" The Daily Mail.

Knebworth See the life of Edward Bulwer – First Lord Lytton by his grandson The Earl of Lytton, published by Macmillan and Co., St Martins Street, London 1913 vols; 1-2.

Bulwer- Long family Heydon Hall.

Insight on the Scriptures 1988, Watchtower Bible and Tract Society of New York Inc.

Blood Line of the Holy Grail by Laurence Gardner* I.S.B.N. 1-85230-870-2

Saxon Chronicles*.

Burkes Peerage [small extracts].

Chrystalis Books [Batsford] The Roman invasion of Britain*.

Chrytalis The Making of Early England.

Penguin Books 1066 The Making of Early England and The Year of the Conquest by David Howarth ISBN 00211845 9*.

Norfolk County Cultural Services.

Norfolk Museum Service.

Norfolk and Norwich Archaeological Society.

Norfolk Public Libraries and Archive Departments.

Public Records Office London for petition N0 SC8 / 96/ 4793.

Open Gate Press 51 Achilles Road, London. NW6 1DZ [Leyland's Itinerary of England and Wales vol. 2. 1535-1543 vol: 16 Edited by Lucy Toulain Smith].

Seeing Roman Britain by Leonard Cotterill.

When, Where, Why and How it Happened by Readers Digest.

Oxford University Press Roman Britain and Carman de Hastings.

E.D.P. Norwich.

BBC Radio 4 Program 'Taking the P**s Out of London'.

with extracts from the book written by Dr. Adam Hart Davis "What the Tudors and Stuarts did for us" contributors, Francis Drew, Derek Johnston, Gary Marshall, Stephen Humphrey, Jennifer Stead and Debra Gosling.

Bloomfield's Norfolk.

Palmers Perlustrations.

Doomsday [Uppsala 1937].

Chronicle Rolls and Chronicle Rolls with Medieval England by Francis Hill.

Internet Sources 1 Merian=Ahen 2 Ahnentafel Rubel-Blass from Internet Dodd of St Quinton http://oaks.nvg.org./abra10him/rollo.

Birth of Europe by Time life Books.

Hereward the Wake by Victor Head.

SOURCES [continued]

Unification and Conquest by Pauline Stafford*.
Peerage and Pedigree vol: 2 page 30 [Wedding Feast at Norwich Castle].
Roman Invasion of Briton by Graham Webster.
Medieval England by Peter Cross.
The Making of England by D.P.Kirby.
The Conquest of Normandy by Charles Crawford and Owen Freelizer.
The History of The Life of Bec. Editor J. Armitage Robinson.
Historical Collection of Staffordshire by William Small.
The Norman Conquest by Freeman [1875 Edition vol2].
William the Conqueror by B.E. Freeman.
Anglo Saxon England by M.S.Stevenson.
Doomsday transcript by Mundford.
Anglo Saxon England by Sir Frank Stenton 2nd Edition.
Medieval England by Sir Frank Stenton.
Whitbread Brewery Archives Chiswell Street London EC1Y 4SD.
Christies Fine Arts Auctioneers London described in Catalogue 'As an extraordinary long band sampler, chaotically worked in coloured wools on a pierced cotton ground' etc. It was featured in Christie's Asian and fine European Costume, Textiles and Fans catalogue 19/11/2002. Lot no 24, illustrated on page 49 [Transcript and other information on Lorena Bulwer's Tapestry.
Burkes Peerage.
The Early Middle Ages by Rosamond McKitterick. Publisher: - Oxford University Press. Great Clarendon Street Oxford.ISBN 0-19-873172-8 [pbk].
A History of Medieval Europe [From Constantine To Saint Louis] By R.C.H. Davis Publisher. Longman Group UK Ltd. Longman House Burnt Mill Harlow Essex. ISBN 0-582-49400-1 [PPR] 2ND Edition.
Early Medieval Europe 300 – 1000 By Roger Collins ISBN 0-333-65808-6 [pbk] Snd. Edition. Published in the U.S.A. 1999 BY St. Martins Press Inc.
Scholarly and reference Div. 175 Fifth Avenue, New York.
Burkes and Savills guide to Country Houses Vol; 111 by John Kenworthy/Browne. Peter Reid, Michael Sayer, David Watkin. ISBN 0 85011 000 0.

POINT OF DISCUSSION EARLY TIMES 1st – 7th CENTURY
FACT OR FICTION ?   [Taken from Charts 2/3]

```
            Matthat                                                   Jesus [many called
              |                                                       by this name those times]
  Anna = Joseph of Arimathea   Heli [High Priest   Arveragus [father of Bran/Bron
                                                    Of Siluna        = * Mary Magdalen
                                                    d. 74 A D
                               Mary = Joseph                      Damaris  ** Jesus 2nd   Joseph
                                                                  b. 33 AD   b 37 AD      b.44 AD
  Anna [Enygeus]  =  Bran/Bron]  Jesus the Christ]  Penardum = King Marius  [The Justice]  Josephes]
  [Some historians   [The Blessed]                  Arthurian descent       Reputedly came to Briton
  regard Anna as                                                            with James in AD 49
  his sister not                                                            see song by William Blake called
    his daughter]      Beli                         Coel 1st[125-170        JERUSALEM
```

As Joseph of Arimathea is a key to our lineage we realise that there is several incidences that are fact or fiction so we have looked into these in depth and leave it for you to decide, although interesting whether he visited England or not, is immaterial to our lineage. It is reputed that he was the uncle of Mary [Jesus the Christ mother] according to Ancient and Classical History and other documents and as can be seen by our chart. Our research shows that Joseph was a rich merchant dealing in metal an important commodity especially for the Romans of that day some documents state he was in the Roman Army. If he was the uncle of Mary then we can continue our lineage from Mary through Heli [Joseph's brother] right through the bible lineage back to Adam which we have done.

So logically thinking

1] After Joseph [Mary's husband] died one would expect Joseph of Arimathea, her rich uncle to look after Mary, and her family [also after as stated in Ancient and Classical History and the bible he placed Jesus in his own family tomb].

2] As Joseph was a merchant dealing in metals one would expect him to visit the rich in metal area of Cornwall to buy metal especially tin thus his reputed visit to England could have been true bringing at times some of his relatives with him building a chapel at Glastonbury.